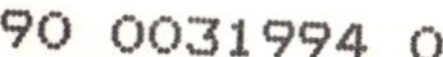

Tolley's

Manual of Accounting

Volume I

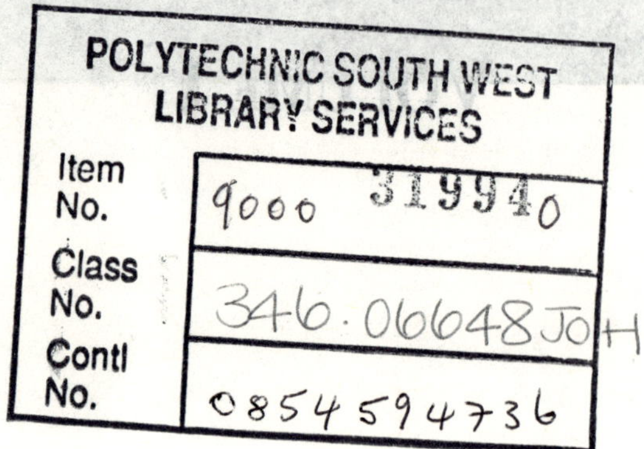

Published by
Tolley Publishing Company Limited
Tolley House
2 Addiscombe Road
Croydon Surrey CR9 5AF England
081 - 686 9141

Typeset by Tek-Art (Typesetting) Ltd, Kent

Printed and bound in Great Britain by
Mackays of Chatham PLC, Chatham, Kent

ISBN 0 85459 473-6

FOREWORD

By Peter Morgan
Director General of the Institute of Directors

In 1985 the Companies Acts were consolidated into one Act. This consolidation meant that company law was slightly easier to follow than it had been for many years. However, the Companies Act 1989, which represents a major piece of legislation, has made the task of reading, let alone interpreting, company law extremely complex.

Ascertaining which provisions of Company Law now apply to a group's annual report and accounts is a major headache. The position becomes even worse when you try to decipher how accounting standards fit in with the legislation, especially where they seem to conflict. Barry Johnson and Matthew Patient must be congratulated at making eminent sense of what is an accounting and legal minefield. Their clear explanations of the accounting provisions of the Companies Acts and of the innumerable other accounting principles and practices adopted by companies show their breadth of experience and knowledge in this technically complicated area.

The accounting and legal world is becoming more regulated each year and it is difficult for the best of finance directors and accountants to keep abreast of the changes. Consequently, a major work like this is to be commended and the authors informed comment and examples taken from published accounts make what is invariably a dry subject come alive.

'Manual of Accounting' is a major reference work and is an extremely useful comprehensive explanatory text, exploring all aspects of UK GAAP. I am therefore only too pleased to commend it to its readers, as I know they will find it invaluable.

Peter Morgan

May 1990

PREFACE

'Manual of Accounting' is the second (much revised) edition of our very successful book on accounting disclosure and measurement, which was previously entitled 'Accounting Provisions of the Companies Act 1985'. This time, we have published in three volumes. The first two volumes cover similar material to that dealt with in our previous edition, but much expanded. Volume I looks primarily at individual companies, whereas volume II deals with groups (and includes many of the provisions that stem from the Companies Act 1989). Volume III considers the varied accounting and disclosure requirements that apply to a number of specialised businesses.

Both volumes I and II give detailed explanations of the accounting provisions of the Companies Acts 1985 and 1989. They also refer throughout to the additional reporting requirements that limited companies have to comply with and that are set out in Statements of Standard Accounting Practice (including exposure drafts) and The International Stock Exchange's Continuing Obligations for listed companies and its General Undertaking for USM companies. The text of volumes I and II includes worked examples and extracts from published financial statements. The financial reporting provisions and Schedules to the Companies Act 1985 (as amended by the Companies Act 1989) are reproduced in the two volumes. The appendices include detailed checklists to those disclosure requirements that apply to company's and to group's financial statements and volume I includes a model set of financial statements.

Volume III is an introduction to the accounting requirements of a number of specialised businesses such as friendly societies, unlimited companies and banking companies. It considers how such entities are incorporated, the different statutes and regulations that apply to them, their filing responsibilities, the accounting requirements that apply to their financial statements and any requirements for audit.

The three volumes of 'Manual of Accounting' also include practical advice and comment we have gained through our work for the Technical Support Section of Coopers & Lybrand Deloitte in advising the Firm's clients, partners and staff.

We hope that finance directors, accountants, legal practitioners, company administrators, financial advisers and auditors will find this manual useful.

We thank Mary Arden, QC (our legal consultant) for her advice once again on the legal content of volumes I and II.

We offer our special thanks to Jyoti Ghosh for his considerable contribution in researching, drafting and checking much of the text. We also thank Eddie Hodgson for his invaluable, voluminous and amusing review comments and William Carver for his contribution and other members of the department for their helpful comments and advice.

Barry Johnson & Matthew Patient

Coopers & Lybrand Deloitte
London
May 1990

CONTENTS

ABBREVIATIONS AND TERMS USED

accounts	=	financial statements.
the Act/the 1985 Act	=	the Companies Act 1985 (as amended by the Companies Act 1989).
the 1989 Act	=	the Companies Act 1989.
ACT	=	advance corporation tax.
AER	=	All England Law Reports.
APC	=	Auditing Practices Committee.
ASC	=	Accounting Standards Committee.
BCLC	=	Butterworths Company Law Cases
CACA	=	Chartered Association of Certified accountants.
CCAB	=	Consultative Committee of Accountancy Bodies Limited.
CC(CP)	=	Companies Consolidation (Consequential Provisions) Act 1985.
Ch	=	Law Reports, Chancery Division.
chapter (1)	=	'Manual of accounting - companies' volume I, chapter (1).
CIMA	=	Chartered Institute of Management Accountants.
CIPFA	=	Chartered Institute of Public Finance and Accountancy.
Cmnd	=	Command Paper.
CO	=	Continuing Obligations, Section 5 of the 'Admission of Securities to listing'.
DP	=	Discussion paper.
EC	=	European Community.
ECU	=	European currency unit.
ED	=	exposure draft.
financial statements	=	accounts.
the 4th Directive	=	EC 4th Directive on Company Law.
GAAP	=	Generally accepted accounting principles (and practices).
GU	=	General Undertaking of the Unlisted Securities Market.
IAS	=	International Accounting Standard.
IAS	=	International Accounting Standards Committee.

ICAEW	=	Institute of Chartered Accountants in England and Wales.
ICAI	=	Institute of Chartered Accountants in Ireland.
ICAS	=	Institute of Chartered Accountants of Scotland.
ICR	=	Industrial Cases Reports.
MR	=	Master of the Rolls.
NASDQ system	=	National Association of Securities Dealers Automated Quotation System.
para(s)	=	paragraph(s) of Schedules to the Companies Acts, or SSAPs, or EDs, or DPs, or text.
QC	=	Queen's Counsel.
RGD	=	Regional development grant.
SC	=	Session Cases
Sch	=	Schedule to the Companies Act 1985 (as amended by the Companies Act 1989) (4 Sch 85 = Schedule 4, paragraph 85).
Sec(s)	=	Section(s) of the 1985 Act (as amended by the Companies Act 1989).
s	=	section of another Act.
SI	=	statutory instrument.
SOI	=	Statement of Intent.
SORP	=	Statement of Recommended Practice.
SSAP	=	Statement of Standard Accounting practice.
TR	=	Technical release.
UK	=	United Kingdom.
US	=	United States of America
USM	=	Unlisted Securities Market.
VAT	=	value added tax.
volume II, chapter (1)	=	'Manual of accounting - groups' volume II, chapter (1).
volume III, chapter (1)	=	'Manual of accounting - specialised businesses', volume III, chapter (1).
WLR	=	Weekly Law Reports.
Yellowbook	=	The International Stock Exchange's 'Admission of Securities to Listing'.

Chapter 1

INTRODUCTION

INTRODUCTION

Manual of accounting

1.1 This 'Manual of Accounting' is the first of three volumes covering many aspects of accounting in the United Kingdom (UK). The books not only cover the accounting provisions included in company law, but also deal with other accounting principles and practices that concern each different entity considered. Each volume covers different aspects of accounting in the UK, and their titles are as follows:

- Manual of Accounting - volume I - Companies.
- Manual of Accounting - volume II - Groups.
- Manual of Accounting - volume III - Specialised businesses.

1.2 This volume of the 'Manual of Accounting' deals primarily, as its title suggests, with the provisions of the Acts that apply to individual companies' financial statements. However, many of these provisions are equally applicable to groups of companies and in certain areas the different rules that apply specifically to groups are also explained.

1.3 Volume II of the manual of accounting concerns groups of companies and the accounting provisions that apply to them. Consequently, that volume considers in detail the requirements for consolidated financial statements which are included in the Companies Act 1989. This legislation, for the most part, reflects existing accounting standards or best practice concerning the preparation of, and the disclosure made in, consolidated financial statement. However, the Companies Act 1989 does make a number of other important changes (for example, the changes to the definitions of subsidiary companies) and these are also dealt with.

1.4 Furthermore, during 1990 the Companies Acts 1985 and 1989 are to be further supplemented by various statutory instruments (SIs). These will relate *inter alia* to the following matters:

- Schedule 6 of the Companies Act 1985, which concerns the disclosure of directors' loans and transactions, is due to be rewritten.
- The Overseas (Accounts) (Modifications and Exemptions) Order 1982 (SI 1982/676), has been rewritten. The SI's provisions have

not altered significantly. This particular SI is considered in 'Manual of Accounting - volume III'

- A new SI to allow listed companies to send summary financial statements of their shareholders. (This SI is considered in 'Manual of Accounting - volume II'.)

- A new SI to require the disclosure of non-audit fees.

- A further SI to deal with other sundry matters stemming from the enactment of the Companies Act 1989.

1.5 These changes to company law are expected to be relatively minor in relation to the totality of accounting provisions included in current legislation. However, it is necessary to bear in mind that there may be additional regulations passed since the publication of this book that have a bearing on particular matters discussed in it.

EC company law harmonisation

1.6 By 1990, the UK had included a substantial number of European Community (EC) Company Law Directives on its statute books. The major directives included in UK legislation are as follows:

- 1st Directive - Publicity requirements, ultra vires and nullity.

- 2nd Directive - Formation of companies and dividend requirements.

- 3rd Directive - Mergers.

- 4th Directive - Company accounts.

- Directive on listing particulars.

- Directive on continuing disclosure of information.

- 6th Directive - 'Scissions'.

- 7th Directive - Group accounts.

- 8th Directive - Auditors.

1.7 The Companies Act 1989 introduced into legislation the latter two directives. A copy of the 4th Directive is included as appendix VIII and a copy of the 7th Directive is included as appendix II to 'Manual of Accounting - volume II'. A summary of EC company law directives and their status in March 1990 is given in appendix III. This appendix also indicates where the directives mentioned above are enacted in UK company law.

1.8 The EC company law harmonisation programme is still far from complete and will continue for many years. As a consequence, the Companies Acts 1985 and 1989 will be further amended and supplemented when further EC Directives are implemented in the UK.

The Companies Act 1989

1.9 The Companies Act 1989 received Royal Assent on 16th November 1989. A major proportion of that Act implements the 7th and 8th Directives. In addition, there were a number of changes made to accounting provisions already dealt with in the Companies Act 1985. The Companies Act 1989 also amended other statutes including, the Fair Trading Act 1973 and the Financial Services Act 1986.

1.10 In order to make the changes to the accounting provisions required to comply with the 7th Directive, Parliament has in Part I of the Companies Act 1989 effectively re-enacted Part VII of the Companies Act 1985. Most of the changes to the Companies Act 1985 are of a minor nature and do not alter greatly existing law, but a few other amendments do introduce substantial changes and these are referred to in detail in the text of this book.

Commencement

1.11 The provisions of the Companies Act 1989 come into force at varying dates during 1990 and 1991. The main accounting provisions were brought into force by The Companies Act 1989 (Commencement No. 4) Order 1990 (SI 1990/355) with effect from 1st April 1990 and apply to accounting periods starting on or after 23rd December 1989. There are a number of transitional provisions that apply to companies' accounting periods that begin before 23rd December 1989 where they have not filed their statutory financial statements by 1st April 1990. Basically, these companies may prepare their financial statements under the accounting provisions set out in the old Part VII of the Companies Act 1985. However, certain provisions of Part I of the Companies Act 1989 also apply, but so as not to affect the content of the financial statements prepared under the old Part VII. Reference should be made to the SI to determine the full extent of the provisions that apply during the transitional period.

1.12 In addition, the commencement order No. 4 includes a number of other provisions of a transitional nature that apply to both the disclosure requirements and the accounting requirements of the Companies Act 1989 (for example, how to determine, for disclosure purposes, the gross amount of goodwill written off in a company).

These transitional provisions are mentioned where applicable in the text of volumes I and II of 'Manual of Accounting'. In cases of doubt, reference should be made to the SI.

The accounting provisions of the Act

1.13 Throughout the 'Manual of Accounting' reference is made to 'the Act'. Such references, unless otherwise stated, are to the Companies Act 1985. As explained above, all of the accounting provisions included in the Companies Act 1989 are substitutions and amendments to the Companies Act 1985. The Companies Act 1985 is split into 27 parts. A summary of these together with the arrangement of sections found in the Act is given on pages 731 to 750. Pages 751 to 946 include a reproduction of the accounting provisions of the Act relating to companies that are considered in this volume of 'Manual of Accounting'. The reproduction is a consolidated version of the Companies Act 1985 as amended by the Companies Act 1989. Volume II of 'Manual of Accounting' includes a reproduction of the accounting provisions of the Act that relate to groups, again amended to include the changes made by the Companies Act 1989.

1.14 This volume deals in particular with the following parts of the Companies Act 1985:

- Part V - Share capital, its increase, maintenance and reduction. (Chapter III of Part V of the Act - Share premiums is considered in 'Manual of Accounting - volume II' chapter 9.)

- Part VII - Accounts and audit. This includes provisions that apply to the financial statements of companies generally. (Provisions that apply to groups are considered in 'Manual of Accounting - volume II' and those that apply to the financial statements of banking and insurance companies are dealt with in 'Manual of Accounting - volume III'.)

- Part VIII - Distribution of profits and assets.

- Part X - Enforcement of fair dealing by directors.

- Schedule 4 - Form and content of company accounts.

- Schedule 5 - Disclosure of information: related undertakings.

- Schedule 6 - Disclosure of information: emoluments and other benefits of directors and others.

- Schedule 7 - Matters to be included in directors' reports.

- Schedule 8 - Exemptions for small and medium-sized companies.

- Schedule 24 - Punishment of offences under the Act. (Those sections that relate to the accounting provisions of the Act are reproduced in appendix IV.)

1.15 The book follows, in general, the order of the accounting provisions in the Act. The Schedules to the Act are introduced (where necessary) into the text when they apply to the provisions of the Act that are being considered.

Other generally accepted accounting principles and practices

1.16 In addition to explaining the accounting provisions of the Companies Acts, the 'Manual of Accounting' summarises also, where appropriate, the other provisions of Generally Accepted Accounting Principles (GAAP) in the UK that are contained in Accounting Standards, exposure drafts, The International Stock Exchange's Continuing Obligations (which apply to listed companies) and The International Stock Exchange's General Undertaking (which applies to companies traded on the Unlisted Securities Market (USM)). A full list of the accounting standards and exposure drafts considered in 'Manual of Accounting' are given in appendix IX of this volume.

1.17 Furthermore, 'Manual of Accounting' also mentions other generally accepted accounting practices that are not covered in specific provisions of the legislation or other accounting regulations, but that are still considered as part of UK GAAP. Consequently, this book serves as a practical guide to applying the accounting provisions of all the major regulations that companies have to consider when they prepare their annual financial statements. Appendix I includes a detailed checklist to the measurement and disclosure requirements that make up UK GAAP and apply to a company's financial statements. A similar checklist that applies to other matters that relate specifically to consolidated financial statements can be found in appendix I to volume II. Volume I also includes a model set of consolidated financial statements for GAAP UK plc (see appendix II).

1.18 'Manual of Accounting' also includes practical comment based on advice given by the Technical Support Group of Coopers & Lybrand Deloitte to the Firm's partners, staff and clients. In order to illustrate matters relating to presentation and disclosure in company financial statements, it includes also extracts from the published financial statements of various companies.

Scope of this book

1.19 Unless otherwise stated, the provisions examined in this book apply to those companies that are defined in section 735 of the Act. The definition in section 735 embraces companies registered under either the Act or a former Companies Act, with an exception for certain Irish companies.

1.20 Companies may be either limited or unlimited. A 'limited' company is a company in which the members' liability is limited by shares or by guarantee. [Sec 1(2)(a)(b)]. An 'unlimited' company is a company that does not limit its members' liability. [Sec 1(2)(c)]. Many of the provisions of this book apply to companies limited by guarantee and to unlimited companies. However, these two types of company are considered further in 'Manual of Accounting - volume III'.

1.21 Limited companies may be either public or private. A 'public' company (plc) is a company limited by shares (or, if incorporated before 22nd December 1980, by guarantee and having a share capital) where its memorandum states that it is a public company. Such a company must also be registered as a public company, and, before it can do business or exercise any borrowing power, it must satisfy the statutory requirements as to its authorised minimum share capital. [Sec 1(3)(4), 117,118]. The current 'authorised minimum' share capital that such a company is required to allot before it can do business or exercise any borrowing power is £50,000, of which a quarter of the nominal value (plus the whole of any premium) has to be paid up. [Sec 118].

1.22 A private company is any company that is not a public company. [Sec 1(3)]. The text of this book draws attention to those requirements of the Act that differ for public companies and private companies respectively.

Chapter 2

ACCOUNTING RECORDS AND REFERENCE PERIODS

Chapter 2

ACCOUNTING RECORDS AND REFERENCE PERIODS

Introduction

2.1 A company must ensure that it keeps proper accounting records. [Sec 221(1)]. A company's directors are under an obligation to present to the company's members, once a year, the company's annual financial statements. [Sec 241(1)]. Those financial statements must include a profit and loss account for the financial year, together with a balance sheet prepared as at the last day of the financial year. [Sec 226(1)(3)]. Schedule 4 to the Companies Act 1985 lays down detailed rules that companies must follow in preparing their financial statements, and Schedule 4A provides the rules for group accounts. The rules in Schedule 4A are considered in detail in 'Manual of Accounting - volume II'. Companies will have to consider also other rules that are contained in SSAPs and in other authoritative accounting statements (for example, SORPs and EDs). In addition, if a company is listed on The International Stock Exchange, it will have to consider the rules outlined in the Continuing Obligations. Similarly, if the company's shares are traded on The International Stock Exchange's USM, it will have to comply with that market's General Undertaking. The accounting records should be sufficient to enable the directors to prepare financial statements that comply with all these rules.

2.2 Furthermore, there may be other legislation that specifies the way in which particular companies should keep their accounting records. For example:

- The Housing Act 1980 gives the Secretary of State power to prescribe accounting requirements for registered housing associations. The Secretary of State took advantage of this provision and imposed certain accounting requirements in the Registered Housing Associations (Accounting Requirements) Order 1982 (SI 1982/828), as amended by SI 1988/395. Housing associations have to comply with these requirements in order to ensure that their financial statements give a true and fair view.

- The Insurance Brokers (Registration) Act 1977 requires all insurance brokers to maintain accounting records that comply with the Insurance Brokers Registration Council (Accounts and Business Requirements) Rules Approval Order 1979 [SI 1979/489] (as amended by the Insurance Brokers Registration Council

(Accounts and Business Requirements) (Amendment) Rules Approval Order 1981 [SI 1981/1630].

2.3 This chapter considers the Act's requirements that relate to keeping proper accounting records, the place where those records should be kept, and the period for which they should be retained. It considers also the responsibilities both of a company's directors and of its auditors, and finally it discusses the accounting period that a company's financial statements must cover.

Accounting records

The requirement to keep proper accounting records

2.4 The requirement that every company shall keep proper accounting records is contained in section 221(1) of the Act. Counsel's interpretation of the meaning of certain words and phrases included in section 221, and shown in italics below, is explained in paragraph 2.6 below. This section of the Act states that the accounting records must be sufficient to show and explain the company's transactions and, consequently, to:

- *Disclose* with reasonable accuracy the company's *financial position at any time*.
- Enable the directors to ensure that any balance sheet and profit and loss account prepared from the *accounting records* comply with the requirements of the Act.

[Sec 221(1)].

2.5 A company's accounting records should detail the following:

- The sums of money the company received and expended on a day-to-day basis, together with explanations of the amounts it received and expended. [Sec 221(2)(a)].
- A record of the assets and liabilities of the company. [Sec 221(2)(b)].
- If the company deals in goods:
  - □ *Statements of stocks* the company held at the financial year end, together with supporting statements of stocktakes.
  - □ *Statements of all goods sold and purchased* by the company, in sufficient detail to enable the goods and the buyers and sellers to be identified. (This requirement, however, does not apply to companies carrying on retail trades.) [Sec 221(3)].

Counsel's opinion on proper accounting records

2.6 Section 221 of the Act derives from section 12 of the Companies Act 1976. The APC took Counsel's opinion on the interpretation of parts of section 12 and published it in 'True and Fair' (Issue No. 6, Winter 1977/78). The interpretation below is based on that opinion and applies equally to section 221 of the 1985 Act, as amended.

- 'Disclose'. The records a company maintains must disclose the basic information from which the financial position can be ascertained. This does not mean that the financial position needs to be displayed in the accounting records after each transaction has been recorded. It does mean, however, that the information from which a statement of the financial position can be prepared is available.

- 'Financial position at any time'. The Act clearly recognises that it is not practicable to draw up financial statements giving a 'true and fair' view of the state of affairs and of the results (as is required to be disclosed in annual financial statements) at any time during the year. However, the Act does require that directors should have available to them an adequate statement at any time of the company's financial position.

  Section 221 seems to indicate that directors should be in a position to prepare, with reasonable accuracy, a statement showing tangible assets, liabilities and pre-tax results at any selected date. Although a company would need to establish its stocks figure to prepare pre-tax results, the Act does not necessarily require that the company undertakes a physical stocktake or maintains continuous stock records. (This is a matter for the directors to decide on, and their decision would depend on the company's particular circumstances.) It appears that a company may estimate the results in any of the following three ways:

  - By applying gross profit margins to sales to arrive at the cost of sales.

  - By maintaining detailed records of the cost of sales.

  - By maintaining detailed stock records to enable a stock valuation to be performed at any time.

- 'Accounting records'. These records need not be in the form of a book. They could, for example, be in a loose leaf binder, or on computer disks or, for prime entry items, in a secure clip of invoices with an add-list attached. The information recorded should be organised and labelled. (A carrier-bag full of invoices is not sufficient.)

- 'Day-to-day'. Clearly, transactions cannot be recorded instantaneously. What is necessary is that, when the entries are made, each transaction should be shown separately and be identified by its date and an explanation of the matter to which it relates. With retail shops, a record of the day's total cash takings will probably suffice.

- 'A record of the assets and liabilities'. The records must include details of all the company's assets and liabilities (such as debtors, creditors and plant and machinery). There is no specific requirement that these records should be updated on a day-to-day basis, but the accounting records should show separately the assets and the liabilities of the company at any particular time. The records must be updated at frequent intervals. They must also contain details of the dates on which assets are acquired and disposed of, and of the dates on which liabilities are incurred and discharged. (Stocks are, however, excluded from these requirements.)

- 'Statements of stocks'. This term is taken to mean a summary supporting the amount included in the financial statements in respect of the stocks held at each financial year end. Also, stocktaking records that support the year-end stocks summary must be retained. The Act imposes an obligation for companies to retain documentation supporting year-end stock valuations, but it allows them considerable flexibility in meeting the requirement to disclose the financial position 'at any time' (see the second point above).

- 'Statements of all goods sold and purchased'. The intention of the Act appears to be to ensure that the substance of transactions is properly recorded. With products where the identity of each individual item of the product is irrelevant to the seller and the purchaser, only the product type of each item is relevant, and it is not necessary for each particular item to be identified. In practical terms, the identity of the seller and the purchaser will normally be available from the purchase and sales ledgers.

Directors' duty to account properly

2.7 The ICAEW issued a technical release (TR 723) in October 1988 that provides guidance on the main duties and responsibilities, particularly of a financial or accounting nature, that directors owe to their company and its shareholders and others. The guidance provided in TR 723 has been incorporated in section 1.401 'Financial and accounting responsibilities of directors' in the ICAEW Members' Handbook.

2.8 This statement sets out what is considered to be best practice rather than what may be acceptable as the legal minimum. It has a section that deals with books of account and other accounting records. The statement gives the following guidance:

> *"In addition to the statutory requirement to keep proper accounting records, the directors have an overriding responsibility to ensure that they have adequate information to enable them to discharge their duty to manage the company's business."*

2.9 A company's normal books of account would include:

- Cash books.
- Sales day book.
- Sales returns book.
- Purchase day book.
- Purchase returns book.
- Creditors ledger.
- Debtors ledger.
- Transfer journal.
- General ledger.

2.10 These books may be retained in book form, or on computer or in any other suitable readable form. Other books of account may be used to assist directors in the preparation of management accounts. These may include stock books to record continuous stock records used in a company's costing systems.

Auditors' duties

2.11 In addition to the requirement that a company must keep proper accounting records, the company has a duty to appoint an auditor, and those auditors must examine any financial statements of the company laid before it in general meeting. They must also report to the members on those financial statements. [Sec 235(1)].

2.12 The auditors have a right of access at all times to the company's accounting records. They also have a right to require such information and explanations from the company's officers as they believe they need in order to form an opinion on those financial statements. [Sec 389A]. In addition, the auditors have a duty to carry out investigations that will enable them to form an opinion both on whether the company has kept proper accounting records, and on whether they have received proper returns adequate for their audit from those branches they did not visit. [Sec 237(1)(a)]. They should also ensure that the company's financial statements are in agreement with the accounting records. [Sec 237(1)(b)]. If the company has not kept proper accounting records (including returns from branches), or if the financial statements are not in agreement with those records, then the auditors must state this fact in their report. [Sec 237(2)]. The Auditing Standard 'The audit report', issued in March 1989, gives examples of audit reports qualified where proper accounting records are not kept.

The place where records are to be kept

2.13 A company must keep its accounting records either at its registered office or at such other place as the directors think fit. The records have to be available for inspection by the company's officers at all times. [Sec 222(1)]. For this purpose, an officer includes a director, or a manager, or the company secretary. [Sec 744].

2.14 If the accounting records are kept outside Great Britain, then accounts and returns must be sent to an appropriate place in Great Britain (for example, the registered office), where they should be available for inspection at all times. [Sec 222(2)]. These accounts and returns should reflect the transactions recorded in the accounting records and disclose the company's financial position at intervals not exceeding six months. They should also enable the directors to ensure that the company's financial statements comply with the form and the content of company financial statements set out in the Act. [Sec 222(2)(3)].

2.15 The requirements as regards accounts and returns to be returned to Great Britain pose no problem for most of the companies that have branches overseas, because their overseas entities will usually return management accounts to Great Britain at regular intervals (normally, monthly). These management accounts will generally satisfy the requirements of section 222(3).

The period of retention of records

2.16 The Act requires that a private company should keep its accounting records for three years from the date when they are prepared and a public company should keep its accounting records for six years. However, where a company is being wound up, this requirement is subject to any provision with respect to the disposal of records that may be contained in the insolvency rules made under section 411 of the Insolvency Act 1986. [Sec 222(5)].

2.17 The period for which companies should keep their accounting records is governed also by various other statutes. These include the Limitation Act 1980, the Latent Damages Act 1986, the Taxes Management Act 1970, and the VAT regulations. These may affect the retention of accounting records in the following ways:

- Limitation Act 1980. The Limitation Act limits the time period during which an action can be brought as follows:

  - An action on a simple (non specialty) contract or in tort (other than in respect of personal injuries) - six years from the date when the cause of the action arose.

  - An action on a contract under seal (specialty contracts) - 12 years from the date when the cause of the action arose.

  - A judgment debt - barred after six years.

  - Interest on a judgment debt - not recoverable more than six years after the date on which it accrued due.

- The Latent Damages Act 1986. The Latent Damages Act amended the Limitation Act 1980 by stating that the overriding time limit for actions for negligence (other than in respect of personal injuries) is 15 years from the occurrence of any act or omission in question.

- Taxes Management Act 1970. The Inland Revenue may generally assess within six years of the chargeable period. But where there is fraudulent or negligent conduct, the period is 20 years. The Taxes Management Act contains two further rules that may be relevant:

  - Production of accounts, books and other information. The Inland Revenue may serve notice and require a company to deliver any documents within the company's possession or power that contain, or may contain, information relevant to, or to the amount of, any tax liability.

  - Time limit for recovery of penalties. Recovery of penalties may be commenced at any time within six years after the date on which the penalty was incurred or at any later time within three years after the final determination of the amount of tax by reference to which the amount of the penalty is to be ascertained.

- VAT regulations. Those companies that are registered for VAT must keep their records and accounts and other related documents for a period of six years. These documents must be open to inspection by H.M. Customs and Excise at all times.

2.18 Consequently, the period of time for which a company should keep its accounting records depends primarily on the type of document involved. As a general rule, most accounting records should be kept for a period of at least six years.

2.19 Further guidance is available in the Accountants Digest number 205, entitled 'Business documents - Management and retention'.

2.20 To overcome the problems of storing accounting records, many companies now microfilm them, and some store them in digital form. For VAT purposes, the Customs and Excise accepts records stored on microfilm, microfiche, and other modes of digital storage. However, prior clearance should be obtained from the Customs and Excise where a company intends to store accounting records in this way. The Customs and Excise would also require the company to provide it with adequate viewing facilities.

2.21 In court proceedings, a court will normally require the production of the original document. However, where the original document is not available, a court will accept other evidence of the document.

2.22 Consequently, before a company destroys any documents that it has microfilmed or stored in digital form, it should consider very carefully whether it should retain the original document. It should remember that certain transactions (for example, a property lease) must be evidenced in writing and, therefore, it should not destroy the original document. Also, before a company destroys any accounting records, it should consult its auditors about whether the microfilmed or digitally stored records will provide them with sufficient audit evidence. The auditors will also want to satisfy themselves that the company imposes adequate controls over the microfilming process.

Penalties for not keeping proper accounting records

2.23 If a company does not keep proper accounting records as required by sections 221 and 222, or does not keep accounts or returns as required by section 222(2), every officer in default will be guilty of an offence and liable to imprisonment or a fine, or both. However, if the officer can show that he acted honestly, and that the default, was excusable in the circumstances in which the company's business was carried on, he will not be guilty of the offence. [Sec 221(5), 222(4) - see appendix IV].

2.24 Similarly, where a director, or a manager or the company secretary fails to take all reasonable steps to ensure that the company keeps these accounting records for the required period, or intentionally causes any default by the company in observing this obligation, he will be guilty of an offence and liable to imprisonment or a fine, or both. [Sec 222 (6) - see appendix IV].

2.25 Failure to keep proper accounting records may be attributable to negligence, incompetence or poor administration. In some cases, there may be fraudulent intent.

2.26 Sections 15 to 17 of the Theft Act 1968 impose penalties for obtaining property by deception and false accounting. Section 18 provides that where a company has committed an offence under section 15, 16 or 17 with the consent or connivance of any director or other officer, he, as well as the company, will be criminally liable. Also, section 19 makes it a criminal offence for any officer of a company to publish, with intent to deceive the company's members or creditors, any written statement or account that he knows is false on a material point.

2.27 In this connection, any document has to be regarded as a whole. Moreover, even though each part of a statement is strictly true, that statement may be false on material points if, by reason of what is omitted from it, it conveys a false impression of the company's position.

The Data Protection Act 1984

2.28 The Data Protection Act has provided individuals with the right to inspect their personal data held on computer systems or other automatic processing systems, and to have that information corrected if necessary.This legislation is, therefore, an important influence on the information companies retain in their accounting records.

2.29 The Act seeks to ensure that personal data is:

- Obtained and processed fairly and lawfully.
- Held only for specified and lawful purposes.
- Not used or disclosed in a manner incompatible with the specified purposes.
- Adequate, relevant and not excessive in relation to specified purposes.
- Accurate and up to date.
- Not retained longer than necessary.

- Available for inspection and correction by the data subject.

  A data subject is an individual who is the subject of personal data. The individual need not be a UK resident. People in business on their own account, however, are individuals and therefore can be data subjects. A company cannot be a data subject because it is not an individual.

- Secure against unauthorised access, or disclosure or destruction.

2.30 The Data Protection Registrar is able to issue notices ordering compliance with the principles of the Data Protection Act, or if necessary to suspend processing or restrict the transfer of data outside the UK. The Registrar possesses limited powers of access to buildings to examine data, and in certain circumstances, to confiscate data.

2.31 This legislation impacts on each company that registers under it in different ways, depending on the type of records kept on computer, and thus it is essential that professional advice is obtained before registration and subsequently, when the records kept on computer are changed.

Accounting reference periods

The requirement to notify the Registrar of Companies

2.32 Within nine months of being incorporated, a company must notify the Registrar of Companies (using Form 224) of the date that it wishes to treat as the date when its accounting reference period comes to an end each year. [Sec 224(2)]. If a company does not give notice of this accounting reference date to the Registrar of Companies within nine months of being incorporated, then, by default, its accounting reference date will become the end of the month in which its anniversary of incorporation falls. If it was incorporated before the commencement of Part 1 of the Companies Act 1989 its accounting reference date will be 31st March, unless the company has registered a different date. [Sec 224(3)].

2.33 A company's first accounting reference period starts on the date of incorporation and ends on the accounting reference date. But the period must not be less than six months and must not exceed 18 months (see also para 2.42). [Sec 224(4)]. Each subsequent accounting reference period will be for 12 months. It will start on the day after the end of the previous accounting reference period and will end with the next accounting reference date. [Sec 224(5)].

2.34 A company's financial statements will cover the period that begins with the first accounting day of the reference period and ends on either one of the following two dates:

- The date on which the accounting reference period ends.
- Another date determined by the directors that is not more than seven days before or after the end of that period.

[Sec 223(3)].

2.35 The date a company chooses for its accounting reference date in the first year after incorporation can alter the accounting requirements considerably. The following two examples illustrate this:

Example 1

Company A is incorporated on 1st January 1991 and the company **did not** inform the Registrar of Companies of an accounting reference date by 30th September 1991. The company's accounting reference period, therefore, starts on the date of incorporation (that is, 1st January 1991), and it is deemed to end 13 months later on 31st January 1992 (see para 2.32). [Sec 224(3)].

Example 2

Company B is incorporated on 1st January 1991 and the company **did** inform the Registrar of Companies by 30th September 1991 that its accounting reference date is to be 31st August. Its first accounting reference period starts on the date of incorporation (that is, 1st January 1991), and it ends eight months later on 31st August 1991. The next accounting reference period is for 12 months, and it ends on 31st August 1992 (see para 2.33). [Sec 224(4)(5)].

2.36 As soon as possible after it is incorporated, a company should decide on a date that it wishes to treat as its accounting year end, and it should inform the Registrar of Companies within the nine-month period allowed. The company should choose the date that is most convenient for it. For example, it should consider carefully the tax implications and also the peak workloads that the business may create (especially in a seasonal business), because it may be inconvenient to have to draw up financial statements at such a time. Unless a company wishes to change its accounting reference date, it is not required to make any further notifications to the Registrar of Companies.

2.37 Although a company's first accounting reference period should not be less than six months, it is possible to have a shorter period. The procedure for achieving a shorter reference period is illustrated in paragraph 2.42 below.

Alteration of accounting reference periods

2.38 A company may, at any time during its accounting reference period, give notice (using Form 225(1) or (2)) to the Registrar of Companies that it wishes to alter its accounting reference date. [Sec 225(1)(2)]. The notice may have the effect of either extending or shortening the current reference period, but a company cannot extend its reference period so as to exceed 18 months, unless an Administration Order is in force under Part II of the Insolvency Act 1986. [Sec 225(6)].

2.39 Consequently, the notice must explicitly specify whether the accounting reference period is to be shortened or lengthened. [Sec 225(3)]. It should be noted, however, that where a company informs the Registrar of Companies of its intention to change its accounting reference date *after* the end of an accounting reference period, the notice of change of the accounting reference date will have effect only where one of the following apply:

- The company is a subsidiary undertaking or a parent undertaking of another undertaking, and the new accounting reference date coincides with the accounting reference date of that other company. [Sec 225(2)(a)]. Furthermore, the period allowed by section 244 of the Act for laying and delivering financial statements (that is, ten months for a private company and seven months for a public company, from the end of the accounting reference period) by reference to the existing accounting reference date must not already have expired at the time the company gives notice. [Sec 225(5)].

- An Administration Order under Part II of the Insolvency Act 1986 is in force. [Sec 225(2)(b)].

2.40 In addition, where the effect of the notice is to extend the accounting reference period this will be allowed only where one of the following applies:

- More than five years has elapsed since an earlier accounting reference period was extended by virtue of section 225.

- The company is a subsidiary undertaking or a parent undertaking of another company, and the new accounting reference date coincides with that of the other company.

- An administration order is in force under Part II of the Insolvency Act 1986.

[Sec 225(4)].

The Secretary of State may waive these conditions.

2.41 The timing of the notice a company gives to the Registrar of Companies of a change in its accounting reference date is crucial to the acceptance of that new date. Consider the following example:

Example

A private company's accounting reference date is 31st December. The company last completed and filed its financial statements for the 12 month period ended 31st December 1987. On 31st October 1989, the company informs the Registrar of Companies that it wishes to change its accounting reference date to 30th June. It can do this only if it is a parent undertaking or a subsidiary of another undertaking of the company, and it is changing its accounting reference date to coincide with the accounting reference date of that other company, or an Administration Order under Part II of the Insolvency Act 1986 is in force.

The company may appear to have two choices: it may either lengthen its accounting reference period and prepare financial statements for the 18 month period to 30th June 1989, or it may shorten its accounting reference period and prepare financial statements for the 6 month period to 30th June 1988. However, if it does the latter, the company will be overdue in filing its financial statements by six months, because, by 31st October 1989, it will be 16 months after the end of its new accounting reference period. This would be an offence under section 242 of the Act and so this option should not be used.

If the facts in the example given above remained the same, except that the company gave notice of the change of accounting reference date to the Registrar of Companies on 1st November 1989, then this notice would not take effect. The reason for this is that the period for filing on the basis of the existing accounting reference date (that is, 31st December 1988), would have already expired (see point 3 in para 2.39).

2.42 As stated in paragraph 2.33 above, a company's first accounting reference period cannot be less than six months. However, it is possible for the company to initially set a longer period and then reduce it by giving notice to the Registrar of Companies under section 225(1). The procedure is illustrated in the following example:

Example

Company C is incorporated on 1st March 1990, and informs the Registrar of Companies, within nine months from date of incorporation, that it wants its first accounting reference period to end on 31st January 1991, 11 months later. It then decides that seasonal factors require an accounting reference date of 31st May. The company may, at any time within the period to 31st January 1991, give notice to the Registrar of Companies that it wishes to alter its accounting reference date to end on 31st May 1990, which gives a reference period of three months.

Chapter 3

ACCOUNTING AND AUDITING PRINCIPLES AND RULES

Chapter 3

ACCOUNTING AND AUDITING PRINCIPLES AND RULES

Introduction

3.1 When companies prepare their annual financial statements, they must comply with a substantial number of accounting principles, rules and regulations. All individual companies' financial statements must comply with the accounting provisions of Schedule 4 to the Companies Act 1985 as to their form and content. [Sec 226(3)]. This applies whatever a company's status (public or private, limited or unlimited) may be. The accounting provisions of the Companies Act 1985 have been increased considerably by the Companies Act 1989. In particular, the Companies Act 1989 introduced a new Schedule 4A that deals exclusively with the form and content of consolidated financial statements. The requirements concerning consolidated financial statements are considered in detail in 'Manual of Accounting - volume II'.

3.2 Companies must also comply with *generally accepted accounting principles* in the UK. These encompass not only the requirements of the Companies Act, but also SSAPs and SORPs and The International Stock Exchange's requirements for listed and USM companies and any other acceptable accounting treatments not included in the official literature. Compliance with generally accepted accounting principles stems from the fundamental need for financial statements to give a true and fair view (see paras 3.9 to 3.12).

3.3 The Act does not define the term 'generally accepted accounting principles' (GAAP), but references are included in section 262(3) (definition of realised profits and realised losses), in Schedule 4A paragraph 2(1) (consolidation adjustments) and paragraph 10(d) (adoption of the merger method of accounting). In addition, the Companies Act 1989 introduced a new requirement for all companies to state whether the financial statements have been prepared in accordance with applicable Accounting Standards and to give particulars of any departures and the reasons for it (see also paras 3.13 to 3.23). [4 Sch 36A].

3.4 Those public limited companies that are listed on The International Stock Exchange have to comply also with the accounting disclosure requirements that are set out mainly in the Continuing Obligations, section 5, chapter 2, paragraphs 20 to 22. Similarly, companies that are traded on the USM have to comply with the disclosure requirements that are set out in the General Undertaking, paragraph 10.

3.5 SSAPs and SORPs are developed by the ASC of the CCAB and are issued by the six governing bodies (ICAEW, ICAS, ICAI, CIMA, CACA and CIPFA). A SORP (that is, a Statement of Recommended Practice) is developed when there is a need for a pronouncement on a specific topic, but when that topic does not require an Accounting Standard. Unlike SSAPs, SORPs are not mandatory, but companies are encouraged to comply with the recommendations contained therein. SSAPs and SORPs are authoritative statements on best accounting practice that aim to narrow the areas of difference and variety in the accounting treatment of the matters they deal with. In addition, a further type of statement, a Franked SORP, provides guidance on best accounting practice in specialised industries. A list of current SSAPs, SORPs, Franked SORPs, and EDs is given in appendix IX. These statements generally apply to all limited companies (see further para 3.13).

3.6 In addition to SSAPs and SORPs, each professional body issues, from time to time, other statements on accounting matters that form part of UK GAAP.

3.7 The auditors must state in their audit report whether, in their opinion, the financial statements have been properly prepared in accordance with the Act. [Sec 235(2)]. The Act also imposes a duty on the auditor to report on the directors' failure to note any departure from applicable Accounting Standards (see further para 3.51). Furthermore, they have a duty, imposed by Auditing Standards, to draw attention in their report to material departures, with which they do not concur, from the requirements of SSAPs (see paras 3.54 to 3.58).

3.8 The first part of this chapter considers the Act's basic requirement that a company's financial statements must give a true and fair view. It also considers the way in which this requirement interacts with the requirement that the financial statements should comply with SSAPs. The chapter goes on to consider some of the more general accounting principles that apply equally to both the historical cost accounting rules and the alternative accounting rules (discussed further in chapters 4 and 5 respectively). Finally, it considers the auditors' duties when reporting on a company's or group's financial statements.

True and fair view

3.9 There is an overriding requirement that all financial statements drawn up under the Act must give a true and fair view. [Sec 226(2)]. Where, however, compliance with the disclosure provisions of the Act (including Schedule 4) would not be sufficient to give a true and fair view, then additional information should be given in the notes to the financial statements. [Sec 226(4)]. This additional information needs to be of sufficient detail to ensure that its disclosure enables the financial statements to give a true and fair view.

3.10 There is a further provision concerning the true and fair view, which provides that if in 'special circumstances' compliance with any of the Act's provisions would be inconsistent with the requirement to give a true and fair view, the directors of the company must depart from that provision to the extent necessary to give a true and fair view. Where such a departure is necessary, the particulars of the departure, the reasons for it and its effect should be given in a note to the financial statements. [Sec 226(5)]. Table 1 illustrates such a departure in respect of investment properties.

Table 1: Illustration of a company that has departed from the statutory accounting rules in order to give a true and fair view.

Extract from Stanhope Properties PLC Report and Accounts 30th June 1989.

Accounting policies extract

Investment properties

In accordance with SSAP19, (i) completed investment properties are revalued annually and the aggregate surplus or deficit is transferred to a revaluation reserve, and (ii) no depreciation or amortisation is provided in respect of freehold and long leasehold investment properties; the directors considering that this accounting policy, which represents a departure from statutory principles, is necessary to provide a true and fair view.

Properties in the course of development are stated at cost less provisions for any permanent diminution in value. Interest and other outgoings attributable to the developments are capitalised in the cost of the properties until the latter are effectivley completed, substantially let and income producing, whereupon they are reclassified as completed investment properties.

3.11 These requirements differ from those that operated before the enactment of the Companies Act 1989. Formerly the financial statements could depart from any of the specific requirements of the Act only if, even with the disclosure of additional information, a true and fair view could not be given. Under the new legislation, departure from any of the specific provisions of the Act will be allowed, but only in special circumstances, if compliance with the Act would be inconsistent with the obligation to give a true and fair view. This means that the true and fair override as provided in section 226(5) can be invoked in special circumstances without having to demonstrate first that a true and fair view cannot be achieved by providing additional disclosure in the notes.

3.12 What is meant by the term 'special circumstances' is not clear, because it is not defined in the Act. Special circumstances are probably most likely to occur where the form and content of financial statements do not reflect adequately the substance of the company's transactions (for example, off balance sheet financing or debt factoring).

Application of Accounting Standards

3.13 The question then arises as to what is meant by a 'true and fair view'. In particular, there is the question of whether the requirement that all financial statements should give a true and fair view includes compliance with the relevant SSAPs. True and fair is a legal concept that can only be interpreted by the courts.

Counsel's opinion on Accounting Standards and 'true and fair'

3.14 The above issues were discussed in the joint opinion the ASC obtained in 1983 from Leonard Hoffmann Q.C. and Mary Arden reproduced in full in appendix V, together with a similar opinion on 'true and fair' that the ICAS obtained from J.A.D. Hope Q.C. of the Scottish bar.

3.15 To obtain a full understanding of Counsel's arguments, the opinions should be read in their entirety. However, the opinions make the following important points:

- The application of the 'true and fair view' involves judgement in terms of degree. There may sometimes be room for differences of opinion over the method to adopt to give a true and fair view. Because questions of degree are involved when a company is deciding on how much information is sufficient to make its financial statements true and fair, it may take account of *(inter alia)* cost effectiveness.

- It is for the court to decide whether the financial statements give a true and fair view in compliance with the Act. But the courts will look for guidance to the ordinary practices of accountants. This is principally because the financial statements will not be true and fair unless the quality and quantity of the information they contain is sufficient to satisfy their readers' reasonable expectations. Those expectations will have been moulded by accountants' practices.

- SSAPs have a two-fold value to the court. First, they constitute an important statement of professional opinion. Secondly, because accountants are professionally obliged to comply with SSAPs, the readers of financial statements expect those statements to conform with the prescribed standards. Departure from a SSAP without adequate explanation may, therefore, result in the financial statements not giving a true and fair view.

- Consequently, the courts will treat compliance with generally accepted accounting principles as *prima facie* evidence that the financial statements are true and fair, and deviations from accepted principles will be *prima facie* evidence that they are not true and fair. These presumptions will be either strengthened or weakened by the extent to which the SSAP is accepted and applied in practice. A SSAP has no direct legal effect, but it will have an indirect effect on the interpretation the courts give to the 'true and fair' concept.

- The fact that Accounting Standards can change over time does not alter the effect they have on the true and fair view. The concept of 'true and fair view' is dynamic.

3.16 The above views are also supported in the judgment given by Woolf J in *Lloyd Cheyham & Co Ltd v Littlejohn & Co* [1987] BCLC 303 in which he stated that:

> *"While they (SSAPs) are not conclusive, so that a departure from their terms necessarily involves a breach of the duty of care, and they are not as the explanatory foreword makes clear, rigid rules, they are very strong evidence as to what is the proper standard which should be adopted and unless there is some justification, a departure from this will be regarded as constituting a breach of duty."*

The Dearing proposals

3.17 In November 1987, the Consultative Committee of Accountancy Bodies (the CCAB) appointed a Review Committee under the chairmanship of Sir Ron Dearing to review and make recommendations on the standard-setting process. The terms of reference were to consider, *inter alia*, the status of Accounting Standards in relation to company law and the procedures for monitoring compliance with standards and their enforcement.

3.18 In discharge of that remit, the Review Committee in their report (the Dearing Report) submitted to the CCAB in September 1988 stated that Accounting Standards should remain, as far as possible, the responsibility of auditors, preparers and users of accounts and there should not be a general move towards incorporating them into law. But in the discharge of the Government's responsibility to facilitate the effective working of the systems of published financial reporting, it should introduce legislation along the following lines:

- For all large companies, directors should be required to state in the notes to the financial statements whether they are drawn up in accordance with applicable Accounting Standards and to draw attention to any material departures, explaining the reasons for the departures.

- There should be a new statutory power under civil law for certain authorised bodies or the Secretary of State to apply to the courts for an order requiring the revision of financial statements that do not give a true and fair view.

- A small levy should be added to the fees paid by all companies to the Companies Registration Office to assist meeting the cost of setting and monitoring standards.

3.19 In addition, the Committee recommended that the task of devising Accounting Standards should be discharged by a newly constituted, expert Accounting Standards Board that would issue standards on its own authority. A Financial Reporting Council should be created that would provide guidance to the Accounting Standards Board on priorities for its work programme and on issues of public interest, and would act as an instrument for promoting good practice in relation to Accounting Standards. In securing compliance with Accounting Standards in support of the 'true and fair' requirement, the Committee recommended establishing a Review Panel to examine contentious departures from Accounting Standards by large companies.

The Companies Act 1989 requirements

3.20 The legislative changes necessary to bring the above recommendations of the Review Committee into effect have been implemented by the Companies Act 1989. Paragraph 36A of Schedule 4 to the Act now requires all companies to state whether the financial statements have been prepared in accordance with applicable Accounting Standards and to give the particulars and reasons for any material departures but not to state the amount or the financial effect of the departure. However, auditors have a duty under the second Auditing Standard to disclose any departures from Accounting Standards that do not have their support (see further para 3.52). It should be noted that The International Stock Exchange's Continuing Obligations require a listed company's directors to give, in the company's financial statements, the reasons for any departure from an applicable SSAP. [CO 21(a)]. This requirement is also found in The International Stock Exchange's General Undertaking for USM companies. [GU 10(a)].

3.21 The obligation to give a true and fair view means that a company should follow any applicable Accounting Standards unless there are good reasons not to do so. 'Accounting Standards' in the Act refers specially to statements of standard accounting practice issued by a body or bodies as may be prescribed by legislation. [Sec 256(1)]. 'Applicable Accounting Standards' means such standards that are, in accordance with their terms, relevant to the company's circumstances and to their financial statements. [Sec 256(2)].

3.22 In providing a framework for the implementation of the Dearing Committee proposals for an independent Accounting Standards Board overseen by a Financial Reporting Council and backed up by a Review Panel, the Act gives the Secretary of State power to make grants to such bodies concerning:

- Issuing Accounting Standards.
- Overseeing and directing the issue of such standards.
- Investigating departures from such standards or from the accounting requirements of the Act and taking steps to secure compliance with them.

[Sec 256(3)].

3.23 In addition, the Companies Act 1989 introduced new procedures enabling directors voluntarily to revise financial statements which are discovered to be defective. [Sec 245]. Further enabling provisions permit the Secretary of State to improve the enforcement of accounting provisions by requiring an explanation from directors of apparent failures to prepare financial statements that comply with the Act. [Sec 245A(1)]. If a satisfactory explanation is not received, the Secretary of State may apply to the court for a declaration that a company's financial statements do not comply with the Act and to order them to be revised. [Sec 245A(3)]. The provisions of the Act relating to the revisions of defective financial statements are dealt with in detail in chapter 25.

Accounting principles and rules included in company law

3.24 Many of the accounting principles and rules that are included in SSAPs appear also in Part II of Schedule 4 to the Act and Schedule 4A.

3.25 Part II of Schedule 4 is divided into three sections:

- Accounting principles. This section covers the fundamental accounting concepts, and they are discussed in paragraphs 3.27 to 3.45 below.
- Historical cost accounting rules. This section covers accounting bases, specific accounting rules, depreciation and amounts necessary to write down cost to a lower net realisable value. These are discussed in chapter 4.

- Alternative accounting rules. This section deals with the accounting treatment of items where the accounting rules applied are designed to take account, in some way, of either inflation or other fluctuations in value (such as the change in a property's value). These are discussed in chapter 5.

3.26 Schedule 4A deals exclusively with the provisions concerning group accounts. The Schedule covers, *inter alia*, the elimination of group transactions, acquisition and merger accounting, the treatment of minority interests, interests of subsidiary undertakings excluded from consolidation, and the consolidation of joint ventures and associated companies. Group accounts are covered in 'Manual of Accounting - volume II'.

Accounting concepts

3.27 SSAP 2 sets out the four fundamental accounting concepts that underlie the preparation of financial statements. These consist of the going concern concept, the consistency concept, the prudence concept and the accruals concept. These, together with a fifth concept that requires assets and liabilities to be valued separately, are reproduced in the Act as the 'accounting principles'. In certain circumstances, however, the economic substance of transactions should be recognised rather than their legal form in a company's financial statements in order to give a true and fair view. The concept of 'Substance over form' is considered in paragraph 3.45 below.

3.28 A company's directors are permitted to depart from any of the accounting concepts where there are special reasons to do so. If they do so, however, the notes to the financial statements must give particulars of the departure, the directors' reasons for it, and its effect. [4 Sch 15].

The going concern concept

3.29 When a company prepares its financial statements, it uses the presumption that it is carrying on business as a going concern. [4 Sch 10]. Of course, this is merely a presumption, and as such it can be rebutted. It would have to be rebutted, for example, if the company were on the brink of being wound up.

3.30 The importance of the going concern concept relates to the bases a company uses to arrive at the amounts at which it states items in the balance sheet. For example, fixed assets are (in effect) valued on the basis of how useful they are to the business as a going concern. If, however, the business is not a going concern, the fixed assets should be valued at their 'break-up' value.

3.31 The following example illustrates this:

Example

A company that manufactures a particular children's toy has the following fixed assets:

	Cost	Depn	Net book value	Break-up value
	£000	£000	£000	£000
Factory buildings	500	25	475	350
Plant and machinery	150	75	75	10
	650	100	550	360

The net book value of the fixed assets is £550,000, whereas their break-up value is £360,000. This difference results from two facts. First, in order to adapt the factory from its present use to a different use, it would need to be altered considerably. Secondly, the plant and machinery would have only a scrap value if the company ceased to manufacture the toy.

So long as the company is a going concern, the financial statements will properly reflect the fixed assets at their net book value of £550,000. If, however, the company ran into severe financial difficulty (so that it could no longer be regarded as a going concern), the fixed assets would have to be written down to their break-up value of £360,000. Therefore, in order to reflect the fact that the company could no longer be regarded as a going concern, there would need to be a provision of £190,000 to reduce the amount at which the fixed assets were stated in the balance sheet.

3.32 With most companies, if the presumption that the company is a going concern is rebutted, it would have a considerable effect. In addition to having to make possible provisions against the book value of fixed and current assets, the company would need to make provision for other costs such as redundancy payments, dilapidations and guarantees.

3.33 In a few situations, the effect of ceasing to regard the business as a going concern may be negligible. The question then arises as to whether the financial statements need to disclose that the company is no longer carrying on business as a going concern. Unless there is a statement to the contrary, the Act allows a reader to *presume* that the company is carrying on business as a going concern. Consequently, where necessary, the company should state that it has prepared its financial statements on a break-up basis, even if the effect of doing so has not been significant.

The consistency concept

3.34 In preparing its financial statements, a company must apply accounting policies consistently within the same financial statements and from one financial year to the next. [4 Sch 11]. Without this rule, it would be difficult to ensure comparability from year to year, or to prevent companies manipulating their results. This is because it is possible for a company to increase or decrease its reported profit merely by changing its accounting policies.

3.35 There are, of course, circumstances where a change of accounting policy is justified. For example, consider a company that has formerly had insignificant development expenditure, which it has always written off at the time the expenditure was incurred. If the company, as a matter of policy, determined to embark on a large-scale programme of research and development, and if the amounts involved were material, it might then decide to defer as much of the development expenditure as it is permitted to defer. Provided that the company satisfies the separate rules that relate to the capitalisation of development expenditure set out in chapter 7, the Act permits the company to change its accounting policy accordingly. SSAP 6 permits a change in accounting policy only if it can be justified on the grounds that the new policy is preferable to the one it replaces because it will give a fairer presentation of the results and of the financial position of the business. [SSAP 6 para 18].

The prudence concept

3.36 A company must use a prudent basis in determining the amount of any item that it includes in its financial statements. [4 Sch 12]. The Act specifies two particular rules in relation to this. The first is that the profit and loss account may include only those profits that have been realised at the balance sheet date. [4 Sch 12(a)]. This means that profits may not be anticipated, and so they should be included only when they are earned. For this purpose, realised profits are defined as:

> *"Such profits or losses of the company as fall to be treated as realised in accordance with principles generally accepted, at the time when the accounts are prepared, with respect to the determination for accounting purposes of realised profits or losses."* [Sec 262(3)].

3.37 A company must determine whether a profit or a loss is realised or unrealised in the light of best accounting practice at the time. In accordance with SSAP 2, 'realised' effectively means realised in the form either of cash or of other assets, whose ultimate cash realisation can be assessed with reasonable certainty. An example of an accounting principle contained in an Accounting Standard (which is the one that is applied in practice and, therefore, 'generally accepted') is taking profits on long-term contracts (which is required subject to certain conditions by SSAP 9). Without this definition of realised profits, such amounts could not be included in the profit and loss account. The concepts of 'realised' and 'distributable' profits are considered further in chapter 19.

3.38 The second rule that the Act specifies in connection with the prudence concept relates to liabilities and losses. A company must take account of all liabilities and losses that either have already arisen, or are likely to arise, in respect of either the financial year in question or a previous financial year. Moreover, they must be included even when they become apparent only in the period between the balance sheet date and the date on which the directors sign the financial statements. [4 Sch 12(b)]. This means, for example, that if a major debtor becomes insolvent after the balance sheet date, and if the directors have not already signed the financial statements in accordance with section 233 of the Act, the resulting loss must be reflected in the financial statements. SSAP 17 specifically requires the disclosure of the date on which the financial statements are approved and signed by the directors (see further chapter 25 para 25.7).

The accruals concept

3.39 The financial statements must reflect all income and expenditure that relate to the financial year in question. This applies irrespective of the dates on which amounts fall due to be received or paid. [4 Sch 13]. The effect of this is that if income and expenditure relate to the current year, they must be accrued in the financial statements. The resulting difference must be shown as either an accrual or a prepayment.

3.40 The Act is silent as to what happens where the accruals concept is inconsistent with the prudence concept, such as where significant uncertainties exist over a possible accrual, as can occur with revenue recognition. SSAP 2, however, makes it quite clear that, in that circumstance, the prudence concept prevails.

The separate valuation of assets and liabilities

3.41 When a company is determining the aggregate amount of any item, it must determine separately the amount of each individual asset or liability that makes up that item. [4 Sch 14]. Although this rule is not described in SSAP 2 as a fundamental accounting concept, it has always been inherent in good accounting practice.

3.42 The treatment of investments is a good example of the separate valuation principle, although the general principle applies equally to other items such as stocks. Those investments that are treated as fixed assets will normally be accounted for at cost, less write-downs for any permanent decrease in value. Before the implementation of the separate valuation rules in the Companies Act 1981, investments (and particularly those in subsidiaries) were often considered as a whole. If one investment had a market value that was less than book value, and all the other investments had an excess of market value over book value that more than compensated, then investments as a whole were not overstated at book value. Usually, a company made no provision against the one overstated investment.

3.43 However, under the 1985 Act, investments have to be considered individually. By law, a provision must be made against an investment if there is a permanent decrease in value below cost. This applies irrespective of the value and the quality of the other investments.

3.44 The only statutory exception to the separate valuation rule is that tangible assets and raw materials and consumables may, in certain circumstances, be included in the financial statements at a fixed quantity and value (see chapter 4 paras 4.39 and 4.40). [4 Sch 25(1)]. In addition, there is a further exception, in that, where there is a legal right of set-off, assets and liabilities may be netted (see chapter 10).

Substance over form

3.45 Accounting for transactions according to their substance rather than their legal form was first adopted in SSAP 21 'Accounting for leases and hire purchase contracts', which capitalised assets held under finance leases rather than just charge lease payments to the profit and loss account. Since then the significance of substance over form for the purposes of arriving at the true and fair view has been recognised more fully, with ED 42 'Special purpose transactions' advocating much greater disclosure and recognition of items in financial statements. ED 42 considered that the need to account for a transaction in accordance with its substance is central to the concept of 'true and fair', so that the accounting effect of the transaction is consistent with its commercial effect. 'Substance over form' or as ED 42 describes it 'Accounting for substance' is not however as yet a fundamental accounting concept and is, therefore, not mentioned in SSAP 2. Mention of this concept is made in the text that follows where the substance of a transaction is relevant to its accounting treatment.

Auditors' duties under the Act

3.46 Every company formed or registered under the Act or its predecessor Acts (except a private company that has passed an elective resolution in accordance with section 379A or a dormant company that has passed a special resolution not to do so) is under an obligation to appoint auditors at each general meeting at which the company's financial statements are presented. The auditors then hold office from the end of that meeting until the end of the next general meeting at which the company's financial statements are presented. [Sec 385(2)].

3.47 The company's auditors are required to report on any financial statements presented at a general meeting. [Sec 235(1)]. Their report has to state whether, in their opinion, the annual financial statements have been properly prepared in accordance with the Act, and in particular whether a true and fair view is given:

- For an individual balance sheet, of the state of affairs of the company as at the end of the financial year.
- For an individual profit and loss account, of the profit and loss of the company for the financial year.
- For consolidated financial statements, of the state of affairs as at the end of the financial year, and the profit or loss for the financial year, of the undertakings included in the consolidation as a whole, so far as concerns members of the company.

[Sec 235(2)].

3.48 The auditors' duties are contained in section 237 of the Act. The auditors have a duty, *inter alia,* to consider whether:

- The company has kept proper accounting records.
- Proper returns adequate for their audit from those branches they did not visit have been received.
- The financial statements they are auditing are in agreement with the accounting records and returns.

3.49 The auditors must report if they are not satisfied that the above requirements have been complied with. [Sec 237(2)]. These duties are discussed further in chapter 2, paragraphs 2.11 to 2.12 .

3.50 In addition, the Act requires the auditors to disclose in their report (so far as they are reasonably able to do so) certain information where that information has not been disclosed elsewhere in the financial statements. This information is as follows:

- The chairman's and the directors' emoluments, pensions and compensation for loss of office (as required by Schedule 6, Part I - see chapter 17).
- Loans and other transactions favouring directors and officers (as required by Schedule 6, Parts II to III - see chapters 21 and 22).

[Sec 237(4)].

Auditors' duties in relation to Accounting Standards

3.51 The auditors' duties in relation to Accounting Standards stem from the application of paragraph 36A of Schedule 4 (see para 3.20).

Paragraph 36A requires the company's directors to state in the notes to the financial statements whether they are drawn up in accordance with applicable Accounting Standards and to draw attention to any material departures, explaining the reasons for the departures. Failure to note a departure will result in the financial statements not complying with Schedule 4. Where a company has not complied with a SSAP, and the directors fail to give the particulars of the departure and the reasons for it in the financial statements, the auditors have a duty to draw attention to this non-compliance in their audit report. This applies irrespective of whether or not the auditor concurs with the departure.

3.52 The explanatory foreword to the SSAPs says that Accounting Standards are authoritative statements on accounting practice, and are approved by the CCAB member Councils. The CCAB member Councils expect their members, who assume responsibilities in respect of financial statements, to observe Accounting Standards. Accordingly, the Councils consider that where members prepare company financial statements, and they find it necessary to depart from applicable Accounting Standards, they should ensure that they disclose the departure and adequately explain it in those financial statements. Unless it would be impracticable or misleading in the context of giving a *true and fair view,* the member should ensure that the company estimates and discloses the financial effect of such a departure.

3.53 In addition, the onus is on the auditors or reporting accountants not only to ensure that any significant departure is disclosed, but also (to the extent that their own concurrence with that departure is either stated or implied) to justify such a departure from any applicable SSAP.

Auditors' duties imposed by Auditing Standards

3.54 Other duties and obligations that auditors must follow are contained in the Auditing Standards and Guidelines. Auditing Standards and Guidelines are developed by the APC, a committee of the CCAB, and are then issued by the councils of five of the governing bodies (that is, the six CCAB bodies excluding CIMA). Members of these bodies that carry out audits must have regard to these Standards in their work. The explanatory foreword to the Auditing Standards and Guidelines explains their scope and authority.

3.55 The foreword says that:

> *"...an 'audit' is the independent examination of, and expression of an opinion on, the financial statements of an enterprise. ....Unless the relevant Auditing Standard or Auditing Guideline indicates to the contrary, the term 'audit' applies:*

a) where there is a statutory requirement for the auditor to express an opinion in terms of whether the financial statements give a true and fair view (for example, audits under the Companies Acts or the Industrial and Provident Societies' Acts);

b) where there is a statutory requirement for the auditor to express an opinion in terms other than whether the financial statements give a true and fair view (for example, audits of government departments or local authorities); and

c) where the terms and scope of the engagement are agreed between the auditor and his client (for example, the audit of a sole trader or partnership) or where they are specified in a legal document (for example, a trust deed)."

3.56 Auditing Standards prescribe the basic principles and practices that members of the bodies of the CCAB are expected to follow when conducting an audit. In observing those standards, the auditor must exercise his judgement both in determining the audit procedures he needs to perform in the circumstances to afford a reasonable basis for his opinion and in determining the wording of his report.

3.57 The second Auditing Standard, 'The audit report', has the following to say about the expression 'true and fair view':

"When expressing an opinion on the financial statements in true and fair or equivalent terms, the auditor should be satisfied , inter alia, that the accounting policies adopted:
(a) are appropriate to the circumstances of the enterprise;
(b) have been consistently applied; and
(c) have been adequately disclosed.

In determining whether the accounting policies are appropriate the auditor should have regard to Statements of Standard Accounting Practice (SSAPs) or any other relevant accounting requirements. In cases where SSAPs apply but there have been departures from their requirements the auditor should have regard to paragraphs 8 and 11 of the Explanatory Foreword to Accounting Standards, which state:

8 'Significant departures from Accounting Standards should be disclosed and explained in the financial statements. The financial effects of such departures should be estimated and disclosed unless this would be impracticable or misleading in the context of giving a true and fair view. If the financial effects of any such departure are not disclosed, the reasons for such non-disclosure should be stated.'

11 *'Where members act as auditors or reporting accountants, they should be in a position to justify significant departures to the extent that their concurrence with the departures is stated or implied. They are not, however, required to refer in their report to departures with which they concur, provided that adequate disclosure has been made in the notes to the financial statements.'"*

3.58 Consequently, the auditors not only have to report that a company's financial statements comply with the Act, but also have to report where those statements do not comply with a relevant SSAP and no disclosure complying with paragraph 36A of Schedule 4 has been made.

Chapter 4

HISTORICAL COST ACCOUNTING RULES

Chapter 4

HISTORICAL COST ACCOUNTING RULES

Introduction

4.1 Companies normally determine the amounts they include in their financial statements in accordance with the historical cost accounting rules. But the Act also permits companies to use certain alternative accounting rules, and these are discussed in chapter 5.

4.2 Paragraphs 16 to 28 of Schedule 4 set out the rules companies must apply in arriving at the amounts at which they must disclose items in their financial statements. These rules cover:

- Fixed assets.
- Current assets.
- Purchase price and production cost of assets.
- Other items.

Each of these is discussed in detail below.

Fixed assets

4.3 The basic rule is that fixed assets are to be shown at either their purchase price or their production cost (see paras 4.22 to 4.27), less any provision for depreciation or diminution in value. [4 Sch 17]. For this purpose, a fixed asset is defined as any asset that is *"intended for use on a continuing basis in the company's activities"*. [Sec 262(1)]. Fixed assets include intangible assets, tangible assets and fixed asset investments.

Depreciation and diminution in value

4.4 Where a fixed asset has a limited useful economic life, a company must write off its purchase price or its production cost less its estimated residual value, if any, systematically over the period of that life. [4 Sch 18]. Although depreciation is not defined in the Act, it is defined in SSAP 12 as *"a measure of the wearing out, consumption or other reduction in the useful economic life of a fixed asset whether arising from use, effluxion of time or obsolescence through technological or market changes"*. [SSAP 12 para 10]. Depreciation is not necessarily intended to result in a company setting aside funds to replace an asset at the end of its useful economic life, but, coincidentally, that may be the result.

4.5 In determining the amount to be written off each asset (other than goodwill) each year, the Act (and also SSAP 12) specifically requires companies to take account of the asset's estimated residual value at the end of its useful economic life. [4 Sch 18(b)]. 'Useful economic life' is defined in SSAP 12 as *"the period over which the present owner will derive economic benefits from* [the asset's] *use"*. [SSAP 12 para 11]. The calculation of depreciation and amortisation is discussed further in chapter 8.

4.6 A company must make provision if *any* fixed asset (including a fixed asset investment) has diminished in value, and this reduction is expected to be permanent. In such a situation, the company must reduce the amount at which it discloses the asset in its financial statements by the amount of this diminution in value. This requirement applies whether or not the asset has a limited useful economic life. [4 Sch 19(2)]. This accords with the treatment required by paragraph 19 of SSAP 12, which says that if, at any time, the directors consider an asset's unamortised cost not to be recoverable in full, the company should write the asset down immediately to its estimated recoverable amount.

4.7 In addition, where a fixed asset *investment* has suffered a diminution in value that the directors consider to be only *temporary*, the Act permits the company to make provision in respect of that diminution in value. Accordingly, it permits it to reduce the amount at which the investment is disclosed in its financial statements. [4 Sch 19(1)]. It should be stressed that this provision is permissive not mandatory. The Act imposes no obligation on a company to make such provision, but it may do so if the directors think it prudent. There is no equivalent provision for a temporary diminution in value of a fixed asset other than an investment (see further chapter 5).

4.8 It may be difficult for a company to determine whether an asset's fall in value is permanent or a temporary or, indeed, whether it has suffered *any* fall in value. For example, as regards its investments, a company will have to consider such matters as the net asset value, liquidity, changes in the nature of the business, future trading difficulties, and other such factors. It may also take advice from stockbrokers and other advisers. On the other hand, it may be easier for a company to determine whether a tangible fixed asset not an investment has suffered a fall in value and, if so, whether that fall is likely to be temporary or permanent. For example, if a machine will not again generate income, the company should write it down to its net realisable value, because any decrease in value to the business will be permanent.

4.9 Where a company has made provision for a diminution in value, but the factors that gave rise to it no longer apply to any extent, then the company must write back the provision to that extent. [4 Sch 19(3)].

4.10 To illustrate these provisions, consider the following example:

Example

The history of a company's fixed assets is as follows:

	Fixed asset investment £000	Tangible fixed asset £000
Cost at 1st January 1989	10	6
Value at 31st December 1991	8	5
Value at 31st December 1992	5*	3*
Value at 31st December 1993	9	4

*Only these reductions in value are expected at the time to be permanent.

Ignoring the normal depreciation rules for the purposes of this example, The Act applies as follows:

- ☐ At 31st December 1991, the directors **could** (if they wish) write down the amount of the fixed asset investment to £8,000. (However, they could not write down the value of the tangible fixed asset to £5,000. This is because the Act allows tangible fixed assets to be written down in value only in circumstances where the diminution in value is expected to be **permanent**.)

- ☐ At 31st December 1992, the directors must write down the amount of the fixed asset investment to £5,000 (whether or not they wrote it down to £8,000 at 31st December 1991). In addition, they **must** write down the value of the tangible fixed asset to £3,000. This is because the fall in value of each of them is expected to be **permanent**.

- ☐ At 31st December 1993, the directors must write back £4,000 in respect of the fixed asset investment and £1,000 in respect of the tangible fixed asset. This is because the reasons that gave rise to the provision for diminution in value of each of them have ceased to apply to that extent.

4.11 Where a company has made any provision for diminution in value, or has written back any provision for diminution in value, it must disclose the amounts involved (either in the profit and loss account or in the notes to the financial statements). [4 Sch 19]. The amounts to be disclosed are:

- Provisions made in respect of the permanent diminution in value of fixed assets (see para 4.6). [4 Sch 19(2)].

- Provisions made in respect of the temporary diminution in value of fixed asset investments (see para 4.7). [4 Sch 19(1)].

- Amounts written back to the extent that the circumstances that gave rise to the provisions no longer apply (see para 4.9). [4 Sch 19(3)].

4.12 The amounts disclosed must be split between these three headings as stated in paragraph 4.11 above, but amounts that fall within the same heading may be aggregated. [4 Sch 19]. To illustrate this, consider the following example:

Example

In the financial year in question, the following events occurred:

- ☐ The company wrote down a building by £15,000 and a machine by £7,000, because they had both fallen in value and the fall was expected to be permanent.
- ☐ The company wrote down an investment in a subsidiary company and a long-term investment by £20,000 and £5,000 respectively, because they had temporarily fallen in value.
- ☐ The company wrote back to cost an overseas investment that it had previously written down by £3,000, because the circumstances that gave rise to the previous write-down had ceased to apply.

4.13 In such circumstances, the aggregate amounts the company must disclose are:

(a) Provisions made in respect of a **permanent** fall in value of fixed assets	£22,000
(b) Provisions made in respect of a **temporary** fall in value of fixed asset investments	£25,000
(c) Write-back of provisions no longer required	£3,000

The amounts in (a) and (b) may not be aggregated together or reduced by the amount in (c).

Other depreciation rules

4.14 SSAP 12 contains two further rules that relate to depreciation. First, where an asset's estimated useful life has been revised, the standard states that normally there will be no material distortion of future results if the asset's unamortised cost is written off over the revised remaining useful life. [SSAP 12 para 18].

4.15 For example, a company purchased an asset on 1st January 1986 for £100,000, and the asset had an estimated useful life of ten years and a residual value of nil. The company has charged depreciation using the straight-line method at £10,000 per annum. On 1st January 1990, when the asset's net book value is £60,000, the directors review the estimated life and decide that the asset will only be useful for a further four years and, therefore, the total life is revised down to eight years. Where the adjustment does not have a material effect on future results, the company should amend the annual depreciation charge to charge the unamortised cost (namely, £60,000) over the revised remaining life of four years. Consequently, it should charge depreciation for the next four years at £15,000 per annum.

4.16 Where, however, the future results would be materially distorted, an adjustment to accumulated depreciation should be made in accordance with SSAP 6. Referring to the example above, the adjustment to accumulated depreciation that should be made for 1990 is £10,000, which is calculated as follows:

Cumulative depreciation to 1st January 1990 (8 year life) =	£50,000
Cumulative depreciation to 1st January 1990 (10 year life) =	£40,000
Adjustment to accumulated depreciation for 1990	£10,000
Current year's charge for 1990	£12,500

In the remaining three years, the depreciation charge in arriving at profit on ordinary activities will be £12,500 each year.

4.17 The adjustment will normally be made in arriving at profit on ordinary activities. It will only be treated as an extraordinary item if it is derived from an extraordinary event. In addition, the nature and amount of the adjustment should be disclosed in the company's financial statements. [SSAP 12 para 18].

4.18 Secondly, if there is a change from one *method* of providing depreciation to another, the unamortised cost of the asset should be written off over the remaining useful life on the new basis, commencing with the period in which the change is made. A change from one method of providing depreciation to another is permitted only if the new method will give a fairer presentation of the enterprise's results and financial position. A change of method does not constitute a change of accounting policy. [SSAP 12 para 21].

4.19 Consequently, in the example given above, the company may decide that, from 1st January 1990, the sum-of-the-digits method of calculation would give a fairer presentation than the straight-line method. If so, the depreciation charge for 1990 would be £24,000 (namely, £60,000 x 4/(4+3+2+1)), because the asset still has a remaining useful life of four years. SSAP 12 states that where the effect of the change is material, it should be disclosed in the year of change. Furthermore, the reasons for the change should also be disclosed. [SSAP 12 para 26]. Such an alteration is not considered a change in accounting policy and, therefore, a prior-year adjustment is not permissible.

Current assets

4.20 In general, current assets are to be shown at the lower of purchase price or production cost (see paras 4.22 to 4.38) and net realisable value. [4 Sch 22, 23(1)]. For example, debtors should be stated after any provision for bad and doubtful debts. For this purpose, current assets are defined as any assets that are not intended for use on a continuing basis in a company's activities. [Sec 262(1)].

4.21 Where a company has written down the value of a current asset to its net realisable value, but the circumstances that gave rise to the write-down cease to apply to any extent (that is, the net realisable value becomes greater than the amount that the asset was written down to), the company must write back the amount of the write-down to that extent. [4 Sch 23(2)]. This means that even where an asset regains only part of its value, the company must write it back to that extent.

Purchase price and production cost of assets

General rule

4.22 The Act sets out detailed definitions of an asset's purchase price and production cost.

4.23 Purchase price is defined as the actual price the company paid for the asset (whether the consideration was in cash or otherwise), plus any expenses that were incidental to its acquisition. [4 Sch 26(1)]. These incidental expenses include, for example, the expenses that the company had to incur in order to get the asset to its present location and into its present condition.

4.24 Production cost is defined as the total of the following amounts:

- The purchase price of the raw materials and consumables the company used in producing the asset.

- The direct costs of production the company incurred (excluding distribution costs in the case of current assets).

- The following other costs that may be included are as follows:

  - ☐ A reasonable proportion of indirect overheads, to the extent that they relate to the period of production.

- ☐ Interest on any capital the company borrowed in order to finance the production of that asset, to the extent that it relates to the period of production. Where such interest has been included in the production cost, the fact that it has been included and its amount must be stated in the notes to the financial statements.

[4 Sch 26(2)-(4)].

4.25 These provisions of the Act are largely consistent with the provisions of SSAP 9 on stocks and long-term contracts. However, with stocks, SSAP 9 *requires* the valuation to include a reasonable proportion of production overheads, whereas the Act merely *permits* it. Therefore, to comply with SSAP 9, companies should take up the option in the Act.

4.26 The Act states that *"in the case of current assets distribution costs may not be included in production costs"*. [4 Sch 26(4)]. A company should not include external distribution costs such as those relating to the transfer of goods from a sales depot to an external customer. It may however include a proportion of the costs that a company incurs in distributing goods from its factory to its sales depot in the valuation. SSAP 9 requires that the costs the company incurs in bringing the goods to their present location and condition should be included in the stocks valuation.

4.27 When determining the purchase price or the production cost of their stocks and other fungible items, companies may apply special rules. These rules are considered in chapter 10.

Inclusion of interest in purchase price or production cost

4.28 The rise in interest rates and the increased use of borrowed funds in recent years, together with the rules for determining the purchase price or the production cost, have caused companies to reconsider the way in which they treat their borrowing costs. Views differ on what the appropriate accounting treatment should be. Some regard such costs as forming part of the cost of the particular asset with which they can be either directly or indirectly identified. Others regard them as essentially period costs that should be charged to income regardless of how the borrowing is applied. As mentioned in paragraph 4.24 above, the Act permits both views.

4.29 The Chartered Association of Certified Accountants published a discussion document in 1983 entitled 'Accounting treatment of capitalised interest', by C.P. Rickwood. The document covers five issues that are relevant to capitalisation of interest, which are listed below:

- That future net benefits are expected to cover any interest capitalised. This is consistent with the principle of matching as any interest carried forward will be expensed in the future period or periods expected to benefit.

- That the interest cost must have a necessary connection with the project (for example, money must have been borrowed to finance the asset). Therefore, interest incurred on money borrowed to finance the acquisition of an asset is regarded as being no different from any other costs associated with the acquisition of the asset.

- That during the period of interest capitalisation there has been continuing activity on the project. Inactivity on the project would indicate that the money borrowed to finance it is being used for some other purpose and, therefore, the related interest charge is no longer a project related cost. Identifying the end of a period of capitalisation is considered in paragraph 4.30 below.

- That there must have been a significant period in which the asset is held prior to its use or its sale, This condition implies that interest costs are a necessary part of the cost of the asset and hence a production input.

- That both the interest impact on the asset, and the time period involved, must be material to the asset and the business. Assets for which only a short time lag occurs between the commitment of funds and full availability of the asset would not warrant interest capitalisation, unless the funds involved were very large in terms of the size of the particular business.

4.30 The period allowed for interest capitalisation would be the time over which the activity on the asset continues. No capitalisation of interest should be made during the period prior to the start of construction, development, or ownership of the asset. Furthermore, for assets intended for resale, the end of the capitalisation period should not extend beyond the completion of any activities that improve the asset's value. Also, the book value of the asset should not exceed its recoverable amount. The interest rate to be used for capitalisation purposes is less easily determined, and the document does not put forward any proposals.

4.31 It must be stressed that the document was issued for discussion only, but it is an indication of generally accepted accounting practice.

4.32 In March 1984, the IASC published IAS 23, 'Capitalisation of borrowing costs'. UK companies are not subject to the requirements of IAS 23 until these requirements are incorporated into a UK

Accounting Standard. However, the contents of IAS 23 may also be regarded as an indication of good accounting practice.

4.33 IAS 23 does not include a firm recommendation on whether borrowing costs should or should not be included in an asset's value. The standard states only how the directors should determine borrowing costs if they wish to capitalise them. It says, *inter alia*, that the directors should calculate a 'capitalisation rate' for the period (by relating, for example, the borrowing costs the company incurred for the period to the borrowings outstanding during that period). They should then apply this capitalisation rate to the expenditure on the acquisition, construction or production of the relevant asset.

4.34 IAS 23 does not address the question of whether the amount to be capitalised should be gross or net of tax relief. There is still no clear consensus of opinion in the UK on this important issue. Accordingly, a company may use either basis, provided that it uses that basis consistently and clearly discloses its policy.

4.35 The International Stock Exchange requires that the financial statements of a listed company or of a company traded on the USM should indicate both the amount of interest capitalised during the year, and the amount and the treatment of any related tax relief. [CO 21(g); GU 10(g)]. Table 2 overleaf illustrates how a company complies with the disclosure requirements for capitalised interest.

Unknown purchase price or production cost

4.36 In certain circumstances, an asset's purchase price or production cost is to be taken as the value the company ascribed to the asset in the earliest available record of its value that the company made on or after it either acquired or produced the asset. These circumstances are where there is no record of either of the following:

- The actual purchase price or the actual production cost.

- Any price, any expenses or any costs that are relevant for determining the purchase price or the production cost.

4.37 This exemption applies also where the relevant record is available, but it could be obtained only with unreasonable expense or delay. [4 Sch 28].

4.38 Where a company has determined, for the first time, an asset's purchase price or production cost according to its earliest known value, the company must disclose this fact in the notes to its financial statements. [4 Sch 51(1)].

Table 2: Disclosure of capitalised interest.

Extracts from J Sainsbury plc Annual Report & Accounts 18th March 1989.

Accounting Policies extract

Capitalisation of Interest
Interest incurred on borrowings to finance specific property developments is capitalised net of tax relief.

Notes extract

1 Tangible Fixed Assets (extract)
The amount included in additions in respect of interest capitalised during the year ended 18th March 1989 amounted to £21.7 million after deducting tax relief of £11.3 million.

17 Net Interest (Payable)/Receivable	Group	
	1989	1988
	£m	£m
Interest receivable	44.3	34.4
Interest payable:		
Bank and Other Interest on loans wholly repayable within five years.	(81.3)	(52.0)
Interest on loans payable by instalments within five years	(1.2)	(0.2)
On loans not wholly repayable within five years		
Debenture Interest	(0.1)	(0.1)
Loan Stock Interest	(0.2)	(0.2)
Other Loans payable by instalments	(1.7)	(1.3)
Finance leases	(2.3)	(1.1)
Interest Capitalised	33.0	29.1
	(53.8)	(25.8)
	(9.5)	8.6

22 Tax on Profit on Ordinary Activities	Group	
	1989	1988
The tax charge for the year is:	£m	£m
Corporation tax at 35%	115.0	97.5
Deferred tax release	(1.6)	—
Overseas tax	6.6	5.0
Share of Associates' tax	5.1	6.5
	125.1	109.0

After deducting tax relief of £11.3 million on interest capitalised the net amount of corporation tax of £103.7 million is payable in December 1989.

The Company is not a Close Company under the terms of the Income and Corporation Taxes Act 1988.

Other items

Assets shown at a fixed amount

4.39 Where certain conditions are satisfied, tangible fixed assets and raw materials and consumables can be shown at a fixed quantity and at a fixed value. These conditions (all of which must be satisfied) are as follows:

- The assets must be assets of a kind that are constantly being replaced.
- Their overall value must not be material to the assessment of the company's state of affairs.
- Their quantity, value and composition must not be subject to material variation.

[4 Sch 25].

4.40 Where this provision applies, all subsequent purchases of the assets in question will be charged direct against profit. This provision enables companies to include (for example) loose tools in either tangible fixed assets or stocks, at a fixed quantity and at a fixed value. However, SSAP 9 says that when valuing stocks, a company must choose a method that produces the fairest practicable approximation to actual cost. It says that base stock and LIFO would not usually bear such a relationship. [SSAP 9 appendix 1 para 12]. Consequently, although permitted by law, the base stock and LIFO methods of valuing stocks are not usually allowed by SSAP 9.

Excess of money owed over value received

4.41 Where the amount that a company owes a creditor exceeds the value of the consideration it received in the transaction that gave rise to the liability, the company *may* treat the amount of the difference as an asset. [4 Sch 24(1)]. If it does so, however, it must write off the amount it shows as an asset by reasonable amounts each year, and it must write off the asset fully before the date on which the debt becomes due for payment. [4 Sch 24(2)(a)].

4.42 Any amount the company includes under assets under this provision must be disclosed separately either on the face of the balance sheet or in the notes to the financial statements. [4 Sch 24(2)(b)].

4.43 An example of the application of this provision is the accounting treatment of 'deep-discounted stock'. This is considered in chapter 11.

Chapter 5

ALTERNATIVE ACCOUNTING RULES

Chapter 5

ALTERNATIVE ACCOUNTING RULES

Introduction

5.1 Paragraphs 29 to 34 of Schedule 4 to the Act set out the rules companies may apply in arriving at the amounts (other than cost) at which they may disclose items in their financial statements. These amounts may reflect changes in the value of assets (for example, the increase in the value of property) that may arise as a result of general or specific price increases.

5.2 These provisions of Schedule 4 are purely permissive in character. That is to say, provided that companies comply with certain conditions, they may (but are not obliged to) adopt any of the alternative accounting rules set out in the Act.

5.3 Legally, companies may adopt all or any of these rules. So for example, a company could include plant and machinery in its balance sheet at current cost, and include every other item on an historical cost basis. However, although it might be reasonable for a company to include certain assets at a valuation, if it mixed the historical cost rules and the alternative accounting rules indiscriminately, it might produce meaningless financial statements. Therefore, the overriding requirement for 'truth and fairness' precludes this approach.

5.4 The combined effect of the historical cost and alternative accounting rules is to allow companies to draw up their financial statements under either the pure historical cost convention, or the historical cost convention modified to include certain assets at a valuation, or the current cost convention.

The alternative accounting rules

5.5 The alternative accounting rules that the Act permits companies to follow when preparing their financial statements are as follows:

- Intangible fixed assets may be stated at their current cost. [4 Sch 31(1)]. This does not apply to goodwill, which can be shown only at the value of the consideration for which it was acquired (less any amounts by which it has been amortised). This exception is supported also by SSAP 22, paragraph 41(a) (see further chapter 7 para 7.82).

- Tangible fixed assets may be stated either at their market value on the date when they were last valued or at their current cost. [4 Sch

31(2)]. Where a policy of revaluing assets is adopted, however, the ASC encourages that such valuations should be kept up to date. [SSAP 12 para 5]. For example, many companies state in their accounting policies that they revalue their properties on a revolving basis to cover all properties once in, say, five years.

- Fixed asset investments may be shown either at their market value on the date on which they were last valued or at a value determined on a basis that the directors think appropriate in the light of the company's circumstances. However, if a company adopts the latter approach, it must state, in the notes to its financial statements, particulars of the method it has adopted, and the reasons for adopting it. [4 Sch 31(3)]. A value determined on a basis that the directors thought appropriate could, for example, include the valuation of unlisted investments on either a net asset basis or an earnings basis. However, it would not be sufficient for the notes merely to state that unlisted investments are included 'at the directors' valuation'.

- Current asset investments may be stated at their current cost. [4 Sch 31(4)].

  A practice, normally adopted by dealing companies is to value current asset investments at market value and any profit or loss arising on the valuation is taken to profit and loss account (*marking to market*). Views differ as to whether such profits and losses are realised or unrealised. Taking unrealised profits to the profit and loss account is a departure from the Act, and it is, therefore, necessary to invoke the true and fair override in section 226(5) of the Act in order to do so. Others consider that because the securities are 'near cash' and readily realisable, the profits could be deemed to be realised and, therefore, there is no departure from the Act. There are published examples of both approaches being used by companies that hold securities for dealing purposes, or other marketable investments such as options, or futures. Either approach appears to be acceptable as no clear guidelines exist at present on when marking to market can, or should, be used and whether a court would determine that such profits are, or are not, realised.

- Stocks may be stated at their current cost. [4 Sch 31(5)].

5.6 The Act does not define 'current cost'. Therefore, where a company chooses to show some assets at their current cost under the alternative accounting rules, their value should normally be determined, in the absence of any agreed Accounting Standard, by considering the guidance given in the ASC's handbook 'Accounting for the effects of changing prices'. Current cost (or value to the business), as defined by the handbook, is the lower of the asset's net current replacement cost and its recoverable amount. Recoverable amount is the higher of the asset's net realisable value and the amount recoverable from its future use. There may in certain circumstances, however, be good reasons for choosing some other method of valuation. For example, properties would generally be valued in accordance with The Royal Institute of Chartered Surveyors' guidance notes.

The revaluation reserve

General rules

5.7 The Act specifies the following rules that relate to the creation and use of the revaluation reserve:

- Any difference between the amount of any item that a company has determined according to one of the alternative accounting rules, and the amount that the company would have disclosed if it had adhered to the historical cost convention, must be credited or debited (as applicable) to a 'revaluation reserve'. [4 Sch 34(1)].

  In determining the amount of this difference, a company should take account, where appropriate, of any provisions for depreciation or diminution in value that it made otherwise than by reference to the value it determined under the alternative accounting rules. It should also take account of any adjustments of any such provisions that it made in the light of that determination. [4 Sch 34(1)].

  When a company values its assets in accordance with the alternative accounting rules, it must:

  - ☐ Value each asset separately. (It must do this in order to comply with the separate valuation principle contained in paragraph 14 of Schedule 4.)

  - ☐ Transfer the surplus or deficit that arises on the revaluation of each asset to the revaluation reserve.

- The Act restricts the circumstances in which a company can transfer an amount from the revaluation reserve. It can do this only where one of the following circumstances exists.

  - ☐ An amount may be transferred to the profit and loss account, if the amount in question was previously charged to that account or represents a realised profit. [4 Sch 34(3)(a)].

  - ☐ An amount may be transferred to capital on capitalisation. Capitalisation means applying the amount standing to the credit of the revaluation reserve wholly or partly to paying up unissued shares in the company to be allotted to the company's members as fully or partly paid shares, thereby allowing bonus and scrip issues to be made out of the revaluation reserve. [4 Sch 34(3)(b), 34(3A)].

These transfers can only be made where the amount standing to the credit of the revaluation reserve is no longer necessary for the purpose of the valuation method used, in which circumstance, the reserve must be reduced accordingly. [4 Sch 34(3)(b)].

Schedule 4 paragraph 34(3B) states that the revaluation reserve shall not be reduced except as mentioned above. This means that it is not available to write off purchased goodwill in individual company's financial statements. This prohibition does not affect goodwill write offs made in consolidated financial statements before the introduction of the Companies Act 1989. However, for companies that become subsidiaries because of the changes in the definitions in the Companies Act 1989, the provisions of the Companies Act 1989 will apply and consolidated goodwill will be prohibited from being written off to the revaluation reserve (see further 'Manual of Accounting - volume II' chapter 8).

- The revaluation reserve must be shown on the face of the balance sheet as a separate amount, although it need not be shown under that name. [4 Sch 34(2)].

- Where any amount has been either credited or debited to the revaluation reserve, its treatment for taxation purposes must be disclosed in a note to the financial statements. [4 Sch 34(4)].

5.8 The implications of these rules in practice are considered in more detail below. The question of whether a revaluation surplus or deficit is realised or unrealised is considered in chapter 19.

Treatment of permanent diminution in value

5.9 Where a revaluation deficit arises because of a permanent diminution in value of an asset below its original cost, it is considered that the alternative accounting rules do not apply. This is because, in such a situation, the historical cost accounting rules require a provision to be made for this permanent diminution in value. [4 Sch 19(2)].

5.10 Paragraph 19(2) of Schedule 4 requires provisions for *permanent* diminution in value that are not shown in the profit and loss account to be disclosed in a note to the financial statements. The requirement of this paragraph is probably to ensure that the provision is separately disclosed, either on the face of the profit and loss account itself, or in the notes to the financial statements.

5.11 However, an alternative interpretation of paragraph 19(2) could mean that where the provision was not charged in the profit and loss account but was charged to another reserve, it would have to be disclosed in a note to the financial statements. If this latter interpretation were correct, it would appear to be acceptable for a company to charge a provision direct to its revaluation reserve, provided that it disclosed that provision in a note to the financial statements.

5.12 Although the treatment of 'provisions for permanent diminution in value' is not clear from the wording of paragraph 19(2) of Schedule 4, the term is not mentioned in paragraph 34(1) of Schedule 4 (treatment of surpluses and deficits on revaluation). Consequently, it appears that provisions for permanent diminution in value should be accounted for through the profit and loss account.

5.13 The prudence concept, contained both in the Act and in SSAP 2, also supports the view that when a company makes a provision for a permanent diminution in an asset's value (in accordance with paragraph 19(2) of Schedule 4), it should charge it to the profit and loss account and not to another reserve. SSAP 2 implies very strongly that a company should charge such provisions to the profit and loss account. Further support is provided by SSAP 12 because paragraph 20 of the standard states that provision for permanent diminution in value of an asset (and any reversals) should be charged (or credited) in the profit and loss account of the period.

5.14 Where an asset has been previously revalued, the alternative accounting rules apply to that part of the deficit that brings the asset's value down to historical cost and, consequently, this should be charged to the revaluation reserve in accordance with paragraph 34(1) of Schedule 4. That part of the deficit below historical cost should be provided for in accordance with paragraph 19(2) and should, therefore, be charged to the profit and loss account. Consequently, the alternative interpretation of paragraph 19(2) of Schedule 4, that of charging a provision for permanent diminution in an asset's value to the revaluation reserve or any other reserve, would only appear to be acceptable where the provision, or part of it, relates to a surplus on a previously revalued asset (see further para 5.19).

Treatment of temporary diminution in value

5.15 When a company applies the alternative accounting rules, it *must* debit to the revaluation reserve *only* those deficits that arise from a *temporary diminution* in value of a fixed asset (other than a fixed asset investment). This is because it would seem that the Act does not permit such revaluation deficits to be charged to the profit and loss account (see para 5.7).

5.16 On a revaluation that gives rise to deficits which are *temporary* (for example, the situation when a diminution arises as part of an annual revaluation exercise), it may be possible for these deficits to be taken to the revaluation reserve and, in effect, netted off against surpluses on other assets. If the net of surpluses and deficits results in an overall deficit, the prudence concept would normally require a provision to be made in the profit and loss account in such a circumstance. This treatment is also consistent with the requirements of paragraph 13 of SSAP 19, 'Accounting for investment properties' (see also para 5.20).

5.17 Also, where a deficit that arises from a *temporary* revaluation of assets has been set off against surpluses on other assets, a problem may arise if those other assets are subsequently sold. The sale of such assets would remove the 'cover' for the deficit. This would leave an overall deficit on the revaluation reserve, and this deficit would also have to be transferred to the profit and loss account on the grounds of prudence.

Treatment of revaluation deficits

5.18 There are a number of ways in which companies have treated revaluation deficits in the past. However, only the last of these approaches described below is now acceptable as the first two are not permitted by the Act.

- A company might take all deficits that arise on the revaluation of individual assets to the profit and loss account.

  Using this method, revaluation deficits that arise from both permanent and temporary diminutions in value would be taken to the profit and loss account. This is not in accordance with paragraph 34(1), which says that, under the alternative accounting rules, revaluation deficits should be debited to the revaluation reserve. Consequently, although prudent, this method does not comply with the Act's provisions.

- Take the *net* amount of revaluation surpluses and revaluation deficits to the revaluation reserve.

  This approach requires that the net amount of revaluation surpluses and revaluation deficits is taken to the revaluation reserve. This method does not comply with paragraph 19(2) of Schedule 4 because, under this method, provisions for permanent diminution in value are not charged in the profit and loss account, nor does it comply either with the provisions of SSAP 12 or with the prudence concept stated in SSAP 2.

- Take those deficits that arise on the revaluation of individual assets to the revaluation reserve to the extent that the revaluation reserve contains surpluses that arose on previous revaluations of the same assets. Any balance of deficits are then taken to the profit and loss account.

This method takes deficits to the revaluation reserve to the extent that the revaluation reserve contains surpluses that arose on previous revaluations of the same asset. Any balance of deficits below historical cost is then taken to the profit and loss account. This method relates to all revaluation deficits that arise from both *permanent* and *temporary* diminutions in value. It also accords with the separate valuation principle outlined in paragraph 14 of Schedule 4.

5.19 Therefore, under the last method outlined in the above paragraph, where an asset has previously been revalued, a deficit on a subsequent revaluation of the same asset that is expected to be *permanent* should be charged to the profit and loss account to the extent that the deficit exceeds any previous surplus. Similar considerations will apply where the deficit is expected to be *temporary.*

Example

If an asset costing £100,000 was revalued in 1989 to £120,000 a surplus would have been credited to the revaluation reserve of £20,000. If in 1992 the same asset is revalued at £90,000, it shows a deficit over its previous valuation of £30,000. If this deficit is expected to be permanent, then a provision for the **permanent** diminution in value of the asset (namely, £10,000) should be charged to the profit and loss account. The provision for **permanent** diminution, therefore, represents the difference between the deficit that arises on the latest valuation after deducting any surplus that may have arisen on a previous revaluation of the same asset that is still standing to the credit of the revaluation reserve (namely, £30,000 - £20,000) and not the total deficit of £30,000. The difference of £20,000 would be debited to the revaluation reserve.

An accounting policy that follows the above method is illustrated in Table 3.

Table 3: Accounting policy explaining the treatment of revaluation surpluses and deficits.

Extract from Lonhro Plc Annual Report 30 September 1988.

Revaluation of fixed assets

Investment properties are revalued annually; the net surplus arising therefrom is credited to revaluation reserve.

For other tangible assets it is Group policy to review regularly their value and, if it is considered appropriate, to obtain independent professional valuations, which are incorporated into the Group accounts. Depreciation is charged to profit before tax on the revised book value from the date of valuation. If the valuation is in excess of the net book value of the relevant asset, the surplus is credited to revaluation reserve. A deficit on valuation of a particular asset is charged to profit before tax to the extent that it is not covered by surpluses arising on prior valuations of that asset which have been previously credited to revaluation reserve.

5.20 Two further problems arise with deficits. First, how should an overall deficit (net of revaluation surpluses) be treated? Secondly, if aggregate revaluation deficits are taken to the revaluation reserve, is it possible to have a debit revaluation reserve balance? As mentioned in paragraph 5.7 above, the Act says that any revaluation deficits that arise when a company adopts the alternative accounting rules must be debited to the revaluation reserve. This implies that it is possible to have a debit balance on the revaluation reserve (for example, where the revaluation reserve has been used to pay up bonus shares and a subsequent revaluation deficit arises). SSAP 12 does not address the problem of the revaluation reserve and the revaluation of assets. The only reference in the Accounting Standards to the way in which companies must treat an overall deficit on the revaluation reserve is in SSAP 19, 'Accounting for investment properties'. Paragraph 13 of that standard says:

> *" Changes in the value of investment properties should not be taken to the profit and loss account but should be disclosed as a movement on an investment revaluation reserve, unless the total of the investment revaluation reserve is insufficient to cover a deficit, in which case the amount by which the deficit exceeds the amount in the investment revaluation reserve should be charged in the profit and loss account."*

Accordingly, when similar circumstances to those outlined in paragraph 13 of SSAP 19 exist, it remains prudent and good accounting practice to charge an overall debit balance on the revaluation reserve to the profit and loss account.

Treatment of accumulated depreciation when assets are revalued

5.21 In the past, companies have adopted two different ways of treating their existing accumulated depreciation when they revalue fixed assets.

5.22 The first method, which is now the only one allowed, is the simple one of comparing the revalued amount with the net book value and taking the difference to the revaluation reserve. This method is illustrated by the following example:

Example

Details of a fixed asset before revaluation are as follows:	£
Fixed asset at cost	1,000
Accumulated depreciation	400
Net book value	600
The asset is revalued to	1,500

Details of the fixed asset after revaluation are as follows:	
	£
Fixed asset at cost	1,000
Surplus on revaluation	500
	1,500
Accumulated depreciation	400
Surplus on revaluation	(400)
	-

The amount transferred to the revaluation reserve is £900 (namely, £1,500 - £600). This includes £400 of accumulated depreciation.

5.23 The second approach, which is now prohibited, is to write back the accumulated depreciation of £400 to the profit and loss account and to transfer the difference between the revalued amount of the asset and its historical cost or previous valuation to the revaluation reserve.

5.24 The proponents of this approach argue that the depreciation charged to date in the light of the revaluation is unnecessary and that the retained profits should reflect this position which would have existed had no such depreciation been charged. This approach appears also to be permitted by paragraph 34(1) of Schedule 4, which says:

> *"With respect to any determination of the value of an asset of a company ... [under the alternative accounting rules] ..., the amount of any profit or loss arising from that determination (after allowing, where appropriate, for any provisions for depreciation or diminution in value made otherwise than by reference to the value so determined and any adjustments of any such provisions made in the light of that determination) shall be credited or (as the case may be) debited to a separate reserve ('the revaluation reserve')."*

5.25 However, the approach is no longer allowed because SSAP 12, paragraph 22 states that:

> *"Depreciation charged prior to the revaluation should not be written back to the profit and loss account, except to the extent that it relates to a provision for permanent diminution in value which is subsequently found to be unnecessary."*

Accordingly, companies should not write back their existing accumulated depreciation when they revalue fixed assets.

Sale of revalued assets

5.26 As noted in the second point of paragraph 5.7 above, the revaluation reserve must be reduced where it is no longer necessary for the purpose of the valuation method that the company has adopted. The most likely situation where this will happen is where the company sells an asset that it has previously revalued.

5.27 Paragraph 34(3) of Schedule 4 allows a company to make a transfer from the revaluation reserve to the profit and loss account where the amount transferred represents a realised profit. Consequently, when a company sells a revalued asset, the Act permits it to credit the profit on the sale (including the amount of the realised revaluation surplus) to the profit and loss account.

5.28 SSAP 6 does not specifically mention how realised revaluation surpluses should be treated. However, in paragraph 20, it does say that the profit and loss account should reflect all profits and losses recognised in the accounts of the year. This implies that realised surpluses *may* be credited to the profit and loss account.

5.29 ED 16, 'Supplement to extraordinary items and prior year adjustments' was issued in 1975, but it never became a standard. Paragraph 14 of this exposure draft stated quite clearly how it proposed that realised revaluation surpluses should be treated. It proposed that:

> *"When fixed assets are realised, the surpluses or deficits compared with book value should be recognised in the profit and loss account for the year and classified as extraordinary items or otherwise according to their nature. Any reserve identified as being in respect of previously unrealised surpluses on the revaluation of those assets thereby becomes a realised surplus, but should not be reported as part of the profit for the year."*

5.30 ED 36 contained the following guidance on the treatment of surpluses or deficits on the disposal of fixed assets that was neither included in the revised SSAP 6 nor in the revised SSAP 12:

> *"When fixed assets are disposed of, the surpluses or deficits recognised in the profit and loss account for the year should be based on the difference between sale proceeds and depreciated original cost. Any reserve identified as being in respect of previously unrealised surpluses on the revaluation of those assets thereby becomes a realised surplus and will be included as part of the profit for the year, but should be disclosed separately where material."*

5.31 On the publication of SSAP 6 (revised) in August 1986, the ASC stated that '*...opinion on this matter does not presently allow one method to be laid down as standard to the exclusion of the other, and that the matter requires further study. Accordingly the matter is not dealt with in SSAP 6 but will be considered in a new project of fixed assets* *and revaluations'*. That project is still under way. But in the meantime, both methods are acceptable, and both comply with the Act.

5.32 The implications of these alternatives can be explained by an example:

Three companies A, B and C buy identical assets on 1st January 1989 for £1,000. Companies B and C revalue their assets at 31st December 1991 to £1,400. Company C again revalues its assets at 31st December 1993 to £1,500. All three companies sell their assets on 31st December 1994 for £2,000. The estimated useful life of the assets at the date of purchase is ten years, and their residual values are nil.

Each company will record the value of the assets in its accounting records as follows:

Fixed asset values

	Co. A	Co. B	Co. C
	£	£	£
Cost 1.1.1989	1,000	1,000	1,000
Three years' depreciation to 31.12.1991	(300)	(300)	(300)
	700	700	700
Revaluation 31.12.1991	-	700	700
Net book value 31.12.1991	700	1,400	1,400
Two years' depreciation to 31.12.1993	(200)	(400)	(400)
	500	1,000	1,000
Revaluation 31.12.1993	-	-	500
Net book value 31.12.1993	500	1,000	1,500
One year's depreciation to 31.12.1994	(100)	(200)	(300)
Net book value 31.12.1994	400	800	1200

The depreciation charges after the first revaluation are calculated as follows:

$$\frac{\text{Net book value}}{\text{Remaining useful life}} = \frac{\pounds 1{,}400}{7 \text{ years}} = \pounds 200 \text{ per annum}$$

The depreciation charge after the second revaluation is calculated as follows:

$$\frac{\text{Net book value}}{\text{Remaining useful life}} = \frac{\pounds 1{,}500}{5 \text{ years}} = \pounds 300 \text{ per annum}$$

If the sale proceeds are compared to the net book values at 31st December 1994, the following surpluses arise. They would be credited to the profit and loss account in 1994.

	Co. A	Co. B	Co. C
	£	£	£
Net book value 31.12.1994	400	800	1,200
Sale proceeds	2,000	2,000	2,000
Surplus on disposal	1,600	1,200	800

If no further adjustments are made to the profit and loss account, the effect on each company's profit and loss account over the life or the assets can be summarised as follows:

	Co. A	Co. B	Co. C
	£	£	£
Depreciation charged	(600)	(900)	(1,000)
Surplus on disposal	1,600	1,200	800
Net surplus over life of asset	1,000	300	(200)
Taken direct to reserves	-	700	1,200

The net surplus shown in the profit and loss account of each company over the life of the assets, therefore, varies considerably. If the surpluses were reported 'above the line' (see para 5.37) as part of the company's normal trading, the earnings per share figure would also vary significantly from company to company.

5.33 This apparent inequity has led many companies, when they sell revalued assets, to transfer their realised revaluation surpluses on the face of the profit and loss account. This would have the following effect on each company's profit and loss account over the life of the assets:

	Co. A	Co. B	Co. C
	£	£	£
Depreciation charged (six years)	(600)	(900)	(1,000)
Surplus of the sale proceeds over net book value	1,600	1,200	800
Realised revaluation surplus	-	700	1,200
Net effect over life of asset	1,000	1,000	1,000

5.34 Consequently, the net effect on the profit and loss account over the life of the assets is the same for each company. However, the companies have charged different amounts of depreciation each year to the profit and loss account as a result of the revaluations. Accordingly, this in turn affects the profit that each company reports when it disposes of the assets in 1994, as follows:

	Co. A	Co. B	Co. C
	£	£	£
Surplus of sale proceeds over net book value	1,600	1,200	800
Realised revaluation surplus	-	700	1,200
Reported profit on disposal	1,600	1,900	2,000

5.35 This will mean that each company's earnings per share figure will differ if the profit on disposal is reported 'above the line' (see para 5.37).

5.36 One question that remains to be answered is how the realised revaluation surplus should be treated if it is credited to the profit and loss account.

5.37 Where the disposal of fixed assets gives rise to a material surplus or deficit, this should be shown separately as either an exceptional item or an extraordinary item, as appropriate. [SSAP 6 para 15]. The surplus or deficit should be shown as an extraordinary item only if the sale of the asset can be said to derive from events outside the company's ordinary activities. This may be so, for example, where a company discontinues a business segment and a profit arises when that part of the business segment is disposed of. This profit on the sale would be treated as an extraordinary item (that is, 'below the line'). However, if, for example, a company carries on a retail trade from a number of retail outlets, and it has a policy of selling a number of old outlets and buying a similar number of new outlets each year, any surpluses on sales of properties could be said to derive from the company's ordinary activities. Consequently, these profits are not extraordinary, and they should be disclosed in the profit and loss account as part of the company's ordinary trading results (that is, 'above the line'). Table 4 overleaf illustrates the situation where the realised revaluation surplus has been transferred directly to profit and loss account reserve. Table 5 overleaf illustrates the situation where the transfer has been made on the face of the profit and loss account.

Disclosure of the revaluation reserve

5.38 As noted in the third point in paragraph 5.7 above, the Act requires that the revaluation reserve must be shown on the face of the balance sheet. However, it may be shown under another name. [4 Sch 34(2)]. This concession is necessary for several reasons, as discussed below.

5.39 Where a company prepares full current cost financial statements in accordance with the ASC's handbook, 'Accounting for the effects of changing prices', the current cost balance sheet includes a reserve that is referred to as the 'current cost reserve'.

5.40 The current cost reserve will include:

- Unrealised revaluation surpluses on fixed assets, stocks and investments.

- Realised amounts equal to the cumulative net total of the current cost adjustments made in accordance with the handbook, namely:

  - The depreciation adjustment (and any adjustments on the disposal of fixed assets).

  - The cost of sales adjustment.

- ☐ The monetary working capital adjustment.
- ☐ The gearing adjustment.

Table 4: Illustration of profit on disposal of a previously revalued asset where the revaluation surplus has been transferred to retained profit.

Extract from Lex Service PLC Annual Report & Accounts 31st December 1988.

Accounting Policies extract

Revaluation Reserve

Net surpluses arising as a result of the incorporation of property valuations in the accounts are taken to the revaluation reserve. On disposal of a property the revaluation surplus or deficit thereon is transferred to retained profit.

Consolidated profit and loss account extract

	Notes	1988 £m	1987 £m
Statement of retained profit			
Opening retained profit		64.4	66.6
Retained profit for the financial year		36.4	18.4
Goodwill arising on acquisitions		(20.1)	—
Transfer from revaluation reserve	23	0.2	0.4
Exchange variations	33	(0.4)	(21.0)
Retained profit carried forward		80.5	64.4

Note extract

23. Revaluation reserve

	Group		Lex Service PLC	
	1988 £m	1987 £m	1988 £m	1987 £m
28th December 1987	10.7	7.3	9.3	6.3
Transfer to profit and loss account	(0.2)	(0.4)	(0.1)	—
Exchange variations	—	(0.1)	—	—
Net surplus on revaluation	—	3.9	—	3.0
31st December 1988	10.5	10.7	9.2	9.3

5.41 In effect, this current cost reserve is very similar to the revaluation reserve outlined in the Act. Consequently, the Act allows the term 'current cost reserve' to be used instead of the term 'revaluation reserve'. The main difference between the current cost reserve and the

Table 5: Illustration of profit on disposal of a previously revalued asset where the revaluation surplus has been dealt with as part of the profit for the year.

Extract from Raglan Property Trust P.L.C. Report & Accounts 31st March 1989.

Accounting policies extract

(d) Tangible fixed assets.
Investment properties are valued annually by independent valuers on the open market value basis and these valuations are incorporated into the financial statements. Surpluses and deficits arising on disposal of investment properties are dealt with in the profit and loss account. The surplus or deficit arising on disposal is the difference between gross sale proceeds and historic cost including selling fees.
No depreciation is provided on investment properties. Other tangible fixed assets are depreciated on a straight-line basis over their estrimated useful lives, ten years for fixtures and fittings, four years for motor vehicles. Short leasehold improvements are depreciated over the unexpired term of the lease.

Note extract

4. Profit on ordinary activities before taxation	1989	1988
The profit on ordinary activities before taxation has been arrived at after crediting:		
Net rents receivable	537,904	546,144
Profit on sale of investment properties (see below)	896,303	330,369
And after charging:		
Depreciation of tangible assets	48,369	52,104
Operating leases:		
Ground rents payable	50,586	50,000
Other	47,355	47,355
Auditor's remuneration	32,440	26,340
Profit on sale of investment properties is arrived at as follows:		
Sale proceeds	1,680,500	1,070,000
Book values including cost of disposal	(1,387,310)	(990,349)
Transfer from revaluation reserve in respect of previous revaluations (note 14)	603,113	250,718
	896,303	330,369

revaluation reserve is that the current cost reserve comprises two parts: an unrealised part that includes surpluses on revaluations, and a realised element that includes items (such as the cost of sales adjustment) that have been either debited or credited to the profit and loss account. The unrealised part of the current cost reserve corresponds to the revaluation reserve under the terms of the Act. To avoid confusion, therefore, it is desirable to present the item in the balance sheet, or in the notes to the balance sheet, as follows:

Current cost reserve	- unrealised	X
	- realised	X
		X

5.42 The disclosure of the 'current cost reserve' is discussed in detail in the ASC's handbook appendices 3 and 9.

5.43 It should also be noted that sometimes a company's articles of association will govern the way in which the company operates its revaluation reserve, and these articles may stipulate also the name of the reserve. Consequently, the company should use that name in its financial statements. Articles of this nature are commonly found in investment companies and pension funds.

Taxation implications

5.44 The Act requires the taxation implications of a revaluation to be noted in the financial statements. [4 Sch 34(4)].

5.45 This does not mean that there must be a statement of whether the amount is taxable or allowable under tax legislation. It means that there must be an explanation of the tax effect of the revaluation.

5.46 The tax effect will often be deferred until a later period. SSAP 15 says that the revaluation of an asset will give rise to a deferred tax timing difference, insofar as the profit or loss that would result from the asset's realisation at the revalued amount is taxable. But this will not apply if the disposal of the revalued asset and of any subsequent replacement assets would not result in a tax liability after taking account of any expected rollover relief. [SSAP 15 para 20].

5.47 The standard requires that tax deferred or accelerated by the effect of timing differences (including any deferred tax on a capital gain) should be accounted for to the extent that it is probable that a liability or asset will crystallise. [SSAP 15 para 25]. In addition to making this provision, a company should disclose, in a note to its financial statements, the total amount of deferred tax (including that on capital gains) that it has not provided for, analysed into its major components. [SSAP 15 para 40]. The standard goes on to say that where the potential amount of deferred tax on a revalued asset is not shown because the revaluation does not constitute a timing difference for the reason explained in paragraph 5.46 above, this fact should be stated. [SSAP 15 para 41].

5.48 Compliance with the disclosure requirements of SSAP 15 will ensure compliance with paragraph 34(4) of Schedule 4.

The depreciation rules

5.49 Where a company has determined an asset's value in accordance with one of the alternative accounting rules, that value (rather than the purchase price or the production cost) is to be (or else is to be the starting point for determining) the amount at which it discloses that asset in its financial statements. Where the asset in question has been subject to a previous valuation, its value according to the latest revaluation supersedes its previous value as the basis the company should use when including it in its financial statements. Accordingly, any references in the depreciation rules to purchase price or production cost must be substituted by a reference to the value determined by the alternative accounting rules the company applied. [4 Sch 32(1)]. This means that, in determining the amount to be written off systematically over a fixed asset's useful economic life, a company must have regard to the asset's value determined according to the latest application of the alternative accounting rules, rather than to its purchase price or its production cost. Even where a company revalues its assets at the end of the year, it is not exempt from providing depreciation against the profits of the year based on the opening cost or valuation and the cost of subsequent additions.

5.50 The Act also says that where the value of any fixed asset has been determined according to the alternative accounting rules, the amount of any provision for depreciation to be charged in the profit and loss account may be either the amount based on the valuation of the asset, or the amount based on its historical cost. However, where the amount so charged is based on historical cost, the difference between that charge and the charge based on the asset's valuation must be disclosed separately. It must be so disclosed either on the face of the profit and loss account or in the notes. [4 Sch 32(2)(3)]. This would appear to allow a company to either debit or credit the difference (as appropriate) direct to the revaluation reserve. This has, however, now been prohibited by SSAP 12.

5.51 SSAP 12 echoes the Act's rules in most respects but it requires all depreciation to be charged to the profit and loss account. Furthermore, the standard requires that where a company revalues assets, and gives effect to the revaluation in its financial statements, it should base the charge for depreciation on the revalued amount. [SSAP 12 para 16]. If this results in a material increase in depreciation compared to previous years' depreciation charges, then the financial statements should disclose in the notes in the year of revaluation the depreciation charge split between that applicable to original cost and that applicable to the change in value on revaluation. [SSAP 12 para 27]. No depreciation previously charged should be written-back to the profit and loss account on revaluation of an asset except to the extent that it relates to a provision for permanent diminution in value which is subsequently found to be unnecessary. [SSAP 12 para 22]. The standard states also that an increase in the value of an asset does not remove the necessity for a company to charge depreciation even where the market value of an asset is greater than its net book value.

5.52 Consequently, it is clear that SSAP 12 requires a company to charge depreciation on the carrying value of the revalued asset in the balance sheet, and to charge it in its entirety to the profit and loss account. The practice of split depreciation, where depreciation on the historical cost is charged to the profit and loss account, and depreciation on the revaluation is charged to the revaluation reserve, has been prohibited. [SSAP 12 para 16].

5.53 Whilst chapter 19 considers realised reserves and distributable profits in detail, it should be noted that section 275(2) of the Act has a bearing on the way in which companies should treat depreciation on revalued assets. This section says that if the revaluation of an asset produces an unrealised profit, then an amount equal to any excess depreciation charged as a result of the revaluation may be treated as a realised profit. This section is concerned only with the determination of distributable profits (and not with the accounting treatment of excess depreciation). Despite this, it means that where a company properly charges the whole of the depreciation based on the revalued assets to the profit and loss account, it may also transfer an amount equal to the excess depreciation from the revaluation reserve to the profit and loss account reserve.

5.54 Because the amount transferred from the revaluation reserve to the profit and loss account reserve represents a realised profit, this treatment would not contravene paragraph 34(3) of Schedule 4.

5.55 The transfer should be made between reserves in the notes. If this transfer was made in the profit and loss account itself, it would be 'below the line' as a transfer from reserves. Where such an adjustment is made, the revaluation reserve is systematically reduced over the asset's life and, consequently, the net profit on the sale of an asset that is credited to the profit and loss account reserve will ultimately be the same whether the asset has been revalued or not.

5.56 The example below shows that where the revaluation reserve is systematically taken to the profit and loss account reserve to compensate for the increased depreciation following a revaluation, rather than being taken to the profit and loss account on sale of the asset, the net effect is the same for the profit and loss account reserve. However there is a significant difference in the reported profits in the year of disposal, which will have an impact on the earnings per share.

Example

The facts are the same as those outlined in paragraph 5.32 except that company C does not again revalue the asset on 31st December 1993. Company A is on a pure historical cost basis and so it is not considered in this example. Company B makes a transfer from the revaluation reserve to the profit and loss account reserve each year, after the asset is revalued, an amount equal to the additional depreciation charged on the revalued asset. Company C makes no such transfer between reserves. Both companies sell the asset on 31st December 1994 for £2,000. The effect on their accounts will be as follows:

Revaluation reserve

	Co. B	Co. C
	£	£
Asset revalued on 31.12.1991	700	700
Three years excess depreciation transferred to the profit and loss account reserve *	(300)	-
Transfer to profit and loss account on disposal, 'above the line'	400	700

*The excess depreciation is calculated as follows:
(Depreciation on revalued asset - depreciation on historical cost) x 3 years = (£200 - £100) x 3 = £ 300

Profit and loss account charge above the line:

	Co. B	Co. C
	£	£
Depreciation charged (six years)	(900)	(900)
Profit on sale of asset*	1,600	1,900
Overall effect on profit and loss account	700	1,000
Reserve movements		
Transfer from revaluation reserve	300	-
Overall effect	1,000	1,000

*The profit on sale of the asset is calculated as follows:

(Sale proceeds - (revalued asset - 3 years depreciation)) + revaluation surplus transferred to the profit and loss account on disposal) that is:

Co. B: (2,000 - (1,400 - 600)) + 400 = £1,600

Co. C: (2,000 - (1,400 - 600)) + 700 = £1,900

Although the effect on company B's and company C's profit and loss account reserve is identical, the effect on the reported profits is quite different.

Additional disclosure required

5.57 Where a company has applied any of the alternative accounting rules, the Act requires it to disclose certain information in the notes to its financial statements. [4 Sch 33(1)].

5.58 First, the notes must state the items affected and the basis of valuation the company has adopted in respect of each such item. [4 Sch 33(2)]. Second, either the balance sheet or the notes must disclose, in respect of every item affected (except stocks), one or other of the following amounts:

- The comparable amounts determined according to the historical cost convention.
- The differences between those comparable amounts and the actual amounts shown in the balance sheet.

[4 Sch 33(3)].

5.59 For this purpose, 'comparable amounts' means the aggregate amount the company would have shown if it had applied the historical cost convention, and the aggregate amount of the cumulative provisions for depreciation or diminution in value that would have been permitted or required in determining those amounts according to that convention. [4 Sch 33(4)].

5.60 To illustrate this requirement, consider the following example:

Example

Details of a company's fixed assets are as follows:

	Cost	Valuation
	£	£
Fixed assets	10,000	15,000
Accumulated depreciation	6,000	4,000
Net book value	4,000	11,000

If the company states the fixed assets in the balance sheet at valuation, the effect of the Act's provisions is to require the balance sheet or the notes to the financial statements to state either the comparable amounts (namely, cost £10,000 and depreciation £6,000) or the difference between the comparable amounts and the amounts at which they are actually stated (namely, £5,000 and £2,000 respectively).

The historical cost net book amount (namely, £4,000) or the difference between the comparable net book amounts (namely, £7,000) is another interpretation of the amounts that are required to be disclosed. This latter disclosure is arguable because the Act refers to the amounts stated in the balance sheet and the amounts so stated will be the net book value of the assets.

5.61 As a result of this requirement, a company that has revalued its fixed assets has to maintain records of both the historical cost and the valuation of those fixed assets. In addition, the company has to calculate depreciation on the historical cost as well as on the valuation.

Table 6 shows how a company complies with these disclosure requirements.

Table 6: Disclosure of historical cost amounts for fixed assets where the assets have been included at a valuation.

Extract from Sketchley plc Report and Accounts 31st March 1989.

Notes extract

11. TANGIBLE ASSETS – COMPANY (extract)

Tenure of land and buildings	Freehold	Long lease	Short lease	Total
	£000	£000	£000	£000
Cost or valuation	8,249	111	2,843	11,203
Depreciation	(162)	(28)	(945)	(1,135)
Net book value at 31 March 1989	8,087	83	1,898	10,068
Net book value at 1 April 1988	4,813	7	552	5,372

For tangible assets included at Valuation, 1987:	£000
Historical cost at 31 March 1989	2,615
Depreciation based on historical cost at 31 March 1989	510
Historical cost net book value at 31 March 1989	2,105
Historical cost net book value at 1 April 1988	2,196

Chapter 6

FORMAT OF FINANCIAL STATEMENTS

FORMAT OF FINANCIAL STATEMENTS

Introduction

6.1 The general provisions that relate to the format and content of company financial statements are detailed in Schedule 4 to the Act. Schedule 4A deals with the format of consolidated financial statements, which are explained in 'Manual of Accounting - volume II'.

6.2 Schedule 4 sets out two alternative formats for the balance sheet and four alternative formats for the profit and loss account. It also lays down certain general guidelines to be followed. These formats and guidelines are discussed below. In addition, the Schedule requires companies to disclose considerable detail both in the notes to the balance sheet and in the notes to the profit and loss account.

General rules

Choice of formats

6.3 Schedule 4 leaves the choice of particular formats to the company's directors. Once the directors have selected the particular formats that they are going to adopt for the balance sheet and the profit and loss account, they should not subsequently change them without good reason. [4 Sch 2(1)]. An example of such a reason might occur if a company changes both its operations and its accounting methods significantly, and considers that, following the changes, its financial statements fit more naturally into a different format.

6.4 In most situations, however, few companies will have good reason to change their formats, and so they must select carefully the formats that they wish to adopt when they prepare their first set of financial statements after incorporation. If a company does eventually change its formats, it may incur a considerable amount of extra work, because it will have to restate the corresponding amounts for the previous year in accordance with the new formats. In addition, the notes to the financial statements must disclose:

- The fact that the company has adopted a different format.
- The directors' reasons for the change.

[4 Sch 2(2)].

Headings and sub-headings

6.5 The formats give a list of items either as main headings or as sub-headings. In the balance sheet, main headings are designated either by letters or by Roman numerals, and sub-headings are designated by Arabic numerals. The object of this notation is for identification purposes only, so that the Act can refer to items by their prefix. There is no requirement for financial statements, when they are prepared, actually to show these letters or numbers. [4 Sch 1(2)]. In the profit and loss account Formats 1 and 2, all items are designated by Arabic numerals.

6.6 Whichever of the balance sheet formats and profit and loss account formats a company chooses, the company must show the items in the fixed order and under the headings and the sub-headings set out in the formats it has adopted. [4 Sch 1(1)]. There are, however, certain exceptions to this rule:

- An item may be shown in greater detail than the prescribed formats require. [4 Sch 3(1)].

  For example, most companies will include motor vehicles under the sub-heading 'Fixtures, fittings, tools and equipment'. Where such motor vehicles are significant in value, additional details may be disclosed as follows:

Fixtures, fittings, tools and equipment:		
Motor vehicles	X	
Other	X	X

- An item representing an asset or a liability, or an item of income or expenditure that is not covered in any of the prescribed formats may be shown separately [4 Sch 3(2)].

  An example is where a company holds stocks that do not fall easily within the sub-headings of raw materials and consumables, work in progress, finished goods and goods for resale, and payments on account (see also Table 7).

- Items that are preceded by Arabic numerals in the Act may be combined in the company's financial statements where either of the following circumstances apply:

  - ☐ Their individual amounts are not material in assessing the company's state of affairs or profit or loss. [4 Sch 3(4)(a)].

- ☐ The combination facilitates the assessment of the company's state of affairs or profit or loss (that is, it results in greater clarity). Where this applies, however, the detailed breakdown of the combined items must be given in the notes to the financial statements. [4 Sch 3(4)(b)].

- ■ A heading or a sub-heading nced not be shown where there is no amount to be included for both the financial year in question and the immediately preceding financial year. [4 Sch 3(5), 4(3)].

- ■ The arrangement, the headings and the sub-headings of items set out in the formats and preceded by Arabic numerals must be adapted if the special nature of the company's business requires this. [4 Sch 3(3)]. Table 8 overleaf shows two examples where companies have adapted the format prescribed by the Act.

Table 7: Use of other headings in the balance sheet.

Extract from Sketchley Plc Annual Report & Accounts 31st March 1989.

Accounting policies extract

Circulating inventory
Circulating inventory comprises rental items in circulation. The basis of valuation is cost less depreciation claculated on a straight line basis over the estimated life of the items in circulation.

BALANCE SHEET (extract)

AT 31 MARCH 1989	NOTE	1989 £000	1988 £000
CURRENT ASSETS			
Circulating inventory		16,435	14,929
Stocks	13	12,706	4,016
Debtors	14	65,979	25,040
Cash at bank and in hand		815	1,469
		95,935	45,454

6.7 The Act requires that companies should use the headings and sub-headings prescribed in the formats except in certain instances where the special nature of the company's business requires their adaption. [4 Sch 1(1), 3(3)]. Nevertheless, some companies in practice, depart from these and from the nomenclature given to other items in both the balance sheet and profit and loss account formats. As the Act does not specifically give companies the freedom to change the wording of the formats except in the one case mentioned above, it is uncertain whether it is allowable for companies to do so. If it is permissible (and for this purpose a distinction may have to be drawn between headings, sub-headings and other items) then clearly there

Table 8: Examples where companies have adapted the format prescribed by the Act.

Extract from British Telecom plc Report and Accounts 31st March 1989.

2 Operating costs	£m	1988 £m
Staff costs		
Wages and salaries	3,357	2,994
Social security costs	246	210
Pension contributions (note 18)	311	288
	3,914	3,492
Own work capitalised	(497)	(410)
Depreciation (note 8)	1,610	1,525
Payments to overseas telecommunications operators	684	655
Other operating costs	2,733	2,498
Other operating income	(180)	(184)
	8,264	7,576
Operating costs included the following:		
Research and development	214	195
Rental costs relating to operating leases, including plant and equipment hire £18m (1988 – £23m)	137	121
Group's share of losses, less profits, of related companies	19	16

Other operating income included profit on disposal of land and buildings of £55m (1988 – £46m)

The auditors' remuneration for the year ended 31 March 1989 for the Group was £2,026,000 (1988 – £1,931,000) including £1,200,000 (1988 – £1,150,000) for the company.

Expenditure charged in operating costs comprises the costs of providing services and selling equipment. The directors believe that the nature of the group's business is such that the analysis of operating costs required by the Companies Act 1985 is not appropriate. As required by the Act the directors have therefore adapted the prescribed format so that operating costs are disclosed, as above, in a manner appropriate to the group's principal activity.

Extract from Ladbrooke Group PLC Annual Report and Accounts 31st December 1988.

16 Debtors	1988 £m	1987 £m
Amounts falling due within one year:		
Trade debtors	122.4	144.9
Other debtors	25.8	45.7
Prepayments and accrued income	47.2	36.7
Films (a)	0.6	0.7
	196.0	228.0
Amounts falling due after more than one year:		
Trade debtors	3.7	4.3
Advance corporation tax recoverable	11.4	–
Other debtors and accrued income	16.0	14.2
	31.1	18.5
	227.1	246.5

(a) Films are shown after deducting the borrowings of £12.8m (1987 £12.5m). These borrowings are repayable only out of future film income or disposal proceeds. This representation does not comply with the requirements of the Companies Act 1985 but is, in the opinion of the directors, appropriate to present a true and fair view.

must be no change other than of pure wording and the new wording must not be misleading in any way.

6.8 A company should consider the presentation of its financial statements in three stages. First, it should consider which of the formats are most suitable for its purposes. Secondly, if the special nature of its business requires it, it must adapt the arrangement and headings and sub-headings of any items designated by Arabic numerals in the selected formats as set out in Schedule 4. Thirdly, it should consider whether it needs to show any item listed in the formats in greater detail, and, if so, it may do so. (Unlike the adaptation of the formats, which is compulsory if the special nature of a company's business requires it, the reporting company has the option to include greater detail under any heading if it wishes to do so.)

6.9 After having considered the presentation of the financial statements, the company must next consider whether compliance with the requirements of Schedule 4 as regards the format of the financial statements, and compliance with other statutory requirements as to the information to be included in the notes to the financial statements, enable the financial statements to give a true and fair view of the company's affairs as at the end of the financial year. If the company decides that compliance with Schedule 4 would not give a true and fair view (see chapter 3 para 3.9), it should examine whether the solution to this problem might be to provide additional information in the financial statements. If in special circumstances, compliance with the Act would be inconsistent with the requirement to give a true and fair view, the directors must depart from the Act's provisions. In such a situation, particulars of the departure, the reasons for it, and its effect must be given in the notes to the financial statements (see further chapter 3 para 3.10).

Corresponding amounts

6.10 Corresponding amounts for the year immediately preceding the year in question must be shown in respect of every item in a company's balance sheet or profit and loss account. [4 Sch 4(1)]. This applies even when no such item exists to be disclosed in respect of the current financial year. [4 Sch 4(3)].

6.11 Also, in general, the corresponding amounts for the previous financial year must be given in respect of each item shown in the notes to the financial statements. [4 Sch 58(2)]. The only exceptions to this relate to:

- Information required under Schedule 4A paragraph 13 (information with respect to acquisition taking place in the financial year).

- The information that must be disclosed in respect of shareholdings in other undertakings under paragraphs 2, 8(3), 16, 21(1)(d), 22(4)(5), 24(3)(4) and 27(3)(4) of Schedule 5.

- The information that must be disclosed in respect of loans and other dealings in favour of directors and others under Parts II and III of Schedule 6 (see chapter 21).

- Opening and closing balances and movements during the year on both the cost (or valuation) and the accumulated provisions for diminution in value of fixed assets (see chapters 7 and 8).

- Movements on provisions for liabilities and charges and reserves (see chapters 11 and 12).

[4 Sch 58(3)].

6.12 Where the amount for the previous year is not comparable with the amount to be shown in respect of the current year, the previous year's amount must be adjusted. Where this applies, particulars of the adjustment and the reasons for it must be disclosed in the notes to the financial statements. This requirement applies in respect of every item in a company's balance sheet or profit and loss account and in respect of each item shown in the notes to the financial statements. [4 Sch 4(2), 58(2)]. This provision accords with the treatment that SSAP 6 recommends. Under SSAP 6, a prior-year adjustment (that has arisen, for example, because there has been a change of accounting policy during the year) is accounted for by restating the previous year's amount, and, where it is affected, by adjusting the opening balance of retained profits accordingly. Where practicable, the effect of the change should be disclosed by showing the amount involved separately in the restatement of the previous year's figures.

Off-setting

6.13 Asset and liability items may not be set off against each other. Similarly, income and expenditure items may not be set off against each other. [4 Sch 5]. Consequently, companies cannot, for example, show hire-purchase liabilities as a deduction from the related asset. (They may, however, deduct from stock the payments they have received on account of orders.) [Note 8 on the balance sheet formats]. This rule, which relates primarily to the presentation of items in the financial statements, is discussed more fully in chapter 10, paragraphs 10.54 to 10.59 on debtors, and in paragraphs 10.68 to 10.78 on bank balances.

The balance sheet

Formats

6.14 The Act sets out two alternative balance sheet formats.

Format 1

6.15 In Format 1, net assets can be shown as equal in total to the aggregate of share capital and reserves. This method of presentation probably represents UK companies' most common practice. The Act does not, however, prescribe the place where the totals should be struck. Consequently, in this format a company can equate total assets less current liabilities, on the one hand, with the aggregate of creditors falling due after more than one year, provisions for liabilities and charges, and capital and reserves, on the other hand. Format 1 is set out on the next two pages and is also illustrated in Table 9.

BALANCE SHEET - FORMAT 1

A Called-up share capital not paid

B Fixed assets
- I Intangible assets
  - 1 Development costs
  - 2 Concessions, patents, licences, trade marks and similar rights and assets
  - 3 Goodwill
  - 4 Payments on account
- II Tangible assets
  - 1 Land and buildings
  - 2 Plant and machinery
  - 3 Fixtures, fittings, tools and equipment
  - 4 Payments on account and assets in course of construction
- III Investments
  - 1 Shares in group undertakings
  - 2 Loans to group undertakings
  - 3 Participating interests
  - 4 Loans to undertakings in which the company has a participating interest
  - 5 Other investments other than loans
  - 6 Other loans
  - 7 Own shares

C Current assets
- I Stocks
  - 1 Raw materials and consumables
  - 2 Work in progress
  - 3 Finished goods and goods for resale
  - 4 Payments on account
- II Debtors
  - 1 Trade debtors
  - 2 Amounts owed by group undertakings

- 3 Amounts owed by undertakings in which the company has a participating interest
- 4 Other debtors
- 5 Called-up share capital not paid
- 6 Prepayments and accrued income

III Investments
- 1 Shares in group undertakings
- 2 Own shares
- 3 Other investments

IV Cash at bank and in hand

D Prepayments and accrued income

E Creditors: amounts falling due within one year
- 1 Debenture loans
- 2 Bank loans and overdrafts
- 3 Payments received on account
- 4 Trade creditors
- 5 Bills of exchange payable
- 6 Amounts owed to group undertakings
- 7 Amounts owed to undertakings in which the company has a participating interest
- 8 Other creditors including taxation and social security
- 9 Accruals and deferred income

F Net current assets (liabilities)

G Total assets less current liabilities

H Creditors: amounts falling due after more than one year
- 1 Debenture loans
- 2 Bank loans and overdrafts
- 3 Payments received on account
- 4 Trade creditors
- 5 Bills of exchange payable
- 6 Amounts owed to group companies
- 7 Amounts owed to undertakings in which the company has a participating interest
- 8 Other creditors including taxation and social security

I Provisions for liabilities and charges
- 1 Pensions and similar obligations
- 2 Taxation, including deferred taxation
- 3 Other provisions

J Accruals and deferred income

K Capital and reserves
- I Called-up share capital
- II Share premium account
- III Revaluation reserve
- IV Other reserves
  - 1 Capital redemption reserve
  - 2 Reserve for own shares
  - 3 Reserves provided for by the articles of association
  - 4 Other reserves
- V Profit and loss account

Table 9: Illustration of a Format 1 balance sheet.

Extract from Hanson PLC Annual Report 30th September 1989.

Balance Sheet
at September 30, 1989

	Note	1989 £ million	1988 £ million
Fixed assets			
Tangible	*20*	12	3
Investments		–	22
Shares in group companies	*18*	8,207	1,015
		8,219	1,040
Current assets			
Debtors including amounts owed by group companies	*11*	6,297	5,067
Cash at bank		192	78
		6,489	5,145
Creditors – due within one year			
Debenture loans		–	15
Bank loans and overdrafts		19	120
Amounts owed to group companies		6,906	2,486
Taxation and social security		114	103
Accruals		272	65
Dividends		238	196
		7,549	2,985
Net current assets (liabilities)		(1,060)	2,160
Total assets less current liabilities		7,159	3,200
Creditors – due after one year	*14*		
Convertible loans		1,045	1,058
Debenture loans		237	150
Bank loans		2,420	–
		3,702	1,208
Capital and reserves			
Called up share capital	*16*	1,024	1,104
Share premium account	*17*	256	145
Profit and loss account	*17*	2,177	743
		3,457	1,992
		7,159	3,200

HANSON *Chairman*
D. C. BONHAM *Finance Director*
November 29, 1989

Format 2

6.16 In Format 2, assets are shown as equal in total to liabilities (which include capital and reserves). Because the information disclosed in

Format 2 is identical in all respects (apart from one) to the information disclosed in Format 1, Format 2 has not been reproduced here but an example is given in Table 10. The only difference between Format 1 and Format 2 is that Format 2 aggregates, on the face of the balance sheet, creditors due within one year and those due after more than one year. However, in respect of each item included in creditors the split between the amount due within one year and the amount due after more than one year, together with the aggregate, must still be disclosed either on the face of the balance sheet or in the notes. [Note 13 on the balance sheet formats]. This method of presentation is more common in some other EC countries (for example, France and Germany) than in the UK

Commentary on specific items

6.17 In determining the amount to be shown under 'Net current assets (liabilities)' in Format 1, a company must take into account any amount that is shown separately under the heading 'Prepayments and accrued income'. [Note 11 on the balance sheet formats]. This applies whether the amount in question is shown as a sub-heading of debtors or as a main heading. But from the layout of Format 1, it seems to be a self-evident requirement. The 4th Directive stated that, in determining the amount to be shown under 'Net current assets (liabilities)' in Format 1, a company should take into account also any amount that is shown separately under the main heading 'Accruals and deferred income'. Presumably the reason for the omission of this requirement from note 11 on the balance sheet formats was that it was considered self-evident.

6.18 Where a company discloses holdings in its own shares under the heading 'Investments', it must show separately the nominal value of the shares it holds. [Note 4 on the balance sheet formats]. A company will generally hold its own shares only where it has acquired them by forfeiture, or by surrender in lieu of forfeiture, or by way of a gift. [Sec 143]. Where a company either purchases or redeems its own shares, it must cancel them (see chapter 9). [Sec 160(4), 162(2)].

6.19 A company must show the amount for creditors in respect of taxation and social security separately from the amount of the other creditors. [Note 9 on the balance sheet formats]. This applies in respect both of creditors payable within one year and of those payable in more than one year (see further chapter 11).

6.20 In determining the split between creditors due within one year and those due after more than one year, a company should normally treat a creditor as being payable on the earliest date on which payment falls due (that is, the date on which the creditor can require payment) rather than on the earliest date on which it expects to make payment.

Table 10: Illustration of a Format 2 balance sheet.

Extract from B.A.T. Industries p.l.c. Annual Report and Accounts 31st December 1988.

B·A·T INDUSTRIES

BALANCE SHEETS

31 December

	Group 1988 £ millions	1987	Company 1988	1987
Assets				
Fixed assets				
Tangible fixed assets (note 11)	2,257	2,178		
Investments in Group companies (note 13)			2,371	2,203
Investments in financial services subsidiaries (note 14)	3,583	1,503		
Investments in associated companies (note 15)	387	302		
Other investments and long term loans (note 16)	173	186		
	6,400	4,169	2,371	2,203
Current assets				
Stocks (note 17)	1,939	1,810		
Debtors (note 18)	960	1,022	1,030	849
Current investments (note 19)	146	312		
Short term deposits	279	954		
Cash at bank and in hand	179	247	1	
	3,503	4,345	1,031	849
Total assets	9,903	8,514	3,402	3,052
Liabilities				
Capital and reserves				
Share capital	380	374	380	374
Share premium account	107	52	107	52
Revaluation reserves	408	295		
Other reserves		387	7	7
Profit and loss account	2,576	2,786	1,187	1,159
Associated companies	130	52		
Interest of B.A.T. Industries' shareholders (note 21)	3,601	3,946	1,681	1,592
Interest of minority shareholders in subsidiaries	340	347		
Shareholders' funds	3,941	4,293	1,681	1,592
Provisions for liabilities and charges (note 22)	709	653		
Creditors				
Borrowings (note 25)	2,661	1,471	500	518
Creditors (note 26)	2,592	2,097	1,221	942
Total funds employed	9,903	8,514	3,402	3,052

On behalf of the Board
P Sheehy, B P Garraway *Directors*
21 March 1989

6.21 Unless a company shows the payments it has received on account of orders as a deduction from stocks, it must show them under creditors. [Note 8 on the balance sheet formats].

6.22 The following items may be shown in alternative positions in the balance sheet:

- Called-up share capital not paid. [Note 1 on the balance sheet formats].
- Prepayments and accrued income. [Note 6 on the balance sheet formats].
- Accruals and deferred income. [Note 10 on the balance sheet formats].

6.23 In addition, two other balance sheet items require further comment:

- 'Payments on account' relate, as appropriate, to payments that a company makes in respect of the acquisition of intangible assets, tangible assets or stocks (see chapter 7 para 7.2, chapter 8 para 8.17 and chapter 10 paras 10.2 and 10.3).
- 'Participating interest' means an interest held by an undertaking in the shares of another undertaking which it holds on a long-term basis for the purpose of securing a contribution to its activities by the exercise of control or influence arising from or related to that interest. A holding of 20 per cent or more of the shares of an undertaking is presumed to be a participating interest unless the contrary is shown. In this context, a participating interest does not include an interest in a subsidiary undertaking. It will however include associated companies as defined in SSAP 1.
- There are certain 'additional items', for example, minority interests, that have to be disclosed in a group's consolidated balance sheet and these are set out in 'Manual of Accounting - volume II' chapter 4 .

The profit and loss account

Formats

6.24 The Act permits companies to use any one of the four alternative formats of the profit and loss account, and it leaves the choice between these formats to the company's directors.

6.25 Unlike the choice between the balance sheet formats, the choice between the profit and loss account formats is significant. A company can choose not only between a vertical presentation (Formats 1 and 2) and a presentation in which it shows charges separately from income (Formats 3 and 4), but also between classifying expenses by function or by type. Thus, depending on which format a company chooses, its financial statements will contain certain additional information, for example, own work capitalised, as well as certain different information.

Classification of expenses by function

6.26 In Formats 1 and 3, expenses are classified by function (for example, cost of sales, distribution costs, administrative expenses). These formats, both of which require identical information, have much in common with the management accounts that many UK companies prepare on a regular basis. Format 1, which is the vertical presentation, is set out below, and illustrated in Table 11 overleaf.

PROFIT AND LOSS ACCOUNT - FORMAT 1

1 Turnover
2 Cost of sales
3 Gross profit or loss
4 Distribution costs
5 Administration expenses
6 Other operating income
7 Income from shares in group undertakings
8 Income from shares in undertakings in which the company has a participating interest
9 Income from other fixed asset investments
10 Other interest receivable and similar income
11 Amounts written off investments
12 Interest payable and similar charges
13 Tax on profit or loss on ordinary activities
14 Profit or loss on ordinary activities after taxation
15 Extraordinary income
16 Extraordinary charges
17 Extraordinary profit or loss
18 Tax on extraordinary profit or loss
19 Other taxes not shown under the above items
20 Profit or loss for the financial year

Classification of expenses by type

6.27 In Formats 2 and 4, expenses are classified by type (for example, raw materials and consumables, staff costs, and depreciation). These formats, both of which require identical information, are in many ways similar to value added statements. Format 2, which is the vertical presentation, is set out below, and also illustrated in Table 12 overleaf.

PROFIT AND LOSS ACCOUNT - FORMAT 2

1 Turnover
2 Change in stocks of finished goods and in work in progress
3 Own work capitalised
4 Other operating income:
5 (a) Raw materials and consumables
(b) Other external charges

6	Staff costs: (a) Wages and salaries (b) Social security costs (c) Other pension costs
7	(a) Depreciation and other amounts written off tangible and intangible fixed assets (b) Exceptional amounts written off current assets
8	Other operating charges
9	Income from shares in group undertakings
10	Income from shares in undertakings in which the company has a participating interest
11	Income from other fixed asset investments
12	Other interest receivable and similar income
13	Amounts written off investments
14	Interest payable and similar charges
15	Tax on profit or loss on ordinary activities
16	Profit or loss on ordinary activities after taxation
17	Extraordinary income
18	Extraordinary charges
19	Extraordinary profit or loss
20	Tax on extraordinary profit or loss
21	Other taxes not shown under the above items
22	Profit or loss for the financial year

Commentary on specific items

6.28 The Act attaches to the formats certain notes and comments on specific profit and loss account items.

6.29 Where expenses are classified by function, the amounts to be shown under cost of sales, distribution costs and administrative expenses are to be stated after taking into account any necessary provisions for depreciation and for diminution in the value of assets. [Note 14 on the profit and loss account formats]. The amounts of the provisions for depreciation, or for the diminution in the value of tangible and intangible fixed assets, must be disclosed separately in the notes to the financial statements. [Note 17 on the profit and loss account formats].

6.30 Income or interest derived from group undertakings must be shown separately from income and interest derived from other sources. [Note 15 on the profit and loss account formats]. Similarly, any interest or similar charges payable to group undertakings must be shown separately. [Note 16 on the profit and loss account formats].

6.31 One other profit and loss account item requires further comment. In the light of present practice in the UK, it is unlikely that any amount would fall to be disclosed under the heading 'Other taxes not shown under the above items'.

Table 11: Illustration of a Format 1 profit and loss account.

Extract from the Burton Group PLC Annual Report and Accounts 2nd September 1989.

CONSOLIDATED PROFIT AND LOSS ACCOUNT

For the financial year ended 2nd September 1989 (£ million)	*Notes*	1989	*1988*
Turnover	2	1,818.5	1,590.2
Cost of sales		(1,520.5)	(1,315.1)
Gross profit		298.0	275.1
Distribution costs		(31.9)	(28.9)
Administrative expenses		(69.9)	(63.1)
Income of related companies		48.6	46.1
Trading profit	2	244.8	229.2
Interest	3	(24.2)	(19.1)
Other income	4	3.2	1.6
Profit on ordinary activities before taxation		223.8	211.7
Taxation	5	(74.1)	(72.3)
Profit on ordinary activities after taxation		149.7	139.4
Extraordinary credit	6	–	0.4
Profit for the financial year	7	149.7	139.8
Dividends	8	(51.2)	(46.6)
Retained earnings		98.5	93.2
Statement of retained earnings			
At 4th September 1988		309.0	216.2
Goodwill written off on acquisitions		–	(0.4)
Retained earnings for the finacial year		98.5	93.2
At 2nd September 1989		407.5	309.0
Earnings per share			
Average shares in issue –actual tax	9	27.0p	25.2p
– fully taxed		26.2p	24.9p
Fully diluted – actual tax		24.7p	23.5p
– fully taxed		24.1p	23.2p

Additional disclosure

6.32 All items in the profit and loss account are preceded by an Arabic numeral and so they may be relegated to the notes to the financial statements. Whichever format of profit and loss account a company adopts, the account must, however, show separately on its face the amount of the company's profit or loss on ordinary activities before taxation. [4 Sch 3(6)].

6.33 Furthermore, whichever format of the profit and loss account a company adopts, the account must show separately as additional items:

- Any amount that has been set aside, or that it is proposed to set aside, to reserves.

- Any amount that has been withdrawn, or that it is proposed to withdraw, from reserves.

- The aggregate amount of any dividends that have been paid and that are proposed.

[4 Sch 3(7)].

Table 12: Illustration of a Format 2 profit and loss account.

Extract from ABB Kent (Holdings) plc Report and Accounts 31st December 1988.

Group Profit and Loss Account

	1988	1987
	£'000	£'000
Turnover	129,985	121,821
Change in stocks of finished goods and work in progress	(875)	502
	129,110	122,323
Other operating income	2,610	3,325
	131,720	125,648
Raw materials and consumables	(47,077)	(45,607)
Other external charges	(4,326)	(4,219)
	80,317	75,822
Staff costs	(48,311)	(46,246)
Depreciation	(3,654)	(3,368)
Other operating charges	(18,416)	(18,209)
Operating profit	9,936	7,999
Interest receivable	993	688
Interest payable	(2,351)	(2,160)
Profit on ordinary activities before taxation	8,578	6,527
Taxation on profit on ordinary activities	(2,850)	(2,481)
Profit on ordinary activities after taxation	5,728	4,046
Minority interests	(430)	(213)
Profit attributable to the members of ABB Kent (Holdings) plc	5,298	3,833
Dividends	(2,660)	(2,280)
Retained profit for the year	2,638	1,553
Earnings per share	7.0p	5.0p
Dividend per share	3.5p	3.0p
Movements in reserves		
Reserves at beginning of the year	40,774	42,731
Exchange translation	(636)	(3,510)
Goodwill on acquisition	(2,285)	—
Property revaluation surplus	6,438	—
Retained profit for the year	2,638	1,553
Reserves at end of the year	46,929	40,774

The notes to the balance sheet and the profit and loss account

6.34 Schedule 4 to the Act requires companies to disclose considerable detail in the notes to their financial statements. The objects of the requirements are:

- To supplement the information given in the financial statements in respect of any particular items that are shown in either the balance sheet or the profit and loss account.
- To give details of anything else that is relevant, in the light of the information so given, to the assessment of the state of the company's affairs.
- To explain any particular circumstances that affect items shown in the profit and loss account.

[4 Sch 37, 52].

Any information that the Act requires to be shown by way of a note to the financial statements may, alternatively, be shown in the company's profit or loss account or balance sheet. [4 Sch 35]. However, the Act does not permit a company to use the directors' report as an alternative method of disclosure.

Accounting policies

6.35 The notes to the financial statements must set out the accounting policies the company has adopted in determining the amounts to be included in the financial statements. [4 Sch 36]. In particular, they must include:

- The method of determining the provision both for depreciation and for diminution in the value of assets. [4 Sch 36].
- The method of translating foreign currency amounts into sterling. [4 Sch 58(1)].

6.36 Accounting policies are defined in SSAP 2 as "*... the specific accounting bases selected and consistently followed by a business enterprise as being, in the opinion of the management, appropriate to its circumstances and best suited to present fairly its results and financial position*". [SSAP 2 para 16]. The consistent application of accounting policy is also required by the Act. Paragraph 11 of Schedule 4 states "Accounting policies shall be applied consistently within the same accounts and from one financial year to the next".

6.37 The standard requires companies to disclose by way of a note to their financial statements the accounting policies they judge to be either material or critical in determining the profit or loss for the year and also in stating the financial position at the end of the year. The explanations should be clear, fair, and as brief as possible. [SSAP 2 para 18].

6.38 The standard gives some examples of matters for which different accounting bases are recognised, and that may have a material effect both on reported results and on the financial position. These matters include:

- Depreciation of fixed assets.
- Treatment and amortisation of intangibles such as research and development expenditure, patents and trademarks.
- Stocks
- Long-term contracts.
- Deferred taxation.
- Hire purchase or instalment transactions.
- Leasing and rental transactions.
- Conversion of foreign currencies.
- Repairs and renewals.
- Consolidation policies.
- Property development transactions.
- Warranties for products or services.

This list is not exhaustive, and it will vary according to the nature of the company's operations. [SSAP 2 para 13].

6.39 Many companies disclose their accounting policies as a separate statement that they locate away from the remainder of the notes. This is generally accepted accounting practice and it has the advantage that the accounting policies are given more prominence and are not lost within the individual notes to the financial statements.

6.40 Paragraph 18 of the standard specifically says: *"The accounting policies ... followed for dealing with items which are judged material or critical in determining profit or loss for the year and in stating the financial position should be disclosed by way of note to the accounts"*. Also, paragraph 36 of Schedule 4 requires that the accounting policies should be given *in the notes* to the financial statements. Consequently, to ensure that the accounting policies are shown in compliance with both SSAP 2 and Schedule 4, the page numbers that identify the financial statements for the purpose of the directors' adoption of the financial statements, and for the purpose of the auditors' opinion, should include the statement of accounting policies.

6.41 Where a company's financial statements have been drawn up under the alternative accounting rules the accounting convention used should be stated in those financial statements (see chapter 5 paras 5.57 to 5.61). However, the company does need to refer to the specific policy for each item that it has accounted for under the alternative rules and this disclosure would normally be made as part of the company's accounting policies.

Compliance with Accounting Standards

6.42 As discussed in chapter 3, paragraphs 3.20 and 3.21, the Companies Act 1989 introduced for the first time the requirement for companies to state whether the financial statements have been prepared in accordance with Accounting Standards that are applicable to the company. In addition, if there are any material departures from these standards, the particulars and the reasons for the departure must be given. [4 Sch 36A]. These requirements do not, however, apply to a company that qualifies as a small or medium-size company in relation to a financial year. [Sec 246(1)(a)].

6.43 Although not required by the Act, the second Auditing Standard, 'The audit report', specifically requires the auditor to disclose the financial effects of the departure unless this would be impracticable or misleading in the context of giving a true and fair view. If the financial effects of the departure are not disclosed, the reasons for such non-disclosure should be stated (see chapter 3 para 3.57).

Statements of source and application of funds

6.44 The Act does not specify formats for, or require companies to include in their financial statements, a statement of source and application of funds. But, SSAP 10 requires that all company financial statements, that are intended to give a true and fair view, should include a statement of source and application of funds both for the period under review and for the corresponding previous period. The only exception to this requirement is that the statement is not required if a company's turnover or gross income is less than £25,000 per annum. [SSAP 10 para 9]. However, if this statement is excluded from the financial statements the company's auditors need only mention in their report that the funds statement has not been given and this will not affect their report on the truth and fairness of those financial statements. In addition, where SSAP 10 is applicable to a company but a statement of source and application of funds is not included in the financial statements (as is often the case with wholly-owned subsidiaries), the directors must state the particulars and reasons for the departure (see para 6.42).

6.45 The standard does not specify a format that a company must use in preparing the statement. It only outlines the object of the statement, which is to show the manner in which the company has financed its operations and used its financial resources. Consequently, the format should be designed to achieve this objective.

6.46 The only stipulations that the standard makes about the format of the statement are that it should show the profit or loss for the period and the adjustments the company has made to it for those items that do not involve the movement of funds. Also, the following sources and applications of funds should be disclosed where they are material:

- Dividends paid.
- Acquisitions and disposals of fixed assets.
- Funds raised by increasing, or funds expended in repaying or redeeming, either medium-term or long-term loans or the company's issued capital.
- Increases or decreases in working capital (sub-divided into its components), and movements in 'net liquid funds'.

[SSAP 10 para 11].

6.47 'Net liquid funds' is defined as cash at bank and in hand and cash equivalents (for example, investments held as current assets), less bank overdrafts and other borrowings repayable within one year of the accounting date. [SSAP 10 para 8].

6.48 The statement is required to be audited, and it should show corresponding amounts for the previous period.

6.49 Although there are no set formats for statements of source and applications of funds, the appendix to SSAP 10 gives various examples of layouts companies may use. Certain of the headings in these examples are, however, now inappropriate, because SSAP 10 was issued before the Companies Act 1981 which introduced the formats. An example of the format of a statement of source and application of funds which does use Companies Act 1985 wording is given below.

STATEMENT OF SOURCE AND APPLICATION OF FUNDS				
	£	£	£	£
Source of funds				
Profit on ordinary activities before taxation		X		X
Extraordinary items		X		X
		X		X
Adjustments for items not involving the movement of funds:				
Depreciation	X		X	
Amounts written off investments	X	X	X	X
Total generated from operations		X		X
Funds from other sources				
Issue of share capital		X		X
Debenture loans		X		X
		X		X
Application of funds				
Dividends paid	(X)		(X)	
Tax paid	(X)		(X)	
Purchase of tangible fixed assets	(X)	(X)	(X)	X
		X		X
Increase or (decrease) in working capital				
Stocks		(X)		X
Debtors		X		X
Creditors		(X)		(X)
		X		X
Movement in net liquid funds:				
Cash at bank and in hand	X		X	
Current asset investments	X		X	
		X		X
		X		X

6.50 The Standard requires also that the statement of source and application of funds in a group's financial statements should be so framed as to reflect the group's operations. [SSAP 10 para 12]. An illustration of a company's source and application of funds statement is given in Table 13 overleaf.

6.51 Where the holding company either acquires or disposes of subsidiary companies, these transactions should be reflected in the statement. The Standard indicates two ways in which these transactions may be disclosed in the statement:

- The first method indicates the funds used or the funds generated from the purchase or sale respectively of subsidiary companies.

- The second method shows the increase or decrease in the individual assets and liabilities the group has acquired or disposed of.

6.52 Whichever method a company uses, it will generally also need to summarise the effect of the acquisition or disposal by way of a footnote to the statement. Where the company has acquired a

Table 13: Illustration of a Source and Application of Funds Statement.

Extract from the Avon Rubber p.l.c. Annual Report 30th September 1989.

SOURCE AND APPLICATION OF FUNDS

for the year ended 30th September 1989

	1989		1988	
	£'000	£'000	£'000	£'000
Source of funds				
From internal sources:				
Profit (excluding minority interests) before taxation		11,438		15,647
Adjustments for items not involving the movement of funds:				
Depreciation	6,314		5,280	
Revaluation surplus now realised	(155)		(23)	
Minority interests	733		365	
Profits retained in associated companies	(172)		(520)	
Disposal of subsidiary companies	(1,137)	5,583	—	5,102
Total generated from operations		17,021		20,749
From external sources:				
Profit on disposal of subsidiary companies		13,370		—
Issue of shares for cash		47		16
Issue of shares to acquire subsidiary company		20,850		—
Issue of shares in subsidiary company for cash		5,700		—
Increase in loans payable		19,667		2,276
Increase in funds		76,655		23,041
Other adjustments for items not involving the movement of funds				
Unrealised exchange gains/(losses) on current assets		164		(307)
		76,819		22,734
Application of funds				
Net increase in fixed assets and investments	21,028		11,149	
Goodwill	35,855		659	
Dividends	2,525		1,856	
Taxation	1,018		951	
Extraordinary items	—	60,426	2,743	17,358
Increase in working capital:				
Stocks	3,645		5,645	
Debtors	3,449		8,329	
Creditors	3,575		(2,919)	
Finance leasing	(1,915)	8,754	(1,494)	9,561
Movement in net liquid funds				
Decrease in bank borrowing	5,574		(3,685)	
Decrease in acceptance credits	2,065	7,639	(500)	(4,185)
		76,819		22,734

The statement includes the effect of acquisitions of the assets of TR Sillinger and the entire share capital of the Caddilac group together with the disposals of 70% of Motorway Tyres and Accessories Limited and the whole of Motorway Tyres and Batteries Limited.

	Acquisitions £'000	Disposals £'000		Acquisitions £'000	Disposals £'000
Goodwill	35,855	—	Issue of shares	20,850	—
Fixed assets	9,795	6,331	Cash	20,301	16,421
Stocks	5,153	7,547	Effect on reserves	—	584
Debtors	8,071	12,805	Transfer to investments	—	800
Creditors	(8,958)	(22,248)			
Borrowings	(8,765)	—			
Profit on disposals	—	13,370			
	41,151	17,805		41,151	17,805

subsidiary company, this footnote should indicate how much of the purchase price has been discharged in cash and how much by the issue of shares. An example of the type of disclosure that should be made in the footnote is shown below:

SUMMARY OF THE EFFECTS OF THE ACQUISITION OF COMPANY A

	£'000
Net assets acquired:	
Tangible fixed assets	200
Goodwill	20
Stocks	50
Debtors	40
Creditors	(45)
	265
Discharged by:	
Issue of shares	150
Cash paid	115
	265

Listed companies' historical summaries

6.53 Although the Act does not require a company to include a historical summary of information in its financial statements, many companies do so. This practice arose because the chairman of The International Stock Exchange wrote to all listed companies in 1964 recommending that they should include a ten-year historical summary in their annual financial statements.

6.54 In practice, because the historical summary is additional voluntary information, many listed companies now give only a five year historical summary, rather than the ten year historical summary recommended by the chairman of the International Stock Exchange.

6.55 There is no set format for historical summaries, but the type of information that listed companies normally give in them is as follows:

Balance sheet

- Tangible assets.
- Other assets.
- Net borrowings.
- Capital and reserves.
- Minority interests.

Profit and loss account

- Turnover.
- Trading profit.
- Interest.
- Profit on ordinary activities before taxation.
- Taxation.
- Profit after taxation.
- Extraordinary items.
- Minority interests and preference dividends.
- Retained earnings.

Statistical information

- Earnings per share.
- Ordinary dividends per share.
- Dividend cover.
- Return on capital employed.

6.56 The historical summary will normally show the actual figures that were reported for each year. However, in certain situations, the reported figures may need to be adjusted. The circumstances where adjustments may be necessary are as follows:

- Where there is a change in accounting policy, SSAP 6 says that amounts relating to past years should be restated if this is necessary to ensure that the reported figures for each year are stated on a consistent basis. If the figures have not been restated, then this fact should be disclosed. If figures have been restated, then it should also be made clear which figures have been restated.
- Where fundamental errors have been corrected by a prior year adjustment, then the historical summary should be changed, and again it should be made clear which figures have been restated.
- Earnings per share figures that are reported should be amended to reflect any:

- ☐ New equity shares that have been issued by capitalising reserves.

- ☐ Equity shares that have been split into shares of a lower nominal value.

- ☐ New equity shares that have been issued by way of rights issues.

The earnings per share figures should be adjusted in the ways explained in chapter 13. Appendix 2 to SSAP 3 says that the resultant figures should be described as the 'adjusted earnings per share'. They should be set out separately (for example, in a separate box) from the other financial information that is not adjusted.

- ■ Dividends per share should also be adjusted where there have been changes in the number of equity shares in issue due to capitalisation of reserves, a rights issue, or a split in the nominal value of shares in issue. Disclosure of the revised dividend in the form of pence per share should be given in a similar way to the adjusted earnings per share.

An example of a five-year historical summary is shown in Table 14 overleaf.

6.57 The ASC stated in chapter 6, paragraph 6.11 of the Handbook, 'Accounting for the effects of changing prices', that companies may prefer to show information on the effects of changing prices separately from the financial statements, as supplementary information, in the five or ten year historical summaries presented with their financial statements. Where a company does adjust its historical summary to eliminate the effects of price changes, it should give the basis of the adjustments that it has made, so as to make the summaries meaningful.

6.58 Because a historical summary is not a requirement of law or of Accounting Standards, and it is not required in order for the financial statements to show a true and fair view, the auditors do not need to report on it. They do, however, have to satisfy themselves that the information shown in the summary is consistent with the audited financial statements and that it is not misleading. [Auditing Guideline, 'Financial information issued with audited financial statements'].

Half-yearly reports and preliminary statements

6.59 The formats set out in the Act apply both to the financial statements of those companies that are limited by either shares or guarantee and to the financial statements of unlimited companies. However, they do not apply to half-yearly reports and preliminary profits statements made by listed companies or by companies traded on the USM, which are *non-statutory* accounts. These reports and statements can be presented in any reasonable form that includes the items that are disclosable under The International Stock Exchange's Continuing Obligations or the USM's General Undertaking. The reason for this is that the formats apply to financial statements drawn up under section 226 of the Act, and section 226 does not apply to half-yearly reports and preliminary profits statements. [Sec 226(1)].

Table 14: Example of a five-year historical summary.

Extract from Norcros p.l.c. Report and Accounts 31st March 1989.

FIVE YEAR SUMMARY

	1989	1988	1987	1986	1985
TURNOVER	£644·7m	£718·1m	£641·1m	£639·7m	£374·9m
OPERATING PROFIT ..	£69·9m	£71·4m	£59·5m	£53·4m	£40·0m
OPERATING MARGIN ..	10·8%	9·9%	9·3%	8·3%	10·7%
PROFIT BEFORE TAXATION ..	£66·9m	£65·3m	£53·2m	£45·1m	£34·3m
EARNINGS FOR ORDINARY SHAREHOLDERS	£44·9m	£42·8m	£35·0m	£26·0m	£19·6m
EARNINGS PER SHARE ..	33·5p	33·0p	28·0p	21·4p	20·2p
DIVIDENDS PER ORDINARY SHARE	16·0p	14·4p	12·0p	9·3p	8·6p
DIVIDEND COVER (TIMES)	2·1	2·3	2·3	2·3	2·3
FUNDS EMPLOYED	£191·7m	£204·6m	£182·5m	£178·5m	£167·3m
RETURN ON FUNDS EMPLOYED	37·8%	35·3%	33·2%	30·9%	24·3%
CAPITAL AND RESERVES ..	£178·2m	£151·8m	£127·7m	£114·8m	£121·4m
NET BORROWINGS	£5·4m	£46·2m	£49·6m	£52·9m	£32·6m
NET DEBT TO EQUITY ..	3·1%	30·5%	38·9%	46·1%	26·9%
INTEREST COVER (TIMES) ..	23·5	11·6	9·4	6·5	7·1
AVERAGE NUMBER OF EMPLOYEES	11,877	13,667	13,478	14,643	11,962
SALES PER EMPLOYEE ..	£50,012	£49,921	£45,050	£41,099	£29,076
OPERATING PROFIT PER EMPLOYEE	£5,882	£5,228	£4,414	£3,646	£3,340

Return on Funds Employed is defined as profit on ordinary activities before taxation and interest payable expressed as a percentage of the total of shareholders' funds, minority interests and borrowings.
Net Debt to Equity is defined as net borrowing expressed as a percentage of capital and reserves (including minority interests).

6.60 The information that The International Stock Exchange requires listed companies to include in their half-yearly reports and preliminary profits statements is as follows:

- An explanatory statement relating to the group's activities and profit and loss during the period (This is required in half-yearly reports only.)

- A statement showing:
  - Net turnover.
  - Profit or loss before taxation and extraordinary items.
  - Taxation.
  - Minority interests.
  - Profit or loss attributable to shareholders, before extraordinary items.
  - Extraordinary items (net of taxation).
  - Profit or loss attributable to shareholders.
  - Rates and amounts of dividends paid and proposed.
  - Earnings per share.
  - Comparative figures.
- An explanation of any significant information required to enable investors to make an informed assessment of the trend of the group's activities. (This is required in half-yearly reports only.)
- A statement as to whether the information reported has been audited. Reference should also be made to section 240 of the Act (see further chapter 25).

[CO 25].

6.61 The General Undertaking requires USM companies to keep the Quotations Department of The International Stock Exchange informed of any information necessary to enable the shareholders and the public to appraise the position of the company. In particular, USM companies are required to notify the Quotations Department of their preliminary profit announcements for any year, half year or other period and to prepare a half-yearly report.

6.62 However, the USM's General Undertaking does not specify what information half-yearly reports and preliminary profits statements that companies traded on the USM prepare should contain, but as a guide they should normally include similar information to that outlined above for listed companies.

Chapter 7

BALANCE SHEET - INTANGIBLE FIXED ASSETS

Chapter 7

BALANCE SHEET - INTANGIBLE FIXED ASSETS

Introduction

7.1 This chapter deals with the disclosure and treatment of intangible fixed assets, which are becoming increasingly important to many enterprises and are assuming greater significance in the balance sheet. It considers, in particular, the disclosure and accounting treatment of research and development expenditure and goodwill. The treatment of computer software costs is also discussed. Goodwill arising on consolidation and brands are considered in 'Manual of Accounting - volume II' chapter 8.

Intangible assets

7.2 Recognition of intangible assets in company balance sheets is specifically permitted by Schedule 4 to the Act. The model formats for the balance sheet include a heading for 'Intangible Assets'. Under that heading there are separate sub-headings for:

- Development costs.
- Concessions, patents, licences, trademarks, and similar rights and assets.
- Goodwill.
- Payments on account.

7.3 Intangible assets may be capitalised subject to the rules set out in the following paragraphs.

7.4 The balance sheet may include amounts for concessions, patents, licences, trade marks and other similar rights and assets only where either of the following conditions is satisfied:

- They were acquired for valuable consideration in circumstances that do not qualify them to be shown as goodwill.
- They were created by the company itself.

[Note 2 on the balance sheet formats].

7.5 Where intangible assets are capitalised, they must always be amortised over their estimated useful economic lives. [4 Sch 18]. Besides applying to those intangibles that are specifically defined in the Act (development costs, concessions, patents, licences, trade marks and goodwill), this requirement applies also to other intangibles such as publishing rights, brands or know-how. Although know-how is not often found in UK financial statements, the bases and the methods of accounting for it should follow generally the accounting principles for development costs.

7.6 The amortisation rules that have to be followed for intangible assets are the same rules that apply to tangible fixed assets, which are discussed in chapter 4, paragraphs 4.4 to 4.19.

7.7 The Act also permits intangible assets, other than goodwill, to be included in financial statements at their current cost. Goodwill on the other hand may not be revalued. [4 Sch para 31(1)].

Technical release 780

7.8 In February 1990, the ASC issued TR 780 which sets out the provisions on accounting for intangible fixed assets.

7.9 TR 780 proposes that an intangible fixed asset should be recognised in the balance sheet as a fixed asset in its own right if and only if all the following conditions are satisfied:

- The historical costs incurred in creating it are known or are readily ascertainable.
- Its characteristics can be clearly distinguished from goodwill and other assets.
- Its cost can be measured independently of goodwill, of other assets and of the earnings of the relevant business or business segment.

7.10 An intangible asset where recognised may only be carried at its historical cost less provisions for depreciation and, if applicable, permanent diminutions in value. TR 780 suggests that an intangible asset can be carried at a valuation only where both of the following conditions are satisfied:

- The carrying amount is based on the depreciated replacement cost of the asset which can be measured with reasonable certainty.
- The depreciated replacement cost represents the current cost of the asset. In order for this condition to be satisfied, there should

be no expectation that the depreciated replacement cost exceeds the net amount recoverable from the asset.

7.11 TR 780 recognises that there are inherent difficulties in determining the useful economic life of intangible assets. As a practical and realistic solution, it proposes that intangible fixed assets should be deemed to have a finite useful economic life not exceeding 20 years except where it can be demonstrated that a longer life is more appropriate. In such circumstances, the cost should be amortised over that longer period subject to it not exceeding 40 years from the date the asset was first brought into use.

7.12 TR 780 recommends that an annual review should be undertaken to determine whether the amortisation period adopted for each intangible fixed asset remains appropriate and whether any permanent diminution in value has occurred.

7.13 Intangible assets, because of their non-physical nature, give rise to particular problems in connection with their recognition, their carrying values and their useful economic lives. The guidance provided by TR 780 is expected to ultimately lead to the formulation of a SSAP (see further 'Manual of Accounting - volume II' chapter 8).

Disclosure

7.14 The disclosure requirements for intangible fixed assets are governed by paragraph 42 of Schedule 4 to the Act. These requirements are identical to those for tangible fixed assets which are discussed in chapter 8. The Act requires the information to be given in respect of each of the sub-headings that are preceded in the formats by Arabic numerals. This means that the required information outlined in chapter 8, paragraphs 8.8 to 8.11 must be disclosed in the financial statements for each of the categories of intangible assets discussed in paragraph 7.2 above (for example, see Table 15 overleaf).

7.15 Where a company has applied one of the alternative accounting rules to any intangible fixed asset, the notes must disclose the years in which the assets were separately valued (so far as the directors know these) and also the separate values. If any assets are valued during the financial year in question, the notes must also disclose the valuers names or particulars of their qualifications and the basis of valuation used by them. [4 Sch 43].

Research and development

7.16 The Act permits only *development costs* (but not research costs) to be capitalised, and then only in *special circumstances*. [4 Sch 20(1)]. Research costs (whether pure or applied) must be written off to the profit and loss account as they are incurred. [4 Sch 3(2)(c)].

Table 15: Disclosure of intangible fixed assets.

Extract from Cooksons Group plc Annual Report 31st December 1988.

Accounting policies extract

Intangible fixed assets

Patents, licences and any such items which can be separately identified and valued are capitalised in the Group balance sheet at cost and are amortised over their estimated useful economic lives.

Note extract

10 Intangible fixed assets

Group	Balance at 1.1.88 £m	Exchange adjustments £m	Acquisitions /transfers £m	Charge for year £m	Balance at 31.12.88 £m
Cost	5.1	0.1	2.8	–	8.0
Amortisation	(0.6)	–	0.6	(0.4)	(0.4)
Net book value	4.5	0.1	3.4	(0.4)	7.6

The intangible fixed assets are mainly comprised of patents, licences and trademarks.

7.17 The Act does not define development. However, SSAP 13 defines development as *"use of scientific or technical knowledge in order to produce new or substantially improved materials, devices, products or services, to install new processes or systems prior to the commencement of commercial production or commercial applications, or to improving substantially those already produced or installed"*. [SSAP 13 para 21]. Therefore, development is the work a company performs after it has planned or designed a new or substantially improved product or service until the time that this is ready either to be manufactured or to be put into operation commercially.

7.18 SSAP 13, which was revised in January 1989, provides examples of activities that would normally be included in research and development. These have been given instead of a detailed discussion of the relevant types of costs that may be included in research and development, as occurs for example in IAS 9, 'Accounting for research and development'. The examples are:

- Experimental, theoretical or other work aimed at the discovery of new knowledge, or the advancement of existing knowledge.

- Searching for applications of that knowledge.

- Formulation and design of possible applications for such work.

- Testing in search for, or evaluation of, product, service or process alternatives.

- Design, construction and testing of pre-production prototypes and models and development batches.

- Design of products, services, processes or systems involving new technology or substantially improving those already produced or installed.

- Construction and operation of pilot plants.

[SSAP 13 para 6].

7.19 The standard also gives examples of activities typically excluded from research and development activities:

- Testing and analysis either of equipment or product for purposes of quality or quantity control.

- Periodic alterations to existing products, services or processes even though these may represent some improvement.

- Operational research not tied to a specific research and development activity.

- Cost of corrective action in connection with break-downs during commercial production.

- Legal and administrative work in connection with patent applications, records and litigation and the sale or licensing of patents.

- Activity, including design and construction engineering, relating to the construction, relocation, rearrangement or start-up of facilities or equipment other than facilities or equipment whose sole use is for a particular research and development project.

- Market research.

[SSAP 13 para 7].

7.20 The original standard specifically permitted market research to be capitalised, if it was incurred in order to determine whether a product under development was commercially viable in terms of market conditions, public opinion, and consumer and environmental legislation. Its exclusion from expenditure that can be carried forward under the revised version, represents a tightening of the rules.

Development costs

7.21 The type of development costs that may be capitalised are not defined either in the Act or in the revised standard, but IAS 9 does give some guidance on the type of costs that may be capitalised. IAS 9 says that development costs may include:

- Salaries, wages and related costs of personnel.
- The costs of materials and services consumed.
- The depreciation of equipment and facilities.
- A reasonable allocation of overhead costs.
- Other related costs, such as the amortisation of patents and licences.

[IAS 9 para 15].

7.22 As an example, a cable television company may wish to capitalise, as development costs, the expenditure it has incurred in:

- Raising capital (excluding preliminary or formation expenses, which it must charge to the profit and loss account).
- Acquiring and installing capital equipment.
- Recruiting personnel and paying their subsequent salary costs.
- Applying successfully for a franchise.
- Laying cables.
- Preparing and purchasing programmes to transmit.

Special circumstances

7.23 As stated in paragraph 7.16 above, the Act permits development costs to be capitalised, but only in *'special circumstances'*. The Act does not define the term *'special circumstances'*. Therefore, it is necessary again to look to SSAP 13 for guidance. It seems reasonable to assume that, if all the conditions set out in paragraph 25 of SSAP 13 are met, special circumstances exist, and so development costs may be capitalised. If any one of the conditions is not met, then development costs must be written off as they are incurred.

7.24 Paragraph 25 of SSAP 13 lays down the following conditions that must all be satisfied if development expenditure is to be capitalised:

- There is a clearly defined project.
- The related expenditure is separately identifiable.
- The outcome of the project has been assessed with reasonable certainty as to both its technical feasibility and its ultimate commercial viability, considered in the light of factors such as likely market conditions (including competing products), public opinion, and consumer and environmental legislation.
- The aggregate of the deferred development costs, any further development costs, and related production, selling, and administration costs, is reasonably expected to be exceeded by related future sales or other revenues.
- Adequate resources exist, or are reasonably expected to be available, to enable the project to be completed, and to provide any consequential increases in working capital.

7.25 Where these conditions are satisfied, a company can defer development expenditure, but only until commercial production begins. SSAP 13 requires a company to amortise the expenditure it has capitalised from the time that commercial production of the product or service begins. Where a company is developing a product, commercial production begins when the company is manufacturing the product with a view to selling it commercially. [SSAP 13 para 28].

Amortisation

7.26 Amortisation of development expenditure must be allocated to each accounting period on a systematic basis. This can be done by reference to the sales or the use of the product or the service, or by reference to the period over which the product or service is expected to be sold or used. However, the period of amortisation may be difficult to determine. In determining this period, the directors must establish a realistic and prudent number of years over which they expect the development expenditure to produce a benefit. They must decide also whether they expect the benefit to occur evenly over these years.

7.27 To continue the example of a cable television company, it would normally write its development expenditure off over a period that begins with the date when it first relays programmes and ends on the date that the franchise period ends. However, if, for example, only a small number of subscribers has signed up during the initial operation period, the company may calculate the amount of amortisation that it charges during that period differently from the amount it charges once the company reaches its projected number of subscribers. The company may, for instance, calculate the amount of amortisation it charges in this initial operation period by reference to the actual number of subscribers to the service, as compared to the estimate of the final number of subscribers.

Disclosure

7.28 SSAP 13 requires the following disclosures to be made in the notes to the financial statements where development costs are deferred and are shown as an asset in the balance sheet:

- The accounting policy should be stated, as required by SSAP 2, and clearly explained.
- The total amount of research and development expenditure written off to the profit and loss account in the period should be disclosed, analysed between the current year's expenditure and amounts amortised from deferred expenditure. No guidance has been given as to where this disclosure should be made, but it would normally be provided in the notes to the accounts, or in the directors' report.
- Movements on deferred development expenditure and the amount carried forward at the beginning and the end of the period should be disclosed. Deferred development expenditure should be disclosed under the heading of 'intangible assets' in the balance sheet.

[SSAP 13 paras 30 to 32].

7.29 In addition, the Act requires that further disclosure should also be made of the period over which the amount of those costs that were originally capitalised is being, or is to be written off, together with the reasons for capitalising the development costs in question (see also para 7.37). [4 Sch 20(2)].

Exemptions from disclosure

7.30 The ASC in 1988 issued TR 690 and TR 706, dealing with the application of Accounting Standards to small companies, and the definition of a 'small company'. SSAP 13 has incorporated these proposals by exempting some companies from certain disclosure requirements.

7.31 A company need not disclose the total amounts of research and development charged in the profit and loss account (see point 2 in para 7.28 above) if it is not:

- A plc.

- A banking company or an insurance company.

- A holding company that has either a plc or a banking or an insurance company as a subsidiary.

- A company that satisfies two of the three criteria for defining a medium-sized company under section 247 of the Act, multiplied by ten. The present medium-sized criteria multiplied by ten would, therefore, provide yardsticks of under 2500 for employees, under £80 million for turnover, and under £39 million for balance sheet totals.

7.32 Where a company adopts Format 1 for its balance sheet, the 'balance sheet total' is the aggregate of the amounts shown under the headings that are preceded by the letters A to D inclusive. Where a company adopts Format 2 for its balance sheet, the 'balance sheet total' is the aggregate of the amounts shown under the general heading 'Assets'. In either case, the effect is to equate 'balance sheet total' to gross assets.

7.33 Consequently, most private companies will not have to disclose the research and development expenditure charged in the profit and loss account. However, they will still have to disclose their accounting policy for research and development and any amounts of deferred development expenditure carried forward in intangible assets. An illustration of a group that capitalises development expenditure is given in Table 16 overleaf.

Provisions for diminution in value

7.34 A company should review at the end of each accounting period the development expenditure it has capitalised. Where the circumstances that justified the original deferral of the expenditure no longer apply, or are considered doubtful, the company should write off immediately the expenditure to the extent that the company considers it to be irrecoverable. [SSAP 13 para 29]. Consequently, a company will have to consider the conditions outlined in paragraph 7.24 above at each year end in order to establish whether it should write off all or some of the previously capitalised development expenditure.

7.35 Where the directors expect the diminution in value of the development expenditure to be permanent, both the Act and SSAP 13 require that provision should be made for the diminution in value of the asset. However, the directors may consider that a diminution in value of development expenditure is only *temporary*. For example, when the financial statements are prepared, the directors may no longer be able to show that the development project is technically feasible, but they may believe that the company will find a solution to the feasibility problem in the future. In the meantime, however, they propose to provide for the diminution in value of the development expenditure (which they consider to be *temporary*) in accordance with SSAP 13. In this situation, the directors should comply with the requirement of SSAP 13 and provide for the temporary diminution in value, even though such a provision may not generally be required to be made under the Act.

Table 16: Disclosure of research and development expenditure.

Extract from The Laing Group Public Limited Company Report and Accounts 31st December 1988.

Accounting policies extract

Research and development

Research costs are written off in the year in which they are incurred.

Development expenditure is written off as incurred except where it is material and is separately indentifiable with a project on which the revenues will be earned in future accounting periods. In such cases, the expenditure is deferred and amortised having regard to production levels achieved and to the ultimate commercial viability of the project.

Note extract

10 Intangible assets

Intangible assets relate to deferred development expenditure less accumulated amortisation.

	1988 £'000	1987 £'000
Gross expenditure	3,659	3,659
Differences on exchange	34	–
	3,693	3,659
Accumulated amortisation	(2,898)	(283)
Net book value	795	3,376

7.36 SSAP 13 no longer states, as did the original standard, that once development costs have been written off, they can no longer be reinstated, even though the uncertainties which has led to their write off no longer apply. Consequently, in determining whether it is now possible to reinstate such costs, it is necessary to consider the requirements of the Act relating to provisions for diminution in the value of fixed assets. These provisions require that where the factors that gave rise to the provision no longer apply to any extent, then the company *must* write back the provision to that extent. [4 Sch 19(3)]. This means that development costs that have been written off in the past may now be reinstated where the reason for making the original provision against them no longer applies. This provision can now, therefore, be applied where development costs were once capitalised and a provision was made for a permanent diminution in value and the reason for that provision no longer applies. However, it is unlikely that this argument can be used where the development expenditure was never capitalised, but was written off as incurred to the profit and loss account.

Effect on realised reserves

7.37 Where development expenditure is deferred by capitalising it, and the unamortised development expenditure is not treated as a realised loss (see chapter 19), the note to the financial statements, that Schedule 4, paragraph 20(2) (see para 7.29) requires, must also state:

- The fact that the amount of unamortised development expenditure is not to be treated as a realised loss for the purposes of calculating distributable profits.

- The circumstances that the directors relied upon to justify their decision not to treat the unamortised development expenditure as a realised loss.

[Sec 269(2)(b)].

Set-up costs

7.38 Some companies incur costs in setting up new branches or businesses. Two possible approaches to this type of expenditure exist:

- Immediate write-off to the profit and loss account.

- Deferral of the costs and their amortisation to the profit and loss account to be matched against revenue in future years.

7.39 As there is no applicable guidance, deferral of such expenditure can only be justified if similar criteria to those of SSAP 13, governing the carry forward of expenditure incurred developing a new product or service, are satisfied (see para 7.24).

7.40 Consequently, the commercial viability of the undertaking must be reasonably assured before deferral of such costs is possible. Where this is not so, prudence requires that the costs should be written off to the profit and loss account as they are incurred. The costs that are likely to be incurred in this area are advertising, both to the trade and to the public, staff training, and costs incurred in establishing reporting and other administrative procedures. Care should be taken to ensure that only costs concerned with the set-up are carried forward where the circumstances justify this. Generally, however, the majority of such costs should be written off to the profit and loss account on the grounds of prudence.

7.41 Where costs are deferred, the accounting treatment should then also follow that outlined in SSAP 13 for development expenditure and the criteria for carry forward should be reconsidered each year. Similarly, there will need to be full disclosure, which will include the accounting policy adopted by the company.

Computer software

Treatment of computer software costs

7.42 Many companies write off the cost of their computer software immediately to the profit and loss account. However, an increasing number of companies capitalise their computer software costs as either tangible fixed assets or intangible fixed assets (for example, see Table 17). These costs may arise in several ways. Consider the following four situations:

Table 17: Illustration of a company that has capitalised software program products.

Extract from STC plc Annual Report 31st December 1988.

Accounting policies extract

Intangible fixed assets

Software program product costs are capitalised once a detailed program design or working model has been established and are amortised on a straight-line basis over the estimated life of the asset, usually between 3 and 4 years. The cost of establishing the design or working model and the costs of maintaining existing products are written off as incurred.

Note extract

12 Intangible fixed assets
Intangible fixed assets comprise the unamortised cost of software program products, as follows:

	Group 1988
	£m
Cost:	
Beginning of year	35.7
Elimination of fully depreciated costs	(10.0)
Additions	7.7
End of year	33.4
Depreciation:	
Beginning of year	17.3
Elimination of fully depreciated costs	(10.0)
Charge for the year	7.9
End of year	15.2
Net book value	18.2

- A company purchases computer software externally (including, for example, packages for applications such as payroll, or general ledger or other similar packages to be used on the company's own computer). The company should capitalise the cost of such software as a tangible fixed asset. This is because the software complies with the Act's definition of a fixed asset, because the company will generally purchase it to use it on a continuing basis in the company's activities. The SSAP 13 criteria do not apply in this situation, because this expenditure is not development expenditure.

  The company should depreciate this software, in common with its other fixed assets, over its estimated useful life. Where a company purchases a software package specifically to run on a particular computer, the software's estimated useful life should generally not exceed the computer's remaining useful life.

  Where a company incurs subsequent expenditure to improve the software, it could either write this expenditure off immediately or capitalise it. If this expenditure is capitalised it should be written off over the remaining useful life of the software package. However, where the improvement costs lead to an extension of the software's useful life, the company will need to revise the depreciation charge, because the asset's life has been extended (see further chapter 4 paras 4.14 to 4.17).

- A company employs programmers to develop software for the company's own use. In this situation, two problems exist:

  - The company will need to analyse the programmers' time and other expenses in order to identify the costs of developing the software.

  - If the software is not operational at the time the financial statements are prepared, the company will have to provide evidence to demonstrate that the software will be completed successfully and have a value to the business.

  Provided that it can overcome both of these problems, a company may capitalise this type of computer software cost as a tangible fixed asset. If the software is not fully developed it should be included under the balance sheet heading of 'Payments on account and assets in the course of construction'.

  SSAP 13 criteria are not relevant in assessing whether this expenditure should be capitalised, because the expenditure is not part of a commercial project. The company is merely producing its own fixed assets.

- A company buys computer software to incorporate into a product that it is developing. This could include software that an external software house writes, and that the company will include in computer-controlled equipment it will produce and sell.

  This expenditure is a form of development expenditure, and so the question of whether this can be capitalised is covered by the criteria included in SSAP 13. Provided that these criteria are satisfied, the company may capitalise the expenditure, and amortise it over the product's estimated useful life (see paras 7.23 to 7.25).

- A company's own programmers write software that the company will include in its products. The question of capitalisation will again depend on whether the criteria set out in SSAP 13 are satisfied.

Difficulties in valuing computer software

7.43 In practice it may be very difficult to value both computer software and computer hardware. This is because substantial advances are being made in technology, and also the cost of high technology products and equipment is continually falling. Where an industry is affected by specific inflation, usually there are Government indices that measure the effect that inflation has had in that industry. However, because the market in high technology products such as computer software and hardware is changing so rapidly, the Government is, apparently, unable to publish a meaningful index for this type of equipment.

7.44 The ASC's handbook on 'Accounting for the effect of changing prices' outlines some of the problems involved in valuing assets where technology has changed significantly since the asset was purchased. It also outlines the following four areas that could change markedly with technological advancement:

- An asset's initial capital cost.
- An asset's operating costs.
- An asset's life.
- An asset's output.

Companies should consider all these areas if they decide to value computer software or hardware.

Goodwill

Introduction

7.45 This section deals only with purchased goodwill arising in an individual company. The treatment of goodwill arising on consolidation, which is another form of purchased goodwill, is covered in 'Manual of Accounting - volume II' chapter 8. Where a company acquires an unincorporated business, it will account for the cost of the business it has acquired by attributing fair values to the separable net assets it has acquired. If the fair value of the consideration the company gave differs from the aggregate of the fair values of the separable net assets it acquired, the difference will be *purchased* goodwill. The company will identify separately this purchased goodwill in its accounting records. This purchased goodwill may be either positive or negative.

7.46 The accounting treatment of purchased goodwill, including goodwill on consolidation, is dealt with in SSAP 22 'Accounting for goodwill' which was issued in December 1984. SSAP 22 was revised by the addition of further disclosure requirements in relation to acquisitions and disposals in July 1989 (see paras 7.72 and 7.73). Furthermore, in February 1990, the ASC published ED 47 in response to criticisms of the current standard. This section discusses the treatment of goodwill in the light of the current standard. The salient features of ED 47 are, however, discussed briefly in paragraphs 7.83 to 7.87.

Definition

7.47 SSAP 22 defines purchased goodwill as the difference between the fair *value of the consideration given* and the aggregate of the *fair values of its separable net assets acquired*. [SSAP 22 para 36].

7.48 The standard defines the term 'fair value' as the amount for which an asset or a liability could be exchanged in an arm's length transaction. [SSAP 22 para 30]. However, the standard gives no guidance on how to ascertain the fair value of the consideration given. Some guidance on fair valuing assets is given in the proposed exposure draft 'Fair value in the context of acquisition accounting', which is considered in detail in 'Manual of Accounting - volume II' chapter 7.

7.49 'Separable net assets' are defined in the standard as those assets (and liabilities) which can be identified and sold (or discharged) separately without necessarily disposing of the business as a whole. They include identifiable intangibles. [SSAP 22 para 27].

Accounting treatment

7.50 Goodwill may be shown as an asset only if it was acquired for valuable consideration. [Note 3 on the balance sheet formats]. This means that companies cannot capitalise goodwill if, for example, it is internally generated. This accords with the requirement in SSAP 22 that companies may recognise goodwill in their financial statements only if it has arisen from a purchase transaction. The Act also requires a company that has capitalised goodwill to write if off over a period chosen by the directors which must not exceed its useful life. [4 Sch para 21(2)(3)]. The standard is, therefore, broadly consistent with the Act, but requires certain additional information to be disclosed (see paras 7.72 and 7.73).

7.51 The standard requires a company to adopt one of the following two policies with regard to purchased goodwill:

- It should normally be eliminated from the financial statements by immediate write-off against reserves. [SSAP 22 para 39].

- It should be carried as an intangible fixed asset in the balance sheet, and amortised to the profit and loss account over its useful economic life. [SSAP 22 para 41].

7.52 SSAP 22 prefers the first approach and this method is illustrated in Table 18. However, ED 47 proposes to prohibit this method and has opted for the amortisation method (see para 7.85). The amortisation method is illustrated in Table 19 overleaf.

Acceptability of using both elimination methods

7.53 An individual company's circumstances may require it to adopt different policies in relation to the goodwill that arises on different acquisitions. For example, a company may generally follow the preferred policy of immediate write-off, but it may need to adopt the policy of amortising goodwill on an unusually large acquisition because of the effect that an immediate write-off would have on its reserves. This treatment is acceptable under SSAP 22 paragraph 42, but the use of several different elimination methods will need to be clearly explained to avoid the financial statements not giving a true and fair view. However, if ED 47 becomes an Accounting Standard, companies will have to adopt a single treatment in relation to goodwill that arises on different acquisitions.

Revaluation of purchased goodwill

7.54 The standard states that where the amortisation treatment is selected, a company should not revalue purchased goodwill. [SSAP 22 para 41(a)]. This accords with the legal requirements for companies and groups, because Schedule 4, paragraph 31(1) does not permit the revaluation of goodwill. The standard effectively introduces a similar prohibition also for banking and insurance companies, which Schedule 4 does not cover.

Table 18: Illustration of a company that has written off goodwill against reserves, which is the method preferred by SSAP 22.

Extract from STC plc Annual Report 31st December 1988.

Accounting policies extract.

Goodwill

Goodwill at cost represents the excess of the cost or value attributed to investments in businesses or subsidiaries over the fair value of the underlying net assets at the date of their acquisition. Goodwill is written off against reserves in the year in which it arises.

Note extract

21 Reserves

	Group		
	Share premium	Other reserves	Profit and loss
	£m	£m	£m
Beginning of year	157.1	94.1	254.1
Change in accounting policy (note 1)	–	–	(3.7)
Beginning of year restated	157.1	94.1	250.4
Arising on share issues	0.3	–	–
Goodwill written off	–	(22.4)	–
Exchange adjustments	–	–	(3.1)
Other movements	–	–	0.7
Retained profit for year	–	–	98.8
End of year	157.4	71.7	346.8

7.55 The standard also states that if there is a permanent diminution in value of purchased goodwill, it should be written down immediately through the profit and loss account to its estimated recoverable amount. [SSAP 22 para 41(a)]. Similarly, Schedule 4, paragraph 19(2) requires a company to make provision for any permanent diminution in value of any fixed asset.

7.56 Under section 275 of the Act, unless a provision for a permanent diminution in value of purchased goodwill results from a revaluation of, or consideration by the directors of the value of, all the company's fixed assets (other than goodwill), it must be treated as a realised loss. However, the immediate write-off of goodwill to reserves as

Table 19: Illustration of disclosure where goodwill is capitalised and amortised over its estimated useful life.

Extract from Juliana's Holdings PLC Annual Report and Accounts 31st December 1988.

Accounting policies extract

(d) Fixed assets and depreciation

Certain freehold land and buildings were revalued at 31st December 1985. Tangible fixed assets and intangible fixed assets are stated at cost and/or valuation less accumulated depreciation. Depreciation is provided to write down the cost of assets over their estimated useful lives.

Principal annual rates of depreciation used are:

Goodwill	5% straight line
Pre-operational expenses	20% straight line
Freehold buildings	2% straight line
Improvements to leasehold premises	Life of lease
Sound and lighting equipment	25% straight line
Fixtures and fittings	20% or 10% straight line
Motor vehicles	20% or 25% straight line
Plant and machinery	20% or 25% straight line
Hire equipment	7½% to 25% straight line

Note extract

12. Intangible fixed assets

Group	Pre-operational expenses	Goodwill arising on consolidation	Purchased goodwill	Total
Cost				
At 1st January 1988	—	724,129	100,363	824,492
Additions during the year	102,412	600,000	2,800	705,212
At 31st December 1988	£102,412	£1,324,129	£103,163	£1,529,704
Amortisation				
At 1st January 1988	—	163,707	15,970	179,677
Charge for the year	4,341	66,204	5,017	75,562
At 31st December 1988	£4,341	£229,911	£20,987	£255,239
Net book value				
At 31st December 1988	£98,071	£1,094,218	£82,176	£1,274,465
At 31st December 1987	£—	£560,422	£84,393	£644,815

recommended by SSAP 22 is not a provision, and so it need not immediately be regarded as a realised loss. (see further paras 7.74 to 7.80).

Useful economic life

7.57 The Act makes no attempt to define the 'useful economic life' of goodwill. However, limited guidance on how to determine the useful economic life of purchased goodwill is given in appendix 1 of SSAP 22.

7.58 Although the standard does not specify either a minimum or a maximum amortisation period, appendix 1 states that the useful economic life of purchased goodwill is the period over which benefits may reasonably be expected to accrue from that goodwill. In the period following the acquisition, the value of the purchased goodwill is considered to diminish, although it may be replaced by non-purchased goodwill. The total goodwill (both purchased and non-purchased) may either remain constant or increase or decrease. However, when a company is determining the useful economic life of purchased goodwill, it should not take into account any actions or expenditure or other circumstances after the date of the acquisition, because these subsequent events create non-purchased goodwill. The purchased goodwill whose useful life is being determined is only that which existed and was recognised at the time of the acquisition.

7.59 Several factors may be relevant in determining the useful economic life of purchased goodwill, and a company should assess these factors at the time it makes the acquisition. They include the following:

- Expected changes in products, markets or technology.
- The expected period of future service of certain employees.
- Expected future demand, competition or other economic factors that may affect current advantages.

7.60 It is not possible to specify general rules regarding the useful economic life over which purchased goodwill should be written off. The ASC considers that it is inappropriate to indicate a maximum number of years for the amortisation period, but ED 47 specifies a maximum amortisation period (see para 7.85). Furthermore, a company may select different useful economic lives for the goodwill that arises on its different acquisitions.

Treatment of negative goodwill

7.61 'Negative goodwill' is the term used for any excess of the aggregate of the fair values of the separable net assets acquired over the fair value of the consideration given. Negative goodwill is the mirror image of positive goodwill. SSAP 22 requires that companies should credit 'negative goodwill' direct to reserves. Whereas the standard permits positive goodwill to be amortised through the profit and loss account, no such option is allowed for negative goodwill. However, ED 47 proposes that negative goodwill, should be treated in the same way as positive goodwill. It, therefore, requires negative goodwill to be credited to the profit and loss account over its estimated useful life. The standard does not require a company to set up a separate reserve for negative goodwill. Where a company does set up a separate reserve, an appropriate description in the financial statements would be 'Negative goodwill' or 'Capital reserve on consolidation'. This item should be included under 'Other reserves' in the balance sheet formats.

Treatment in the holding company's financial statements

7.62 Where one company acquires another company, the separable net assets from the point of view of the acquiring company will be the shares in the acquired company, not the individual assets and liabilities of the acquired company. The fair value of the consideration given will normally equal the fair value to the purchaser of the shares acquired. Consequently, when one company acquires another company, purchased goodwill will not normally arise in the holding company's balance sheet.

7.63 The standard does not require an adjustment to be made in the holding company's financial statements to the carrying value of the shares in the acquired company in respect of any consolidation goodwill written off either in the group accounts or in the subsidiary's or associate's financial statements. However, the holding company should write down the investment's carrying value to reflect any permanent diminution in value.

7.64 This accords with the legal requirements both for the purchased goodwill that companies carry, and for the purchased goodwill that groups carry (see further 'Manual of Accounting - volume II' chapter 6).

Disclosure

7.65 The notes to the financial statements should explain the accounting policy the company follows in respect of goodwill. [SSAP 22 para 43].

7.66 Where a company has made any acquisitions during the year, it should show the amount of purchased goodwill, where this is material, separately for each acquisition. [SSAP 22 para 44].

7.67 Where a company selects the amortisation method, it should show purchased goodwill as a separate item under intangible fixed assets in the balance sheet until the time it is fully written off. [SSAP 22 para

45]. The disclosure requirement in paragraph 45 of the standard accords with the Schedule 4 formats, which require that a company should show purchased goodwill (to the extent that it has not been written off) separately under the heading of intangible fixed assets.

7.68 Paragraph 45 of SSAP 22 requires a company also to show the movement on the goodwill account during the year. Paragraph 42 of Schedule 4 contains a similar requirement. A company should show the cost, the accumulated amortisation and the net book value of goodwill both at the beginning and the end of the year (see Table 19 above).

7.69 In addition, a company must show in respect of goodwill:

- The effect that any acquisitions, any disposals and any transfers have had on cost during the year.
- The amount of goodwill amortised during the year.
- The amount of any adjustments to accumulated amortisation that have arisen from any disposals.
- The amount of any other adjustments to accumulated amortisation.

[4 Sch 42].

7.70 Furthermore, paragraph 21(4) of Schedule 4 and paragraph 45 of SSAP 22 both require a company to disclose the period it has selected for amortising the goodwill relating to each of its major acquisitions. Paragraph 21(4) of Schedule 4 to the Act requires the company also to disclose its reasons for choosing that period.

7.71 As noted in paragraph 7.53 above, the standard permits a company to select different useful economic lives for the goodwill that arises on different acquisitions. Consequently, a company may need to disclose several amortisation periods, with each one relating to different elements of the goodwill total.

7.72 For each material acquisition and in aggregate for other acquisitions where these are material in total although not so individually, the following information should be given:

- The fair value of the consideration and the amount of purchased goodwill arising during the period, identifying the method of dealing with the goodwill arising and whether it has been set off against a merger reserve or any other reserves or has been carried forward as an intangible asset.

- A table showing the book values, as recorded in the acquired company's books, and the fair values of each major category of assets and liabilities acquired.

- An analysis, with suitable explanations, of the fair value adjustments made for:

  - Achieving uniform accounting policies.

  - Revaluations.

  - Establishing provisions, with separate disclosure of provisions made in respect of future trading losses.

  - Any other major items.

- Details of movements on provisions established in respect of acquisitions and analysed between the amounts used and the amounts released unused or applied for another purpose, together with sufficient details to identify the extent to which provisions have proved unnecessary. This requirement is designed to mitigate, by disclosure, the practice of over-prudent provisioning at the time of an acquisition which is followed by the release of those excess provisions to profit and loss account in later years.

- A statement and reasons for using provisional values in fair valuing assets and liabilities or the consideration, together with sufficient disclosure and explanations of any adjustments subsequently made to such provisional values and to goodwill.

[SSAP 22 paras 47 to 51].

7.73 Where a previously acquired business or business segment is later sold, separate disclosure of the financial effect should be given, which should include the following:

- The profit or loss on the disposal.

- The amount of purchased goodwill attributable to the business or business segment disposed of and how it has been treated in determining the profit or loss on disposal.

- Details of proceeds where no profit or loss is recorded on a disposal because the proceeds were accounted for as a reduction in the cost of the acquisition.

[SSAP 22 paras 52, 53].

Effect on realised profits of writing off goodwill

7.74 The effect on realised profits of writing off goodwill is particularly relevant in the case of an individual company, because distributions are made from the profits of individual companies not groups.

7.75 As mentioned in the first point of paragraph 7.51 above, paragraph 39 of SSAP 22 states that companies should normally eliminate purchased goodwill (other than negative goodwill) immediately on acquisition against reserves. Paragraph 2 of appendix 2 to SSAP 22 discusses whether this elimination reduces realised reserves. That paragraph concludes that an immediate write-off of goodwill (excluding, therefore, consolidation goodwill) does not constitute an immediate reduction of realised reserves (unless the goodwill is considered to have suffered a permanent diminution in value). However, even where goodwill is not immediately written off against realised reserves, the elimination of purchased goodwill by an individual company must ultimately result in a realised loss. This eventual realised loss arises because purchased goodwill has a limited useful life.

7.76 The effect of this paragraph is to give a choice of two options to a company that writes goodwill off immediately to reserves. The first option is that the company may write the goodwill off immediately to reserves and deem it a realised loss. The second option is that the company may write the goodwill off immediately and either deem it unrealised, or write it off to a suitable unrealised reserve. It will then transfer the amount written off from unrealised reserves, or deemed to be unrealised, to realised reserves on a systematic basis over the useful economic life of the goodwill. The second option will have the same effect ultimately on distributable reserves as the amortisation method that paragraph 41 of SSAP 22 permits.

7.77 A company may wish to use the second option above where it has for distribution purposes insufficient realised reserves to cover the immediate write-off of the purchase cost of the goodwill.

7.78 In practice, the most common unrealised reserve is the revaluation reserve that arises when a company revalues some or all of its fixed assets. However, paragraph 34(3) of Schedule 4 has the effect that this reserve should not be used to write off goodwill. A suitable unrealised reserve may exist in the form of a 'Merger reserve' where the company has previously taken advantage of the relief provided under section 131 of the Act. Another suitable reserve could be a reserve created as a result of the crediting to reserves negative goodwill arising on prior acquisitions (see para 7.80). Both these reserves are available to write off goodwill arising on the acquisition of unincorporated businesses.

7.79 For a public company, however, the write-off of goodwill initially to a suitable unrealised reserve may have a significant effect on its ability to pay dividends. This is because a public company cannot make a distribution which reduces its net assets below the aggregate of its share capital plus its non-distributable reserves. The write-off of goodwill may well bring this restriction into play.

7.80 Where negative goodwill arises in the financial statements of an individual company, it should credit it initially to an unrealised reserve. [SSAP 22 appendix 2 para 3]. The company may then transfer the negative goodwill from that unrealised reserve to realised reserves. This transfer should be in line with the depreciation or the realisation of the assets acquired in the business combination that gave rise to the goodwill in question. This transfer may not be necessary if ED 47 is adopted as an Accounting Standard, as it will require negative goodwill to be credited directly to the profit and loss account over its estimated useful life (see para 7.61). The determination of distributable profits is considered further in chapter 19.

Difference between goodwill and other intangible assets

7.81 SSAP 22 defines goodwill as the difference between the value of a business as a whole and the aggregate of the fair values of its separable net assets. Separable net assets include intangible assets other than goodwill. Companies are increasingly trying to identify intangible assets when they acquire a business so that the figure of goodwill that arises on consolidation is kept to a minimum. Intangible assets are concessions, patents, licences, trade marks and similar rights and assets. [4 Sch formats]. Other examples include brands, publishing titles, franchise rights and customer lists.

7.82 Where a company identifies intangible assets (excluding purchased goodwill) on the acquisition of a business, it should incorporate them in its balance sheet at their fair value (see paras 7.47 to 7.49). In subsequent years, companies may revalue these intangible assets to their current cost (see para 7.7). Some companies may wish to have the option of revaluing as many of their intangible assets as possible (for example, in order to strengthen their balance sheets). Consequently, these companies should ensure that they identify all intangible assets when they acquire a business. In this respect brands are becoming an increasingly important intangible asset, and these are considered in detail in 'Manual of Accounting - volume II' chapter 8.

The requirements of ED 47

7.83 In February 1990, the ASC published ED 47 which proposes important changes to SSAP 22.

7.84 As stated in paragraph 7.51 above, SSAP 22 at present requires goodwill to be eliminated by either immediate write off to reserves or capitalisation and amortisation through the profit and loss account. The current standard, however, encourages companies to account for purchased goodwill by writing it off immediately against reserves. The main reason for this treatment is that it achieved consistency of treatment between purchased and non-purchased goodwill. The ASC now considers, however, that goodwill is no different from any other capital assets, either tangible or intangible, that a business may acquire in order to generate a stream of economic benefits. It should, therefore, be treated consistently with other purchased intangible and tangible fixed assets and, in addition, purchased and non-purchased goodwill should be treated consistently. Consideration of the range of intangible assets, for example franchise rights, trade marks and know-how, and their similarities to goodwill (except that goodwill lacks identifiability) has led the ASC to the view that presenting goodwill arising on acquisition as an asset in the balance sheet will provide more useful information than its elimination against reserves immediately on acquisition.

7.85 ED 47, therefore, proposes to prohibit companies from eliminating purchased goodwill immediately on acquisition against reserves. Instead, it proposes that purchased goodwill should be recognised as an asset and carried in the balance sheet. The ASC considers that purchased goodwill does not have an indefinite life and, therefore, the cost of purchased goodwill should be written off to the profit and loss account over the useful economic life. Purchased goodwill is proposed to be written off over 20 years. However, in exceptional circumstances (which companies would have to justify in their financial statements), a longer period of up to 40 years may be appropriate.

7.86 ED 47 also proposes that the directors should review the goodwill carried on the balance sheet annually to determine whether the carrying value is excessive. If there is a permanent diminution in the value of purchased goodwill, it should be written down immediately through the profit and loss account. Purchased goodwill should not be revalued upwards.

7.87 The proposals in ED 47 have aroused considerable controversy particularly among listed companies. There is a consensus of opinion that where the 'amortisation method' is used, the effect of amortisation has been to depress reported profits by a figure that is often arbitrary, as the useful economic life of goodwill cannot be accurately determined. It remains to be seen whether the proposals will eventually become standard accounting practice.

Chapter 8

BALANCE SHEET - TANGIBLE FIXED ASSETS

Chapter 8

BALANCE SHEET - TANGIBLE FIXED ASSETS

Introduction

8.1 Intangible fixed assets are dealt with in chapter 7. This chapter considers the disclosure of tangible fixed assets in a company's financial statements, excluding investments which are examined in chapter 9. It considers, in particular, the measurement and disclosure of government grants, investment properties and leased assets.

8.2 The rules for determining the purchase price or the production cost of an asset is discussed earlier in chapter 4, paragraphs 4.22 to 4.38.

Definitions

8.3 Schedule 4 defines all assets as either fixed or current. Assets are fixed assets if the company intends to use them on a continuing basis in its activities. Any assets the company does not intend to use in that way are current assets. [Sec 262(1)].

8.4 The Act specifically states, however, that the following three items cannot be treated as assets in any company's balance sheet:

- Preliminary expenses.
- Expenses of, and commission on, any issue of shares or debentures.
- Costs of research.

[4 Sch 3(2)].

8.5 Consequently, these items should not be capitalised, and they must be written off to the profit and loss account, except where a company has a share premium account, in which case, the first two items can be written off to that account [Sec 130(2)].

8.6 There is very little room for flexibility in relation to the general definition of fixed and current assets. A company must include all its assets under one or other of the two main headings of fixed assets and current assets, unless this would mean that its financial statements would not give a true and fair view. So, for example, assets such as investments or a vehicle hire fleet must be categorised as either fixed or current assets, or else be split between the two categories. By contrast, banks which are governed by the disclosure requirements of Schedule 9 generally do not separate fixed from current assets.

8.7 Where a company intends to dispose of a fixed asset, the asset is not 'intended for use on a continuing basis in the company's activities'. If the asset needs to be reclassified as a current asset, then it is not appropriate that it should be included in the balance sheet at an amount that exceeds cost, unless it is disclosed as stocks or a current asset investment. This is because the alternative accounting rules can only be adopted for stocks and current asset investments and not other current asset items. [4 Sch 31(4)(5)]. However, SSAP 9 does not allow stocks to be stated at current cost in either historical cost financial statements or financial statements modified to include the revaluation of only certain assets. When a company intends to dispose of a fixed asset, it may be more appropriate for it to retain the asset under fixed assets in a new sub-heading 'assets held for resale'.

Disclosure

8.8 In respect of either the cost or the valuation (before any provisions for depreciation or diminution in value) of each item in the format that is included under the general heading 'Fixed assets' (whether the item is shown on the face of the balance sheet or in the notes), the notes to the financial statements must disclose:

- The aggregate amount of that item at both the beginning and the end of the financial year in question.

- The effect of any application of the alternative accounting rules during that financial year (see chapter 5).

- The amount of any acquisitions, and the amount of any disposals, during that financial year.

- The amount of any transfers of assets to or from that item during that financial year.

[4 Sch 42(1)(2)].

8.9 It should be noted that these requirements apply to all categories of fixed assets (whether intangible assets, tangible assets or investments). Moreover, they require the information to be given in respect of each of the sub-headings that are preceded in the formats in the Act by Arabic numerals.

8.10 In addition, the Act requires details to be disclosed about any provisions made in respect of each fixed asset category. The need for, and the calculation of, provisions both for depreciation and for the diminution in value of assets are discussed earlier in chapter 4, paragraphs 4.4 to 4.13. In particular, the notes must disclose:

- The cumulative amount of provisions for either depreciation or the diminution in value of assets at both the beginning and the end of the financial year in question.
- The amount of any such provisions that have been made during that financial year.
- The amount of any such provisions that have been eliminated during that financial year on the disposal of the fixed assets to which they related.
- The amount of any other adjustments made in respect of any such provisions during that financial year.

[4 Sch 42(3)].

8.11 Where a company has applied one of the alternative accounting rules to any fixed asset other than listed investments, the notes must disclose the years in which the assets were separately valued (so far as the directors know these) and also the separate values. If any assets were valued during the financial year in question, the notes must also disclose:

- The valuers' names or the qualifications of the persons who acted as valuers.
- The bases of valuation that the valuers applied.

[4 Sch 43].

Tangible assets

8.12 The Act sets out in the formats the following four categories of tangible assets:

- Land and buildings.
- Plant and machinery.
- Fixtures, fittings, tools and equipment.
- Payments on account and assets in course of construction.

8.13 The Act also requires that land and buildings should be split between freehold, long leasehold and short leasehold. [4 Sch 44]. For this purpose, a lease includes an agreement for a lease. It will be a long lease if it still has 50 years or more to run at the end of the financial year in question. Otherwise, it will be a short lease. [4 Sch 83].

8.14 Many companies face practical problems when categorising their tangible assets into these four fairly restrictive headings. In particular, some companies find it difficult to decide whether certain assets should be described as 'plant and machinery' or 'fixtures, fittings, tools and equipment'. Some companies also have difficulty in deciding the category in which to include motor vehicles.

8.15 In practice, companies categorise their assets according to the nature of their particular business. As a general rule, companies treat major manufacturing assets (including motor vehicles involved in the manufacturing process - for example, fork-lift trucks and cranes) as plant and machinery'. They include other assets not involved in the manufacturing process in 'Fixtures, fittings, tools and equipment'. The assets on which a company charges depreciation in the manufacturing account will normally be 'plant and machinery'.

8.16 Because the Act allows a company to show any item in greater detail than the format it adopts requires, a company may, for example, disclose the amount for motor vehicles as a subdivision of either plant and machinery or fixtures, fittings, tools and equipment. [4 Sch 3(1)]. However, where an asset does not fall under any of the headings given in the formats, paragraph 3(2) of Schedule 4 allows a company to include the amount of it under a separate heading. Consequently, motor vehicles could be included in the balance sheet as a separate item.

Payments on account and assets in course of construction

8.17 'Payments on account' represent payments a company makes in respect of tangible assets of which it has not yet taken delivery. 'Assets in course of construction' will represent the cost of purchasing and installing fixed assets ahead of their productive use. The timing of the transfer of an asset from this category to the appropriate heading will vary. A company will not normally charge depreciation on an asset that is in the course of construction until it is completed and it is transferred to an asset heading that is appropriate (see Table 20).

Depreciation of tangible assets

8.18 A company will normally include those tangible fixed assets that have a limited useful economic life in its balance sheet at their purchase price or production cost less a provision for depreciation. [4 Sch 17,18]. If a company adopts the alternative accounting rules, these assets may be shown in the balance sheet at market value or current cost. [4 Sch 31(2)].

Table 20: Disclosure of payments on account and assets under construction (where no depreciation is charged).

Extract from The General Electric Company p.l.c. Report & Accounts 31st March 1989.

8. TANGIBLE FIXED ASSETS	Freehold property £ million	Leasehold property Long £ million	Leasehold property Short £ million	Plant and machinery £ million	Fixtures, fittings, tools and equipment £ million	Payments on account and assets under construction £ million	Total £ million
Group							
Cost at 1st April, 1988	320.5	50.7	16.7	1,031.8	364.9	33.0	1,817.6
Exchange rate adjustment	12.0	–	1.2	12.8	9.6	.7	36.3
Additions at cost	26.8	2.1	1.8	140.9	110.4	Net 4.3	286.3
Additions from acquisitions	18.6	.5	3.8	7.4	7.7	–	38.0
Disposals at cost	*9.6*	*1.5*	–	*30.8*	*42.3*	–	*84.2*
Cost at 31st March, 1989	368.3	51.8	23.5	1,162.1	450.3	38.0	2,094.0
Depreciation at 1st April, 1988	102.1	13.4	7.7	672.3	197.5		993.0
Exchange rate adjustment	3.0	–	.6	7.3	4.9		15.8
Charged to profit and loss account	12.1	2.0	1.7	125.7	81.3		222.8
On disposals	*1.0*	*.4*	–	*26.0*	*37.5*		*64.9*
Depreciation at 31st March, 1989	116.2	15.0	10.0	779.3	246.2		1,166.7
Net book value at 31st March, 1989	252.1	36.8	13.5	382.8	204.1	38.0	927.3
Net book value at 31st March, 1988	218.4	37.3	9.0	359.5	167.4	33.0	824.6
Company							
Cost at 1st April, 1988	14.8	1.3	.1	79.2	27.2	3.0	125.6
Additions at cost	5.2	1.2	–	3.8	5.6	Net 2.4	18.2
Disposals at cost	*10.5*	*.1*	–	*29.8*	*11.1*	*1.9*	*53.4*
Cost at 31st March, 1989	9.5	2.4	.1	53.2	21.7	3.5	90.4
Depreciation at 1st April, 1988	3.5	.1	.1	49.1	12.8		65.6
Charged to profit and loss account	.2	–	–	7.3	4.9		12.4
On disposals	*.4*	–	–	*19.8*	*6.2*		*26.4*
Depreciation at 31st March, 1989	3.3	.1	.1	36.6	11.5		51.6
Net book value at 31st March, 1989	6.2	2.3	–	16.6	10.2	3.5	38.8
Net book value at 31st March, 1988	11.3	1.2	–	30.1	14.4	3.0	60.0

Depreciation rates:
Freehold buildings – 2% to 4% per annum
Leasehold property – over period of lease or 50 years for long leases
Plant, machinery, fixtures, fittings, tools and equipment – on average, in excess of 10% per annum.

	GROUP 1989 £ million	GROUP 1988 £ million	COMPANY 1989 £ million	COMPANY 1988 £ million
Capital expenditure				
Commitments contracted at 31st March	72.7	69.4	2.2	4.9
Authorised but not committed at 31st March	59.6	61.1	.8	4.2

8.19 The calculation of depreciation and the rules that relate to depreciation that are contained both within the Act and in SSAP 12 are discussed in more detail in chapter 4, paragraphs 4.4 to 4.13 and chapter 5, paragraphs 5.49 to 5.56.

8.20 The provision for depreciation will be based on the difference between cost (or valuation) and residual value. In an extreme situation, if the residual value is high, it is possible that very little depreciation will be required (for example, see Table 21). If a company fails to provide a small amount of depreciation because it is not material, the company can nevertheless regard itself as complying in principle with both the Act and SSAP 12 on accounting for depreciation.

Table 21: Example of a company whose directors do not depreciate properties because the resultant depreciation charge would be immaterial.

Extract from Allied-Lyons PLC Report and Accounts 4th March 1989.

Accounting policies extract

DEPRECIATION

No depreciation is provided on land or on licensed and other properties which are freehold or held on lease for a term of or exceeding 100 years unexpired. Other buildings, plant and equipment are depreciated over their estimated useful lives. The rates used are given in note 16 to the accounts. It is the group's policy to maintain properties comprising the licensed estate in such condition that the value of the estate, taken as a whole, is not impaired by the passage of time. Such expenditure is charged to profits in the year in which it is committed. As a consequence, any element of depreciation would, in the opinion of the directors, be immaterial and no provision for depreciation has been made.

8.21 Where a company does not wish to depreciate a particular asset because it considers the charge for depreciation would not be material, it should first consider the following two matters:

- Although a depreciation charge may not be material in any one year, the cumulative depreciation can, within a few years, have a material effect on the financial statements. Consequently, materiality will need to be judged in connection with other key items (for example, retained profits and the book values of the relevant assets).

- Although a depreciation charge may not be significant in a particular year, a similar charge may have a significant effect on the financial statements of a following year. This can occur, for example, where a company's profit decreases.

8.22 The standard also states that the depreciation methods used should be those that are the most appropriate having regard to the types of assets and their uses in the business. [SSAP 12 para 8]. There is a range of acceptable depreciation methods that are used in practice.

Although the straight-line method is the simplest one to apply, it may not always be the most suitable.

8.23 In addition, the standard defines an asset's useful economic life as the period over which the *present* owner will derive economic benefits from using it. [SSAP 12 para 11]. Any useful economic life remaining at the end of the present owner's period of ownership should be taken into account in determining the residual value. The reason for this is that the residual value to be used in calculating depreciation should be the asset's estimated value at the end of this period. However, the estimated residual value should exclude the effects of inflation. [SSAP 12 para 12].

Government grants

8.24 SSAP 4 says that grants relating to fixed assets should be credited to revenue over the asset's expected useful life. This may be achieved by either of the following two means:

- Reducing the fixed asset's cost of acquisition by the amount of the grant (for example, see Table 22).

Table 22: Example of an accounting policy where capital expenditure grants are deducted from the cost of the fixed assets.

Extract from Cape Industries PLC Annual Report 31st March 1989.

10.Capital expenditure grants
Grants in respect of capital expenditure are deducted from the cost of fixed assets to which they relate, and are consequently credited to revenue over the expected useful lives of those assets.

- Treating the amount of the grant as a deferred credit, and transferring a proportion of this to revenue annually.

8.25 ED 43, issued in June 1988, and not yet converted into a standard, proposes radical changes to SSAP 4. The proposed standard applies to all types of government grants, excluding other forms of government assistance such as equity finance, soft loans and advisory assistance.

Recognition of grants

8.26 SSAP 4 does not specifically address the question of when grants should be recognised. ED 43 explicitly stipulates that government grants should not be recognised until they have been received, or until the conditions for their receipt have been complied with and there is reasonable assurance that the grant will be received, whichever is the earlier. [ED 43 para 26].

8.27 The 'accruals' concept implies that government grants should be recognised in the profit and loss account to match them with the expenditure towards which they are intended to contribute. [ED 43 para 6]. The relationship between the grant and the related expenditure is, therefore, of paramount importance in establishing the accounting treatment to be adopted.

Grants related to revenue expenditure

8.28 SSAP 4 offers no ruling on grants related to revenue expenditure, since it is assumed that these are credited to revenue in the same period in which the related expenditure is incurred. ED 43 is far more explicit than SSAP 4 and applies to a wide range of government grants. The overriding principle is that grants received should be matched with the expenditure towards which they are intended to contribute. If a grant is made as a contribution towards revenue expenditure, then it should be credited to the profit and loss account of the period in which the related expenditure is incurred. This means that where revenue expenditure has been incurred before the receipt of the grant, the grant should be credited to the profit and loss account immediately on receipt. Where, however, a grant has been received but not all revenue expenditure has been incurred in the period in which the grant was received, a proportion of the grant will have to be deferred so as to match it with the related expenditure in the period in which they are subsequently incurred.

Grants related to capital expenditure

8.29 Perhaps the most significant change proposed by ED 43 is the accounting treatment of grants related to fixed assets. As stated in paragraph 8.24 above, under SSAP 4, a grant aiding the purchase of a fixed asset can be accounted for either as a deduction from the cost of the asset or as a deferred credit. However, the deferred credit approach is the method adopted by ED 43 (for example, see Table 23). Consequently, the alternative treatment at present allowed in SSAP 4 (to deduct the grant from the cost of the asset) will not be available if ED 43 is adopted as a standard.

8.30 In its revision of SSAP 4, the ASC felt that the deduction of capital based grants from the cost of fixed assets may be in conflict with Schedule 4 to the Act which requires that (subject to any provision for depreciation or diminution in value) fixed assets should be stated, under the historical cost accounting rules, at their purchase price or production cost. The statutory definitions of purchase price or production cost make no provision for any deduction from the amount in respect of a grant or subvention received from a third party. In addition, the general rule in paragraph 5 of Schedule 4, that amounts in respect of items representing assets or income may not be set off against amounts in respect of items representing liabilities or expenditure, might be interpreted as specifically forbidding the netting approach.

Table 23: Illustration of the disclosure of government grants where the deferred income alternative is followed.

Extract from Sidlaw Group plc Annual Report and Accounts 30th September 1989.

Accounting Policies extract

Grants

Revenue grants are credited to the profit and loss account. Capital grants are credited to deferred grants and amortised in the profit and loss account over the estimated lives of the qualifying assets.

Balance sheet extract

		Group		Company	
		1989	1988	1989	1988
	Note	£000	£000	£000	£000
Deferred income					
Deferred grants	22	101	114	–	–
Net assets employed		30,413	28,002	15,184	15,100

Note extract

	Group		Company	
	1989	1988	1989	1988
	£000	£000	£000	£000
22 DEFERRED GRANTS				
At 30 September 1988	114	103	–	–
Receivable less repayable	30	34	–	–
Transfer to profit and loss account	(43)	(23)	–	–
At 30 September 1989	101	114	–	–

8.31 The Institute's publication 'A Survey of UK Published Accounts' over the five year period 1978/79 to 1983/84 indicates that roughly half of the companies in receipt of capital based grants adopted the policy of deducting them from the cost of the related assets, which ED 43 proposes to prohibit. It, therefore, remains to be seen whether the netting approach will be re-instated in the revised standard.

Grant not attributable to specific expenditure

8.32 In certain circumstances, the terms of the grant may not specify precisely the expenditure it is intended to meet, for example, where a grant is intended to defray project costs that comprise both revenue and capital expenditure. In such situations, ED 43 proposes that in the absence of persuasive evidence to the contrary, government grants should be assumed to contribute towards the expenditure which forms the basis for its payment. [ED 43 para 28].

8.33 ED 43 states that certain grants are based not on the incurring of specific expenditure but on other criteria such as the creating of jobs. Such grants should be recognised in the profit and loss account so as to match them as closely as possible with the costs involved in meeting the specified criteria, for example in providing the jobs. [ED 43 para 29]. The cost of creating new jobs may entail the purchase of significant amount of fixed assets, such as, warehouse facilities, plant and equipment, etc. In such cases it may be possible to match the grant received with the capital expenditure incurred in creating the jobs. An example of a company that has adopted this type of policy is given in Table 24.

Table 24: Disclosure of accounting policy for non-expenditure related grants.

Extract from VSEL Consortium PLC Annual Report 31st March 1989.

Accounting policies extract

12 Non-expenditure related grants
Grants received which are not based on the incurring of specific expenditure, but rather the meeting of specified criteria are rcognised in the profit and loss account, so as to match them as closely as possible with the specified criteria. Any amounts not so recognised in the year are included in creditors.

Repayment of grants

8.34 Government grants sometimes become repayable because certain conditions are not fulfilled. A government grant that becomes repayable gives rise to a revision to an accounting estimate and not to a prior year adjustment. The repayment should be accounted for by first setting off the repayment against any unamortised deferred credit relating to the grant. To the extent that the repayment exceeds any such deferred credit, or where no deferred credit exists, the repayment should be charged immediately to the profit and loss account.

Tax treatment of grants

8.35 The treatment for taxation purposes of government grants will depend upon the terms of the grant and the particular statute or regulation under which it is made. Some grants are tax free. They are not deductible from costs of fixed assets when calculating capital allowances and are not treated as income receipts assessable to corporation tax. Other grants are treated as trading receipts and, therefore, fall to be treated as income.

8.36 It is generally accepted that the treatment of an item for tax purposes does not necessarily determine its treatment for accounting purposes. For instance, a grant which is taxed as a receipt may have to be amortised to income over the period in which the related expenditure is recognised. To follow the tax treatment and take the grant immediately to income on receipt will lead to a departure from the matching principle. In such situations, the correct accounting treatment would be to follow the matching principle and to deal with the timing difference arising between the tax charge and the recognition of the corresponding credit in the profit and loss account in accordance with SSAP 15 (see further chapter 11).

Disclosure

8.37 SSAP 4 only requires the amount of the deferred credit, if material, to be shown separately in the balance sheet where the deferred income alternative is followed. The disclosure requirements of ED 43 are more specific and are stated as follows:

- The accounting policy adopted for government grants should be disclosed (this is already required by SSAP 2).
- Deferred credits in respect of grants received should be included in the balance sheet under the heading 'Accruals and deferred income' and identified separately in a note to the balance sheet.
- The total amount credited to the profit and loss account in respect of grants should be disclosed in a note to the profit and loss account.
- Potential liabilities to repay grants in specified circumstances should, if necessary, be disclosed in accordance with paragraph 16 of SSAP 18 (some of these disclosures are also required by paragraph 50(2) of Schedule 4).

[ED 43 paras 34-37].

8.38 In the explanatory note section, ED 43 further proposes that the accounting policy note should include the period or periods over which grants are credited to the profit and loss account, as precisely as is practicable given the number and variety of grants that are received. It is not clear, however, why this requirement was not included in the standard section of the exposure draft and, therefore, its status remains unclear.

Investment properties

8.39 The Act does not use the term 'investment property'. However, SSAP 19 defines it as:

"an interest in land and/or buildings:
(a) in respect of which construction work and development have been completed; and
(b) which is held for its investment potential, any rental income being negotiated at arms length." [SSAP 19 para 7].

8.40 Moreover, the standard gives the following two examples of properties that should not be treated as investment properties:

- A property that is owned and occupied by a company for its own purposes.

- A property that is let to, and occupied by, another group company.

[SSAP 19 para 8].

8.41 Where a property is held for its investment potential, but it is either partly occupied by the company or partly let to and occupied by another group company, it would normally be appropriate to apportion the property between an 'investment' element and a 'non-investment' element. This apportionment could, for example, be done on the basis of arm's length rentals. However, before a company apportions properties in this way, it should consider materiality. For example, if a company has a number of investment properties and one small 'split' property, all the properties could be treated as investment properties.

8.42 The standard requires that investment properties should be included in the balance sheet at their open market value. [SSAP 19 para 11]. In addition, investment properties (excluding leases with less than 20 years to run) should not normally be depreciated. Therefore, the application of SSAP 19 will be a departure from the depreciation rules in the Act. Such a departure is, however, permitted in order for the financial statements to give a true and fair view. [Sec 226(4)]. This section, in turn, requires the financial statements to show, in a note, particulars of the departure, the reasons for it, and its effect. [Sec 226(5)]. However, if a company is to show the *effect* of *not* depreciating investment properties, it must, by implication, calculate and disclose the depreciation.

8.43 There may, however, be circumstances in which the amount of depreciation cannot be identified or quantified. With this in mind, the accountancy bodies discussed with the DTI the potential conflict between SSAP 19 and the Act that arose when this provision was originally brought into company law by the 1981 Act. Issue No. 20 of the APC Bulletin 'True and Fair' stated:

"The Department of Trade has reviewed the text of the following note and has indicated that it meets the requirements of (section 226 of the Act) where SSAP 19 is applied:

'Investment Properties

In accordance with SSAP 19, (i) investment properties are revalued annually and the aggregate surplus or deficit is transferred to a revaluation reserve, and (ii) no depreciation or amortisation is provided in respect of freehold investment properties and leasehold investment properties with over 20 years to run. The Directors consider that this accounting policy results in the accounts giving a true and fair view. Depreciation or amortisation is only one of many factors reflected in the annual valuation and the amount which might otherwise have been shown cannot be separately identified or quantified'."

Accordingly, where this note is included, it will not be necessary for the financial statements to show the effect of not providing for depreciation or amortisation.

8.44 The Standard does not require the valuation of investment properties to be made by qualified or independent valuers. But it does call for the disclosure of the names or qualifications of the valuers, the bases they used, and a statement of whether the person who made the valuation is an employee or an officer of the company. [SSAP 19 para 12].

8.45 However, where investment properties represent a substantial proportion of the total assets of a *major* company (for example, a listed company), the valuation should normally be carried out:

- Annually by persons holding a recognised professional qualification and having recent post-qualification experience in the location and with the category of properties concerned.
- At least every five years by an external valuer.

[SSAP 19 para 6].

8.46 The standard requires companies to display prominently in their financial statements both the carrying value of investment properties and the investment revaluation reserve. [SSAP 19 para 15]. An example of how a company discloses its investment properties is shown in Table 25 overleaf.

8.47 The treatment of the revaluation deficits or surpluses that may arise on the revaluation of investment properties is discussed in chapter 5, paragraph 5.20.

Table 25: Disclosure of Investment Properties.

Extract from Speyhawk Public Limited Company Report & Accounts 30th September 1989.

Accounting policies extract

INVESTMENT PROPERTIES

Interest and other outgoings in respect of investment properties under construction are capitalised until the property is substantially income producing or for a maximum period of one year after practical completion.

Completed investment properties and land held for inverstment are stated at open market value in accordance with Statement of Standard Accounting Practice No. 19. No depreciation is provided as required by the Companies Act 1985 as the Directors consider that the valuation results in the accounts giving a true and fair view.

11 INVESTMENT PROPERTIES

	Freehold properties	Long leasehold properties	Short leasehold properties	Total
	£'000	£'000	£'000	£'000
Cost or valuation at 1st October 1988	23,714	390	429	24,533
Additions	32,789	9,000	—	41,789
Disposals	(1,105)	—	—	(1,105)
Transfer from fixed assets	400	—	—	400
	55,798	9,390	429	65,617
Revaluation surplus	3,459	2,169	(36)	5,592
Cost or valuation at 30th September 1989	59,257	11,559	393	71,209
Divided between:				
Property in the course of construction at cost	15,087	—	—	15,087
Properties at valuation	44,170	11,559	393	56,122

The properties were valued on the basis of open market value at 30th September 1989 by:

Weatherall Green & Smith, Chartered Surveyors	53,165
Christopher Kennedy FRICS, a Director of the Company	2,957
	56,122

The cost to the Group of the freehold properties at 30th September 1989 was £43,394,000 (1988 — £14,884,000) and the leasehold properties £9,165,000 (1988 — £356,000)

8.48 A further problem that arises with investment properties is whether they should be treated as tangible fixed assets or as fixed asset investments. Neither the Act nor SSAP 19 gives any clear guidance on this question.

Leased assets

8.49 Although the Act contains no specific requirement for it, SSAP 21 requires that, where a company finances a significant amount of its capital investment through leasing, its financial statements should properly reflect the full impact of its leasing transactions. The standard details the accounting treatment that both lessors and lessees should adopt.

8.50 A lease is defined in SSAP 21 as a contract between a lessor and a lessee for the hire of a specific asset. The lessor retains ownership of the asset, but he conveys to the lessee the right to use the asset in return for paying specific rentals. In addition, the definition of a lease in the standard also includes other arrangements, not described as leases, in which some party retains ownership, but conveys to another party the right to use the asset for an agreed period of time in return for specific rentals. For example, a 'bare boat charter' (that is, a charter of a boat without a crew) will normally have all the characteristics of a lease, and it should be accounted for as such.

8.51 The scope of SSAP 21 does not include either lease contracts concerning rights to explore or exploit natural resources or licensing agreements (for example, agreements to lease motion pictures, video recordings, manuscripts, plays, patents and copyrights).

8.52 The accounting treatment that a company adopts for a leased asset (whether the company is a lessor or a lessee) will depend on whether the lease is a finance lease or an operating lease. The standard defines a finance lease as a lease that transfers to the lessee substantially all the risks and rewards of owning an asset. All other leases are classified as operating leases.

8.53 Because the subject of lease accounting is highly complex, the rest of this section looks only at the disclosure that SSAP 21 and the Act require in company financial statements of both lessors and lessees.

Treatment and disclosure of finance leases by lessees

8.54 The standard requires that a finance lease (including a hire purchase contract that is of a financing nature) should be recorded in a lessee's balance sheet both as an asset and as an obligation to pay future rentals. At the inception of the lease, the sum to be recorded both as an asset and as a liability should be the present value of the minimum lease payments, derived by discounting them at the interest rate implicit in the lease. [SSAP 21 para 32].

8.55 An asset leased under a finance lease should be depreciated over the shorter of the lease term and its useful life. The lease term, as defined in SSAP 21, is the period for which the lessee has contracted to lease the asset and any further terms for which the lessee has the option to continue to lease the asset, with or without further payment. The option period would only be taken into account if it is reasonably certain at the inception of the lease that the lessee will exercise the option. With a hire purchase contract that has the characteristics of a finance lease, the asset should be depreciated over its useful life. [SSAP 21 para 36].

8.56 Rentals payable should be apportioned between the finance charge and a reduction of the outstanding obligation for future amounts payable. The total finance charge under a finance lease should be allocated to accounting periods during the lease term, so as to produce either a constant periodic rate of charge on the remaining balance of the obligation for each accounting period or a reasonable approximation to it. [SSAP 21 para 35].

8.57 In respect of finance leases (including hire purchase contracts that have the same characteristics as finance leases), SSAP 21 requires the following information to be disclosed in the lessee's financial statements:

- The gross amount, the related accumulated depreciation and the total depreciation allocated for the period, analysed by each major class of asset capitalised under finance leases. [SSAP 21 para 49].

  Alternatively, this information may be included within the totals disclosed by each major class of asset for owned assets. However, where this alternative is adopted, the total of the net amount of assets held under finance leases, and the total amount of depreciation allocated for the period in respect of finance leases, need to be disclosed separately. [SSAP 21 para 50].

- The liability for net obligations under finance leases (net of finance charges allocated to future periods), shown separately from other liabilities. This liability should be disclosed either on the face of the balance sheet or in the notes to the financial statements. [SSAP 21 para 51].

- The liability for net obligations under finance leases, analysed between amounts payable in the next year, amounts payable in the second to fifth years inclusive from the balance sheet date, and the aggregate amounts payable after the fifth year. [SSAP 21 para 52].

  Where the lessee discloses the analysis of obligations under finance leases separately, he may, as an alternative to analysing the net obligations, analyse the gross obligations, and show future finance charges as a separate deduction from the total. [SSAP 21 para 52]. Companies that are either listed on The International Stock Exchange or traded on the USM also have to comply with the disclosure requirements that are outlined in chapter 11 paragraph 11.5.

- The aggregate finance charge allocated to the period. [SSAP 21 para 53].

- The commitments under finance leases existing at the year end that have been entered into, but whose inception occurs after the year end. [SSAP 21 para 54]. (This requirement is analogous to the legal requirements in Schedule 4, paragraph 50(3) in respect of capital commitments for fixed assets (see chapter 11).) These disclosure requirements are illustrated in Table 26.

Table 26: Illustration of the disclosure of finance leases in a lessee's financial statements in accordance with SSAP 21.

Extract from Racal Electronics PLC Annual Report & Accounts 31st March 1989.

Accounting policies extract

6. Leases

Tangible fixed assets held under finance leases and the related lease obligations are recorded in the balance sheet at the fair value of the leased assets at the inception of the lease. The excesses of the lease payments over the recorded lease obligations are treated as finance charges which are amortised over each lease term to give a constant rate of charge on the remaining balance of the obligations. Rental costs under operating leases are charged to profit and loss account in equal annual amounts over the periods of the leases.

Notes extract

4	Group interest payable less investment income	1989 £000	1988 £000
	Interest payable:		
	Bank overdrafts, loans and other borrowings repayable within five years	33,716	24,668
	Loans and other borrowings repayable wholly or in part after five years	5,084	9,531
	Finance charges on hire purchase contracts and finance leases	1,528	–
		40,328	34,199

12	Tangible fixed assets (extract)	Freehold premises £000	Leasehold premises Long term £000	Short term £000	Plant machinery furniture and vehicles £000	Equipment on lease or hire £000	Cellular radio, paging, data & navigation transmitting networks £000	Total £000
	Net book value							
	31 March 1989	105,207	3,455	8,212	169,084	37,756	187,880	511,594
	31 March 1988	91,629	1,886	6,367	133,499	29,564	116,537	379,482

The net book value of the Group's tangible fixed assets includes £9,093,000 of assets held under finance leases and hire purchase contracts.

Table 26 continued

17	Creditors: amounts falling due within one year (extract)	1989 Group £000	1989 Company £000	1988 Group £000	1988 Company £000
	Current instalments due on loans and mortgages	12,423	–	7,958	1,286
	Bank overdrafts and short term borrowings (Note 18)	216,100	216,508	190,869	152,009
	Trade creditors	178,322	–	152,288	–
	Amounts owed to subsidiaries	–	1,015	–	410
	Amounts owed to associated companies	4,841	–	6,580	–
	Advance receipts	29,817	–	32,982	–
	Current corporation tax	73,271	14,319	51,368	12,333
	Obligations under finance leases (Note 20)	3,614	–	–	–

19	Creditors: amounts falling due after more than one year (extract)	1989 Group £000	1989 Company £000	1988 Group £000	1988 Company £000
	Loans (Note 21)	39,386	20,710	133,540	120,010
	Mortgages (Note 22)	221	–	378	–
	Loan stock (Note 23)	70,776	70,776	71,155	71,155
	Trade creditors	2,291	–	2,562	–
	Advance receipts	3,173	–	3,335	–
	Corporation tax	576	–	4,978	–
	Obligations under finance leases (Note 20)	6,369	–	–	–

20	Obligations under finance leases	1989 £000	1988 £000
	Obligations under finance leases fall due as follows:		
	(a) between one and two years	2,316	–
	(b) between two and five years	3,196	
	(c) in more than five years	857	–
		6,369	–
	(d) in one year or less	3,614	–
		9,983	–

8.58 It is evident from the above that the lessee has several choices regarding the way he can disclose both his obligations under finance leases and assets he holds under finance leases. For example, the lessee can show his obligations under finance leases as a separate item on the balance sheet under the heading of 'Creditors'. Alternatively, he can combine that item within the total of another liability under the same heading, and analyse it in the notes to the financial statements. Similarly, the lessee can show assets he holds under finance leases as fixed assets separately on the balance sheet under the heading 'Tangible assets'. Alternatively, he can combine those assets with other owned tangible assets on the face of the balance sheet, and disclose the appropriate information in the notes to the financial statements. All these options are available to the lessee, and they are also permitted under the Act's balance sheet formats. The lessee's choice of methods will, normally, depend on the materiality of the amounts concerned.

8.59 The standard does not address the question of whether assets held under finance leases should be disclosed as tangible fixed assets or as intangible fixed assets. However, the fact that the standard allows the lessee to combine such assets with owned assets gives the impression that the lessee should treat such assets as tangible fixed assets. It may seem strange that the standard treats assets held under finance leases as tangible fixed assets when in fact it argues that it is the rights in the assets, and not the assets themselves, that are capitalised. However, there is very little difference in substance between assets held under finance leases and owned assets and this view is supported by ED 42. Also, because the disclosure requirements leave the reader in no doubt as to the true nature of leased assets, there is little to be gained by describing such assets as intangibles. The standard, therefore, takes a commonsense view, and it does not take too literal an interpretation of the word 'tangible'.

Treatment and disclosure of operating leases by lessees

8.60 Operating leases should not be capitalised, and the lease rental should be charged on a straight-line basis over the lease term, unless another systematic and rational basis is more appropriate. This applies even if the payments are not made on such a basis. [SSAP 21 para 43].

8.61 In respect of operating leases (including hire purchase contracts that have the same characteristics as operating leases), SSAP 21 requires the following information to be disclosed:

- The total of operating lease rentals charged as an expense in the profit and loss account, and analysed between amounts payable both in respect of the hire of plant and machinery and in respect of other operating leases. [SSAP 21 para 55].

- The payments that the lessee is committed to make during the next year, analysed between those in which the commitment expires within that year, those in which the commitment expires within the second to fifth years inclusive, and those in which the commitment expires more than five years after the balance sheet date. This analysis should show the commitments in respect of land and buildings separately from those of other operating leases. [SSAP 21 para 56]. This requirement is sometimes misunderstood, the intention is to show only the annual commitment not the total amount that will be payable until the end of the lease.

These disclosure requirements are illustrated in Table 27.

Table 27: Illustration of the disclosure of operating leases.

Extracts from The Burton Group PLC Annual Report and Accounts 2nd September 1989.

Accounting policies extract

(g) Leased assets
Assets used by the Group which have been funded through finance leases are capitalised and the resulting lease obligations are included in creditors. Rentals payable under operating leases are charged to the profit and loss account as incurred over the lease term.

Notes extract

	1989 *£'m*	*1988* *£'m*
2 *Turnover and trading profit*		
An analysis of turnover and trading profit is set out on page 10.		
Trading profit is stated after charging		
Wages and salaries	260.7	225.4
Social security costs	18.9	16.1
Other pension costs	11.5	12.8
Depreciation	58.9	43.9
Operating lease rentals	129.1	98.8
Hire of plant	0.4	0.7
Employee profit sharing scheme	3.0	3.7
Auditors' remuneration	0.7	0.7

21 *Lease obligations*	*Group* *1989* *£'m*	*Group* *1988* *£'m*	*Company* *1989* *£'m*	*Company* *1988* *£'m*
Finance lease obligations expiring:				
Between one and two years	2.4	3.4	1.1	2.0
Between two and five years	0.6	2.9	0.2	1.4
	3.0	6.3	1.3	3.4
Operating lease commitments in respect of land and buildings for the 1990 financial year, on leases expiring:				
Within one year	0.7	0.4	0.1	0.3
Between one and five years	5.3	4.3	0.4	2.7
Over five years	112.0	102.8	6.5	64.5
	118.0	107.5	7.0	67.5
Operating lease commitments in respect of other assets for the 1990 financial year, on leases expiring:				
Within one year	1.2	–	0.1	–
Between one and five years	2.7	–	0.1	–
Over five years	0.4	–	0.1	–
	4.3	–	0.3	–

8.62 The disclosure requirements for operating leases may present particular practical problems. Under the disclosure requirements, the payments that the lessee is committed to make during the next year are analysed according to the time when the commitment expires. Two situations that have to be provided for are a rental pause during the next year (where no rentals are due), and a significant rent review that is expected during the period. In either of these situations, and in order to avoid misleading the user of the financial statements, the basic disclosure will need to be supplemented with an explanation.

Additional disclosure required in a lessee's financial statements

8.63 In respect of both finance leases and operating leases, the accounting policies that the lessee has adopted must be disclosed in the financial statements. [SSAP 21 para 57].

8.64 An example of the accounting policy that a company may adopt is as follows:

Example

Accounting policy note

Where assets are financed by leasing agreements that give rights approximating to ownership ('finance leases'), the assets are treated as if they had been purchased outright. The amount capitalised is the present value of the minimum lease payments payable during the lease term. The corresponding leasing commitments are shown as obligations to the lessor and reported under creditors.

Depreciation on the relevant assets is charged to the profit and loss account on a straight-line basis to write the assets off over their expected useful lives.

Lease payments are treated as consisting of capital and interest elements, and the interest is charged to the profit and loss account using the annuity method.

All other leases are 'operating leases', and the annual rentals are charged to the profit and loss account on a straight-line basis over the lease term.

8.65 In addition to the standard's disclosure requirements, the Guidance Notes to the standard indicate that other details about a company's leases may need to be disclosed in order to give a true and fair view of the company's state of affairs. These include, for example, contingent rentals, profit participation arrangements, significant restrictions on future borrowing or leasing, and contingent liabilities. The information will depend on whether the user's appreciation of the company's state of affairs would be affected if he was aware of that information. The criteria to be applied to that information are no different from those to be applied to any other information about the company's financial affairs.

8.66 Where a lessee sub-leases assets to a third party, he will also need to consider the disclosure requirements appropriate to lessors.

Property leases

8.67 Under the standard, leases of land and buildings are subject to the same accounting requirements as other leased assets. This means that they should either be classified as finance leases or as operating leases, and should be accounted for accordingly.

8.68 If the lessee has a short-term lease, it is unlikely to satisfy the criteria as a finance lease. This is because the lessor will retain the benefits of ownership, such as increases in value and rent reviews that adjust lease payments to market rate on a regular basis.

8.69 Situations can occur, however, where a short lease can be a finance lease. An example could be a building with a relatively short life, perhaps built to a customer's specification or for a specific use, or certain types of sale and leaseback arrangements (see paras 8.71 and 8.72).

8.70 Longer leases are more likely to be finance leases. Such leases are often at a peppercorn rental, but may involve the payment of a lease premium. The lease premium represents, in effect, the present value of the minimum lease payments, which is the amount required to be capitalised as a fixed asset under SSAP 21. However, in many situations, the peppercorn rentals under long-term leasehold properties are immaterial and, as such, their present value need not be capitalised under SSAP 21.

8.71 Leasing transactions of property can be complicated where, for example, sale and leaseback arrangements exist. A sale and leaseback transaction occurs where the owner of an asset sells it and immediately acquires the right to use it again through a lease agreement. If the lessee fulfils the normal criteria for a finance lease, by for example, taking on again substantially all the risks and rewards of ownership of the asset, the lease will be a finance lease, and should be capitalised in accordance with SSAP 21. Many of these types of transaction are purely financing arrangements and should be treated as such.

8.72 Non-subsidiary dependent companies were used in the past to, in effect, take leased assets off the group's balance sheet, using sale and leaseback arrangements. Companies used to sell assets to a non-subsidiary dependent company, which leased them back under the terms of an operating lease. The group's financial statements would not consolidate the assets of the non-subsidiary dependent company. The changes incorporated in the Companies Act 1989 mean that such a company is now likely to satisfy the criteria for consolidation as a subsidiary, as it will probably be subject to dominant influence or unified management. Consequently, such subsidiaries will no longer avoid consolidation and, therefore, the leased assets will return to the group's balance sheet (see further 'Manual of Accounting - volume II' chapter 3).

Treatment and disclosure of finance leases by lessors

8.73 The amount due from the lessee under a finance lease should be recorded in the lessor's balance sheet as a debtor at the amount of the net investment in the lease, after making provisions for items such as bad and doubtful rentals receivable. [SSAP 21 para 38].

8.74 The lessor should normally allocate his total gross earnings under a finance lease to accounting periods to give a constant periodic rate of return on his net cash investment in the lease (after taking account of all cash flows including tax). In arriving at the constant periodic rate of return, the lessor may make a reasonable approximation. [SSAP 21 para 39]. A finance company will normally allocate gross earnings from a hire purchase contract to give a constant periodic rate of return on its net investment (ignoring any tax effects). This is because the tax effects of a hire purchase contract are rarely significant as the lessee takes all of the benefit and so the company's net investment in a hire purchase contract will approximate to its net cash investment in that contract.

8.75 In respect of finance leases and hire purchase contracts that have similar characteristics, the following need to be disclosed:

- The net investment in finance leases at the balance sheet date. This figure should show separately the amount in respect of finance leases and the amount in respect of hire purchase agreements. [SSAP 21 para 58].

- The accounting policy adopted for recognising finance lease income. [SSAP 21 para 60(a)].

- The cost of assets acquired in the period (whether by purchase, finance lease or hire purchase) for the purpose of letting under finance leases or hire purchase contracts. [SSAP 21 para 60(c)].

These disclosure requirements are illustrated in Table 28 overleaf.

Treatment and disclosure of operating leases by lessors

8.76 SSAP 21 requires that a lessor should record, as fixed assets, the assets he holds for leasing under operating leases. It also requires that he should depreciate those assets over their useful economic lives. [SSAP 21 para 42].

8.77 The lessor should recognise his rental income from operating leases (excluding charges for services such as insurance and maintenance) on

Table 28: Illustration of the disclosure of finance leases in a lessor's financial statements in accordance with SSAP 21.

Extract from Anglo Leasing plc Annual Report 31st March 1989.

Accounting policies extract

(b) Finance agreements
Finance agreements are accounted for on the basis of gross receivables less related unearned income and are included in debtors.

(c) Recognition of profit on finance agreements
Profit on finance agreements is recognised over the period in which receivables are due using the sum of the digits method after allowing for a proportion of initial costs.

Note extract

2 GROSS EARNINGS UNDER FINANCE AGREEMENTS

(a) Gross earnings
This represents income arising from finance agreements, as set out in the accounting policy note on the "Recognition of profit on finance agreements".

(b) Receivables
The rentals and instalments receivable during the year from which gross earnings are derived are as follows:

	1989 £'000	1988 £'000
Lease rentals	78,555	57,699
Instalments under credit agreements	16,090	10,672
	94,645	68,371

13 DEBTORS

	Group		Company	
	1989 £'000	1988 £'000	1989 £'000	1988 £'000
Net investment in finance agreements				
– leases	204,654	148,008	163,638	131,645
– credit agreements	29,347	17,742	28,802	17,201
Trade debtors	2,068	1,040	1,449	986
Amounts owed by subsidiary companies	—	—	38,560	15,277
Other debtors	795	1,091	781	1,069
Prepayments and accrued income	7,175	3,586	6,539	3,386
	244,039	171,467	239,769	169,564
The above includes amounts falling due after more than one year in respect of:				
Net investment in finance agreements				
– leases	150.055	107,216	119,277	95,519
– credit agreements	18,639	10,165	18,357	9,848
Amounts owed by subsidiary companies	—	—	28,949	10,430
The cost of assets acquired for the purpose of letting under finance leases in the year	115,771	80,301	83,279	69,988
Value of credit agreements advanced in the year	25,054	13,849	24,770	13,471
	140,825	94,150	108,049	83,459

a straight-line basis over the period of the lease, irrespective of when the payments are due. [SSAP 21 para 43]. This requirement does not apply, however, if another systematic and rational basis is more representative of the time pattern in which the lessor receives the benefit from the leased asset (for example, the time pattern of the related depreciation charge).

8.78 The lessor needs to disclose the gross amount and the accumulated depreciation of the assets he holds for use under operating leases or hire purchase contracts that have similar characteristics. [SSAP 21 para 59].

<u>Additional disclosure required in a lessor's financial statements</u>

8.79 In respect of both finance leases and operating leases (including hire purchase contracts that have similar characteristics), the following need to be disclosed also:

- The policy adopted for accounting for operating leases and finance leases.

- The aggregate rentals receivable in the accounting period, analysed between amounts receivable under finance leases and amounts receivable under operating leases.

[SSAP 21 para 60(a)(b)].

8.80 Where a lessor adopts a policy of 'grossing up' the amount of regional development grant (RDG) that is credited to his profit and loss account, he will need to disclose the amount by which both his profit before tax and his taxation have been increased.

8.81 The term 'grossing up' means that the lessor prefers to gross up the amount of RDG he credits to the profit and loss account in each period (as if he had received the RDG net of tax), and to increase the tax charge accordingly. In this way he spreads the tax benefits from the RDG over the life of the lease in the same way as the RDG itself (that is, in proportion to the net cash investment in the lease).

8.82 The Guidance Notes to SSAP 21 indicate that the lessor may also need to disclose further information about his leases and hire purchase contracts that is of particular significance to the users of the financial statements. (This includes, for example, details of arrangements that could affect his future profitability, such as contingent rentals or new-for-old guarantees.)

Implications of the Act on the disclosure lessors make

8.83 A leasing company's financial statements will need to comply with the Act's requirements, and they must give a true and fair view. Consequently, they must comply with the specific requirements of either Schedule 4 or, if the company is a banking or an insurance company, with Schedule 9.

8.84 Although some banks that comply with Schedule 9 may carry out leasing activities themselves, most banks prefer, for tax reasons, to carry out their leasing through separate subsidiaries. Consequently, most lessors, whether they are related to a bank or not, will not be a banking company that is, a company which is authorised under the Banking Act 1987 and so they will have to comply with the requirements of Schedule 4 to the Act (as opposed to Schedule 9).

8.85 Lessor companies may have various problems in following the balance sheet formats and the profit and loss account formats detailed in the Act.

8.86 The balance sheet formats set out in Schedule 4 do not show any specific category for leased assets. Paragraph 3(2) of Schedule 4, however, permits (with certain exceptions) a company's balance sheet or profit and loss account to include an item that is not otherwise covered in the formats.

8.87 Leased assets can, therefore, be shown on the face of the balance sheet as a separate item. However, leased assets will have to be shown under the heading of either fixed assets or current assets. They can be shown in one or other of the following two ways:

- As a category of tangible fixed assets (for example, 'Assets out on operating leases').

- As a category of debtors under current assets (for example, 'Amounts receivable under finance leases').

8.88 Schedule 4 states that a company's assets are fixed assets if the company intends to use them on a continuing basis in its activities. It states also that any assets the company does not intend to use in that way are current assets. Assets leased out under operating leases are certainly intended to be used on a continuing basis in a company's activities. Consequently, they should be shown as tangible fixed assets. Assets leased out on finance leases are more difficult to classify, and they could be classified either as current assets or as fixed assets under the definition in the Act. However, SSAP 21 requires that amounts due under finance leases should be shown under current assets as a category of debtors. This means also that the amounts due under finance leases must be analysed between amounts receivable within one year and those receivable after more than one year (see Table 28). [Note 5 on the balance sheet formats].

8.89 Irrespective of whether leased assets are classified under Schedule 4 as fixed or current, a lessor will need to follow the appropriate valuation rules of Schedule 4 (discussed further in chapter 4). Therefore, unless the alternative accounting rules are applied, those leased assets that are shown as tangible fixed assets will need to be shown at purchase price or production cost, less depreciation. Those leased assets that are shown as debtors will need to be shown as amounts receivable, less (where appropriate) a provision to reduce the amount to the net realisable value.

8.90 The profit and loss account formats set out in Schedule 4 are not particularly well suited to a leasing company. For example, a leasing company has neither 'Turnover' nor 'cost of sales' in the normal sense of these words. Paragraph 3(3) of Schedule 4, however, provides that, in any situation where the special nature of the company's business requires such adaptation, the directors should adapt the arrangement and the headings of those items that are preceded by Arabic numerals. This allows the lessor to adapt the profit and loss account formats to reflect the special nature of his business. For example, a finance lessor should normally show, as his turnover, his 'gross earnings' from leasing. Similarly, where interest costs are a direct cost of leasing, these costs could be deducted from gross earnings to show 'gross profit'. Alternatively, interest costs could be shown in their normal position in the profit and loss format (that is, below 'Administrative costs').

Chapter 9

BALANCE SHEET - INVESTMENTS

Chapter 9

BALANCE SHEET - INVESTMENTS

Introduction

9.1 This chapter considers the disclosure required for all types of investments, including investments in subsidiary undertakings where consolidated financial statements are not prepared. These requirements are included in Schedule 5 to the Act, which deals with the disclosure in companies' financial statements of information concerning related undertakings. The Schedule is split into two parts. The first part sets out the disclosure requirements for undertakings that are not required to prepare consolidated financial statements, and the second part deals with the disclosure requirements for those undertakings that must prepare consolidated financial statements. The latter requirements are covered in 'Manual of Accounting - volume II'.

All investments

9.2 A company can treat investments in its balance sheet as either fixed asset investments or current asset investments depending on how it intends to use them. The model formats for the balance sheet include a heading for 'Investments' under the general heading of both 'Fixed assets' and 'Current assets'. Moreover, there are separate sub-headings for investments under both the fixed and the current categories.

9.3 For each of the sub-headings of fixed asset investments, a company has to disclose the information required for other fixed assets under Schedule 4, paragraphs 42(1)(2). These include disclosure of the aggregate amount of that item at both the beginning and the end of the financial year and certain other information about the purchase and sale of those investments. These requirements are discussed in chapter 8, paragraph 8.8.

9.4 In addition, Schedule 4, paragraph 42(3) requires details to be disclosed about any provisions made in respect of each fixed asset investment category. Again the rules are the same as for other fixed assets as discussed in chapter 8, paragraph 8.10.

9.5 Furthermore, the Act requires the notes to the financial statements to include certain information about any investments a company holds (irrespective of whether these are shown as fixed assets or as current assets). In particular, the notes must disclose:

- The amount that relates to listed investments. [4 Sch 45(1)(a)].

- The amount relating to listed investments split between those listed on a recognised investment exchange, and any other listed investments. [4 Sch 45(1)(b)].

- The aggregate market value of listed investments, where it differs from the amount at which they are stated in the balance sheet. [4 Sch 45(2)(a)].

- Both the market value and the stock exchange value of any listed investments must be disclosed, where the former value is taken as being higher than their stock exchange value. [4 Sch 45(2)(b)]. This disclosure is required because the market value and the stock exchange value may differ according to the size of the investment and its marketability. For example, a controlling stake could be worth proportionately more than a minority interest in a company, because stock exchange prices traditionally reflect the values of small parcels of shares.

9.6 For this purpose, a 'listed investment' means any investment that is listed either on a 'recognised investment exchange' other than an overseas investment exchange within the meaning of the Financial Services Act 1986 or on any stock exchange of repute outside Great Britain. [4 Sch 84]. All other investments are to be regarded as unlisted, including those traded on the USM, and no additional information is required to be disclosed for these investments. A 'recognised investment exchange' means any body of persons that is a recognised investment exchange for the purposes of the Financial Services Act 1986. Currently, the only body designated in Great Britain as a recognised investment exchange is The International Stock Exchange.

9.7 There is no definition of 'stock exchange of repute' in the Act. In practice, whether a stock exchange outside Great Britain is reputable or not will depend both on its status in its own country and on the circumstances surrounding its operation.

9.8 The disclosure requirements outlined above are best illustrated by an example (see also Table 29 overleaf):

Details of investments held:

	Co.	Balance sheet value £'000	Market value £'000	Stock exchange value £'000
Listed on The International Stock Exchange (a recognised investment exchange)	A	100	250	300
	B	150	110	110
	C	130	150	125
	D	75	25	20
		455	535	555
Listed on The New York Stock Exchange (A stock of repute outside Great Britain)	E	190	200	225
	F	65	110	100
	G	15	25	25
		270	335	350
Quoted on The Unlisted Securities Market		30	70	75
Total of investments		755	940	980

This disclosure may be summarised in the notes to the financial statements as follows:

Listed investments	£'000
Listed on a recognised investment exchange	455
Other listed investments	270
Total - balance sheet value	725
Total - market value	870

Listed investments include certain investments for which the market value is considered to be higher than the stock exchange value. The market value of these investments is £285,000 (that is £150,000+£25,000+£110,000) and their stock exchange value is £245,000 (that is, £125,000+£20,000+£100,000).

Significant holdings - 10 per cent or more

9.9 Where a company at the end of its financial year has a *'significant holding'* of shares of any class in another *undertaking*, other than a subsidiary undertaking, the Act requires the company to disclose certain information. [5 Sch 7].

9.10 For the purposes of the disclosure requirements, it is necessary to consider the meanings of the terms *'significant holding'*, *'undertaking'* and *'shares'*.

- The Act defines a 'significant holding' as a holding of ten per cent or more of the nominal value of any class of shares in the undertaking, or a holding that exceeds one tenth of the amount of the company's assets, as disclosed in its balance sheet. [5 Sch 7(2)].

- 'Undertaking' means a body corporate or partnership or an unincorporated association carrying on a trade or business, with or without a profit. [Sec 259(1)].

- Reference to 'shares' is taken to mean:

  - The allotted shares in relation to an undertaking that has a share capital. This applies to bodies corporate with a share capital.

  - The rights to share in the capital of an undertaking which has capital, but has no share capital. This would apply to partnerships.

  - Interests that confer any right to share in the profits, or liability to contribute to the losses, of the undertaking, or that give rise to an obligation to contribute to the debts or expenses of the undertaking in the event it being wound up. This includes most other undertakings that are not bodies corporate or partnerships.

[Sec 259(2)].

9.11 The notes to the financial statements of the investing company must disclose in respect of such undertakings:

- Its name.

- Its country of incorporation, where it is incorporated outside Great Britain.

- If it is incorporated in Great Britain, whether it is registered in England and Wales or in Scotland.

- If it is unincorporated, the address of its principal place of business.

- The identity of each class of shares the investing company holds.

- The proportion of the nominal value of the shares of each class that the investing company holds.

[5 Sch 8].

Table 30 overleaf illustrates the type of information that should be disclosed in this situation.

Table 29: Disclosure of listed and unlisted investments (treated as current assets)

Extract from The General Electric Company p.l.c. Report & Accounts 31st March 1989.

Note extract

13. CURRENT INVESTMENTS	GROUP 1989 £ million	GROUP 1988 £ million	COMPANY 1989 £ million	COMPANY 1988 £ million
Short-dated securities at market value*				
Listed in the United Kingdom	2.0	14.4	–	12.3
Listed overseas	198.9	174.8	–	–
Other investments at lower of cost and market value†				
Listed in the United Kingdom	68.7	56.3	34.6	37.0
Listed overseas	12.7	53.5	12.7	53.5
Unlisted	–	2.5	–	2.5
Finance leases receivable	–	90.8	–	–
	282.3	392.3	47.3	105.3
Note				
*At cost: listed in the United Kingdom	2.1	14.1	–	12.0
listed overseas	203.0	173.7	–	–
†Market value: listed in the United Kingdom	75.7	57.4	39.0	37.0
listed overseas	12.8	53.6	12.8	53.6
unlisted	–	2.5	–	2.5

9.12 In interpreting the Act's disclosure requirements, shares held on behalf of the company by any person should be attributed to it. However, shares held on behalf of a person other than the company should not be attributed to it. Furthermore, shares held by a company (company A) by way of security should be treated as held by the company providing them as security (company B), where both the following conditions apply:

- The rights attached to the shares (other than the right to exercise them for the purpose of preserving the security or of realising it) are exercisable only in accordance with the instructions of company B.

- Where the shares are held by way of security in connection with the granting of loans by way of normal business activities, those rights are exercisable only in the interests of company B.

[5 Sch 13(3)(4)].

Table 30: Disclosure of information about significant holdings of 10 per cent or more.

Extract from The Independent Investment Company, Public Limited Company, Annual Report and Accounts 30th June 1989.

Note extract

11. Significant Interests

(b) Other interests of 10% or more of any class of equity share capital:

Name	*Country of Incorporation or Registration*	*Class of Capital*	*% of Class Held*	*% of Equity Held*
Ashlar	USA	Preferred Series A	22.5	11.9
Caledonian Trust	Scotland	Ordinary	24.1	17.6
Castelle	USA	Preferred Series A	15.0	9.0
		Preferred Series B	14.0	
The Center for Humanities	USA	Preferred Series B	40.0	8.0
Cinema Group	USA	Common	16.3	13.9
Codeworks	USA	Common	33.0	5.0
		Preferred Series C	10.0	
Financial Benefit Group	USA	Common Class A	12.7	10.0
Frame Technology	USA	Preferred Series A	15.0	2.0
Gillow	England	Ordinary	12.5	12.8
		CCRP	13.8	
Hewetson	England	CCRP	18.1	12.4
Magna Computer	USA	Preferred Series B	25.0	7.0
Professional Healthcare	USA	Preferred Series A	13.0	4.0
Read-Rite	USA	Preferred Series BB	16.0	5.5
Redwood International	England	CRP	76.0	9.7
Surveillance by Objectives	USA	Preferred Series B	37.0	11.0
Syntellect	USA	Preferred Series F	25.0	2.0
Teksyn	USA	Preferred Series B	21.0	9.0
Vencor	USA	Preferred Series A	22.0	3.0
WangDat	USA	Preferred Series A	35.0	17.0
		Preferred Series B	17.0	

9.13 The particulars to be disclosed may relate to *inter alia* either an undertaking that is established under the law of a country outside the UK or an undertaking that carries on its business outside the UK. Where, in either of these two situations, the directors believe that disclosure of the information detailed in paragraph 9.11 above would be *seriously prejudicial* to the business of that undertaking, or to the business of the company or any of its subsidiary undertakings, and the company has obtained the Secretary of State's agreement, that information need not be disclosed. [Sec 231(3)]. The previous legislation had a similar exemption that applied if, in the opinion of the directors, disclosure would be *harmful* to the business of the company or any of its subsidiaries. The wording in the new legislation has been tightened to apply now in situations where disclosure would be seriously prejudicial. Where advantage is taken of this exception, this must be stated in the notes to the financial statements. [Sec 231(4)].

9.14 Where a company has a significant holding in a number of undertakings and, in the directors' opinion, compliance with the above disclosure requirements would mean that particulars of excessive length would have to be disclosed in the financial statements, the company is not required to disclose the information detailed above for every undertaking. In this circumstance, the directors still have to give in the notes to the financial statements the information relating to those undertakings whose results or financial position principally affect the figures shown in the company's financial statements and similar information for those undertakings excluded from consolidation under section 229(3) or (4). [Sec 231(5)(a)(b)].

9.15 Where a company takes advantage of the exemption outlined in the above paragraph, the financial statements must state that the information is given only for those investments that principally affect the company's annual financial statements. [Sec 231(6)(a)]. In addition, the full information (including both the information that is disclosed in the notes to the financial statements and the information that is not) should be annexed to the company's next annual return. [Sec 231(6)(b)]. This differs from the previous requirement which only required details for those investments not included in the financial statements to be annexed to the annual return. Where a company fails to annex this information to its next annual return, the company and any officer of it who is in default is liable to a fine, and for continued contravention, to a daily default fine. [Sec 231(7)]. Obviously, under these provisions the information required to be given in the annual return could be lengthy and company secretaries should take care in compiling this information.

Significant holdings - 20 per cent or more

9.16 Where a company has a 'significant holding' in an undertaking (which is not a subsidiary) amounting to 20 per cent or more of the nominal value of the shares in the undertaking, the following information should be given in the financial statements in addition to the information required by paragraph 9.11 above:

- The aggregate amount of the capital and reserves of the undertaking at the end of its relevant financial year.

- The profit or the loss of that undertaking as disclosed by those financial statements.

[5 Sch 9(1)(a)(b)].

These amounts are to be ascertained from the undertaking's financial statements prepared for the year ending with, or last before, the company's financial year. [5 Sch 9(5)]. Table 31 illustrates the type of information to be disclosed when a company has an investment holding of 20 per cent or more.

Table 31: Disclosure of information about significant holdings of 20 per cent or more.

Extract from The Independent Investment Company, Public Limited Company, Annual Report and Accounts 30th June 1989.

Note extract

11. Significant Interests

(a) As at 30 June 1989, The Independent Investment Company held between 20% and 50% of the allotted share capital of the following companies:

Name	*Country of Incorporation or Registration*	*Class of Capital*	*% of Class Held*	*% of Equity Held*	*Latest Available Accounts*	*Share Capital and Reserves £'000*	*Profit/ (Loss) for year £'000*
Autoclenz	England	CCPPO	31.0				
		CRP	31.0	27.3	27.8.88	(5,178)	313
		B Ordinary	31.0				
Bankside Underwriting	England	B Voting	65.4				
Agencies		B Non-voting	60.1	20.8	30.9.88	3,236	1,219
		Loanstock	63.3				
Business Sales Group	England	CCPPO	100.0				
		CRP	100.0	20.0	31.12.88	412	7
		Ordinary	20.0				
P.I. Research	USA	Preferred Series A	20.0	20.0	N/A	N/A	N/A
Seattle Silicon	USA	Preferred Series A	26.0	23.0	31.12.88	1,657	(3,331)
Wharfedale	England	CCPPO	64.0				
		CCRP	64.0	35.2	30.6.88	(1,154)	(372)
		Ordinary	33.1				
Wolfson Microelectronics	Scotland	Ordinary	24.6	24.6	31.12.88	245	(262)
		Preference	35.9				

Percentage of equity held assumes that any profit related ratchet will operate so as to reduce Independent's equity holding to its minimum level. Equity percentages shown are fully diluted based on the latest audited accounts available.

9.17 If this additional information is immaterial, it need not be disclosed. [5 Sch 9(4)]. Also, the exemptions in paragraphs 9.13 and 9.14 above are available but the information required by paragraph 9.15 above must still be given in the company's next annual return.

9.18 Moreover, the additional information in paragraph 9.16 above does not need to be given in either of the following two situations where:

- The company is exempt by virtue of section 228 from the requirement to prepare consolidated financial statements (see below). Where this exemption applies, the company's investment in all such undertakings must be shown, in aggregate, in the notes to the company's financial statements by way of the equity method of valuation (that is, by stating the company's share of the net assets of the undertaking).

  Section 228 exempts a company from the requirement to prepare consolidated financial statements in the following circumstances:

  - ☐ The company is a wholly-owned subsidiary of an EC parent.

  - ☐ The company is a subsidiary of an EC parent and that parent holds more than 50 per cent of the shares in the company and notice requesting the company to prepare financial statements has not been served on the company by shareholders holding in aggregate more than half of the remaining shares or 5 per cent of the total shares in the company.

- The company's investment is in an undertaking that is not required by any of the Act's provisions to deliver a copy of its balance sheet to the Registrar of Companies and it does not otherwise publish that balance sheet in Great Britain or elsewhere. Where this situation exists, the information need not be given, provided the company's holding is less than 50 per cent of the nominal value of the shares in the undertaking.

[5 Sch 9(2)(3)].

Stock Exchange requirements

9.19 The International Stock Exchange's Continuing Obligations require that the following information should be given by listed companies that have interests in equity share capital that exceed 20 per cent of another *company's* capital (where that company is not a subsidiary):

- The company's principal country of operation.

- Particulars of its issued capital and debt securities.

- The percentage of each class of debt securities attributable to the company's interest (either direct or indirect).

[CO 21(e)].

9.20 If the number of such investments is large and, consequently, the details to be disclosed would be excessive, then in a similar way to the

Act, The International Stock Exchange requires details to be disclosed of only the more material investments.

9.21 The USM's General Undertaking contains a similar requirement, except that it requires one further detail to be disclosed. Unless the group's interest in the company is dealt with in the consolidated balance sheet as an associated company, the financial statements must disclose the total amount of the company's reserves. [GU 10(e)]. The General Undertaking, however, gives no exemption from disclosure if the number of such investments is large. However, in practice, only the more material investments would be disclosed.

Participating interests

9.22 One specific category of investments that the Companies Act 1981 introduced was 'shares in related companies'. The definition of a related company closely corresponded to SSAP 1's definition of an associated company, although the two definitions were not identical. The term 'related companies' has been removed by the Companies Act 1989, which deletes paragraph 92 of Schedule 4 to the Act. In its place the Act now talks of 'undertakings in which the company has a participating interest'.

9.23 'Participating interest' is defined in section 260(1) of the Act to mean:

> *"an interest held by an undertaking in the shares of another undertaking which it holds on a long-term basis for the purpose of securing a contribution to its activities by the exercise of control or influence arising from or related to that interest".*

9.24 A holding of 20 per cent or more of the shares of an undertaking is presumed to be a participating interest unless the contrary is shown. In this context, a participating interest does not include an interest in a subsidiary undertaking. It will, however, include associated undertakings as defined in both the Act and SSAP 1 (see para 9.30 below).

9.25 The definition of participating interest as stated above is very similar to the previous definition of a related company but with one important difference. Participating interest only refers to 'shares' of another undertaking, no mention is made of voting rights. In contrast, the previous definition of a related company referred to a *qualifying capital interest* which was defined to be an interest in a class of equity shares that *carries rights to vote in all circumstances at general meetings.*

9.26 The removal of the reference to voting rights from the definition of participating interest is intentional. The Companies Act 1989 introduced the term 'associated undertaking' which is dependent on holding shares which give 'voting rights'. In the definition of an associated undertaking (considered more fully in 'Manual of Accounting - volume II' chapter 11), an undertaking is presumed to exercise significant influence if it holds 20 per cent or more of the voting rights in another undertaking, unless the contrary is shown. By contrast, a holding of 20 per cent or more of the non-voting shares in an undertaking will not indicate an investment in an associated undertaking, but will nevertheless be a participating interest, unless the contrary is shown.

9.27 The term 'associated undertaking' is defined in the Act for consolidated financial statements purposes. Consequently, this term does not appear in any of the balance sheet formats of an individual company. Therefore, where an investing company that is not required to prepare consolidated financial statements holds 20 per cent or more of the shares, whether voting or non-voting, in another undertaking, that investment will generally be shown as a 'participating interest' in the company's balance sheet. Participating interests will include associated companies as defined in SSAP 1. If, however, the company is included in the consolidated financial statement of a larger group, in the group's consolidated balance sheet, its holding of 20 per cent or more of the voting shares in an undertaking (that is, in an associate) will be shown under the sub heading 'interests in associated undertaking' and, its holding of 20 per cent or more of the non-voting shares in an undertaking will be shown under the sub heading 'other participating interests'.

9.28 Further information about participating interests is required to be disclosed in the investing company's financial statements in addition to the information about investments outlined in paragraphs 9.16 and 9.19 above.

9.29 'Participating interests' and 'loans to undertakings in which the company has a participating interest' appear as separate sub-headings under the fixed asset main heading of 'investments' in both balance sheet formats. Also, both balance sheet formats require the disclosure of 'amounts owed by undertakings in which the company has a participating interest' under 'debtors', and the disclosure of 'amounts owed to undertakings in which the company has a participating interest' under 'creditors'. In addition, 'amounts owed by and to undertakings in which the company has a participating interest' that are due for payment within one year must be shown separately from amounts due after one year. [Notes 5 and 13 to the balance sheet formats]. These format requirements effectively prohibit companies from showing participating interests and investments in associated companies as one figure, including the cost of the shares in the undertakings, loans to them and after deducting loans from them. The same argument applies to investments in subsidiaries. This disclosure also fulfils the requirements contained in paragraphs 27 and 28 of SSAP 1.

Associated companies

9.30 As stated in paragraph 9.24 above, participating interests include investments in associated companies. Companies that have investments in associated companies have to comply with the requirements of SSAP 1.

9.31 The standard requires that investments in associated companies should be shown in the investing company's own financial statements as follows:

- Income from associated companies should be shown as dividends received and receivable. [SSAP 1 para 18(a)].

- Unless it is shown at a valuation, the amount at which the investing company's interests in associated companies should be shown is the cost of the investment less any amounts written off. [SSAP 1 para 25].

The treatment of an investing group's interests in associated companies is covered in 'Manual of Accounting - volume II' chapter 11.

9.32 If the investing company does not prepare consolidated financial statements because it has no subsidiaries, then it only has to report its own profit and loss account and balance sheet. The only income that can properly be included in that profit and loss account will be dividends received from the associated company. This treatment is consistent with the Act's requirement that only realised profits can be included in a company's profit and loss account. For this reason SSAP 1 suggests that a company should equity account by presenting a separate pro-forma profit and loss account in addition to its own profit and loss account. Alternatively, the company could add the information in supplementary form to its own profit and loss account in such a way that its share of the associated company's profits is not treated as realised for the purposes of the Act.

9.33 Similarly, as the company's balance sheet will carry the investment at cost less amounts written off, SSAP 1 suggests that a separate pro-forma balance sheet should be given in which the associated company will be presented on the equity method of accounting. Alternatively, the information could be added in supplementary form to the company's own balance sheet.

9.34 However, the above information need not be given if the company itself is a wholly-owned subsidiary of another undertaking, because in that situation, the investing group's interest in the associated company will be accounted for on the equity basis in the ultimate group's consolidated financial statements.

Investments in subsidiary undertakings

9.35 Where, at the end of a financial year, a company does not prepare consolidated financial statements, but has subsidiary undertakings, the investing company's financial statements have to disclose the information outlined in paragraph 9.11 above for each of its subsidiary undertakings. [5 Sch 1, 2(1)]. For this purpose, an undertaking is a subsidiary of a parent undertaking where, in any of the five situations that follow, the parent:

- Holds a majority of the voting rights in the undertaking.
- Is a member of the undertaking and can appoint or remove directors having the majority of the votes on the board.
- Has a right to exercise a dominant influence over the undertaking by virtue of provisions either in its memorandum or articles, or in a 'control contract'.
- Is a member of the undertaking and controls the majority of voting rights in it via an agreement with other shareholders.
- Owns a participating interest in the undertaking and actually exercises a dominant influence or operates unified management.

The five situations are considered in detail in 'Manual of Accounting - volume II' chapter 3.

9.36 The disclosure requirement in the last two points of paragraph 9.11 above is extended to include, in addition, the shares held by any subsidiaries of the investing company. Consequently, the identity and nominal values of the shares in each class that the investing company and its subsidiaries holds in a subsidiary undertaking has to be shown, distinguishing between those held by the company itself and those held by any of its subsidiaries. [5 Sch 2(2)]. It is not sufficient to show just the identity and the proportion of shares that the investing company holds in the subsidiary undertaking.

9.37 The Act also requires the company to state the reasons for not preparing consolidated financial statements. [5 Sch 1(4)]. If the reason why the company is not required to prepare consolidated financial statements is that its subsidiary undertakings fall within the exclusions from consolidation provided for in section 229, the reason for exclusion should be stated for each subsidiary undertaking. [5 Sch 1(5)]. Section 229 exclusions are covered in detail in 'Manual of Accounting - volume II' chapter 3.

9.38 Except where one of the conditions below is satisfied, the information outlined in paragraph 9.16 above must also be given for each subsidiary: [5 Sch 3(1)].

- The company is exempt by virtue of section 228 from the requirement to prepare consolidated financial statements (see para 9.18 above). [5 Sch 3(2)].

- The company's investment is in a subsidiary undertaking that is not required by any provision of the Act to deliver a copy of its balance sheet to the Registrar of Companies and that does not otherwise publish that balance sheet in Great Britain or elsewhere. Where this situation applies, the information need not be given, provided the company's holding is less than 50 per cent of the nominal value of the shares in the subsidiary undertaking. [5 Sch 3(3)].

- The information to be disclosed is not material. [5 Sch 3(4)].

9.39 In addition, the company can take advantage of the exemptions outlined in paragraphs 9.13 and 9.14 above, either where the information would be seriously prejudicial or would be of excessive length, in which case, the information required by paragraphs 9.11 and 9.16 above need not be given. Where the company has taken exemption by virtue of paragraph 9.14 above, the full information must still be given in the company's next annual return (see para 9.15).

9.40 Where the financial year of one or more subsidiary undertakings does not coincide with that of the company, the notes to the company's financial statements must disclose:

- The reasons why the company's directors consider it inappropriate for the subsidiary's financial year to coincide with that of the company.

- The balance sheet date of the subsidiaries involved or where there are more than one subsidiaries, the earliest and latest of those dates.

[5 Sch 4].

For example see Table 32.

9.41 Paragraph 5 of Schedule 5 to the Act requires further information to be disclosed about subsidiary undertakings in circumstances where a company is not required to prepare consolidated financial statements. These disclosure requirements are as follows:

- Any qualifications contained in the auditor's reports on the financial statements of subsidiary undertakings for financial years ending with or during the company's financial year.

- Any note contained in the financial statements that draws attention to a matter that, if the note had not been given, would have been referred to in the qualification.

[5 Sch 5 (1)].

This provision applies unless the matter that is the subject of the qualification is covered in the parent company's own financial statements, or is immaterial from the point of view of the parent company's members.

Table 32: Disclosure of information where the financial year ends of subsidiaries and associates do not coincide with that of the holding company.

Extract from Mekechnie PLC Report and Accounts 31st July 1989.

Accounting policies extract

e) ACCOUNTING DATES

(i) HOLDING COMPANY AND SUBSIDIARIES

Financial statements are made up to 31 July with the exception of certain Australian subsidiaries which are made up to 30 June in order to meet Group's reporting requirements.

(ii) ASSOCIATES

Associates which do not prepare audited financial statements up to 31 July are treated as follows:

UK AND EUROPE

The year end of the associates is 31 December and the results included are based on unaudited financial statements to the following 31 July.

SOUTH AFRICA AND JAPAN

The year end of the associates is 31 December and the results included are based on unaudited financial statements to the following 30 June.

AUSTRALIA

The results are based on audited financial statements for the year to 30 June.

9.42 Furthermore, the aggregate amount of the total investment of the company in the shares of subsidiary undertakings must be stated using equity accounting, unless both the following conditions apply.

- The company is exempt from the requirement to prepare consolidated financial statements, because its parent is included in the financial statements of a larger group.

- The directors state their opinion that the aggregate value of the company's assets consisting of shares in, or amounts due from, subsidiary undertakings, is not less than the aggregate of the amounts at which the assets are included in the company's balance sheet.

[5 Sch 5(2)].

9.43 If the information required by paragraphs 9.41 and 9.42 above cannot be obtained, this fact should be stated. [5 Sch 5(3)]. In addition, information required by paragraph 9.42 above must be disclosed even where the disclosure of that information would be seriously prejudicial. [Sec 231(3)].

9.44 Further information about group undertakings is required to be disclosed in the financial statements of the investing company that does not prepare consolidated financial statements in addition to the information about investments in subsidiaries outlined in paragraphs 9.35 to 9.43 above.

9.45 Both the balance sheet formats specify the place where the aggregate amounts should be shown of any amounts owed to and from, and any interests in, group undertakings. In addition, a parent or a subsidiary must disclose separately (either on the face of the balance sheet or in the notes to the financial statements) any item required to be shown in the balance sheet formats in relation to group undertakings, split between the amounts owed to or from, and any interests in:

- Any parent or any fellow subsidiary.
- Any subsidiary.

[4 Sch 59].

9.46 Because amounts owed by and to group undertakings have to be shown in specific positions in the formats, it is not acceptable for undertakings to net these balances off and to disclose the net balance, together with the cost of the investments, in the balance sheet as 'Investments in subsidiaries'. This applies even where a note to the financial statements gives additional information that explains the net balance.

9.47 Moreover, the amounts owed and owing have to be ascertained on an undertaking by undertaking basis. [4 Sch 5]. Consequently, for accounting disclosure purposes, amounts that one subsidiary owes to the parent cannot be offset against amounts the parent owes to another subsidiary. Set-off can be allowed only in circumstances where a legal right of set-off exists, for example, between loans.

9.48 Furthermore, undertakings have to analyse 'amounts owed by (and to) group undertakings' between amounts that will fall due within one year and amounts that will fall due after more than one year. [Notes 5 and 13 on the balance sheet formats]. The results of this analysis will largely depend both on the way in which group undertakings are financed and on the terms of any formal or informal agreements between the undertakings.

Parent company information

9.49 Where, at the end of a financial year, a company is a subsidiary of another undertaking, the following information should be provided about the company's ultimate holding company (which includes any corporate body):

- Its name.
- Its country of incorporation (if known), if incorporated outside Great Britain.
- If it is incorporated in Great Britain, whether it is registered in England and Wales or in Scotland.

[5 Sch 12].

9.50 In addition to the above, information relating to two further parent undertakings may have to be disclosed where the ultimate holding company (or other body corporate) does not prepare consolidated financial statements. The disclosure relates to the parent of the largest and smallest group of undertakings for which consolidated financial statements are prepared, and of which the company is a group member. [5 Sch 11(1)].

9.51 The information to be disclosed in respect of both these parent undertakings is as follows:

- The name of the parent undertaking.
- The country of incorporation, if incorporated outside Great Britain.
- If it is incorporated in Great Britain, whether it is registered in England and Wales or in Scotland.
- The address of its principal place of business, if it is unincorporated.
- The address from which copies of the undertaking's consolidated financial statements can be obtained, if these are available to the public.

[5 Sch 11(2)(3)(4)].

9.52 Where the ultimate holding company does prepare consolidated financial statements, the above information need be given only for the ultimate holding company (the parent company of the largest group of undertakings) and for the parent company of the smallest group of undertakings that prepares consolidated financial statements which include the company. [5 Sch 11(1)].

9.53 The disclosure requirements of paragraphs 9.49 to 9.51 above are illustrated by the example that follows. Consider the simple group structure set out in the diagram below:

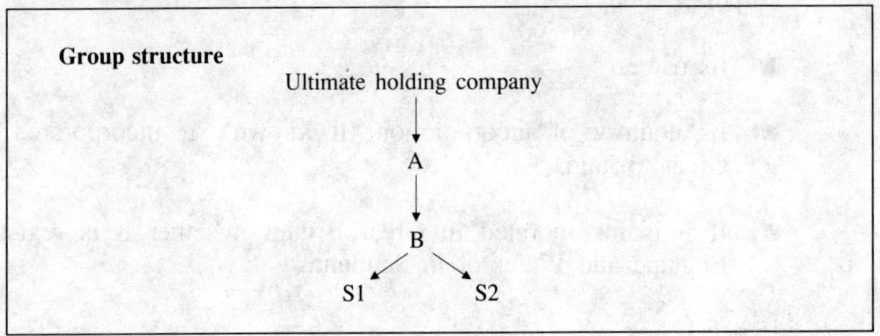

In the situation where the ultimate holding company **prepares** consolidated financial statements, the parent company of the largest group will be the ultimate holding company. The notes to the financial statements of companies A, B, S1 and S2 will have to disclose for the ultimate holding company the information set out in paragraphs 9.49 and 9.51 above by virtue of paragraphs 12 and 11 of Schedule 5.

In addition, the notes to the financial statements of companies B, S1 and S2 will have to disclose the information, set out in paragraph 9.51 above by virtue of paragraph 11 of Schedule 5, about the parent company of the smallest group depending on whether company A or company B prepares consolidated financial statements. The circumstances that arise are as follows:

- ☐ If company A prepares consolidated financial statements but company B does not, then companies B, S1 and S2 will have to disclose the relevant information for company A (the parent of the smallest group).
- ☐ If company B prepares consolidated financial statements but company A does not, then companies S1 and S2 will have to disclose the relevant information for company B (the parent of the smallest group).
- ☐ If companies A and B both prepare consolidated financial statements, then company B will have to disclose the relevant information about company A (the parent of the smallest group) and companies S1 and S2 will similarly have to disclose the relevant information about company B (the parent of the smallest group).

In the situation where the ultimate holding company **does not prepare** consolidated financial statements, the notes to the financial statements of companies A, B, S1 and S2 will have to disclose for the ultimate holding company the information set out in paragraph 9.49 above by virtue of paragraph 12 of Schedule 5.

In addition, the notes to the financial statements of companies B, S1 and S2 will have to disclose the information, set out in paragraph 9.51 above by virtue of paragraph 11

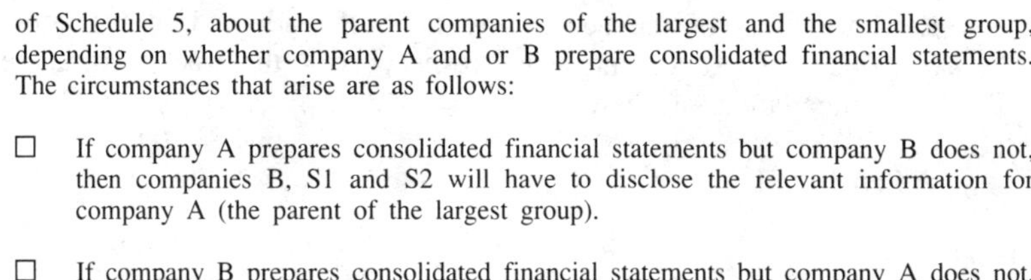

of Schedule 5, about the parent companies of the largest and the smallest group, depending on whether company A and or B prepare consolidated financial statements. The circumstances that arise are as follows:

- ☐ If company A prepares consolidated financial statements but company B does not, then companies B, S1 and S2 will have to disclose the relevant information for company A (the parent of the largest group).

- ☐ If company B prepares consolidated financial statements but company A does not, then companies S1 and S2 will have to disclose the relevant information for company B (the parent of the largest group).

- ☐ If companies A and B both prepare consolidated financial statements, then all three companies B, S1 and S2 will have to disclose the relevant information about company A (the parent of the largest group). In addition, companies S1 and S2 will have to disclose the relevant information about company B (the parent of the smallest group). This means that in the situation described, companies S1 and S2 will have to disclose information concerning three parent companies (that is, the ultimate holding company, company A and company B).

9.54 The information required by paragraphs 9.49 and 9.51 above need not be disclosed with respect to a parent undertaking that is established outside the UK or carries on business outside the UK, and if it would, in the opinion of the directors, be seriously prejudicial to the business of its parent undertakings, or to the business of the company or any of its subsidiaries, and the Secretary of State agrees that the information need not be disclosed. [Sec 231(3)(b)]. Some companies have taken advantage of this concession where they have reasons to believe that the ultimate holding company's nationality would be unacceptable or offensive to its own customers.

Arrangements attracting merger relief

9.55 In certain circumstances, a company may be relieved from the obligation to carry any share premium to a share premium account required under section 130. The provisions that give this relief are known as the merger relief provisions and appear in section 131 and 132 of the Act. Merger relief and merger accounting are discussed in detail in 'Manual of accounting - volume II' chapter 9,.

9.56 Where a company does not prepare consolidated financial statements, but has allotted shares during the financial year in consideration for the issue, transfer or cancellation of shares in another corporate body under arrangements attracting merger relief, it must disclose in its financial statements:

- ■ The name of the other company.

- ■ The number, nominal value and class of shares allotted.

- ■ The number, nominal value and class of shares in the other company issued, transferred, or cancelled.

- Particulars of the accounting treatment adopted in the company's financial statements in respect of the issue, transfer or cancellation of shares.

[5 Sch 10(2)]

9.57 If the company has, during the financial year or during either of the two preceding financial years, allotted shares in the circumstances described above, then the notes to the financial statements may need to disclose further information in the following two circumstances:

- The company disposes of either of the following:
  - ☐ Shares in the 'merged company'.
  - ☐ Fixed assets that, *at the time of the arrangement*, were assets of either the 'merged company' or any of its subsidiaries.

  If the company realises a profit or loss on such a disposal, and that profit or loss is included in the company's profit and loss account, the amount of that profit or loss has to be disclosed. [5 Sch 10(3)(a)].

- The company disposes of shares in any company (other than the merged company), and the profit or loss that it makes on this disposal is to some extent attributable to the fact that the company whose shares have been sold (or one of its subsidiaries) owned as assets either of the following:
  - ☐ Shares in the 'merged company'.
  - ☐ Fixed assets that, *at the time of the arrangement*, were assets of either the 'merged company' or any of its subsidiaries.

  In this situation, the profit or loss attributable to the sale of those assets that is included in the company's profit and loss account has to be disclosed. [5 Sch 10(3)(b)].

9.58 In both the above situations, the notes to the financial statements must give an explanation of the transaction to which the information relates. Such explanations may alert those shareholders who have acquired shares in a new company in exchange for their shares in another company, of any substantial disposals of the assets of the company that they originally owned or whether the company's management is pursuing a policy of 'asset stripping'. Such a policy would conflict with the basic concept of a merger as discussed in 'Manual of Accounting volume II' chapter 9.

9.59 These provisions of the Act apply from *the time of the arrangement*, which is determined as follows:

- Where as a result of an arrangement the other company becomes a subsidiary, the time is the date on which it becomes a subsidiary, or if the arrangement becomes binding on the fulfilment of a condition, the date on which that condition is satisfied.

- Where the company is already a subsidiary, the first day on which the shares are allotted.

[5 Sch 10(4)].

Own shares and shares in own parent

9.60 The main heading of 'investments' has a sub-heading 'own shares'. When a company purchases its own shares, it must cancel them at the time it purchases them. [Sec 160(4), 162(2)]. Thus, unlike the practice that is generally permitted both in the USA and also by the 2nd Directive, a company cannot purchase its own shares and then treat them as 'treasury shares' until the time it resells them.

9.61 A company will generally hold its own shares only where it has acquired them by forfeiture, or by surrender in lieu of forfeiture, or by way of gift. The Act sets out certain rules to govern situations where companies hold their own shares. In particular, a public company that acquires shares by forfeiture must generally dispose of them within three years. Otherwise, it must cancel them and so effectively bring about a capital reduction (see also chapter 6 para 6.18). [Sec 146].

9.62 A subsidiary company cannot normally own shares in its holding company. [Sec 23(1)]. However, this prohibition does not apply where the subsidiary is acting as a personal representative for a third party, or as trustee and the holding company or a subsidiary of it has no beneficial interest under the trust. [Sec 23(2)]. This provision also does not extend to market makers. [Sec 23(3)]. However, the prohibition does include those shares that might be held on behalf of the subsidiary by another person as its nominee. [Sec 23(7)].

9.63 Where a corporate body becomes a subsidiary company because of the changes in the definition of subsidiaries included in section 736 of the Act, it may retain any shares that it already held in its parent. However, where shares are held in this way, they will carry no right to vote at company meetings. [Sec 23(4)].

9.64 In certain situations, a subsidiary may find that it does hold shares in its parent. This may arise, for example, where the parent has recently acquired the subsidiary which owned shares in the parent before it became a group member. Before the introduction of the Companies

Act 1989, such holdings were in breach of section 23(1) of the Act. Now, however, where a company acquires shares in its parent after the commencement of the new section 23(1), but before it becomes a subsidiary of the parent, it may retain those shares. Also in this circumstance, those shares will carry no right to vote at company meetings. [Sec 23(5)].

9.65 The notes to the parent's financial statements must disclose the number, description and the amount of the shares or debentures that subsidiaries or their nominees hold. [5 Sch 6(1)]. This information is not required, however, where the subsidiary holds the shares or debentures as personal representative or as trustee. [5 Sch 6(2)]. However, the exemption for a subsidiary acting as a trustee will not be available if the company or any of its subsidiaries is beneficially interested under the trust, unless the beneficial interest is by way of security for the purpose of a transaction entered into by it in the ordinary course of business, which includes the lending of money. [5 Sch 6(3)].

Loans for acquisition of own shares

9.66 Where any outstanding loans made in respect of the acquisition of the company's shares under either section 153(4)(b) or (c) or section 155 of the Act (various situations of financial assistance by a company for purchase of its own shares) are included under any item in the balance sheet, these must be disclosed in aggregate for each item. [4 Sch 51(2)].

Other investments

9.67 The category 'other investments' will normally include the following items (other than investments in subsidiaries and companies in which the investing company has a participating interest):

- Listed and unlisted securities.
- Life assurance policies.
- Joint ventures, and partnerships if they are not subsidiaries or participating interests.

9.68 Building society deposits and bank deposits could be included either as 'other investments' (either under fixed assets or under current assets - depending on the nature of the deposits) or as 'cash at bank and in hand'. If the amount is material, the accounting policies should disclose where such items are included.

Chapter 10

BALANCE SHEET - CURRENT ASSETS

Chapter 10

BALANCE SHEET - CURRENT ASSETS

Introduction

10.1 This chapter deals with the accounting treatment and disclosure of current assets other than current asset investments which are considered in chapter 9. In particular, it looks at problems that arise in the disclosure and the valuation of stocks and long-term contracts following the revision of SSAP 9. Some special purpose transactions that relate to stocks and debtors are also considered.

Stocks

Disclosure

10.2 The Act requires that stocks should be analysed between the following four categories:

- Raw materials and consumables.
- Work in progress.
- Finished goods and goods for resale.
- Payments on account.

[4 Sch Formats].

10.3 A company should follow this categorisation so long as it produces true and fair financial statements. However, in certain circumstances, the special nature of a company's business may mean that the company needs to adapt the formats. 'Payments on account' represent the payments a company makes on account of stocks, and not the payments it receives from customers.

10.4 SSAP 9 requires that the figure of stocks disclosed in the financial statements should be the total of the lower of cost and net realisable value of the separate items of stock or of groups of similar items. The original version of SSAP 9 required that the accounting polices used in calculating cost, net realisable value, attributable profit and foreseeable losses should be stated. In practice, however, such details were rarely given and the revised version has recognised this fact. Consequently, the revised version merely requires that the accounting policy that has been applied to stocks should be stated and applied consistently within the business and from year to year. [SSAP 9 para 32].

10.5 The Act allows companies to use certain methods for arriving at the purchase price or the production cost of stocks and other 'fungible items'. For this purpose, 'fungible items' are those items that are indistinguishable one from another (for example, identical nuts and bolts). [4 Sch 27(6)]. A company may adopt any of the following methods:

- First-in, first-out (FIFO).
- Last-in, first-out (LIFO).
- Weighted average price.
- Any other similar method.

[4 Sch 27(1)(2)].

10.6 When choosing a method, the directors must ensure that the method they choose provides the fairest practicable approximation to 'actual cost'. SSAP 9 considers that the LIFO method does not usually bear a reasonable relationship to actual cost, and so LIFO is not an acceptable method of valuation in the UK.

Replacement value of stocks

10.7 Paragraph 27 of Schedule 4 says that, where the historical cost of stocks or fungible assets is calculated using a method (such as those mentioned in para 10.5), and that valuation differs materially from the 'relevant alternative amount' of those items, then the difference should be disclosed in a note to the financial statements (for example, see Table 33 overleaf).

10.8 The 'relevant alternative amount' will normally be the amount at which the assets would have been disclosed if their value had been determined according to their replacement cost as at the balance sheet date. [4 Sch 27(4)]. The replacement cost of these types of assets will normally be their current cost. However, a company may instead determine the relevant alternative amount according to the most recent actual purchase price or the most recent actual production cost of assets of that class before that date. But it can do this only where this method gives a more appropriate standard of comparison for assets of the class in question. [4 Sch 27(5)]. The Act leaves it to the company's directors to form an opinion as to whether the method does this.

Table 33: Disclosure of the replacement value of stocks.

Extract from The British Petroleum Company p.l.c. Annual Report & Accounts 31st December 1988.

Note extract

19 Stocks

	1988	1987
	£m	£m
Petroleum	1,433	1,765
Chemicals	334	284
Minerals	119	111
Nutrition	177	143
Other	98	135
	2,161	2,438
Stores	342	278
	2,503	2,716
Replacement cost	2,570	2,694

10.9 The example below illustrates the calculation of the value of stocks on both a FIFO basis and a weighted average price basis. It also considers how the replacement cost of stocks should be disclosed:

Example

Two companies, A and B, have identical opening and closing stocks figures and purchases in a particular year, as follows:

	Units	Values
		£
Opening stocks	100	835
Purchases March	50	500
July	100	1,150
September	50	600
December	150	2,000
Closing stocks	250	

Company A chooses to determine the value of its closing stocks by the FIFO method, and company B does so by the 'weighted average price' method. In these circumstances, the amount to be included in the balance sheets would be calculated as follows:

Company A:

		£
150 at £2,000/150	=	2,000
50 at £600/50	=	600
50 at £1,150/100	=	575
		3,175

Company B:

$$\frac{£835 + £500 + £1,150 + £600 + £2,000}{100 + 50 + 100 + 50 + 150} \times 250 = 2,825$$

The value of the stocks at replacement cost is, say, £3,300.

If the difference between the balance sheet value of stocks and their replacement cost is material in the context of their balance sheet value, it must be disclosed under the requirement outlined in paragraph 10.7. The difference for company A is £125 (£3,300 - £3,175), which is unlikely to be considered material. The difference for company B is £475 (£3,300 - £2,825), which may, in certain circumstances, be considered material. If it is, it must be disclosed.

10.10 Counsel has advised that a 'method' is not used when stocks are valued at either their actual purchase price or their production cost. It would appear, therefore, that where companies value their stocks at actual purchase price or production cost, they do not need to disclose, in their financial statements, the difference between this value and the replacement value of those stocks.

10.11 In many situations, it is likely that some items of stocks will be valued by one of the methods mentioned above, and that other items will be valued at actual purchase price or production cost. Where a company does this, the company will need to disclose not only the difference between the figure of stocks valued by a method and their replacement cost, but also the actual purchase price or production cost of the stocks it has valued by that method. Otherwise, it could be misleading for the company to disclose the figure that represents the difference, without also giving an indication of the proportion of the total stock value to which this difference relates.

10.12 For those stocks valued by a 'method', the Act effectively requires two stock valuations: one for normal balance sheet purposes and the other for arriving at the relevant alternative amount. Where a company has to calculate the current replacement cost of stocks for current cost accounting purposes, this calculation should impose no additional burden on the company in complying with the Act. In such situations the current replacement cost may be arrived at by using indices. A company should use indices that are sufficiently relevant to each line of its stocks, the result when it applies them globally is, in accounting terms, equivalent to the result produced when it applies them to each individual line.

Long-term contracts

10.13 Paragraphs 22 and 23 of Schedule 4 requires that *"the amount to be included in respect of any current asset shall be its purchase price or production cost. If the net realisable value of any current asset is lower than its purchase price or production cost, the amount to be included in respect of that asset shall be the net realisable value"*. However, paragraph 27 of the original SSAP 9 required that *"the amount at which long-term contract work in progress is stated in periodic financial statements should be cost plus any attributable profit, less any foreseeable losses and progress payments received and receivable"*.

10.14 The inclusion of 'attributable profit' in the carrying value of long-term contract work in progress resulted in a conflict with the Act. This conflict affected only the inclusion of attributable profit in the balance sheet valuation of current assets, not its inclusion in the profit and loss account. However, it was possible for companies to comply with the requirements of the original standard by invoking the 'true and fair override'. The DTI, however, argued that the 'true and fair override' (included in section 226(5)) should only be used as a last resort. They encouraged the ASC to accommodate compliance with section 226(5) and the EC 4th Directive (valuation rules for current assets) within a revised standard. The ASC set up a working party to consider how this matter could be resolved. Their work culminated in September 1988 in the issue of SSAP 9 (revised), which has made significant changes to the presentation of long-term contracts in financial statements to avoid this conflict with the law.

Definition

10.15 With three exceptions there are only minor changes concerning the definitions given in the revised standard. The exceptions are the definition of 'long-term contracts', the addition of a definition of 'payments on account' and the widening of the definition of 'attributable profit'.

10.16 A 'long-term contract' is defined in SSAP 9 as follows:

> *"A contract entered into for the design, manufacture or construction of a single substantial asset or the provision of a service (or of a combination of assets or services which together constitute a single project) where the time taken substantially to complete the contract is such that the contract activity falls into different accounting periods. A contract that is required to be accounted for as long-term by this accounting standard will usually extend for a period exceeding one year. However, a duration exceeding one year is not an essential feature of a long-term contract. Some contracts with a shorter duration than*

one year should be accounted for as long-term contracts if they are sufficiently material to the activity of the period that not to record turnover and attributable profit would lead to a distortion of the period's turnover and results such that the financial statements would not give a true and fair view, provided that the policy is applied consistently within the reporting entity and from year to year." [SSAP 9 para 22].

10.17 The original definition of long-term contracts only related to contracts that extended for more than one year. The intention of the revised definition is that companies engaged in short-term contracts will now be able to recognise profits on such contracts, if not to do so would distort the period's turnover and results. Such a situation might arise, for example, when a company completes a material short-term contract just after the year end, but a substantial amount of work on the contract had been completed before the year end. If an element of profit is not attributable to the current period, this might distort that period's turnover and results to such an extent that they do not give a true and fair view.

10.18 'Payments on account' are defined as *"all amounts received and receivable at the accounting date in respect of contracts in progress"*. [SSAP 9 para 25].

10.19 The definition of attributable profit requires that it should be calculated, specifically, after estimating 'remedial and maintenance costs'. [SSAP 9 para 23]. In practice, for example, these costs will include the usual snagging clause of a building contract (that is, the clauses covering completion of the finishing touches to a building). They would also include provision for costs incurred under a 'guarantee' period for maintenance that is part of the original contract.

Turnover

10.20 Paragraph 28 of the revised standard states that long-term contracts should be assessed on a contract by contract basis and reflected in the profit and loss account by recording turnover and related costs as contract activity progresses. No definition of turnover is provided in the revised standard, it merely states that turnover is ascertained in a manner appropriate to the stage of completion of the contract, the business and the industry in which it operates.

10.21 The approach that the revised standard adopts is that the profit and loss account and the balance sheet should be fully articulated. In essence, this means that amounts recorded as turnover in respect of a contract are treated as debtors to the extent that they are unpaid, and amounts recorded as costs of sales are deducted from the balance sheet work in progress figure. This is based on the theory that once a transaction has been recorded as turnover, it cannot then also be carried as stocks and must, consequently, be a receivable.

10.22 The standard does not prescribe a method of calculating turnover and this is left for individual companies to determine according to their own circumstances. However, amounts taken through the profit and loss account in an accounting period would normally relate to separate or measurable parts of the contract completed within that period. Appendix 1 to the standard states that turnover may sometimes be ascertained by reference to the valuation of work carried out to date. In other situations, there may be specific points during a contract where individual elements of work done will have separately ascertainable sales values, where costs can be identified and, therefore, turnover can be recorded as appropriate. This could be, for example, when delivery or when customer acceptance takes place.

10.23 Although there is no definition of turnover in the revised standard, the standard does require that, in particular, the means of ascertaining turnover, should be disclosed as an accounting policy (for example, see Table 34). [SSAP 9 para 32].

Table 34: Illustration of accounting policy for turnover in respect of long term contracts.

Extract from Countryside Properties PLC Report and Accounts 30th September 1989.

Accounting policies extract

Turnover

Turnover comprises sales of properties where building has been completed and the property has been legally conveyed to the purchaser. In the case of long-term contracts, turnover includes amounts invoiced during the year for work certified as completed under the contract. Disposals of land, partially developed land and gross rents receivable from investment properties are also included in turnover. Sales of second-hand properties acquired solely to assist the sale of new properties under the Group's part-exchange scheme are not included in turnover.

Recognition of profit

10.24 The profit and loss account should only include profit when the outcome of a particular contract can be ascertained with reasonable certainty (that is, where it is reasonable to foresee profits in advance of the completion of a contract). This is often a difficult exercise to undertake in practice. In addition, the standard comments that this judgement of future profitability should be exercised with prudence. [SSAP 9 para 29].

10.25 Therefore, the turnover recognised on a particular contract will depend on the state of completion of that contract. For example, when, in the contract's early stages, it is not possible to foresee its outcome with reasonable certainty, turnover will equal the costs incurred that are charged to cost of sales. Therefore, no profit will be recognised in the profit and loss account. However, when in the later stages of a contract, the outcome can be assessed with reasonable certainty, turnover should include profit prudently recognised as earned at that stage of completion.

10.26 When a company determines the amount of attributable profit to be included in turnover, it should take account of the company's type of business, the nature of the contract and the contractual relationship with its customer. Appendix 1 to the revised standard states that when estimating profit:

> *"it is necessary to take into account not only the total costs to date and the total estimated further costs to completion...but also the estimated future costs of rectification and guarantee work, and any other future work to be undertaken under the contract. These costs are then compared with the total sales value of the contract."* [SSAP 9 appendix 1 para 25].

10.27 In practice, there appear to be two basic approaches to determining attributable profit:

- The actual profit calculated by comparing the priced 'bill of quantities' to a contractor's own internal costing of the project. The 'bill of quantities' is a document prepared at the tender stage showing specifications set out in terms of quantities and values.

- By calculating total anticipated profit to completion of the contract and 'attributing' a reasonable portion to the work carried out. This might be done by reference to the cost of work incurred to date and the cost estimated to complete the contract.

In addition, some companies prefer to take a more prudent approach, and show profit only on that portion of work inspected and accepted by the contracting parties.

10.28 No matter what method of determining attributable profit is adopted, it should be applied consistently and from year to year. Paragraph 32 of SSAP 9 requires that the *method* of ascertaining attributable profits should be stated in the accounting policies. This means that the basis of calculation should be disclosed.

Cost of sales

10.29 The associated costs of achieving the turnover that is recorded in the profit and loss account on a contract by contract basis is deducted from the total costs incurred to date and charged in the profit and loss account as 'cost of sales'. Consequently, the reported result is attributed to the proportion of work completed.

10.30 The standard requires that where it is anticipated that a loss might result on a particular contract, the whole of the loss should be provided for as soon as it is foreseen. [SSAP 9 para 11]. This provision would normally be charged to cost of sales (see also para 10.39).

Disclosure

10.31 The disclosure requirements of the revised standard have effectively removed the conflict between the original requirement in SSAP 9 to include attributable profit in work in progress and the Act's requirement to show stocks at the lower of cost and net realisable value. The revised SSAP 9 requires that long-term contracts should be disclosed in the balance sheet as follows (see also Table 35 overleaf):

- The amount by which recorded turnover exceeds payments on account should be classified as 'amounts recoverable on contracts' and separately disclosed within debtors.

- The balance of payments on account (in excess of amounts matched with turnover, and offset against long-term contract balances) should be classified as 'payments on account' and separately disclosed within creditors.

- The amount of long-term contracts at costs incurred, net of amounts transferred to cost of sales, after deducting foreseeable losses and payments on account that exceed turnover, should be classified as 'long-term contract balances' and separately disclosed within the balance sheet heading 'stocks'. The balance sheet note should disclose separately the balances of:

  - Net cost less foreseeable losses.

  - Applicable payments on account.

- The amount by which the provision or accrual for foreseeable losses exceeds the costs incurred (after transfers to cost of sales) should be included within either 'provisions for liabilities and charges' or 'creditors' as appropriate.

[SSAP 9 para 30].

Table 35: Illustration of the disclosure of accounting policy on long-term contracts

Extract from John Laing PLC Annual Report and Accounts 31st December 1988.

Accounting policies extract

(f) Long-term contracts

Amounts recoverable on contracts which are included in debtors, are stated at cost, plus attributable profit to the extent that this is reasonably certain after making provision for contingencies, less any losses incurred or foreseen in bringing contracts to completion, and less amounts received as progress payments. Cost for this purpose includes valuations of all work done by sub-contractors, whether certified or not and all overheads other than those relating to the general administration of the relevant companies. For any contracts where receipts exceed the book value of work done, the excess is included in creditors as payments on account.

10.32 Each of the above balance sheet disclosure requirements is illustrated in the examples that follow:

Example 1

Turnover exceeds payments on account	£'000
Turnover (value of work done)	52
Cumulative payments on account	45
Excess	7
Balance of costs on this contract not transferred to cost of sales	10
Balance sheet (extract)	£'000
Stocks	
Work in progress	
Net cost less foreseeable losses	10
Debtors	
Amounts recoverable on contracts	7

10.33 In the above example, the value of work included in turnover for the particular contract exceeds the progress payments received and receivable to date on that same contract. In accordance with SSAP 9, the excess amount is classified as 'amounts recoverable on contracts' and is shown separately under the heading 'debtors' in the balance sheet formats.

10.34 Treating amounts recoverable on contracts as an unbilled debtor is a relatively new concept in the UK and has been criticised by some members of the profession. They believe that this unbilled amount should remain in work in progress and that to describe amounts not yet invoiced to customers as a 'debtor' is wrong.

10.35 The ASC realised that there was concern over its suggested treatment and sought Counsel's opinion before issuing the revised standard. Counsel's opinion stated that there was nothing in the proposals that conflicted with the law. A long-term contract bears the characteristics of any legally binding contract so that the contractor may sue for any monies rightfully owed by the customer. This implies that amounts receivable for work completed under a long-term contract can, correctly, be regarded as realisable. Consequently, to regard amounts recoverable on contracts (which are by definition legally binding) as a debtor is not contrary to the Act, and the balance may be disclosed separately under debtors in the balance sheet formats. In addition, there is no necessity to disclose any further details, such as the profit element included in the debtor, in the notes to the financial statements.

Example 2

Payments on account exceed turnover and balance of costs on contracts

	£'000
Turnover (value of work done)	52
Cumulative payments on account	60
Excess	8
Balance of costs on this contract not transferred to cost of sales	5
Balance sheet (extract)	
Stocks	
Work in progress	
Net cost less foreseeable losses	5
Applicable payments on account	(5)
	-
Creditors	
Payments on account (£8,000 - £5,000)	3

10.36 In the second example, payments on account exceed both the amount of recorded turnover and costs incurred to date. The excess amount is classified as 'payments on account' and separately disclosed in 'creditors'.

Example 3

Payments on account exceed turnover

	£'000
Turnover (value of work done)	52
Cumulative payments on account	60
Excess	8
Balance of costs on this contract not transferred to cost of sales	10

Balance sheet (extract)

Stocks	
Work in progress	
Net cost less foreseeable losses	10
Applicable payments on account	(8)
	2

10.37 In this example, long-term contracts comprise the total costs incurred to date less:

- Amounts transferred to the profit and loss account in respect of work carried out to date.
- Any foreseeable losses.
- Any applicable payments on account.

10.38 The balance sheet note should disclose separately both the net cost less foreseeable losses and the applicable payments on account.

10.39 As mentioned in paragraph 10.29 above, the amount transferred to the profit and loss account for a particular contract is the costs incurred to date in reaching that contract's stage of completion recognised in turnover. In most circumstances, this amount represents the cost of sales figure for a contract. However, where a provision is made for foreseeable losses, this charge also becomes part of cost of sales. The amount to be included in respect of applicable payments on account is the amount, if any, by which the payments on account on a particular long-term contract exceed the cumulative turnover recorded on that particular contract.

Example 4

Provision for foreseeable losses

	£'000
Turnover (value of work done)	52
Cumulative payments on account	45
Excess	7
Total costs on this contract	50
Transferred to cost of sales	40
Balance	10
Provision/accrual for foreseeable losses	30

Profit and loss account (extract)	£'000
Turnover	52
Costs of sales (£40,000 + £30,000)	(70)

Balance sheet (extract)	
	£'000
Stocks	
Work in progress	
Net cost less foreseeable losses (£10,000 - £10,000)	-
Debtors	
Amounts recoverable on contracts	7
Liabilities	
Provision/accrual (£30,000 - £10,000)	20

10.40 In this example, foreseeable losses exceed net costs incurred to date by £20,000 and, as mentioned in the fourth point of paragraph 10.31 above, such excesses should be included in either accruals or provisions.

10.41 The revised standard provides no guidance on when these losses should be shown as an accrual and when they should be shown as a provision. The treatment used would appear to depend on the contract's state of completion at the time the financial statements are finalised. A provision is defined in the Act as:

> "*..any amount retained as reasonably necessary for the purpose of providing for any liability or loss which is either likely to be incurred, or certain to be incurred but uncertain as to the amount or as to the date on which it will arise.*" [4 Sch 89].

10.42 The definition of a provision given in the Act implies that there is some argument for disclosing a loss as an accrual if a loss can be quantified with certainty. Losses that cannot be calculated with accuracy at the time of signing the financial statements should be disclosed as a provision.

10.43 The revised standard's definition of foreseeable losses requires also that remedial and maintenance costs should be estimated and included in the determination of any future losses on a contract. [SSAP 9 para 24].

Special purpose transactions involving stocks

10.44 ED 42, 'Accounting for special purpose transactions' was issued in 1988 and deals with how to account for certain transactions that are often not included in a company's or group's balance sheet. The proposals in the exposure draft stemmed from TR 603 which had been issued by the ICAEW's Technical Committee in the previous year. The exposure draft's proposals deal with certain types of transactions concerning stock, and these are considered in the paragraphs that follow.

Sale and repurchase of stock

10.45 Sale and repurchase of stock was one of the types of off balance sheet transaction described in appendix 1 to TR 603. The Technical Release described the situation where stock is sold with the option to buy it back, the option being so constructed that it is reasonably certain that it will be exercised. The arrangement may run for months, or even years, during which time the company that sold the stock will use the sale proceeds as a form of finance. The stock and the related purchase obligation (that is, the liability to repay the finance provided by the temporary holder of the stock) are often excluded from the balance sheet, the difference between the original selling price and the buy-back price (which is effectively a finance charge) being debited to cost of sales when the item is finally sold to an independent party.

10.46 A good example of this type of arrangement is a scheme that is operated by a number of banks. These banks are not allowed to earn interest by lending money. Consequently, they have devised a scheme whereby they will enter into an agreement with a company to purchase stocks (or other assets) from the company at book value and then to resell that stock back to the company after a predetermined period at a slightly higher fixed price. Clearly, the price differential is equivalent to interest, because the scheme is a means of financing stocks or other assets). Often the assets themselves remain physically with the company.

10.47 The exposure draft covers these types of transaction under the heading 'non-monetary items'. ED 42's proposals confirm that sale and repurchase agreements where the repurchase price is predetermined and covers primarily interest and holding costs should be treated as a financing arrangement. [ED 42 para 39]. However, it also mentions an example where this treatment would not be appropriate.

10.48 It states that an agreement to sell commodity stocks at the current spot market price and to buy them back at the spot market price applicable three months hence should be accounted for on the relevant separate occasions as a sale and repurchase. [ED 42 para 39]. This is because control over the amount of the net future cash flows available from the commodities has been relinquished during the transaction. In other words, the seller is exposed to market risk, rather than just interest cost, during the period.

10.49 With other sale and repurchase transactions, to accord with the proposals in ED 42, the price differential in such transactions should be charged to the profit and loss account as interest. During the existence of the scheme, the stock or other assets should remain on the balance sheet and the related finance should be shown as a liability. [ED 42 para 10]. It will also be necessary to explain the nature of the transaction where the finance is effectively secured on the related asset. Even where the reporting company lacks legal ownership of the asset, this fact may need to be disclosed.

Example

A company sells stock in year 1 for £100,000 and at the same time enters into an agreement to repurchase it a year later for £110,000. The £10,000 should not be treated as part of the cost of the stock, but represents interest, and should be charged to the profit and loss account. If the company's year end fell half way through the transaction, the company should show in its balance sheet stock of £100,000 and a financing liability of £100,000. Assuming interest accrues evenly throughout the period £5,000 of interest should be accrued and charged to the profit and loss account.

Consignment stock

10.50 Consignment stock was a type of off balance sheet transaction that was identified in appendix 1 to TR 603. The technical release dealt with financing schemes whereby dealerships frequently obtain stock on consignment from the manufacturer. The purchase price for such stock is generally payable immediately on sale or after a set period and is calculated to take account of the length of time that the stock has been held. The manufacturer is, therefore, effectively financing the trading stocks of the dealership, but neither the stock nor the 'loan' is reflected in the dealer's balance sheet.

10.51 ED 42 specifically mentions consignment stock also, but states that its accounting treatment will depend very much on the provisions of the consignment arrangement. [ED 42 para 41]. ED 42 makes the distinction between arrangements where the dealer has no risks attaching to the stockholding and other arrangements. For example, a dealer may be able to return the stock to the manufacturer without incurring any penalties and, therefore, carries little or no risk in holding the stock. Clearly, it would not be necessary to include the relevant stock in the balance sheet in this situation. However, it may be necessary to reflect such stock and the related finance in the balance sheet of a dealer who is ultimately obliged to purchase consignment stock and where he has to bear any stockholding gains or losses.

10.52 The exposure draft further points out that such transactions are commonly complicated by deposit arrangements, but it maintains that the appropriate treatment under the proposals should still be determined by analysing the rights and obligations attaching to the arrangement. [ED 42 para 42].

Goods with reservation of title

10.53 It is quite common for a company that sells goods to other companies to have a reservation of title clause included in their contracts. This enables the selling company to retain ownership of those goods until the purchaser has paid for them. It is common practice for the purchaser to recognise such stocks in its balance sheet, although the supplier retains legal title to the goods. The liability to the supplier is also recognised, and a note indicating the amount of liabilities that are subject to reservation of title clauses is given. However, in practice, this note is often not given where the purchasing company is a going concern. This is an example of a transaction where it has become generally accepted practice to record the economic substance of the transaction, rather than its legal form. Where this practise is followed, consideration should be given to whether the notes to the financial statements need to comply with section 226(5).

Debtors

Disclosure

10.54 The amount of each item to be shown under the heading 'Debtors' must be split between those receivable within one year of the balance sheet date and those receivable later than that. [Note 5 on the balance sheet formats]. For this purpose, a debtor is considered to be receivable on the earliest date on which payment is due, rather than on the earliest date on which payment is expected.

10.55 The Act requires that all debtors should be disclosed as current assets, no matter when they fall due for payment. The Act draws a distinction only between fixed assets and current assets. If a company intends to use assets on a continuing basis in its activities, then they are fixed assets. If the assets do not comply with this definition, they are deemed to be current assets. [Sec 262(1)]. Consequently, long-term debts are current assets, because the company does not use them on a continuing basis in its activities. However, a situation may arise where a company has a particular long-term debt that is very material, such as a deferred consideration receivable in respect of a subsidiary it has sold. If it has such a debt, it may be misleading to include this debt under current assets, and the company may have to insert an intermediate asset heading between 'Fixed assets' and 'Current assets'. The company may need to do this in order that its financial statements give a true and fair view.

Valuation

10.56 One problem that arises with the valuation of debtors is where a company invoices customers at provisional prices that may be higher than the prices that eventually will be agreed. The customers usually pay all or some of the amount of the provisional invoices, and the company sets up a provision for possible repayment. The provision is deducted from debtors in respect of the same customer, and the net price is recorded as sales. This situation may also arise where a company gives a discount to its debtors for the early settlement of debts, although this type of discount would not normally be deducted from sales, but would be included under 'Administrative expenses' as it is more in the nature of a finance charge.

10.57 This accounting treatment is basically acceptable. The provision that prohibits set-off (paragraph 5 of Schedule 4) does not inhibit normal accounting for assets and liabilities. Debts should be shown net of provisions to reduce them to their net realisable value. This treatment is not in any way affected by the fact that set-off is prohibited.

10.58 The three following situations may arise:

- If the customer pays only part of the provisional amount, and the part he pays is equal to the subsequently agreed price, the deduction of the provision from debtors quite properly states the debtor at the net sum. This is in accordance with the Act, which requires that current assets should be stated at the lower of cost and net realisable value.

- If the customer pays the whole of the provisional amount, the fact that a provision has been deducted from the debtor will cause the account, or that part of it, to be in credit. Consequently, the company's account will show, at least in part, a liability payable to the customer. Assume that the company settles this liability by either issuing a credit note or using some similar method. The account is therefore settled by a series of invoices, credit notes and cash. If, in the normal course of the company's dealing with the customer he has one account that, in normal circumstances, will represent a net debtor at any one stage, there is no reason for the company to include the credit balance in creditors, rather than to net it against debtors.

- In some situations, refunds may be so substantial as to turn a normal debtor relationship into a normal creditor relationship (for example, the liability may be settled in due course by a cheque). In that circumstance, it would be incorrect to leave the negative amount in debtors. In this situation, it would be more appropriate to include the amount in creditors, rather than in debtors (provided that the amount concerned is material).

10.59 The company is adopting a course of trading that it is then following faithfully in its accounting. The company would not be invoking the 'true and fair' override the Act envisages. Consequently, it would not need to disclose any further information.

Factoring

10.60 Factoring is a transaction which is capable of different accounting treatments. It involves raising money from the sale of a company's debtor balances before the debt is collected. ED 42 points out that there are many forms of debt factoring, but that only some types will be affected by the proposals in the exposure draft. [ED 42 para 37]. Debt factoring arrangements can range between extremes, from the total sale of the debtor balance without further recourse to the company, to providing finance until the debt is collected with the company bearing the risks of slow paying debtors and bad debts.

10.61 In the former situation, the risks associated with the debt are transferred from the company to the factor. The risk of non-collection are reflected in the price that the factoring company will pay for the debt. Consequently, when the debts are sold, the company has no further risks associated with them and it would be consistent with the proposals in the exposure draft to exclude these amounts from the company's balance sheet.

10.62 In the latter situation, where there is effectively full recourse, the risk of non-collection remains with the company and would need to be provided for as with any other debt. Also the finance raised would need to be reflected in the balance sheet as a liability and the cost of such finance expensed as interest in the profit and loss account. It may also be necessary to explain in the notes to the financial statements whether the finance is secured on the debts.

10.63 The key question to be asked is whether there is any recourse to the company concerned for any of the debt. If there is *full* recourse, then the debt should be retained on balance sheet. By contrast, in many factoring agreements treated as off balance sheet, there is only *limited* recourse to the company selling the debt. The exposure draft proposes that where there is only limited recourse, that such debt should be excluded from the balance sheet with provision being made for expected doubtful debts. Any remaining risk should be disclosed as a contingent liability.

10.64 There is an element of inconsistency here in the exposure draft's proposals, because it suggests that for other special purpose transactions even a limited amount of recourse might mean that the item should be brought back onto the balance sheet. The proposed revision to ED 42 may remove this inconsistency by requiring that factored debts should be retained on the balance sheet to the extent that recourse arrangements apply.

Sale and repurchase of assets

10.65 The overnight sale and repurchase of assets was identified in appendix 1 to TR 603 as a 'window dressing' transaction. In such transactions, a company agrees to sell certain assets shortly before the accounting year end and arranges to repurchase them early in the following accounting year. The effect is to improve certain balance sheet ratios.

10.66 This type of transaction is referred to in ED 42 as a linked transaction, where the legal title to the property may have passed, but the benefits and risks associated with it have not. The transaction should be treated as a financing arrangement rather than a sale, leaving the asset and a corresponding liability on the balance sheet of the original owner. [ED 42 para 10].

Prepayments and accrued income

10.67 Prepayments and accrued income may be disclosed in one of two alternative positions. [Note 6 on the balance sheet formats]. They may be disclosed either as a category of debtors or as a separate category in their own right. Where prepayments and accrued income are disclosed under debtors, they must be analysed by age. If, however, they are included as a separate category, no such analysis is required.

Cash at bank and in hand

Disclosure

10.68 Traditionally, balances at bank are included in the financial statements of companies at the balance shown in the cash book, and the uncleared cheques and lodgements are reconciled to the balance shown in the bank statements. In the normal situation, this would represent the prudent view, in that the company is anticipating the bank's clearance of its cheques. Debtors and creditors are likewise reflected as though outstanding cheques or lodgements have in fact been cleared. Cheques issued are usually no longer in the control of the issuing company, and the balance at bank is deemed to be the balance shown in the cash book.

10.69 In certain situations, however, there may be an abnormal period of time between the date on which the cheques are drawn and recorded in the company's cash book and the date on which they are cleared through the bank account.

10.70 Some companies, therefore, now choose to include in their financial statements the balance shown on the bank statement. This raises the question of the appropriate form of presentation for uncleared banking items (that is, cheques issued or received before the year end but not cleared by the bank). Where this policy is adopted, cheques issued or received before the year end, but not cleared by the bank should normally be included in creditors and debtors respectively. The rationale for this treatment is that the company is not recognising the cash transaction until it is reflected by the bank. An alternative treatment that may be appropriate if the amounts are material would be to disclose such uncleared cheques as 'Cash in transit' or 'Uncleared banking items'. The effect of this treatment is that the balance at bank is shown as the balance on the bank statement, and creditors and debtors are shown after reflecting cheques issued or received respectively before the year end and the net amount being processed by the bank is shown as 'Cash in transit' or 'Uncleared banking items' (for example, see Table 36).

10.71 For the purposes of disclosure in the financial statements, either method is acceptable, provided that a company uses the same method from one year to the next. If a company changes its method, it should, in that year, adjust the comparatives and give an explanation. If the balance at bank is the balance shown on the bank statements, it is desirable that this fact is noted in the accounting policies (see Table 36).

Right of set-off

10.72 Because the Act does not allow set-off between either assets and liabilities or income and expenditure, there has been considerable debate about the situation where there is a legal right of set-off of debit and credit bank balances. The question that arises is whether it is acceptable, in such circumstances, to offset the balances for balance sheet disclosure under the Act.

10.73 The answer to this offset question will depend on the particular circumstances of each situation. However, the following comments may provide useful guidance.

10.74 Paragraph 5 of Schedule 4 provides that:

> *"Amounts in respect of items representing assets or income may not be set off against amounts in respect of items representing liabilities or expenditure (as the case may be), or vice versa."*

10.75 As explained below, it seems that this provision does not preclude recognition of the effect of a legally-enforceable right of set-off, and the resulting sum the company owes is the true amount of its 'liability' for the purposes of Schedule 4. There is no definition, for this purpose, of the word 'liability'. A reasonable definition would be that it is an amount that a company would be held liable to pay in legal proceedings, on the assumption that those proceedings are commenced on the balance sheet date.

Table 36: Illustration of disclosure where bank loans and overdrafts have been stated after adjusting for uncleared banking items.

Extract from Wm Morrison Supermarkets PLC 28th January 1989.

Accounting Policies extract

(j) Bank loans and overdrafts

Bank loans and overdrafts are stated after adjusting for uncleared banking items.

Note extract

	1989 £000's	1988 £000's
31 Creditors—amounts falling due within one year		
Commercial paper programme	8,000	
Multi option facility	30,000	20,000
Bank loans and overdrafts	9,011	(183)
Uncleared banking items (see below)	5,170	9,195
Payments received on account	283	184
Trade creditors	47,603	33,374
Fixed asset creditors	3,089	4,198
Lease finance	139	139
Corporation tax	7,683	8,519
Other taxes and social security	2,810	2,634
Accrued preference dividend	920	738
Proposed ordinary dividend	1,641	1,403
	116,349	80,201

The multi option facility was represented entirely by bills of exchange

Uncleared banking items		
Cheques issued but not received at bank	15,002	17,176
Less credits not cleared by bank	9,832	7,981
	5,170	9,195

10.76 Applying this definition, a company should, if there is no special arrangement that precludes set-off, show in its balance sheet the net amount it owes to its bank at that date in each of the following situations:

- Both the amount it has deposited with the bank and the amount it owes to the bank are due on demand.
- Both such amounts are due for payment on the same date.
- The amount that it owes to the bank has either fallen due for payment or will fall due for payment before the deposit it made with the bank matures. For set-off to be allowed, it is necessary that such a deposit will either mature or can be made to mature before the expiration of the minimum period within which the bank could obtain judgment against the company, commencing on the balance sheet date.

10.77 In all these situations, it is likely that the amount that a court would find was due from the company on the date on which it gave judgment (or would be due from the company on the due date for the payment of its debt, if that is later) would be the net amount. It should be noted that the situations described above are all circumstances where the company that makes the deposit is also the company that is the debtor to the bank. It is not in general possible in the consolidated financial statements for an amount that one group company owes to the bank to be set-off against the amount of a deposit that another member of the group has lodged.

10.78 Equally, the liability of one member of a group to a bank cannot be reduced or extinguished because the company that made the deposit has guaranteed the liability of the debtor company. However, this situation would be different if both of the following conditions applied:

- Each and every member of the group that borrowed money from, or deposited money with, the bank was jointly and severally liable to the bank for the amounts owed to the bank.
- The bank, accordingly, was liable to repay deposits to such companies jointly and severally.

In this circumstance, set-off would be acceptable.

Chapter 11

BALANCE SHEET - LIABILITIES

Chapter 11

BALANCE SHEET - LIABILITIES

Introduction

11.1 This chapter deals with the general disclosure requirements for creditors including loans and debentures, provisions for liabilities and charges including deferred taxation, and contingent liabilities. It also considers some of the problems that arise in accounting for items such as deep discounted stocks and other financial instruments.

Creditors

Disclosure

11.2 The Act specifies a considerable amount of detail that a company's financial statements must give in respect of its indebtedness.

11.3 All items included under creditors must be analysed between amounts that will fall due within one year of the balance sheet date and amounts that will fall due after more than one year. [Note 13 on the balance sheet formats].

11.4 In addition, the notes must, in respect of each item that is shown under the heading 'Creditors: amounts falling due after more than one year' in Format 1 (or 'creditors' in Format 2), state:

- The aggregate amount that is included under the item which:

  - Is payable or repayable (other than by instalments) in more than five years, beginning with the day after the end of the financial year.

  - Is payable or repayable by instalments, any of which will fall due for payment after the end of that five-year period. In this situation, the aggregate amount of the instalments that will fall due for payment after the end of the five-year period must also be disclosed.

  These amounts must be shown separately. [4 Sch 48(1)].

- The terms of payment or repayment, and the applicable rate of interest for the debts payable or repayable in more than five years by instalments or otherwise. Where the number of debts is such that, in the directors' opinion, this requirement would result in a statement of excessive length, this information need be given only in general terms. [4 Sch 48(2)(3)].

11.5 A company that is either listed on The International Stock Exchange or traded on the USM must analyse its liabilities still further. The International Stock Exchange's Continuing Obligations and the USM's General Undertaking require bank loans and overdrafts, and other borrowings, to be analysed between amounts repayable:

- Within one year, or on demand.
- Between one year and two years.
- Between two and five years.
- After five years.

[CO 21(f); GU 10(f)].

Of these, only the second and third items represent additional analysis to that required by the Act.

11.6 For the purpose of the Act, a loan falls due for repayment (or an instalment falls due for payment) on the earliest date on which the lender could require repayment (or payment) if he were to exercise all options and rights available to him. [4 Sch 85]. This rule would apply also for the purpose of The International Stock Exchange's Continuing Obligations and the USM's General Undertaking.

11.7 Where any item that is shown under the heading 'Creditors' includes liabilities for which the company has given security, these liabilities must be disclosed in aggregate. Also, the notes must give an indication of the nature of the securities given. [4 Sch 48(4)]. For this requirement to be meaningful, the financial statements should show some disaggregation of the relevant liabilities. This is because it could be misleading merely to disclose the aggregate of a basket of securities compared with the aggregate of a basket of liabilities.

11.8 This requirement to disclose securities does not apply to the situation where an unpaid supplier has supplied the company with stock that is subject to a reservation of title clause. The reason for this is that, in this situation, the person who reserves title does not pass ownership in the goods, and so his rights are not in the nature of security. The ICAEW published in July 1976 an accounting statement, 'Accounting for goods sold subject to reservation of title' (V24 - now section 2.207 of the ICAEW Members' Handbook). This statement recommends that, if the amount of creditors that are covered by reservation of title clauses is material, the accounting policies should describe how these creditors have been treated. Also, the financial statements should disclose, if practicable, the amount of creditors that are covered by reservation of title clauses. Reservation of title is dealt with further in chapter 10 paragraph 10.53.

Analysing creditors due

11.9 It should not be too difficult to analyse creditors on the basis outlined in paragraph 11.4 above. However, with a bank loan or an overdraft, it is not always obvious how that analysis should be made.

11.10 The age or the repayment term of a bank overdraft will usually be determined by reference to the terms of repayment, rather than by the facility period. If the overdraft is repayable on demand, it will clearly fall into the category of being repayable within one year. However, a company may have a medium-term bank facility for, say, five years. It uses this facility by drawing bills that the bank then discounts. When these bills become repayable, other bills are drawn, and so on. Normally, these would also fall into the category of being repayable within one year. But, if there is no way that the bank can recall the money as long as the amounts outstanding remain within the facility, the loans may be treated as medium-term borrowings (that is, loans that will fall due after more than one year). If the bank has the ability to terminate the facility and not to discount the new bills, the loans should then be shown as loans that will fall due within one year. Either way, the amounts may be shown either as 'Bank loans and overdrafts' or as 'Bills of exchange payable'.

Debentures

Definition

11.11 The term 'debenture' is defined in section 744 of the Act as including *"debenture stock, bonds and any other securities of a company, whether constituting a charge on the assets of the company or not"*. This definition is very wide. It does not distinguish clearly between a debenture loan and any other loan. Whether a particular loan is a debenture or not will depend on the documentation. A formal loan agreement, whether containing security or not, will often constitute a debenture. Although a bank loan may be a debenture loan, the balance sheet formats distinguish between bank loans and other debenture loans. Consequently, the disclosure requirements that are set out in paragraphs 11.35 to 11.39 below apply only to those other debenture loans and not to bank loans.

Accounting treatment

11.12 Debenture loans can be issued with a wide variety of terms relating to interest, conversion and redemption. Consequently, they can be particularly difficult to account for in practice. The accounting rules that apply to such instruments have been discussed in an ICAEW Technical Release (TR 677), issued in December 1987. The guidance is not mandatory and only indicates current thinking on accounting for complex capital issues. The following paragraphs summarise the main points of TR 677.

- Raising equity or loan capital.

When equity or loan capital is raised, the amount of capital shown in the balance sheet should increase by the net proceeds of the issue, after deducting proper expenditure incurred with third parties in the course of the issue. Expenses on the issue of shares or debentures, however, may be written off to the share premium account.

- Cost of capital exceeds issue proceeds.

Where the cost of repaying loan capital is greater than the proceeds of the issue, the difference should be charged to the profit and loss account in instalments. These instalments should be calculated on an appropriate basis, over the period from the date of the issue to the date of repayment.

- Profit and loss account charge.

Unless there are good economic reasons for taking another approach, the total charged to the profit and loss account in any year should be based on the effective annual cost of borrowing throughout the whole period of the loan. Where the date or the amount of the repayment is uncertain, the charge in the profit and loss account should be related to best estimates available each time financial statements are prepared.

- Constituent parts of financial instruments.

Where a transaction has a number of constituent parts the accounting treatment of each should be considered separately, but having regard to the true commercial effect of the transaction taken as a whole.

- Disclosure.

The financial statements should disclose sufficient information about a complex capital issue for a reader to appreciate its nature and impact. In particular, where instruments, or parts of instruments, representing complex capital issues are quoted on the market, disclosure of market value at each balance sheet date may be useful.

Convertible loan stock

11.13 Convertible loan stock is a form of debenture and comes with a range of varying conversion rights. These stocks offer the option to holders of either converting the loan stock at a specified event or date into shares of the company at a fixed price, or redeeming them at a certain date. The advantage to a company in issuing a convertible loan stock is that the right of conversion increases the value of the loan stock and so reduces the cost of borrowing by the company. It, therefore, enables a company to raise finance at keen rates of interest.

11.14 Convertible loan stocks may be issued with no variation of rights (fixed terms) and those with variation of rights (conversion or redeemable options). Convertible stocks with fixed terms normally carry a coupon rate of interest which is less than the prevailing market rate and are convertible into equity at the end of their lives. The economic effects of such an issue are that a company's equity shareholders allow shares to be taken up in the future at less than full value. This will, therefore, dilute their future shareholdings in exchange for a reduction of interest costs in the intervening period. Consider the following example:

Example

The particulars of a convertible loan stock with fixed terms are as follows:

☐ Ten year bond of £100,000 nominal value.
Convertible to equity after ten years.
Issue price £100,000 with 6 per cent interest.
Current market rate of interest 10 per cent.

Accounting treatment

Using the principles of TR 677 (see para 11.12), the market rate (that is, 10 per cent) for the bond should be charged to the profit and loss account. Consequently, in addition to the 6 per cent interest paid each year, an additional 4 per cent would be accrued over the life of the bond (that is, ten years). This is necessary in order to show a true cost of capital. The difference between the market rate charged in the profit and loss account and the rate of interest paid should be treated as capital and disclosed separately as part of shareholders funds.

When the shares are issued, the additional interest of 4 per cent per annum that has been built up as capital (in this example accumulating at £4,000 per annum) should be treated as proceeds of the issue of those shares and credited to the share premium account.

11.15 Convertible loan stocks that are issued with alternative redemption or conversion options normally give the stockholder the choice of either redeeming the stock for cash at a future specified date, or range of dates, or opting for conversion into equity shares. Consider the following example:

Example

The particulars of the stock are identical to those in the previous example, except that the stockholder has a redemption option, as well as an option to convert.

☐ Ten year bond of £100,000 nominal value.
Convertible to equity after ten years at £2 per share (that is, convertible into 50,000 shares).
Issue price £100,000 with 6 per cent interest.
Redeemable in five years to give a 10 per cent return.

After five years the stockholder has the opportunity to redeem the stock at an amount that will give him a 10 per cent return on his investment. If the share price after five years is below the £2 price per share, the stockholder will logically take the redemption option.

Accounting treatment

Where redemption is probable it is clear that the full redemption value of the stock needs to be accrued. Consequently, the 4 per cent additional interest should be charged in the profit and loss account and credited to a redemption reserve.

Where conversion is likely, some companies in practice do not accrue the additional interest. However, there is an argument that even where conversion is likely interest should be accrued, because this will represent part of the consideration from the issue of the shares when conversion takes place. There is also a possibility that the difference between the nominal value of the stock and the conversion value (that is in the example, £2) is the true premium on the shares that should be recognised in the accounts. As yet neither of these arguments has been tested legally.

In practice, however, in the past many companies with such debt have provided for redemption, where it is unlikely that there will be sufficient incentive at the end of the option period for shareholders to opt for conversion into equity shares. This will apply if the price per share that the options are exercisable at, is far in excess of the current listed price per share, with little hope that the listed price will reach the exercisable price in time to make conversion into equity shares favourable. A number of companies that made such stock issues before the Stock Exchange 'crash' have found themselves in this situation. Since the crash it has become more likely that the stockholders will opt for redemption, because share prices have not performed as well as expected.

In addition, an alternative treatment that has been adopted in practice to avoid the necessity to provide for redemption is to extend the option period with the hope that the share price will rise sufficiently during that period to make conversion attractive. Where provision is not made for the additional interest payable on redemption, the amount of the contingent liability that this additional interest represents must, nevertheless, be disclosed in the financial statements.

Interest rate bonds

11.16 Another type of stock that is quite common in volatile interest rate markets is the interest rate bond. These bonds have complex interest arrangements and two such bonds, the variable rate bond and the stepped bond are discussed below.

11.17 As the name suggests, the rate on a variable rate bond is fixed to a particular index or interest rate and moves in line with the movement of that index or interest rate. For example, bonds may be issued with their rate fixed to either of the following:

- Retail Prices Index (RPI).
- London Inter-bank Offered Rate (LIBOR).

For these types of bond there is no need to make any adjustment to the interest charge, because the amount of interest payable in respect of the year is a fair charge against the profits for the year. The variations in interest payments are caused by external events outside the management's control and should, consequently, be reflected in the profit and loss account during the year in which the variation occurs.

11.18 A stepped bond is one where the interest rate is not fixed, but where it increases in steps over a period of time. There may be good economic reasons why a company might find it attractive to issue a stepped bond rather than a normal floating rate bond.

Example

The particulars of a stepped bond are as follows:

- Interest increases by steps of 2 per cent every two years.
  5 per cent in the first two years.
  7 per cent in the next two years etc.
  Increasing to 23 per cent at year 20.

Accounting treatment

It is not appropriate for the earlier years to benefit from the lower rate of interest. The effective rate computed over the anticipated life of the bond should be charged in each annual profit and loss account irrespective of the amount paid in each year.

In this example, the charge to the profit and loss account should be the effective rate calculated as follows:

On a straight line basis

(5 + 7 + 9 + 11 + 13 + 15 + 17 + 19 + 21 + 23) x 2/20 = 14%

This method should generally be used unless there are good economic reasons for believing that the cost of finance to the company should be spread on an alternative basis. An example of this would be where the market rate of interest is very different from the calculated average rate.

Perpetual loan stock

11.19 Perpetual loan stock exists where no repayment date is given in the terms of the instrument. The stock's terms can differ, but a common condition is that a high rate of interest is paid for the first years of the stock, which then falls to a negligible figure. If the interest were simply debited to the profit and loss account, the company would bear an artificially high rate for the first years, and then would suffer no significant profit and loss charge for the rest of the life of the perpetuity. Such treatment might reflect the form of the loan agreement, but it would not deal with its substance. The substance of such transactions, in practice, is that the excessive interest the stock yields is intended to pay back the stock's nominal value over the initial interest period. Consider the following example:

Example

A typical stock could raise say £100,000 and might pay interest at 14 per cent for the first ten years of its life, but may pay only a nominal rate of interest, say 0.125 per cent in subsequent years. Consequently, at the end of the first ten years, the bond has little value.

Accounting treatment

The capital element of the stock is, in effect, repaid over the initial ten year period of high interest payments. Consequently, the interest payment during the initial period of 14 per cent represents a payment of interest and a repayment of capital. Therefore, the profit and loss account should only bear a normal interest charge (equivalent to market rate) and the balance of the 14 per cent interest will, therefore, represent a repayment of capital. This repayment of capital should be debited to an asset account. At the end of the ten year period, the balance sheet will show an asset of £100,000 and a corresponding liability of £100,000. The stock's market value is then likely to be immaterial. However, there is still an actual liability of £100,000 that will crystallise should the company go into liquidation. In practice, however, what is likely to happen at the end of ten years is that the company will go into the market and repurchase the stock for a nominal amount and, therefore, extinguish any liability on it.

Deep discounted stock

11.20 A deep discounted stock is a form of loan stock (that is, a debenture loan) that is issued at a discount and repayable at par. Deep discounted stocks are issued by a company for a number of reasons. For example, there may be cash flow advantages, as these instruments pay a lower rate of interest than market. In effect, payment of part of the interest is deferred until the stock is repaid. The accounting treatment of deep discounted stocks should generally follow the guidance given in TR 677 in respect of debentures (see paras 11.12). The disclosure provisions outlined in paragraphs 11.35 to 11.39 below apply equally to deep discounted stocks. The paragraphs that follow outline the accounting treatment that should be adopted by both the company issuing the loan stock and the company acquiring the loan stock.

The issuing company

11.21 To a company that issues this type of stock, the discount it gives when it issues the stock is effectively its cost of borrowing the money. The company should, therefore, treat the discount as interest payable, and write it off in stages as a charge against income in arriving at the company's profit or loss on ordinary activities before taxation. Consider the example that follows:

Example

Particulars of bond

Ten year bond of £100,000 nominal value.
Issue price £60,000 with 6 per cent interest.

	£'000
Discount	40
Additional charge each year	4
Total charge to the profit and loss account	
Interest	6
Discount	4
Total interest	10

11.22 In the above example, the discount of £40,000 is in substance a rolled-up interest charge, and should be written off to the profit and loss account, on an appropriate basis, over the period to maturity of the bond. The annual write-off (that is, the deemed interest) can be calculated either on a straight-line basis over the period of the loan (to give a constant charge each year), or on an actuarial basis (to give a constant rate on the amount outstanding at any one time). The charge should be included under the heading of 'interest payable and similar charges' in the profit and loss account. This treatment complies with paragraph 24 of Schedule 4 to the Act, which states

> *"Where the amount repayable on any debt owed by a company is greater than the value of the consideration received in the transaction giving rise to the debt, the amount of the difference may be treated as an asset"*. [4 Sch 24(1)].
>
> *"Where any such amount is so treated-*
>
> *(a) it shall be written off by reasonable amounts each year and must be completely written off before repayment of the debt"*. [4 Sch 24(2)(a)].

11.23 The question also arises as to whether the amount of £40,000 in the above example can be regarded as a discount arising on the issue of the debentures for the purposes of section 130(2) of the Act and, therefore, available for write off against the share premium account. As explained in paragraph 11.22 above, the amount of £40,000, although called a discount by the market, is in effect a rolled-up interest charge and, as such, is probably not a discount for the purposes of the Act. It should not, therefore, be written off to the share premium account.

11.24 If the terms of the issue are that the stock is repayable at par (either at the end of a set period or, in specific circumstances, on an earlier date), it would be appropriate to show in the balance sheet the liability at par and the unamortised discount as an asset. In accordance with paragraph 5 of Schedule 4 to the Act, a company cannot show the asset as a deduction from the liability. Where a company shows the unamortised discount as an asset, paragraph 24 of Schedule 4 requires the company either to show that asset separately on the face of the balance sheet or to disclose it in the notes to the financial statements. Continuing with the example above:

As £4,000 of the £40,000 discount has been charged to the profit and loss account, the balance sheet at the end of the year should disclose the outstanding balances related to deep discounted stocks in the following way:

Balance sheet disclosure

	£'000
Asset	
Unamortised discount (£40,000 - £4,000)	36
Liability	
Ten-year stock	100

11.25 If the terms of the issue specify that, for example, the stock can be repaid at a date earlier than the redemption date, but at less than par, it may be appropriate to show the liability in the balance sheet at that lower amount. In this situation, the liability may increase progressively over the years as the date of redemption at par draws closer.

11.26 In addition to making the disclosures noted in paragraphs 11.37 and 11.38 below, the company should disclose also the accounting policy that it has adopted in respect of the treatment of deep discounted stock in both the profit and loss account and the balance sheet.

11.27 Generally (subject to various conditions), a company that issues this type of stock will obtain tax relief in each accounting period for the discount that accrues over that period. The special tax rules that apply to deep discounted stock are set out in section 57 and Schedule 4 of the Income and Corporation Taxes Act 1988.

11.28 The issuing company will also have to consider the need to provide or disclose any deferred tax that may arise from any timing difference between the amount of the discount charged in the company's profit and loss account and the amount of discount allowed in its tax computation.

The investing company

11.29 To the company that acquires the loan stock, the discount is effectively the interest it will receive on the loan. Although it does not receive the 'interest' until the stock is redeemed, the company should treat it as interest receivable on an annual basis. The company should credit it in arriving at its profit or loss on ordinary activities before taxation. It may, however, consider the amount not realised, and therefore not distributable, until it has actually been received.

11.30 The deep discounted stock should be included in the balance sheet as an investment loan at cost plus the amount of interest that has been credited to the profit and loss account.

11.31 However, where a company holds the deep discounted stock as a fixed asset, but it does not intend to hold the stock to redemption, and where the market value at the balance sheet date is lower than cost plus accrued interest, the company will need to make a provision if it expects the diminution in value to be permanent. [4 Sch 19(2)]. Where the company holds the deep discounted stock as a current asset, and the market value is lower than cost plus accrued interest, the company will need to make a provision to ensure that the deep discounted stock is shown at the lower of cost and net realisable value. [4 Sch 23].

11.32 It is important that the notes to the financial statements clearly state the company's policy in respect of deep discounted stock.

11.33 As mentioned in paragraph 11.27 above, the special tax rules that apply to deep discounted stock are set out in section 57 and Schedule 4 of the Income and Corporation Taxes Act 1988. The investing company will be taxed only when it either redeems or disposes of the stock. The company will be taxed as if it had received investment income equal to the accrued discount over the period for which it has held the security. There will be a timing difference between the treatment of the discount in the company's profit and loss account and the treatment in its tax computation. Consequently, the company may have to account for deferred taxation on this timing difference.

Other discounted stock

11.34 As an alternative to issuing deep discounted stock, companies may issue other forms of stock at a discount. With other discounted stocks, the rate of interest can be very low (the most extreme of which is the 'zero coupon bond') or it can be deferred for the first few years and become payable only over the last few years to redemption, or alternatively, the interest can be stepped, as explained in paragraph 11.18. Another possibility is that stock may be redeemable at a premium. The discount on such stock will be lower than the discount on deep discounted stock, but the principles outlined in paragraphs 11.20 to 11.33 above still apply.

Disclosure

11.35 A company that has debenture loans must split them between convertible and non-convertible loans. [Note 7 on the balance sheet formats].

11.36 Where a loan is classified as a debenture loan, section 130(2) of the Act permits debenture issue expenses and any discount arising on the issue to be written off against the share premium account (as to what constitutes a discount for this purpose, see para 11.23). In addition, any premium payable on redemption can be similarly written off against the share premium account (subject to the rules considered in paras 11.37 to 11.39).

11.37 If a company has issued any debentures during the financial year, the notes to the financial statements must disclose:

- The reason for making the issue.
- The classes of debentures issued.
- The amount issued, and the consideration the company received in respect of each class of debentures issued.

[4 Sch 41(1)].

11.38 Moreover, the notes must also disclose:

- Particulars of any redeemed debentures that the company has power to reissue.
- The nominal amount and the book value of any debentures that are held by either a nominee of, or a trustee for, the company.

[4 Sch 41(2)(3)].

11.39 In addition, the general disclosure requirements for creditors set out in paragraphs 11.2 to 11.10 above apply to all debentures. An illustration of the disclosure requirements for debentures is given in Table 37.

Trade creditors

11.40 'Trade creditors' could comprise either all items included in the creditors ledger or simply those items that relate to the cost of sales. Most companies classify all creditors ledger items as trade creditors, although such treatment could distort the cost of sales/trade creditors ratio. A company should ensure that, whatever treatment it adopts, it is consistent from year to year.

Table 37: Disclosure of debentures.

Extract from Next PLC Accounts 31st January 1989.

Note extract

17 CREDITORS DUE AFTER ONE YEAR

	GROUP		COMPANY	
	31.1.89	31.1.88	*31.1.89*	*31.1.88*
	£m	£m	*£m*	*£m*
7.00% Debenture stock 1986/91	0.5	0.5	*0.5*	*0.5*
7.75% Debenture stock 1987/92	0.5	0.5	*0.5*	*0.5*
6.75% Convertible bonds due 2002	47.9	47.9	*47.9*	*47.9*
5.75% Convertible bonds due 2003	100.0	100.0	*100.0*	*100.0*
Bank loan	1.7	3.8	–	–
Obligations under finance leases	6.8	3.8	–	–
	157.4	156.5	*148.9*	*148.9*
UK corporation tax	7.1	10.4	–	–
Other creditors and accruals	9.0	–	*8.1*	–
	173.5	166.9	*157.0*	*148.9*

	GROUP				COMPANY	
	Debentures	Convertible Bonds	Bank Loan	Finance Leases	*Debentures*	*Convertible Bonds*
	£m	£m	£m	£m	*£m*	*£m*
Due within 1 to 2 years	–	–	1.7	2.9	–	–
Due within 2 to 5 years	1.0	–	–	3.9	*1.0*	–
Due after 5 years	–	147.9	–	–	–	*147.9*
	1.0	147.9	1.7	6.8	*1.0*	*147.9*

The debentures are secured by a fixed charge on certain named properties. They are repayable at par in the last year quoted. Redemption can be made between the earlier and the later dates at the option of the Company or at any time by purchase in the open market.

The convertible bonds are unsecured. Further details of these bonds are:

	6.75% Convertible Bonds due 2002	5.75% Convertible Bonds due 2003
Bondholders may convert into ordinary shares at a price per share of	286p	430p
Bondholders may redeem on	15.1.92	14.10.92
at an interest yield to redemption of	11.55%	10.46%
The company may redeem subject to a minimum share price of	372p	559p

Other creditors including taxation and social security

11.41 The line 'other creditors including taxation and social security' must be analysed between other creditors, and taxation and social security. [Note 9 on the balance sheet formats]. These headings should include the following items:

- Other creditors
  - ☐ Dividends (see para 11.44).
  - ☐ Any items that cannot appropriately be analysed elsewhere.
- Taxation and social security
  - ☐ Corporation tax.
  - ☐ VAT.
  - ☐ ACT payable on dividends (see paras 11.46 to 11.50).
  - ☐ Social security and other amounts (such as PAYE owed in respect of wages and salaries).
  - ☐ Excise duty.

11.42 'Other creditors including taxation and social security' contrasts with the line under provisions for 'taxation, including deferred taxation'. The latter item will comprise all deferred tax liabilities (see further paras 11.59 to 11.63).

11.43 'Other creditors including taxation and social security', like other categories of creditors, has to be split between amounts that will fall due within one year and amounts that will fall due after more than one year. From 1990 all companies will be paying corporation tax within nine months, and so no corporation tax balances payable in over one year should arise.

Dividends and related ACT

11.44 Dividends are not specifically referred to in either of the balance sheet formats. Schedule 4 requires the disclosure in the profit and loss account of the aggregate amount that is recommended for distribution by way of dividend. [4 Sch 3(7)(b)]. Paragraph 51(3) of Schedule 4 requires the proposed dividends to be disclosed also in the balance sheet or in the related notes. A proposed dividend is not a liability in law until it has been declared, and so it would not be appropriate to include it within any of the items listed in the formats. In practice it is normally included as a separate item under 'creditors'.

11.45 In addition, the notes to the financial statements must state:

- The amount of any arrears in the payment of fixed cumulative dividends on the company's shares.

- The period for which these dividends are in arrear. Where there is more than one class in arrear, this period must be given in respect of each class.

[4 Sch 49].

11.46 Furthermore, SSAP 8 requires that proposed dividends should be included in creditors without the addition of the related ACT. The ACT payable on proposed dividends (whether recoverable or irrecoverable) should be included under 'taxation and social security'.

11.47 Where there is unrelieved ACT on proposed dividends that is deemed to be recoverable, it should be treated as an asset. Unless the unrelieved ACT can be set off against the deferred tax account, it should be included in 'prepayments and accrued income'.

11.48 This treatment complies with SSAP 8. However, SSAP 15 states that debit balances arising in respect of ACT on dividends payable or proposed at the balance sheet date should be carried forward only to the extent that it is foreseen that sufficient corporation tax will be assessed on the profits or income of the next accounting period, against which the ACT is available for offset. [SSAP 15 para 31]. Debit balances arising in respect of ACT other than on dividends *payable or proposed* at the balance sheet date should be written off unless their recovery is assured beyond reasonable doubt. Such recovery will normally only be assured where the debit balances are recoverable (without replacement by equivalent debit balances) out of the corporation tax that is expected to arise on the profits or income of the next accounting period. [SSAP 15 para 32].

11.49 The provisions of the standard, detailed above, that apply to the carry forward of ACT are based on the same logic as the provisions that apply to the need to provide for deferred taxation. That is, ACT should be carried forward as an asset only to the extent that it is expected to be recoverable, in the same way that deferred taxation should be provided as a liability only to the extent that it is likely to become payable.

11.50 The following example emphasises the importance of the SSAP 8 requirement that in order to carry forward ACT, it should not be replaced by an equivalent asset.

Example

A company has paid a large dividend and cannot relieve ACT against corporation tax in the current accounting period. It, therefore, wishes to carry forward the related ACT to the next accounting period as an asset. It is likely to recover the ACT by reducing the expected corporation tax liability on trading profits of the next period. However, the ACT asset will be replaced by another as the present level of dividend payout is anticipated to continue.

As the ACT will be replaced next year by an equivalent amount, it should not be carried forward, but should be written off to the profit and loss account and included in the current year tax charge. However, if the ACT relates to a dividend proposed at the balance sheet date, it would be possible to carry it forward as an asset to be set off against corporation tax profits of the next accounting period.

Accruals and deferred income

11.51 In the same way that 'prepayments and accrued income' may be shown in either of two positions in the formats, the item 'accruals and deferred income' may be disclosed either as a category of creditors or as a separate category in its own right. [Note 10 on the balance sheet formats]. Where 'accruals and deferred income' is disclosed under creditors, it must be analysed between those amounts that will fall due within one year and those amounts that will fall due after more than one year. [Note 13 on the balance sheet formats]. No such analysis is required if 'accruals and deferred income' is included as a separate category.

11.52 'Accruals and deferred income' could include government grants of a capital or revenue nature that are accounted for as deferred credits.

Provisions for liabilities and charges

11.53 There is sometimes confusion whether items should be disclosed under provisions, or creditors or accruals. In this connection, the treatment of provisions for taxation has already been considered under 'Other creditors including taxation and social security' (see para 11.41). For some provisions (for example, those for bad and doubtful debts), it is correct to net them against the assets to which they relate. This treatment is correct because the assets have to be stated, in accordance with the statutory accounting rules, at their net realisable value. [4 Sch 19(2), 23(1)].

11.54 'Provisions for liabilities or charges' is defined in the Act as:

> *"Any amount retained as reasonably necessary for the purpose of providing for any liability or loss which is either likely to be incurred, or certain to be incurred but uncertain as to amount or as to the date on which it will arise."* [4 Sch 89].

11.55 Creditors, by contrast, normally comprise those amounts that are actually owing to third parties, and not amounts retained that are reasonably necessary for providing for any liability or loss that is likely to be incurred. Also, accruals generally include those amounts representing costs and charges (possibly apportioned at the balance sheet date) that are not yet actually owing to third parties.

11.56 Where there has been any transfer to or from any provision for liabilities or charges other than a transfer from that provision for the purpose for which that provision was set up, the Act requires certain information to be disclosed in respect of each provision for liabilities or charges that is shown either on the face of the balance sheet or in the notes. This information is as follows:

- The aggregate amount of the provision at both the beginning and the end of the financial year.
- Any amounts transferred either to or from the provision during the financial year.
- The source and the application of any amounts so transferred.

[4 Sch 46(1)(2)].

An example of such a disclosure is given in Table 38.

Table 38: Disclosure of provisions for liabilities and charges.

Extract from Vickers P.L.C. Annual Report and Accounts 31st December 1988.

Note extract

Notes

16 PROVISIONS FOR LIABILITIES AND CHARGES Extract

	Warranty £m	Dilapidations £m	Reorganisation £m	Other liabilities £m	Deferred taxation £m	Total £m
Group						
At 1 January 1988	14·1	0·6	4·7	9·0	0·6	29·0
Exchange adjustment	0·1	–	–	(0·1)	(0·1)	(0·1)
Provided	10·7	0·1	2·5	2·4	0·2	15·9
Used	(7·6)	–	(1·8)	(2·2)	–	(11·6)
Released	(1·8)	–	(0·1)	(1·8)	–	(3·7)
Disposals of businesses	(1·2)	(0·3)	(1·8)	(0·9)	(0·5)	(4·7)
Release to revaluation reserve	–	–	–	–	(0·1)	(0·1)
At 31 December 1988	14·3	0·4	3·5	6·4	0·1	24·7
Company						
At 1 January 1988	1·7	0·3	2·6	3·1	–	7·7
Provided	0·9	–	1·2	–	–	2·1
Used	(0·4)	–	(0·4)	(2·2)	–	(3·0)
Released	(0·5)	–	–	(0·5)	–	(1·0)
Disposals of businesses	(0·1)	–	(1·4)	–	–	(1·5)
At 31 December 1988	1·6	0·3	2·0	0·4	–	4·3

11.57 Where an amount is shown under 'Other provisions', and it includes any individual provision that is itself material, the information detailed above must be given in respect of each such provision. [4 Sch 46(3)]. Possible examples are provisions for future rationalisation, for redundancy, for dilapidations, or for warranty claims.

11.58 If the provision for liabilities and charges includes any provision for taxation (other than deferred taxation, which is discussed below), it must be disclosed separately. [4 Sch 47].

Deferred taxation

Actual liability

11.59 The provision for deferred taxation should be included under the balance sheet heading 'Taxation, including deferred taxation'. In addition, SSAP 15 requires any provision for deferred taxation to be shown separately. The standard says that tax deferred or accelerated by the effect of timing differences should be accounted for to the extent that a liability or an asset will probably crystallise. [SSAP 15 para 25]. The deferred tax balance, its major components, and transfers to and from the deferred tax account should be disclosed in the notes to the balance sheet (for example, see Table 39). [SSAP 15 paras 37, 38].

Table 39: Disclosure of deferred taxation.

Extract from Thorn EMI plc Annual Report 31st March 1989.

17. Deferred Taxation

	Group		*Company*	
	1989	1988	1989	1988
	£m	£m	£m	£m
Excess of accumulated taxation allowances over depreciation provided against tangible fixed assets	46.8	39.9	36.7	39.0
Other timing differences	30.8	22.8	30.6	19.4
Advance corporation tax	(42.8)	(36.5)	(42.8)	(36.5)
	34.8	26.2	24.5	21.9
Movements during the year:				
At 31 March 1988	26.2		21.9	
Currency retranslation	(1.2)		–	
Arising during the year	18.7		5.2	
Other movements	(8.9)		(2.6)	
At 31 March 1989	34.8		24.5	
Deferred taxation which has not been provided comprises the following:				
Excess of accumulated taxation allowances over corresponding depreciation provided against tangible fixed assets	4.3		–	
Other timing differences	5.6		2.7	
	9.9		2.7	

No provision has been made for further taxes which could arise if subsidiary or related companies are disposed of or if overseas companies were to remit dividends to the UK in excess of those anticipated in these accounts: it is considered impracticable to estimate the amount of such taxes.

The Company has undertaken to discharge the liability to corporation tax of the majority of its wholly-owned UK subsidiaries; their deferred tax liabilities are, therefore, dealt with in the accounts of the Company.

11.60 The provision for deferred tax should be calculated by the liability method, and it should be reduced by any deferred tax debit balance that arises from separate categories of timing differences. It should also be reduced by any ACT that is available for offset against the deferred tax provision. [SSAP 15 paras 24, 29]. However, it is incorrect to offset ACT against a deferred tax balance to a greater extent than it is actually recoverable against that deferred tax liability when it becomes payable. For example, if a company has a deferred tax balance of £20,000 that has been calculated at a corporation tax rate of 35 per cent, then the maximum amount of ACT that can currently be offset against that deferred tax balance is £14,286 (namely, £20,000 x 25%/35%). The 25 per cent used in the calculation is the current basic rate of income tax.

Contingent liability

11.61 Where a company does not provide for some or all of any deferred tax (because the directors do not consider that a liability will crystallise), paragraph 40 of SSAP 15 requires that the total amount of any unprovided deferred tax should be disclosed in a note to the financial statements, analysed into its major components. In addition, where the potential amount of deferred tax on an asset that has been revalued is not shown (because the revaluation does not constitute a timing difference), this fact (but not necessarily the amount) should be stated in the financial statements (see further chapter 5 paras 5.44 to 5.48).

11.62 When the value of an asset is shown in a note to the financial statements (because it differs materially from its book amount), the note should show the tax effects, if any, that would arise if the asset were realised at that value at the balance sheet date. [SSAP 15 para 42]. In this situation, the 'tax effect' means that the potential amount of tax should be disclosed.

11.63 The deferred tax disclosure requirements that relate to the profit and loss account are considered in more detail in chapter 14. The Act requires that the deferred tax provision in the balance sheet should be disclosed separately from any other taxation provision. [4 Sch 47].

Contingent liabilities

Guarantees and other financial commitments

11.64 The notes to the financial statements must give details of:

- Any charge on the company's assets that has been given in order to secure the liabilities of any other person.

- The amounts so secured (where practicable).

[4 Sch 50(1)].

An example is given in Table 40.

Table 40: Disclosure of contingent liabilities.

Extract from Granada Group PLC Annual Report 30th September 1989.

Note extract

		Group 1989 £m	Parent 1989 £m	Group 1988 £m	Parent 1988 £m
Note 23	*Contingent liabilities*				
a)	Under guarantees of bank overdrafts, mortgages and loans to overseas subsidiaries	–	2.7	–	2.6
	Under a group registration, joint and several liability for VAT	–	13.0	–	8.7
	Bank performance guarantee	–	–	27.1	27.1

b) There are also contingent liabilities in respect of the due performance of leases entered into by subsidiaries and certain forward foreign exchange contracts entered into by the parent company and subsidiary companies.

c) The parent company and certain of the Group's travel subsidiaries have entered into a travel bond with the Tour Operators Study Group. At 30 September 1989 this contingent liability amounted to £13.8 million (1988 – £13.3 million).

d) In 1987 proceedings were started in England by Amev International NV against Granada in respect of the sale in 1985 of the L'Etoile group of insurance companies, in which Amev claims damages against Granada. The claim is being vigorously defended and lawyers acting on Granada's behalf in the proceedings are highly confident of a successful outcome for Granada.

11.65 This requirement is particularly relevant for groups of companies. Therefore, where (for example) a company has guaranteed a subsidiary's overdraft to the extent of £10m by way of a charge on the company's assets, the actual overdraft of the subsidiary at the year end should be disclosed (up to a maximum, in this situation, of £10m).

11.66 In respect of any other contingent liability that has not been provided for in the financial statements, the notes must disclose:

- The amount, or the estimated amount, of that liability.
- Its legal nature.
- Whether any valuable security has been provided by the company in connection with that liability. Where this is so, details of the security provided must be given.

[4 Sch 50(2)].

11.67 Consequently, if a company has given an unlimited guarantee for an overdraft of its subsidiary, and there is no charge on its assets, the fact that it is unlimited and that no valuable security has been provided and the actual amount of the overdraft, need to be disclosed.

11.68 In addition to the Act's requirements, SSAP 18 requires a company to accrue all its material contingent losses in its financial statements. This requirement applies only if it is probable that a future event will confirm a loss that can be estimated with reasonable accuracy at the date on which the board of directors approves the financial statements. [SSAP 18 para 15]. For example, the company may have entered into an uncovered forward foreign currency contract during the year. If this contract matures before the date when the board approves the financial statements, and it results in a loss, the company should provide for this loss in its financial statements. In other situations, material contingent losses must merely be disclosed in the notes to the financial statements (unless the possibility of loss is remote, in which case no disclosure is required). [SSAP 18 para 16].

11.69 To comply with SSAP 18, the notes to the financial statements must state:

- The nature of the contingency.
- The uncertainties that are expected to affect the ultimate outcome.
- A prudent estimate of the financial effect, or a statement that such an estimate is not practicable. For this purpose, the amount to be disclosed is the potential financial effect (before taking account of taxation) after deducting any amounts accrued and the amounts of any contingencies that have only a remote possibility of loss.

[SSAP 18 paras 18, 19, 20].

11.70 The Act requires the notes to the financial statements also to disclose, where practicable, either the aggregate amount or the estimated amount of capital expenditure that:

- Has been contracted for, but not provided for, at the balance sheet date.
- Has been authorised by the directors, but not contracted for, at that date.

[4 Sch 50(3)].

An example of such a disclosure is given in Table 41 overleaf.

11.71 Any other financial commitments that have not been provided for must be disclosed in the notes to the financial statements to the extent that they are relevant to a proper understanding of the company's state of affairs. [4 Sch 50(5)]. An example of such a commitment might be where a company has agreed in principle to enter into a major joint venture with another company. In this situation, the company should disclose the amount of money that it has agreed in principle to contribute to the venture. It is not envisaged that this provision of the Act will normally require the disclosure of financial commitments that relate to a company's day-to-day trading operations (such as, commitments under supply contracts).

Table 41: Disclosure of capital commitments.

Extract from Allied-Lyons PLC Report and Accounts 4th March 1989.

14 CAPITAL COMMITMENTS	UNITED KINGDOM	OTHER COUNTRIES	1989 TOTAL	1988 TOTAL
	£m	£m	£m	£m
Expenditure authorised at 5th March 1988	367	88	455	326
Authorised during the year less withdrawals	297	53	350	416
	664	141	805	742
Expenditure during the year	(251)	(52)	(303)	(287)
Expenditure authorised at 4th March 1989	413	89	502	455
Contracted for but not provided in the accounts	47	14	61	51
Authorised by the directors but not contracted for	366	75	441	404
	413	89	502	455
Beer and retailing division	275	26	301	277
Wines and spirits division	56	37	93	74
Food division	78	26	104	102
Central companies	4	—	4	2
	413	89	502	455

11.72 Where any of the commitments referred to in paragraphs 11.64, 11.66, 11.70 and 11.71 above relate to group companies, these must be shown separately. In particular, they must be analysed between those relating respectively to:

- Any parent company or any fellow subsidiary of the company.
- Any subsidiary of the company.

[4 Sch 59(A)].

Pension commitments

11.73 The notes to the financial statements must show separately pension commitments that have respectively been provided for and not provided for. The notes must give a separate indication of any such commitments that relate to a company's former directors. [4 Sch 50(4)].

11.74 The Act does not specify the basis a company should use to measure pension costs or pension commitments that it has not provided for. In the absence of a standard accounting practice on pension costs and the very limited disclosure provisions required by the Act, UK companies typically provided little information about pension costs or the extent of potential future liabilities. The concerns about the quality of disclosure were partly addressed by the ASC when it issued ED 32 'Disclosure of pension information in company accounts', in May 1983.

11.75 However, following the exposure period, the ASC decided to deal with both measurement and disclosure aspects of accounting for pension costs in the same Accounting Standard. SSAP 24 'Accounting for pension costs' was issued in May 1988. SSAP 24 prescribes extensive disclosure including accounting policy, actuarial valuation methods and assumptions, actuarial valuations and explanation of variations in cost. The provisions of SSAP 24 are considered in chapter 14.

Chapter 12

BALANCE SHEET - SHARE CAPITAL AND RESERVES

Chapter 12

BALANCE SHEET - SHARE CAPITAL AND RESERVES

Introduction

12.1 This chapter deals with the general disclosure requirements for share capital and reserves. It also considers the situation where a company can have shares in more than one currency.

Classification of shares

12.2 Shares can be divided into numerous different types, including ordinary shares, equity shares, preference shares, non-voting shares, and redeemable shares. The classification depends on the rights that the shares are given in the company's memorandum and articles of association.

- *Ordinary shares* normally confer on their holders the residue of the rights of the company which have not been conferred on other classes. Therefore, subject to the rights of other classes (which are normally, though not always limited), the rights of the ordinary shares are generally unlimited. Ordinary shares normally carry the voting powers of the company.

- *Equity shares* comprise the issued share capital of a company excluding any part which, neither as respects dividends nor as respects capital, carries any right to participate beyond a specified amount in a distribution. [Sec 744].

- *Preference share* is the term given to any share that has some preferential rights in relation to other classes of shares, particularly in relation to ordinary shares. These preferential rights are of great variety, but refer normally to the right to a fixed *dividend*, although they could also refer to the right on winding up to receive a proportionate part of the *capital* or otherwise to participate in the distribution of the company's assets. Preference shares generally carry limited voting rights, although they can be constructed to carry the same or greater voting rights than the ordinary shares or be given no voting rights at all. Also they can be constructed to be either equity or non-equity. In order to make preference shares equity, it is necessary to give them, in addition to their fixed dividend rights, some right to participate beyond a specified amount in the capital of the company on liquidation.

- *Non-voting shares* are normally ordinary shares that do not carry any voting rights.

- *Redeemable shares* may be redeemed either at a set date or event, or at the option of the company or the shareholder, and may be issued if authorised by the company's articles. [Sec 159]. At present the requirements of the Companies Act 1985 is that the terms amd manner of redemption of redeemable shares must be provided by the articles. However, section 133 of the Companies Act 1989 introduced a new section 159A in the Companies Act 1985 which will, when brought into force by a SI, provide the more detailed requirements as follows. The date on or by which, or dates between which the shares are to be redeemed must be specified in the company's articles. Where the articles give the directors power to fix the date of redemption, such date or dates must be fixed before the shares are issued. Furthermore, the amount payable on redemption must also be specified in the articles or determined in accordance with those articles. In the latter situation, the articles must not contain any provisions for the redemption amount to be determined by reference to any person's discretion or opinion. Any other circumstances in which the shares are to be or may be redeemed and any other terms and conditions of redemption must also be specified in the articles. [Sec 159A].

12.3 For tax purposes, *ordinary share capital* has a special meaning that is defined in the Income and Corporation Taxes Act 1988 as *"in relation to a company,... all the issued share capital (by whatever name called) of the company, other than capital the holders of which have a right to a dividend at a fixed rate, but have no other right to share in the profits of the company."* [Sec 832 ICTA 1988]. Consequently, preference shares although they may be equity cannot be ordinary share capital for tax purposes where they carry the right to a fixed dividend.

Disclosure of share capital

12.4 The amount of allotted share capital and the amount of called-up capital that has actually been paid up must be shown separately. These amounts must be shown either under the heading 'called-up share capital' in the balance sheet, or in a note to the financial statements. [Note 12 on the balance sheet formats]. 'Called-up share capital' means:

- That proportion of a company's share capital as equals the aggregate amount of the calls made on its shares (whether or not those calls have been paid).

- Any share capital that has been paid up without being called.

- Any share capital that is to be paid on a specified future date under the Articles of Association, or under the terms of allotment, or any other arrangements for paying for those shares.

[Sec 737(1)].

12.5 The following example illustrates the disclosure requirements for called-up share capital:

Example

On 30th November 1990, a company allots 100,000 ordinary shares of £1 each. By 31st December 1990, the company has made calls amounting to 75p per share. At 31st December 1990, the holders of 10,000 shares have not paid the last call of 25p per share. In the financial statements at 31st December 1990, the company would have to make the following disclosures:

Allotted share capital	£100,000
Called-up share capital	£75,000
Paid-up share capital	£72,500
Called-up share capital not paid	£2,500

12.6 Called-up share capital is part of the double entry, and it will appear under capital and reserves (KI in Format 1 or AI in Format 2). Similarly, called-up share capital not paid forms part of the double entry, and it will appear in the balance sheet format either as a separate item (A in Format 1 or 2) or under debtors (C II 5 in Format 1 or 2). Neither the allotted share capital nor the paid-up capital forms part of the double entry. However, they must still be disclosed either on the face of the balance sheet or in a note to the financial statements.

12.7 Where shares are partly paid, no rules exist for a private company to determine the minimum amount of the consideration, by reference to nominal value and share premium. For example, a private company can issue (say) a 20p share at £1 and have only 30p paid up. A public company must, however, have paid up at least a quarter of the nominal value plus the whole of any premium. [Sec 101]. Consequently, in the example the minimum amount paid up would represent 85p (that is 20p x ¼ + premium of 80p).

12.8 The notes to the financial statements must also show the amount of a company's authorised share capital. In addition, where shares of more than one class have been allotted, the notes must show the number and the aggregate nominal value of the shares of each class that have been so allotted. [4 Sch 38(1)].

12.9 In practice, companies will generally be able to refer to share capital that is 'allotted, called up and fully paid', because these items will often be the same amount.

12.10 Where any part of the allotted share capital consists of redeemable shares, the notes to the financial statements must show:

- The earliest and the latest dates on which the company may redeem those shares.
- The fact whether or not the company is obliged to redeem those shares, or either it or the holder merely has an option to do so.
- The amount of any premium payable on redemption, or the fact that no such premium is payable.

[4 Sch 38(2)].

12.11 Where a company has allotted any shares during the financial year, the notes to the financial statements must state:

- The reason for making the allotment.
- The classes of shares allotted.
- The number of shares allotted, their aggregate nominal value, and the consideration received in respect of each class of shares allotted.

[4 Sch 39].

12.12 In addition to the particulars required by the above paragraph, the International Stock Exchange's Continuing Obligations require a company to disclose:

- The names of the allottees, if less than six in number, and in the case of six or more allottees, a brief generic description of them.
- The market price of the securities concerned on a named date, being the date on which the terms of the issue were fixed.

[CO 21(q)].

12.13 Furthermore, information has to be given about any 'contingent rights to the allotment of shares' that may exist. These rights could be options to subscribe for shares, or rights on the conversion of loan stock or any other rights where a person may require the allotment of shares (whether, in the latter case, the rights arise on conversion of any other type of security, or otherwise). The information to be given is:

- The number, the description and the amount of the shares in respect of which the right is exercisable.

- The period during which the right is exercisable.

- The price to be paid for the shares allotted.

[4 Sch 40].

12.14 Consequently, the financial statements have to include details of the rights of conversion of convertible loan stock. The disclosure requirements for share capital are illustrated in Table 42 overleaf.

Serious loss of capital

12.15 If the value of a public company's net assets falls to half or less of its called-up share capital, the directors have a duty to convene an extraordinary general meeting, in order to determine what action, if any, to take to remedy the situation. Proper notice must be given, and the directors must convene the meeting not later than 28 days from the earliest date the difficulties of the company were known to a director. The meeting itself must be held within 56 days of that earliest date. If the company fails to convene the meeting, each of the directors of the company permitting the failure is liable to a fine. [Sec 142].

Multi-currency share capital

12.16 In recent years a number of companies have issued share capital denominated in foreign currencies. One of those companies was the Scandinavian Bank Group Plc. In 1986 it petitioned the court for confirmation of a special resolution to cancel part of its existing sterling share capital in order to increase its share capital to £30m, $30m, SFr 30m and DM 30m (see *Re Scandinavian Bank Group plc,* [1988] Ch 87).

12.17 The court confirmed that a company can have shares in more than one currency. Any particular share, however, must be denominated in one particular currency, but different shares can be denominated in different currencies. This does not conflict with the requirement in the Act because section 5(a) states that *"the memorandum must...state the amount of the share capital...and the division of the share capital into shares of a fixed amount"*. By fixed amount the Act does not mean a fixed value in sterling terms.

Table 42: Disclosure of called up share capital.

Extract from the Burton Group plc Annual Report and Accounts 2nd September 1989.

Note extract

18 Called up share capital		*1989 £'m*	*1988 £'m*
Ordinary shares of 50p each Allotted and fully paid		278.3	276.8
Authorised		400.0	350.0

	Number	Nominal Value £	Consideration £
Shares allotted during the year:			
On exercise of options between 33½p and 273½p	946,779	473,390	1,168,688
On conversion of 5¾% Guaranteed Loan	6,573	3,286	2,103
On conversion of 8% Convertible Unsecured Loan Stock	53,478	26,739	149,740
Employee profit sharing scheme	1,978,609	989,305	3,700,000
	2,985,439	1,492,720	5,020,531

i) During the year options were granted to purchase 11,290,459 shares at 171p per share including options granted to the following Directors: Mr L. Cooklin 294,806 shares, Mr D. N. Legg 912,288 shares and Mr. P. G. Plant 294,806 shares. These options may be exercised between 1991 and 1998. Options granted in previous years, and still outstanding, were in the price range 104 to 324p per share and may be exercised between 1989 and 1998. The aggregate number of shares covered by options capable of being exercised is 26,545,072, the total consideration being £57,954,643.

ii) During the year options were granted to participants in the savings related share option scheme to purchase 633,456 shares at 158p. The aggregate number of shares covered by such options cabable of being exercised is 2,163,093, the total consideration being £3,824,898.

iii) Holders of the 8% Convertible Unsecured Loan Stock 1996/2001 have the right, at any time during January in any year up to and including 1996, to give notice of conversion into shares of The Burton Group plc at a price of £2.80 nominal stock for each share.

iv) The holders of FF 665,000 5¾% Convertible Guaranteed Loan 1992 of Burton BV have the right at any time until 1st July 1992 to give notice of conversion into shares of The Burton Group plc at a price of 32p per share. For the purpose of calculating the number of shares to be issued on conversion the exchange rate of £1 = FF 11.88225 will be used throughout the life of the loan.

v) As part of the terms of the issue of the US $80 million 9¾% Guaranteed Notes 1991, warrants are outstanding carrying rights to subscribe for 26,752,000 shares in The Burton Group plc at a price of 272p per share, exercisable at any time during the period ending 27th February 1991 or at such later date as the Company may, at its discretion, determine.

vi) The holders of £110 million 4¾% Convertible Bonds 2001 have the right at any time until 17th August 2001 to give notice of conversion into Ordinary Shares of The Burton Group plc at a price of 315p per share. The market price of the Ordinary Shares when the Bonds were issued was 259p per share.

12.18 However, sections 117 and 118 of the Act require a public company to have an authorised minimum allotted share capital of £50,000. This requirement stems from article 6 of the 2nd Directive. The court held (obiter) that this 'authorised minimum' must be in pounds sterling.

12.19 Consequently, a private company can issue any amount of shares in a foreign currency. However, a public limited company can only express its shares in more than one currency if at least £50,000 of its share capital is in sterling.

Disclosure of reserves

12.20 Certain information must be included in the notes to the financial statements in respect of each reserve that is shown either on the face of the balance sheet or in the notes to the financial statements (for example, see Table 43). This information is as follows:

- The aggregate amount of the reserve both at the beginning and the end of the financial year.
- Any amounts transferred to or from the reserve during the financial year.
- The source and application of any amounts transferred.

[4 Sch 46(1)(2)].

Table 43: Disclosure of reserves.

Extract from London & Edinburgh Trust PLC Annual Report 31st December 1988.

Note extract

23. RESERVES (extract)	Share premium account £m	Capital redemption reserve £m	Other reserves (unrealised) £m	Revaluation reserve (unrealised) £m	Capital reserve (realised) £m	Profit and loss account £m
Company:						
At 1st January, 1988	1.3	–	(0.1)	3.7	2.4	39.7
Premium on shares issued	7.2	–	–	–	–	–
Purchase of own shares	–	0.3	–	–	–	(3.6)
Share issue costs	(0.9)	–	–	–	–	–
Surplus on revaluation of investment properties	–	–	–	1.1	–	–
Retained profit for the year	–	–	–	–	–	12.6
At 31st December, 1988	7.6	0.3	(0.1)	4.8	2.4	48.7

Revaluation reserve

12.21 Where a company has valued an item in accordance with one of the alternative accounting rules, the Act states that the revaluation surplus or deficit *must* be credited or debited to a revaluation reserve. [4 Sch 34(1)].

12.22 Furthermore, a company can transfer an amount from the revaluation reserve to the profit and loss account, if the amount was previously charged to that account or represents realised profit, or on capitalisation. These transfers can only be made where the amounts are no longer necessary for the purpose of the valuation method that the company has adopted. [4 Sch 34(3)]. The aim of the requirements concerning the use of the revaluation reserve is that the balance sheet should represent unrealised and uncapitalised profits relating to fixed assets carried at a valuation which are still being used by the company.

12.23 The revaluation reserve must be disclosed on the face of the balance sheet. However, it may be described by a different name, although it is generally preferable for companies to keep to the terminology in the Act. [4 Sch 34(2)].

12.24 Where an amount has been credited or debited to the revaluation reserve, its treatment for taxation purposes must be disclosed in a note to the financial statements. [4 Sch 34(4)].

12.25 The revaluation reserve and some of the problems surrounding it are considered in the discussion on the alternative accounting rules in chapter 5, paragraphs 5.7 to 5.48, and in 'Manual of Accounting - volume II' chapter 8.

Other reserves

12.26 The main heading 'other reserves' includes four sub-headings: 'capital redemption reserve', 'reserve for own shares', 'reserves provided for by the articles of association' and 'other reserves'. The last heading will include all reserves, both realised and unrealised, that do not fit elsewhere in the formats. If they are material, they should be specifically described.

Profit and loss account

12.27 Many companies do not use the wording 'profit and loss account'. They use instead terms such as 'revenue reserves'. The possibility of changing the wording of headings and sub-headings from those prescribed in the formats is discussed in chapter 6, paragraph 6.7. The Act does not expressly allow different wording to be used unless the special nature of the company's business requires otherwise (for example, investment trusts publish a 'revenue account' instead of a 'profit and loss account', because of the special nature of their business).

Realised and distributable reserves

12.28 The Act contains no specific requirement for reserves to be disclosed as either realised or unrealised, or as distributable or non-distributable. However, where a company has significant non-distributable reserves, it may need, in order to give a true and fair view, to disclose the amount of the reserves that it may not legally distribute under the Act.

12.29 Realised and distributable reserves are dealt with in detail in chapter 19.

Chapter 13

THE PROFIT AND LOSS ACCOUNT - INCOME

Chapter 13

THE PROFIT AND LOSS ACCOUNT - INCOME

Introduction

13.1 The profit and loss account is one of the statements that a company must include in its financial statements. The Act requires the profit and loss account to comply with one of the four alternative formats of profit and loss account: Formats 1 and 3 are vertical presentations and Formats 2 and 4 show charges separately from income. These formats are set out in more detail in chapter 6. The format a company chooses can be significant because, depending on the format, some of the information the company discloses in its profit and loss account will be different. Some of the items that are discussed below may relate only to one pair of formats. In addition, the Act lays down certain rules that relate to the disclosure of information in the notes to the profit and loss account, and also certain rules regarding the measurement of items that are included in the profit and loss account and these requirements are also considered below.

13.2 This chapter deals with revenue recognition and also considers the disclosure requirements for segmental information and the calculation and disclosure of earnings per share.

Revenue recognition

13.3 Revenue recognition is mainly concerned with the timing of recognition of revenue in the profit and loss account of an enterprise. At present, there is no Accounting Standard on the recognition of revenue earned from operations. The only direct reference to revenue recognition is contained in SSAP 2's definition of prudence and in paragraph 12(a) of Schedule 4 to the Act. In accordance with SSAP 2, revenue and profits should not be anticipated but should be recognised by inclusion in the profit and loss account only when realised in the form either of cash or other assets whose ultimate cash realisation can be assessed with reasonable certainty. The concept of prudence is further embodied in paragraph 12(a) of Schedule 4 to the Act which states that *"only profits realised at the balance sheet date shall be included in the profit and loss account"*. For the purpose of defining realised profits, reference should be made to *"principles generally accepted, at the time when the accounts are prepared, with respect to the determination for accounting purposes of realised profits or losses"*. [Sec 262(3)]. The term 'principles generally accepted' for the determination of realised profits is not defined in the Act, although guidance on its meaning is contained in TR 481, which is reproduced as appendix VII (see further chapter 19 para 19.24).

13.4 Other than the above two specific references to revenue recognition and realised profits, there is no guidance in the UK on generally accepted recognition criteria. IAS 18, 'Revenue Recognition', however, does provide some guidance.

13.5 IAS 18 is concerned with the recognition of revenue arising in the course of the ordinary activities of an enterprise from:

- The sale of goods.
- The rendering of services.
- The use by others of resources of the enterprise that yield interest, royalties, and dividends.

[IAS 18 para 1]

Sale of goods

13.6 IAS 18 states that revenue from a transaction involving the sale of goods should be recognised when the seller has transferred to the buyer the significant risks and rewards of ownership of the asset being sold. The standard specifies the following three considerations as being relevant in deciding whether significant risks and rewards of ownership have been transferred to the buyer:

- Whether any significant acts of performance remain to be completed.
- Whether the seller retains any continuing managerial involvement in, or effective control of, the goods transferred to a degree usually associated with ownership.
- Whether the payment of the debt relating to the goods transferred is dependent on the derivation of revenue by the buyer from the goods.

[IAS 18 para 23(a)].

13.7 IAS 18 recognises that there may be uncertainties associated with measuring the amount of revenue arising from a transaction and states that revenue should not be recognised until such uncertainties are removed. For transactions involving the sale of goods the standard provides that no significant uncertainty should exist in respect of:

- The consideration that will be derived from the sale of the goods. This means that where there is uncertainty regarding the amount of consideration that can be determined within reasonable limits, the recognition of revenue should be postponed.

- The associated cost incurred, or to be incurred in producing or purchasing the goods. In most situations, such costs can reasonably be determined and provided for in the financial statements. Where, however, costs still to be incurred cannot reasonably be determined, revenue recognition should be postponed.

- The extent to which the goods may be returned. Revenue recognition should also be postponed where an enterprise is exposed to significant or unpredictable amounts of goods being returned. However, where the volume of goods being returned is predictable, provision can be made and revenue can be recognised.

[IAS 18 para 23(b)].

Services

13.8 Where a transaction involves rendering services, IAS 18 states that the performance of those services should be the deciding factor for the recognition of revenue. IAS 18 specifies that performance of a service should be measured either by the percentage of completion method or under the completed contract method, whichever relates the revenue to the work accomplished. [IAS 18 para 24].

13.9 The percentage of completion method is relevant where performance consists of executing more than one act. In this type of circumstance, revenue is recognised proportionately by reference to the performance of each act. [IAS 18 para 10(a)]. This is the basis used for recognising revenue on long-term contracts under SSAP 9 (see further chapter 10 paras 10.24 to 10.28).

13.10 The completed contract method is used where performance consists of executing a single act. Alternatively, services are performed in more than a single act, and the services yet to be performed are so significant in relation to the transaction taken as a whole that performance cannot be deemed to have been completed until the execution of those acts. [IAS 18 para 10(b)].

13.11 Whichever method is adopted, IAS 18 states that performance should only be regarded as being achieved when no significant uncertainty exists regarding both the following:

- The consideration that will be derived from rendering the service.

■ The associated costs incurred (or to be incurred) in rendering the services.

[IAS 18 para 24].

<u>The use by others of an enterprise's resources</u>

13.12 IAS 18 states that revenues arising from others using an enterprise's resources, which yield interest, royalties and dividends should only be recognised when no significant uncertainty concerning measurability or collectability exists. These revenues are recognised on the following bases:

■ Interest.

On a time proportion basis taking account of the principal outstanding and the rate applicable.

■ Royalties.

On an accrual basis in accordance with the terms of the relevant agreement.

■ Dividends from investments not accounted for under the equity method of accounting.

When the shareholder's right to receive payment is established.

[IAS 18 para 25].

<u>Revenue recognition examples</u>

13.13 The appendix to IAS 18 contains a number of examples that illustrate and clarify the guidance provided by the standard. The appendix is illustrative only and does not form part of the Accounting Standard but is of considerable interest as it illustrates clearly the principles set out in the statement. The examples included in the appendix are reproduced below.

A. Sale of Goods

☐ 'Bill and hold' sales, i.e. delivery is delayed at buyer's request but buyer takes title and accepts billing.

Revenue should be recognised notwithstanding that physical delivery has not been completed so long as there is every expectation that delivery will be made. However, the item must be on hand, identified and ready for delivery to the buyer at the time the sale is recognised rather than there being simply an intention to acquire or manufacture the goods in time for delivery.

☐ Shipped subject to conditions

- Installation and inspection i.e. goods are sold subject to installation, inspection, etc.

  Revenue should normally not be recognised until the customer accepts delivery and installation and inspection are complete. In some cases, however, the installation process may be so simple in nature that it may be appropriate to recognise the sale notwithstanding that installation is not yet completed (e.g. installation of a factory tested television receiver normally only requires unpacking and connection of power and antennae); in other cases, the inspection may only be performed for purposes of final determination of contract prices (e.g. shipments of iron ore, sugar, soya beans etc.) and it may be appropriate to recognise the estimated amount of the revenue at the date of shipment or other suitable time.

- On approval

  Revenue should not be recognised until the shipment has been formally accepted by the buyer or the time period for rejection has elapsed.

- Guaranteed sales i.e. shipment is made giving the buyer an unlimited right of return.

  Recognition of revenue in such circumstances will depend on the substance of the agreement. In the case of normal retail sales (e.g. chain store offering 'money back if not completely satisfied') it may be appropriate to recognise the sale but to make a suitable provision for returns based on previous experience. In other cases, the substance of the agreement may amount to a sale on consignment, in which case it should be treated as indicated below.

- Consignment sales i.e. a shipment is made whereby the recipient undertakes to sell the goods on behalf of the shipper.

  Revenue should not be recognised until the goods are sold to a third party.

- Cash on delivery sales

  Revenue should not be recognised until cash is received by the seller or his agent.

☐ Lay away sales, i.e. those sales where the purchaser makes a series of instalment payments to the seller, and the seller delivers the goods only when the final payment is received.

Revenue from such sales should not be recognised until goods are delivered. However, when experience indicates that most such sales are consummated, revenue may be recognised when a significant deposit is received.

☐ Special orders and shipments, i.e. where payment (or partial payment) is received for goods not presently held in stock e.g. the stock is still to be manufactured or is delivered directly to the customer from a third party.

Revenue from such sales should not be recognised until goods are delivered to the buyer.

- ☐ Sale/repurchase agreements (other than swap transactions) i.e. where seller concurrently agrees to repurchase the same goods at a later date.

  For such transactions that are in substance a financing arrangement, the resulting cash inflow is not revenue as defined and should not be recognised as revenue.

- ☐ Sales to intermediate parties, i.e. where goods are sold to distributors, dealers or others for resale.

  Revenue from such sales can generally be recognised if significant risks of ownership have passed. However, in some situations the buyer may in substance be an agent and in such cases the sale should be treated as a consignment sale.

- ☐ Publication and record subscriptions.

  Revenue received or billed should be deferred and recognised either on a straight line basis over time or, where the items shipped vary in value from period to period, revenue should be based on the sales value of the item shipped in relation to the total sales value of all items covered by the subscription.

- ☐ Instalment sales.

  When the consideration is receivable in instalments, revenue attributable to the sales price exclusive of interest should be recognised at the date of sale. The interest element should be recognised as revenue, proportionately to the unpaid balance due to the seller. If collection is not reasonably assured, revenue should be recognised as cash instalments are received.

- ☐ Real estate sales.

  When property is sold, revenue is usually recognised when the buyer takes possession. However, the buyer's down payment or other commitment may be insufficient to provide assurance of the eventual completion of payment. Although the security of the vendor is usually assured by the ability to foreclose the property or to apply other remedies in the event of default by the buyer, it would be inappropriate to recognise revenue in full at the time of the sale. In these circumstances the transaction should be accounted for as cash instalments are received.

- ☐ Trade discounts and volume rebates.

  Trade discounts and volume rebates received are not encompassed within the definition of revenue, since they represent a reduction of cost. Trade discounts and volume rebates given should be deducted in determining revenue.

B. Rendering of Services

- ☐ Installation fees.

  In cases where installation fees are other than incidental to the sale of a product, they should be recognised as revenue only when the equipment is installed and accepted by the customer.

- ☐ Servicing fees included in the price of the product.

  Where the selling price of a product includes an identifiable amount for subsequent servicing for, say, a warranty period, it will normally be appropriate to defer the relevant portion of the selling price and to recognise it as revenue over the appropriate period.

☐ Advertising and insurance agency commissions.

Revenue should be recognised when the service is completed. For advertising agencies, media commissions will normally be recognised when the related advertisement or commercial appears before the public, as opposed to production commission, which will be recognised when the project is completed. Insurance agency commissions should be recognised on the effective commencement or renewal dates of the related policies. In some circumstances the commission may be adjusted depending upon the claims experience in respect of the policies written by the agent. In cases where it is expected that the policy will need servicing during its life, the commission or a relevant part thereof may be recognised over that period.

☐ Financial service commissions.

A financial service may be rendered as a single act or may be provided over a period of time. Similarly charges for such services may be made as a single amount or in stages over the period of the service or the life of the transaction to which it relates. Such charges may be settled in full when made or added to a loan or other account and settled in stages. The recognition of such revenue should therefore have regard to

- Whether the service has been provided 'once and for all' or is on a 'continuing' basis.
- The incidence of the costs relating to the service.
- When the payment for the service will be received.

In general, commissions charged for arranging or granting loan or other facilities should be recognised when a binding obligation has been entered into. Commitment, facility or loan management fees which relate to continuing obligations or services should normally be recognised over the life of the loan or facility having regard to the amount of the obligation outstanding, the nature of the services provided and the timing of the costs relating thereto.

☐ Admission fees.

Revenue from artistic performances, banquets and other special events should be recognised when the event takes place. When a subscription to a number of events is sold, the fee should be allocated to each event on a systematic and rational basis.

☐ Tuition fees.

Revenue should be recognised over the period of instruction.

☐ Initiation, entrance and membership fees.

Revenue recognition from these sources will depend on the nature of the services being provided. If the fee permits only membership, and all other services or products are paid for separately, or if there is a separate annual subscription, the fee should be recognised when received. If the fee entitles the member to services or publications to be provided during the year, it should be recognised on a systematic and rational basis having regard to the timing and nature of all services provided.

☐ Franchise fees.

Generally, franchise fees may cover the supply of any combination of initial and subsequent services, equipment and other supplies, know-how etc. Frequently, the determination of such matters, and the allocation of the franchise fee thereto, is difficult and requires considerable judgement. As a general guidance, however, the following methods of fee recognition may be appropriate:

- The proportion of the initial franchise fee that relates to tangible assets (if any) should be recognised when the items are delivered.
- The portion that applies to future services (if any) should be deferred and recognised as revenue when the services are rendered.
- If continuing fees receivable under the agreement are inadequate to cover the cost and a reasonable profit level for the continuing services, recognition of some or all of the initial franchise fee should be delayed.

13.14 There are, in addition, many other issues that arise in specific industries, that present particular problems of revenue recognition. The examples that follow highlight two such issues and the related accounting practices that have achieved general acceptance.

Sale of Property

13.15 The date on which the sale of a property is effected is crucial to deciding in which period the revenue from the sale should be recognised. Where an unconditional and irrevocable contract has been entered into for the sale of a property, the profit arising on the sale can be recognised at the time when the contract is exchanged (for example, see Table 44). This is because the equitable and the beneficial interests already vest in the purchaser, who has a legal commitment for the outstanding purchase consideration. The situation is, therefore, no different from goods sold on credit.

Table 44: Example of an accounting policy where profit is recognised when unconditional contracts have been exchanged.

Extract from Associated British Port Holdings Plc Annual Report and Accounts 31st December 1988.

Accounting policies extract

RECOGNITION OF PROFIT ON PROPERTY DEVELOPMENTS

Profits or losses arising on the sale of sites or completed developments are recognised when contracts for sale have been exchanged and have become unconditional. Profit on pre-sold property developments is recognised on a proportion of completion basis; full provision is made for any foreseeable losses.

13.16 However, many companies do not take credit for such sales until legal completion has taken place, as is illustrated in Table 45. This policy is, therefore, more conservative than the one outlined above. The application of either of these methods will usually depend on the circumstances of the sale. In practice, both of these policies are used to recognise the sale proceeds arising from either completed developments or completed houses.

Table 45: Example of an accounting policy where profit is recognised on legal completion of sale.

Extract from Countryside Properties PLC Report and Accounts 30th September 1989.

Accounting policies extract

Profit

Profit is taken on legal completion of sale of each property, except in the case of long-term contracts where attributable profit is taken having regard to the proportion of the contract completed at the balance sheet date.

13.17 Where, however, a development is substantially complete and a binding and unconditional contract of sale has been entered into prior to the year end, it is acceptable to recognise the profit at the date of the relevant contract provided legal completion takes place shortly thereafter (for example, see Table 46). However, this will only be possible where legal completion has taken place before the financial statements are signed by the directors. It is important to note that where significant uncertainties exist on exchange of contracts, revenue recognition should always be delayed until legal completion. This will, therefore, reduce the risk of recognising profits that may not have been earned.

Table 46: Example of an accounting policy where revenue is recognised on exchange of contracts and legal completion takes place shortly thereafter .

Extract from Crest Nicholson PLC Annual Report and Accounts 31st October 1988.

1. Accounting policies

iv Income recognition (extract)

Profit is recognised on commercial property developments or units of development which, at the year end, are substantially complete and subject to binding and unconditional contracts of sale and where legal completion has occurred shortly thereafter. Where the sale price is conditional upon letting, profit is restricted by reference to the space unlet at the year end.

Profit in respect of construction and leisure related activities, is recognised when the contract is complete.

In the case of contracts that are regarded as long term, profit is recognised during construction provided a binding contract for sale exists and the outcome can be foreseen with reasonable certainty.

Sale of software and related services

13.18 In the software industry, the timing of revenue recognition poses a number of problems. Software houses normally earn their revenue *inter alia* from three principal sources:

- Sale of off-the-shelf or ready made software where the licensing arrangement gives the customer the right to use the software for a specified period.

- Sale of customised software developed for specific application by the customer.

- Sale of software support services related to either own software or customised software.

13.19 The sale of ready made software can be recognised when the licensing agreement is signed or when a copy of the master is delivered to the customer. Normally, however, recognition of revenue takes place when the licensing agreement is signed. This is because the software house will have incurred all the costs associated with the development, production and marketing of the product and, therefore, revenue recognition need not be postponed as long as there is every expectation that delivery will be made. On the other hand, it could be argued that the sale of software under a licensing agreement is no different from the sale of any other goods. If this argument is followed, revenue should be recognised on delivery, as it is at this stage that significant risks and rewards of ownership are transferred to the customer. Whichever method is used, full provision should be made for any further costs that are likely to be incurred in connection with the sale.

13.20 The creation of software specifically developed for use by a customer normally requires executing a number of separate acts over a period of time. The product has to be designed and developed according to the customer's specification, adequately tested and finally installed on the customer's hardware. Where a contractual obligation is performed by an indeterminate number of acts over a period of time, revenue should normally be recognised in accordance with the principles outlined in SSAP 9. Consequently, the software house should recognise profits in a manner appropriate to the stage of completion of the contract, provided that the outcome can be assessed with reasonable certainty (see further chapter 10 paras 10.24 to 10.28].

13.21 The procedure to recognise profit is to include an appropriate proportion of total contract value as turnover in the profit and loss account as the contract activity progresses. The costs incurred in reaching that stage of completion should be matched with this turnover, resulting in the reporting of results that can be attributed to the proportion of work completed. Where, however, the outcome cannot be assessed with reasonable certainty before the conclusion of the contract, or where the contract is of a relatively short duration, the completed contract method should be applied and, accordingly, revenue should be recognised when final completion takes place (for example, see Table 47).

Table 47: Example of an accounting policy illustrating the recognition of revenue on software contracts.

Extract from Alphameric plc Report & Accounts 31st March 1989.

Accounting policies extract

Turnover

Turnover represents the amount receivable for goods sold and services provided to external customers during the year, excluding value added tax.

Revenue on systems contracts, involving the supply of hardware and software, is recognised in proportion to the completion of the contract, once the contract outcome can be forseen with reasonable certainty.

13.22 Where the software house provides an after sales support service (for example, product enhancement) through a separate maintenance contract, the question arises as to whether the maintenance income is capable of being regarded as earned 'up front' or whether the income should be deferred and recognised on a straight line basis over the period of the contract.

13.23 It can be argued that if the cost of maintenance is negligible, the maintenance contract effectively provides the company with income with no material costs of earning that income. In this situation, it might be acceptable to recognise the income when it becomes due, that is, usually all at the start of the maintenance period. However, it may be necessary to accrue any related maintenance costs. Alternatively, if the cost of maintenance is material, the likelihood is that such costs will be incurred over the period of the agreement. In such a situation, it will be prudent to spread the income over the period to which it relates, that is, the period of the maintenance agreement. Both these approaches are illustrated in Table 48 overleaf.

13.24 The above extracts provide some evidence of current practice in the UK concerning accounting for computer software. Although stated policies are sometimes brief and uninformative, it is clear that there is considerable diversity of practice in the UK.

Table 48: Examples of accounting policies illustrating the different treatment of software support costs.

Extract from Kewill Systems PLC Report and Financial Statements 31st March 1989.

Accounting policies extract

g) Turnover
Turnover is calculated net of value added tax and represents the total amount receivable by the group in respect of goods sold and services supplied during the year. Non refundable income from annual licences and software support is taken into account at the date of invoicing while income from charges for hardware support is apportioned over the period to which it relates.

Extract from Electronic Data Processing PLC Annual Report and Accounts 30th September 1989.

Accounting policies extract

Deferred income
Deferred income represents that portion of maintenance contracts taken out by customers but relating to a future period.

Turnover

13.25 The Act clearly defines the amount a company must include in its profit and loss account under the heading of 'Turnover'. It comprises the amounts a company derives from providing goods and services that fall within its ordinary activities, after deducting trade discounts, VAT and any other taxes based on the amounts it so derives. [Sec 262(1)]. This definition accords with the requirement in SSAP 5 that turnover should exclude VAT on taxable outputs. However, SSAP 5 goes further: it says that, if a company intends to show also its gross turnover, it should show the VAT relevant to that turnover as a deduction in arriving at the turnover exclusive of VAT.

13.26 The Act's definition does give rise to some unexpected results, particularly in specialised businesses. Three examples are given below:

Example 1

Where a company sells certain items either FOB (free on board) or CIF (cost, insurance, freight), it may wish to reduce the CIF items to FOB by deducting these expenses from turnover. However, because there is usually a profit element in the CIF charges and because there is no right of set-off of expenditure against income under the Act, the amount for turnover should include the full CIF selling price.

Example 2

Where a company acts as an agent or a dealer (for example, a commodity broker) it should not include the gross value of its contracts in turnover. It should, however, include the commission or margin that it makes on each deal in turnover.

Example 3

In the past advertising agencies grossed up their fee income by a factor of 6⅔ to obtain an effective turnover figure. This practice assumed that an average commission of 15 per cent was earned on all advertising business. After the introduction of the 1981 Act, advertising agencies started to base their turnover on commission earned, gross fees earned being disclosed by way of note.

Segmental Reporting

Introduction

13.27 There have been requirements for segmental reporting for many years in the UK. Segmental reporting involves the reporting of disaggregated financial information such as turnover, profits and capital employed. The requirement to disclose segmental information is set out in the Act. For listed companies and companies traded on the USM, there are additional requirements in The International Stock Exchange's Continuing Obligations and the USM's General Undertaking respectively.

13.28 At present, there is no Accounting Standard on segmental reporting. However, the ASC, as long ago as 1984, had on its work programme a project on segmental reporting. Work commenced in 1986 and this culminated in the publication of ED 45, 'Segmental reporting', in November 1988. Its proposals are more limited than those of the consultative paper which preceded it and are very similar to the requirements of IAS 14, 'Reporting financial information by segment'.

The Companies Act requirements

13.29 The Act requires the notes to the profit and loss account to include certain information analysed by both class of business and geographical market.

13.30 Where a company has carried on two or more classes of business during the financial year in question, and these, in the directors' opinion, differ substantially from each other, the notes must give:

- A description of each class.
- The amount of turnover that is attributable to each class.

- The amount of profit or loss before taxation that is, in the directors' opinion, attributable to each class.

[4 Sch 55(1)].

13.31 'Turnover' has the same meaning for this purpose as that given in paragraph 13.25 above.

13.32 The Act states that, in determining either the turnover or the profit or loss attributable to each class, the directors must have regard to the way in which the company's activities are organised. [4 Sch 55(3)]. Where classes of business do not, in the directors' opinion, differ substantially, they are to be treated as one class. Similarly, where the directors believe that markets do not differ substantially, those markets are to be treated as one market. [4 Sch 55(4)].

13.33 Where a company has supplied goods or services within two or more markets during the financial year in question, the turnover (but not the profit or loss before taxation) must also be disaggregated between markets. This is necessary, however, only if the directors believe that the markets differ substantially. For this purpose, 'market' means a market delimited by geographical bounds. [4 Sch 55(2)]. It is important that companies maintain adequate records to enable them to meet these requirements.

13.34 The disaggregated information need not be disclosed where the directors consider that its disclosure would be seriously prejudicial to the company's interests. In these circumstances, however, the fact that any such information has been omitted must be stated, although the reasons need not be given. [4 Sch 55(5)].

13.35 As an extreme example, if a company or a group supplies only customers in two countries that are politically opposed to each other, a published geographical split of turnover could well be prejudicial to the interests of the company or the group. Provided that the notes to the profit and loss account disclose the fact that this analysis has not been given, no further information is required.

<u>The International Stock Exchange requirements</u>

13.36 With listed companies and companies that are traded on the USM, The International Stock Exchange's Continuing Obligations and the USM's General Undertaking respectively require a geographical analysis of both the net turnover and the contribution to trading results of those trading operations the company or the group carries on outside the UK and the Republic of Ireland. [CO 21(c); GU 10(c)]. Although the Act specifically refers to turnover attributable to each different geographical market that the company has supplied, and not the country of supply, the Continuing Obligations state that:

> *"A broad geographical analysis of net turnover by way of figures or percentages, given by market (not necessarily given country by country), will be acceptable."* [CO 21(c)].

13.37 Transactions within a group should be excluded. Where fifty per cent of total overseas operations relates to one continent a further analysis, by country within that continent, should be given. The analysis of the contribution to trading results is required only where the contribution from a specific area is 'abnormal' in nature. Abnormal is defined as substantially out of line with the normal ratio of profit to turnover. For example, if a forty per cent profit is earned by a group in relation to turnover in one continent, compared with ten percent on turnover elsewhere, this fact should be made apparent.

13.38 There is no exemption from disclosure on the grounds that such disclosure would be seriously prejudicial. For this reason a listed company may still be required by the International Stock Exchange to give such disclosure. Where a listed company does not disclose the information on these grounds, it could be required to explain the circumstances to the International Stock Exchange direct. Similar restrictions are imposed on companies trading on the USM.

13.39 The requirements of the Act and the Continuing Obligations are less extensive than those of IAS 14. IAS 14 requires not only segmental information on sales and profit, but also information on capital employed by business segment and geographical region.

ED 45 requirements

13.40 ED 45 was published in November 1988. The proposals in ED 45 go beyond what is required by the Act and the International Stock Exchange by introducing several new disclosure requirements (for example, see Table 49 overleaf). Insofar as it repeats the requirements of the Act, ED 45 will apply to all companies. However, the additional requirements proposed in ED 45 will only have to be given by:

- All public companies or holding companies that have a public company as a subsidiary.
- All other companies that meet at least two of the following three criteria for defining a medium-sized company under section 247 of the Act multiplied by ten:
  - Turnover in excess of £80m.
  - Balance sheet total in excess of £39m.
  - Number of employees in excess of 2,500.

Table 49: Disclosure of segmental information.

Extracts from The BOC Group plc Report & Accounts 30th September 1989.

Notes Extract

1. Segmental information

a) Turnover by business – 1989

	Gases and related products £ million	Health care £ million	Special products and services £ million	Discontinued £ million	Total by origin £ million	Total by destination £ million
Europe[1]	351.8	166.6	185.0	1.4	704.8	673.9
Africa	137.7	38.1	21.6	–	197.4	203.7
Americas[2]	556.7	403.1	77.3	–	1 037.1	996.7
Asia/Pacific	696.2	60.4	78.9	46.7	882.2	947.2
Turnover including related companies	1 742.4	668.2	362.8	48.1	2 821.5	2 821.5
Less turnover of related companies						
BOC Group share	215.4	13.8	15.8	0.7	245.7	245.7
External share	236.4	13.8	15.8	0.7	266.7	266.7
Turnover	1 290.6	640.6	331.2	46.7	2 309.1	2 309.1
Turnover by business – 1988						
Europe[1]	314.5	143.0	167.9	0.9	626.3	612.5
Africa	118.3	28.0	19.4	3.5	169.2	173.3
Americas[2]	450.3	369.3	63.4	118.7	1 001.7	963.9
Asia/Pacific	610.4	44.9	59.4	50.3	765.0	812.5
Turnover, including related companies	1 493.5	585.2	310.1	173.4	2 562.2	2 562.2
Less turnover of related companies						
BOC Group share	186.8	11.0	11.5	2.2	211.5	211.5
External share	206.4	11.1	11.5	2.2	231.2	231.2
Turnover	1 100.3	563.1	287.1	169.0	2 119.5	2 119.5

[1]Turnover and profit before tax relating to the UK amounted to £557.1 million (1988: £499.4 million) and £136.1 million (1988: £112.3 million) respectively.
[2]The US turnover and profit before tax were £957.3 million (1988: £923.8 million) and £62.9 million (1988: £78.5 million) respectively.

b) Profit, capital employed and capital expenditure

	Operating profit		Capital employed		Capital expenditure	
(i) Business analysis	1989 £ million	1988 £ million	1989 £ million	1988 £ million	1989 £ million	1988 £ million
Gases & related products	254.2	219.4	1 429.3	1 172.9	265.0	201.7
Health care	106.5	90.8	384.3	343.7	50.4	47.6
Special products & services	45.2	43.1	202.2	186.5	23.0	35.1
Corporate	(14.9)	(17.4)	35.8	39.9	3.6	4.1
Continuing business	391.0	335.9	2 051.6	1 743.0	342.0	288.5
Discontinued business	4.6	17.5	(27.7)	15.5	2.8	5.7
	395.6	353.4	2 023.9	1 758.5	344.8	294.2

Table 49 continued

(ii) Regional analysis	Profit before tax 1989 £ million	1988 £ million	Capital employed 1989 £ million	1988 £ million	Capital expenditure 1989 £ million	1988 £ million
Europe	143.8	121.7	704.0	599.5	135.5	109.0
Africa	38.7	34.3	103.1	70.0	34.4	22.6
Americas	74.1	89.4	842.0	735.9	130.4	124.6
Asia/Pacific	73.9	56.1	374.8	353.1	44.5	38.0
	330.5	301.5	2 023.9	1 758.5	344.8	294.2

13.41 The exposure draft proposes that information contained in the financial statements to be segmented in two principal ways by:

- Class of business.
- Geographical segments.

13.42 A 'class of business' is defined as a distinguishable component of an enterprise that provides a separate product or service or a separate group of related products or services.

13.43 A 'geographical segment' is a geographical area comprising an individual country or group of countries in which a company operates.

13.44 The Act recognises both of the above two bases in paragraph 55 of Schedule 4 referring to geographical areas as 'markets'. The explanatory note to the exposure draft states that the determination of a company's classes of business must depend on the judgement of the directors. In this regard, the exposure draft supports the provisions of the Act, but provides further guidance on factors that should influence the determination of segments.

13.45 The exposure draft proposes that a company should define each of the reported classes of business and indicate the composition of each of the reported geographical segments. [ED 45 para 35]. For each reported class of business and geographical segment, it is proposed that a company will be required to disclose:

- Turnover.
- Segment results.
- Capital employed.

[ED 45 paras 37, 38].

13.46 Disclosure of turnover has to be given on both a source and destination basis, unless there is no material difference between the two. [ED 45 para 40]. The source basis means the geographical area from which goods and services are supplied. In contrast, the destination basis means the geographical area to which goods and services are supplied. The analysis may then have to distinguish between external turnover and 'inter-segment turnover'. Inter-segment turnover means sales made to or from a geographical or business segment If, for example, sales from a geographical segment (source basis) are £100m and this figure includes £10m of sales from that segment to group companies in other geographical segments, £10m would be disclosed as inter-segment sales. If, on the other hand, sales to a geographical segment (destination basis) were £80m and this included sales to group companies of £5m, then £5m would be disclosed as inter-segment sales. The inter-segment turnover may then be required to be analysed segmentally and shown separately and the basis of inter-segment pricing is likely also to require disclosure. [ED 45 paras 37(a), 38(a)].

13.47 Segment results may be required to be disclosed before accounting for taxation, minority interests and extraordinary items and before or after accounting for interest as appropriate. [ED 45 paras 37(b), 38(b)].

13.48 Whether or not it is appropriate to disclose segment results before or after interest will depend on the nature of the business. The exposure draft concludes that where the nature of the business is such that interest income and expense are fundamental to the nature of the business the segment result should be shown after interest. [ED 45 para 20]. In the majority of companies, however, segments are financed by a mixture of equity and debt. In such situations, interest earned or incurred will be the result of the company's overall policy rather than reflecting the result of individual segments of the company's business. For this reason, the segment result should be disclosed before interest with interest shown separately. Disclosure of the segment result before interest also conflicts with the Act, which requires disclosure of the profit or loss before taxation. However, for the reasons explained in the exposure draft, the ASC is of the view that disclosure of the results before interest may in the majority of situations be more meaningful. It may be permissible for companies to depart from the Act's requirements in order to give a true and fair view, however, in that event, the particulars of the departure, the reasons for it and its effect would have to be given in the notes to the financial statements.

13.49 The exposure draft also deals with the treatment of common costs. These are defined as costs that relate to more than one segment. It is proposed that such costs should be treated in the way that the directors consider appropriate. If, for instance, common costs are apportioned among segments for the purposes of internal reporting then it may be appropriate to apportion them in a like manner for external reporting purposes. Some companies may, however, not wish to apportion common costs, as any such apportionment may, in many situations, be on an arbitrary basis. In such circumstances, the common costs should be deducted from the total of the segment results. [ED 45 para 22].

13.50 The capital employed in each business segment and geographical segment should be disclosed. The exposure draft permits flexibility in the definition of capital employed, but suggests that in most situations it is likely that non-interest bearing operating assets less non-interest bearing operating liabilities would be the most appropriate measure. However, where interest income or expense has been included in arriving at segment results, then the related interest bearing assets and liabilities should be included in determining capital employed. In addition, the method of calculating capital employed should be disclosed. [ED 45 paras 37(c), 38(c)]

13.51 The exposure draft suggests that in most situations, the disclosure of results and the analysis of capital employed by geographical segments should be based on the areas from which goods or services are supplied (source basis).

13.52 In addition to the above disclosure requirements, the exposure draft suggests the disclosure of segmental information for associated companies, unless such information cannot be obtained. The ability of a company to obtain such information will obviously depend on whether or not the associated companies are prepared to provide it. This fact is recognised in the exposure draft, which suggests that disclosure of segmental information on associated companies is only necessary where, in total, they account for at least 20 per cent of the total result or 20 per cent of the total capital employed of the reporting company (including the company's share of the results and net assets of the associated companies). [ED 45 para 27].

13.53 The information required in respect of associates is a segmental analysis of both of the following:

- The company's share of profits or losses of associates before accounting for taxation, minority interests and extraordinary items.

- The company's share of the net assets of associated companies (including goodwill to the extent that it has not been written off) stated where possible after attributing fair values to the net assets at the date of acquisition by the company of the interest in each associated company.

[ED 45 para 41].

13.54 The segmental disclosure should be of the aggregate data for all associated companies for which the information is available and should be shown separately in the segmental report. [ED 45 para 41].

13.55 The total of the information disclosed by segment should agree with the related figure in the financial statements. If it does not, the company should provide a reconciliation between the two figures. [ED 45 para 42].

13.56 Comparative figures for the previous accounting period should be provided. There is, however, no need to provide comparative information on the first occasion on which a company provides a segmental report, if the necessary information is not readily available. [ED 45 para 43].

13.57 If a change is made to the definition of segments or to the accounting policies that are adopted for reporting segmental information, the nature of the change should be disclosed. The reason for the change and the effect of the change should be stated. The previous year's figures should be restated to reflect the change. [ED 45 para 44].

13.58 The exposure draft provides a similar exemption from disclosing segmental information to that contained in paragraph 55(5) of Schedule 4, where such disclosure would be seriously prejudicial to the interests of the company. However, the fact that any such information has not been disclosed must be stated. [ED 45 para 34]. In addition, it is not necessary to disclose information segmentally if the disclosure of that information is not required by the Act; the fact that such information has not been disclosed should be stated. [ED 45 para 39]. An example of this is turnover attributable to banking in the case of a banking company.

13.59 ED 45 has not yet been adopted as standard accounting practice and, therefore, the proposals contained in the exposure draft may be subject to further amendments.

Gross profit

13.60 The gross profit or loss has to be shown as a separate item in Format 1, and it can be readily ascertained from the items that are disclosed in Format 3. Formats 2 and 4 analyse expenditure in a different manner. Therefore, if a company wishes to avoid disclosing its gross profit, it should adopt either Format 2 or Format 4.

Own work capitalised

13.61 Where a company has constructed some of its own tangible fixed assets, and it adopts either Format 2 or Format 4 for its profit and loss account, it should include the costs of direct materials, direct labour and overheads it has capitalised as a credit under the heading 'own work capitalised'. The costs of direct materials, direct labour and overheads are charged in the profit and loss account, by including these amounts under the relevant expenditure headings. The amount capitalised is then credited in the profit and loss account as own work capitalised, and it is debited to tangible fixed assets. Thus, items such as raw material costs in the profit and loss account will include the costs connected with such work.

Other operating income

13.62 'Other operating income' will include income that is associated with a company's normal activities, but that falls outside the definition of turnover. Such income could (for example) include the profit on the sale of fixed assets. However, if the profit on the sale of fixed assets is not material, it could be applied in reducing the depreciation charge.

13.63 'Other operating income' could include also rents from land (net of outgoings). In addition, however, the notes to the profit and loss account must disclose the amount of rents from land, after deducting ground rents, rates and other outgoings. This requirement applies only if a substantial part of the company's revenue for the financial year in question consists of such rents. [4 Sch 53(1)(5)].

Income from investments

Dividends

13.64 The notes must disclose separately the amount of income from listed investments. [4 Sch 53(1)(4)]. SSAP 8 requires that dividends received from UK resident companies should be included in the profit and loss account at the amount of cash received or receivable, plus the related tax credit. The amount of the tax credit is then disclosed under UK corporation tax as 'tax attributable to franked investment income'.

13.65 Dividends received and receivable from both subsidiary and fellow subsidiary companies will be included in 'income from shares in group undertakings'. Traditionally, dividends are included in the receiving company's financial statements, even though they may not be declared or paid by the paying company until the subsequent year. In a group's consolidated financial statements, this line will appear only if dividends are received or receivable from subsidiaries that have not been consolidated.

Income from participating interests

13.66 'Income from shares in undertakings in which the company has a participating interest' will include, for example, income from the following undertakings in which the investing company holds on a long-term basis 20 per cent or more of the shares in that undertaking.

- Income from bodies corporate (including dividends received from associated undertakings).
- Share of profits from partnerships.
- Share of profits from unincorporated associations carrying on a trade or business, with or without a profit.

Where dividends have been received solely from associated companies, the wording of the formats may be amended to read 'income from shares in associated undertakings'. Participating interest is defined in section 260(1) of the Act (see also chapter 9 paras 9.22 to 9.34).

Earnings per share

13.67 The Act does not require information to be given in respect of earnings per share (EPS). However, SSAP 3 requires listed companies and companies traded on the USM to show the figure of earnings per share on the face of the profit and loss account (for example, see Table 50). [SSAP 3 para 13]. This requirement does not apply, however, to banking and insurance companies.

13.68 The earnings per share is the profit or loss (in pence) that is attributable to each equity share. The profit or loss to be used in this calculation is the consolidated profit or loss for the period both after tax and after deducting minority interests and preference dividends, but before taking into account extraordinary items. It should also include associated companies' earnings. The earnings figure should be divided by the number of equity shares that are in issue and that rank for dividend in respect of the period. Both of these figures should be shown in a note to the profit and loss account.

13.69 The earnings per share figure disclosed on the face of the profit and loss account for both the period under review and the corresponding previous period should be calculated using the 'net basis'. [SSAP 3 para 14]. On this basis, the charge for taxation used in determining the earnings figure should include:

- Any irrecoverable ACT.
- Any unrelieved overseas tax that arises from the payment or the proposed payment of dividends.

[SSAP 3 para 11].

13.70 The profit and loss account tax charge should be used even where it has been reduced by losses brought forward. However, where this has a material effect on the earnings per share figure that is disclosed, an explanation of the effect should be given. Also, SSAP 3 considers the effect of using the 'nil basis' for calculating earnings per share. Under this basis, the charge for taxation that should be used excludes:

- Irrecoverable ACT.
- Any unrelieved overseas tax that arose from the payment or the proposed payment of dividends. above, except in so far as these arise in respect of preference dividends.

[SSAP 3 para 12].

Table 50: Illustration of the calculation and disclosure of earnings per share.

Extract from the Burton Group plc Annual Report and Accounts 2nd September 1989.

Consolidated profit and loss account extract

		Notes	1989	1988
Earnings per share				
Average shares in issue	– actual tax	9	27.0p	25.2p
	– fully taxed		26.2p	24.9p
Fully diluted	– actual tax		24.7p	23.5p
	– fully taxed		24.1p	23.2p

Note extract

9 *Earnings per share*

The calculations of earnings per share is based on the profit for the financial year using the average number of shares in issue of 555,463,000 (1988 – 553,214,000).

The fully diluted earnings per share calculations is based on a profit of £163.0 million (1988 – £152.7 million) after adjusting for:

(a) a sum equivalent to the yield net of corporation tax from 2½% Consols on:
  (i) the consideration receivable on the surrender of warrants to subscribe for shares and
  (ii) the consideration receivable in the event of employees exercising the options granted to them.

(b) interest net of corporation tax on:
  (i) 5¾% Convertible Guaranteed Loan 1992.
  (ii) 8% Convertible Unsecured Loan Stock 1996/2001.
  (iii) 4¾% Convertible Bonds 2001.

The total number of shares in issue on surrender of warrants, exercise of options and conversion of loans would be 659,566,715 (1988 – 649,900,034).

13.71 SSAP 3 says that, if there is a material difference between the earnings calculated using the nil basis and the earnings calculated using the net basis, then it is desirable to disclose the earnings per share calculated on both bases. [SSAP 3 para 9].

Treatment of changes in equity share capital

13.72 Where there is only one class of equity share capital, and this remains constant throughout the period, the calculation of the earnings per share is simple. If, however, there is more than one class of equity shares or (perhaps) some of the shares are not fully paid, the calculation becomes more difficult. In these circumstances, the earnings should be apportioned over the different classes of shares in issue in accordance with either their dividend rights or their other rights to participate in profits.

13.73 If new equity shares are issued during the year, either for cash at full market price or as consideration for the acquisition of an asset, the earnings should be apportioned over the average number of shares that rank for dividend during the period, and weighted on a time basis. When a subsidiary is acquired for shares, the new shares should be taken into account from the day on which the new subsidiary's profits are included in the group's earnings. Where a company makes a bonus issue (or subdivides the shares into shares of a smaller nominal value), the earnings should be apportioned over the number of shares that rank for dividend after the capitalisation. The corresponding earnings per share figure disclosed for the previous year should be recalculated using the new number of shares in issue.

13.74 Where equity shares are issued during the year by way of a rights issue at less than full market price, SSAP 3 recommends that the factor used to adjust the earnings per share for the previous period (and all earlier periods) should be based on the closing price on the last day of quotation of the shares cum rights. The factor it recommends is

$$\frac{\text{Theoretical ex rights price}}{\text{Actual cum rights price on the last day of quotation}}$$

The theoretical ex rights price is effectively the average price per share after the rights issue. Consider the following example:

Example

At 31st December 1990, the issued capital of a company consisted of 1.8m ordinary shares of 10p each, fully paid. The profit on ordinary activities for the year ended 31st December 1990 and 1991 amounted to £630,000 and £875,000 respectively. On 31st March 1991, the company made a rights issue on a 1 for 4 basis at 30p. The actual cum rights price on the last day of quotation cum rights was 60p.

Calculation of theoretical ex rights price

	No		Pence
Initial holding	4	market value	240
Rights taken up	1	cost	30
New holding	5	theoretical price	270

Theoretical ex rights price $= \frac{270}{5} = 54p$

Market value relates to actual cum rights price.
Cost relates to rights issue price.

13.75 For the earnings per share of the current year, it is necessary to adjust the weighted average share capital. This can be done by adding the proportion of the capital in issue before the rights issue (after applying the bonus element factor set out below) to the proportion of the capital in issue after the rights issue. Referring to the above example, the bonus element of the rights issue is given by the fraction

$$\frac{\text{Actual cum rights price}}{\text{Theoretical ex rights price}} = \frac{60}{54} = \frac{10}{9}$$

The weighted average share capital is calculated as follows:

Weighted average share capital:

The number of shares in issue before the rights issue, adjusted for the bonus element would be:

$1.8m \times \frac{10}{9} = 2,000,000$

The number of shares after the rights issue would be:

$1.8m \times \frac{5}{4} = 2,250,000$

Therefore, the weighted average number of shares would be:

$2.0m \times \frac{3}{12}$	=	500,000
$2.25m \times \frac{9}{12}$	=	1,687,500
Weighted average number		2,187,500

Calculation of EPS following a rights issue

EPS for 1991 $= \frac{£875,000}{2,187,500} = 40p$

An adjustment is necessary to correct the earnings per share figure of the previous year to reflect the effective bonus element in the rights issue. This can be done by adjusting the earnings per share figure of the previous year by the **reciprocal** of the bonus element factor as shown below.

EPS for 1990 (was)	=	$\frac{£630,000}{1,800,000}$	=	35p
EPS for 1990 (now) as adjusted for bonus element	=	$35p \times \frac{9}{10}$	=	31.5p

Fully diluted earnings per share

13.76 Companies often have equity shares in issue that do not rank for a dividend in the period, although they may do so in the future. They may also have debentures, or loan stock or preference shares that are convertible into the company's equity shares. Furthermore, there may be options or warrants to subscribe for shares in the company.

13.77 Where these situations exist, SSAP 3 requires that the fully diluted earnings per share (calculated on the basis outlined in paragraph 13.79 below) should be shown also on the face of the profit and loss account (for example, see Table 50). Where this figure is disclosed, SSAP 3 requires that:

- The basis of calculation should be disclosed.
- The corresponding amount should be given (unless the assumption on which the calculation is based did not exist in the previous period).
- Equal prominence should be given to the basic and fully diluted earnings per share figures.

[SSAP 3 para 16].

13.78 The fully diluted earnings per share figure need not be given if either the dilution amounts to less than 5 per cent of the basic earnings per share figure or the basic earnings per share figure is negative. [SSAP 3 para 16].

13.79 The fully diluted earnings per share should be calculated in the following ways:

- Where equity shares exist that will rank for a dividend in the future, the fully diluted earnings per share figure should be calculated using the assumption that these shares ranked for dividend from the beginning of the period (or on the date of their issue, if this was during the period). [SSAP 3 appendix 1 para 29].

- Convertible loan stock should be brought into the calculation as if it had been converted into the maximum number of new equity shares at the beginning of the period (or on the date of the issue of the loan stock, if this was during the period). Also, the earnings for the period should be adjusted to take account of the saving of interest on the stock (net of corporation tax) that would have arisen if the conversion had occurred. [SSAP 3 appendix 1 para 30]. Similar considerations apply to convertible preference shares, that is, the dividend is added back to earnings and the maximum number of ordinary shares that could be issued on conversion is brought into the calculation.

- Where options or warrants exist, the calculations should be made using the maximum number of equity shares that would have been in issue if the options and warrants had been exercised on the first day of the period (or on the date of issue, if this was during the period). The earnings for the period should also be adjusted using the assumption that the proceeds of subscription were invested in 2.5 per cent Consolidated Stock on the day on which the options or warrants were exercised (see also Table 50 above). [SSAP 3 appendix 1 para 31].

13.80 For both convertible loan stock and options and warrants, the fully diluted earnings per share figure will still have to be given in the year in which either the loans are converted or the options and warrants are exercised. This will be necessary unless the conversion or the exercise was carried out on the first day of the period.

Chapter 14

THE PROFIT AND LOSS ACCOUNT - EXPENDITURE

Chapter 14

THE PROFIT AND LOSS ACCOUNT - EXPENDITURE

Introduction

14.1 The previous chapter dealt with the measurement and disclosure of income items in the profit and loss account. This chapter considers the measurement and disclosure of expenditure items, including pension costs.

Cost of sales, distribution costs and administrative expenses

14.2 These headings give rise to many questions concerning the allocation of costs and overheads. The following lists are intended to provide guidance as to the items that may be included under each heading.

14.3 *Cost of sales* will normally comprise:

- Opening (less closing) stocks.
- Direct materials.
- Other external charges (such as the hire of plant and machinery or the cost of casual labour).
- Direct labour.
- All direct production overheads, and indirect overheads that cannot be related specifically to the distribution and administrative functions.
- Research and development costs.
- Cash discounts received on 'cost of sales' expenditure (this is not a set-off, but an effective reduction in the purchase price of an item).
- Stock provisions.

14.4 *Distribution costs* will normally comprise:

- Payroll costs of the sales, marketing and distribution functions.
- Advertising.

- Salesmen's travel and entertaining.
- Warehouse costs for finished goods.
- Transport costs concerning the distribution of finished goods.
- All costs of maintaining sales outlets.
- Agents' commission payable.

14.5 *Administrative expenses* will normally comprise:

- Payroll costs of the administrative function.
- All costs of maintaining the administration buildings.
- Bad debts.
- Professional costs.
- Cash discounts on sales.

14.6 As stated in chapter 6, if Format 1 or 3 is adopted, charges for depreciation or the diminution in value of assets have to be analysed under the above headings. [Note 14 on the profit and loss account sheet formats]. The type of analysis will depend on the function of the related assets (see also para 14.24).

14.7 In some specific instances, the above analyses may not be appropriate. For example, in the context of a mail order company, agents' commission payable may be regarded as a cost of sale rather than as a distribution cost.

14.8 The way in which a company analyses its costs will depend very much on the nature of its business. Where a company incurs significant operating expenses that it considers do not fall under any one of the headings 'cost of sales', 'distribution costs' and 'administrative expenses', there is nothing to prevent the company including an additional item for these expenses in Formats 1 or 3. The overriding consideration is that a company should analyse its operating expenses consistently from year to year.

14.9 Some companies have adapted these items or shown additional items. However, these companies seem to be in a minority. This is probably because the items are general enough to apply to most companies' expenditure. Examples of adaptations and additional items that companies have used in their financial statements are shown below.

Examples of adaptation of items:

- ☐ Selling and distribution costs.
- ☐ Marketing, selling and distribution costs.
- ☐ Administrative and selling expenses.
- ☐ Selling and general administration expenses.

Examples of additional items:

- ☐ Sales commission (shown in addition to distribution costs).
- ☐ Major reorganisation costs, including redundancy.

Deferred costs

14.10 Costs should only be deferred where the matching principle is not superseded by prudence. In general, this means that costs should only be carried forward where they will be recovered from future related revenues. The following three examples illustrate the types of principle that must be considered before costs can be deferred.

Example 1

A company introduces new technology and incurs redundancy costs. It wishes to defer these costs and match them against the future benefits to be obtained from the new technology.

This is a situation where the prudence concept should prevail over the matching concept, and consequently, it is not acceptable to carry forward redundancy costs to match against the benefit to be obtained from new technology. Although the SSAP 13 definition of 'development' includes the words **"produce new or substantially improved . . . processes"** [SSAP 13 para 21 (c)], redundancy costs would not fall into this definition.

Example 2

A company negotiated a long-term facility and pays a substantial commitment fee. It wants to defer this cost and amortise it over the term of the facility.

Normally such costs should be written off immediately on the grounds of prudence. However, if for example, the fee were taken into account in setting the interest rate, it might be acceptable to spread the fee if the annual cost of borrowing that results is equivalent to a market rate of interest.

Example 3

A company has capitalised internally developed software for use in its own business. It now wishes to capitalise 'installation costs' which include a large element of staff training costs.

The cost of training staff to use the software should not be capitalised as there is no clear matching of such costs against future revenue. On the grounds of prudence they should be written off.

Staff costs and numbers

Employee costs

14.11 Staff costs are defined in paragraph 94 of Schedule 4 to the Act as being the costs a company incurs in respect of the persons it employs under contracts of service. A contract *of service* (or a contract of employment as it is also called) is an agreement under which the employer agrees to employ the employee for a wage or a salary in return for the employee's labour. This agreement must be made in writing. However, self-employed persons are not employed by the company, but merely have contracts to perform specific services for that company. The costs of self-employed people should normally be excluded from staff costs, because their contracts will be contracts *for services*. Examples of such persons are consultants and contractors. Their costs should normally be included under 'other external charges'.

14.12 Normally, casual employees should also be excluded from 'staff costs'. In certain circumstances, however, it may be necessary to include casual employees in order for the financial statements to give a true and fair view. An example of such a circumstance would be where a company employs significant levels of casual staff (such as in the retail, newspaper and hotel industries).

14.13 The item 'staff costs' does not appear in the profit and loss account Formats 1 and 3. This is because expenses are classified in these formats by function, rather than by type. However, where a company prepares its profit and loss account in the style of either Format 1 or Format 3, it has to disclose, in the notes to the profit and loss account, the equivalent information to that given when Formats 2 and 4 are used.

14.14 In summary, either the profit and loss account format or the notes must disclose, in aggregate, each of the following amounts:

- The wages and salaries that were either paid to employees or are payable to them, in respect of the financial year in question.

- Social security costs that the company has incurred on behalf of its employees. For this purpose, social security costs are any contributions the company makes to any social security or pension scheme, or fund or arrangement that the State runs. These costs will include the employer's national insurance contributions.

- Other pension costs the company has incurred on behalf of employees. For this purpose, pension costs include:

- ☐ Any contributions a company makes for the purposes of any non-State occupational pension scheme that is established to provide pensions for employees.

- ☐ Any sums the company has set aside for that purpose.

- ☐ Any amounts the company has paid in respect of pensions, without those amounts having first been so set aside.

Pension costs will, therefore, include the company's contributions to any pension scheme other than the State scheme. An illustration of these disclosure requirements is given in Table 51.

[4 Sch 56(4), 94].

Table 51: Illustration of the disclosure of employee costs and numbers.

Extract from WH Smith Group PLC Annual Report 3rd June 1989.

21 Staff

Analysis of staff by activity

The average number of persons employed by the Group analysed by activity was as follows:

	53 weeks to 3 June 1989			52 weeks to 28 May 1988		
	Male	Female	Total	Male	Female	Total
Retailing						
Books, stationery, news, recorded music, travel, etc	7,106	16,887	23,993	6,699	15,129	21,828
Do it yourself	2,103	2,304	4,407	1,820	1,906	3,726
Distribution						
News, office supplies, books, etc	3,967	2,100	6,067	3,447	1,736	5,183
Television services	33	30	63	23	20	43
	13,209	21,321	34,530	11,989	18,791	30,780

Analysis of staff by geographical area

The average number of persons employed by the Group analysed by geographical area was as follows:

	53 weeks to 3 June 1989			52 weeks to 28 May 1988		
	Male	Female	Total	Male	Female	Total
United Kingdom						
Full time	8,999	8,876	17,875	8,186	7,936	16,122
8–29 hours per week	1,971	7,103	9,074	1,592	6,482	8,074
Less than 8 hours per week	967	1,610	2,577	709	1,485	2,194
	11,937	17,589	29,526	10,487	15,903	26,390
Europe	36	75	111	29	69	98
USA	759	1,895	2,654	668	1,756	2,424
Canada	477	1,762	2,239	805	1,063	1,868
	13,209	21,321	34,530	11,989	18,791	30,780

	53 weeks to3 June 1989	52 weeks to28 May 1988
	£m	£m
Staff costs		
Wages and salaries	228.5	193.2
Social security costs	19.1	16.3
Other pension costs	2.9	8.0
Staff share ownership scheme	3.3	2.4
	253.8	219.9

14.15 The Act says that wages and salaries should be determined by reference to either the payments the company makes or the costs it incurs in respect of all persons it employs. [4 Sch 94(3)]. There is no definition in the Act of 'costs incurred'. It is likely that this term would include the money value of benefits in kind, as in the case of directors' remuneration under paragraph 1(4) of Schedule 6 to the Act (see further para 14.20), however, companies sometimes charge the cost of staff benefits to other items in the profit and loss account and not to staff costs.

Average number of employees

14.16 In addition to requiring that the notes to the profit and loss account should disclose employee costs, the Act requires that those notes should include information in respect of the number of employees.

14.17 The two disclosures that the notes must contain in connection with the number of employees are:

- The average number of employees in the financial year. The number must be calculated by:

  - Ascertaining the number of persons employed under contract of service, whether full-time or part-time, for each week in the year.

  - Adding together all the weekly numbers.

  - Dividing the resulting total by the number of weeks in the financial year.

  The average number of employees includes persons who work wholly or mainly overseas, as well as persons who work in the UK.

- The average number of employees by category. This number must be calculated by applying the same method of calculation as outlined above to each category of employees. For this purpose, the categories of persons employed are to be such categories as the directors select, having regard to the way in which the company's activities are organised.

  Because the guidance on how to select categories is rather vague, directors of companies have chosen a variety of different categories. Some companies split between part-time employees and full-time employees, others between hourly-paid, weekly-paid and salaried staff, or between production, sales and administration staff.

[4 Sch 56].

These disclosure requirements are illustrated in Table 51 (page 289).

14.18 Consolidated financial statements should include the information outlined above only for the group as a whole. This applies to all profit and loss account disclosures for a company that avails itself of the exemption not to publish its own profit and loss account.

14.19 There is no exemption from disclosure where the number of employees is small, or (for example) where a company is a wholly-owned subsidiary.

Directors

14.20 Directors who have a contract of service with the company are to be regarded as employees. Therefore, their salaries, their social security costs and their other pension costs must be included in the required analysis under staff costs, even if a note is included stating that directors' emoluments are shown elsewhere (as illustrated in Table 51 above). In addition, directors' emoluments have also to be disclosed separately in accordance with the requirements of Part I of Schedule 6 to the Act. In this situation, their emoluments will exclude those social security costs that the company bears, because such amounts are neither paid to the director nor paid in respect of a pension scheme. The disclosure of directors' aggregate emoluments, will, however, include the estimated money value of any benefits in kind.

14.21 In contrast to payments under a contract *of service* (where the director is employed), amounts paid to directors under contracts *for services* (equivalent to the director being self-employed) should not be disclosed under staff costs. But, under Part I of Schedule 6 to the Act, they must be disclosed as directors' emoluments in the notes to the financial statements. Whether a director's contract with the company is a contract *of service* or a contract *for services* is a question of fact in each circumstance. Usually, however, executive directors will have contracts *of service,* whereas non-executive directors will have contracts *for services.* Contracts for services might include, for example, consultancy arrangements. Directors' emoluments are dealt with further in chapter 17.

Practical problems relating to employee costs

14.22 In practice, there may be problems in deciding on the employees to include in staff costs and in identifying the average number of employees. One of the most frequent problems arises where employees clearly work for one company, but their contracts of service are with another company (for example, the holding company). Also, further complications arise when that other company pays the wages and salaries of these employees. If paragraph 56 of Schedule 4 to the Act was strictly interpreted in these situations, it could lead to the disclosure of misleading information in the financial statements. Accordingly, a company may need to depart from the strict interpretation of paragraph 56 to enable its financial statements to give a true and fair view. In those situations where a departure is necessary, the financial statements should disclose particulars of the departure, the reasons for it, and its effect.

14.23 Some of the more common problems that arise in this respect are considered in the examples that follow:

Example 1

Employees work full time for, and are paid by, a subsidiary company, but their contracts of service are with the holding company.

It would be misleading if there were no disclosure of staff costs or numbers in the subsidiary company's financial statements. Consequently, the wages and salaries the subsidiary company pays to those employees should be disclosed as 'staff costs' in its financial statements, and those employees should be included in the calculation of the average number of staff employed.

The notes to the subsidiary company's financial statements should explain that those staff have contracts of service with another company. They should also explain why their remuneration and average number are disclosed in the financial statements.

The holding company's consolidated financial statements normally will not be affected (unless the subsidiary is not included in the consolidated financial statements), because they will show the average number of employees and staff costs of the group as a whole, but not those of the holding company separately. Consequently, no additional disclosure should be necessary in the holding company's financial statements. (However, if the contracts of service are with a fellow subsidiary company, then that fellow subsidiary company's financial statements should disclose the fact that certain employees have service contracts with the company. But those financial statements should state that, because those employees work for, and are paid for wholly by, a fellow subsidiary company, their staff costs and average number are disclosed in the fellow subsidiary company's financial statements.)

Example 2

Employees work full time for the subsidiary company, but they are not paid by the subsidiary company, and they do not have service contracts with it. However, the subsidiary company bears a management charge for their services from the company that pays the employees, and it can ascertain the proportion of the management charge that relates to staff costs.

Again, in this situation it could be misleading if the subsidiary company's financial statements disclosed no information about staff costs or numbers. Accordingly, the proportion of the management charge that relates to staff costs should be disclosed in the subsidiary company's financial statements as 'staff costs'. The employees concerned should be included in the calculation of the average number of employees. The notes to the financial statements should explain that the employees do not have contracts of service with the company, and they should also explain why their costs and average number are disclosed in the financial statements. For the reason outlined in example 1 above, the holding company's financial statements should not be affected. (If the contracts of service are with, and the employees are paid by, a fellow subsidiary company, then that fellow subsidiary's financial statements should contain the same information as outlined in example 1).

Example 3

The facts are the same as in example 2 except that the subsidiary company is unable to break down the management charge and ascertain the part of it that relates to staff costs.

In this situation, for the same reason as explained in example 2, the holding company's consolidated financial statements will be unaffected. The notes to the subsidiary company's financial statements should explain that the employees' contracts of service are with the holding company and that their remuneration is included in the holding company's financial statements. The notes should also explain that the management charge that the holding company makes includes the cost of these employees, but that it is impossible to ascertain separately the element of the management charge that relates to staff costs. (If the employees' contracts of service are with a fellow subsidiary, rather than with the holding company, and that fellow subsidiary also pays the employees, the fellow subsidiary's financial statements should disclose the employees' remuneration in its staff costs, and should also include the employees in the calculation of average number employed. The notes should explain that these employees work for a fellow subsidiary company, and that the company recharges the cost of their employment to that fellow subsidiary as part of a management charge.)

Example 4

The facts are the same as in example 2 above, except that no management charge is made for the employees' services. This will often apply where staff work either full-time or part-time for small companies.

In this situation, the notes to the subsidiary company's financial statements should explain that the company is not charged for the services provided by the employees that work for it. If appropriate, the notes should also indicate that the cost of these employees and their average number are included in the holding company's consolidated financial statements. For the same reason as given in example 1 above, however, the holding company's consolidated financial statements should not be affected. (Once again, if it is a fellow subsidiary that employs and pays the employees, its financial statements should include the cost of these employees in its staff costs, and should include these employees in the average number employed. If appropriate, the notes to the financial statements should explain that these employees work for a fellow subsidiary company, but that no management charge is made for their services to that company.)

Depreciation (including other amounts written off assets)

14.24 Where the company prepares its profit and loss account in accordance with either Format 1 or Format 3, expenses are classified by function. Consequently, any provisions for either depreciation or the diminution in value of tangible and intangible fixed assets will not be disclosed in the profit and loss account format. Accordingly, the Act requires that this information must be disclosed separately in the notes to the financial statements (for example, see Table 52 overleaf). [Note 17 on the profit and loss account formats].

Other operating charges (including other external charges)

14.25 The relevant formats (Formats 2 and 4) link 'other external charges' with 'raw materials and consumables'. Therefore, such charges are likely to include any production costs from external sources that are not included under other headings (for example, equipment rentals and the costs of subcontractors). 'Other operating charges' tends to be a residual class of all charges relating to the ordinary activities of a business that do not fall into any other category. 'Other external charges' may also include losses on exchange.

Table 52: Illustration of the analysis of the provision for depreciation and for diminution in value of assets where expenses are classified by function.

Extract from The British Petroleum Company p.l.c. Annual Report and Accounts 31st December 1988.

Note extract

5 Depreciation and amounts provided

	1988 £m	1987 £m
Included in the income statement under the following headings:		
Depreciation:		
Replacement cost of sales	1,687	1,515
Distribution	198	191
Administration	39	39
	1,924	1,745
Depreciation of capitalised leased assets inlcuded above	27	46
Amounts provided against fixed asset investments:		
Replacement cost of sales	11	2
Exploration expenditure	8	22
	19	24

Pension costs

Introduction

14.26 SSAP 24, 'Accounting for pension costs' was issued in May 1988. Before its issue the Act provided the only guidance on the disclosure required concerning pension commitments, although it provided no guidance on the correct accounting treatment that should be adopted.

14.27 SSAP 24, however, deals with both the measurement of pension costs and the disclosure of pension information in company financial statements. It applies to all situations where a company has a legal, contractual or implied obligation to provide pensions for its employees.

14.28 Most pension schemes in the UK are funded. This means that the future liabilities for benefits are provided for by the accumulation of assets held independently from the employing company's own assets. The principles of SSAP 24 apply, however, whether a scheme is funded or unfunded. [SSAP 24 para 73].

14.29 Pension schemes may be 'defined contribution' or 'defined benefit' schemes and the standard applies to both. [SSAP 24 para 74].

- Defined contribution schemes are schemes where the future benefits payable to members are determined by the accumulated value of contributions paid in to the scheme. [SSAP 24 para 62]. The employers' obligations are, therefore, normally discharged by an agreed level of contributions.

- Defined benefit schemes are schemes where the rules determine the benefits to be paid, irrespective of the contributions paid in respect of each member. [SSAP 24 para 61]. Employers' obligations are not capable of being defined in an absolute sense, but actuarial expertise is required to determine an appropriate level of contributions to fund those obligations.

14.30 The main impact of the standard is on those companies that provide defined benefit schemes.

Accounting objective

14.31 The following principle underlies the accounting requirements of the standard. Because the cost of providing pensions is part of the remuneration of employees, the cost should be allocated as fairly as possible so as to match the benefit derived from the services of the employees. Hence the accounting objective in SSAP 24 is stated to be that *"the employer should recognise the expected cost of providing pensions on a systematic and rational basis over the period during which he derives benefit from the employees' services"*. [SSAP 24 para 77].

Defined contribution schemes

14.32 In a defined contribution scheme, the employer's obligation at any point in time is restricted to the amount of the contributions payable to date. Consequently, the company will meet the accounting objective by charging against profits the amount of contributions payable to the pension scheme in respect of the accounting period. [SSAP 24 para 78]. Accounting for the cost of such schemes under SSAP 24 is, therefore, straightforward.

Defined benefit schemes

14.33 The standard requires that the method of providing for pension costs *"should be such that the regular pension cost is a substantially level percentage of the current and expected future pensionable payroll in the light of the current actuarial assumptions"*. [SSAP 24 para 79]. The actuarial valuation method used to calculate the cost should, therefore, be consistent with the objective.

Actuarial considerations

14.34 In a defined benefit scheme, the members' benefits are not directly related to the value of contributions and the fund's investment performance, but are typically determined by a formula based on pensionable service and salary. The majority of schemes operated by larger companies are 'final salary' schemes, where an employee's retirement pension will be based on the level of his salary at, or near, retirement date. Actuarial techniques are required to value pension liabilities. There are several methods that an actuary can use to determine a contribution rate that will provide a scheme with sufficient assets to meet its liability to pay the promised benefits. Some methods will produce a different contribution level each year, others will provide a level rate of contribution for all future years.

14.35 Further, the actuary must make key assumptions about such factors as return on investments in a scheme, increases in wages and salaries and increases in pension payments. SSAP 24 does not specify any particular actuarial method and assumptions that should be used. The standard is deliberately flexible and leaves the choice of methods to be adopted to the company's actuary in consultation with his client. It does, however, require that the chosen valuation method and assumption used for accounting purposes should satisfy the accounting objective described in paragraph 14.31 above and should make full provision over the employees' service lives for the expected costs of their pensions.

Regular pension cost and variations in cost

14.36 The total cost of pensions in a year can notionally be divided into the regular cost and variations from regular cost. The 'regular cost' is the consistent ongoing cost that is recognised under the actuarial method used. [SSAP 24 para 72]. Where a stable percentage contribution rate is determined, which makes full provision for the expected benefits over the anticipated service lives of employees, then this will normally be the appropriate amount to charge in the profit and loss account. [SSAP 24 para 20].

14.37 'Variations from regular cost' arise in the following circumstances:

- Experience surpluses or deficiencies arising from actuarial valuations. These are differences between the actuarial value of the assets and of the liabilities of a scheme. As new valuations are carried out, they take account of the fact that actual events may not have coincided with the assumptions made at the time of the previous valuation (for example, the actual return on investments may differ from that which was assumed). These differences will give rise to a surplus or a deficiency in the scheme.

- Increases to pensions in payment or to deferred pensions for which provision has not previously been made (see para 14.46).

- Changes in actuarial methods or assumptions that affect the actuarial value of accrued benefits.

- Improvements in benefits or changes in conditions for membership. These generally increase the cost of providing the pension benefits and have an element of past service cost which gives rise to a variation.

[SSAP 24 para 21].

These sources of variations from regular costs are referred to below.

Accounting for experience surpluses and deficiencies

14.38 The general rule is that variations from regular cost caused by surpluses or deficiencies should be spread forward over the expected remaining service lives of current employees in the scheme. SSAP 24 does not suggest a period but says it will be determined by the actuary. [SSAP 24 para 23].

14.39 Variations from regular cost may, however, in cash terms be reflected in the form of one or more of the following:

- Contribution holidays.

- A period of reduced contributions.

- Cash refunds to employers.

- Additional lump sum contributions or a period of increased contributions.

14.40 The general rule for allocating variations from regular cost in the profit and loss account represents a departure from the widespread practice previously adopted by most companies, which is to recognise such variations as they arise. Paragraph 80 of the standard states that variations should be allocated over the expected or average remaining service lives of current employees in the scheme. The standard does not specify how the variation from regular cost should be spread, and different methods can produce very different reported pension costs. Common methods are

- Straight line basis over the expected remaining service life.

  Under this method, the surplus to be reduced, or deficiency to be funded, will be allocated on a straight-line basis, so that the annual pension cost would be calculated as follows:

  $$\text{Regular cost} - \frac{\text{Surplus to be reduced}}{\text{Average remaining service life}}$$

  $$\text{Regular cost} + \frac{\text{Deficiency to be funded}}{\text{Average remaining service life}}$$

  In this situation, the annual profit and loss account charge expressed as a percentage of total pensionable payroll, will tend to vary over the chosen number of years if the payroll cost rises annually.

- Level percentage of current and future pensionable payroll.

  Under this method, the adjustment to the regular cost in respect of the allocation of the surplus or deficiency is weighted so that the net pension cost is expected to be a stable percentage of pensionable payroll each year. In practice, this will probably be the preferred method.

14.41 The straight line method of spreading a variation from regular cost is illustrated in the following example.

The actuarial valuation at 31st December 1989 of the pension scheme of a company showed a surplus of £240,000. The actuary recommended that the company eliminate the surplus by taking a contribution holiday in 1990 and 1991 and then paying contributions of £45,000 for the next eight years. After the end of the eight year period, the standard contributions of £60,000 will become payable. The average remaining service life of employees in the scheme at 31st December 1989 was ten years.

The regular cost is £60,000.
The variation to be spread is £240,000. On a straight line basis this is equivalent to £24,000 per annum, leaving a net pension cost of £36,000 per annum.

The financial statements of the company for the next ten years will show the following:

Year	Funding £'000	P & L charge £'000	Provision £'000
1990	-	36	(36)
1991	-	36	(72)
1992	45	36	(63)
1993	45	36	(54)
1994	45	36	(45)
1995	45	36	(36)
1996	45	36	(27)
1997	45	36	(18)
1998	45	36	(9)
1999	45	36	-

SSAP 24 follows the 'income approach' to accounting for pension costs that focuses on the profit and loss charge. The balance sheet asset or liability is then derived as a consequence. A net pension provision will arise where the cumulative pension cost charged exceeds contributions paid. This will happen, as in the example above, where a company takes a contribution holiday. The profit and loss account will be charged each year with the regular pension cost less a proportion of the total reduction in contributions given by the contribution-free period. A provision will accumulate each contribution-free year. The amount provided in this way will be reversed over the chosen period of employees' service lives as the regular contributions paid following the holiday exceed the annual profit and loss charge.

Conversely, a prepayment will arise where contributions paid over a limited period to fund a deficit exceed the cumulative annual charge to profit and loss account.

14.42 There are, however, three exceptions to the general rule of spreading surpluses and deficiencies as described above:

- Where a surplus or deficiency that causes a 'significant change' in the level of contributions has resulted from a significant reduction in the number of employees, then the profit and loss charge should reflect the reduced level of contributions as it occurs. [SSAP 24 para 81]. This treatment recognises the fact that a surplus arising from, say, a major redundancy programme, falls outside the normal process of revising estimates of contribution levels. Consequently, it would be inappropriate to spread the benefit forward over the service lives of remaining employees. This different treatment is a requirement, not an option. What is 'significant' in this context may be open to argument, but clearly the actuary will need to be involved in isolating the cause of a surplus and quantifying the effect on contribution levels of a significant reduction in the number of employees.

- Where a company takes a cash refund as part of a scheme to reduce a surplus in accordance with the provisions of the Finance Act 1986, then it may depart from the spreading principle and credit the refund to profit and loss account in the period in which it occurs. [SSAP 24 para 83].

- Where prudence requires it, a material deficiency should be recognised over a shorter period. This is expected to arise, however, only in very limited circumstances. SSAP 24 states that the deficiency must have been caused by a major event outside the normal scope of actuarial assumptions, and must have resulted in significant additional contributions being paid into the scheme. One example given is where there has been a major mismanagement of pension scheme assets. In most situations where deficiencies give rise to additional 'top up' funding, the standard requires that the additional payments should be allocated over the expected remaining service lives rather than written off when paid. [SSAP 24 paras 28, 82].

Extraordinary items

14.43 Where a material surplus or deficiency is caused directly by an extraordinary event, the requirements of SSAP 6 may override the provisions outlined above. SSAP 6 requires that individual elements of income and expenditure that derive from a single extraordinary event should be aggregated, and they would normally be recognised in the profit and loss account in the same period. [SSAP 24 para 26].

14.44 If a company closes a business segment and makes a large number of employees redundant, then the effect of any resulting pension scheme surplus should be recognised immediately as part of the extraordinary item. This applies even though the surplus may give rise to a contribution holiday or reduced contribution rate over a number of years. This differs from the treatment of a surplus caused by a significant reduction in the number of employees that is not attributed to an extraordinary event. In the latter situation, the benefit should be recognised as the reduced contributions occur.

14.45 A practical problem may arise where an extraordinary event occurs that is likely to materially affect the actuarial valuation of the pension scheme. It may be difficult or impossible to obtain appropriate actuarial information on a timely basis. Consequently, it may be impractical to include an extraordinary charge or credit in respect of future pension contributions in the financial statements of the period in which the extraordinary event took place. A special actuarial valuation may be required if the event falls between normal valuations. Alternatively, the effect on pension costs of, for example, a terminated activity, may have to be recognised as an extraordinary item in a subsequent year when it is quantified. SSAP 6 allows items, if they relate to one extraordinary event, to be treated as extraordinary even though they may be recognised over more than one accounting period. [SSAP 6 para 12].

Increases to pensions in payment and deferred pensions

14.46 Increases to pensions in payment and deferred pensions were mentioned earlier as one source of variation from regular cost. If the cost of additional benefits is covered by a surplus in the scheme, no additional charge is required. Otherwise, according to SSAP 24, costs should be accounted for as follows:

- Where an employer grants a one-off *ex-gratia* increase that affects pensions paid in the current period, but that will not affect pensions paid in future periods, the cost should be charged against profits in the period in which the increase is granted.

- Where an employer grants an *ex-gratia* pension to an employee on retirement, that is outside the benefits provided by a scheme, the capital cost should be charged against profits in the period in which it is granted.

- Where an employer grants a single discretionary improvement to pensions in payment for the current and future periods, without creating an expectation of similar increases in the future, the capitalised value of the improvement should be charged against profits in the period in which it is granted.

- Where discretionary increases are granted periodically, the preferred treatment is for such increases to be allowed for in the actuarial assumptions. This applies even though there is no contractual commitment to award future increases, but there is a reasonable expectation that they will be forthcoming on a regular basis. The cost would then be charged over the service lives of the employees. However, if no allowance has been made in the actuarial assumptions, the capitalised value of each increase should be provided for in the period in which it is granted. Increases that are specified in the rules of a pension scheme or by law will be taken into account in the actuarial assumptions. Therefore, the cost of such increases will be charged over the service lives of the employees.

[SSAP 24 paras 33 to 38].

Other variations

14.47 Variations from regular costs that are caused by changes in actuarial methods or assumptions, or by retroactive changes in benefits or membership, should be spread forward according to the general rule outlined in paragraph 14.38 above . [SSAP 24 para 30, 31].

Discounting

14.48 Notional interest arises because discounting is implicit in the methods used by actuaries to value pension funds. Any surpluses or deficits reported by the actuary are discounted amounts which increase with the passage of time. For example, where a surplus of (say) £200,000 is to be absorbed by a contribution holiday, the holiday might extend over a period to save (say) £230,000. The amount of £30,000, therefore, represents notional interest and arises because if the surplus is not withdrawn from the scheme immediately, the underlying assets continue to earn interest. A question arises as to whether a notional interest benefit or cost should be accounted for and, if so, what rate of interest should be used. There is little guidance on this issue in the standard since discounting in financial statements is considered to be a general issue and not unique to pensions. [SSAP 24 para 40]. However, general guidance on the use of discounting in financial statements is given in TR773.

14.49 In general, the interest effects arising from short-term timing differences between the payment of contributions and the recognition of cost are not likely to be material and can be ignored. [SSAP 24 para 40]. Where, however, the difference is long-term, (for example, where a surplus giving rise to a contribution holiday is spread for accounting purposes over a much longer period) it would be correct, in principle, to account for any notional interest on balance sheet assets or liabilities arising.

14.50 The interest rate that should be applied will be the long-term rate inherent in the actuarial assumption, because this rate is used by the actuary to project the unwinding of the surplus or deficit in the scheme. Consequently, the actuary should have information concerning notional interest that can be used to account each year for such interest as it arises.

14.51 It is preferable that the treatment of interest *should be* disclosed in the company's accounting policy on pension costs. If the interest payable or receivable is material and it is included as part of the pension cost, then that fact should be stated.

Foreign schemes

14.52 SSAP 24 offers a practical concession to companies and groups that operate foreign pension arrangements in respect of overseas operations. Although in principle, adjustments should be made to account for the costs of foreign schemes in accordance with the UK standard, SSAP 24 paragraph 91 recognises that in some situations it may be impractical and costly to obtain the necessary actuarial information. In such circumstances, compliance is encouraged but not mandatory. The consolidated financial statements should disclose as a minimum the amount charged against profit in respect of the foreign scheme, and the basis of that charge. The appendix to the standard includes an example of how such disclosure might be incorporated into the notes.

Deferred tax

14.53 In most companies, prior to SSAP 24, there were no material differences between pension costs charged in the profit and loss account and contributions paid (allowing for normal opening and closing accruals). The basis for obtaining tax relief on pension costs is that contributions should only be allowed as an expense when paid. Under SSAP 24 it is likely, therefore, that pension costs charged will differ from costs available for tax relief. This means that timing differences will arise in situations where there are pension holidays, short term funding of deficiencies and where pension fund assets or liabilities are recognised under the transitional provisions of the standard. They will also arise in respect of unfunded schemes.

14.54 Although timing differences arising from a pension holiday or pension deficit will probably reverse over a long time scale (for example, the average remaining service life), it still needs to be considered whether a corresponding deferred tax liability or asset should be required in accordance with SSAP 15. Similar considerations apply to the application of the transitional provisions.

14.55 In respect of unfunded schemes, however, the charge for pension costs is made during employees' service lives and tax relief obtained when pensions are paid during retirement. The individual timing differences will ultimately reverse, but the aggregate liability of an unfunded scheme may well continue to grow because new provisions are made each year. In such a situation, it needs to be considered whether a deferred tax asset may be recognised, since SSAP 15 does not allow recognition of deferred tax assets where their recoverability is permanently deferred.

Disclosure of pension information

14.56 The standard requires sufficient information to be disclosed to give the user a proper understanding of the impact of the pension arrangements on a company's financial statements. [SSAP 24 para 45]. In contrast, company law contains very limited disclosure provisions in respect of pensions. The Act requires disclosure of:

- The pension costs charged.

- Any pension commitments included under any provision shown in the company's balance sheet.

- Any such commitments for which no provision has been made.

[4 Sch 50(4)].

14.57 In addition, SSAP 24 prescribes extensive disclosure which is detailed in the paragraphs that follow.

Defined contribution schemes

14.58 A company should disclose the following:

- The nature of the scheme (that is, defined contribution).

- The accounting policy.

- The pension cost charge for the period.

- Any outstanding or prepaid contributions at the balance sheet date.

[SSAP 24 para 87].

The appendix to the standard gives an example of disclosure in respect of a defined contribution scheme.

Defined benefit schemes

14.59 Because the obligation of an employer providing such a scheme is greater and more uncertain, more extensive disclosures are required. Examples are provided in the appendix to SSAP 24. In particular, a good deal of precise actuarial information is required. The standard requires the following information to be disclosed:

- The nature of the scheme (that is, defined benefit).

- Whether it is funded or unfunded.

- The accounting policy and, if different, the funding policy.

- A statement as to whether the pension cost is assessed in accordance with the advice of a professionally qualified actuary and, if so, the date of the most recent formal actuarial valuation. If the actuary is an employee or officer of the company or group, then this fact should be disclosed.

- The pension cost charge for the period together with explanations of significant changes in the charge compared to that in the previous accounting period.

- Any provisions or prepayments in the balance sheet resulting from a difference between the amounts recognised as cost and the amounts funded or paid directly.

- The amount of any deficiency on a current funding level basis, together with the action taken to rectify it. This is analogous to a discontinuance valuation. It is a measure of solvency that compares the assets of the scheme with the actuarial value of liabilities, in respect of benefits that would arise if all the members were to leave the scheme at the valuation date. There is no requirement to disclose a surplus on a current funding level basis.

- An outline of the results of the most recent actuarial valuation on an ongoing basis. An 'ongoing valuation' is defined as a valuation that assumes the scheme will continue in existence, new members will be admitted (if appropriate), and that allows for expected increases in earnings in valuing its liabilities. The actuarial information to be disclosed includes:

  - The actuarial method used and the main actuarial assumptions.

  - The market value of the scheme assets at the date of their valuation or review.

  - The level of funding expressed in percentage terms, and comments on any material surplus or deficit revealed by this.

- Any commitment to make additional payments over a limited number of years.

- The accounting treatment adopted in respect of a refund made under deduction of tax (see second point in para 14.42) where a credit appears in the financial statements in relation to it.

- Details of the expected effects on future costs of any material changes in the group's and/or company's pension arrangements.

[SSAP 24 para 88].

These disclosure requirements are illustrated in Table 53 overleaf.

14.60 The requirement for companies to disclose their actuarial methods and principal assumptions is quite onerous. It includes, for example, assumptions relating to the future rate of return on investments, and

Table 53: Disclosure of pension costs and pension scheme information.

Extract from The BOC Group plc Report & Accounts 30th September 1989.

Note extract

16. Retirement benefits

a) Pension costs

The Company and its subsidiaries operate a number of pension schemes throughout the world. The total pension cost for the Group was £9.3 million (1988: £11.4 million).

The principal schemes are of the defined benefit type. Those located in the UK and Australia are based on final salary and in the US on annual salary. The schemes are self administered and the schemes' assets are held independently of the Group's finances.

The pension cost is assessed in accordance with the advice of professionally qualified actuaries and, in respect of the principal schemes, the pension cost for the year ended 30th September was:

	£ million
Regular Pension cost based on a constant percentage of earnings over the employees' service lives with the Group	(22.8)
Variations from regular cost based on a constant percentage of current and estimated future earnings over the average remaining service lives of current employees	24.1
Net Pension credit to operating profit	1.3

NOTE 16 CONTINUED

The results of the most recent valuations of the principal schemes were:

	UK	US	AUSTRALIA
Date of most recent valuation or review	5th April 1987	1st January 1988	30th September 1987
Method used	Profected Unit	Projected Unit	Attained Age
Main assumptions:			
Rate of price inflation	5.0%	6.0%	6.0%
Real return on investments relative to price inflation	4.0%	3.0%	3.0%
Increase in earnings relative to price inflation	1.5%	0.5%	1.0%
Market Value of investments at last valuation date	£480m	£201m	£108m
Actuarial surplus at last valuation date	£142m	£36m	£34m
Level of funding being the actuarial value of assets expressed as a percentage of the accrued service liabilities	150%	124%	177%

Acting on the advice of the respective actuaries, Group funding of these schemes remains suspended and further Group funding is unlikely to be required during the next financial year.

Table 53 continued

b) Other Retirement benefits

The Group has a commitment in the US to provide post-retirement medical benefits to former employees. The cost incurred for the year was £2.8 million which includes a provision of £1.3 million to meet future liabilities.

future increases in salaries and pensions (as illustrated in Table 53). Relatively small changes in the forecast rates could substantially affect the size of any surplus or deficit arising.

14.61 The level of funding that must be disclosed for the most recent valuation is an actuarial measure of the extent to which the assets of the scheme are sufficient to cover its liabilities (as illustrated in Table 53). [SSAP 24 para 66]. It compares the actuarial obligations with the actuarial valuation of assets. This requirement has not been without controversy, because disclosure of surpluses could be sensitive information. This would especially be so, for example, when a company is subject to a possible takeover.

Subsidiary companies

14.62 A subsidiary that is a member of a group pension scheme and whose holding company is registered in the UK or the Republic of Ireland is exempted from disclosing most of the actuarial information required by the standard. [SSAP 24 para 90]. Instead, it need in effect only disclose the nature of the group scheme to which it belongs, together with the name of the holding company in whose financial statements the actuarial particulars relating to the group are given. The remaining disclosure requirements of SSAP 24 are applicable to all group companies. Further, the standard apply to all participating companies.

Combined disclosure

14.63 Where a company or group operates more than one pension scheme, SSAP 24 allows disclosure to be given on a combined basis. This is so unless disclosure of information about individual schemes is necessary for a proper understanding of the financial statements. [SSAP 24 para 89]. However, where one scheme produces a deficiency on a current funding level basis, disclosure of the deficiency should not be avoided by setting it off against a surplus in another scheme.

Transitional arrangements

14.64 The accounting and disclosure requirements of SSAP 24 are effective for accounting periods beginning on or after 1st July 1988.

14.65 Where the implementation of the accounting provisions of SSAP 24 necessitates a change of accounting policy in dealing with experience surpluses or deficiencies, special considerations apply. These will be where an employer is in the middle of a contribution holiday, or period of reduced or increased contributions to reduce a surplus or fund a deficiency. SSAP 24 refers to a 'cumulative adjustment' which is essentially an estimate of the surplus or deficiency in the scheme at the beginning of the accounting period in which the standard is first applied.

14.66 The transitional provisions of SSAP 24 give companies the option of either of the following methods of dealing with the cumulative adjustment:

- Spreading forward any surplus or deficiency over the employees' expected remaining service lives.

- Making a prior year adjustment (the common interpretation is that the resulting adjustment would only be made to opening reserves and no attempt would be made to restate the previous years' profit and loss account).

The way in which the transitional provisions have been applied should be disclosed in the financial statements for the period in which SSAP 24 is first implemented (for example, see Table 54). [SSAP 24 para 92].

14.67 Where the company has a surplus in its fund, the choice of method may depend on whether the company is more interested in improving earnings per share by reducing the future pension cost to be charged, or in improving gearing by increasing assets and reserves immediately. Similar considerations will apply for deficiencies. The following example illustrates both these approaches. The figures used are the same as in the previous example. For the sake of simplicity, the example ignores the effect of interest on balance sheet figures.

Example

The actuarial valuation at 31st December 1986 of the pension scheme of a company showed a surplus of £240,000. The actuary recommended that the company eliminate the surplus by taking a contribution holiday in 1987 and 1988 and then paying contributions of £45,000 for the next 8 years to 1996. From 1997 the standard contributions of £60,000 will become payable. The average remaining service life of employees in the scheme at 31st December 1988 was 10 years. The company is adopting SSAP 24 for the first time in their financial year to 31st December 1989.

The contribution holiday for the two years will have the effect of reducing the surplus of £240,000 at the beginning of 1989 to £120,000. The company may choose to spread the surplus over the average remaining service life of employees or make a prior year adjustment by incorporating the surplus of £120,000 as a prepayment in the balance sheet and adjusting the opening reserve accordingly.

Table 54: Disclosure of accounting policy on pension costs and pension scheme information following adoption of SSAP24.

Extract from Granada Group PLC Annual Report 30th September 1989.

Note extract

10 *Pension costs*

The expected cost of pensions in respect of the Group's defined benefit pension schemes is charged to the profit and loss account so as to spread the cost of pensions over the service lives of employees in the schemes. Variations from the regular cost are spread over the remaining service lives of current employees in the schemes. The pension cost is assessed in accordance with the advice of qualified actuaries. This is a change of accounting policy following adoption of SSAP24. In previous years, the charge to the profit and loss account was the actual amount of contributions made by the Group to the schemes.

Note 3 *Pension Scheme*

The Group operates a number of pension schemes around the world. The major schemes are of the defined benefit type with assets held in separate trustee administered funds.

The Group's main UK schemes, which cover the majority of UK employees, were assessed by Minet Consultancy Services and William M Mercer Fraser, consulting actuaries, as at 31 December 1988 using the projected unit method. The principal actuarial assumptions adopted were that, over the long term, the annual rate of return on investments would be 2% higher than the annual increase in total pensionable remuneration and 4.5% higher than the annual increase in present and future pensions in payment. With effect from 1 October 1989 the Group's main UK schemes have been merged. Based on the 31 December 1988 assessment the actuarial value of the assets of the merged scheme was sufficient to cover 190% of the benefits that had accrued to members, after allowing for benefit improvements and expected future increases in pensionable remuneration. The actuarial surplus is being spread over the average remaining service lives of current employees with the exception of that relating to the Electronic Rentals Group plc at the date of acquisition which has been credited to goodwill. On the recommendation of the actuaries no company contributions will be made to the scheme for at least three years. The market value of the scheme's assets as at 31 December 1988 was £345 million.

The net pensions credit for the Group was £1.6 million (1988 – cost of £6.2 million). The credit arises principally as a result of the actuarial surplus in the main UK schemes. A prepayment of £88.9 million is included in debtors representing the surplus on the assessment of the Electronic Rentals Group pensions scheme at 31 December 1988 and the excess of the pension credit to profit over the amounts funded during the year.

Transitional provisions

	Spreading		Prior Year adjustment	
Year	P&L charge £'000	Provision £'000	P&L charge £'000	Prepayment £'000
Opening balance		Nil		120
1989	48	(3)	60	105
1990	48	(6)	60	90
1991	48	(9)	60	75
1992	48	(12)	60	60
1993	48	(15)	60	45
1994	48	(18)	60	30
1995	48	(21)	60	15
1996	48	(24)	60	-
1997	48	(12)	60	-
1998	48	-	60	-

Note: Under the spreading method, the annual pension cost = £60,000 - $\frac{£12,000}{10,000}$ = £48,000

The prepayment reduces each year by £60,000 - £45,000 = £15,000

Interest payable and similar charges

14.68 'Interest payable and similar charges' appears as a separate item in all the profit and loss account formats. Furthermore the Act requires certain additional disclosures in respect of interest. Note 16 to the profit and loss account format requires that interest payable to group undertakings must be disclosed separately. In addition, Schedule 4 requires the disclosure of the amount of the interest on or any similar charges in respect of:

- Bank loans and overdrafts, and other loans that are repayable:
  - Otherwise than by instalments wholly within five years of the balance sheet date.
  - By instalments wholly within five years of the balance sheet date.
- Loans of any other kind made to the company.

[4 Sch 53(2)].

This paragraph can be interpreted in several different ways. However, the DTI has confirmed that it is intended that each of the items above should be separately disclosed. Table 55 illustrates these disclosure requirements.

14.69 The requirement to give the above analyses does not apply to either interest or charges on loans from group undertakings. But it does apply to interest or charges on all other loans, whether or not these are made on the security of a debenture (see Table 55). [4 Sch 53(2)].

Table 55: Disclosure of interest payable and similar charges.

Extract from J Sainsbury plc Annual Report & Accounts 18th March 1989.

Note extract

17 Net Interest (Payable)/Receivable

	Group 1989 £m	1988 £m
Interest receivable	44.3	34.3
Interest payable:		
Banks and Other Interest on loans wholly repayable within five years.	(81.3)	(52.0)
Interest on loans payable by instalments within five years	(1.2)	(0.2)
On loans not wholly repayable within five years		
Debenture Interest	(0.1)	(0.1)
Loan Stock Interest	(0.2)	(0.2)
Other Loans payable by instalments	(1.7)	(1.3)
Finance Leases	(2.3)	(1.1)
Interest Capitalised	33.0	29.1
	(53.8)	(25.8)
	(9.5)	8.6

Taxation

Disclosure

14.70 The notes to the profit and loss account must disclose the following amounts in respect of taxation:

- The amount of the charge for UK corporation tax. Where this amount would have been greater but for double taxation relief, the gross amount must also be disclosed.

- The amount of the charge for UK income tax.

- The amount of the charge for taxation that has been imposed outside the UK on profits, income and (to the extent to which it has been charged to income) capital gains.

[4 Sch 54(3)].

14.71 SSAP 8 requires that the UK corporation tax should specify:

- The charge for corporation tax on the income of the year. (Where such corporation tax includes transfers between the deferred taxation account and the profit and loss account, and these transfers are material, they should be separately disclosed.)

- Tax attributable to franked investment income (see chapter 13 para 13.64).

- Irrecoverable ACT (see chapter 11, paras 11.44 to 11.50).

- The relief for overseas taxation (that is, double taxation relief).

[SSAP 8 para 22(a)].

14.72 The notes to the profit and loss account must disclose the basis on which the charges to both UK corporation tax and income tax have been computed. They must disclose also details of any special circumstances that affect any liability to taxation (whether for the financial year in question or for future years, and whether in respect of profits, income or capital gains). [4 Sch 54(1)(2)]. 'Special circumstances' could include (for example) the effect on the tax charge (if this is material) of losses either utilised or carried forward. In addition, the rate of taxation that has been used in calculating the above figures should be disclosed. (SSAP 8 requires this disclosure only if the rate of corporation tax is not known for all or part of the financial year. [SSAP 8 para 23]. However, it is generally accepted accounting practice to disclose the rate in all circumstances.)

14.73 In addition to the requirement to disclose the amount of double taxation relief in the fourth point of paragraph 14.71 above, SSAP 8 requires that the financial statements should disclose the total overseas taxation figure (including both relieved and unrelieved overseas taxation) and also that part of the unrelieved overseas taxation that arises from either the payment or the proposed payment of dividends. [SSAP 8 para 22(b)].

14.74 Further to the requirements of both the Act and SSAP 8, SSAP 15 requires that the amount of deferred tax that relates to the company's ordinary activities should be disclosed separately as part of the tax on the profit or loss on ordinary activities. [SSAP 15 para 33]. SSAP 15 also requires that the notes to the financial statements should disclose any amounts of deferred tax that have not been provided in the year, analysed into the major components (see also chapter 11 paras 11.59 and 11.60). [SSAP 15 para 35].

14.75 Where deferred tax is not provided on earnings that are retained overseas, this fact should be noted. [SSAP 15 para 44]. Table 56 illustrates the taxation disclosure requirements detailed above.

Table 56: Disclosure of the profit and loss account taxation charge on ordinary activities.

Extract from Thorn EMI plc Annual Report 31st March 1989.

Note extract

4. Taxation

	1989	1988
	£m	£m
Taxation on profit on ordinary activities:		
United Kingdom:		
Corporation tax at 35% (1988: 35%)	(30.5)	(35.5)
Double taxation relief	1.7	1.0
	(28.8)	(34.5)
Overseas taxation	(39.6)	(32.1)
Deferred taxation:		
United Kingdom	(7.5)	(10.7)
Overseas	(13.6)	0.1
Related companies' taxation:		
United Kingdom	(5.3)	(4.0)
Overseas	(6.0)	(4.6)
Prior year adjustments	4.7	6.8
	(96.1)	(79.0)

The charge for taxation has been reduced by £1.5m (1988: £2.7m) in respect of taxation likely to be deferred for the foreseeable future in respect of timing differences.

14.76 Where a company has incurred an extraordinary profit or loss, the notes must disclose separately the taxation on the profit or loss on ordinary activities and the taxation on the extraordinary profit or loss. [4 Sch 54(3)]. The tax treatment of extraordinary items are further considered in chapter 15 para 15.20 to 15.24.

14.77 The Act does not indicate the type of information that must be included under the profit and loss account heading 'other taxes not shown under the above items'. At present, no such 'other taxes' are collected in the UK, and so this heading in the format appears to be superfluous for the time being.

Group relief

14.78 Where a company that is a member of a group is determining the amount of deferred taxation to be provided, SSAP 15 requires that it should take into account any group relief that it expects (on reasonable evidence) to be available and also any charge for that relief. Any assumptions the company has made in anticipation of either the receipt or the surrender of group relief should be noted. [SSAP 15 para 43]. When group relief gives rise to special circumstances that affect the liability to taxation of either the year or future years, it ought (if it has a material effect) to be disclosed to comply with paragraph 54 of Schedule 4 to the Act (see para 14.72).

14.79 Group relief may be obtained without a payment passing between the companies concerned. Where it is not proposed that the claimant company should pay the surrendering company for the tax loss, the trading loss may be financed in another way (for example, by way of a loan). However, non-payment or underpayment for group relief received is objectionable if there are minority interests in the company. The reason for this is that if a company that has minority shareholders surrenders its losses for group relief purposes without receiving an adequate compensation payment, the minority shareholders' interests will be impaired. Non-payment or underpayment for group relief is also objectionable if the company is insolvent or unable to make a distribution of the amount in question. Likewise, overpayment for group relief is objectionable if there are minority interests in the receiving company.

14.80 The claimant company may make a payment to the surrendering company of any amount that does not exceed the gross amount of the group relief that it receives. The payment may take one of the following forms:

- The payment may be of the amount of the corporation tax saving by reason of group relief. Such a payment would normally be appropriate where a partly-owned subsidiary is involved (whether as the claimant company or as the surrendering company) in order to preserve the minority shareholders' interests.

- The payment may be of the gross amount of the group relief, but no more than that. Any part of a payment in excess of the gross amount of the group relief (for example, to finance the balance of a loss) is not a payment in respect of group relief, and it should not be dealt with as such in the financial statements.

- The payment may be made of any other amount up to a maximum of the gross amount of the group relief (as in the second point above) if it is desired to finance only part of the surrendering company's loss.

14.81 With group relief where no payment passes between the companies concerned, the companies' financial statements should normally disclose the facts and the impact.

14.82 Where a payment passes between the companies concerned, the accounting treatment will depend upon the nature of the payment, as follows:

Example 1

Where the payment represents the amount of the tax saving, it should be dealt with as part of the tax charge to bring this into proper relationship with the profits, and it should be disclosed as shown below.

The claimant company

	£000	£000
Profit on ordinary activities before taxation		110
Tax on profit on ordinary activities	18	
Amount payable to holding company (subsidiary or fellow subsidiary) in respect of tax saved by group relief	21	
(that is, £110,000 x 35%)		39
Profit for the financial year		71

The surrendering company

	£000
Loss on ordinary activities before taxation	(60)
Amount receivable from subsidiary (holding company or fellow subsidiary) in respect of tax saved by group relief	21
Loss for the financial year	(39)

Example 2

Where the payment is equivalent to the gross amount of group relief, and the companies adopt Format 1 or 2 for the profit and loss account, it should be dealt with in arriving at the profit before taxation, and it should be disclosed as shown below.

The claimant company

	£000
Payable on ordinary activities	110
Amount payable to holding company (subsidiary or fellow subsidiary) in respect of group relief	(60)
Profit before taxation	50
Tax on profit on ordinary activities (being £50,000 x 35%)	18
Profit for the financial year	32

The surrendering company

	£000
Loss on ordinary activities (of which £10,000 disallowed for tax purposes)	(70)
Amount receivable from subsidiary (holding company or fellow subsidiary) in respect of group relief	60
Loss for the financial year	(10)

> Note: All the company's tax losses have been used by group relief claimed by a subsidiary (the holding company or a fellow subsidiary). Therefore, they are not available to be set off against the company's future profits in computing the tax liability on those profits.

Example 3

Where the payment is of any other amount up to a maximum of the gross amount of the group relief, it should be dealt with in arriving at the profit before taxation, and it should be suitably described and amplified by a note, as shown below.

The claimant company

	£000
Profit on ordinary activities	110
Contribution towards loss of holding company (subsidiary or fellow subsidiary) payable by way of group relief	(40)
Profit before taxation	70
Tax on profit on ordinary activities (see note below) (being, (£70,000 x 35%) - £7,000)	18
Profit for the financial year	52

Note: The charge for taxation has been reduced by £7,000 (being (£60,000 - £40,000) x 35%) by reason of group relief receivable in addition to that appropriate to the contribution towards the loss of the holding company (subsidiary or fellow subsidiary) that is charged against the company's profits.

The surrendering company

	£000
Loss on ordinary activities	(60)
Contribution towards loss receivable from subsidiary (holding company or fellow subsidiary) by way of group relief	40
Loss for the financial year	(20)

Note: The whole of the company's losses for taxation purposes have been absorbed by way of group relief claimed by a subsidiary (the holding company or a fellow subsidiary). Consequently, they are not available to be set off against the company's profits future profits in computing the liability to taxation on those profits.

Example 4

Where the group relief payment is for an amount that is less than the amount of the tax saving, the disclosure in the company's financial statements should be as follows.

	£000
Profit on ordinary activities	110
Tax on profit on ordinary activities (being, (£110,000 x 35%) - £10,000)	29
	81

Note: The charge for taxation has been reduced by £10,000 by reason of group relief receivable from the holding company for which no payment has been made.

In this situation, the treatment in the surrendering company would be similar to that shown in example 3.

14.83 ACT can also be surrendered from one group company to another for a payment of any amount up to the amount of the ACT surrendered. Where the payment is for an amount that is less than the ACT surrendered, then the difference should be credited to the tax charged in the profit and loss account. A note similar to that shown above should explain the treatment that has been adopted.

14.84 Where a payment for group relief is brought into account in a year subsequent to that to which it relates, it should be appropriately described (depending upon the nature of the payment) as set out in examples 1 and 2, with the addition of words indicating that it relates to previous years. If the tax relief appropriate to the payment is brought to account at the same time, that too should be described appropriately.

14.85 The claimant company's profit that is available for group relief may include capital gains that have been taken to extraordinary items, rather than to the profit before taxation. Without a claim for group relief, the corporation tax on the capital gain would normally be charged to extraordinary items as a deduction from the gain. If a claim for group relief is made in these circumstances, the claimant company's accounting treatment should normally be as follows:

- The loss that is being surrendered should be applied to the profits on the following basis. The tax charge should be calculated with and without including extraordinary items, and the difference between these two amounts will then be effectively due to the extraordinary items [SSAP 6 para 8]. The loss surrendered should be apportioned first to the profit on ordinary activities up to the extent of the attributable tax charge and any remaining relief against the tax charge on the extraordinary items. The payment for the relief given should then be dealt with by apportioning the payment between ordinary and extraordinary items, on the same basis as the relief surrendered.

- If the amount of corporation tax chargeable on extraordinary items is reduced by a claim for group relief, and no payment is made for this, it may be desirable, on consolidation, for a transfer to be made (equivalent to the amount of that reduction), from extraordinary items to reduce the tax charge on ordinary activities in the profit and loss account.

Provided that some other group companies are making profits, such a transfer would have the effect, on consolidation, of bringing the group tax charge into proper relationship with the group profit on ordinary activities before taxation as shown in the consolidated profit and loss account. At the same time, it would leave a charge which, in the consolidated profit and loss account, will represent corporation tax on the capital gain.

- Where the charge to extraordinary items in respect of corporation tax on a capital gain is reduced by group relief, and no compensating set-off against the tax charge is made on consolidation, a note explaining the treatment should be appended to extraordinary items.

- Certain types of company whose articles of association contain restrictions on the distribution of capital profits (for example, investment companies), need to take care that they do not effectively pay away a capital gain as a group relief payment of the gross amount of the group relief to a subsidiary or a fellow subsidiary, because this would defeat the purpose of the articles. There is, however, nothing to prevent payment being made of an amount equivalent to the tax that would otherwise have been paid on the gain.

Other profit and loss disclosure items

14.86 In addition to the items required to be disclosed by the formats, the following three further amounts require to be disclosed:

- Any amounts that have been set aside for redeeming either share capital or loans. [4 Sch 53(1)(3)].

- Any amounts that have been charged in respect of the hire of plant and machinery. [4 Sch 53(1)(6)].

- The amount of the auditors' remuneration paid in cash (including any expenses the auditors incurred and the company reimbursed) and the nature and estimated money value of any benefits in kind paid to the auditors. [Sec 390A].

Chapter 15

THE PROFIT AND LOSS ACCOUNT - EXCEPTIONAL AND EXTRAORDINARY ITEMS

Chapter 15

THE PROFIT AND LOSS ACCOUNT - EXCEPTIONAL AND EXTRAORDINARY ITEMS

Introduction

15.1 This chapter deals with the accounting treatment and disclosure of extraordinary and exceptional items. This area of accounting has caused considerable difficulties over the years, not least because a company's earnings per share is calculated on the profit before extraordinary items. Whether or not particular items are classified as extraordinary will depend on the particular circumstances. Items that are extraordinary in one company will not necessarily be extraordinary in another. SSAP 6 'Extraordinary items and prior year adjustments', which was revised in 1986, now provides much clearer rules for determining whether an item is extraordinary or not by clarifying the distinction, by defining each of the terms and providing lists of examples of items which might fall into each category. Prior year adjustments are considered in chapter 16.

Exceptional items

15.2 Formats 2 and 4 have a specific position for the item 'exceptional amounts written off current assets'. However, the Act does not indicate the place where other exceptional items should be shown, although, in accordance with the requirements set out in paragraph 15.6 below, they must be disclosed in the notes to the financial statements.

15.3 The original standard did not define exceptional items, but SSAP 6 (revised) does contain a definition that follows closely the description in paragraph 57 of Schedule 4 to the Act (see para 15.6 below). The definition in SSAP 6 states that exceptional items are those

> *"material items which derive from events or transactions that fall within the ordinary activities of the company, and which need to be disclosed separately by virtue of their size or incidence if the financial statements are to give a true and fair view."* [SSAP 6 para 29].

15.4 SSAP 6 gives the following examples of items that may be classified as exceptional if they are material:

- Redundancy costs relating to continuing business segments.

- Reorganisation costs unrelated to the discontinuance of a business segment.
- Previously capitalised development expenditure on intangible fixed assets written off other than as part of a process of amortisation.
- Amounts transferred to employee share schemes.
- Profits or losses on the disposal of fixed assets.
- Abnormal charges for bad debts and write-offs of stock and work in progress. (These items would be included in 'exceptional amounts written off current assets' in Formats 2 and 4.)
- Surpluses arising on the settlement of insurance claims.
- Amounts received in settlement of insurance claims for consequential loss of profits.

15.5 SSAP 6 states that it should be acceptable to relegate exceptional items of this nature to a note to the profit and loss account (for example, see Table 57). However, the standard requires that where the profit before exceptional items needs to be shown separately in order to give a true and fair view, exceptional items should be disclosed as a separate item on the face of the profit and loss account. [SSAP 6 para 3].

Table 57: Disclosure of exceptional items.

Extract from Bass plc Annual Report 30th Sept 1989.

Note extract

4. EXCEPTIONAL ITEMS

Exceptional surplus on disposal of fixed assets and subsidiaries of £64m (1988 £20m) is in respect of the sale of certain European hotels.

Exceptional reorganisation costs of £34m (1988 Nil) arise from the restructuring of the Group's brewing and pub retailing activities.

15.6 The notes to the profit and loss account must disclose particulars of any amounts that fall within the company's ordinary activities, but are exceptional by virtue of either their size or their incidence. Examples of such items are abnormal charges for bad debts or stock write-offs, abnormal provisions for losses on long-term contracts, and significant adjustments of prior-year taxation provisions. [4 Sch 57].

Extraordinary items

15.7 The Act does not define the term 'extraordinary'. But SSAP 6 defines it as follows:

> *"those items which derive from events or transactions that fall outside the ordinary activities of the company and which are therefore expected not to recur frequently or regularly. They do not include exceptional items nor do they include prior year items merely because they relate to a prior year."* [SSAP 6 para 30].

15.8 The profit and loss account formats require extraordinary items to be analysed under the four headings of: 'extraordinary income', 'extraordinary charges', 'extraordinary profit or loss' and 'tax on extraordinary profit or loss'. It is not correct simply to list all such items under one main heading 'extraordinary items'. However, the detailed breakdown may be given in a note, rather than on the face of the profit and loss account, and in practice, many companies adopt this form of disclosure (for example, see Table 58 overleaf). [4 Sch 57]. SSAP 6, however, requires only the net amount of extraordinary items to be disclosed. [SSAP 6 para 6].

15.9 Whether or not particular items are classified as extraordinary will depend on the particular circumstances and the nature of a company's business. Subject to this, SSAP 6 gives some examples of items that may be classified as extraordinary. They are:

- The discontinuance of a significant business segment, either through termination or disposal.
- The sale of an investment not acquired with the intention of resale (such as investments in subsidiary and associated companies).
- Profits or losses on the disposal of fixed assets.
- Provision made for the permanent diminution in value of a fixed asset because of extraordinary events during the period.
- The expropriation of assets.
- A change in the basis of taxation, or a significant change in Government fiscal policy.

[SSAP 6 para 4].

Table 58: Disclosure of extraordinary items.

Extract from Hogg Robinson Gardener Mountain PLC 31st December 1988.

Note extract

10 EXTRAORDINARY ITEMS	*Year to 31.12.88 £000*	*Unaudited year to 31.12.87 £000*	*9 months to 31.12.87 £000*
Provision for out of court settlement in relation to Rotterdamse litigation	(4,000)	–	–
Profits less losses on disposal, after provision for reduction in value, of associated companies	735	801	84
PCW settlement	(100)	–	–
Release of tax provision no longer required on cost of previously unlet floors of the Group's headquarters	413	850	850
Release of tax provision no longer required on the sale of the Group's previous headquarters due to the availability of roll-over relief	–	2,006	–
Costs and other amounts written off on the divestment of Lloyd's agencies	–	(764)	–
Demerger, defence and abortive merger costs	(174)	(1,594)	(1,594)
Provision for reorganisation of the Group's headquarters following demerger	–	(1,601)	(1,601)
	(3,126)	(302)	(2,261)
Related taxation: Current	700	(633)	(375)
Deferred	700	–	–
Extraordiany loss	(1,726)	(935)	(2,636)

15.10 It should be noted that SSAP 6 includes profits or losses on the disposal of fixed assets in the examples of items that may be classified as exceptional and extraordinary (see paras 15.4 and 15.9). A material surplus or deficit of a fixed asset, including property may be either exceptional or extraordinary, according to the nature of the event which gave rise to the disposal. [SSAP 6 para 15]. Examples of the extraordinary treatment might include the profit or loss on the sale of property which is surplus to requirements as a result of the closure of a business segment which formerly used that property. The exceptional treatment might include sales of surplus properties to raise working capital, but which do not result from the closure of a business segment.

Terminated activities and reorganisations

15.11 SSAP 6 draws a sharp distinction between exceptional and extraordinary items in respect of terminated activities and reorganisations. The distinction is based on whether or not the relevant costs are related to a continuing or a discontinuing business segment (for example, see Table 59).

Table 59: Disclosure of an accounting policy for the treatment of closure, disposal and reorganisation costs.

Extract from Guinness PLC Report and Accounts 31st December 1988.

Accounting policies extract

Closure, disposal and reorganisations costs

The costs of closure, disposal and related major reorganisation programmes arising through discontinuance of a significant part of a Group business activity are charged as extraordinary items. Other reorganisation costs, in continuing business activities, are charged against profit before taxation and separately disclosed if material. Amounts charged include provision for foreseeable future costs.

8. Extraordinary items

	1988	*1987*
	£m	*£m*
Gain on businesses sold	16	230
Other	–	29
	16	259
Taxation relating to gain on businesses sold	–	(42)
	16	217

15.12 A business segment is defined as:

> *"A material and separately identifiable component of the business operations of a company or group whose activities, assets and results can be clearly distinguished from the remainder of the company's activities. A business segment will normally have its own separate product lines or markets."* [SSAP 6 para 32].

15.13 The above definition of a business segment is still open to different interpretations. It may mean that the product lines and the markets should be different from the rest of the company's operations or it may mean that the product lines and the markets should be 'separately identifiable' (that is, that the assets and results can be clearly distinguished from those of the company as a whole). The accounting treatment will, therefore, depend both on the particular circumstances and on the interpretation placed on the definition of a business segment.

Example

A company closes one factory, which makes product A, and reorganises its second factory, which makes product B. The company wishes to treat the closure costs of both factories as extraordinary because they stem from the same decision.

The fact that these two events are the consequence of the same decision should not affect their treatment. If product A can be identified as a business segment it would qualify as extraordinary. The same considerations would apply to product B. If the reorganisation involves both the closure of separately identifiable departments and other costs relating to continuing business segments, part of the reorganisation costs may be extraordinary and part exceptional.

15.14 Where a decision has been made to discontinue a business segment or where a significant business segment has been terminated, SSAP 6 states that a provision is necessary for the consequences of all decisions taken up to the balance sheet date. This compliments the requirement of SSAP 17 which includes, as a non-adjusting post balance sheet event, the closure of a significant part of the trading activities, if this was not anticipated at the year end. SSAP 17, however, also provides that a material post balance sheet event should be an adjusting event if it indicates that the application of the going concern concept to the whole or a material part of the company is not appropriate. Therefore, there still remains some room for the exercise of judgement. SSAP 6 states that the provision will usually include some or all of the following items:

- Redundancy costs (net of government contributions).
- Costs of retaining key personnel during the run-down period.
- Profits or losses arising from the disposal of assets, including anticipated ongoing costs such as rent, rates and security.
- Pension costs.
- Bad and doubtful debts arising from the decision to close.
- All debits and credits arising from trading after the commencement of implementation.
- Any losses due to penalty clauses in contracts.

[SSAP 6 para 11].

15.15 Where such provisions occur over a number of periods, they are not prevented from being treated as extraordinary. This means that where a company has experienced a long period of rationalisation (for example, more than five years) which has involved the closures of major business segments, the costs of rationalisation can still be treated as extraordinary over a number of years notwithstanding that they occurred frequently. Also, it does not matter whether the costs result from either a single decision or a number of separate unrelated decisions. [SSAP 6 para 12].

15.16 All debits and credits arising from trading after the date of implementation should be included in the provision for termination. The date of implementation was chosen rather than the decision date because it was felt that it was less likely to be manipulated. It does pose problems in practice because closures are often implemented gradually with trading continuing virtually as normal until the last few weeks or months before closure. There is likely to be some variation in practice on the interpretation of 'implementation date' but it is difficult to envisage any better yardstick that might be chosen.

15.17 It is important to distinguish profits or losses arising on terminated activities from profits or losses which arise up to the date of disposal of a subsidiary. In the former situation, trading profits or losses arising from the date of implementation of a closure may be shown as part of the extraordinary item. In the latter situation, SSAP 14 on Group Accounts requires that the consolidated profit or loss account should include the subsidiary's results up to the date of disposal. SSAP 14 distinguishes these results from the gain or loss on the sale of the investment in the subsidiary, which under SSAP 6, may be shown as an extraordinary item.

15.18 Profits and losses which arise up to the date of disposal of a subsidiary are thus treated as part of the profits and losses on ordinary activities. Usually there is separate disclosure of such results if they are material in order to show the effect of the disposal on the consolidated results (see further 'Manual of Accounting - volume II' chapter 5). SSAP 6 requires similar disclosure for results of terminated activities up to the date of implementation. Paragraph 13 of the standard explains that profits or losses arising before the commencement of implementation are part of the trading for the year and are not extraordinary. However, because these results derive from a business segment that has been discontinued, they may require separate disclosures to enable the results of continuing activities to be ascertained. Most companies already do this in practice.

15.19 Reorganisation programmes which do not represent a discontinuance of a business segment are part of the normal business process and so their related costs should be included in the results of the company's ordinary activities (for example, see Table 60 overleaf). [SSAP 6 para 14].

Tax treatment of extraordinary items

15.20 The treatment of taxation on extraordinary items was not dealt with in the original standard. The revised standard states that the taxation attributable to extraordinary items should be calculated by computing the tax on the profit or loss on ordinary activities as if the extraordinary items did not exist. This notional tax charge may then be compared with the total estimated tax charge on the profit and loss for the financial year. Any additional tax charge or credit (including deferred tax) that arises should be attributed to the extraordinary items. [SSAP 6 para 38].

Table 60: Illustration of accounting policy for reorganisation costs.

Extract from Lucas Industries plc Annual Report 31st July 1989.

Accounting policies extract

REORGANISATION COSTS

When a decision to reorganise a business is made the anticipated costs are provided. Costs relating to the reorganisation of continuing businesses are charged in arriving at the profit before taxation and those relating to withdrawal from business segments are charged as extraordinary items. The operating results of business segments from which the group is withdrawing are excluded from the date the decision is taken and are shown separately in the notes to the accounts.

15.21 The same principles apply to group relief. If one company in a group has a large extraordinary loss, any tax relief that results could, for tax computation purposes, be surrendered as group relief, and then be set off against ordinary profits before tax in other group companies. For financial statements purposes, however, the same principles apply to consolidated financial statements as apply to individual financial statements. The tax attributable to a group's ordinary profits should, therefore, also be calculated as if the group's extraordinary items did not exist (see also chapter 14 para 14.85).

15.22 The principle of consistency requires that the tax effects of an extraordinary item should be treated as extraordinary even when the extraordinary item and the tax effects are recognised in different accounting periods. [SSAP 6 para 9]. For example, where there are tax losses brought forward, and those losses are attributable to extraordinary items in previous years, they should be disclosed as an extraordinary credit in the year in which they are used. In this situation, the extraordinary loss would be disclosed in one period and the tax relief attributable to that loss would also be disclosed as an extraordinary credit when it is utilised. Furthermore, a tax charge or credit may itself be an extraordinary item, for example in the case of significant adjustments to the deferred tax account arising from a change in the basis of taxation or a significant change in Government fiscal policy. [SSAP 6 para 10].

15.23 Where a company has incurred an extraordinary profit or loss, the notes must disclose separately the taxation of the profit or loss on ordinary activities and the taxation on the extraordinary profit or loss. [4 Sch 54(3)]. The profit and loss account formats also require separate disclosure of the taxation on an extraordinary item, because the formats include the heading 'tax on extraordinary profit or loss'. In addition, any deferred tax that relates to the extraordinary item should be shown separately as part of the taxation on the extraordinary item. [SSAP 15 para 34].

15.24 Where a deferred tax adjustment arises that is due to a change in either the rate of tax or tax allowances, it should normally be disclosed as part of the tax charge for the period and not as a prior year adjustment. However, where an adjustment arises because of a significant change in government fiscal policy, it should, where it is material, be treated as an extraordinary item. [SSAP 15 para 36 and SSAP 6 para 10]. SSAP 6 precludes such an adjustment from being treated as either a prior-year adjustment or an adjustment to opening reserves.

Preliminary profit statements, half-yearly reports and historical summaries

15.25 The International Stock Exchange requires listed companies and companies quoted on the USM to publish preliminary profits statements, half-yearly reports and historical summaries. It requires that extraordinary items should be disclosed in such reports. SSAP 6 also encourages companies to disclose extraordinary items in such statements. In addition, exceptional items should be disclosed where they have a material effect on the trend of profits and losses.

Chapter 16

THE PROFIT AND LOSS ACCOUNT - APPROPRIATIONS

Chapter 16

THE PROFIT AND LOSS ACCOUNT - APPROPRIATIONS

Introduction

16.1 This chapter deals with amounts appropriated from the profit and loss account in the form of dividends and transfers to and from reserves. The accounting treatment and disclosure of shares issued in lieu of cash dividends are examined. The treatment of prior year adjustments, that is prior year items that are adjusted against the opening balance of retained profits or reserves, and which are limited to items arising from changes in accounting policies and from the correction of fundamental errors, is also considered.

Dividends

16.2 'Dividends' is not an item that is found in the detailed profit and loss account formats. However, paragraph 3(7)(b) of Schedule 4 to the Act requires that a company's profit and loss account shall show separately the aggregate amount of any dividends paid and proposed. Dividends cannot be relegated to the notes to the profit and loss account: they must be disclosed on the face of it. The amount of dividends paid and proposed that is disclosed should exclude any amount of related ACT. [SSAP 8 para 4].

16.3 A question arises as to where dividends should be disclosed in the profit and loss account formats. SSAP 6 requires that dividends should be shown after tax and extraordinary items and also be deducted from the profit or loss for the financial year. [SSAP 6 para 34].

16.4 In order to pay a dividend, a company has to have sufficient distributable reserves. Distributable reserves are considered in detail in chapter 19.

16.5 In addition to the Act's requirements regarding dividends, The International Stock Exchange's Continuing Obligations for listed companies and the USM's General Undertaking for companies traded on the USM require particulars to be disclosed of any arrangements under which a shareholder has either waived or agreed to waive any dividends. [CO 21(o); GU 10(l)].

Shares in lieu of cash dividends (scrip dividends)

16.6 Many listed companies choose to make arrangements for ordinary shareholders to elect to receive their dividends in the form of additional ordinary shares rather than in cash. The share equivalent is sometimes referred to as a scrip dividend or a stock dividend and consists of shares fully paid up out of the company's profits. The advantages of issuing scrip dividends are that in the short-term, the company's cash position would be improved. Secondly, no ACT is payable in respect of those dividends taken in the form of shares. This can be of significant benefit to the company where ACT would otherwise be irrecoverable.

16.7 The paragraphs that follow consider the way that such dividends, and the corresponding issue of additional shares, should be treated in the company's financial statements.

16.8 Whether or not shares are offered in lieu of a final dividend, prudence requires that full provision for the dividend payment in cash should be made on all allotted shares at the year end. This is because the number of shareholders who will accept the offer is unknown. After the year end when some shareholders accept the offer to take additional shares instead of a cash dividend, the remaining credit balance in respect of the provision for the dividend has to be dealt with. There are two alternative bases which can be adopted and these are as follows:

- *The Bonus share basis:*

  This approach is based on dividing the scrip dividend into two separate events, namely the waiver of the dividend by the shareholder and the subsequent issue of bonus shares to that shareholder by the company. In this situation, the total excess provision is written back to the profit and loss account reserve, the bonus issue being made at par out of capital reserves (usually the share premium account or the revaluation reserve).

- *The Re-investment basis:*

  This approach recognises that the economic reality of an issue of shares under a scrip dividend scheme is not the issue of bonus shares, but rather the payment of a dividend. In substance, the issue of shares can be regarded as the payment of cash dividends with shareholders simultaneously reinvesting the proceeds in an issue of new shares. The dividend foregone by the shareholder in electing to take a scrip dividend of shares may, therefore, be treated as being the consideration paid for those new shares. Normally the consideration for the new shares will exceed their nominal value. Accordingly, the nominal value of the shares issued would be credited to the share capital account and the balance of the deemed consideration credited to the share premium account. The whole of the deemed consideration would be charged against the excess provision.

16.9 There are published examples of both methods being used in practice, as are illustrated overleaf in Tables 61 and 62. The choice of which method should be used would, however, depend on the provisions relating to scrip dividends that are contained in the company's articles of association. It should also be noted that the 'bonus issue' basis has a beneficial effect to the company in maximising the level of distributable reserves that remain available after the issue.

Reserve movements

General disclosure

16.10 The Act requires that any amounts set aside to, or proposed to be set aside to, or withdrawn from, or proposed to be withdrawn from, reserves should be shown separately in the company's profit and loss account. [4 Sch 3(7)(a)].

16.11 SSAP 6 further requires that all reserve movements, including the movement on the retained profit and loss account, should be disclosed in a single statement of movements on reserves. A reference should be made on the face of the profit and loss account to where the statement can be found, where it does not immediately follow that account. [SSAP 6 para 25]. An example of an acceptable disclosure is shown below.

Extract from profit and loss account

	£'000
Profit for the financial year	40
Dividends	(15)
Retained profit for the year	25

Movements on reserves are set out in Note X.

Extract from notes to the financial statements

Note X: Movements on reserves

	Profit and loss account £'000	Revaluation reserve £'000
Balance brought forward	75	150
Retained profit for the year	25	-
Transfer from revaluation reserve	10	(10)
Balance carried forward	110	140

Table 61: Treatment of scrip dividend under the 'Bonus share' basis.

Extract from The Hammerson Property Investment and Development Corporation plc Report and Accounts 31st December 1988.

Notes extract

19 Share capital (extract)

(a) Authorised and issued

	Ordinary shares of 25p each	'A' Ordinary (limited voting) shares of 25p each
	£000	£000
Authorised at 1st January 1988		
36,627,292 Ordinary shares of 25p each	9,157	
138,364,506 'A' Ordinary (limited voting) shares of 25p each		34,591
Unissued shares at 1st January 1988	346	2,986
Issued at 1st January 1988		
35,245,157 Ordinary shares of 25p each	8,811	
126,419,052 'A' Ordinary (limited voting) shares of 25p each		31,605
Movements during the year:		
(i) Issues under scheme to permit shareholders to receive shares in lieu of cash dividend (note 20)		
35,486 Ordinary shares of 25p each	9	
166,340 'A' Ordinary (limited voting) shares of 25p each		41

20 Share premium account

	£000
Balance 1st Janaury 1988	212,284
Premium on shares issued	25,292
	237,576
Scrip dividend [note 19 (a) (i)]	(50)
Balance 31st December 1988	237,526

23 Profit and loss account

	Group	Holding company
	£000	£000
Balance 1st January 1988	74,815	206,346
Adjustment in respect of 1987 final dividend elected to be taken in the form of additional shares	666	666
	75,481	207,012
Retained profit/(loss) for the year	32,637	(26,608)
Adjustment in respect of 1988 interim dividend elected to be taken in the form of additional shares	830	830
Transfer from foreign exchange fluctuation reserve (note 22)	23,814	457
Balance 31st December 1988	132,762	181,691

Table 62: Treatment of scrip dividend under the 'Re-investment' basis.

Extract from The Boots Company PLC Report and Accounts 31st March 1989.

Notes extract

19 Share capital (extract)

	1989 £m	1988 £m
Ordinary shares of 25p each:		
Authorised	300.0	
Allotted, called up and fully paid	231.7	230.7

Details of ordinary shares allotted during the year are as follows:

	Scrip dividends	Profit sharing scheme	Option schemes	Total
Number of shares allotted (million)	2.5	.7	.6	3.8
	£m	£m	£m	£m
Nominal value	.6	.2	.2	1.0
Share premium	4.7	1.4	.6	6.7
Consideration	5.3	1.6	.8	7.7

During the year appropxmately 27% of shareholders, owning 6.5% of shares, elected to take all or part of their dividends in shares.

20 Reserves (exctract)

	Parent			
	Share premium account £m	Revaluation reserve £m	Profit and loss account £m	Total £m
At 31st March 1988	7.4	–	477.1	484.5
Profit retained	–	–	80.6	80.6
Issue of shares	6.7	–	–	6.7
Share issue expenses	(.1)	–	–	(.1)
Surplus on property valuation	–	32.7	–	32.7
At 31st March 1989	14.0	32.7	557.7	604.4

Prior-year adjustments

16.12 'Prior-year adjustments' is not a statutory expression but the Act requires disclosure of the particulars of any amounts relating to a previous financial year that are included under any item in the profit and loss account. [4 Sch 57]. However, SSAP 6 defines them *"as those material adjustments applicable to prior years arising from changes in accounting policies or from the correction of fundamental errors. They do not include normal recurring corrections and or adjustments of accounting estimates made in prior years"*. [SSAP 6 para 31].

16.13 One of the fundamental accounting concepts is that there should be consistency of treatment of like items from one accounting period to the next. [SSAP 2 para 14]. A change in accounting policy should, therefore, not be made unless the new policy can be justified as being preferable to the one that it replaces. Where a company changes an accounting policy, SSAP 6 requires that those cumulative adjustments that apply to previous years and that have no bearing on the current year's results should be accounted for by restating those previous years. The object of this restatement is to adjust the opening balance of retained profits on to the new basis of accounting. Where it is practicable to do so, the effect of the change should be disclosed, by showing the amount involved separately in the restatement of the previous year (for example, see Table 63). [SSAP 6 paras 18, 19].

16.14 A fundamental error is an error that is significant enough to affect the truth and fairness of a company's financial statements. It has to be so fundamental that it would have led to the withdrawal of those financial statements if the error had come to light before those financial statements had been laid before the members at a general meeting (see further para 16.17). The correction of such an error should not be included in the current year's profit and loss account. Instead, it should be adjusted by restating previous years' results.

16.15 Where either a change in accounting policy or a correction of a fundamental error affects the corresponding profit and loss account and balance sheet for the immediately preceding period, that profit and loss account and the balance sheet should be adjusted onto the same basis as for the current period.

16.16 Under the original SSAP 6, prior-year adjustments were required to be shown in a statement of reserves immediately following the profit and loss account. Under the revised standard, the statement of reserves may be contained in a note, provided that there is a cross reference to the note from the profit and loss account (see para 16.11). The example that follows illustrates how a prior-year adjustment may be presented.

Table 63: Illustration of the disclosure of a prior year adjustment.

Extract from Cray Electronics Holdings P.L.C. Report and Accounts 29th April 1989.

Accounting policies extract

(d) Research and development

In previous years up to 30th April, 1988, the policy has been as follows:

"Research and development expenditure is written off as incurred, except that development expenditure incurred on an individual project is carried forward when its future recoverability can be foreseen with reasonable assurance. Any expenditure carried forward is amortised during the years following completion of the development in line with the sales from the related projects. The period of write off is a maximum of 3 years."

This policy has been changed with effect from 1st May, 1988 to:

"Expenditure on research and development is charged against income in the period in which it is incurred except to the extent that such expenditure is recoverable on contracts with third parties."

The result of this change in accounting policy which has been applied retrospectively has been to reduce the retained profit at 30th April, 1987 and the profit for the financial period 1987/88 by £2,476,000 and £1,537,000 respectively.

Additionally this change in accounting policy has impacted the results for the year to 29th April, 1989 to the extent that profits have been reduced on ordinary activities before taxation by £4,196,000 inclusive of costs in work-in-progress compared with the results that would have been stated had this policy not been changed.

Statement of Group Retained Profits

	1989 £000	1988 £000
Retained profit at 1st May, 1988 as previously reported	16,738	12,960
Adjustments for mergers	290	346
Prior year adjustment on change of accounting policy for development expenditure	(4,013)	(2,476)
Restated retained profit at 1st May, 1988	13,015	10,830
Share Capital Reserve release	7	–
Premium on redemption of shares in subsidiary	–	(22)
Acquisition costs*	1,516	(1,516)
Exchange gain/(loss) on restatement of investment in overseas subsidiaries	166	(36)
Revaluation Reserve release	11	–
Retained (deficit)/profit for the period	(1,576)	3,759
Retained profit at 29th April, 1989	13,139	13,015

*This relates to costs now written off to the Special Reserve.

Profit and loss account

	1992 £'000	1991 £'000
Turnover	115	102
Cost of sales	90	82
Profit on ordinary activities before taxation	25	20
Tax on profit on ordinary activities	10	8
Profit on ordinary activities after taxation	15	12
Extraordinary items	2	1
Profit for the financial year	13	11
Dividends	5	5
Retained profit for the financial year	8	6

Movements on reserves are set out in note X

Extracts from notes to the financial statements

Note X: Movements on reserves

	Profit and loss account £'000	Revaluation reserve £'000
At 1st January 1992 - as previously reported	44	38
Prior year adjustment (see note below)	(25)	-
As restated	19	38
Retained profit for the year	8	6
At 31st December 1992	27	44

Note: The prior year adjustment represents an overstatement of the 1991 stock valuation caused by an error in the stock records. The comparative profit and loss account and balance sheet have been restated accordingly.

16.17 The Companies Act 1989 also introduced a new requirement that permits directors to revise financial statements that are subsequently found to be defective. The procedures to be followed in revising defective financial statements are discussed further in chapter 25.

Chapter 17

DIRECTORS' REMUNERATION

Chapter 17

DIRECTORS' REMUNERATION

Introduction

17.1 The disclosure of directors' remuneration can be considered under six headings:

- Aggregate emoluments.
- Banding of emoluments.
- Emoluments waived.
- Pensions.
- Compensation for loss of office.
- Sums paid to third parties in respect of directors' services.

These areas are considered in turn in paragraphs 17.11 to 17.43 below. First, however, certain general rules are outlined, and these apply to all forms of directors' remuneration.

General rules

17.2 A company's directors have a duty to give information about their remuneration to the company so that the information discussed below can be disclosed in the financial statements. This requirement applies also to a person who has been a director of the company within the preceding five years. If a director does not give notice of the required information to the company, he is liable to a fine. [Sec 232(3)(4) - see also appendix 4].

17.3 If the required information is not disclosed in the financial statements, the auditors have a duty to include the information (so far as they are reasonably able to do so) in their audit report. [Sec 237(4)].

17.4 The remuneration to be disclosed should include all amounts paid to a director (whether those payments are made by the company, or by a subsidiary undertaking of the company or by any other person), unless the director has to account in turn to another group company for the receipt of the remuneration. [6 Sch 10(2)]. (This provision, however, does not apply to emoluments a director has waived. [6 Sch 10(1)].)

Example

Mr. Smith spends part of his time as an executive director of company A and part of his time as an employee of company B (company B is not connected with company A). Company B pays Mr. Smith's salary, and it invoices company A for an amount to cover that part of the time that Mr. Smith spends working for company A. Although Mr. Smith is paid by company B (and not by company A of which he is a director), the amount that he receives from company B is partially in respect of his services as a director of company A. Consequently, he should disclose to company A, as remuneration, the proportion of his salary that relates to his services as a director of company A. This figure may or may not be the same as the amount that company B has invoiced company A. This will depend on whether the invoiced amount is intended to cover an amount that is either more or less than the actual cost of the director's services (for example, it may cover in addition other management services provided by company B to company A).

17.5 There is also nothing in the Act to suggest that the director must receive payments personally in order that they should be subject to disclosure as remuneration. In addition, amounts paid to or receivable by a director will include amounts paid to or receivable by a person connected with him, or a body corporate controlled by him (but such amounts should not be counted twice). [6 Sch 10(4)]. Consequently, even where a director sets up another company specifically to receive his remuneration, that remuneration will be deemed to be remuneration received by him if that company is controlled by him.

17.6 Furthermore, if the company has nominated (either directly or indirectly) the director to be a director of another company, the director's remuneration should include any amount he receives as a director of that other company (whether or not that other company is a subsidiary of the company). [6 Sch 13(2)(a)].

Example

Company A has nominated one of its directors to the board of company B (company A and B are not connected). Company B pays £20,000 per year to the director in respect of his services. In this situation, the director must disclose to company A, as remuneration, the amount of £20,000 that he receives from company B. Company A will need to disclose, as directors remuneration, the aggregate of the amount paid to the director in respect of his services as director of company A and the amount of £20,000 he receives from company B. If, on the other hand, the amount of £20,000 is paid to company A (that is, as a sum to be accounted for to the company, see para 17.4) and not to the director personally, then this amount need not be included as directors emoluments in the financial statements of company A. In either situation, company B will need to disclose the payment of £20,000 as directors' emoluments in its own financial statements.

17.7 A director's remuneration (excluding any emoluments he waives) that should be disclosed in the financial statements for a particular year is the remuneration receivable by him in respect of that year, regardless of when it is paid to him. If any remuneration is not receivable in respect of a period, then it should be disclosed in the financial statements of the period in which it is paid. [6 Sch 11(1)]. For example, long-term performance related bonuses, which are not normally paid in respect of a particular financial year, should be disclosed as directors emoluments in the year in which they are paid (for example, see Table 64).

Table 64: Disclosure of performance related profit participation scheme in directors' remuneration.

Extract from Sedgewick Group plc Annual Report 31st December 1988.

Note extract

4 Employee information (extract)

Remuneration of directors:

The remuneration of the directors is determined by the compensation committee of the board comprised of non-executive directors.

Remuneration includes performance-related profit participation. Provision is made in financial statements for performance-related profit participation in the year to which it relates although it may not become payable until some future period. The accumulated provision at 31 December, 1988, is £684,000 (1987 £305,000). The years in which such future performance-related profit participation payments are expected to be made and the number of directors expected to receive those payments in each year are set out below. Such amounts will be included within the disclosed remuneration of directors in the year of payment.
1989, 1; 1990, 1; 1992, 2; 1994, 1; 1995,5.

17.8 If it is necessary to apportion remuneration paid to a director (for example, if the person was appointed a director part way through the year), the directors may apportion it in any way that they consider appropriate. [6 Sch 12].

17.9 In certain situations, directors' remuneration might not be included in the notes to the financial statements of a period because either the director is to account for it to another group company, or an expense allowance is not chargeable to UK income tax. Where this is so, and these reasons are subsequently found not to be justified, the remuneration must be disclosed in a note to the first financial statements in which it is practicable for this to be done, and the remuneration must be identified separately. [6 Sch 11(2)].

17.10 Common problems arise with the disclosure of directors' emoluments in a group context. Consider the following examples where a director of a parent company has also been nominated to the board of one of its subsidiaries. In all the situations, it is assumed that the director is remunerated by the parent company in connection with his services as director of the parent company.

Example 1

Where the subsidiary pays the director directly in respect of his services as a director of the subsidiary.

In this situation, the director must disclose to the parent company the remuneration that he receives from the subsidiary. The parent company will need to disclose, as directors' emoluments, the aggregate of the amount paid to the director in respect of his services as a director of the parent company and the amount he receives in respect of his services as a director of the subsidiary. [6 Sch 10(2)]. The subsidiary will also need to disclose the amount paid to the director by the subsidiary, as directors' emoluments, in its own financial statements.

Example 2

Where the subsidiary pays the director, but the director is liable to account for the remuneration he receives in respect of his services as director of the subsidiary company to the parent company.

In this situation, the notes to the financial statements of the parent company need only disclose, as directors' emoluments, the amounts paid to the director in respect of his services as director of the parent company. The amount paid by the subsidiary needs to be disclosed, as directors' emoluments, in the subsidiary's financial statements. Where however, the director is subsequently released from the obligation to account for the remuneration, the remuneration must be disclosed in a note to the first financial statements of the parent company in which it is practicable to show it, and the remuneration must be distinguished from other remuneration. [6 Sch 11(2)].

Example 3

Where the parent company pays the director directly and recharges the subsidiary for his services as a director of the subsidiary.

The aggregate amount that needs to be disclosed, as directors' emoluments, in the parent company's financial statements is the same as in example 1. The notes to the subsidiary's financial statements must disclose, as directors' emoluments, the amounts paid to the parent company in respect of the director's services.

Example 4

Where the parent company pays the director directly, but no recharge is made to the subsidiary.

Again, the aggregate amount that needs to be disclosed, as directors' emoluments, in the parent company's financial statements is the same as in example 1. The notes to the financial statements of the subsidiary, however, must include details of the remuneration paid by the parent company in respect of the director's services. An explanation to the effect that the charge for director's remuneration has been borne by the parent company may be useful, although there is no requirement in the Act to do so. If it is necessary for the parent company to apportion the director's remuneration, the directors may apportion it in any way they consider appropriate. [6 Sch 12].

Aggregate emoluments

17.11 The notes to the profit and loss account must disclose the aggregate amount of the directors' emoluments. [6 Sch 1(1)].

17.12 Directors' emoluments mean emoluments paid to or receivable by any person in respect of:

- His services as a director of the company.
- His services as a director of any subsidiary of the company, during the time in which he is a director of the company.
- His services in connection with the management of either the company or any subsidiary undertaking of the company.

[6 Sch 1(2)(a)(b)].

If an undertaking is a subsidiary undertaking at the time the service is rendered by the directors, it should be included even where the undertaking is no longer a subsidiary at the reporting date. [6 Sch 13 (2)(b)].

17.13 For this purpose, 'emoluments' paid to or receivable by a director include his normal remuneration salary, but also include the following:

- Fees and percentages.
- Any expense allowances (to the extent that they are chargeable to UK income tax).
- Contributions paid in respect of him under any pension scheme.
- The estimated money value of any benefits received otherwise than in cash.
- Emoluments in respect of a person accepting office as director.

[6 Sch 1(4)].

17.14 The Act also requires that the emoluments earned for services as a director of a company or a subsidiary, while a director of the company, should be aggregated and disclosed (that is, points one and two in para 17.12). In addition, emoluments earned for services in connection with the management of either the company or any subsidiary of the company must also be separately disclosed (that is, point three in para 17.12). [6 Sch 1(3)]. Generally speaking, 'emoluments in respect of services' will include fees for attendance at board meetings and other duties in connection with the office of a director that are normally paid to both executive and non-executive directors. Emoluments in respect of services in connection with the management of the company will include salaries and other benefits that are only paid to executive directors. If the strict wording of the Act is followed, such emoluments, which were generally disclosed as 'other emoluments' in the past, could be described as 'management remuneration' or 'remuneration as executives'. Table 65 illustrates the disclosure requirements for directors' emoluments.

Table 65: Example of the disclosure of directors' emoluments.

Extract from Glaxo Holdings p.l.c. Annual Report and Accounts 30th June 1989.

Note extract

5 REMUNERATION OF DIRECTORS AND EMPLOYEES extract	1989 £'000	1988 £'000
a) Remuneration of Directors of the Holding company for services to the Company, its subsidiary and associated companies:		
Fees	73	*42*
Other emoluments	2,713	*2,699*
Pension scheme contributions	780	*993*
Compensation for loss of executive office to a former Director	–	*180*

b) Emoluments, excluding pension scheme contributions, of:

i) The Chairman, £598,081 (1988 – £396,931)
ii) Other Directors of the Holding company, including overseas Directors

Exceeding £	Not exceeding £	1989 Number	1988 Number	Exceeding £	Not exceeding £	1989 Number	1988 Number
–	5,000	1	–	170,000	175,000	–	*1*
10,000	15,000	1	*2*	185,000	190,000	–	*1*
15,000	20,000	3	*2*	230,000	235,000	1	*1*
30,000	35,000	1	*1*	275,000	280,000	1	*1*
100,000	105,000	–	*1*	320,000	325,000	1	–
115,000	120,000	–	*2*	450,000	455,000	–	*2*
130,000	135,000	–	*1*	490,000	495,000	1	–
155,000	160,000	1	–	600,000	605,000	1	–

17.15 Whether the director receives emoluments for services as a director of the company or otherwise in connection with the management of its affairs is a question of fact. There is a presumption that all payments made to a director, except for reimbursement of expenses, will generally fall within both these categories, unless it can clearly be demonstrated otherwise. However, an exception could be where payments have been made to a director in a self employed or professional capacity. Consider the following example:

Example

A director of a company is paid for technical services supplied on a 'self employed persons' basis. How should this be disclosed.

Provided that it can be clearly established that the fees are genuinely for technical services and that they are not connected with management services (which they might be if the director were a technical director), then the amounts paid need not be disclosed as emoluments. However, the transaction may need to be disclosed as one in which the director has a material interest (see further chapter 22). In practice, however, it is often difficult to make such a precise distinction and the remuneration for other services is often included with directors' remuneration.

17.16 A 'pension scheme' in point three of paragraph 17.13 above means a scheme for the provision of pensions in respect of services as a director or otherwise, which is maintained wholly or partly by means of contributions. [6 Sch 13(3)(b)]. A contribution to a pension scheme means any payment (including an insurance premium) paid for the purposes of the scheme. However, it does not cover payments made in respect of two or more persons, if the amount paid in respect of each of them cannot be ascertained separately. [6 Sch 13(3)(c)]. For example, if a company either makes a lump sum payment to a pension scheme or pays a premium to an insurance company for a pension scheme, and the contribution in respect of each director cannot be separately identified, no amount is required to be disclosed as directors' emoluments in respect of pension contributions. But, where the payment is in respect of a number of directors, then the question whether the emoluments can be separately identified for each director should probably be treated as irrelevant. This is because the disclosure required by the Act is of the aggregate amounts paid to pension schemes and, consequently, the additional amounts paid for all directors would have to be disclosed in aggregate.

17.17 Emoluments in respect of a person accepting office as director (see the last point in para 17.13) is a new category brought in by the Companies Act 1989. Its effect is to require disclosure of various incentive payments (so-called 'golden hellos') that are made by companies to attract people to join the company's board of directors.

17.18 Directors' emoluments should not include the employer's national insurance contributions, because the amounts are neither paid to the director nor paid in respect of a pension scheme.

17.19 When considering directors' emoluments, there is no need to distinguish between a director's service contract and a contract for services that a director has with the company. Remuneration received in either capacity will fall to be disclosed in the company's financial statements as directors' emoluments. However, a director's service contract makes him essentially an employee of the company and, therefore, such emoluments will have to be included in staff costs. On the other hand, a contract for service puts the director in essentially the same position as a third party hired to do a particular job. Amounts invoiced to the company should be charged to the profit and loss account, but should not be classified as 'staff costs' (see further chapter 14 paras 14.20 and 14.21).

17.20 The estimated money value of a benefit in kind that must be included in directors' emoluments should be taken as the market value of the facility that is provided for the director's private benefit, less any contribution the director pays (for example, see Table 66). The amount used to assess the taxable benefit should be used only where it is not possible to ascertain the market value of the benefit. However, in practice the value of the taxable benefit is often a good starting point for considering the value that should be placed on the amounts for accounting disclosure purposes.

Table 66: Disclosure of taxable benefits in directors' remuneration.

Extract from Allied-Lyons PLC Report and Accounts 4th March 1989.

6 EMOLUMENTS OF DIRECTORS AND HIGHER PAID EMPLOYEES (extract)

The emoluments of the chairman (including incentive bonus) were £377,477 (£303,975) and the emoluments of the highest paid director apart from the chairman (including incentive bonus) were £442,571.

During the year ending 4th March 1989 the service agreement between Mr. H.C. Hatch, Jr and Hiram Walker-Gooderham & Worts Limited dated 25th March 1986 relating to Mr. Hatch's former capacity as president and chief executive officer of that company was terminated, on payment of a bonus of one year's salary (Cdn$320,000) in accordance with the terms thereof. In its place, Mr. Hatch and the company have entered into a service agreement for the employment of Mr. Hatch as finance director of Allied-Lyons PLC. The bonus is included within the emoluments shown in this note. Also included within Mr. Hatch's emoluments is the sum of £33,980 attributable as a taxable benefit to his occupation of a residential property he owns jointly with the company as detailed in last year's annual accounts.

Banding of emoluments

17.21 The directors' emoluments (*excluding* contributions paid to a pension scheme) must also be analysed in the following way:

- Chairman's emoluments. [6 Sch 3(1)].
- Highest-paid director's emoluments, if this exceeds the chairman's emoluments. [6 Sch 4(3)].
- Banding of all directors' emoluments. [6 Sch 4(2)]

These requirements are considered further in the paragraphs that follow and an example of the disclosure requirements is given in Table 65 above.

17.22 This information must be given if the company is either a parent company or a subsidiary of another company. However, other companies need not give the information where the aggregate amount of the directors' emoluments for the financial year is less than £60,000. [6 Sch 2]. For the purposes of calculating the £60,000 threshold, directors' pension contributions should be included. Consequently, where the company is either a subsidiary or a parent company, it must still give the information outlined above, even where the aggregate directors' emoluments are below £60,000. In this context, the 'financial year' means the company's reporting period. [Sec

742(1)(d)]. Therefore, even if the profit and loss account covers a period of, say, only nine months, or 15 months, the limit for disclosure is still £60,000.

17.23 A 'chairman' means, in this context, the person elected to chair directors' meetings. If a chairman is not elected, then the chairman is deemed to be the person who carries out this function at directors' meetings. [6 Sch 3(2)].

17.24 If more than one person has been chairman during the year, each such person's total emoluments for the year must be attributed to that part of the year during which he was chairman, and these amounts must be disclosed separately. [6 Sch 3(3)]. The notes do not have to disclose the emoluments of a chairman who worked either wholly or mainly outside the UK. [6 Sch 3(4)].

17.25 The notes must disclose the emoluments of the highest-paid director who did not work either wholly or mainly outside the UK during the year, if his emoluments exceed those of the chairman. [6 Sch 4(3)(5)]. The highest-paid director's emoluments need not be disclosed again if he was the chairman. Where there has been more than one chairman during the year, the emoluments of those chairmen in respect of the period during which they were chairmen should be aggregated in order to determine whether another director has received emoluments in excess of the aggregate chairmen's emoluments. [6 Sch 4(4)].

17.26 The bands into which the emoluments of all directors (including both the chairman and the highest-paid director but excluding any directors who worked either wholly or mainly outside the UK) fall must be disclosed in the notes to the financial statements. The Act defines the 'bands' as £0 to £5,000, £5,001 to £10,000, and bands of £5,000 beyond that. The notes must give the number of directors whose emoluments fell within each band. [6 Sch 4(2)]. No matter how long the company's reporting period is, the bands do not change. For example, if the profit and loss account covers a period that exceeds 12 months, the bands still remain as multiples of £5,000. Companies may, however, wish also to give as additional information the amounts in bands, on an annualised basis. Some companies disclose also, as supplementary information, the number of directors whose emoluments net of tax (basic rate less tax allowances) fall into the appropriate bands.

Emoluments waived

17.27 If any director has waived his right to receive emoluments, the notes to the financial statements must give the following information:

- The number of directors who have waived their rights to receive emoluments.

- The aggregate amount of the emoluments they have waived.

[6 Sch 6(1)].

17.28 In determining these figures it should be assumed that a sum not receivable for a particular period would have been paid at the time that it was 'due', and if a sum was payable only on demand, it would have been 'due' at the time of the waiver. [6 Sch 6(2)].

17.29 The International Stock Exchange's Continuing Obligations and the USM's General Undertaking require listed companies and companies traded on the USM respectively to disclose also particulars of any arrangement under which a director has either waived or agreed to waive any future or current emoluments. This applies in respect of emoluments from either the company or any of its subsidiaries. [CO 21(n); GU 10(k)].

Pensions

17.30 The notes must disclose the aggregate amount of the present directors' pensions and any past directors' pensions. [6 Sch 7(1)]. This amount must be divided between pensions in respect of services as a director (whether of the company or of a subsidiary undertaking), and other pensions. [6 Sch 7(3)]. A subsidiary undertaking includes an undertaking which is a subsidiary undertaking at the time the services were rendered, even though it is not a subsidiary undertaking of the company at the reporting date. [6 Sch 13(2)(b)].

17.31 Where a pension paid to a director includes benefits otherwise than in cash, the value of such a pension should be determined according to its estimated money value. In addition, the nature of any such benefits must be disclosed. [6 Sch 7(4)]. The term 'pensions' also includes any superannuation allowance, or superannuation gratuity or similar payment. [6 Sch 13(3)(a)].

17.32 If the contributions paid under a pension scheme are substantially adequate for maintaining that scheme, the amount of pensions disclosed should not include any pension paid or receivable under that scheme. [6 Sch 7(2)]. In practice, this means that if the contributions a company paid under an occupational pension scheme were adequate to fund those pensions, the pensions payable under that scheme need not be disclosed. However, 'top hat' or other additional pensions that are not provided from the standard occupational scheme would have to be disclosed. Otherwise, the term 'pension' includes any pension paid to, or receivable by, either a director or a past director in respect of services he has provided to either the company or another group company. It includes also any pension paid to or receivable by any other person (for example, a dependant or nominee) in respect of the services of either a director or a past director.

Compensation for loss of office

17.33 Disclosure must be made of the aggregate amount of any compensation paid to directors or past directors in respect of loss of office. [6 Sch 8(1)]. This amount should include not only payments made in respect of the loss of office by the director of the reporting company, but also payments in respect of the loss of any other office the person concerned held. It will, therefore, include compensation for the loss of office as a director of any subsidiary or of any other office that involved the management of the company or of any subsidiary undertaking. The amount should include any compensation paid either while the person was a director, or on his ceasing to be so, or otherwise in connection with his ceasing to be a director of the company. [6 Sch 8(2)]. Compensation for loss of office also includes any amount paid in connection with a director's retirement from office. That is to say, it includes any payments made when the director leaves the company, either on reaching retirement age or in any other circumstances. [6 Sch 8(4)]. Because pensions are separately disclosed, they should not be included in this category of payment, but a top up to the pension scheme might well be disclosable.

17.34 Compensation for loss of office includes benefits received or receivable otherwise than in cash. The value of the benefit should be determined according to its estimated money value. [6 Sch 8(3)]. Where compensation is given in kind, the company's financial statements should disclose its nature. [6 Sch 8(3)]. For example, the compensation might be the gift to the director of a car that he had previously used, but that was owned by the company. In this situation, the money value of the car and the fact that the compensation is in the form of a car will have to be disclosed. Normally, the market value of the car at the time of transfer should be used for this purpose.

17.35 The statutory description of 'payments made in compensation for loss of office' is widely drawn. In deciding whether a payment made to a director or a former director is required to be disclosed, regard should be had to both the nature and the circumstances of the payment, rather than to just the description the company gives to it. For example, most '*ex-gratia*' payments made on either a director's retirement or his removal from office could well be regarded not as gratuitous payments, but as payments in compensation for loss of office. And, as such, they should be disclosed.

17.36 A company must disclose details (including the amount) of any payment by way of compensation for loss of office, or as consideration for or in connection with retirement from office, to members of the company, and the proposal must be approved by the company at its general meeting. Otherwise the payment is unlawful. [Sec 312]. Similarly, a payment to a director in connection with the transfer of any part of a company (for example, following a management buy-out) or property of a company, must also be disclosed and approved at its general meeting. Otherwise again the payment is unlawful and, in this situation, section 313(2) provides that the amount received by the director is deemed to be received by him in trust for the company.

17.37 However, bona fide compensation or consideration paid to a director for damages for breach of contract or as a pension for past services, does not require approval at a general meeting or disclosure to shareholders. [Sec 316(3)]. Approval may still however be required under section 320 (substantial property transactions involving directors). Whether or not the payment is made in respect of a breach of contract or as a pension for past services, it is still required to be disclosed in the company's financial statements as compensation for loss of office.

17.38 The amount disclosed for compensation for loss of office must distinguish both between:

- Compensation in respect of the office of director (whether of the company or any of its subsidiaries).

- Compensation in respect of other offices (whether of the company or any of its subsidiaries).

[6 Sch 8(2)].

These amounts have to be further analysed between compensation paid by, or receivable from, the company or from any of its subsidiaries or from any other person. [6 Sch 10(3)].

17.39 For this purpose, a subsidiary includes a company that was a subsidiary immediately before the date on which the director lost office. [6 Sch 13(2)(b)].

17.40 Compensation paid to a director for loss of office is a category of payment different from an 'emolument'. Consequently, it should not be included in that person's emoluments for banding purposes.

Sums paid to third parties in respect of directors' services.

17.41 Paragraph 9 of Schedule 6 has introduced a new requirement for companies to disclose in their financial statements any consideration paid to or receivable by third parties for making available the services of any person:

- As a director of the company.

- While a director of the company, as director of any of its subsidiary undertakings, or otherwise in connection with the management of the affairs of the company or any of its subsidiary undertakings.

[6 Sch 9(1)].

17.42 In this context, third parties do not include

- The director himself or a person connected with him or body corporate controlled by him.

- The company or any of its subsidiary undertakings.

[6 Sch 9(3)].

17.43 For the purposes of this disclosure, the definition of consideration includes non-cash benefits. Where a benefit is given, its amount should be determined with reference to its estimated money value. The nature of the non-cash benefit must also has to be disclosed. [6 Sch 9(2)].

Example

A company borrows money from a venture capital company. As part of the financing arrangement, a director of the venture capital company has been appointed to the board of directors of company A. Company A pays £10,000 per year to the venture capital company in respect of the director's services. The director is remunerated by the venture capital company and does not receive the money paid in respect of his services by company A personally. In this situation, the amount of £10,000 would be disclosed in the financial statements of the company as sums paid to third parties in respect of directors' services in accordance with paragraph 9 of Schedule 6.

Chapter 18

FOREIGN CURRENCY TRANSLATION

Chapter 18

FOREIGN CURRENCY TRANSLATION

Introduction

18.1 The Act does not include any provisions that deal with either the translation of foreign currency transactions or the translation of foreign currency financial statements, other than to require the basis on which such sums are translated into sterling to be stated. [4 Sch 58(1)]. However, SSAP 20, 'Foreign currency translation', does cover these matters. The standard's requirements are intended to produce results that are generally compatible with the effects of rate changes on both a company's cash flows and its equity. Furthermore, the intention of the standard is that translation should also ensure that the financial statements give a true and fair view.

18.2 The standard deals separately with the translation of foreign currency transactions by individual companies and with the translation of foreign currency financial statements for consolidation purposes. The standard also contains a number of disclosure requirements. This chapter explains the provisions of SSAP 20 that affect individual companies. The provisions of SSAP 20 that relate to consolidations are considered in 'Manual of Accounting - volume II' chapter 12.

Transactions arising during the year

18.3 The standard covers the translation of any currency transactions and balances that arise from the operations of a company. A company should translate currency transactions carried out during the year (for example, fixed assets or stock purchased from overseas) using the rate of exchange at the date of the transaction. [SSAP 20 para 46]. Where a company makes regular purchases of, say, stock from overseas and exchange rates do not fluctuate significantly, it may use an average rate for the period as an approximation. Where, however, the company is to settle a transaction at a contracted rate, it should use that rate. Where a trading transaction is covered by a related or matching forward contract, the rate specified in the contract may be used. [SSAP 20 para 46].

18.4 Once a company has translated and recorded a non-monetary asset, it will not normally need to translate that asset again. [SSAP 20 para 47]. Examples of non-monetary assets are intangible fixed assets, tangible fixed assets, equity investments, and stocks and work-in-progress. In certain circumstances, however, the provisions set out in this paragraph will not apply to foreign equity investments. The treatment of such investments is considered in paragraph 18.17 below.

18.5 As mentioned above, a company will normally translate the currency transactions it has completed during the year at the exchange rate that was ruling on the date on which each transaction occurred. There is no guidance in SSAP 20, however, as to whether the date of the transaction should be taken as the date on which the contract for the purchase or the sale was signed, or whether it should be taken as the date of delivery. An example of a company that uses a mid-market rate of exchange for translating subscription receipts is given in Table 67.

Table 67: Illustration of an accounting policy that describes the translation of subscription receipts.

Extract from Maxwell Communications plc Report and Accounts 31st March 1989.

Foreign currencies

Subscriptions received in advance in foreign currencies are translated at the mid-month rate of exchange in the month of receipt, or, where covered by a matching forward contract, at the rate of exchange specified in that contract.

All foreign currency monetary assets and liabilities, with the exception of subscriptions received in advance, are translated into sterling at the rates of exchange ruling at the balance sheet date, or, if appropriate, by reference to the rate of exchange fixed under the terms of related or matching foreign exchange contracts.

The results of overseas subsidiaries are translated at the average rate of exchange for the period.

Differences on exchange arising from the translation of the opening net investments in subsidiary and associated companies and related net currency borrowings at the period end exchange rates, together with the differences arising from the translation of the results at the average rate compared to the period end exchange rate, are taken directly to reserves.

18.6 In the US accounting standard on foreign currency translation (FAS 52), the relevant date is "*the date at which a transaction is recorded in accounting records in conformity with generally accepted accounting principles*". Accordingly, the date on which the transaction occurred should normally be taken as the date on which the transaction is recorded.

18.7 The examples that follow illustrate the principles explained above:

Example 1

In March 1990, a UK company purchased plant for use in the UK from a French company for FF 500,000. At the date the company purchased the plant, the exchange rate was £1 = FF 10.00. The purchase price is to be settled in three months time, although delivery is made immediately. The UK company should record the plant in its accounting records at £50,000. The company will not need to translate the plant again. At the settlement date, the exchange rate is £1 = FF 10.25 so the actual amount the UK company paid was £48,780. The company should include the gain on exchange of £1,220 (that is, £50,000 - £48,780) in arriving at its profit or loss on ordinary activities.

Example 2

In March 1991, a UK company purchased plant for use in the UK from a German company for DM 750,000. The transaction is contracted to be settled at £1 = DM 3.00. The UK company should record the plant in its accounting records at £250,000. The company will not need to translate the plant again, and no exchange differences will arise.

Example 3

In January 1991, a UK company sold goods to a Dutch company for fl 400,000. The Dutch company paid for the goods in March 1991. At the time of the sale, the exchange rate is £1 = fl 3.2, and at the time of the payment, the exchange rate is £1 = fl 3.5. The UK company, however, had covered the transaction by a matching forward contract. The exchange rate specified in the forward contract is £1 = fl 3.35. The relevant translations are as follows:

fl 400,000 at fl 3.2 =	£125,000
fl 400,000 at fl 3.5 =	£114,286
fl 400,000 at fl 3.35 =	£119,403

The UK company could record the sale in one of the following ways:

- ☐ It could record the sale and the debtor at £125,000, that is, at the exchange rate ruling at the date of the sale. Because the company has entered into a matching forward contract, the amount received from the debtor is fl 400,000 which it sells for £119,403. Consequently, the company would have a loss on exchange on the transaction of £5,597 (that is, £125,000 - £119,403) to include in its profit or loss on ordinary activities.

- ☐ It could record the sale and the debtor at £119,403, that is, at the exchange rate specified in the matching forward contract. Because the company has entered into a matching forward contract, the amount receivable and ultimately received from the debtor is £119,403. Consequently, the company would not recognise a loss on exchange on the transaction.

Whichever method the company chooses to record the sale, its profit or loss on ordinary activities will be the same.

Year end balances

18.8 A company should translate its monetary assets and liabilities denominated in foreign currencies outstanding at the end of the year using the rate of exchange at the balance sheet date (that is, the closing rate). [SSAP 20 para 48]. Examples of monetary assets and liabilities are debtors, cash at bank and in hand, creditors and loans. An accounting policy that covers the translation of monetary assets and liabilities is given in Table 68.

Example 1

In January 1990, a UK company purchased goods from a Spanish company for Pts 10,000,000. At the date the company took delivery of the goods, the exchange rate was £1 = Pts 180. The UK company should record the purchase and the creditor at £55,555.

At 31st March 1990, the UK company's year end, it had not paid for the goods. The exchange rate at 31st March 1990 was £1 = Pts 190. The company should include the creditor in its balance sheet at £52,632. The company should include the gain on exchange of £2,381 (that is, £55,555 - £52,632) in its profit or loss on ordinary activities.

Example 2

A company rents a property in the US and has made a deposit of the sterling equivalent of $100,000 in respect of dilapidations etc., which is returnable in dollars when the lease ends in 25 years time. The company will have to translate this amount at the end of each financial year at the closing rate of exchange, because it is a monetary asset. A note to the financial statements should also explain that the cash balance includes an amount of £X that is on long-term deposit and not, therefore, freely available for use in the company's business.

Table 68: Illustration of an accounting policy that explains the treatment of monetary assets and liabilities.

Extract from Thorn EMI plc Annual Report 31st March 1989.

Foreign Currencies Transactions denominated in foreign currencies are recorded at the rate of exchange ruling at the dates of the transactions. Monetary assets and liabilities denominated in foreign currencies are translated into sterling either at year end rates or, where there are related forward foreign exchange contracts, at contract rates. The resulting exchange differences are dealt with in the determination of profit for the financial year.

On consolidation, the assets, liabilities and results of overseas subsidiaries and related companies are translated into sterling at year end rates. Exchange differences arising from the retranslation of the opening net investment in overseas subsidiaries and related companies and from foreign currency borrowings, in so far as they are matched by those overseas operations, are dealt with in Group reserves.

18.9 Where the rate of exchange is fixed under the terms of the relevant transaction, the company should use that rate. When an outstanding trading transaction is covered by a related or matching forward contract, the rate specified in that contract may be used (for example, see Table 69). [SSAP 20 para 48]. Consequently, no exchange gain or loss would arise in respect of a currency transaction outstanding at the end of the year. This is because the company should record the creditor or debtor initially and at the balance sheet date at the same rate of exchange.

18.10 Furthermore, where an outstanding trading transaction is covered by a related or matching forward contract and the company chooses to use the rate specified in that contract, rather than the closing rate, no exchange gain or loss will arise until the transaction is settled.

Example

A company issues a Eurobond of $50M which it swaps with a bank for a sterling equivalent loan of £35M, together with an agreement to swap back in ten years time when the bond becomes due.

The company should show a liability to repay £35M as this amount is fixed by the agreement to swap back into $50M in 10 years time. A note to the financial statements should explain the transaction in some detail in order to give a true and fair view.

Table 69: Illustration of an accounting policy that explains the translation method used where forward exchange contracts exist.

Extract from Marks & Spencers p.l.c. Annual Report and Financial Statements 31st March 1989.

Foreign currencies

The trading results of overseas subsidiaries have been translated using average rates of exchange ruling during the financial year.

The balance sheets of overseas subsidiaries have been translated into sterling at the rates of exchange ruling at 31 March, except for those assets and liabilities where a forward exchange contract has been arranged, in which case this forward rate is used. Exchange differences arising between the translation into sterling of the net assets of these subsidiaries at rates ruling at the beginning and end of the year are dealt with through reserves.

The cost of the Company's investment in overseas subsidiaries and tangible fixed assets of overseas branches are translated at the rate ruling at the date of investment. All other foreign currency assets and liabilities of the Company and its United Kingdom subsidiaries are translated into sterling at the rate ruling at 31 March, except in those instances where a forward exchange contract has been arranged in which case this forward rate is used. These exchange differences are dealt with through the profit and loss account.

Treatment of gains and losses

18.11 Exchange gains and losses will arise both on the currency transactions a company completes during the year and on its currency transactions or balances outstanding at the end of the year. The company should include all such exchange differences in its profit or loss for the year from ordinary activities (for example see Table 68 above). The only exception to this rule is that an exchange difference on a currency transaction that is itself treated as an extraordinary item should be included as part of that item. [SSAP 20 para 49].

18.12 In certain exceptional situations a company may have doubts as to either the convertibility or the marketability of the currency of a long-term monetary item outstanding at the end of the year. Where this is so, on the grounds of prudence such a company should restrict the amount of any gain (or the amount by which any gain exceeds past exchange losses on the same item) that it recognises in its profit and loss account. [SSAP 20 para 11, 50]. A long-term monetary item is an item that falls due more than one year after the balance sheet date. [SSAP 20 para 44].

18.13 Where a UK company raises a long-term currency borrowing and converts it into sterling to finance operations in the UK, such a restriction would not normally be necessary. This is because, in the absence of exchange controls, when the currency loan falls due for repayment there should be no problem in converting sterling into the currency of the loan.

18.14 Where a UK company makes a long-term currency loan to, say, an overseas supplier, such a restriction may be necessary. This is because from time to time certain overseas countries impose restrictions on the remittance of funds. As a result of these restrictions, there may be a problem in converting the currency of the loan into sterling when the loan falls due for repayment.

18.15 To determine the extent of any restriction, the company should retranslate the currency loan at the closing rate. It should then consider the loan's realisable value in the light of any restrictions on the remittance of funds from the country concerned. If the company considers that loan's realisable value is less than the retranslated amount, it should write the loan down. The company should offset the write down against the exchange gain that arises when it retranslates the loan, and it should include the net amount in the profit and loss account as an exchange gain.

18.16 To illustrate this type of situation, consider the example that follows:

Example

In April 1990, company A, which is incorporated in the UK, used surplus currency to make a long-term loan of Fc 20,000,000 (Fc being a fictional currency) to its overseas supplier. The loan was made when the exchange rate was £1 = Fc 5.00. Initially, the loan would be translated and recorded in company A's books at £4,000,000. The amount that company A will ultimately receive will depend on the rate of exchange ruling on the date when the loan is repaid.

At 31st March 1991, company A's year end, the exchange rate is £1 = Fc 4.00. If the loan of Fc 20,000,000 was translated at this rate it would give an asset of £5,000,000 and an exchange gain of £1,000,000. There are, however, doubts as to the convertibility of Fc. Therefore, company A considers that, on the grounds of prudence, it should limit the gain so that the sterling value of the loan is shown at its present estimated realisable value of £4,500,000. Accordingly, company A restricts the exchange gain that it includes in its profit and loss account for the year ended 31st March 1991 to £500,000.

Hedging equity investments

18.17 Where a company has used foreign currency borrowings either to finance, or to provide a hedge against, its foreign equity investments, and where, also, the conditions set out below apply, the company may denominate its equity investments in the appropriate foreign currency. This means that the investment will be regarded as a currency investment and the company will need to translate the carrying amount at the closing rate each year for inclusion in its financial statements. Where a company treats investments in this way, it should take to reserves any exchange differences that arise when the investments are retranslated. It should also take the exchange differences on the related foreign currency borrowings to reserves. It would then offset the exchange differences as a net increase or a net decrease to unrealised reserves. (SSAP 20 does not require companies to maintain a separate reserve for exchange differences, however such adjustments are required to be disclosed separately (see further para 18.40). The conditions for offset, all of which must apply, are as follows:

- In any accounting period, a company may offset exchange differences on its borrowings only to the extent of the exchange differences that arise when the investments are retranslated.
- The borrowings must not exceed, in aggregate, the total amount of cash that the investments are expected to be able to generate from profits or otherwise.
- A company should apply consistently the accounting treatment it adopts.

[SSAP 20 para 51].

Offset restriction

18.18 To illustrate the first condition in paragraph 18.18 above, consider the following example:

Example

Some years ago, company B, incorporated in the UK, raised a loan for US$ 7,500,000 to finance an equity investment amounting to FF 36,800,000 in a French company. The relevant rates of exchange are:

		At 31st March 1990	At 31st March 1991
£1	=	US$ 1.7	US$ 1.6
£1	=	FF 10.3	FF 10.0

The loss on exchange on the loan for the year ended 31st March 1991 is:

US$ 7,500,000 at 1.7	4,411,765
US$ 7.500,000 at 1.6	4,687,500
	£275,735

The gain on exchange on the retranslation of the French franc investment for the year ended 31st March 1991 is:

	£
FF 36,800,000 at 10.3	3,572,816
FF 36,800,000 at 10.0	3,680,000
	£107,184

In this example, the amount of the exchange loss on the loan that company B can offset as a reserve movement against the exchange gain on the investment is limited to £107,184. It must include the balance of the exchange loss on the loan (that is, £168,551) in its profit or loss on ordinary activities for the year.

18.19 If, in the example, there had been a gain on exchange on the loan for the year ended 31st March 1991 of, say, £250,000 and a loss on exchange on the investment of, say, £100,000, the amount of the exchange gain on the loan that company B could have offset as a reserve movement against the exchange loss on the investment would have been limited to £100,000. Company B would have had to include the balance of the exchange gain on the loan (that is, £150,000) in its profit or loss on ordinary activities for the year.

18.20 On the other hand, if in the example there had been a loss on exchange on the retranslation of the French franc investment as well as a loss on exchange on the loan, company B would have had to include the whole of the loss on exchange on the loan in its profit or loss on ordinary activities for the year. Company B would still treat, as a reserve movement, the loss on exchange on the retranslation of the investment.

18.21 Furthermore, if in the example there had been a gain on the loan as well as a gain on exchange of the French franc investment, company B would have included the gain on exchange on the loan in its profit or loss on ordinary activities. Company B would still treat, as a reserve movement, the gain on exchange on the retranslation of the investment.

Borrowing restriction

18.22 The second condition for the offset procedure detailed in paragraph 18.17 above does not specify a time scale that the foreign undertaking is given to generate sufficient profits. The condition should not cause a problem in a straight forward situation, such as the purchase of a US dollar investment portfolio with a US dollar borrowing. Similarly, the condition should not cause a problem where a borrowing that is invested in a profitable company is sufficiently long-term to enable that company to generate sufficient profits to cover the borrowing. In borderline situations, however, it may be difficult for a company to quantify cash flows and so ensure that it has complied with the condition. Problems may arise also where the borrowing is for a significantly shorter term than the expected useful life of the investment to the investing company.

18.23 The second condition outlined in paragraph 18.17 above states that the borrowings must not exceed, in aggregate, the total amount of cash that the investments are expected to be able to generate from profits or otherwise. The next example illustrates this provision.

Example

In 1985, company C, incorporated in the UK, raised a DM loan to finance a DM equity investment in a German company. Both at 31st March 1990 and at 31st March 1991, the loan amounted to DM 15,000,000, and the equity investment amounted to DM 17,000,000. Company C, however, considers that the total amount of cash that the investment is able to generate will be DM 12,000,000.

At 31st March 1990, the exchange rate is £1 = DM 3.0, and at 31st March 1991 the exchange rate is £1 = DM 2.8. In the year ended 31st March 1991, the amount of the exchange loss on the loan that company C can offset as a reserve movement against the exchange gain on the investment is calculated as follows:

	£
DM 12,000,000 at 3.0	4,000,000
DM 12,000,000 at 2.8	4,285,715
	£ 285,715

Company C must report the exchange loss on the remaining DM 3,000,000 of the loan as part of the profit or loss on ordinary activities for the year. It would also have to write down the investment to DM 12,000,000 as it has suffered a permanent diminution in value.

Consistent accounting treatment

18.24 The third condition in outlined in paragraph 18.17 above is that a company should apply consistently the accounting treatment it adopts. The objective of the condition is to prevent a company from changing its accounting treatment depending on the way in which exchange rates move. Where exchange rate movements give rise to exchange losses on borrowings, and the first two conditions apply, it is obviously advantageous for a company to be able to use the offset procedure. If, however, in a subsequent year, exchange rate movements give rise to exchange gains on those borrowings, and the first two conditions still apply, the company must still use the offset procedure. It cannot include the exchange gains in its profit on ordinary activities. Also where a company sells a foreign currency investment it should apply the offset procedure up to the date of sale and not stop at the previous year end. This applies in particular where the related loan gives rise to an exchange gain between the previous accounting year end and the date of sale. Consider the following example.

Example

A company's accounting policy is to take unrealised exchange differences on long-term borrowings, that are matched with currency equity investments, direct to reserves . In previous years unrealised gains on a particular matched borrowing amounted to £100,000. In the current period the borrowing is being repaid and there is a gain in the period up to the date of repayment of £25,000. The company wishes to know whether it can take any of these gains to its profit and loss account.

Where the matching principle is used it should normally be continued on a consistent basis until the date of repayment of the loans. Consequently, none of the profits in the example would be available to be taken to the profit and loss account.

General guidance

18.25 Because it may not be advantageous for a company to adopt the offset procedure, the use of the procedure is optional under the standard.

18.26 SSAP 20 does not require a company to designate the purpose for which each foreign loan is raised at the commencement of the loan. Consequently, provided that the conditions apply, a company could apply the offset procedure to aggregate foreign currency borrowings that either finance, or provide a hedge against, aggregate foreign equity investments. Where, however, there is an economic link between certain loans and certain investments, it is best practice for a company to apply the offset procedure separately, rather than in aggregate.

18.27 The net investment that a company has in a foreign undertaking is its effective equity stake. In appropriate circumstances, intra-group loans and other deferred balances may be regarded as part of the effective equity stake. [SSAP 20 para 20]. The standard states that, where such loans are intended to be as permanent as equity, they should be treated as part of the investing company's net investment in the foreign undertaking. The requirement in Schedule 4 to the Act for a company to analyse amounts owed by or to group companies between amounts that will fall due within one year of the balance sheet date and other amounts may well indicate intra-group loans and other deferred balances that it should properly treat as part of its effective equity stake.

Treatment in formats

18.28 The profit and loss account formats in Schedule 4 to the Act distinguish between operating income and expenses and other income and expenses. Therefore, a company will need to consider the nature of each exchange difference. A company should normally show gains and losses that arise from trading transactions as 'other operating income/charges'. Where arrangements that can be considered as financing give rise to exchange gains and losses, a company should disclose these separately as part of 'other interest receivable and similar income' or as part of 'interest payable and similar charges'. Exchange gains and losses that arise from events that themselves fall to be disclosed as exceptional items should be included as part of such items. Similarly, exchange gains and losses that arise from events that fall to be treated as extraordinary items should be included as part of such items.

18.29 In practice, there are probably few instances where exchange differences will fall to be treated as part of an extraordinary item. One example, however, is where a company sells an overseas subsidiary and there is a delay between the date of the sale and the date on which the buyer remits the currency proceeds. If the company treats the profit or loss on the sale of its overseas subsidiary as an extraordinary item, it should treat the exchange gain or loss on the remittance as an extraordinary item.

18.30 The exchange gain or loss that arises when a currency loan is retranslated should not be treated as extraordinary. With floating exchange rates, companies must expect gains or losses on currency loans.

Post balance sheet events

18.31 If a company enters into a currency transaction before its year end, and then settles it after the year end at a different rate, an exchange gain or loss may arise. If an exchange loss arises that is not covered by a hedging transaction, and it is material in the circumstances of the company, it may be prudent for the company to note the loss, in its financial statements, in accordance with the provisions of SSAP 17 on accounting for post balance sheet events. Normally, such a loss would not be an adjusting event, so a provision would not be required.

Treatment of unrealised gains

18.32 Paragraph 12 of Schedule 4 to the Act states that *"only profits realised at the balance sheet date shall be included in the profit and loss account"*. Exchange gains on the translation of some currency transactions are not realised.

18.33 Where exchange gains arise on short-term monetary items, their ultimate cash realisation can normally be assessed with reasonable certainty. Therefore, applying the prudence concept defined in SSAP 2, such profits are properly recognised in the profit and loss account. Furthermore, these profits are treated as realised in accordance with generally accepted accounting principles and, accordingly, they constitute realised profits for the purposes of Part VII of the Act. [Sec 262(3)].

18.34 Exchange gains that arise on long-term monetary items are not realised, but there is a 'special reason' for a company to include them in its profit and loss account. The special reason is that the company needs to treat exchange gains and exchange losses symmetrically. Exchange gains can be determined no less objectively than can exchange losses.

18.35 The consideration of how exchange gains and losses affect distributable profits is detailed in chapter 19 paragraphs 19.54 to 19.62.

Example

A group has a US subsidiary. A loan account from the UK parent to the subsidiary is denominated in US dollars and is for the long-term. The parent has shown a profit on the loan during the year, which it has included in reserves. It is intended in the next period that the loan will be converted into sterling.

When the loan is converted into a sterling loan a gain or loss will arise from the previous year end to the date on which the loan is converted. This gain or loss will be realised by the parent for distribution purposes. In addition, any exchange gains or losses on translation of the loan that have previously been taken to reserves will also become realised.

Major realignments of currencies

18.36 SSAP 20 does not refer to major realignments of currencies. Therefore, a company should treat those translation differences that arise as a result of a major realignment in the same way that it treats the translation differences that arise from a gradual movement in exchange rates. Where the translation differences that arise from a major realignment of currencies are significant, the company may need to disclose them separately in its profit and loss account as an exceptional item.

Translation of multi-currency share capital

18.37 The issue of shares by a company in more than one currency is considered in chapter 12 paragraphs 12.16 to 12.19. The question arises as to how such foreign currency share capital should be translated for reporting purposes at the company's year end. Two possibilities are considered below:

- Translate such share capital using the closing rate of exchange.

- Translate such capital using the historical rate at the date that the shares were issued.

Views differ on which method should be used, and both are acceptable. The former method moves the value of share capital in line with exchange rate movements. The latter method preserves the historical value of the capital, any translation difference being reported as a reserve movement. Consequently, both methods have the same effect on shareholders funds.

Example

A parent company denominates its share capital in US dollars with effect from 31st January 1990. The group's reporting date is 31st December. The company wishes to present its consolidated financial statements for the year to 31st December 1990 in US dollars (having previously reported in Sterling) and wonders what rate should be used to translate their opening reserves.

There are no hard and fast rules on the rate that should be used in this type of situation, but it is acceptable to use the rate that applied at 31st December 1989. The group should also disclose in a note to their consolidated financial statements an explanation of the rate used for translating the share capital and the rate used for translation the opening reserves.

Disclosure requirements

18.38 The extent of the disclosure requirements depends on whether or not the company is an exempt company. An exempt company is a banking company or an insurance company that chooses not to prepare its financial statements in accordance with section 226 of, and Schedule 4 to, the Act.

18.39 However, all companies to which SSAP 20 applies must disclose the translation methods they have used and also the way in which they have treated the resulting exchange differences. [SSAP 20 para 59]. They must disclose also the net movement on reserves that have arisen from exchange differences. [SSAP 20 para 60(b)].

18.40 In addition, companies that are not exempt companies (as outlined in para 18.38) must disclose the net amount of their exchange gains and losses on their foreign currency borrowings less deposits, and they must separately identify the following:

- The amount they have offset in reserves under the offset procedure explained in paragraphs 18.17 to 18.27 above.

- The net amount they have charged or credited to the profit and loss account.

[SSAP 20 para 60(a)].

18.41 Where a company departs from the historical cost rules, Schedule 4 to the Act requires it to make certain additional disclosures on a historical cost basis. Translation at closing rates does not, however, constitute a departure from the historical cost rules in Schedule 4. Consequently, a company is not required under the provisions of the Act to make additional disclosures on a historical cost basis.

Chapter 19

REALISED AND DISTRIBUTABLE PROFITS

Chapter 19

REALISED AND DISTRIBUTABLE PROFITS

Introduction

19.1 Companies may make a distribution to their shareholders only out of profits that are available for distribution. Part VIII of the Act, 'Distribution of profits and assets', imposes conditions that companies must satisfy before they can make distributions. Some of these conditions apply only to public companies. Also, special provisions apply to investment companies and insurance companies, and these provisions are considered in 'Manual of Accounting - volume III'.

19.2 The statutory rules in Part VIII of the Act supplement the common law requirements as to distributions. For example, under common law, a distribution can be made only in accordance with any conditions in a company's memorandum or articles of association.

Definition of distribution

19.3 For the purposes of Part VIII of the Act, 'distribution' is defined as any distribution of a company's assets to its shareholders (whether or not it is made in cash), *other than* a distribution that is made by way of any one of the following:

- The issue of either fully-paid or partly-paid bonus shares.

- The redemption or the purchase of any of the company's own shares, either out of capital, or out of the proceeds of a fresh issue of shares, or out of unrealised profits in accordance with Part V, Chapter VII of the Act.

- The reduction of share capital by either of the following means:

    - Extinguishing or reducing the liability in respect of share capital that is not paid up.

    - Paying off paid-up share capital.

- The distribution of assets to shareholders on a winding-up.

[Sec 263(2)].

Basic conditions applying to all companies other than investment companies and insurance companies

19.4 Any company (whether public or private) may make a distribution only out of 'profits available for the purpose'. [Sec 263(1)]. In this sense, the word 'make' means 'pay'. Therefore a company must have available sufficient profits at the time it pays a dividend not at the time it declares one.

19.5 For any company other than an investment company or an insurance company, profits available for distribution are the company's accumulated realised profits that have not previously been either distributed or capitalised, less its accumulated realised losses (insofar as they have not been previously written off in either a reduction or a re-organisation of capital). [Sec 263(3)]. The origin of these profits and losses may be either revenue or capital. [Sec 280(3)].

Additional conditions that public companies have to satisfy

19.6 In addition to the condition that it can make a distribution only out of profits available for the purpose, a public company can make a distribution only to the extent that the distribution does not reduce the amount of the company's net assets below the aggregate of its called-up share capital (defined in chapter 12, para 12.4) plus its undistributable reserves. [Sec 264(1)].

19.7 In this context, 'undistributable reserves' include:

- The share premium account.
- The capital redemption reserve.
- The excess of accumulated unrealised profits that have not previously been capitalised over accumulated unrealised losses that have not previously been written off by a reduction or a re-organisation of capital. For this purpose, capitalisation includes the issuing of bonus shares, but it excludes transfers of profits to the capital redemption reserve that have been made after 22nd December 1980.
- Any reserve that the company, for any other reason, is prohibited from distributing.

[Sec 264(3)].

19.8 The effect of this additional condition is that whereas a private company can make a distribution provided only that it has realised profits available, a public company can do so only if it has profits available after it has provided for any net unrealised losses.

19.9 The example below, which sets out extracts from the balance sheets of four companies, gives examples of the method of calculating distributable profits as outlined in paragraphs 19.4 to 19.6 above:

		Company 1		Company 2		Company 3		Company 4	
		£	£	£	£	£	£	£	£
A	Share capital		1,000		1,000		1,000		1,000
B	Unrealised profits	150		150		150		-	
C	Unrealised losses	-		(200)		(200)		(200)	
D	Net unrealised profits		150		-		-		-
E	Net unrealised losses		-		(50)		(50)		(200)
F	Realised profits	300		300		300		300	
G	Realised losses	-		-		(120)		(120)	
H	Net realised profits		300		300		180		180
I	Share capital and reserves		1,450		1,250		1,130		980
	Maximum distributable profit:								
	Private company (H)		300		300		180		180
	Public company (H - E)		300		250		130		Nil

The relevant accounts

19.10 The Act states that, in order to determine whether a company has profits available, and (if it is a public company) whether the additional condition in paragraph 19.6 above has been satisfied, reference must be made to certain items in the company's 'relevant accounts'. [Sec 270(2)].

19.11 The items to be referred to in the 'relevant accounts' are:

- Profits, losses, assets and liabilities.
- Provisions as defined in chapter 11 paragraph 11.54.
- Share capital and reserves (including undistributable reserves).

[Sec 270(2)].

19.12 The 'relevant accounts' are normally the company's latest audited financial statements that have been laid before the company in general meeting. [Sec 270(3)]. However, where a distribution would exceed the amount that is distributable according to the latest audited financial statements, *interim accounts* must be prepared and used in addition to the latest financial statements to justify the payment. These additional financial statements are necessary to enable a proper judgement to be made of the amounts of any of the relevant items referred to in paragraph 19.11 above. [Sec 270(4)(a)]. These interim accounts are different to those required under the International Stock Exchange's

Continuing Obligations. Furthermore, *initial accounts* must be prepared and used where a company proposes to make a distribution during its first accounting reference period (see further chapter 2 para 2.32) or before the date on which it lays its first audited financial statements before the shareholders. [Sec 270(4)(b)].

19.13 The Act lays down strict requirements in respect of the relevant accounts used for the purposes of testing the legality of a distribution. Failure to comply with these requirements will mean that the distribution will be illegal. [Sec 270(5)]. The shareholders cannot agree to waive the requirements. [*Re Precision Dippings Ltd v Precision Dippings Marketing Ltd* [1985] Ch 447]. These requirements do not apply to a private company's interim or initial accounts. However, the Act still requires a private company to prepare such accounts to enable the directors to make a reasonable judgement as to the profits available for distribution. [Sec 270].

19.14 The requirements for relevant accounts, including interim and initial accounts of public companies, are as follows:

- They must be 'properly prepared', or they must be so prepared at least to the extent that is necessary in order to decide whether or not a proposed distribution is legal. In particular, the items referred to in paragraph 19.11 above must be determined. [Sec 271(2), 272(2), 273(2)].

  For annual financial statements, 'properly prepared' means that they must comply with Part VII of the Act. For either *interim or initial* accounts, it means that they must comply with section 226 of the Act (that is, both the form and the content must comply with Schedule 4). It also means that the balance sheet comprised in those accounts has to be signed by the directors in accordance with section 233 of the Act. [Sec 272(3), 273(3)].

- They must give a true and fair view of both the state of the company's affairs and its profit or loss. [Sec 271(2), 272(3), 273(3)].

- They must not include, for a public company, any uncalled share capital as an asset. [Sec 264(4)].

- With annual financial statements, the auditors must have given their opinion on them in accordance with section 235 of the Act. [Sec 271(3)]. So far as *initial accounts* are concerned, the auditors must have reported whether, in their opinion, those accounts have been properly prepared. [Sec 273(4)]. *Interim accounts* need not be audited.

- If the auditors have qualified their opinion, they must state, in writing, whether the subject matter of their qualification is material in determining the legality of the proposed distribution. [Sec 271(3)(4), 273(4)(5)]. With annual financial statements, this statement will suffice if it relates to other distributions, provided that it covers, *inter alia,* distributions of the same description as the distribution proposed (see para 19.63). [Sec 271(5)].

- With annual financial statements, such statements must have been laid before the shareholders in general meeting. [Sec 271(4)]. With *initial* accounts, a copy of those accounts, together with a copy of the auditors' report and such statement (where applicable), must have been delivered to the Registrar of Companies. [Sec 273(6)]. With *interim* accounts, it is required only that a copy of the accounts should be delivered to the Registrar of Companies. [Sec 272(4)].

19.15 If any document in a set of accounts that must be delivered to the Registrar of Companies is in a foreign language, a certified translation of that document must also be delivered to the Registrar of Companies. [Sec 242(1), 272(5), 273(7)]. However, the Registrar of Companies will accept financial statements in a currency other than sterling, provided that they include the exchange rate between that currency and sterling at the balance sheet date.

19.16 Both *interim* and *initial* accounts delivered to the Registrar of Companies in accordance with the above requirements are unlikely to need to include a directors' report in order to give a true and fair view.

19.17 A company may find that it does not have sufficient distributable reserves shown in its last relevant accounts to justify paying an interim dividend. Where this is so, the company will have to prepare *interim* accounts and, with a public company, will have to deliver them to the Registrar of Companies (in the way outlined above) to justify the payment of the interim dividend. In this situation, if the company is listed on The International Stock Exchange, it is advisable that the company should also release the interim accounts to The International Stock Exchange. This is because the interim accounts may contain price-sensitive information, and the Continuing Obligations include a general requirement that such information should be released to The International Stock Exchange as soon as it is available. A similar requirement in the USM's General Undertaking makes it advisable that a company traded on the USM should do the same.

19.18 A particular set of financial statements may have been used to determine whether a distribution can be made. If it is proposed to determine the legality of a subsequent distribution by reference to the same financial statements, the amount of the proposed distribution must be notionally increased by the amount of the earlier distribution. [Sec 274(1)]. The object of this requirement is to prevent a company avoiding the restrictions by making several small distributions that are permissible individually, but which, when taken in aggregate, exceed the amount available for distribution.

19.19 Consider the two situations below:

	A	B
	£	£
Distributable profits, per relevant accounts	30,000	20,000
Distribution already made by reference to those accounts	15,000	15,000
Proposed further distribution	10,000	10,000

If the proposed further distribution is considered in isolation, then it is permissible in both situations. However, section 274(1) of the Act requires the proposed distribution to be added to those distributions that have already been made by reference to the same financial statements. This means that, in both situations, the amount to be compared with the profits available for distribution is £25,000 (that is, £15,000 + £10,000). In situation A, this is less than the distributable profits (£30,000) and so the further distribution is permissible. In situation B, however, the distributable profit is only £20,000. Consequently, the proposed further distribution of £10,000 is not permissible, and only £5,000 remains to be distributed.

Distinction between realised and unrealised profits and losses

19.20 Although section 263(3) of the Act provides that a company's available profits for distribution are *"its accumulated, realised profits ... less its accumulated, realised losses"*, the exact meaning of the term 'realised' is not defined in the Act (see also section 742(2)). Section 262(3) merely gives an indication of the interpretation of the term. It says that *"references to realised profits and realised losses, in relation to a company's accounts, are to such profits or losses of the company as fall to be treated as realised in accordance with principles generally accepted, at the time when the accounts are prepared, with respect to the determination for accounting purposes of realised profits or losses"*.

19.21 Moreover, there is little indication in case law of what is meant by 'realised'. The few cases that there have been mainly relate to tax law, rather than to company law. All that can really be derived from the cases is that the judges have interpreted 'realised' as meaning something wider than 'realised in cash', and also that they, like the legislature, see realisation as an accounting, rather than a strictly legal, concept.

19.22 Because of these difficulties of interpretation, the CCAB issued, in September 1982, the following guidance statements:

- TR 481 - The determination of realised profits and the disclosure of distributable profits in the context of the Companies Acts 1948 to 1981.

- TR 482 - The determination of distributable profits in the context of the Companies Acts 1948 to 1981.

19.23 These two guidance statements are reproduced as appendix VII. Although they both refer to the Companies Acts 1948 to 1981, they apply equally to the Companies Act 1985 (as amended by the Companies Act 1989), and all references below refer to the equivalent sections of the 1985 Act.

Technical release 481

19.24 The main purpose of TR 481 is to give guidance on the interpretation of the term 'principles generally accepted', as used in section 262(3) of the Act. The phrase is not defined in the Act. But it has been given a judicial interpretation, as being *"principles which are generally regarded as permissible or legitimate by the accountancy profession. That is sufficient even though only one company actually applies it in practice"*. [*Lord Denning, MR, in Associated Portland Cement Manufacturers Ltd v Price Commission.* [1975] ICR 27]. The main conclusions that TR 481 sets out are as follows:

- Unless an Accounting Standard specifically indicates that a profit should be treated as unrealised, a profit that is required by an Accounting Standard to be recognised in the profit and loss account should normally be treated as a realised profit. For example, SSAP 9, 'Stocks and long-term contracts', requires that attributable profit should be included in the value of long-term contracts (see chapter 10 paras 10.16 and 10.17). Consequently, this attributable profit should be treated as realised.

- A profit may be recognised in the profit and loss account in accordance with an accounting policy that is not the subject of an Accounting Standard, or (exceptionally) that is contrary to a standard. Such a profit will normally be a realised profit if the accounting policy is consistent with the two concepts of accruals and prudence as set out in both SSAP 2 and Schedule 4 to the Act (see chapter 3 paras 3.36 to 3.40).

- Where, in special circumstances, a company could not give a true and fair view (even if it provided additional information) without including an unrealised profit in its profit and loss account, the Act requires a company to include that unrealised profit. Moreover, where the directors have special reasons for doing so, Schedule 4 allows them to include an unrealised profit in the profit and loss account. Where unrealised profits are thus recognised in the profit and loss account, a note to the financial statements must give particulars of this departure from the statutory accounting principles, the reasons for it, and its effect (see chapter 3 para 3.28). [4 Sch 15].

19.25 In 1989 Professor Bryan Carsberg and Christopher Noke (of the London School of Economics) published a report entitled 'The reporting of profits and the concept of realisation'. The report was commissioned by the ICAEW's Research Board at the request of the ASC. The report's objective was to discuss the meaning of 'realised profits' and the reporting of unrealised items and to identify possible courses of action and to produce some recommendations.

19.26 First, they surveyed and analysed existing academic literature. This analysis led them to conclude that *"no single definition of the term 'realised profits' commands general acceptance"*. They went on to say that *"The British standard SSAP 2 contains definitions that are unclear. The US literature refers to variability of practice and avoids taking a firm position to end that variability"*.

19.27 Secondly, they used ideas from their survey of the literature to identify meanings of the term 'realisation' and to analyse the relative merits of those meanings. This work identified the following six possible meanings of 'realisation':

- Conversion into cash

  Under this approach, a profit (or loss) would be said to be realised whenever an asset is exchanged for cash. This option provides a narrow concept of realisation, much narrower than the one implied by current practice or required by the Act.

- Conversion into one of a set of specific assets

  This possibility allows conversion into assets other than cash, (for example, debtors) in order to recognise a realised profit on the sale of an asset on credit (in which circumstance the profit is marked by ownership of a debt). To justify this option, it is necessary to consider the intrinsic merits of the assets or invoke the reliability test which is considered below.

- Resulting from an exchange

  Under this approach, a profit is said to be realised whenever one asset is exchanged for another, regardless of the nearness-to-cash of the asset acquired. The asset acquired would presumably be measured at fair value and profit could be recognised even if the transaction was a straight swop of stock for stock.

- Earned by undertaking services

  Profit would be regarded as realised in step with the completion of the work required under a contract. This option might be used, for example, to indicate when profit could be recognised on a service where payment has been made in advance. This option can only be applied in situations where the net assets of a business have increased as a result of the undertaking's activities and not in situations where the focus is on the appreciation of assets while they are held.

- Represented by assets, whose values can be measured with acceptable reliability

  Under this option, no exchange transaction would necessarily be needed. A realised profit could result from holding an asset while its price increases. The sole criterion to recognise a realised profit would be the ability to measure the asset with confidence. Consequently, the asset measurement would have to be verifiable.

- Represented by a freely disposable store of wealth

  Profit would be recognised when an exchange or holding results in the ownership of an asset that could be disposed of without affecting the continuity of the business. However, the criterion of free disposability, if strictly interpreted, is a very restrictive test.

19.28 Professor Carsberg and Christopher Noke established a preference for the approach based on the reliability of measurement as outlined in the fifth point above. This approach would mean that a surplus or a gain should be included in profit only if its occurrence can be established from sufficiently reliable measurements. All gains as well as losses that can be recognised on the grounds of reliability carry useful information about financial performance. They suggested that only if such gains and losses are brought together for reporting purposes can adequate reporting take place.

19.29 Their overall conclusion was that they had failed to identify any currently accepted clear meaning of realisation. Indeed, they concluded that a clear meaning cannot be decided from current practice. Consequently, they recommended that the ASC should prepare a statement that would produce a general definition of realisation (probably by revising SSAP 2). They considered that the main purpose underlying the concept of realisation is to secure reliability of measurement to ensure that profits are recognised only when they can be said to have occurred with reasonable certainty. They also considered that a definition based on this concept should be explored. They suggested that, once realisation has been defined generally, individual standards should indicate the application of this general definition to specific situations. In addition, they considered that the traditional profit and loss account should be limited to legally distributable profits, and also that companies should be encouraged to publish an additional statement (perhaps a statement of 'total gains') to indicate the overall financial performance by bringing together all profits and gains. Finally, they recommended that the ASC should consider expressing a view about whether financial capital maintenance or physical capital maintenance is the preferable concept to form the basis for profit measurement in the main financial statements.

19.30 Until the ASC revises Accounting Standards to take account of Carsberg and Noke's research, TR 481 is the principal guidance available on determining which profits are realised and which are not.

Technical release 482

19.31 TR 482 gives guidance on the way in which a company should determine distributable profits in the context of current legislation. It states that, in general, companies are allowed to make distributions only out of realised profits, less realised losses (as outlined in para 19.5). In addition, a public company must deduct any net unrealised losses from net realised profits before making a distribution.

19.32 When determining the profits from which a company is allowed to make distributions, the starting point (the *"accumulated realised profits ... less accumulated realised losses"*) will normally be the accumulated balance on the profit and loss account. This figure may need adjusting to take into account any items that the company is required to exclude in determining its distributable profits (such as, the additional restrictions imposed on public companies referred to above).

19.33 Increasingly, there are differences between the balance on a company's profit and loss account and the amount that is realised (and so is distributable in law). A company may or may not need to highlight, in its financial statements, the fact that there is a difference between the balance on the profit and loss account and the amount that is legally distributable. Where the difference is material, the financial statements may need to disclose the amounts of distributable and undistributable reserves respectively, in order to give a true and fair view.

19.34 This requirement may also apply when the size of a dividend paid or proposed is substantial, as compared to the total of distributable reserves, and there is the risk that the shareholders may be under the mistaken impression that the same level of dividends can be maintained in the future without unrealised profits being turned into realised profits. In these circumstances, companies should disclose the difference between the balance on the profit and loss account and the amount that is legally distributable, in order that their financial statements should give a true and fair view.

Effect that revaluations of fixed assets have on distributable profits

19.35 An example of an adjustment that may be necessary to arrive at the profit available for distribution arises when fixed assets have been revalued. Consider the following situations:

19.36 First, provisions for the depreciation of revalued fixed assets require special treatment to the extent that they *exceed* the amounts that would have been provided if the assets had not been revalued. For the purpose of calculating the amount of profit that is legally available for distribution, a company is required to treat an amount equivalent to the excess depreciation on the revaluation surplus as a realised profit. [Sec 275(2)]. In this way, the provision for depreciation that is charged in the profit and loss account is reduced to the amount that would have been charged on the asset's original cost.

19.37 As a result, when fixed assets have been revalued, the depreciation of the 'surplus element' will not normally affect the amount of a company's accumulated distributable profits. However, it will affect its annual profits as stated in the published financial statements (see also chapter 5 paras 5.49 to 5.56).

19.38 The example that follows, which ignores the effect of taxation, illustrates the implications of section 275(2).

	Cost	Valuation	Difference between cost and valuation
	£	£	£
Fixed assets	1,000	2,500	1,500
Profit before depreciation	5,000	5,000	N/A
Depreciation at 10% a year	100	250	150
Profit after depreciation	4,900	4,750	N/A

If the Act did not contain section 275(2), the distributable profit for the period would be £4,750, because the profit that the financial statements disclosed would be the profit after charging depreciation on the revalued amount. The effect of section 275(2) is to add back the additional depreciation of £150 (that arises because the assets have been revalued) in determining the profits available for distribution. Without this provision, companies might be discouraged from revaluing their fixed assets, because the extra depreciation to be charged on the resulting surplus would have the effect of reducing their profits available for distribution.

This provision is illustrated in Table 70.

Table 70: Illustration of the excess depreciation on revalued assets being transferred from the revaluation reserve to the profit and loss account.

Extract from Thomas Locker (Holdings) plc Report and Accounts 31st March 1989.

Note extract

20 Reserves

	Revaluation reserve £000	Other non-distributable reserves £000	Profit and loss account £000
Group			
At 1st April 1988	4,055	258	10,140
Unrealised exchange adjustments	229	(4)	534
Profit for the year		12	718
Surplus on revaluation of fixed asset investments	145		
Purchased goodwill written off			(303)
Transfers	(167)	(5)	172
At 31st March 1989	4,262	261	11,261
Parent company			
At 1st April 1988	1,154		5,034
Unrealised exchange adjustments			4
Profit for the year			177
Transfer	(13)		13
At 31st March 1989	1,141	–	5,228

Goodwill written off relates to the acquisition of the business of the Synthetic Screening Section of Robinson Milling Systems Limited.

The transfer from revaluation reserve to profit and loss account relates to depreciation provided during the year on the revaluation surplus as at 1st April 1988 and to the revaluation surplus realised on disposals.

The group reserves include £4,636,000 (1988, £3,906,000) in respect of certain subsidiaries operating overseas which, if distributed as dividends, would involve additional taxation liabilities for which no provision has been made.

The profit and loss account at 31st March 1989 incluides £274,000 (1988, £297,000) which is frozen temporarily by South African government regulations.

Commercial rates of exchange have been used in translating the accounts of the South African and Belgian subsidiaries.

19.39 Secondly, adjustments will be required also for any items taken to reserves that may properly be included in the determination of distributable profits. For example, an unrealised profit on an asset revaluation will originally be credited direct to a revaluation reserve.

When the asset is subsequently disposed of, the whole profit is clearly realised, notwithstanding the fact that all or part of it may not have been passed through the profit and loss account. In addition, where a revalued asset is disposed of any deficit over cost that has previously been treated as unrealised should be redesignated as a realised loss.

19.40 Where an asset's original cost is not known, or where it is not possible to ascertain it without unreasonable delay or expense, its cost is taken to be the value shown in the company's earliest available record of its value. [Sec 275(3)].

19.41 The CCAB guidance statement TR 482 also discusses the writing-back of past depreciation when an asset is revalued. However, opinion is divided as to whether the amount of depreciation written back represents a realised or an unrealised surplus, and the guidance statement gives no firm guidance. SSAP 12 paragraph 22 comments that this depreciation should not be written back to the profit and loss account, except to the extent that it relates to a provision for permanent diminution in value which is subsequently found to be unnecessary. However, this comment does not necessarily answer the question of whether the profit is realised or not. Where a company places reliance on such a profit being realised in order to make a distribution, the directors may find it appropriate to seek legal advice.

19.42 Thirdly, unless it offsets a previous unrealised surplus on the same asset, a deficit on the revaluation of an asset gives rise to a provision, and that deficit must be treated as a realised loss. Such a realised loss cannot be reduced by being offset (either wholly or in part) against revaluation surpluses on other assets (whether or not they are of the same class). There is, however, an exception to this. The Act says that where a provision for the diminution in value of a fixed asset arises on a revaluation of *all* the fixed assets, such a provision may be treated as unrealised. [Sec 275(1)]. A revaluation of all of the company's fixed assets may exclude the revaluation of goodwill. [Sec 275(1)]. Furthermore, in this connection, the directors may *consider* the value of a fixed asset and treat that consideration as a revaluation of that asset. [Sec 275(4)]. This means that the directors do not need to have all of the fixed assets professionally valued in order to take advantage of the provision in section 275(1). But they must consider the value of all those assets that have not been revalued, and they must comply with the other conditions that are listed in paragraphs 19.47 and 19.48 below.

Treatment of revalued assets in relevant accounts

19.43 The interpretation of the provisions in section 275 has caused numerous problems. Guidance on some of these problems is set out in paragraph 19.51 below. However, this guidance needs to be read with an understanding of sections 275(1), 275(4), 275(5) and 275(6) of the Act. These are, therefore, summarised in paragraphs 19.44 to 19.50 that follow.

19.44 Section 275(1) of the Act states that a diminution in value of a fixed asset that appears when all the company's fixed assets are revalued, need not be treated as a realised loss.

19.45 In determining whether a revaluation of a company's fixed assets has taken place for the purposes of section 275(1), the directors' *consideration* of the value at any particular time of any fixed asset may be treated as a revaluation. [Sec. 275(4)]. However, a company may, in such circumstances, take advantage of the exemption contained in section 275(1) only where the conditions in paragraphs 19.47 and 19.48 below are satisfied.

19.46 For this purpose, 'consideration' does not necessarily mean the directors' valuation of the asset as an individual item. It simply means that the directors should have addressed themselves to the question of the asset's value for the purpose of determining the legitimacy of distributions.

19.47 The conditions referred to in paragraphs 19.42 and 19.45 above that must be satisfied are as follows:

- All the company's fixed assets (or all those other than goodwill) have been revalued, either by an actual revaluation or by the directors' consideration of their value.

- The directors are satisfied that the aggregate value of the fixed assets that they have treated as having been revalued only because they considered the assets' value at the time in question, is not less than the aggregate amount at which those assets are, for the time being, stated in the company's financial statements. [Sec 275(5)]. However, the directors will not be able to use this consideration to justify treating a provision as unrealised unless the notes to the relevant accounts state that:

  - ☐ The directors have considered the value of some of the company's fixed assets, without actually revaluing those assets.

  - ☐ The directors are satisfied that the aggregate value of those assets whose value they have considered was not less than the aggregate amount at which those assets are or were stated in the company's accounts.

- ☐ The asset or assets that have diminished in value are recorded in the company's relevant accounts after providing for that diminution in value.

[Sec 275(6)].

19.48 In addition, the directors' consideration of the value of those fixed assets that have not been revalued must take place at the same time as, and must consider the value at the same date as, the revaluation that recognised the particular asset's diminution in value. The notes must also state this fact. [Sec 275(6)(c)].

Example

In December 1989, a professional valuer values as at 30th June 1989 a company's land and buildings, then the directors must, also in December 1989, consider the value of all the other fixed assets (with the exception of goodwill) as at 30th June 1989. This means that where, to justify a distribution in (say) early 1991, the directors prepare relevant accounts (the last relevant accounts being those to December 1989), they are not allowed to consider retrospectively the value as at 30th June 1989 of all the company's assets that were not revalued in December 1989.

19.49 Surprisingly, where a company revalues all of its fixed assets, then even where an actual revaluation shows an overall deficit, the diminution in value of the asset that is being accounted for can still be treated as an unrealised loss for distribution purposes. This interpretation appears to be inconsistent with normal accounting convention which would treat such deficits as a charge to the profit and loss account, that is, as if it were a realised loss. However, the diminution in value of the asset that is being accounted for will reduce a public company's distributable profits if, as a result of the provision, there is a net deficit on the revaluation reserve. This is because a public company's distribution must not reduce its net assets to less than its share capital plus undistributable reserves (see para 19.6).

19.50 The information that follows is used to illustrate four situations that may arise when directors consider the value of a company's assets.

	Book value £000	Market value £000	Deficit £000
Land and buildings	1,000	750	250
Plant and machinery	50	40	10
	1,050	790	260

The four situations are as follows:

- The market value of all the fixed assets has been determined by a professional valuation. The diminutions in value may, therefore, be treated as unrealised losses, even though there is an overall deficit of £260,000. The reason for this is that the deficit results from a revaluation of all the fixed assets. [See 275(1)].

- The market value of the land and buildings has been determined by a professional valuation, but the market value of the plant and machinery results from the directors' consideration of its value. Because the aggregate value of the assets that the directors have considered is £40,000, which is less than their book value of £50,000, the directors cannot claim to be satisfied that those assets' aggregate value is not less than their book value. The directors are, therefore, not able to rely on the exemption in section 275(1) and so they must treat the deficit on the revaluation of the land and buildings as well as the deficit on the plant and machinery as a realised loss. [Sec 275(5)].

- If the directors considered that the plant and machinery's market value was £60,000 (not £40,000), then they would be able to treat the deficit on the land and buildings of £250,000 as unrealised. This applies even though the fixed assets have an overall deficit of £240,000.

- However, in both the first and the third situations, if the company was a public company, it might still be prevented from making a distribution even if it could treat the loss as unrealised. This is because a distribution must not reduce the amount of a public company's net assets below the aggregate of its called-up share capital plus its undistributable reserves.. [Sec 264(1)].

Interpretation of the provisions of section 275

19.51 Paragraph 19.43 above refers to the fact that these provisions of section 275 have caused many problems when companies determine their distributable profits. The responses to the questions discussed below are based on guidance given by Counsel.

- Where a provision has been charged to realised profits, and it is subsequently released, does this restore the realised profits in question?

  Where an asset has been either written down or provided against and it is then written up again, the initial reaction is that the write-up constitutes a profit that *prima facie* appears to be unrealised. However, it seems correct that the write-up should be treated as a realised profit to the extent that the previous reduction was charged to realised profits. (This view is supported by *Bishop v Smyrna and Cassaba Railway Co.* [1895] 2 Ch 596, in particular at page 601, and by *Stapley v Read Bros.* [1924] 2 Ch 1.) Furthermore, paragraph 19(3) of Schedule 4 requires a company to write back such a provision no longer required to the profit and loss account. The write back to the profit and loss account will fall to be treated as realised.

- In what order should releases of provisions be applied where provisions have been made in previous years, and where some of these have been treated as realised losses and some as unrealised losses?

The principle expressed above is easy enough to apply when all provisions have been charged against the same reserve, and where the whole of a particular provision is restored at the same time. It seems that there is no established authority or principle that lays down any rule where the position is less simple. The best solution would seem to be to apply common sense. This solution leads to the conclusion that the more recent parts of the provision should normally be regarded as being released before the earlier parts.

- What is the meaning of the words 'value' and 'the company's accounts' in sections 275(4) and 275(5) respectively?

It seems clear that the word 'value' in section 275(4) means market value, and not book value.

The question arises whether the 'company's accounts' that are referred to in section 275(5), are those financial statements (to, say, 30th September 1989), which are in the course of preparation, and in which the directors have adjusted the assets' book values (by taking into account depreciation, for example), or the previous financial statements (that is, those to 30th September 1988).

When section 275(4) is relied on, section 275(6) deals with the contents of the note to the financial statements where the directors have considered the value of any of the company's fixed assets, without actually revaluing those assets. Section 275(6)(b) requires the notes to state:

> *"That they (the directors) are satisfied that the aggregate value of those assets at the time in question is or was not less than the aggregate amount at which they are or were for the time being stated in the company's accounts."*

This note makes it clear that the company's accounts for the purpose of section 275(5) are those in which the revaluation is incorporated. Thus the directors must compare actual values with the values at which the relevant assets are to be incorporated in the accounts.

This view is supported by the fact that the section 275(4) procedure, including the requirement for a section 275(6) note, applies also to *initial* accounts being prepared.

- If no dividend is to be paid by reference to the relevant accounts, but the directors have considered the value of the company's fixed assets in accordance with section 275(6), does that section require that the note that is needed if a distribution is to be made should be included in those relevant accounts?

Relevant accounts are those financial statements that contain the entries that justify a particular distribution, either because they show adequate distributable profits or because they have been specially prepared in order to justify the distribution. (This interpretation seems clear from section 270 generally and, in particular, from subsections (2) and (3) and the introductory words of sections 271(1), 272(1) and 273(1)).

Consequently, it appears to follow that, if a company does not propose to justify a particular distribution by reference to a particular set of financial statements, section 275(6) does not require those financial statements to contain the special note, because those financial statements are not *relevant accounts*.

Accordingly, it seems that the note that section 275(6) requires need not appear in the financial statements either for the year in which the section 275(4) revaluation took place, or for a subsequent year, unless those financial statements are to be relied upon for the purpose of justifying a distribution.

However, if the note is excluded from the financial statements, the directors cannot use those financial statements to justify a distribution in the future. Although the directors may have no plans at that time to make a distribution, they may wish to do so at some time before the next audited financial statements are prepared. If they have not included the note required by section 275(6) in their last set of financial statements, then they will need to prepare *interim accounts* to justify the proposed distribution. Consequently, it will be sensible to include in the financial statements the note that section 275(6) requires, even where the directors do not intend at that time to make a distribution.

However, for a private company, the note need not appear in the *interim* or the *initial* accounts that the directors rely upon to justify making a distribution. This is because sections 272 and 273 do not apply to private companies.

- Where the note that section 275(6) requires is not included in a company's financial statements, does this omission convert a provision on a revaluation that is made in those financial statements into a realised loss for all future financial statements that are to be used as relevant accounts?

It appears that any financial statements that are used to justify a distribution are *relevant accounts*. And, for the purposes of section 275(6), they are the relevant accounts, even if the directors do not need to rely on the particular section 275(4) revaluation in order to justify a current distribution. Accordingly, if a set of financial statements that does not contain a note relating to a section

275(4) revaluation that took place in either that year or a previous year, become *relevant accounts* (because they are used to justify a distribution), it seems that the provision that is made on that revaluation becomes, and must remain, a realised loss. Where it becomes necessary to rely on section 275(4) to justify a subsequent distribution, it will be too late to include the section 275(6) note in a subsequent set of financial statements.

This last point, however, is a difficult issue, and it is still the subject of debate. Consequently, this is another reason why it is advisable to include in any financial statements the note that section 275(6) requires, even where a distribution is not to be made by reference to those financial statements.

Summary of desirable action

19.52 To summarise, therefore, when the directors have some of the company's assets valued, and the deficits that arise on this revaluation affect the company's ability to pay a dividend, the directors should:

- Consider the value as at the same date of all other assets (excluding goodwill) themselves at the same time that the valuation of the assets that shows the deficit is made.

- Include the note referred to in the second point of paragraph 19.47 above in the financial statements for the year in which the valuation took place. The directors should do this even if they do not intend to make a distribution by reference to those financial statements.

- Repeat that note in all subsequent financial statements, because they may become *relevant accounts* for the purpose of making a distribution in the future.

19.53 If the directors take these three steps, any deficits that arise from a revaluation of the company's assets may be treated as unrealised for the purpose of making distributions.

Effect that foreign currency translation has on distributable profits

19.54 SSAP 20 requires that a company should translate those of its currency transactions that are outstanding at the end of the year (for example, creditors for fixed assets purchased from overseas, and currency loans) using the rate of exchange at the balance sheet date (that is, the closing rate). Where, however, the rate of exchange is fixed under the terms of the relevant transaction, the company should use that rate. Where an outstanding trading transaction is covered by a related or a matching forward contract, the rate specified in that contract may be used. [SSAP 20 para 48].

19.55 Exchange gains and losses will arise both on the currency transactions a company completes during the year and on its currency transactions outstanding at the end of the year. The company should include all such exchange differences in its profit or loss for the year from ordinary operations. The only exception to this rule is that an exchange difference on a currency transaction that is itself treated as an extraordinary item should be included as part of that item. [SSAP 20 para 49].

19.56 However, not all exchange gains on the translation of currency transactions that are included in the profit and loss account are realised. There is a conflict here with paragraph 12 of Schedule 4 to the Act, because this paragraph states that *"only profits realised at the balance sheet date shall be included in the profit and loss account"*.

19.57 Where exchange gains arise on short-term monetary items, their ultimate cash realisation can normally be assessed with reasonable certainty. Monetary items are defined in SSAP 20 as money held and amounts to be either received or paid in money. [SSAP 20 para 44]. Where a company is not an exempt company (as defined in SSAP 20), monetary items should be categorised as either short-term or long-term items. Short-term monetary items are those that fall due within one year of the balance sheet date. Therefore, such gains are realised in accordance with the prudence concept defined in SSAP 2. Accordingly, if they are included in the profit and loss account, this treatment does not conflict with paragraph 12 of Schedule 4 to the Act.

19.58 Exchange gains that arise on long-term monetary items are not realised, but there is a special reason for a company to include these gains in its profit and loss account. The special reason is that the company should treat exchange gains and exchange losses symmetrically. Exchange gains can be determined just as objectively as exchange losses. Consequently, it would be illogical to account for adverse movements in exchange rates and then not to account also for favourable movements. [SSAP 20 para 10]. Paragraph 15 of Schedule 4 to the Act states that, where there is a special reason, companies may depart from the accounting principles in Schedule 4. Where a company does include exchange gains on long-term monetary items in its profit and loss account, it must state, in its financial statements, the particulars of, the reasons for, and the effect of, the departure from the Act. [4 Sch 15].

19.59 However, SSAP 20 does recognise that, in exceptional circumstances, it may be prudent for a company to restrict the amount of the exchange gain on long-term monetary items (or the amount by which the gain exceeds past losses on the same items) that it recognises in the profit and loss account. This restriction would be appropriate where the company has doubts about either the convertibility or the marketability of the currency in question. [SSAP 20 para 50].

19.60 Where exchange gains on long-term monetary items are included in the profit and loss account, they will be unrealised to the extent that they exceed past losses on the same items. Where exchange losses on long-term monetary items are included in the profit and loss account, they will be realised to the extent that they exceed past unrealised gains on the same items. To illustrate this, consider the following example.

Example

In 1989, a UK company took out a long-term US dollar loan. It did not use the loan to finance a foreign equity investment. Consequently, the company must include in its profit and loss account the exchange gains and losses that arise when the loan is retranslated at the closing rate. (There are no doubts as to either the convertibility or the marketability of US dollars.)

Assuming that the exchange differences were as shown below, they should be treated either as unrealised or as realised in the way indicated below.

Year ended 31 December	Exchange gain/(loss) included in profit and loss account	Unrealised	Realised	Note
	£	£	£	
1989	250,000	250,000	-	(a)
1990	(300,000)	(250,000)	(50,000)	(b)
		-	(50,000)	
1991	75,000	25,000	50,000	(c)
		25,000	-	
1992	50,000	50,000	-	(d)
		75,000	-	

Notes to the example above:

(a) The company must treat the whole of the exchange gain as unrealised.

(b) On the basis that the exchange loss reverses the previous exchange gain on the loan, it would appear equitable that the company can treat £250,000 of the loss as unrealised. The company must treat the balance of the loss as realised.

(c) The company can treat the gain as realised to the extent that it reverses a past loss on the loan. It must treat the balance of the gain as unrealised.

(d) The company must treat the whole of the exchange gain as unrealised.

19.61 In order to identify unrealised exchange gains on the translation of long-term monetary items, a company will need to keep detailed records of the exchange gains and losses that arise over the life of each long-term monetary item.

19.62 Where the exchange difference on a borrowing is a loss, it can be argued that the loss is not a provision because it is not a loss *"either likely to be incurred, or certain to be incurred but uncertain as to amount or as to the date on which it will arise"* [4 Sch 89]. On the basis of this argument, a company would not have to take such a loss into account when determining its distributable profits. Because of the uncertainty that exists, the ASC's Technical Release that accompanies SSAP 20 suggests that, if sufficient distributable profit exists only as a result of the company offsetting a loss on its currency borrowings against a gain on its related foreign equity investments, it may be appropriate for the directors to obtain legal advice. Foreign currency translation is also considered in chapter 18.

Qualified audit reports and distributions

19.63 As mentioned in the fifth point of paragraph 19.14 above, if the auditors have qualified their opinion, they must state in writing whether the subject matter of their qualification is material in determining the legality of the proposed distribution. [Sec 271(3)(4), 273(4)(5)].

19.64 Therefore, where auditors qualify their report on the annual financial statements of a company that is proposing to pay a dividend, they will need to make an additional statement to the shareholders. This statement must be laid before the company in general meeting. [Sec 271(4)].

19.65 Many companies pay interim dividends, and the annual financial statements that the auditors report on will constitute the *relevant accounts* for the purposes of those interim dividends. Accordingly, auditors should, whenever possible, word their report in the annual financial statements to cover any future distributions.

19.66 The implication of a qualified audit report may be either *favourable* or *unfavourable*. An audit qualification may be material for distribution purposes, but in a favourable sense. For example, it may be possible to say that if any adjustment was to be made to eliminate the need for the qualification, it could have the effect only of increasing the company's net assets or realised profits. In this situation, the qualification is regarded as *favourable* for distribution purposes. An *unfavourable* qualification means that the profits available for distribution could be less than the amount shown in the financial statements.

19.67 Where the effect of the auditors' qualification is *favourable,* the auditors could include the following additional statement in their report:

> In our opinion, the qualification is not material for the purpose of determining whether any distribution payable by reference to these financial statements is permitted under the Companies Act 1985.

19.68 Where the auditors can quantify the effect of an audit qualification that is *unfavourable* but not material for this purpose, they could word the additional statement in their report as follows:

> In our opinion, the qualification is not material for the purpose of determining whether distributions not exceeding £X in total payable by reference to these financial statements are permitted under the Companies Act 1985.

19.69 If the auditors can word their statement on these lines, and not restrict it to the legality of the proposed final dividend only, they will not need to make a further statement in respect of the next interim dividend. If, however, the auditors do have to make a further statement, the company will have to hold a general meeting to lay the statement before the shareholders.

Other matters

Bonus issues

19.70 Some companies have found that they have utilised past revaluation reserves for bonus issues. The question has then arisen as to whether, in order to comply with the Act, they need to reinstate the revaluation reserves out of distributable reserves.

19.71 Although the position is not entirely clear, there is a strong argument against the need to reinstate the revaluation reserve. Section 264(3) of the Act defines a company's undistributable reserves as including *"the amount by which the company's accumulated unrealised profits, so far as not previously utilised by capitalisation ... exceed its accumulated, unrealised losses (so far as not previously written off in a reduction or reorganisation of capital duly made)"*. Capitalisation is defined as including every description of capitalisation except a transfer of the company's profits to its capital redemption reserve on or after 22nd December 1980. This definition implies that a company may utilise its undistributable reserves, such as a revaluation reserve, for bonus issues. In addition, there is no specific provision in the Act that requires the revaluation reserve to be reinstated if it has been utilised in a manner the law permits.

19.72 Companies may not make bonus issues unless their articles of association expressly permit them to do so. Therefore, newly-incorporated companies must take express power in their articles to make bonus issues out of unrealised profits (for example, as detailed in article 110 of Table A, SI 1985/805). However, companies that existed before 22nd December 1980 need not alter their articles to do this if immediately before that date they had power under their articles to capitalise unrealised profits. With companies that existed at 22nd December 1980, this means that a power in the articles to make bonus issues out of profits available for dividend will be deemed to include a power to make bonus issues out of unrealised profits. [Sec 278].

Amounts unpaid on debentures and shares

19.73 A company may not apply an unrealised profit to pay up debentures or any amounts that are unpaid on its issued shares. [Sec 263(4)]. The purpose of this prohibition is to prevent profits that are not available for distribution being made available indirectly for dividend purposes.

Profits and losses made before 22nd December 1980

19.74 Where the directors are unable to determine whether a profit or a loss that was made before 22nd December 1980 is realised or unrealised, they may treat the profit as realised and the loss as unrealised. [Sec 263(5)].

Capitalisation of development costs

19.75 Where development costs are capitalised and are shown as an asset in a company's balance sheet (see chapter 7 paras 7.16 to 7.37), any amount capitalised *must* nevertheless be treated as a realised revenue loss. [Sec 269(1)]. This does not apply to any part of the amount in the balance sheet that represents an unrealised profit on a revaluation of the development costs. It does not apply also if there are special circumstances that justify the directors deciding not to treat the capitalised development costs as a realised (revenue) loss. In this situation, the note that states the reasons for capitalising development costs must state also that the development costs have not been treated as a realised revenue loss. In addition, the note must state the justification the directors used for adopting this treatment. [Sec 269(2)].

Consolidated financial statements

19.76 Where consolidated financial statements are prepared, the relevant distributable profits will be the parent company's realised profits. This is because distributable profits must be established for individual companies, and by definition, groups of companies are not individual companies. However, some groups disclose also aggregate distributable reserves of the group (for example, see Table 71).

19.77 Consequently, a situation may arise where the group has sufficient distributable profits in aggregate to make a desired distribution, but the parent company itself has insufficient distributable profits. In this situation, a distribution may not be made to the parent company's shareholders without distributions first being made from the subsidiaries to the parent company to pass the distributable profits to the parent company. The parent company must then prepare *relevant accounts* that account for the receipt of these distributions in order to justify a distribution to its shareholders (see further paras 19.10 to 19.19). However, these relevant accounts need only include the parent company's financial statements (not the consolidated financial statements), because it is the parent company that will make the distribution.

Table 71: Illustration of a group that discloses the reserves that are distributable for both the group and the holding company.

Extract from British Airways Plc Report & Accounts 31st March 1989.

Note extract

19 RESERVES	Distributable	Non-distributable		Total	
	Profit and loss account £m	Revaluation reserve £m	Other reserve £m	1989 £m	*1988 £m*
a GROUP					
Balance 1 April	248	212	(7)	453	*425*
Retained profit for the year	119			119	*101*
Valuation of aircraft fleets					*277*
Transfers related to valued assets	45	(45)			
Exchange adjustments – Fleet assets *(note 10a)*	(1)			(1)	*6*
Purchased goodwill written off					*(357)*
Other movements			(2)	(2)	*1*
Balance 31 March	411	167	(9)	569	*453*

	Distributable	Non-distributable		Total	
	Profit and loss account £m	Revaluation reserve £m	Other reserve £m	1989 £m	*1988 £m*
b COMPANY					
Balance 1 April	258	212		470	*415*
Retained profit for the year:					
Trading results	101			101	*26*
Absorption of BCal liabilities on transfer of the business to British Airways Plc	(36)			(36)	*(253)*
Valuation of aircraft fleets					*277*
Transfers relating to valued assets	45	(45)			
Exchange adjustments – Fleet assets *(note 10a)*	(1)			(1)	*6*
Other movements	2			2	*(1)*
Balance 31 March	369	167		536	*470*

19.78 If a parent company or a subsidiary has assets that have been revalued in accordance with the alternative accounting rules, the revaluation reserve is unrealised. However, if the company concerned sells these revalued assets to another company within the same group, the revaluation reserve becomes realised. It then appears *prima facie* that these reserves are available for distribution. Similarly, a parent company could sell one of its subsidiaries to another subsidiary to create distributable reserves. If these transactions are carried out at arm's length and are supported by proper legal documentation, the resulting surpluses appear to be realised. The fact that a transaction is undertaken between companies in the same group need not prevent the profit on the transaction being realised, and therefore distributable. If the transaction is entirely artificial, however, it may be unlawful to make a distribution from the resulting profit. This point has not yet been tested in the courts. As an example, however, Counsel has advised that, where the consideration is left outstanding because the group company that was purchasing the asset did not have sufficient funds to complete the transaction, then the transaction would not be legally valid for the purpose of creating realised profits. Where a company wishes to create distributable profits by an intra-group transaction, it would be wise for it to seek legal advice if it has any doubts about the legality of the proposed distribution.

19.79 Such transactions create problems on consolidation. Consider the following two examples:

Example 1

A subsidiary has a property that originally cost £100,000 but it has been revalued in the subsidiary's books to £500,000. Ignoring any depreciation, the revaluation reserve balance is £400,000. The subsidiary then sells the property to a fellow subsidiary in an arm's length transaction for £500,000 (its open market value). Consequently, the subsidiary will show in its profit and loss account the surplus on disposal of the property of £400,000. If the transaction is legally valid, the subsidiary may then distribute this realised profit to its parent company. However, as far as the group is concerned, there is no disposal. Therefore, on consolidation, the revaluation surplus that has been realised should be reinstated as an unrealised revaluation reserve. An additional problem may arise if the parent company decides to distribute these funds to its shareholders. In these circumstances, funds have left the group, and the transaction may need to be explained further if the consolidated financial statements are to give a true and fair view.

Example 2

The situation is similar to that described above, except that the realised profit in the subsidiary represents pre-acquisition reserves. Pre-acquisition reserves are a company's retained earnings at the date on which that company becomes a subsidiary of another company. Before the enactment of the Companies Act 1981, where a subsidiary paid a dividend to its parent company out of its pre-acquisition profits, the parent company would treat the dividend received as a reduction of the cost of its investment in that subsidiary. Consequently, dividends the subsidiary paid to the parent company out of pre-acquisition profits were not available for distribution to the parent company's shareholders.

However, the Companies Act 1981 amended paragraph 15(5) of the then Schedule 8 to the Companies Act 1948. This change had the effect that where a subsidiary now pays a dividend to its parent company out of pre-acquisition profits, that dividend need not necessarily be applied as a reduction in the cost of the investment in the subsidiary. [SSAP 23 appendix para 3]. Such a dividend should be applied to reduce the carrying value of the investment to the extent that it is necessary to provide for a diminution in value of the investment in the subsidiary as stated in the parent company's financial statements. To the extent that this is not necessary, it appears that the amount received will be a realised profit in the hands of the parent company. However, in this example on consolidation, any part of the dividend received by the parent company that has not been applied to reduce the cost of the investment, will need to be adjusted on consolidation by taking out of the parent company's realised reserves an amount that will cause the goodwill on consolidation to remain the same as in previous years. If, as in the first example, the parent company decides to distribute these funds to its shareholders, the transaction may need to be explained further if the consolidated financial statements are to give a true and fair view.

19.80 The elimination of unrealised profits or losses resulting from intra-group transactions are discussed further in 'Manual of Accounting - volume II' chapter 5.

Memorandum and articles of association

19.81 Distributions are not only influenced by the provisions of the Act. They may also be subject to any enactment, or any rule of law or any provision in the memorandum or articles of association that may restrict either the amounts available for distribution or the circumstances in which a distribution may be made. [Sec 281].

19.82 For example, investment companies are restricted by their memorandum and articles of association from distributing realised capital profits (see 'Manual of Accounting - volume III').

19.83 It is important, therefore, for the directors to have regard to the memorandum and articles, as well as to the statutory rules, before making a distribution. Also, a company cannot lawfully pay a dividend if, as a result, the company would either become insolvent, or have insufficient working capital to carry on its business.

Distributions in kind

19.84 A company may make a distribution that includes a non-cash asset. Where the asset to be distributed has been included in the relevant accounts, and part of the amount at which it is stated represents an unrealised profit, the Act allows that profit to be treated as realised for the purpose of the distribution. [Sec 276(a)]. The Act also allows that unrealised profit to be taken to the profit and loss account if this is done for the purpose of making the distribution. [Sec 276(b)]. However, the company's articles must contain a power to make such distributions. Table A contains this power in article 105, and it requires the dividend to be approved at a general meeting. [SI 1985/805]. The dividend is declared as a cash amount, and it is for the directors to satisfy themselves as to the asset's value.

19.85 The directors may have difficulty in determining a value to be placed on the asset that is being distributed. They should value the asset that is being distributed at its fair value in order to show the dividend at its fair value. The asset's fair value would, in most situations, be its open market value and the asset should, therefore, be valued at arm's length. Consequently, a surplus or a deficit (which is the difference between the asset's net book value and its fair value) may have to be accounted for in the company's financial statements. This surplus (or deficit) should be recorded as an extraordinary item in the company's profit and loss account. Consider the following example.

Example

A company wishes to distribute to its shareholders an asset that has a net book value of £9,000. The directors have obtained an independent open market valuation of the asset that assesses its value as £10,000. In order to give the true cost of the dividend, the company should record the unrealised profit of £1,000 (namely, £10,000 - £9,000) as an extraordinary item in its profit and loss account, and it should increase the asset's recorded value by £1,000. The company should then disclose a dividend of £10,000 in the profit and loss account and show the asset as having been disposed of. The company is not permitted to show the dividend as a deduction from reserves, because paragraph 3(7)(b) of Schedule 4 to the Act requires it to be shown in the company's profit and loss account.

19.86 The views expressed in the paragraph above are also supported in the judgment given by Hoffmann J in *Aveling Barford v Perion Ltd and others* [1989] 1 WLR 360. In that case, the plaintiff company sold property at considerably less than its fair value to the company's sole shareholder at the time when it had no distributable reserves. In delivering his judgment, the judge stated that:

> *"The sale to Perion was not a genuine exercise of the company's power under its memorandum to sell its assets. It was a sale at a gross undervalue for the purpose of enabling a profit to be realised by an entity controlled and put forward by its sole beneficial shareholder. This was as much a dressed-up distribution as the payment of excessive interest in Ridge Securities or excessive remuneration in Halt Garage. The company had at the time no distributable reserves and the sale was therefore ultra vires and incapable of validation by the approval or ratification by the shareholder."*

Liability for an unlawful distribution

19.87 Any shareholder of a company who receives an unlawful distribution is liable to repay it to the company if, at the time he received it, he knew, or he had reasonable grounds to believe, that it was made in contravention of the Act. [Sec 277(1)]. This provision is without prejudice to any other liability of a shareholder to repay distributions that have been unlawfully made to him. [Sec 277(2)].

19.88 Even where a distribution has been made that is apparently permitted by the relevant accounts, the directors may be personally liable in respect of payments made out of undistributable reserves. This situation may arise where the company makes a distribution that is covered by the distributable reserves shown in the last relevant accounts, but the company no longer has distributable reserves because they have been consumed by losses the company has made since those accounts were drawn up.

19.89 In these circumstances, the creditors may seek to have the company wound up. The liquidator may then sue the directors for making a distribution out of capital. Consequently, the directors should not only refer to the relevant accounts when they authorise a dividend: they should also take into account the company's results since the date on which those accounts were drawn up.

Chapter 20

DIRECTORS' REPORT

Chapter 20

DIRECTORS' REPORT

Introduction

20.1 The principal objective of the directors' report is to supplement the financial information in the profit and loss account and the balance sheet with certain narrative information about the company's activities and its future. The purpose of that narrative information is to give the user of the financial statements a more complete picture of the company than he would otherwise obtain.

20.2 A banking company or an insurance company does not have to include in its directors' report all the information stipulated in this chapter. The directors' report of such a company is considered in 'Manual of Accounting - volume III'.

The company's activities and its future

20.3 The directors must include in their report a fair review of the development of the business of the company and its subsidiaries during the financial year (for example, see Table 72 overleaf), and of their position at the end of it. [Sec 234(1)(a)]. The Act goes on to require the directors' report also to give particulars of any *important events* affecting the company or any of its subsidiaries that have occurred *since the end of the financial year* [7 Sch 6(a)], and to indicate likely *future developments* in the business of the company and its subsidiaries. [7 Sch 6(b)]. The Act also requires the directors' report to indicate the activities (if any) of the company and its subsidiaries in the field of *research and development.* [7 Sch 6(c)].

20.4 The Act does not indicate the form that this review of the business should take, nor does it indicate the detail the directors must include in their review. This provision is expressed in broad terms only, so as to allow directors as much freedom as possible to decide how best to meet the requirement.

20.5 Many public companies do not, in practice, include in their directors' report the review of the business and indications of likely future developments. Instead, they include the required information either in the chairman's statement or in a detailed review of operations. Provided that the directors' report refers to the place where the information appears, it still complies with the Act (for example, see Table 72 overleaf).

Table 72: Illustration of the disclosure of group's businesses in the directors' report and reference to where the detailed information can be found.

Extract from Berisford International plc Annual Report 30th September 1989.

Directors' report extract

1 Principal Activities and Business Review

Over the last two years the Group's principal activities have been restructured into four divisions: Food, Property, Financial Services and Commodities. Given the competing needs for cash and management resources the Board believes that in future it would be in the best interests of shareholders to concentrate on the food and food-related sector of the business. This strategy will make the greatest use of our management talents and provide high quality earnings for the Group.

The Group's turnover, profit before interest and profit before exceptional items are shown by division in Note 2 to the accounts.

Details of the average number of persons employed by the Group and the aggregate remuneration of such persons are shown in Note 4 to the accounts.

A review of the business and future development plans are contained in the Chairman's Statement and Review of Operations on pages 2 to 25.

Important post-balance-sheet events

20.6 SSAP 17 also covers the disclosure of any important events that have occurred since the end of the financial year (see also chapter 25 paras 25.28 to 25.30).

20.7 SSAP 17 distinguishes between events that require changes in the amounts to be disclosed in the financial statements ('adjusting events') and events that only require to be disclosed ('non-adjusting events'). Basically, a material post-balance-sheet event requires changes in the amounts disclosed in the financial statements where either of the following applies:

- It is an adjusting event (that is, it is an event that provides additional evidence relating to conditions that existed at the balance sheet date).

- It indicates that it is not appropriate to apply the going concern concept to either the whole or a material part of the company.

[SSAP 17 para 22].

20.8 On the other hand, a material post balance sheet event does not require changes in the financial statements (but it does require to be disclosed in the notes to the financial statements) in either of the following cases:

- It is a non-adjusting event. That is, it is an event that arises after the balance sheet date, and it concerns conditions that did not exist at that time but it is of such materiality that its non-disclosure would affect the ability of users of the financial statements to reach a proper understanding of the financial position.

- It is either a reversal or a maturity after the year end of a transaction entered into before the year end, and the substance of that transaction was primarily to alter the appearance of the company's balance sheet (that is, window dressing).

[SSAP 17 para 23].

20.9 In such circumstances, the information to be disclosed is the nature of the event and an estimate of its financial effect. Where it is not possible to make such an estimate, that fact must be disclosed. [SSAP 17 para 24].

20.10 However, an important difference between the Act and SSAP 17 is that the Act requires material post balance sheet events to be disclosed in the *directors' report* (as illustrated in Table 73), whereas SSAP 17 requires that either the financial statements must be adjusted or the effect must be disclosed in the *notes to the financial statements*. If a company decides to disclose the information only in one place, there should be a cross-reference from the directors' report to the notes, or *vice versa*.

Table 73: Illustration of the type of information required in the directors' report on significant post-balance sheet events.

Extract from Berisford International plc Annual Report 30th September 1989.

Directors' report extract

13 Post Balance Sheet Events

By an Agreement dated 9 October 1989 Bristar (Overseas) Limited purchased a 51% stake in Sugarpol (Torun) Sp.Zo.O, a joint venture with Torun Enterprise Zone and Rolimpex, to operate 2 sugar factories in Poland. The Group contributed US$102,000 in capital and has a commitment to a further US$5m in supplementary payments.

By an Agreement dated 15 November 1989 the Company purchased Pinecraven Developments plc, a property development company. The purchase price of £7.2m was satisfied by the issue of 5,000,000 ordinary shares of 10p each.

By an Agreement dated 29 December 1989, the Company disposed of its holding in Cresvale Holdings S.A., being its remaining interest of 25% in the Cresvale Group, to Pallas Group S.A. for US$30m.

Likely future developments

20.11 The Act requires the directors' report to contain an indication of likely future developments in the business of the company and its subsidiaries. [7 Sch 6(b)]. As with the provisions relating to a review of the company's business during the year, the Act contains no amplification as to the extent and the scope of this commentary on likely business developments. The reason why this provision is expressed in broad terms only is to allow directors as much freedom as possible to decide how best to meet the requirement.

20.12 With either listed companies or companies that are traded on the USM, the wording for the note on future developments will have to be chosen very carefully. Otherwise, there is the danger that the note could, at some later stage, be construed as a profit forecast. This could have the following consequences for such companies:

- The Council of The International Stock Exchange issued a statement in August 1975 that stated that *"whenever it becomes possible, by using* (the wording of any statement) *in conjunction with published data, to arrive at an approximate figure for future profits by an arithmetical process, the Council will take the view that a forecast has been made and require it to be reported on"*. This means that, if the directors' report is construed as including a profit forecast, accountants must report on that forecast.

- The following year's financial statements will have to explain any material differences (if any exist) between the actual results and the forecast. [CO 21(b), GU 10(b)].

- The City Code on Take-Overs and Mergers states that, if a company has issued any statement that constitutes a profit forecast, and that forecast relates to a period during which a takeover bid arises, then that forecast must be repeated in any offer or defence document, and accountants must report on it.

Research and development activities

20.13 The requirement to give an indication of the research and development activities of the company and its subsidiaries does not mean that the accounting policy for research and development should be disclosed in the directors' report. This should remain as part of the financial statements. The Act requires instead a narrative statement that considers the commercial aspects of the research and development, and that supplements the accounting policy and the information that SSAP 13 requires (see also chapter 7 para 7.16). Some companies may be reluctant to disclose too much information on research and development to competitors. However, the Act does not indicate how much detail needs to be given, and so a broadly-worded note should be sufficient to comply with the Act's requirements. An illustration of this disclosure is shown in Table 74.

Table 74: Illustration of the type of information to be given in the directors' report about the group's research and development activities.

Extract from Avon Rubber p.l.c. Annual Report 30th September 1989.

Directors' report extract.

11. Research and development

Research and development work is undertaken by all companies in the group to provide the best product designs and materials and is supported by a central team providing specialist assistance in areas such as the use of finite element analysis in the design of products and statistical systems for the development of rubber formulations.

The Teaching Company Scheme with Bristol University combined with research programmes with Bath, Brunel and Warwick Universities provides expertise and generates important data.

The strength of our research and development plays a vital role in the drive for Total Quality Management and the satisfaction of the exacting technological requirements of international customers.

The company's acquisition of its own shares

20.14 The directors' report of a UK listed company must give particulars of any authority given by the shareholders in general meeting for the company to purchase its own shares that is still effective at the year end (for example, see Table 75). [CO 21(p)].

Table 75: Illustration of a company's directors seeking power to purchase the company's own shares.

Extract from John I. Jacobs PLC Report and Accounts 31st December 1988.

Purchase by the Company of its own stock units. The directors believe that it is desirable that the Company should continue to have authority to purchase its own stock units and accordingly a Special Resolution will be proposed at the annual general meeting of the Company to renew the existing authority. Stockholders will also be invited to renew such authority at subsequent annual general meetings. The directors will only undertake purchases of the Company's own stock units after paying due attention to the effects on assets and earnings per unit for the remaining stockholders and when it is advantageous for the Company to do so. Purchases by the Company of its own stock units reduces the number of units in issue, giving the remaining stockholders a greater interest in the assets and profits of the Company. The resolution proposed would only enable the Company to purchase its own units on The Stock Exchange and there is no intention to stand in the market. The Company would not be able to enter into contracts with individual stockholders directly for the purchase of stock units.

20.15 If the company has acquired some of its own shares, Part II of Schedule 7 to the Act requires the directors' report to include certain information. The directors' report must contain the details set out in paragraph 20.16 below where any of the following circumstances occur:

- A company acquires its own shares by purchase, or by forfeiture, or by surrender in lieu of forfeiture, or by way of a gift, or redemption, or in a reduction of capital duly made, or by order of the court. [7 Sch 7(a); Sec 143(3)].

- A nominee of a public company acquires shares in the company from a third party without the company providing any financial assistance, and the company has a beneficial interest in those shares. [7 Sch 7(b); Sec 146(1)(c)].

- Any person acquires shares in a public company with the financial assistance of the company, and the company has a beneficial interest in those shares. [7 Sch 7(b); Sec 146(1)(d)].

- A company takes a lien or a charge (either express or implied) on its own shares for any amount that is payable in respect of those shares. [7 Sch 7(c); Sec 150(2)].

- A company that remained an 'old public company' after 22nd March 1982, and did not apply before that date to be re-registered under section 8 of the Companies Act 1980 as a public company, holds a lien or a charge (either express or implied) on its own shares, and that lien or charge existed on 22nd March 1982. [7 Sch 7(c); CC(CP) s 6(3)].

- A company that either existed on 2nd November 1862 or was formed after that date in pursuance of either any Act of Parliament (other than the 1985 Act) or letters patent, or was otherwise legally constituted and has registered under section 680 of the Act as a public company or a private company that has re-registered under Section 43, holds a lien or a charge (either express or implied) on its own shares, and that lien or charge existed immediately before the company was re-registered or registered as a public company. [7 Sch 7(c); Sec 150(4)].

20.16 Where any of the above circumstances has occurred, the directors' report must state the following details:

- The number and the nominal value of the shares that the company has purchased in the financial year.

- The aggregate consideration the company paid and the reasons it purchased the shares.

- The number and the nominal value of the shares the company has at any time either acquired or charged as mentioned in the points in paragraph 20.15 above.

- The maximum number and the nominal value of shares the company has at any time either acquired or charged as mentioned in the points in paragraph 20.15 above that the company or the other person held at any time during the financial year.

- The number and the nominal value of shares the company has at any time either acquired or charged as mentioned in paragraph 20.15 above that, during the financial year, either the company or the other person has disposed of or the company has cancelled.

- The percentage of the called-up share capital that the shares of that description represent, if the number and the nominal value of the shares of any particular description are disclosed pursuant to the first five points in paragraph 20.15 above.

- The amount of any charge.

- The amount or the value of any consideration for any shares that either the company or the other person disposed of during the financial year that the company or the other person acquired for money or money's worth.

[7 Sch 8].

20.17 The directors should take care in drafting the note that explains the reason for any purchase by the company of its own shares (as required above). The reason should be consistent with that put forward for tax purposes.

20.18 The directors' report of a UK listed company must give the following additional information concerning purchases or proposed purchases of the company's own shares:

- In relation to purchases other than either through the market or by tender or by partial offer to all shareholders, the names of the sellers of the shares that have been purchased, or are to be purchased, by the company.

- If the company has purchased any of its own shares since the year end, or has either been granted an option or entered into a contract to purchase its own shares since the year end, then the directors' report should disclose the equivalent information to that detailed in paragraph 20.16 above.

[CO 21(p)].

Employee information

20.19 Parts III, IV and V of Schedule 7 require the directors' report to contain information regarding the company's policy in respect of the employment of disabled persons, of the health, safety and welfare at work of employees, and of the involvement of employees in the management of the company.

20.20 If a company is required to prepare consolidated financial statements, the directors' report needs to contain the employee information required by Schedule 7 only in respect of the parent company. However, in practice, most parent companies include the required employee information in respect of the whole group.

Employment of disabled persons

20.21 If the company employed, on average, 250 or more employees in the UK in each week of the financial year, the directors' report must contain a statement that describes the company's policy during the year in respect of the following:

- Giving full and fair consideration (having regard to the persons' particular aptitudes and abilities) to applications for employment that disabled persons (as defined in the Disabled Persons (Employment) Act 1944) make to the company.

- Continuing the employment of, and arranging appropriate training for, any of the company's employees who have become disabled during the period in which the company employed them.

- Otherwise providing for the training, the career development and the promotion of those disabled persons the company employs.

[7 Sch 9].

An illustration of this disclosure is given in Table 76.

Health and safety of employees

20.22 The Secretary of State may make regulations that require certain classes of company to include in their directors' report information concerning employees' health and safety. [7 Sch 10(1)(3)]. The information should include details of the arrangements in force in the financial year both for securing the health, safety and welfare at work of employees of the company and its subsidiaries, and for protecting other persons against risks to their health or safety connected with the work of those employees. [7 Sch 10(1)].

Table 76: Illustration of the information required in the directors' report on the employment of disabled persons.

Extract from Portsmouth and Sunderland Newspapers plc Annual Report 1st April 1989.

Employment of Disabled Persons

The Company has continued to make positive efforts—through voluntary and statutory organisations—to encourage disabled people to apply for suitable jobs. Contacts with local Disablement Resettlement Officers have been maintained at each centre . Other initiatives, particularly through local organisations, and training establishments, are pursued to try to increase the number of disabled persons actually applying for vacancies. Applications which are received from disabled persons are always given full consideration, but the number of applicants is disappointing.

The Company's policy on training, career development, and promotion of disabled people is, as far as possible, identical to that for other employees, and if employees become disabled every effort is made to ensure their continued employment, with appropriate training where necessary. The Company's buildings and offices are designed, where possible, to provide facilities and amenities for disabled people.

20.23 To date, March 1990, the Secretary of State has not made any such regulation, and so there is no requirement at present for companies to disclose in the directors' report information on employees' health and safety. Nevertheless, some companies have done so on a voluntary basis.

Employee involvement

20.24 Paragraph 11 of Schedule 7 requires the directors' report to describe the action the company has taken during the financial year to introduce, maintain, or develop arrangements aimed at:

- Providing employees systematically with information on matters of concern to them as employees.
- Consulting employees or their representatives on a regular basis, so that the company can take the views of employees into account in making decisions that are likely to affect their interests.
- Encouraging the involvement of employees in the company's performance through (for example) an employees' share scheme.
- Achieving a common awareness on the part of all employees of the financial and the economic factors that affect the company's performance.

[7 Sch 11(3)].

20.25 This requirement applies only to the directors' report of a company that employs, on average, more than 250 employees in the UK each week during the financial year. [7 Sch 11(1)]. Table 77 gives an example of the information to be shown.

Table 77: Illustration of the information required in the directors' report on employee involvement.

Extract from Midland Bank plc Annual Report and Accounts 31st December 1988.

Employee communication and involvement

United Kingdom
Midland Group has continued to show its commitment to effective communication between management and employees. Extensive use of video and computer-based communication and training materials has complemented our overall efforts in these areas, and has encouraged employees to contribute directly to product development, quality of service, and cost containment initiatives.

While responsibility for day-to-day communication rests with line management, the Group regularly uses such media as the in-house Group newspapers and bulletin to keep all employees involved in strategic and tactical business decisions. A further review of the framework of management/employee communications will be conducted in 1989 to ensure that it remains fully effective and responsive to our changing business needs.

The employee share schemes were reviewed in 1988 and a revised Profit Sharing Scheme was approved by shareholders at the annual general meeting on 28 April 1988. The new scheme will increase significantly the number of employees who receive their profit sharing in shares. In 1988, as a result of the special profit sharing payment approved by shareholders, almost 8,600 employees elected to invest in the future of the Group by taking shares instead of cash. Also, nearly 6,000 eligible staff accepted options under the Savings-Related Share Option Scheme.

During the year, the Group introduced a range of initiatives designed to promote equal opportunities for all employees including improved remuneration, benefit and pension arrangements for part-time staff. In addition, the Group has recently announced the intention to introduce a substantial number of workplace nurseries over the next four years; a radical step amongst clearing banks.

Consultation and negotiations have continued on a range of issues between management and representatives of recognised unions within the Group. The principal unions involved during 1988 were the Banking, Insurance and Finance Union, and the Manufacturing, Science and Finance Union (MSF) in which the Association of Scientific, Technical and Managerial staffs was merged in 1988. However, in February 1989 the Bank gave notice of termination of its agreements with MSF because their membership level within the Bank was considered too small to justify continued recognition for collective bargaining purposes.

Political and charitable gifts

20.26 If a company that is not the wholly-owned subsidiary of another company incorporated in Great Britain has given money for either political purposes or charitable purposes during the year, and the amount given for both purposes exceeds £200 in aggregate, the company must disclose certain information in its directors' report. [7 Sch 3(1)(2)].

20.27 The information that must be disclosed is as follows:

- The amount given for both political purposes and charitable purposes. These amounts must be disclosed separately. [7 Sch 3(2)(a)].

- If the company has given money for political purposes (including a subscription to a political party), the name of each person or political party to whom the company has donated more than £200 during the year, together with the actual amount donated. [7 Sch 3(2)(b)].

20.28 With a group, the parent company directors' report needs to give the information in paragraph 20.27 above only in respect of the group as a whole. It has to give the information only if the amount the company and its subsidiaries have given for both political purposes and charitable purposes exceeds £200 in aggregate. [7 Sch 4].

20.29 Money a company gives for 'charitable purposes' means any money it gives for purposes that are exclusively charitable. [7 Sch 5(4)]. Donations for purposes that include either a political or a commercial element do not come within the definition. The definition also excludes charitable donations a company gives to a person who, at the time of the gift, was ordinarily resident outside the UK. [7 Sch 5(3)].

Directors' interests

20.30 The financial statements must disclose information about the directors' interests in the company's shares or debentures. For this purpose, an interest in shares or debentures includes any interest of any kind whatsoever in shares or debentures. [13 Sch 1(1)]. The information on directors' interests may be disclosed either in the directors' report or in the notes to the financial statements. [7 Sch 2(1)].

20.31 The notes to the financial statements or the directors' report must state whether or not anyone who was a director of the company at the end of the financial year was interested, at the end of the financial year, in any shares in, or any debentures of, the company, or any subsidiary, or any parent company or any fellow subsidiary. This statement should be based on the information contained in the register the company maintains in accordance with section 325 of the Act (director's obligation to notify his interests in the company and in companies in the same group). [7 Sch 2(1)]. Interests in shares or debentures has the same meaning as in section 324. [7 Sch 2A(4)].

20.32 If any director had such an interest at the end of the financial year, the financial statements must give also the following information:

- A statement as to whether or not the director had an interest in either that company or any other body corporate in the same group (that is, the company itself, or a subsidiary, or a parent company or a fellow subsidiary) at the end of the financial year. This is taken to mean that also the name of the company in question must be stated. In addition, the number of shares in, and the amount of debentures of, the particular company must be disclosed. [7 Sch 2A(1)(2)].

- If the director was interested in shares or debentures at the end of the year, a similar statement must be given as to whether or not the director had an interest in either that company or any other body corporate in the same group at the beginning of the financial year. Where the director has such an interest, the number of shares in, and the amount of debentures of, the company in question must be stated. If he became a director during the financial year, the information should be given on the date he became a director. Again, the name of the company in question must be specified. [7 Sch 2A(3)].

20.33 If a person was appointed a director on more than one occasion during the year, the information should be given as at the date he was first appointed. [7 Sch 2A(5)]. This requirement covers a situation where, for example, a person is appointed a director between the end of the preceding financial year and the date of the annual general meeting. Under article 79 of Table A (if applicable), this person would have to be reappointed as a director at the annual general meeting. However, the financial statements should give the information required under the second point of paragraph 20.32 above as at the date he was first appointed.

20.34 The financial statements must disclose information about the interests of the company's directors in the company's shares, where such interests take the form of a 'put' or a 'call' option that a director holds otherwise than under a trust. [13 Sch 6(1)].

20.35 The financial statements should also state whether, according to the register, a director or member of his 'immediate family' exercised any *right* to subscribe for shares in, or debentures of, the company or another body corporate in the same group. If any such right were granted or exercised, the number of shares or the amount of debentures should be stated, also disclosing the name of the company involved. [7 Sch 2B(1)(2)]. A director's 'immediate family' includes a spouse and infant children, including step-children. In Scotland the term 'infant' means a pupil or minor. [7 Sch 2B(3)]. 'Immediate family' does not include a person who is also a director of the company. [7 Sch 2B(4)]. Consequently, the financial statements will have to disclose whether a director or a member of his immediate family has any options to subscribe for shares in the company or in any other group company.

20.36 In addition, the International Stock Exchange's Continuing Obligations specifically require all listed companies to disclose directors' interests in any options in the capital of the company. [CO 21(h)].

20.37 The information that the financial statements should disclose in respect of a director's option to subscribe for shares consists of the number and amount of shares that the director has an option over and the name of the company to which the shares relate. However, the financial statements do not have to disclose the price at which the director can exercise his option. But, the notes to the financial statements must disclose, in summary, both the option price at which, and the period during which, *any* options are exercisable in respect of the company's shares (see chapter 12 para 12.13). [4 Sch 40].

20.38 Where a director of a wholly-owned subsidiary is also a director of the parent company, The Companies (Disclosure of Directors' Interests) (Exceptions) Regulations 1985 (SI 1985/802) give relief from the disclosure requirements in paragraphs 20.30 to 20.35 above. In this situation, the director's interest needs to be disclosed only in the parent company's financial statements, and not in the subsidiary's.

20.39 Furthermore, those same regulations exempt a director from notifying certain interests in shares to his company where that company is a wholly-owned subsidiary of a body incorporated outside Great Britain. The exemption extends to interests in shares in, or debentures of, the parent company that is incorporated outside Great Britain, or any other body incorporated outside Great Britain. Consequently, such interests are not required to be disclosed in a company's financial statements, because they are not required to be notified to the company.

20.40 In addition, a company that is either listed on The International Stock Exchange or traded on the USM must disclose any change in the directors' interests between the end of the financial year and a date not more than one month before the date of the notice of the general meeting at which the financial statements are to be presented. Where there has been no such change, this fact should be stated in the directors' report. Also, the interests that are disclosed for these companies must distinguish between beneficial interests and non-beneficial interests. [CO 21(h); GU 10(h)].

An illustration of how a company discloses its director's interests is given in Table 78 overleaf.

Table 78: Illustration of the disclosure of the directors' interests and other major interests in the capital of the company.

Extract from the Savoy Hotel PLC Directors' Report & Annual Accounts 31 December 1988.

Directors' Interests and other Major Shareholdings

Interests at 31st December, 1988, and (shown in italic) at 1st January, 1988.

	Ordinary Share Capital			
Directors' Beneficial Interests	A Shares		B Shares	
Sir Anthony Tuke	1,500	*1,500*	—	—
G. R. C. Shepard	12,173	*12,023*	11	*11*
M. B. Radcliffe	3,233	*3,233*	—	—
M. J. de R. Richardson	1,500	*1,500*	—	—
V. S. Emery	50	*50*	—	—
H. Morton Neal	5,324	*5,324*	—	—
Sir George Christie	1,500	*1,500*	—	—
J. Kemp-Welch	3,000	*3,000*	—	—
Sir J. Oliver Wright	500	*500*	—	—
Interests as Trustees				
G. R. C. Shepard	—	—	630	*630*
M. B. Radcliffe	1,044,758	*1,044,758*	329,021	*329,021*
H. Morton Neal	715	*715*	28	*28*

	Debenture and Loan Stocks					
	4% First		8¼%		8½%	
Directors' Beneficial Interests	£	£	£	£	£	£
V. S. Emery	—	—	—	—	50	*50*
Interests as Trustees						
G. R. C. Shepard	600	*600*	2,000	*2,000*	—	—
M. B. Radcliffe	1,000	*1,000*	—	—	18,835	*18,835*

Mr. G. R. C. Shepard and Mr. V. S. Emery have beneficial interests of £307 (£307) and £100 (£100) respectively in the 4% First Mortgage Debenture Stock of Savoy Theatre Limited.

Between the end of the year and 11th April, 1989, Mr. G. R. C. Shepard has ceased to ahve a beneficial interest in 419 A Ordinary Shares registered in his daughter's name, she having reached the age of eighteen.

Other Major Interests at 11th April, 1989.
The Company has been notified that Trusthouse Forte PLC is interested in 19,479,880 A Ordinary Shares and 164,960 B Ordinary Shares equal to 69.02 per cent. of the ordinary capital of The Savoy Hotel PLC, which carries the right to 42.32 per cent. of the total votes. Under the terms of the Companies Act 1985, The Savoy Hotel PLC is a subsidiary of Trusthouse Forte PLC, but Trusthouse Forte PLC does not control The Savoy Hotel PLC.

The Company has also been informed of the interests as shown below of the trustees of The D'Oyly Carte Charitable Trust, which amounts to 25.19 per cent. of the issue of B Ordinary Shares and 3.77 per cent. of the A Shares (equivalent to 14.17 per cent. of the total votes), the trustees of The Wontner Family Settlement, which amounts to 20.88 per cent. of the B Ordinary Shares (equivalent with A Shares to 10.86 per cent. of the total votes) and of the trustees of The Savoy Educational Trust, which amounts to 18.82 per cent. of the B Ordinary Shares and 4.62 per cent. of the A Shares, giving a total of 11.51 per cent. of the total votes.

The individual interests of each trustee, as notified to the Company, being their total interest in B Ordinary Shares is as follows:– Sir John Batten 329,021, Sir Martyn Beckett 329,021, Sir Denys Buckley 272,831, E. J. P. Elliott 245,819, Mrs J. A. C. O. Martin French 245,830, J. A. McCracken 329,021, M. B. Radcliffe 329,021, Mrs J. Sibley 245,819, The Honourable John Sinclair 245,822, K. P. J. Strange 273,377, Mrs J. K. Thorne 329,026, Lady Wontner and Sir Hugh Wontner 277,988.

A. G. I. Wontner and J. I. H. Wontner are interested in 68,186 and 90,915 B Ordinary Shares respectively representing 5.22% and 6.96% of the B Ordinary Shares in issue.

La Fondation pour la Formation Hotelière has notified the Company of its interest in 155,163 B Ordinary Shares (equivalent with A Shares to 5.77 per cent. of the total votes). M. B. Radcliffe and V. S. Emery are members of its Conseil d'Administration.

Other information to be disclosed in the directors' report

20.41 The directors' report must disclose also the following information:

- The amount (if any) that the directors recommend should be paid as a dividend, and the amount (if any) that they propose to carry to reserves. [Sec 234(1)(b)].

- The name of anyone who was a director of the company at any time during the financial year. [Sec 234(2)].

- The principal activities of both the company and of its subsidiaries during the year, and details of any significant change in those activities. [Sec 234(2)].

- Particulars of any significant changes in the fixed assets of both the company and any of its subsidiaries that have occurred during the year. [7 Sch 1(1)].

- The difference between the market value and the balance sheet value of any interest in land and buildings, if the market value of the interest differs substantially from the value at which it is included in the balance sheet, and if, also, the directors are of the opinion that the difference is of such significance that it should be brought to the shareholders' or debenture holders' attention. The difference has to be shown with such degree of precision as is practicable (for example, see Table 79). [7 Sch 1(2)].

Table 79: Illustration of the type of information required to be given in the directors' report about the value of the group's properties.

Extract from WH Smith Group PLC Annual Report 3rd June 1989.

Report of the directors (extract)

Fixed Assets

Details of tangible fixed assets and capital expenditure for the year are shown in note 12 to the financial statements on page 45.

The most recent valuation of the Group's properties in the United Kingdom, other than those held under leases containing provision for rent reviews at seven year intervals or less, was made by Messrs Edward Erdman, Surveyors, as at 30 May 1987, in the adjusted sum of £152,354,000. The valuation of the properties was made on the basis of their open market value within their existing use and with vacant possession of those properties, or parts of properties, which were in the Group's occupation, but otherwise subject to the lettings then existing. The resulting surplus of £51,899,000 over book value was incorporated in the 1987 financial statements. The Board believes that the existing value of the Group's properties in the United Kingdom at 3 June 1989 was in excess of the current book value. In accordance with the Group's practice, these properties will be formally revalued for next year's accounts.

- The fact that the company has purchased or maintained any insurance during the financial year for any officers or auditors against any liability which otherwise attach to them in respect of any negligence, default, breach of duty or trust in relation to the company as is mentioned in section 310(3)(a) of the Act. [7 Sch 5A].

Approval and signing of directors' report

20.42 The board of directors has to approve the directors' report and it must be signed on behalf of the board by a director or the secretary of the company. [Sec 234A(1)].

20.43 In addition, a director or the secretary of the company is required to sign, on behalf of the board, a copy of the directors' report that is to be delivered to the Registrar of Companies. [Sec 234A(3)].

20.44 Every copy of the directors' report that is laid before the company in general meeting, or that is otherwise circulated, published or issued, must state the name of the person who signed the balance sheet on behalf of the board. [Sec 234A(2)].

Liability for contravention

20.45 Every person who was a director of the company at the end of the period within which the company's financial statements must be laid before the company in general meeting and must be delivered to the Registrar of Companies (see chapter 25), is guilty of an offence if the directors' report fails to comply with the Act's requirements. In addition, every such person is liable to a fine (see appendix IV). [Sec 234(5)].

20.46 It is a defence in such a situation for a director to prove that he took all reasonable steps to ensure that the directors' report complied with all the Act's requirements. [Sec 234(6)].

20.47 Furthermore, where the company does not comply with the requirements for the approval and signing of the directors' report as set out in paragraphs 20.42 to 20.44 above, the company and every officer of it who is in default will be guilty of an offence and liable to a fine (see appendix IV). [Sec 234A(4)].

Additional requirements for listed companies and USM companies

20.48 The International Stock Exchange's Continuing Obligations and the USM's General Undertaking require the directors' report (or the notes to the financial statements) of listed companies and companies traded on the USM respectively to give information on further matters in addition to those the Act covers. These additional matters are considered in the paragraphs that follow.

20.49 The directors should state whether, so far as they are aware, the company is a 'close company' for taxation purposes. They should also state whether there has been any change in that respect since the end of the financial year. [CO 21(j), GU 10(j)].

20.50 The directors' report (or the notes to the financial statements) should disclose particulars of any 'substantial interest' in the company's share capital that any person other than a director holds as at a date not more than one month before the date of notice of the meeting at which the financial statements are to be presented. [CO 21(i); GU 10(i)]. For this purpose a 'substantial interest' is any holding of 3 per cent or more of the nominal value of any class of share capital that carries voting rights. Such interests are required to be notified to the company by the shareholder within two days of the obligation to notify arising so that the interest can be included in the company's register. Consequently, the information required to be disclosed should be contained in the register the company maintains in accordance with sections 198 to 220 of the Act.

20.51 The directors' report (or the notes to the financial statements) *for listed companies only* should state the unexpired period of any service contract of more than one year's duration of any director who is proposed for re-election at the annual general meeting. If the director has a service contract for a term of less than one year, the directors' report must state that fact. [CO 43(c)].

20.52 If a director's service contract does not specify a term, the term can be ascertained in one of the following ways:

- If the contract is determinable on the giving of notice, the expiration of the notice period will indicate the earliest date at which the contract could end.

- If no notice period is stated in the contract, the term may be implied. This implication may be given either by custom and practice, or by the company's articles of association, or in some other way.

- If the contract contains no express or implied provision as to notice, there would be a presumption that the term is for a period of five years. A longer period cannot be agreed without the approval of the company in general meeting.

20.53 Where the length of the unexpired period of a director's service contract has been determined in one of the ways above, the details should be fully disclosed in the directors' report. The notice convening the annual general meeting of companies listed on The International Stock Exchange and also of companies traded on the USM must give the place where, and the time at which, copies of service contracts can be examined. If there are no such contracts, the notice must state the fact. [CO 43(b); GU 11].

20.54 The directors' report should disclose particulars of any contract of significance between the company (or one of its subsidiaries) and a corporate substantial shareholder. For this purpose, a 'contract of significance' is one which represents in value a sum equal to one per cent or more of:

- The company's net assets, for a capital transaction or for a transaction of which the principal purpose is the granting of credit.
- The company's total purchases, sales, payments or receipts, as appropriate, for other transactions.

[CO 21(l)].

Where the company has subsidiaries these comparisons should be made on a group basis.

20.55 A 'corporate substantial shareholder' is defined as any body corporate who either is entitled to exercise, or control the exercise of, at least 30 per cent of the voting power at the company's general meetings or is in a position to control the composition of a majority of the company's board of directors. [CO 21(l)].

20.56 In addition, the directors' report should disclose details of any contract with a corporate substantial shareholder (as defined above) to provide services to the company or to one of its subsidiaries. This information is not required if the shareholder is providing services that it normally provides as part of its principal business and it is not a contract of significance that is required to be disclosed. [CO 21 (m)].

20.57 The identity of independent non-executive directors must be disclosed, together with a short biographical note on each. [CO 21(t)].

20.58 Guidance on the appointment of non-executive directors can be found in the Code of Recommended Practice, published by PRONED (Promotion of non-executive directors) in April 1987. This guidance states that quoted companies with a turnover in excess of £50 million, or employing more than 1,000 employees, should normally include at least three independent non-executive directors, comprising about a third of the Board. The guidance suggests that independent non-executive directors:

- Should not have been employed as executives of the company within the last five years.

- If they are professional advisers, they should not be retained by the company, either personally, or through their firm, on a continuing or regular basis.

- Should not be, personally or through their company, a significant customer or supplier of the company.

20.59 Shareholders who are sent a notice of a meeting that is to occur on the same day as an AGM, which includes business that is considered not to be routine business of an AGM must be provided with an explanation in the directors' report of such business. In addition, an explanatory circular must also accompany any notice of such a meeting sent to holders of listed debt securities. [CO 32].

Auditors' consideration of the directors' report

20.60 The auditors have a statutory duty to carry out such investigations during the course of their audit of the financial statements as are necessary for them to form an opinion on whether or not the information that the directors' report contains is consistent with the financial statements on which they are reporting. The Act requires auditors to draw attention in their report to the fact that in their opinion there is an inconsistency between the directors' report and the company's financial statements for the year in question. [Sec 235(3)]. However, the Act does not require the directors' report to be audited as such. If the information contained in the directors' report is consistent with that in the financial statements, the audit report does not have to include any specific comment.

20.61 The directors' report does not form part of the financial statements on which the auditors report. Consequently, the pages referred to in the 'scope' paragraph of the audit report should not include the pages on which the directors' report is printed.

20.62 Where companies choose to disclose in some other statement certain of the statutory information that is required to be included in the directors' report (see para 20.5), the auditors have to consider whether all of the financial information that is contained in that other statement is consistent with the information disclosed in the financial statements. If the auditors are to do this, they may have to perform considerably more work than if they merely reviewed the limited information that the directors' report should give.

20.63 The Auditing Guideline, 'Financial information issued with audited financial statements', includes the following extract from an example of an audit report qualified on the grounds of inconsistency between the directors' report and the audited financial statements:

> *"In our opinion, the information given in the directors' report is not consistent with the company's financial statements for the financial year. Paragraph 7 of the directors' report states without amplification that the company's trading resulted in a profit before tax of £X. The profit and loss account, however, states that the company incurred a loss before tax for the year of £Y and, as an extraordinary item, a profit from the sale of land of £Z."*

20.64 Auditors should also review the chairman's statement and any other supplementary financial information that is disclosed (for example, five-year summaries), in order to ensure that the information disclosed is neither misleading nor inconsistent with the financial statements on which they are reporting.

Chapter 21

LOANS TO DIRECTORS AND OFFICERS

Chapter 21

LOANS TO DIRECTORS AND OFFICERS

Introduction

21.1 The Act imposes restrictions on dealings between a company and its directors by making loans and certain credit-related transactions and arrangements unlawful. The purpose of these restrictions is to prevent a conflict of interest arising between the directors and the company. In addition (and whether they are lawful or not) the Act requires that most transactions and arrangements that may favour directors should be disclosed. The Act also requires certain transactions with officers of the company to be disclosed.

21.2 The Act's requirements relating to transactions between the company and its directors or officers are, perhaps, the main legal safeguard available against directors or officers abusing their position in a company. The disclosure requirements, in particular, ensure that shareholders and others that have an interest in the company (for example, creditors) will be informed about all the significant transactions the company enters into with those responsible for the company's management that might (either directly or indirectly) benefit those individuals. The intention is to encourage directors and officers to take care before entering into such transactions, because the shareholders will be fully informed of them. There has been a certain amount of controversy surrounding the disclosure requirements relating to directors' transactions and, consequently, the disclosure requirements that are dealt with in Schedule 6 of the Act may be amended by further legislation.

21.3 Appendix VI contains decision tables that determine whether a loan to a director is prohibited by the Act. These tables should be read in conjunction with this chapter.

21.4 This chapter deals with loans, quasi-loans and credit transactions as they apply to relevant and non-relevant companies. It explains their legality, the sanctions imposed if the rules are breached, and the disclosure requirements. It also deals with the special provisions that apply exclusively to money lending companies and banking companies

Definitions

21.5 The definitions that follow are essential to an understanding of the types of transaction that the Act prohibits.

Director

21.6 The definition of a director includes any person who occupies the position of director by whatever name called. [Sec 741(1)]. This means that it is the person's responsibilities and duties and not his title that determines whether or not he is a director. A director is a person who actively takes part in board meetings and votes at them.

Shadow director

21.7 A 'shadow director' is a person in accordance with whose instructions the directors are accustomed to act. [Sec 741(2)]. An exception to this definition exists where the directors follow advice given in a professional capacity, such as may be received from the company's accountant. A professional adviser acting in that capacity alone would not, therefore, be a shadow director.

Example

The principal shareholder (owning 60 per cent) of a company ceased to be a director before the beginning of the year, but continues to direct the operations of the company as he still controls and dominates the company.

The principal shareholder falls within the definition of a shadow director and should be treated as a director of the company. Any transactions that he enters into that are covered by the Act's requirements should, therefore, be disclosed

Alternate director

21.8 The position of an 'alternate director' is determined by the articles of association of a company. If the articles adopted are those of Table A, the alternate director has the following position:

- He is appointed and can be removed by the same director of the company.
- If the potential alternate director is not already a director, his appointment must be approved by a resolution of the board.
- If the director who appointed the alternate director ceases to be a director, the appointment of the alternate ceases immediately.
- The alternate director is a full director of the company, and can, at meetings of the board, fulfil all the functions of the director appointing him, in the absence of that director. Attendance and voting at board meetings is only permitted when the appointing director is absent.

21.9 Where the term 'director' is used in this chapter, it includes references to directors, shadow directors and alternate directors.

Connected person

21.10 A 'connected person' is a person who is connected with a director and is either an individual or a legal person (for example, a company). A connected person includes any of the following:

- The director's wife, or husband, or child (including an illegitimate child), or step-child, but excludes any child who is at least 18 years of age. [Sec 346(2)(a),(3)(a)].

- A body corporate with which the director is associated except in certain situations. [Sec 346(2)(b)]. (See further para 21.11 on 'associated' relationship).

- A person acting in his capacity as a trustee of any trust that is in either of the following situations:

  - It includes as a beneficiary the director or his spouse, children, step children, or a body corporate with which he is associated.

  - It confers a power on the trustees to benefit the director or his spouse, children, step children, or a body corporate with which he is associated.

  [Sec 346(2)(c)].

  However, trustees of either an employee share scheme or a pension scheme are not to be regarded as connected with a director merely by virtue of that trusteeship. [Sec 346(3)(b)].

- A partner of either the director or certain of his connected persons. [Sec 346(2)(d)].

- A Scottish firm in which one of the following applies:

  - The director is a partner, or certain persons connected with him, are partners.

  - Another Scottish firm is a partner, and the director or any such connected persons are partners of that other Scottish firm.

  [Sec 346(2)(e)].

  Scottish partnerships, unlike English ones, have legal personality.

However, none of the above persons are connected if they themselves are also directors of the company. [Sec 346(2)].

Association with a director

21.11 A body corporate is 'associated' with the director if, and only if, the director, together with the persons connected with him, satisfy either of the following two conditions:

- *Interested* in at least 20 per cent of the equity share capital.
- Able to *exercise or control* at least 20 per cent of the voting power at any general meeting.

[Sec 346(4)].

For simplicity, a body corporate (that is, an entity incorporated in Great Britain or elsewhere) is referred to below as a company.

21.12 In the definition of 'associated' a director's interest in shares, or his control of the voting power, may be either direct (that is, he himself owns the shares or controls the votes) or indirect (that is, a company that he controls owns the shares or controls the votes). In determining whether the director and those connected with him can control the exercise of more than 20 per cent of the voting power of a company in general meeting, any votes held indirectly by a director through another company are to be included in the calculation, but only if the director 'controls' that second company. [Sec 346(8)]. A director of a company is deemed to control that second company if, but only if, the following two conditions are satisfied:

- He or any person connected with him is *interested* in any part of the equity share capital of that second company, or is entitled to exercise or control the exercise of any part of the voting power at any general meeting of that company.
- That director, the persons connected with him *and the other directors of that company,* together, are interested in more than 50 per cent of the second company's share capital or are entitled to exercise or control the exercise of more 50 per cent of that voting power.

[Sec 346(5)].

21.13 Under the above provisions, the interests of a director must be aggregated with those of his connected persons. The rules that the Act lays down for determining whether a person is interested in shares provide, *inter alia,* that a person is to be treated as interested in shares if a company is interested in them and where either of the following two conditions are met:

- The person is entitled to exercise, or control the exercise of, more than 50 per cent of that company's voting power at general meetings.

- That company or its directors are accustomed to act in accordance with his directions or instructions.

[13 Sch 4].

21.14 For the purpose *only* of determining whether a company is associated with a director, another company with which the director is associated is not regarded as a connected person (see para 21.10), except where that company is a partner of the director or a trustee of a trust the beneficiaries of which include, or may include, the director or a member of the director's family (see third and fourth point of para 21.10). [Sec 346(6)]

21.15 The following examples illustrate an 'association' through an interest in shares and an 'association' through control of voting power:

Association through an interest in shares

Example 1

Mr. Jones owns 18 per cent of company A's equity share capital, and he also owns 25 per cent of company B's equity share capital. Company B owns 19 per cent of company A's equity share capital..

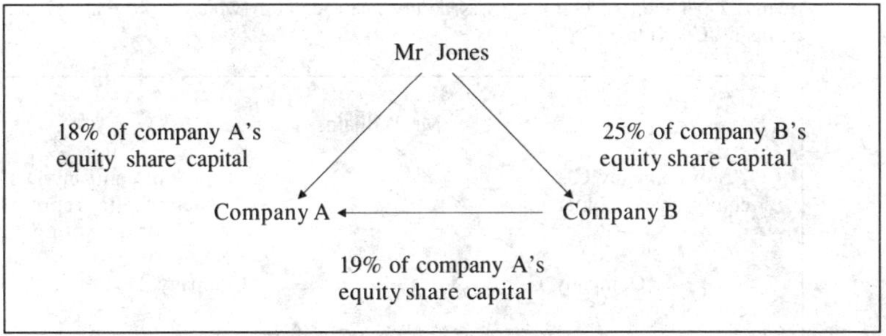

Mr. Jones is associated with company B, because he has an interest in more than 20 per cent of the equity share capital of that company. [Sec 346(4)].

In the situation of company A, despite Mr Jones having an effective holding of 22.75 per cent (that is, 18% + 25% x 19% = 22.75%), company A is not associated with him. This is because in deciding whether company A is associated with Mr Jones, company B's interest in company A's shares should be ignored. [Sec 346(6)(a)].

Example 2

The facts are the same as in example 1 except that Mr Jones owns 5 per cent of company A and he also owns 51 per cent of company B.

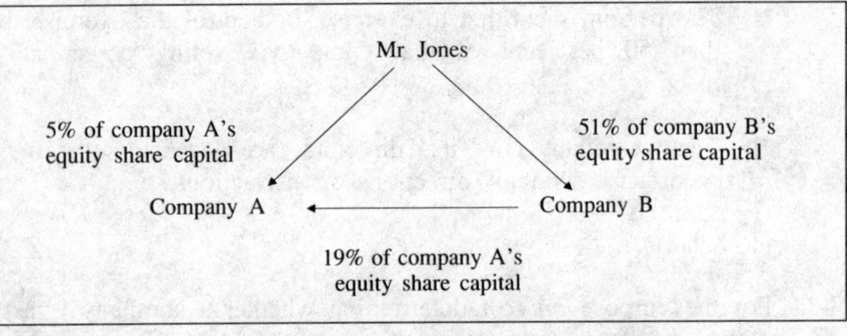

In this situation, although Mr Jones has an effective holding of 14.69 per cent (that is, 5% + 51% x 19% = 14.69%), company A is associated with him. This is because, although company B's interest in company A's shares should be ignored, [Sec 346(6)(a)], nevertheless, Mr. Jones is taken to be interested in the shares of company A held by company B, because he is entitled to exercise, or control the exercise of, more than 50 per cent of the voting power of company B. [13 Sch 4]. Consequently, company A is connected with Mr. Jones via the operation of section 346(4)(a), because he has an interest in 24 per cent (all of the 19 per cent and not a proportion of it, together with a direct holding of 5 per cent) that is greater than 20 per cent of company A's equity share capital.

Association through control of voting power

Example 3

Mr. Williams owns 2 per cent of company C's equity share capital . He also owns 100 per cent of company D's £1 'A' equity shares but none of the £1 'B' equity shares. The issued share capital of company D consists of 5,000 £1 'A' equity shares and 45,000 £1 'B' equity. Each 'A' share carries 3 votes and each 'B' share carries 1 vote. Company D owns 25 per cent of company C's equity share capital (which represents 25 per cent of company C's votes).

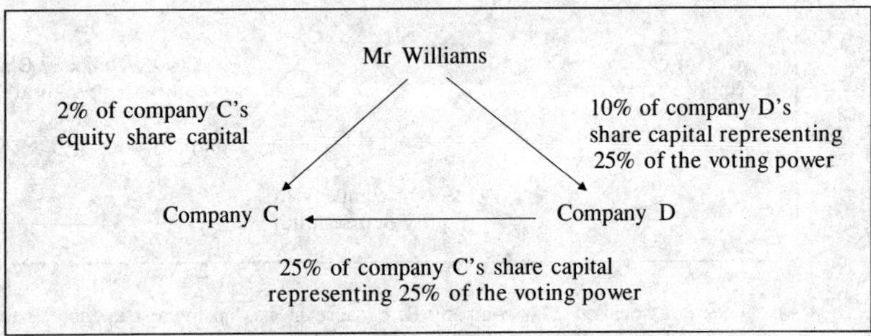

Although Mr. Williams holds only 10 per cent of the equity share capital of company D, he is able to exercise 15,000 votes out of a maximum of 60,000 votes, which represent in total 25 per cent of the voting power. Therefore, Mr Williams is associated with company D, because he is able to control more than 20 per cent of the voting power of that company. [Sec 346(4)(b)].

In determining whether company C is associated with Mr Williams, the interest of company D in the shares of company C should be disregarded. [Sec 346(6)(a)]. However, unlike in the second example above, Mr. Williams is also not interested in the shares in company C held by company D via the operation of paragraph 4 of Schedule 13, because he is only entitled to exercise, or control the exercise of, 25 per cent of the voting power of company D. Because Mr Williams neither controls nor is presumed to control company D, company C is not associated with Mr. Williams by the operation of section 346(4).

Example 4

The facts are the same as in example 3, except that Mr Williams has acquired a further 18,000 £1 'B' equity shares from some of the existing 'B' equity shareholders.

Mr Williams is now able to exercise 33,000 votes out of a maximum of 60,000 votes, which represent in total 55 per cent of the voting power of company D. Therefore, Mr Williams is not only associated with company D, but he is also interested in part of its equity share capital and is able to exercise more than 50 per cent of its voting power. [Sec 346(5)]. Because Mr Williams controls company D, he is regarded as controlling company D's exercise of its voting power in company C. [Sec 346(8)]. Because company D's voting power exceeds 20 per cent of the potential voting power at company C's general meeting, company C is regarded as being associated with Mr Williams by the operation of section 346(4).

Relevant company

21.16 A 'relevant company', for the purpose of the provisions of the Act that relate to directors' transactions, is either of the following types of company:

- A public company.
- A company that belongs to a group in which either the parent company or any subsidiary is a public company.

[Sec 331(6)].

A non-relevant company is effectively a residual class, which includes all companies other than relevant companies.

Prohibited transactions with directors

21.17 Section 330 of the Act prohibits companies from entering into certain transactions, such as loans, quasi-loans and credit transactions, for the benefit of their directors or persons connected with those directors. Its provisions are amplified in sections 332 to 338 of the Act. The extent of these restrictions varies according to whether or not the company concerned is a relevant company. The Act also includes exemptions from these restrictions that are available in certain circumstances, and these are considered in detail in the paragraphs that follow.

Loans

Definition

21.18 Although the expression 'loan' is not defined in the Act, it was interpreted in a case brought under the Companies Act 1948. In that case it was held that the dictionary definition should be applied. The dictionary definition of a loan is *"a sum of money lent for a time to be returned in money or money's worth"*. [*Champagne Perrier-Jouet S.A. v H.H. Finch Ltd.* [1982] 1 WLR 1359]. It is, therefore, apparent that a loan arises wherever monies are advanced on the understanding that they will be repaid.

Value of loans

21.19 The value of a loan is the principal amount of the loan. [Sec 340(2)]. For these purposes, the interest due on the loans may be ignored.

General Prohibition

21.20 The general prohibition for making loans to directors and persons connected with them is as follows:

- Relevant companies

  A relevant company may not make a loan to either its own directors or its parent company's directors or a person connected with such directors. [Sec 330(2)(a), 330(3)(b)].

  Equally, a relevant company may not enter into any guarantee or indemnity, or provide any security, in connection with the loan a third party makes to either a director of the company or a director of its parent company or a person connected with such directors. [Sec 330(2)(b), 330(3)(c)].

- Non-relevant companies

  A non-relevant company may not make a loan or enter into a guarantee or provide any security in connection with a loan made by a third party, to or for either a director of the company or a director of its parent company. [Sec 330(2)(a)(b)]. However, non-relevant companies may make a loan to a person who is connected with a director.

Exemptions

Small loans

21.21 There is a general exemption for small loans. Any company (whether relevant or non-relevant) may make a loan to a director of either the company or its parent company, provided that the aggregate of the 'relevant amounts' immediately after the loan is made to him does not exceed £5,000. [Sec 334]. The amounts to be aggregated are:

- The value of the proposed transaction.

- The amount outstanding under any other transaction that was made under the same exception permitting the transaction.

- The value of any existing arrangement within section 330(6) or (7) (described in paras 21.38 to 21.43), that was made under the same exception.

[Sec 339(2)].

21.22 The amounts outstanding under any other transaction and the value of any existing arrangement that have to be taken into account under the last two points of paragraph 21.21 above are those made by the company or any subsidiary for the following people:

- The director in question (or, where the proposed transaction is to be made for a connected person of a director, the director with whom that person is connected).

- Any person connected with the director.

[Sec 339(3)].

21.23 Where the proposed transaction is to be made by a company for a director of its parent company (or a person connected with such a director) there must also be taken into account the amounts outstanding under any other transaction and the value of any existing arrangement referred to in paragraph 21.21 above that were made by the *parent company or any subsidiary* for the director or a person connected with him. [Sec 339(2)].

Example

A subsidiary wishes to loan £3,000 to the director of its parent company, which has already lent him £2,500. It is unsure whether this proposed loan is legal.

Section 339(2) requires that amounts lent by the parent company or any subsidiary should be added to any proposed additional loan to the director of the parent company in order to determine whether the new loan falls within any available exemption. In this situation the small loans exemption is £5,000, which is less than the total of the two loans combined (£3,000 plus £2,500). The subsidiary should, therefore, restrict its loan by £500 to fall within the small loans exemption.

21.24 Amounts lent by a company which at the time of making the loan was a subsidiary or fellow-subsidiary but which is no longer a subsidiary or fellow subsidiary when the calculation under section 334 later has to be done, need not be taken account into such calculation. [Sec 339(5)].

21.25 The small loans exemption does not apply, however, to loans that relevant companies make to persons who are connected with a director and accordingly loans to such persons are not aggregated with those to the director for the purpose of determining whether the small loans exemption has been utilised. [Sec 339(1)]. It also does not apply to guarantees, or indemnities or securities that such companies provide to directors or their connected persons. [Sec 334].

Groups

21.26 The second exemption relates to inter-company loans in the same group. A relevant company may make a loan (or enter into a guarantee, or provide any security in connection with a loan) to another company within the same group. This applies even where a director of the relevant company is associated with that other group company. [Sec 333].

21.27 A parent company, whether relevant or non-relevant, is not prohibited from making loans to a director of its subsidiary. Similarly, a subsidiary may lend to a director of a fellow subsidiary. Also the Act does not prohibit loans being made to a director before he became a director of the company.

Quasi-loans

Definition

21.28 Quasi-loans are transactions where one party (the creditor) either agrees to pay, or pays, a sum for another (the borrower). It also covers transactions where the creditor agrees to reimburse, or reimburses, expenditure another party incurs for the borrower. A quasi-loan exists where either of the following two conditions apply:

- The transaction's terms are such that the borrower (or a person on his behalf) will reimburse the creditor.
- The circumstances surrounding the transaction give rise to a liability on the borrower to reimburse the creditor.

[Sec 331(3)].

21.29 The following are common examples of a quasi-loan:

Example 1

A director uses a company credit card to buy goods, and he does so on the understanding that the company will settle the liability and he will reimburse the company at a later date.

Example 2

Companies in a group pay for goods and services for the personal use of a director of the parent company, on the basis that he will reimburse those companies at a later date.

Value of quasi-loans

21.30 The value of a quasi-loan is the amount, or maximum amount, that the person to whom it is made is liable to reimburse the creditor. [Sec 340(3)].

General prohibition

21.31 The general prohibition for making quasi-loans to directors and persons connected with them applies only to relevant companies.

- Relevant companies

  Relevant companies are prohibited from making quasi-loans to either the company's directors or its parent company's directors, or to a director's connected persons. [Sec 330(3)(a)(b)].

  Relevant companies may not enter into a guarantee or provide security for a quasi-loan a third party makes to a director or a person connected with him. [Sec 330(3)(c)].

- Non-relevant companies

  The above restrictions do not apply to non-relevant companies. Non-relevant companies may make quasi-loans of any amount to either the company's directors or its parent company's directors, or to the connected persons of such directors. They may also guarantee or provide security in respect of a quasi-loan to such a person.

Exemptions

Small quasi-loans

21.32 Relevant companies may make quasi-loans to a director (but not to his connected persons), provided the following two conditions are satisfied:

- The amount of the proposed quasi-loan and the amounts outstanding under existing quasi-loans in favour of that director do not exceed £5,000.

- The director is required to repay each relevant quasi-loan within two months.

[Sec 332(1)].

The total amount of relevant quasi-loans will include such loans made by the relevant company or by any of its subsidiaries, or, if the director is a director of a parent company of that relevant company, by any other subsidiary of the parent company. [Sec 332(2)].

Groups

21.33 Where a relevant company is a member of a group, it is not prohibited either from making a quasi-loan to another member of that group, or from entering into a guarantee or providing security for any such quasi-loan, by reason only that a director of one of the group companies is associated with another group company. [Sec 333].

Credit transactions

Definition

21.34 A credit transaction is any transaction where a creditor:

- Supplies any goods or sells any land under either a hire purchase agreement or a conditional sale agreement.
- Leases or hires any land or any goods in return for periodic payments.
- Otherwise disposes of land, or supplies goods or services, on the understanding that payment (whatever form it takes) is to be deferred.

[Sec 331(7)].

'Services' means anything other than goods or land. [Sec 331(8)].

Value of credit transactions

21.35 The value of this type of transaction is the price that it would be reasonable to expect could be obtained for the goods, land or services to which the transaction relates if they had been supplied in the ordinary course of the company's business and on the same terms (apart from price). [Sec 340(6)]. If the value of the transaction cannot be ascertained, then it is deemed to exceed £50,000. [Sec 340(7)].

General prohibition

21.36 The general prohibition for making credit transactions to directors and persons connected with them is as follows:

- Relevant companies

  A relevant company may not enter into a credit transaction for the benefit of a director of either the company or its parent company, or a person connected with such a director. [Sec 330(4)(a)].

  A relevant company may not either guarantee such a transaction that somebody else enters into, or provide security in respect of such a transaction. [Sec 330(4)(b)].

- Non-relevant companies

  Non-relevant companies are not affected by the above rules relating to credit transactions.

Exemptions

21.37 A credit transaction that is made to either a director of the company or its parent company or to a person connected with such directors is not prohibited if one of the following conditions is satisfied:

- The aggregate value of the proposed transaction, taken with the value of any other credit transactions, guarantees and securities thereof that are still outstanding plus any existing arrangements that fall within section 330(6) and 330(7) and that were made in connection with a credit transaction and made to any one director or his connected persons, does not exceed £5000. [Sec 335(1)]. (Arrangements that fall within section 330(6) and 330(7) are discussed in paragraphs 21.38 to 21.43 below.)

- The transaction in question was entered into in the ordinary course of its business, and the value and the terms on which the company offers the credit transaction to the director are no more favourable than the value and the terms the company would have offered to a person who was of similar financial standing, but was unconnected with the company. [Sec 335(2)].

The value of a credit transaction is considered in paragraph 21.35 above.

Assignment or assumption of rights, or obligations or liabilities

General prohibition

21.38 Both *relevant companies* and *non-relevant companies* are not permitted to arrange to have assigned to them, or to assume responsibility for, any rights, or obligations or liabilities under loans, or quasi-loans or credit transactions (or any guarantee or provisions of security in respect of such loans or transactions). This applies if the transactions concerned would have been unlawful had the company itself entered into them. For the purpose of this section, the transaction will be treated as having been entered into on the date of the arrangement. [Sec 330(6)].

21.39 An illustration of an 'assignment', and an illustration of an 'assumption of liabilities' are given in examples 1 and 2 respectively below:

Example 1

A third party makes a loan to a director of a company and, subsequently, the director's company purchases the third party's rights to the loan. In this situation, the company has (illegally) paid out resources to acquire an asset, and the company purports to become a creditor of the director just as if it had advanced the loan itself.

Example 2

A third party guarantees a loan that a fourth party makes to a director of a company and, subsequently, the director's company enters into an arrangement with the third and the fourth parties, whereby the third party is released from his guarantee, and the company purports to assume the liability. Again, in this situation, the company's resources are (illegally) tied up by a contingent liability when the company purports to assume the guarantee on behalf of the director.

Value of assignment or assumption

21.40 The value of this type of arrangement is the value of the transaction to which the arrangement relates less any amount by which the person's liability has been reduced. [Sec 340(5)]. If the value of the transaction cannot be ascertained, then it is deemed to exceed £50,000. [Sec 340(7)].

Indirect arrangements

General Prohibition

21.41 The Act prohibits those indirect arrangements whereby another person enters into a transaction that would have been unlawful had the company itself entered into it. This prohibition applies only if that person has obtained, or is to obtain, under the arrangement any benefit from the company, its parent company, its subsidiary or its fellow subsidiary. [Sec 330(7)]. This provision is designed to prevent a company's resources from being used to procure another person to provide one of the various forms of prohibited credit without the company itself either entering into, or subsequently becoming a party to, the transaction.

21.42 This provision is very widely drafted, and it is intended to cover the wide variety of forms that these types of arrangement can take. For example, it covers the situation where a company agrees to make a loan to another company's director in return for that other company making a loan to one of the first company's directors. It also covers the situation where a director persuades a bank to make a loan on favourable terms to him in return for his company placing business with the bank.

Value of indirect arrangements

21.43 The value of an indirect arrangement is ascertained in the same way as the value of an assignment or an assumption of rights considered in paragraph 21.40 above.

General exemptions from prohibited transactions

21.44 In addition to the exemptions that apply only to particular types of transactions (for example, the *de minimis* exemption for a loan of less than £5,000), the Act includes more general exemptions in respect of:

- Transactions between a subsidiary and its parent company.
- Directors' business expenditure.

Transactions between a subsidiary and its parent company

21.45 The following transactions between a subsidiary and its parent company are not affected by the restrictions that the Act imposes on loans, quasi-loans and credit transactions:

- A loan or a quasi-loan a company makes to its parent company, or a company's guarantee or provision of security to a third person who has made a loan or quasi-loan to the company's parent company.
- A credit transactions a company enters into as creditor for its parent company, or a guarantee or security that a company provides in connection with a credit transaction a third party makes for the company's parent company.

[Sec 336].

These types of transactions are, therefore, lawful.

Directors' business expenditure

21.46 The Act permits a company to give a director funds to meet expenditure incurred or to be incurred by him for the purposes of the company, or to enable him to perform his duties properly as an officer of the company. [Sec 337(1)]. Furthermore, the company is not prohibited from doing anything to enable a director to avoid incurring such expenditure of the kind described in section 337(1). [Sec 337(2)]. The company may provide these funds by way of a loan, or a quasi-loan or a credit transaction, or by any other similar arrangement. This exemption applies, however, only if one of the following two conditions is satisfied:

- The transaction has been approved in advance by the company in general meeting. [Sec 337(3)(a)]. At that general meeting, the purpose of the expenditure, the amount of funds to be provided, and the extent of the company's liability under the transaction must all be made known. [Sec 337(4)].

- It is a condition of the transaction that, if the company does not subsequently approve the transaction at, or before, the next annual general meeting, the director will discharge, within six months, any liability that arises under the transaction. [Sec 337(3)(b)].

21.47 A relevant company may not enter into such a transaction if the aggregate of the relevant amounts (see para 21.21) exceeds £10,000. [Sec 337(3)]. However, with non-relevant companies there is no upper limit on transactions of this type.

21.48 The most common form of transaction of this nature is a bridging loan a company gives to a director who changes location within the company, and so is required to move house.

21.49 Section 337 of the Act does not restrict advances of an appropriate amount a company makes to a director for business expenditure. Consequently, these types of transaction are permitted without first needing to be approved in general meeting. This is because the funds the company provides to the director in this way are not lent to him.

Disclosure requirements

Introduction

21.50 The Act requires considerable detail to be disclosed in the notes to a company's financial statements regarding transactions with directors whether they are lawful or not. The circumstances in which disclosure is required and the particulars regarding disclosure are set out in Parts II and III of Schedule 6 to the Act. [Sec 232(1)(2)].

21.51 Details of the transactions that require to be disclosed must be given in the notes to the consolidated financial statements of a parent company, or if it is not required to prepare consolidated financial statements, its individual financial statements, or in the financial statements of any company other than a parent company. Such transactions are required to be disclosed for shadow directors as well as for other directors. [6 Sch 27(2)].

Disclosure of section 330 transactions

21.52 Unless they are specifically exempted from being disclosed (see paras 21.59 to 21.61), any transaction or arrangement of a type described in section 330 (that is, loans, quasi-loans, credit transactions, related guarantees, assignments and indirect arrangements) and agreements to enter into such transactions must be disclosed in the notes to the financial statements. [6 Sch 15(a)(b), 16(a)(b)].

21.53 The transactions, arrangements and agreements which are required to be disclosed by all companies (that is, both relevant and non-relevant) are those entered into by a company or (if it is a parent company) by its subsidiaries:

- For a person who was a director at any time during the financial year of either the company or its parent company.
- For a person who was connected with such a director.

[6 Sch 15(a)(b), 16(a)(b)].

21.54 The disclosure provisions apply irrespective of whether or not:

- The transaction is either prohibited by section 330 of the Act, or falls within one of the exemptions given in sections 332 to 338.
- The person for whom the transaction was made was a director, or was a person connected with a director, at the time the transaction was made. This is provided, however, that the person has subsequently become a director, or has become connected with a director.
- The company that entered into the transaction was a subsidiary of the company of which the person was a director at the time the transaction was made.

[6 Sch 19].

Disclosure applicable to all transactions

21.55 Accordingly, the following details must be given for each disclosable transaction, arrangements or agreements:

- Particulars of the transaction's principal terms. [6 Sch 22(1)]. The 'principal terms' will include those terms that relate to the provision of either the cash or the non-cash asset and also the arrangements for repaying the value of that asset (including any interest component, together with any related security or guarantees).

- A statement that the transaction either was made during the financial year or existed during that period. [6 Sch 22(2)(a)].

- The name of the director concerned in the transaction and where applicable, the name of the connected person. [6 Sch 22(2)(b)].

- The additional disclosures, as appropriate, set out below.

Additional disclosure for loans

21.56 For any loan, or of any arrangement relating to a loan, the following information has to be disclosed:

- The amount of the liability (in respect of both principal and interest), at both the beginning and the end of the financial year.

- The maximum amount of the liability during that period.

- The amount of any due but unpaid interest.

- The amount of any provision that the company has made against the failure or the anticipated failure of the borrower to repay the whole, or any part, of the principal or interest.

[6 Sch 22(2)(d)].

The 'value' of such loans is considered in paragraph 21.19 above. The above disclosure requirements are illustrated in Table 80.

Additional disclosure for guarantees or securities

21.57 For any guarantee or security, or of any arrangement relating to any guarantee or security, the following information has to be disclosed:

- The amount of the company's or its subsidiary's liability, at both the beginning and the end of the financial year.

- The maximum amount for which the company or its subsidiary may become liable.

- Any amount the company or its subsidiary has paid, and any liability it has incurred, either in fulfilling the guarantee or in discharging the security.

[6 Sch 22(2)(e)].

The 'value' of such guarantees or securities is the amount guaranteed or secured. [Sec 340(4)].

Table 80: Illustration of the disclosure of loans to directors.

Extract from Allied-Lyons PLC Report and Accounts 4th March 1989.

Note extract

LOANS TO DIRECTORS

On appointment as directors on 19th April 1988, Mr. C.E. Arnett and Mr. D. Beatty were in receipt of loans from subsidiary companies as follows:–

Mr. C.E. Arnett — a loan of US$150,000 at a rate of interest of 4% per annum taken over by the group on the acquisition of the Tetley Inc. tea business in 1972 and utilised for the purchase of shares in a former employing company. The loan was repaid in full on 3rd June 1988.

Mr. D. Beatty — a loan of £318,000, interest free, as short-term housing finance in connection with a company-initiated employment move. The loan was repaid in full on 15th July 1988.

Additional disclosure for quasi-loans, credit transactions and related arrangements or agreements

21.58 For quasi-loans, credit transactions and related arrangements or agreements (including indirect arrangements for such transactions), disclosure has to be made of the 'value' of the transaction or arrangement, or the 'value' of the transaction or arrangement to which the agreement relates. [6 Sch 22(2)(f)]. The effect of this provision is to require, for example, the disclosure of:

- The amount to be reimbursed where a company buys goods on behalf of a director, or the maximum amount to be reimbursed in respect of quasi-loans. [Sec 340(3)].

- The arm's length value of any goods and services purchased in credit transactions. [Sec 340(6)].

- The value of arrangements for assignments and back-to-back deals. [Sec 340(6)].

The meaning of 'value' for these types of transactions is considered in paragraphs 21.30, 21.35, 21.40 and 21.43 above.

Exemptions from disclosure

21.59 Some of the additional information outlined in the above paragraphs need not be disclosed for loans and quasi-loans where a company makes them to another wholly-owned company in the same group, or to the parent company where the company is wholly-owned, and where the information would otherwise have been disclosable only on the grounds that the director of the company that made the loan was also associated with the company that received the loan. [6 Sch 23]. But where this type of transaction does exist, the financial statements still have to give particulars of the transaction's principal terms, a statement that the transaction was made or existed during the year, and the name of the company concerned (see para 21.55). This exception means that, where certain *intra-group loans* are made by the company, only those details are required to be disclosed.

21.60 The disclosure requirements above do not apply to the following circumstances:

- A transaction between two companies, where a director of one of the companies (or of its subsidiary or its parent company) is interested only by virtue of the fact that he is also a director of that other company [6 Sch 18(a)]. This exemption means that, among other things, details of many general *intra-group trading* transactions between companies are not required to be disclosed.

- A transaction that was not entered into during the period to which the financial statements relate, and that did not exist at any time during that period. [6 Sch 18(c)].

- The following transactions that a company or its subsidiary has made for a person who was a director of the company or its parent company, or was connected with any such director, at any time during the financial year, provided that the outstanding aggregate value of the transactions did not exceed £5,000 at any time during the period.

  - □ Credit transactions.

  - □ Guarantees or security relating to credit transactions.

  - □ Assignments, or assumptions or arrangements of the type referred to in sections 330(6) and (7) of the Act that relate to credit transactions (see paras 21.38 to 21.43).

  - □ Agreements to enter into credit transactions.

  [6 Sch 24(1)(2)].

The reference to 'aggregate value' means the value of all transactions for a particular director, including those made to a person connected with him. In addition, the amount by which any liability of the person for whom the transaction was made has been reduced should be deducted. [6 Sch 24(1)].

Without this threshold limit, a company's financial statements would sometimes contain an excessive amount of information about directors' transactions. Petty transactions involving deferred payment by directors are very common, and it is not the Act's intention to require disclosure of these. The Act intends that disclosure should prevent abuse where the transactions involve larger sums.

21.61 The Secretary of State has power to increase by statutory instrument the financial limits mentioned in the last point of the paragraph above. [6 Sch 26].

Penalties for failure to disclose

21.62 The Act imposes a penalty on the company's directors for failure to disclose information about directors' transactions in the company's financial statements. If the financial statements that are approved by the directors do not disclose the required information, then every director of the company who is party to their approval and who knows that they do not comply or is reckless as to whether they comply is guilty of an offence and is liable to a fine (see appendix IV). [Sec 233(5)]

21.63 Moreover, where the financial statements do not disclose the information required, the auditors must include, in their report (so far as they are reasonably able to do so), a statement giving the details that have been omitted. [Sec 237(4)]. The auditors are not required to draw attention to an unlawful transaction by stating that it either is illegal or contravenes the Act, but they should, of course, consider the effect of any illegal transaction on the truth and fairness of the financial statements. This consideration will include the question of whether the debt is recoverable.

Notification to the board

21.64 In addition to the substantial amount of disclosure that is required to be made in the financial statements in respect of transactions or arrangements of the kind described in section 330, the Act requires a director to disclose these transactions to the board. This is because section 317(6) of the Act regards such transactions and arrangements, whether they are lawful or not, as transactions or arrangements in which a director is interested. The notification procedures that should be followed are discussed further in chapter 22 paragraphs 22.14 to 22.19.

Transactions with officers

Introduction

21.65 In contrast to its substantial number of provisions that relate to transactions with directors, the Act does not prohibit a company from entering into transactions with its officers other than directors. However, the Act does require disclosure in respect of the following types of transaction, arrangement and agreement made by the company or any of its subsidiaries for persons who at any time during the financial year were officers of the company (but not directors or shadow directors):

- Loans (including any guarantees or security for loans), or arrangements of the types described in section 330(6) or (7) of the Act that relate to loans, or agreements to enter into any such transactions.

- Quasi-loans (including any guarantees or security for quasi-loans), or arrangements of the types described in section 330(6) or (7) of the Act that relate to quasi-loans, or agreements to enter into any such transactions.

- Credit transactions (including any guarantees or security for credit transactions), or arrangements of the types described in section 330(6) or (7) of the Act that relate to credit transactions, or agreements to enter into any such transactions.

[Sec 232(2); 6 Sch 28].

21.66 For this purpose, the term 'officer' should be interpreted as including the company secretary and the company's senior managers. [Sec 744].

Disclosure requirements

21.67 In respect of the transactions to be disclosed, the consolidated financial statements, or (if consolidated financial statements are not prepared) the parent company's financial statements, or the financial statements of any company other than a parent company, must disclose:

- The aggregate amounts outstanding at the end of the financial year under such transactions, made by either the company or (if it is a parent company) its subsidiaries. The aggregate amounts must relate to each category of transaction described in paragraph 21.65 above.

In this respect, 'amounts outstanding' means the amount of the outstanding liabilities of the person for whom the transaction was made. With a guarantee or a security, it means the amount guaranteed or secured. [6 Sch 30].

- The number of officers with whom the company made those transactions.

[6 Sch 29(1)].

Exemptions from disclosure

21.68 The transactions outlined in paragraph 21.65 above need not be disclosed where the aggregate amount outstanding at the end of the financial year for an officer of the company does not exceed £2,500. [6 Sch 29(2)]. The Secretary of State has power to increase this limit by statutory instrument. [6 Sch 29(3)].

Penalty for failure to disclose

21.69 There is a penalty on the company's directors if they fail to make the disclosure the Act requires in respect of a company's officers (see para 21.62). [Sec 233(5)] . In addition, the auditors must include a statement in their audit report giving the required particulars, so far as they are reasonably able to do so (see para 21.63). [Sec 237(4)].

Money-lending companies

Introduction

21.70 The Act defines a 'money-lending company' as *"a company whose ordinary business includes the making of loans or quasi-loans, or the giving of guarantees in connection with such loans"*. [Sec 338(2)]. Money-lending companies are not banking companies under the Banking Act 1987 and they have special rules. A money-lending company may be either a relevant or a non-relevant company. All the general provisions of the Act that prevent relevant and non-relevant companies from making loans and quasi-loans to directors or their connected persons are applicable to relevant and non-relevant money-lending companies. However, money-lending companies (both relevant and non-relevant) may take advantage of a number of further exemptions. The relevant exemptions and disclosure requirements are considered in the paragraphs that follow.

Exemptions

21.71 Section 338(1) of the Act permits money-lending companies (both relevant and non-relevant) to make loans or quasi-loans, or to guarantee such transactions, to any director or his connected persons, subject to the following two conditions:

- The company makes the transaction in the ordinary course of its business. [Sec 338(3)(a)].

- The amount involved is not greater than, and the terms of the contract are not more favourable than, those that the company might reasonably be expected to have offered to, or in respect of, a person who was unconnected with the company, but who had a similar financial standing to that of the director (that is, on normal commercial terms).. [Sec 338(3)(b)].

21.72 A further condition applies to a money-lending company that is a relevant company. Such a company may not enter into a transaction if the aggregate of the relevant amounts (see para 21.21) concerned exceeds £100,000. [Sec 338(4)]. In determining that aggregate, loans to companies that the director is connected with, but that he does not control, may be excluded. [Sec 338(5)].

21.73 However, money-lending companies do not benefit from any special provisions that apply to the following types of transaction:

- The provision of security in connection with a loan or a quasi-loan.

- Credit transactions, or the provision of a guarantee or security in connection with them.

- The assignment of rights, or obligations or liabilities under any transaction.

- Indirect arrangements under any transaction.

The exception in respect of quasi-loans and credit transactions mentioned in the first and second point above is applicable only to relevant companies because it is only for such companies that they are restricted. Consequently, in all these situations, money-lending companies are in the same position as any other company, and the rules detailed in sections 330 to 337 of the Act (as outlined in paras 21.17 to 21.49) apply to them.

Loans on beneficial terms for house purchase

21.74 In contrast to the provisions set out above in respect of loans on normal commercial terms, money-lending companies (both relevant and non-relevant) may make loans on beneficial terms to directors of either the company or its parent company, only for the purpose of house purchase or improvement. Provided that all the following conditions are satisfied, loans for the above purposes will be allowed:

- The loan is to assist the director either to purchase or to improve his only or main residence, or of land enjoyed with it. This type of loan will also include a loan the company has made to take over any similar loan that any other person has made to the director.
- The company makes similar loans of that type available to its employees on no less favourable terms.
- The aggregate of the relevant amounts does not exceed £100,000.

[Sec 338(6)].

21.75 The aggregate of the relevant amounts in the last point of the preceding paragraph is determined as follows:

- Relevant company

  The following transactions must be taken together with the proposed housing loan for the purposes of determining the relevant amount:

  - The value of any house loans or guarantees thereof made on beneficial terms that are still outstanding.
  - The value of any loans or guarantees thereof made on commercial terms and that are still outstanding.
  - The value of any arrangements falling within section 330(6) and 330(7) that are made either in connection with a house loan made on beneficial terms or a loan made on commercial terms.

Consequently, a company may make a director a loan on beneficial terms or a loan on commercial terms to the value of £100,000, or any combination of them, provided that the aggregate value of the transaction relating to that director does not exceed £100,000.

- Non-relevant company

  The same consideration applies to non-relevant companies as above. However, since there is no financial limit upon the value of a transaction that a non-relevant money-lending company may make on commercial terms, a non-relevant company may make a house loan on beneficial terms to the value of £100,000, and it may then go on to make loans on commercial terms to any value. But, if a non-relevant company makes a loan on commercial terms to the value of £100,000 in the first instance, it may not then make a house loan on beneficial terms. The reason for this is that the £100,000 limit allowable under section 338(6) will then have been exhausted.

Disclosure requirements

21.76 A money-lending company (unless it is a banking company's parent company) is bound by the same disclosure requirements as any other company. Therefore, the information set out in paragraphs 21.50 to 21.58 above will have to be disclosed in the notes to the financial statements.

Banking Companies

Introduction

21.77 Those provisions of the Act that prevent companies from making loans and quasi-loans to directors or their connected persons are relaxed to some extent for banking companies. The special rules that cover the legality of these transactions for such companies are set out in section 338 of the Act.

21.78 A banking company means a company that is authorised under the Banking Act 1987. [Sec 744]. These companies also fall within the definition of 'money-lending companies' (see para 21.70).

Exemptions

21.79 There is no limit to the amount of loans, quasi-loans and guarantees in respect of such loans and quasi-loans that a banking company can make to a director or his connected persons, provided the following two conditions are satisfied:

- The company makes the transaction in the ordinary course of its business.

- The amount involved is not greater than, and the terms of the contract are not more favourable than, those that the company might reasonably be expected to have offered to, or in respect of, a person who was unconnected with the company, but who had a similar financial standing to that of the director (that is on normal commercial terms).

[Sec 338(1)(3)(4)].

21.80 However, like money-lending companies, banking companies do not benefit from any special provisions that apply to the following types of transaction:

- The provision of security in connection with a loan or a quasi-loan.

- Credit transactions, or the provision of a guarantee or security in connection with them.

- The assignment of rights, or obligations or liabilities under any transaction.

- Indirect arrangements under any transaction.

21.81 In all these situations, banking companies are in the same position as any other company, and the rules detailed in sections 330 to 337 of the Act (as outlined in paras 21.17 to 21.49) apply to them.

Loans on beneficial terms for house purchase

21.82 Banking companies may make loans on beneficial terms to directors for house purchase and house improvement on the same basis and conditions as set out in paragraph 21.74 above.

21.83 Banking companies may ignore loans made on commercial terms in computing whether or not a house loan on beneficial terms falls within the £100,000 limit. Therefore, only the amount of any previous house loans that were still outstanding should be brought into the aggregation. [Sec 339(4)]. In effect, a banking company may make house loans to either its directors or its parent company's directors on beneficial terms to the value of £100,000. In addition, they may make loans to such directors on commercial terms up to any value.

Disclosure requirements

21.84 A banking company, or a banking company's parent company, is exempted from some of the disclosure requirements that apply to other companies. The provisions of Schedule 6 have effect subject to Part IV of Schedule 9. [Sec 255B(2)].

21.85 A banking company or the parent company of a banking company does not have to disclose the detailed information outlined in paragraphs 21.56 to 21.58 above in respect of loans, quasi-loans and other dealings in favour of directors and connected persons in relation to a transaction or arrangement of a kind mentioned in section 330, or an agreement to enter into such a transaction or arrangement. to which *that banking company is a party*. [9 Sch Part IV, 2].

21.86 However, a banking company or the parent company of a banking company does have to disclose the aggregate information outlined in paragraph 21.89 below in respect of loans, quasi-loans, credit transactions and related guarantees, securities and indirect arrangements of the kind described in paragraph 21.41 above made by that banking company for:

- A director, shadow director, or his connected person.
- A person who was a chief executive or manager (within the meaning of the Banking Act 1987) of that company or parent company.

[9 Sch Part IV 3(1)]

21.87 The Banking Act 1987 defines a chief executive as *"a person who, either alone or jointly with one or more persons, is responsible under the immediate authority of the directors for the conduct of the business of the institution"*. If the principal place of business is outside the UK, the chief executive includes a person who alone or jointly with other persons, is responsible for the conduct of its business in the UK [BA 1987 Sec 105(7)(8)].

21.88 A manager is defined by the Banking Act 1987 as a person (other than a chief executive) who, under the immediate authority of a director or chief executive of the institution, undertakes one of the following tasks:

- Exercises managerial functions.
- Is responsible for maintaining accounts or other records of the institution.

[BA 1987 Sec 105(6)].

21.89 The details to be disclosed are as follows:

- The aggregate amounts outstanding at the end of the financial year, analysed under loans, quasi-loans and credit transactions.
- The number of persons for whom the bank made those transactions.

[6 Sch 29, 9 Sch Part IV 3(1)].

An illustration of this disclosure is given in Table 81.

21.90 For the purpose of these provisions insofar as they relate to loans and quasi-loans, a company that a person does not control should not be treated as being connected with him. [9 Sch Part IV 3(4)]. The interpretation of a person connected with a director or controlling a company is given in section 346 (see also para 21.10). [9 Sch Part IV, 3(5)].

Table 81: Illustration of the disclosure of loans made to directors and officers of a banking company.

Extract from Midland Bank plc Annual Report and Accounts 31st December 1988.

Note extract

30 Directors' and officers' loans

In accordance with the requirements of sections 233 and 234 of the Companies Act 1985, the aggregate amounts outstanding at 31 December 1988 from persons who were directors or officers (or connected with directors or officers) during the year, and the number of persons concerned, were as follows

	£m	
	Aggregate amount outstanding	Number of persons
Directors		
Loans	1.5	11
Quasi-loans	*	27
Credit transactions	–	–
Officers		
Loans	0.1	2
Quasi-loans	#	1
Credit transactions	–	–

* aggregate amount outstanding was £15,839
# aggregate amount outstanding was £375

Register of transactions

21.91 A banking company, or a banking company's parent company, must maintain a register that contains a copy of every transaction whose particulars would have been disclosed in the financial statements had the company not been a banking company. The register must contain this information for the current year and for the ten preceding years. If the transaction is not recorded in writing, the register must contain a written memorandum setting out the transaction's terms. [Sec 343(1)(2)(3)].

21.92 However, no entries need be recorded in the register where the aggregate value of transactions, arrangements or agreements for a director or a connected person does not exceed £1,000 at any time during the financial year. [Sec 344(1)].

Special statement

21.93 In addition, unless the banking company is a wholly-owned subsidiary of another UK company [Sec 344(2)], it must prepare a statement that includes particulars of those transactions for the financial year preceding its annual general meeting. This statement must be made available for inspection by the company's members for at least 15 days before the annual general meeting, and also at the meeting itself. [Sec 343(4)(5)].

21.94 The auditors must examine this statement. They must also submit a report to the shareholders stating whether or not all the particulars the Act requires have been included in it. Where any required particulars have been omitted, the auditors must include a statement of the required particulars in their report (so far as they are reasonably able to do so). Their report must be annexed to the company's statement. [Sec 343(6)(7)].

21.95 The disclosure of particulars in the special statement need not be made where the outstanding aggregate value of those transactions, arrangements or agreements for a director or a connected person does not exceed £1,000 at any time during the financial year. [Sec 344(1)].

21.96 For the purpose of these provisions insofar as they relate to loans and quasi-loans, a company that a person does not control should not be treated as being connected with him. [Sec 343(9)].

Liability for contravention

21.97 Where a banking company fails to comply with the requirements set out in paras 21.91 to 21.96 above, any person who is a director at the time (other than a shadow director) is both guilty of an offence and liable to a fine. In these circumstances, however, it will be a sufficient defence for a person to show that he took all reasonable steps to ensure that the bank complied with the requirements (see appendix IV). [Sec 343(8)].

Criminal sanctions and civil remedies

21.98 The penalties the Act imposes on a company that contravenes the Act's provisions that relate to the legality of directors' transactions vary according to whether or not the company is a relevant company. A relevant company will incur both criminal and civil liability, whereas a non-relevant company will incur only civil liability.

21.99 As regards criminal liability, a relevant company that contravenes section 330 of the Act will be guilty of an offence. [Sec 342(2)]. A director will also be guilty of an offence if he either authorises or permits the transaction concerned. This provision will also apply to any other person who causes the company to enter into such a transaction. [Sec 342(1)(3)]. In this situation, the director's or the other person's state of mind is relevant in deciding whether an offence has been committed. To be guilty of an offence, he must have known, or have had reasonable cause to believe, that the transaction contravened section 330. A relevant company may escape liability if it can prove that it did not know of the facts at the time it entered into the transaction. [Sec 342(5)]. The criminal penalty is imprisonment or a fine, or both (see appendix IV). [Sec 342(4)].

21.100 A company may choose to regard an unlawful transaction as voidable. [Sec 341(1)]. This means that a company does not need to regard itself as bound by any agreement that it has entered into with the director or any other person. However, because a transaction is not actually void, a company may wish to elect to affirm the agreement instead. Also, the company will not be entitled to treat the transaction as voidable if the subject matter of the transaction cannot be restored (for example, where the sum a company has lent has been used to buy goods which have been consumed), or if the person who benefited under the transaction has indemnified the company. [Sec 341(1)(a)].

21.101 Similarly, a transaction will not be voidable if a third party has, *bona fide* and without actual notice, acquired rights under the agreement, and these rights would be affected if the company avoided the liability. [Sec 341(1)(b)].

21.102 The person who benefited from the unlawful transaction may not himself elect to treat it as voidable. Moreover, he, and any other director who authorised the transaction, are (without prejudice to any other liability imposed by law) liable to account to the company for any gain they have made (whether directly or indirectly) and also to indemnify the company for any loss or damage it incurs as a result of the transaction. [Sec 341(2)(3)]. Where a director took all reasonable steps to ensure that the transaction did not contravene the Act, he need not either account to the company or indemnify it, if the transaction in question was made for a person connected with him. [Sec 341(4)]. A connected person (and a director who authorised the transaction) will avoid civil liability if they can show that, at the time the company entered into the agreement, they did not know of the circumstances that amounted to a contravention. [Sec 341(5)].

Chapter 22

TRANSACTIONS WITH DIRECTORS AND RELATED PARTIES

Chapter 22

TRANSACTIONS WITH DIRECTORS AND RELATED PARTIES

Introduction

22.1 The Act and The International Stock Exchange's Continuing Obligations and General Undertaking cover a range of transactions and arrangements in which the director has, directly or indirectly, a material interest (for example, contracts between a director and a company for the sale of non-cash assets). These transactions are in addition to those specified in section 330 of the Act, which are dealt with in the previous chapter. The Act and The International Stock Exchange's Continuing Obligations specify certain information that has to be made available to shareholders, either by disclosure in the company's financial statements or in some other way. The emphasis is placed on disclosure to enable interested parties to determine the benefit a director gains through his relationship with the company.

22.2 This chapter is, therefore, concerned with the disclosure requirements of contracts or substantial property transactions in which a director has a material interest. It also covers the disclosure requirements relating to transactions that a company may enter into with related parties other than directors. In particular, it considers the proposals in ED 46, 'Related Party Transactions', which was published in April 1989.

Material interests in transactions or arrangements

Introduction

22.3 The Act states that a director has an interest in a transaction or arrangement for the supply or transfer of any interest in goods, land or services, where he is the person to whom the goods, land or services, or the interest, are supplied or transferred. [Sec 331(9)(e)].

22.4 An interest in such a transaction or arrangement is not 'material' if in the board's opinion it is not material, but this is without prejudice to whether or not such an interest is material in a situation where the board has not considered the matter. 'The board' means the directors of the company who prepare the financial statements, but it excludes the particular director who has the interest in the transaction. [6 Sch 17(2)].

22.5 Although the Act does not say so explicitly, it is, of course, implicit that the directors' opinion on the materiality of a transaction must have been formed in good faith. Where the directors have not considered the question of materiality, the materiality of a transaction will be a matter of fact. This does not mean that the transaction will be regarded as material. It simply means that, in the absence of an opinion from the directors, it cannot be presumed not to be material.

Interpretation of 'material interest'

22.6 In practice, the interpretation of the words 'material interest' has caused considerable debate. Although the test of materiality is not clear, two tests, the 'relevant' test and the 'substantial' test, are regarded as having some authority. The 'relevant' test considers a transaction to be material if it is likely to be of interest or relevance either to the shareholders or to the other users of the financial statements. The 'substantial' test considers a transaction to be material if the director's interest in the transaction is substantial.

22.7 The 'substantial' test can be illustrated by the following example:

Example

Where a director buys a bar of chocolate in the company's shop, he is the other party to the contract, and accordingly his interest in the transaction (his purchase of the bar of chocolate from the company) is material.

22.8 The expression 'material' has not yet been interpreted in case law in the context of directors' transactions. However, of the two tests referred to above, Counsel has advised that the 'relevant' test is to be preferred. Counsel has said that the correct approach should be to find out whether the existence of the arrangement would be significant to a shareholder. It could be significant either because it is one of importance to the company or because it is one of importance to the individual director. Where the transaction is of importance either to the company or to the individual director, then a material interest does exist, and it should be disclosed. On the other hand, it should be borne in mind that other Counsel have advised that the substantial test is preferred.

22.9 Because of this confusion, the Law Society's Standing Committee on Company Law proposed an amendment to paragraph 17(2) of Schedule 6 to the Act (see para 22.4) to try to clarify the meaning of 'material interest'. It suggested that the definition should be altered to include the following:

> *"An interest is material if, and only if, knowledge thereof might reasonably be expected to influence the judgement:*

> *(a) of a person in determining whether he will enter into any transaction or arrangement with the relevant company and, if so, upon what terms or whether he will deal in securities of the company; or*
>
> *(b) of a member of the company in determining whether he will exercise any of his rights in that capacity."*

22.10 Although no amendment on these lines has yet been adopted, the rules on the disclosure of material interests in transactions as they affect transactions in groups of companies were relaxed in 1984. These changes have been included in the Act and are those described in paragraph 22.20 and 22.21 below.

22.11 There is still considerable uncertainty about the meaning of this term. Therefore, if a director has an interest in a transaction that may or may not be material, legal advice should be taken.

22.12 Certain other types of transaction involving a director (or his connected persons) and the company may not be regarded as material, and if so, they do not have to be disclosed in the financial statements. These are considered in paragraph 22.23 below.

Disclosure requirements

22.13 The Act requires considerable detail to be disclosed, regarding transactions in which a director has, directly or indirectly, a material interest. The Act requires that directors must disclose their interest to the company. [Sec 317]. The Act also requires disclosure of such interests in the notes to the companies financial statements. [6 Sch 15(c), 16(c)].

Notification to the board

22.14 Where a director has an interest in a contract that involves the company, section 317 of the Act imposes a specific obligation on the director to disclose his interest in the contract at a meeting of the company's directors. A contract for this purpose includes any transaction or arrangement. This applies whether the director is either directly or indirectly interested in the contract, or the proposed contract, with the company. A director must disclose his interest in a proposed contract at one of the following:

- At the directors' meeting at which the contract is first considered.

- If, however, the director acquires an interest in the contract at a later date, he must disclose his interest at the next subsequent meeting.

[Sec 317(2)].

22.15 When a director is, for example, a member of another company that might enter into significant transactions with the company, then he can give a general notice that he is interested in that other company. If he does this, it will be regarded as giving sufficient notice to cover all further transactions with that company. [Sec 317(3)]. The director must either give the notice at a meeting of the directors or take reasonable steps to ensure that it is brought up and read at the next directors' meeting. [Sec 317(4)].

22.16 These notification requirements apply to those transactions and arrangements favouring directors or their connected persons that are covered by section 330 (see chapter 21 para 21.64). [Sec 317(6)]. Consequently, a director, for example, must declare at a directors' meeting his interest in any loan that he, or one of his connected persons, receives from the company. Again, a general notice of an interest may be given.

22.17 The general principles of section 317 apply also to shadow directors. However, a shadow director must disclose his interest by notice, in writing, to the directors, not at a meeting of the directors. Such notice can be in either one of the following forms:

- Specific, and given before the date of the meeting at which he would have been required to declare his interest, had he been a director.

- General (as described in para 22.15).

[Sec 317(8)].

22.18 If a director fails to disclose an interest in accordance with section 317 of the Act, this will be a criminal offence, and he will be liable to a fine. [Sec 317(7) - see appendix IV]. Also, this section does not prejudice the operation of any rule of law that may restrict a director from being interested in contracts with the company. [Sec 317(9)]. This means that the contract may be voidable, and the director may be liable to account to the company for any gain he has made as a result of the transaction, and to indemnify the company for any loss it incurs.

22.19 In addition to the statutory requirement to disclose interests in contracts, the company's articles of association may also contain other specific requirements for the disclosure of interests in contracts. For example, the revised Table A deals, in articles 85 and 86, with directors' material interests in contracts. The requirements of these articles are as follows.

> *"Subject to the provisions of the Act, and provided that he has disclosed to the directors the nature and extent of any material interest of his, a director notwithstanding his office-*
>
> *(a) may be a party to, or otherwise interested in, any transaction or arrangement with the company or in which the company is otherwiseinterested;*
>
> *(b) may be a director or other officer of, or employed by, or a party to any transaction or arrangement with, or otherwise interested in, any body corporate promoted by the company or in which the company is otherwise interested; and*
>
> *(c) shall not, by reason of his office, be accountable to the company for any benefit which he derives from any such office or employment or from any such transaction or arrangement or from any interest in any such body corporate and no such transaction or arrangement shall be liable to be avoided on the ground of any such interest or benefit.*
>
> *For the purposes of [the above] regulation 85*
>
> *(a) a general notice given to the directors that a director is to be regarded as having an interest of the nature and extent specified in the notice in any transaction or arrangement in which a specified person or class of persons is interested shall be deemed to be a disclosure that the director has an interest in any such transaction of the nature and extent so specified; and*
>
> *(b) an interest of which a director has no knowledge and of which it is unreasonable to expect him to have knowledge shall not be treated as an interest of his."*
>
> [Table A articles 85, 86].

Disclosure in financial statements

22.20 The Act requires that any transaction involving the company or its subsidiary in which a person who was, at any time during the financial year, a director of either the company or its holding company had, either directly or indirectly, a material interest should be disclosed. [6 Sch 15(c), 16(c)] This requirement also applies if a person who is connected with a director has an interest in such a transaction. [6 Sch 17(1)].

22.21 This disclosure has to be made either in the consolidated financial statements, or in the financial statements of any company other than a holding company. [Sec 232(1)(2)]. Where a company with subsidiaries has not prepared consolidated financial statements (either because it is a wholly-owned subsidiary or because its subsidiaries are excluded from consolidations), the notes to the financial statements must give the equivalent information that would have been given if those consolidated financial statements had been prepared. [6 Sch 15]. Such transactions are required to be disclosed for shadow directors as well as for other directors. [6 Sch 27(2)]. Where a company has entered into a transaction of one of the types described in paragraph 22.20 above that is required to be disclosed in the financial statements, the financial statements must contain the following information:

- Particulars of the transaction's principal terms. [6 Sch 22(1)]. The 'principal terms' will include those terms that relate to the provision of either the cash or the non-cash asset and also the arrangements for repaying the value of that asset (including any interest component, together with any related security or guarantees).

- A statement that the transaction either was made during the financial year or existed during that period. [6 Sch 22(2)(a)].

- The name of the director concerned in the transaction. Where a transaction is made for a director's connected person, the name of the connected person and the director concerned have to be given. [6 Sch 22(2)(b)].

- The name of the director who has the material interest in the transaction, and the nature of the interest. [6 Sch 22(2)(c)].

- The 'value' of the transaction or arrangement or, where applicable, the 'value' of the transaction or arrangement to which the agreement relates. [6 Sch 22(f)]. The value of the transaction is the arm's length price of the goods, land and services. [Sec 340(6)].

The above disclosure requirements are illustrated in Tables 82 and 83 below.

22.22 In addition to the statutory disclosure requirements outlined above, The International Stock Exchange's Continuing Obligations require listed companies to give particulars in their statutory financial statements of an contract of significance that a director was materially interested in and that existed during the financial year. [CO 21(k)]. The International Stock Exchange Regulations are dealt with in paragraphs 22.38 to 22.42 below.

Table 82: Disclosure of directors' interests in contracts.

Extract from Laing Properties Annual Report 31st December 1988.

Note extract

5 Interests in contracts

(a) By virtue of their shareholdings in John Laing plc, B. O. Chilver, D. Edwards, C. M. Laing and D. E. Laing are indirectly interested in the contracts under which Laing Properties plc employs the John Laing group to undertake construction and other services. Payments under contracts of this nature made during the year ended 31 December 1988 totalled £387,000 (1987 £151,000).

In addition, wholly-owned subsidiaries of John Laing plc and Laing Properties plc have entered into a joint venture for the redevelopment of an industrial site at Maple Cross, near Rickmansworth owned by the John Laing group, under which the partners have agreed to contribute to costs and share profits in approximately equal proportions.

(b) During 1988 there subsisted a number of General Partnerships formed by the US subsidiary, Laing Properties, Inc., under a participation plan established as a management incentive scheme. The conditions of each partnership provided (a) for the interests held by the Limited Partners to be purchased at full value, and (b) for Laing Properties, Inc., to receive a special payment out of any net proceeds resulting from the sale of assets before any surplus was available for distribution to the partners.

Certain assets were sold during the year, and from the proceeds a distribution was made to the partners in proportion to their respective interests; of this distribution, the amount due to G. L. Aulbach, a director of Laing Properties plc, over and above the return of his capital investment was $174,582.

As of 31 December 1988, the capital investments in all but one of the General Partnerships were refunded to the Limited Partners pursuant to the termination of the partnerships. The aggregate interests of the participating executives in the remaining partnership at that date was 6.3%, comprising $64,000 of residual distributions due from the sale of an asset. G. L. Aulbach's share of this sum, amounting to $25,513, was paid to him in January 1989.

Exemptions from disclosure

22.23 The disclosure requirements set out in paragraph 22.21 above do not apply in the following situations:

- A transaction between two companies, where a director of one of the companies (or of its subsidiary or its holding company) is interested only by virtue of the fact that he is also a director of that other company. [6 Sch 18(a)]. This exemption means that, among other things, details of many general intra-group trading transactions between companies are not required to be disclosed.

- A contract of service between a company and one of its directors, or between a company and a director of its holding company, or between a director of the company and any of its subsidiaries. [6 Sch 18(b)]. The inspection of such contracts by the company's members is regulated by section 318 of the Act. A listed company must disclose details of service contracts under the requirements of The Stock Exchange's Continuing Obligations. This requirement is considered in chapter 20, paragraph 20.51. There is a distinction between a *contract of service,* where a director is employed by the company, and a *contract for services,* where a director is an independent contractor. There is *no exemption* from disclosure for the latter type of contract.

Table 83: Example of the disclosure of substantial contracts with directors.

Extracts from Abingworth plc Annual Report 30th June 1989.

Directors' report extract

Board of Directors (extract)

Certain Directors of the Company were the principal promotors of and are shareholders in Interven Capital S.A., Interven II S.A., Tetraven Fund S.A. and Biotechnology Venture Fund S.A. ("the Luxembourg companies") to each of which Abingworth Management Limited provides investment advice, under the terms of separate investment advisory contracts, for which it is remunerated on the basis of its cost plus ten per cent thereof. Each such contract subsisted throughout the course of the year. Details of the Directors' approximate percentage interests in the equity capital of each of the Luxembourg companies at 30 June 1989 are shown below:

	Interven Capital S.A.	Interven II S.A.	Tetraven Fund S.A.	Biotechnology Venture Fund S.A.*
Hon. A.T.S. Montagu	7.63	5.90	5.69	3.61
P.F. Dicks	7.50	5.30	5.17	3.33
S.M. Gray	2.56	2.05	0.63	0.36
Dr. N.W. Horne	—	0.13	0.13	0.08
D.F.J. Leathers	—	—	—	5.00
D.J. Morrison	—	0.13	1.75	1.13
D.W. Quysner	0.54	3.65	4.10	2.38
Sir James Spooner	1.50	1.30	0.31	0.15

* Fully diluted for committed subscriptions outstanding.

On 17 August 1989, the Company entered into a conditional contract for the sale of Abingworth Management Limited to a company owned by Messrs. Montagu, Bunting, Dicks, Leathers, Morrison and Quysner. The sale was approved by shareholders at an Extraordinary General Meeting held on 13 September 1989, at which time the Company also entered into a revised Investment Advisory Agreement with Abingworth Management Limited.

Save as disclosed, there was no contract of significance subsisting during the year ended 30 June 1989 in which a Director of the Company had a material interest.

- A transaction that was not entered into during the period to which the financial statements relate, and that did not exist at any time during that period. [6 Sch 18(c)].

- There is a *de minimis* exception for any transactions or arrangements with a company or any of its subsidiaries in which a director of the company or its holding company had, directly or indirectly, a material interest if the aggregate value did not exceed £1,000 at any time during the relevant period. The aggregate value includes:

  - ☐ The value of each such transaction which was made after the commencement of the financial year.

  - ☐ The value of each such transaction that was made before the commencement of the financial year, less the amount (if any) by which the liability of the person for whom the transaction was made has subsequently been reduced.

  Alternatively, if that value did exceed £1,000, it did not exceed the lower of £5,000 and 1 per cent of the value of the company's net assets at the end of the relevant period. [6 Sch 25]. For this purpose, 'net assets' are the aggregate of the company's assets less the aggregate of its liabilities (including provisions for liabilities and charges). This minimum figure is flexible in order that it should take account of the needs of different sizes of company. The Secretary of State has power to increase by statutory instrument the financial limits mentioned above.

- Transactions that, in the opinion of the board, are not material (see para 22.4).

- Transactions involving other members of the same group which are entered into by those group companies in the ordinary course of their business and at arm's length and which would otherwise be disclosable under Schedule 6, paragraphs 15(c) or 16(c) (that is, those transactions outlined in para 22.20 above). [6 Sch 20(a)(b)]. There is some confusion on the interpretation of this section and it has been suggested that the exemption can be read without invoking the words 'group'. Consequently, if this interpretation is correct the exemption also applies to any transactions in the ordinary course of business and at arm's length.

- A transaction or arrangement that would otherwise be disclosable under paragraph 15(c) or 16(c) of Schedule 6 because the director had a material interest, but only on account of the fact that he was associated with the company. ('Associated' is defined in chapter 21 paragraph 21.11.) This exemption applies only if the company is a member of a group of companies and if one of the following situations exists:

  - ☐ The company is a wholly-owned subsidiary.

- □ No company within the same group, other than the company itself or one of its subsidiaries, was a party to the transaction or arrangement.

[6 Sch 21].

These conditions mean that the exemption from disclosure is available only if minority interests in the company are not affected. The effect of this provision is that, provided the conditions are satisfied, a director who is associated with the company and who would therefore have an interest in every contract that the company is party to that may be disclosable, does not have to disclose that interest.

Penalties for failure to disclose

22.24 The Act imposes a penalty on the company's directors for failure to disclose information about transactions in which the directors had, directly or indirectly, a material interest. If the company's financial statements that are approved by the directors do not disclose the required information, then every director of the company who is party to their approval and who knows that they do not comply or is reckless as to whether they comply is guilty of an offence and is liable to a fine (see appendix IV). [Sec 233(5)].

22.25 Moreover, where the financial statements do not comply with the relevant disclosure, the auditors must include, in their report (so far as they are reasonably able to do so), a statement giving the details that have been omitted. [Sec 237(4)]. The auditors are not required to draw attention to an unlawful transaction by stating that it is either illegal or contravenes the Act, but they should, of course, consider the effect of any illegal transactions on the truth and fairness of the financial statements.

Substantial property transactions

Introduction

22.26 Unlike transactions such as loans, quasi-loans and credit transactions that (for relevant companies at least) are *prima facie* unlawful, the Act does not prohibit a company (whether a relevant company or not) from entering into an arrangement for the acquisition of substantial non-cash assets from (or their transfer to) a director of the company or its holding company or their connected persons, provided prior approval of the shareholders is obtained. [Sec 320(1)].

22.27 Substantial non-cash assets are those whose value is not less than £1,000 and also exceeds the lesser of £50,000 and ten per cent of the company's asset value. [Sec 320(2)]. For this purpose, 'asset value' means the value of the company's net assets as disclosed in its latest financial statements. Alternatively, where there are no such financial statements, 'asset value' means the amount of the company's called-up share capital (as defined in section 737(1)). [Sec 320(2)].

22.28 In this context, 'non-cash asset' means any property, or any interest in property other than cash. (For this purpose, 'cash' includes foreign currency.) The acquisition of a non-cash asset also includes the creation of an interest in property (for example, a lease) and the discharge of any person's liability other than a liability for a liquidated sum. [Sec 739(1)(2)].

Shareholders' approval of transactions

22.29 As stated in paragraph 22.26 above, the Act requires that any arrangement for the acquisition of non-cash assets should first be approved by the company in general meeting (for example, see Table 84). [Sec 320(1)]. If, alternatively, the arrangement is with a director of the holding company or a person connected with him, it must also be first approved by a general meeting of the holding company. [Sec 320(1)].

Table 84: Example of a company seeking shareholders' approval to enter into a substantial property transaction with one of its directors.

Extract from Amec p.l.c. Annual Report and Accounts 31st December 1988.

PROPOSED TRANSACTION BY A DIRECTOR

To comply with section 320 of the Companies Act 1985, any arrangement entered into between a director and the company, or one of its subsidiaries, to acquire a non-cash asset in excess of £50,000 in value must be approved by shareholders.
Mr CI Bateman is proposing to purchase a house built by a subsidiary company, Fairclough Homes Limited. The purchase price will be the open market price as determined by a reputable third party valuer.
Resolution 4 in the notice of the annual general meeting authorises the company to proceed with this transaction.

22.30 The arrangements that this section of the Act covers are those where:

- A director of either the company or its holding company, or a person connected with such a director, acquires (or is to acquire) a non-cash asset from the company.

- A company acquires (or is to acquire) a non-cash asset from a director of either the company or its holding company, or from a person connected with such a director.

[Sec 320(1)].

22.31 The same rules also apply to those transactions of this nature that involve a shadow director or his connected persons. [Sec 320(3)].

22.32 Section 320 also affects certain intra-group transactions. Where, for example, a director of a company owns or controls a certain percentage of the shares in another group company, that other group company may fall within the definition of a connected person (see chapter 21 para 21.10 and 21.11). In these circumstances, and unless the company in general meeting first approves them, all dealings between the company and any company that falls within the definition of a connected person will require approval (see para 22.33).

Exemptions from obtaining approval

22.33 However, although the company will still have to comply with the disclosure requirements set out in paragraph 22.36 below, the shareholders' approval is not required for an arrangement of the type described in paragraph 22.26 above where one of the following conditions is satisfied:

- The value of the non-cash asset at the time of the arrangement is less than £1,000 (or, if the value is greater than £1,000, it is less than the lower of £50,000 and 10 per cent of the company's asset value). [Sec 320(2)].

- The body corporate in question is neither a company within the meaning of the Act, nor a body registered under section 680. [Sec 321(1)].

- The company in question is a wholly-owned subsidiary of any company, wherever incorporated. [Sec 321(1)]. In these circumstances, in practice, the holding company's directors have control over the subsidiary's directors.

- The non-cash asset is to be acquired:

  - By a holding company from any of its wholly-owned subsidiaries.

  - By a wholly-owned subsidiary from its holding company.

  - By a wholly-owned subsidiary from a fellow wholly-owned subsidiary.

  [Sec 321(2)(a)].

  In effect, this exemption relieves companies that would otherwise be required by section 320 of the Act to obtain approval at a general meeting for intra-group transactions that take place in a wholly-owned group.

- The arrangement is entered into by a company that is being wound up, and the winding-up is not a members' voluntary winding-up. [Sec 321(2)(b)].

- The following two conditions are satisfied:

  - A member of the company acquires an asset from the company.

  - The arrangement was made with that person in his capacity as a member of the company.

  [Sec 321(3)].

- The transaction is effected on a recognised investment exchange by a director, or a person connected with him, through an independent broker. [Sec 320(4)].

Liability for contravention

22.34 A director who contravenes section 320 of the Act is not guilty of a criminal offence, but he may incur civil penalties. The arrangement (and any transaction pursuant thereto) may be treated as voidable by the company unless at least one of the following three conditions is satisfied:

- It is impossible to obtain restitution of the subject matter of the transaction, or else the company has been indemnified for any loss or damage it has suffered.

- A third party has acquired rights, *bona fide* and for value, and without having notice of the contravention.

- The arrangement is affirmed by the company in general meeting (and/or by the holding company, as the case may be) within a reasonable period of the arrangement being made.

[Sec 322(1)(2)].

22.35 The director who entered into the arrangement, or a person connected with him, or a director who authorised it may all be liable to account to the company for any gain they have received. They may also be liable to indemnify the company from any resultant loss or damage it has incurred. [Sec 322(3)]. However, a director will not be liable if the arrangement was made with a person connected with him, and if he himself took all reasonable steps to ensure that the company obtained the required approval. [Sec 322(5)]. This liability is without prejudice to any other liability which may have been incurred and arises whether or not the arrangement has been avoided. [Sec 322(4)]. A connected person or a director who authorised the transaction will not be liable if they can show that they did not know the relevant circumstances that formed the contravention. [Sec 322(6)].

Disclosure requirements

22.36 The disclosure requirements outlined in paragraphs 22.13 to 22.21 above (disclosure notification to the company and in financial statements) apply equally to substantial property transactions and arrangements of a kind described in paragraph 22.26 above. The requirements apply irrespective of whether the transactions and arrangements have been approved by the company in general meeting.

22.37 The International Stock Exchange's requirements that relate to substantial property transactions (and other transactions with directors) are considered in the paragraphs that follow.

The International Stock Exchange's requirements

22.38 The International Stock Exchange's Continuing Obligations for listed companies and its General Undertaking for companies traded on the USM contain further disclosure requirements that relate to substantial property transactions and other transactions with directors. The principal requirement that relates to a company's transactions with its directors and former directors is that the company is obliged to circulate to its shareholders information about, and usually to obtain their prior approval of, those transactions that fall within the definition of Class IV transactions. Class IV transactions are defined in chapter I of section 6 of the 'Admission of Securities to Listing'. A Class IV transaction is any transaction that involves a director, or any associate of a director, or a past director (or certain other persons stipulated in that section).

22.39 Although the proposed transaction may be legal within the meaning of the Act, The International Stock Exchange may, nevertheless, require that the company should observe certain additional procedures. The basic requirement is stated in paragraph 14 of The International Stock Exchange's Continuing Obligations. That paragraph requires, *inter alia,* that details of any acquisitions or realisations of assets that fall within the definition of a Class IV transaction, must be notified to The International Stock Exchange and to the shareholders, and shareholders prior approval must be obtained.

22.40 The USM's General Undertaking contains a similar requirement. Note 1(d) to the General Undertaking requires that *"transactions which involve, or involve an associate of, a director ... should be subject to prior approval of the company in general meeting and the issue of an explanatory circular".*

22.41 The Continuing Obligations also require particulars of any contract of significance (including substantial property transaction) which existed during or at the end of the financial year in which a director of the company is, or was, materially interested (for example, see Table 85 overleaf). [Co 21(k)]. In this context, 'a contract of significance' is one that represents a sum equal to one per cent or more of:

- The company's net assets, for a capital transaction.
- The company's net assets, for a transaction whose principal purpose is the granting of credit.
- The total purchases, sales, payments or receipts of the company, for other transactions.

22.42 Where a listed company's directors have not had a material interest in any significant contracts of the company during the financial year, they must disclose this fact in the financial statements (for example, see Table 86 overleaf). [CO 21(k)].

Related party transactions

Introduction

22.43 Although there are extensive Companies Act and International Stock Exchange requirements and reliefs regarding the disclosure of transactions with related parties, neither the scope of the current legislation nor the requirements of the International Stock Exchange is considered comprehensive. For example, the Act places considerable emphasis on the disclosure of transactions with directors and the disclosure of group companies. Similarly, The International Stock Exchange requires listed companies to disclose certain additional details about substantial shareholdings. But neither of these documents is concerned with, for example, economic dependence and management charges.

22.44 In order to provide a more comprehensive guidance on the disclosure of transactions with related parties, the ASC published ED 46 'Disclosure of related party transactions', in April 1989. The ASC's rationale for ED 46 is explained in paragraph 2 of the exposure draft, which states that *"financial statements are generally prepared on the basis that enterprises are separate and distinct from their owners and from other entities and that transactions reflected in the financial statements are effected on an arm's-length basis between independent parties. These assumptions cannot be relied upon in the presence of relatedparties".*

Table 85: Disclosure of transactions with directors required by The International Stock Exchange's Continuing Obligations.

Extract from Berisford International plc Annual Report 30th September 1989.

29 Disclosable Transactions

Juicy Lucy Limited/Juicy Lucy International B.V.

By an Agreement dated 8 September 1989 S & W Berisford (Investments) Limited invested £700,000 in Juicy Lucy Limited, including £92,000 by way of convertible loans over which A Tapnack and A Birnbaum (Directors of Group subsidiary companies) have been granted an option. In addition, Sandown Investment Holdings, a partnership in which the Group has a 70% interest, the remaining 30% being held by A Tapnack and A Birnbaum acquired 50% of Juicy Lucy International B.V. for £75,000.

Paul Salgo Limited

By an Agreement dated 26 July 1989 Sandown Investment Holdings purchased 15% of the share capital of Paul Salgo Limited (in which the Group had a 53.55% interest) held by G Franklin (formerly a Director of Paul Salgo Limited) for £75,000.

J. H. Rayner (España) S.A.

By Agreements dated 10 February and 23 March 1989 respectively Rayner Coffee International Partnership purchased the remaining 40% shareholdings in Alpha Commodities Corporation for US$399,000 and J H Rayner (España) S.A. for US$245,000 not already owned from Bocksberg Corporation a company representing A Madeira (then a Director of J H Rayner (España) S.A.).

Holmes Halls Tanners Limited

By an Agreement dated 6 March 1989 Holmes Halls Tanners Limited was sold for £3.5m to Profitwell Limited, a company representing E Stanners and T Ulliot (formerly Directors of Holmes Halls Tanners Limited).

Banco Sterling S.A.

On 28 February 1989 Pauline Marie Brasil increased its investment in Banco Sterling S.A., a Brazilian multiple bank, by US$5.5m to maintain a 47.5% stake, the balance being held by the Garcez Group, representing, among others, A Garcez and H Saffer (Directors of Group subsidiary companies).

Ketlon (UK) Limited

By Agreements to lease dated 30 May 1989, Ketlon (UK) Limited in which the Group has a 76% investment, has agreed to take the following leases:

(a) for a term of 22 years of a new building to be known as the Heat Treatment Shop extending to approximately 20,000 square feet at an initial rental of £3.50 per square foot from Dana Properties Limited,

(b) of a new building known as Units 5, 6 and 7, Dana Estate, extending to approximately 23,000 square feet at an initial rent of £6.00 per square foot from Dana Properties Limited, a company representing among others, A Simon (Director and minority shareholder of Ketlon (UK) Limited).

22.45 The definition of related parties is widely drawn and the exposure draft requires disclosure only of 'abnormal transactions' with related parties. Therefore, in some situations, the proposals in the exposure draft go further than the requirements of Act and The International Stock Exchange, whereas in other respects the reverse is true.

Table 86: Example of the disclosure required by The International Stock Exchange's Continuing Obligations where there were no contracts of significance with the directors of the company.

Extract from Allied-Lyons PLC Report and Accounts 4th March 1989.

Report of the directors extract

Contracts

No director, either during or at the end of the financial period, was materially interested in any contract that was significant in relation to the company's business.

Definitions

22.46 ED 46 uses many defined terms that are important in understanding the proposals. These are considered in the paragraphs below.

Related parties

22.47 Two or more parties are considered to be related parties when for all or part of the financial period either of the following applies:

- One party is able to exercise either direct or indirect control, or significant influence, over the other party or over the assets or resources of the other party.
- Such parties are subject to common control or significant influence from the same source.

22.48 In deciding whether parties are related, it is necessary to consider the substance of the relationship . This is determined by identifying all its aspects and implications and by giving greater weight to those likely to have commercial effect in practice. [ED 46 para 22]. For example, a party might be a related party under the above definition if it has an option that it is likely to exercise. Conversely, a party that holds an option which is structured such that it is unlikely to be exercised would probably not be a related party on the basis of that option alone.

22.49 ED 46 states that the following are presumed to be related parties of the reporting enterprise, unless there is evidence to the contrary:

- Its ultimate or intermediate parent company or companies, subsidiary companies, fellow subsidiaries, associated companies, related companies, and fellow associated and related companies.

- Companies controlled for voting purposes, in terms of votes exercisable by the shareholders or by the directors, by the same enterprise or persons who controls the reporting company.
- Its directors and the directors of its parent company or companies and members of their immediate families.
- A company or person owning, or able to exercise effective control over, 10 per cent or more of the voting rights of the company, whether directly or through nominees, and members of the immediate family of any such person.
- Partnerships, companies or trusts or entities in which any person in the two points directly above has a controlling interest or which they have the ability to influence significantly.
- The other party when a management contract exists and the reporting enterprise is either the managing or the managed party.

[ED 46 para 23].

22.50 The above list of related parties is not intended to be exhaustive. Another example of a party that might be related in some circumstances is a major provider of finance.

22.51 For the purposes of paragraph 22.49 above, the term 'directors' includes any persons having authority or responsibility for planning, directly or controlling the activities or resources of the reporting enterprise. Therefore, in addition to those holding that title, it includes shadow directors, officers and other persons with a similar authority or responsibility (see further chapter 21 paras 21.6 to 21.9). [ED 46 para 23].

22.52 The term 'immediate family' includes any family member whom a director, or person owning 10 per cent or more of the voting rights, might influence, or be influenced by, because of the family relationship. [ED 46 para 23]. The notion of immediate family could be extended, presumably, to adult children, parents, and brothers and sisters. Perhaps cousins and other relations are not intended to be regarded as immediate family. The lack of a precise definition is presumably intentional. Consequently, whether a family member is in a position to influence, or to be influenced, will be a question to be answered on the facts of each particular situation.

Control

22.53 Control is defined as determining, or having the ability to determine, the financial or operating policies of an enterprise. [ED 46 para 24].

Therefore, control exists where another company or individual holds more than half the voting rights in a company, whether or not that voting power is used to determine the company's policies. The definition is very similar in effect to the Companies Act 1989 definition of a subsidiary (see further 'Manual of Accounting - volume II' chapter 3). However, the definition in ED 46 will encompass control by individuals and, for example, partnerships as well as holding companies, and so is broader in scope.

Significant influence

22.54 Significant influence involves participation in, or the ability to participate in, the financial or operating policy decisions of an enterprise, but not necessarily to have control of them. [ED 46 para 25]. As with the definition of control, this definition has the effect that there is deemed to be significant influence where an investor holds, say, 25 per cent of the shares in an enterprise whether or not he actively uses that holding to exert influence. This contrasts with SSAP 1, which defines significant influence in terms of actual participation.

Related party transaction

22.55 A related party transaction is a transfer or granting of benefits or obligations between related parties, irrespective of whether the transactions are recognised in the accounting records or whether consideration passes. Such transactions would include:

- Sales, purchases and transfer of goods.
- Other assets and services.
- Transactions related to management.
- Royalty and licence agreements.
- Leases.
- Guarantees and loans.

[ED 46 para 26].

22.56 The above definition envisages that some related party transactions might not be entered in a company's accounting records or might not involve any consideration passing. Examples of this might include:

- Transfer of assets for nil consideration.
- Managements services that are provided by one company to another free of charge.

- Guaranties to third parties in respect of other group companies. Letters of support.
- Interest free loans (the principal would be entered in the accounting records but no interest would be charged).
- Rent-free accommodation or loan of vehicles or other assets at no charge.

Normal and abnormal transactions

22.57 A 'normal' transaction is defined as one which is undertaken by the reporting enterprise in the ordinary course of business on normal commercial terms except where it is so material that it has a significant impact on the financial statements. Transactions entered into in the ordinary course of business are those which are usually, or frequently, or regularly, undertaken by the enterprise. [ED 46 para 27]. Normal commercial terms are defined as terms that are no more or less favourable than it would be reasonable to expect if the transaction had not been with a related party. [ED 46 para 28].

22.58 An 'abnormal' transaction is any transaction other than a normal transaction. [ED 46 para 29]. The effect of the definition is that a transaction is abnormal if it is either:

- Outside the enterprise's ordinary course of business, irrespective of the terms on which they are undertaken.
- Not on normal commercial terms, although entered into in the ordinary course of business.
- So material as to size or nature that (despite being in the ordinary course of business and on normal commercial terms) it has a significant impact on the financial statements.

[ED 46 para 14].

Disclosure of transactions

22.59 ED 46 proposes that certain information should be disclosed for each *abnormal* transaction with, or on behalf of, or for the benefit of, a related party whether or not consideration passes. The information it suggests should be disclosed is as follows:

- The name of the related party.
- The relationship between the parties.

- The extent of any ownership interest (in percentage terms) in the related party or by it in the reporting enterprise.
- The nature of the transaction.
- The amounts involved, either in percentage or in monetary terms.
- The amount due to or from the related party at the balance sheet date.
- The basis on which the transaction price has been determined.
- Any other information necessary to understand the commercial substance of the transaction and of its effects on the financial statements.

[ED 46 para 32].

Illustrations of the above disclosure are given in Table 87.

Table 87: Disclosure of related party transactions.

Extract from Lit Holdings PLC Report and Accounts 31st December 1988.

Note extract

28. Contracts with related parties

The following contracts with related parties existed during the year.

During the period the Company occupied premises on a temporary basis which involved payment of rental of £27,500 to Botts & Company Limited, a company in which JC Botts has a significant shareholding. The arrangements were on arms length commercial terms.

A sum of £25,000 was paid to Botts & Company Limited during the period in respect of advisory services under an agreement which was rescinded on 30th September 1988.

Extract from London & Edinburgh Trust PLC Annual Report 31st December 1988.

Note extract

27. RELATED PARTY TRANSACTION
In December 1988, Alarpar Ltd, a subsidiary company of which G J Bowes and D G P Walsh are directors and in which they indirectly hold 25% of the issued share capital, sold the long leasehold interest in Sheddingdean Small Business Centre, Units 1-15, Burgess Hill for £800,000 to BNW Holdings Ltd., a company in which G J Bowes and D G P Walsh indirectly hold a 66% interest. The property was carried in Alarpar Ltd at a book value of £500,000.

22.60 As stated above, ED 46 proposes that only abnormal transactions with related parties should be disclosed. Inevitably, therefore, the implementation of the 'abnormal only' rule will be subjective. Despite the definitions that are provided in paragraphs 22.57 and 22.58 above, there is bound to be some ambiguity in any consideration of what is normal and what is abnormal.

Exemptions from disclosure of transactions

22.61 In some companies or groups, the above disclosure requirements, although applicable only to abnormal transactions, could give rise to very extensive disclosures. Consequently, ED 46 contains the following proposals which are designed to reduce the amount of disclosure.

Aggregation

The disclosure of individual transactions with a particular related party may be aggregated. However, this does not apply if disclosure of an individual transaction is necessary for an understanding of the impact of related party transactions on the financial statements, or is required by other regulations. [ED 46 para 33].

Group exemptions

Disclosure is not required:

- In consolidated financial statements of any transactions or balances between group companies that have been eliminated on consolidation.
- In the parent company's own financial statements where consolidated financial statements are presented at the same time.
- In the financial statements of wholly-owned subsidiaries, of transactions with other group companies if the identity of the ultimate parent company is disclosed.

[ED 46 para 34].

Disclosure of control

22.62 Due to the potential influence that a controlling related party might have on the results and/or the financial position of the reporting undertaking, the exposure draft proposes to require additional information to be disclosed where such a controlling relationship exists. The disclosures proposed are:

- The existence and nature of controlling related party relationships, whether or not any transactions between the parties have taken place.
- The name of the controlling enterprise and, if different, that of the ultimate controlling enterprise.
- The name of the intermediate controlling enterprise in the UK or the Republic of Ireland, where the ultimate controlling enterprise is situated outside the UK or the Republic of Ireland.

[ED 46 para 35].

22.63 The above disclosure requirements are proposed to apply where control exists, but not where there is just significant influence. This contrasts with the provisions relating to the disclosure of transactions, which it is proposed would apply when there is either control or significant influence.

Disclosure of dependence

22.64 The exposure draft contains some proposals for disclosing dependence. It recognises that there may be situations where an undertaking, although not related, may be economically dependent on one or a few parties with which it transacts a significant amount of its business. Consequently, the viability of the reporting undertaking may rest on such economic dependence. Such parties could include a major customer, supplier, franchiser, franchisee, agent, borrower or lender. In these situations, it is considered that users of financial statements need to be made aware of the nature and extent of that dependence.

22.65 ED 46, therefore, proposes that where the transactions between an enterprise and another party, or other facts arising from a relationship with another party, have a pervasive influence on the enterprise, the identity of that party and a general indication of the nature and extent of the dependence should be disclosed. [ED 46 para 36].

Examples of disclosure

22.66 The appendix to the exposure draft sets out 11 different types of examples of disclosure that might be given. Examples 1 to 8 relate to disclosure of transactions. Example 9 suggests the type of disclosure where control exists. Examples 10 and 11 relate to economic dependence.

Materiality

22.67 As for other Accounting Standards, ED 46 includes the provision that it need not be applied to immaterial items. While the proposals cannot over-ride legal requirements, the guidance in paragraph 19 of the exposure draft is that information may often be most useful if it is aggregated by type of transaction and nature of relationship, for example, details of total sales to related companies. On the other hand, the disclosure of some transactions, for example with management and shareholders, may be required for the purposes of giving a true and fair view, irrespective of their materiality. The Act takes a similar approach. Materiality governs the accounting and disclosure requirements of Schedule 4 to the Act, but does not extend to the requirements to directors' remuneration and transactions.

Invalidity of certain transactions involving directors

22.68 Where a company enters into a transaction with its directors or its parent company directors, and the board of directors of the company exceed any limitation on their powers under the company's articles in connection with the transaction, the company may choose to regard the transaction as voidable. This also applies where the party to the transaction includes a person connected with such a director or a company with which a director is associated. [Sec 322A(1)(2)].

22.69 Whether or not the transaction can be treated as voidable, any party to the transaction as mentioned in the above paragraph and any director of the company who authorised the transaction (without prejudice to any other liability imposed by law) is liable to:

- Account to the company for any gain which he has made directly or indirectly by the transaction.

- Indemnify the company for any loss or damage resulting from the transaction.

[Sec 322A(3)].

22.70 A person other than the director of the company is not liable to account to or indemnify the company if he can show that at the time the transaction was entered into he did not know that the directors were exceeding their powers. [Sec 322A(6)].

22.71 The transaction ceases to be voidable in any of the following situation.

- Restitution of any money or other asset which was the subject matter of the transaction is no longer possible.

- The company is indemnified for any loss or damage resulting from the transaction.

- Rights acquired *bona fide* for value and without actual notice of the directors' exceeding their powers by a person who is not party to the transaction would be affected by the avoidance.

- The transaction is ratified by the company in general meeting, by ordinary or special resolution or otherwise as the case may require.

[Sec 322A(5)].

22.72 However, where the transaction is voidable in any of the above situations but is valid under section 35A (power of directors to bind the company) because the person dealing with the company has acted in good faith, the court may (on the application of that person or the company) make an order either affirming, severing, or setting aside the transaction, on such terms, as appears to the court to be just. [Sec 322A(7)].

Chapter 23

SMALL AND MEDIUM-SIZED COMPANIES

Chapter 23

SMALL AND MEDIUM-SIZED COMPANIES

Introduction

23.1 The Act includes certain concessions that permit small and medium-sized companies to file abbreviated financial statements. It also provides exemption for such companies from the requirements of paragraph 36A of Schedule 4 (disclosure with respect to compliance with Accounting Standards). [Sec 246(1)(a)]. Companies that take advantage of these concessions will be able to file financial statements that do not comply with all the detailed provisions of the Act as to their form and content.

23.2 It is important to appreciate that the available concessions relate only to the financial statements that a company must deliver to the Registrar of Companies under section 242 of the Act. [Sec 246(1)(b)]. The concessions do not affect the financial statements that a company must provide to its shareholders. Accordingly, even if a small or a medium-sized company wishes to take advantage of the concessions in respect of the financial statements that it must file, it must still prepare full financial statements. These full financial statements must comply with all the provisions of the Act. In addition, the company must give those financial statements to its shareholders and (unless the company is a private company and has taken advantage of section 252, see also chapter 25 paras 25.20 to 25.27) also lay them before the company in general meeting in accordance with sections 238(1) and 241(1) of the Act.

23.3 The practical result of these concessions is that, if a company chooses to file abbreviated financial statements, it must prepare two sets of financial statements: one for the Registrar of Companies and one for the shareholders. Consequently, although it is a concession as to disclosure of information to outsiders, it has no cost advantage. Indeed, it is likely to be more costly to prepare two different sets of financial statements.

23.4 The concessions relating to abbreviated financial statements are not available to any company that is, or was, at any time during the financial year that the financial statements relate to, one of the following types of company:

- A public company.

- A banking company, being a company which is authorised under the Banking Act 1987.

- An insurance company under Part II of the Insurance Companies Act 1982.

- An authorised person under the Financial Services Act 1986.

- A member of an ineligible group. An ineligible group is a group in which any of its members is one of the types of companies stated in points one to four above. In addition, an ineligible group includes a body corporate that is able lawfully to issue shares or debentures to the public.

[Sec 246(4)].

23.5 With the exception of dormant companies (see chapter 24), the 'unabbreviated' financial statements (that is, those financial statements prepared under section 226 of the Act) of small and medium-sized companies must be audited.

Definitions of small and medium-sized companies

23.6 A company qualifies as a small company for a financial year if it satisfies any two of the following three conditions during that year:

- The amount of its turnover did not exceed £2,000,000.

- The balance sheet total (see para 23.8) did not exceed £975,000.

- The average number of employees the company employed in the financial year (defined as in para 23.9) did not exceed 50.

[Sec 247(3)].

23.7 A company qualifies as a medium-sized company for a financial year if it satisfies any two of the following three conditions during that year.

- The amount of its turnover did not exceed £8,000,000.

- The balance sheet total (see para 23.8) did not exceed £3,900,000.

- The average number of employees the company employed in the financial year (defined as in para 23.9) did not exceed 250.

[Sec 247(3)].

23.8 Where a company adopts Format 1 (see chapter 6) for its balance sheet, the 'balance sheet total' is the aggregate of the amounts shown under the headings that are preceded by the letters A to D inclusive. Where a company adopts Format 2 for its balance sheet, the 'balance sheet total' is the aggregate of the amounts shown under the general heading 'assets'. [Sec 247(5)]. In either case, the effect is to equate 'balance sheet total' to gross assets.

23.9 The number of employees means the average number of persons employed by the company in the year (determined on a weekly basis). The method prescribed by paragraph 56(2)(3) of Schedule 4 (see further chapter 14 para 14.17) should be adopted for the calculation (adding up those defined as employed for each week and dividing by the number of weeks in the year). [Sec 247(6)].

23.10 The Act lays down the following four rules that must be applied in determining whether a company may file abbreviated financial statements:

- In respect of a company's first financial year, the company will qualify to deliver the abbreviated financial statements that apply to a small or a medium-sized company, provided that it satisfies the appropriate size conditions under section 247(3) in respect of that year. [Sec 247(1)(a)].

- In subsequent years, a company will be able to file abbreviated financial statements, provided that it satisfies the appropriate size qualifications under section 247(3) both in the year in question and in the preceding year. [Sec 247(1)(b)].

- A company that qualifies to be treated as either a small or a medium-sized company in one year, may file abbreviated financial statements in the following year, even if it does not satisfy the conditions in that year. However, if it does not satisfy the conditions in the year after that, then, at that time, it must file the kind of financial statements in that subsequent year that are appropriate to the company's size. If, on the other hand, the company reverts to satisfying the conditions in that year, then it may continue to file abbreviated financial statements. [Sec 247(2)(a)(b)].

- Where a company has not prepared its financial statements in respect of a 12-month period, the turnover threshold must be proportionately adjusted in order to establish whether the appropriate condition has been satisfied. [Sec 247(4)]. For example, if a company prepares financial statements for a nine-month period, the turnover threshold will be £1.50m (that is, 9/12 x £2.0m) for a small company, and £6.0m (that is, 9/12 x £8.0m) for a medium-sized company.

23.11 The application of these provisions is complicated and, perhaps, is best illustrated by an example.

Example

Consider the following details relating to two companies (A and B). Company A has existed for many years, and in the year immediately before year 1 it qualified as a medium-sized company. Company B is incorporated on the first day of year 2.

	Year 1	Year 2	Year 3	Year 4
Company A:				
Turnover	£8.0m	£8.1m	£8.1m	£9.5m
Gross assets	£3.9m	£4.0m	£4.2m	£3.9m
Average number of employees	240	255	255	250
Company B:				
Turnover	-	£1.9m	£2.1m	£2.0m
Gross assets	-	£0.975m	£1.0m	£0.97m
Average number of employees	-	55	60	63

Company A

In year 1, company A satisfies all the criteria that enable it to be treated as a medium-sized company. It is assumed that it did so also in the previous year. Consequently, it can file abbreviated financial statements for a medium-sized company for year 1.

In year 2, company A ceases to qualify as a medium-sized company because both its turnover and its number of employees exceed the criteria. However, it can still file the abbreviated financial statements of a medium-sized company, because the Act permits it to do so if it was able to file the abbreviated financial statements in the preceding year.

In year 3, company A ceases to qualify as a medium-sized company for a second consecutive year. Consequently, it is no longer entitled to file 'medium-sized company' financial statements.

In year 4, company A reverts to satisfying the criteria of a medium-sized company. However, it is not entitled to take advantage of the concessions. This is because it must satisfy the criteria for two consecutive years before it changes its classification.

Company B

In year 2 (which is its first year after incorporation), company B qualifies as a small company. Therefore, under the Act, it can file 'small company' financial statements, because the Act permits it to do so if it satisfies the criteria in its first financial year. (It satisfies the criteria both for turnover and gross assets, but not for number of employees.)

In year 3, company B also ceases to qualify as a small company, because it has exceeded all the three conditions. However, it can still file 'small company' financial statements, because it qualified to do so in the preceding year.

In year 4, company B satisfies the criteria of a small company. Despite the fact that it did not satisfy the criteria in respect of year 3, it can still continue to file 'small company' financial statements, because it failed to satisfy the criteria for only one year.

23.12 For parent companies, there is a further condition that they must satisfy before filing abbreviated financial statements. A parent company should not be treated as qualifying as a small or medium-sized company in relation to a financial year, unless the group headed by it qualifies also as a small or medium-sized group. [Sec 246(5)]. Consequently, if the parent is a small company, it can only file abbreviated financial statements if it is also the parent of a 'small group'. If it were the parent of a 'medium-sized group', it could only file abbreviated financial statements applicable to a medium-sized group. Similarly, a medium-sized parent can only file abbreviated financial statements if it is the parent of a 'medium-sized group'. Small and medium-sized groups are also exempt in certain circumstances from preparing consolidated financial statements (see further 'Manual of Accounting - volume II' chapter 2).

Exemptions for small companies

23.13 Where a company qualifies as a small company, its directors need deliver only abbreviated financial statements to the Registrar of Companies. These abbreviated financial statements need to contain only an abbreviated version of the full balance sheet and abbreviated notes. [8 Sch 1(1), 3].

23.14 The directors of a small company need not deliver either a profit and loss account, or a directors' report, or any information relating to emoluments, pensions and compensation for loss of office of directors and chairman. [8 Sch 2, 4, 3(3)].

23.15 The abbreviated balance sheet referred to in paragraph 23.13 above is a balance sheet that discloses only those items that are preceded in the appropriate format by either a letter or a Roman numeral. [8 Sch 1(1)]. However, the aggregate amounts of debtors and creditors must be split between the amounts receivable or payable within one year and the amounts receivable or payable in more than one year. The split must be disclosed either on the face of the balance sheet or in the notes. [8 Sch 1(2)(a)(b)].

23.16 Only the requirements of Schedule 4 relating to the following matters apply in respect of the notes to the financial statements of a small company:

- Accounting policies.
- Share capital.
- Particulars of allotments.
- Fixed assets, so far as it relate to items to which a letter or Roman number is assigned in the adopted balance sheet format.

- Particulars of debts.
- The basis used in translating foreign currency amounts into sterling.
- Corresponding amounts for the previous year must also be given in respect of each of the above items.

[8 Sch 3(1)].

23.17 The following information required by Schedule 5 need not be given:

- The financial years of subsidiary undertakings.
- Additional information about subsidiary undertakings.
- Shares and debentures of the company held by subsidiary undertakings.
- Arrangements attracting merger relief.

[8 Sch 3(2)].

23.18 However, disclosure requirements imposed by other sections of, and schedules to, the Act still apply (for example, Part III of Schedule 6 - particulars of transactions with directors and officers).

23.19 A small company's abbreviated financial statements will not disclose the amount of its profit for the year. The nearest that a user of the financial statements can get to this figure will be the difference between the 'profit and loss account' in the balance sheet at both the beginning and the end of the period that the financial statements cover. This amount may be very misleading, because it is arrived at not only after the deduction of undisclosed directors' fees, but also after the deduction of undisclosed dividends. This means that the detail of profit will not be placed on public record with the Registrar of Companies, and so it will not be available to the company's competitors. However, this detail will be disclosed to shareholders, because the company must give shareholders 'unabbreviated' (that is, full) financial statements even though it files abbreviated statements.

23.20 The abbreviated balance sheet that is required to be delivered to the Registrar of Companies must be signed on behalf of the board by a director of the company in accordance with section 233(4). [8 Sch 1(3)]. An example of a abbreviated vertical balance sheet for a small company (based on Format 1) is set out on the next page.

Exemptions for medium-sized companies

23.21 The modifications that the Act permits, regarding the financial statements that a medium-sized company must deliver to the Registrar of Companies, relate principally to the profit and loss account. They allow the following items to be combined and shown as one item under the heading of 'Gross profit or loss':

- In the formats where expenses are classified by function: turnover, the cost of sales, gross profit or loss and other operating income.
- In the formats where expenses are classified by type: turnover, the change in stocks of finished goods and in work in progress, own work capitalised, other operating income, raw materials and consumables, and other external charges.

[8 Sch 5].

23.22 In addition, the notes to the financial statements may omit the disaggregated information in respect of both turnover and profit or loss before tax that would otherwise be required. [8 Sch 6].

ABBREVIATED BALANCE SHEET FOR A SMALL COMPANY

	£	£
Fixed assets		
Intangible assets		X
Tangible assets		X
Investments		X
		X
Current assets		
Stocks	X	
Debtors	X	
Investments	X	
Cash	X	
	X	
Creditors (amounts falling due within one year)	X	
Net current assets		X
Total assets less current liabilities		X
Creditors (amounts falling due after more than one year)		(X)
Provisions for liabilities and charges		(X)
Net assets		X

Abbreviated Balance Sheet for a Small Company continued	
Capital and reserves	
Called-up share capital	X
Share premium account	X
Revaluation reserve	X
Other reserves	X
Profit and loss account	X
	X

Directors' statement on abbreviated financial statements

23.23 For small and medium-sized companies, each abbreviated balance sheet a company delivers to the Registrar of Companies must be signed by the directors in accordance with section 233 of the Act. Moreover, where the directors of either a small company or a medium-sized company have relied on the exemptions for individual financial statements, they must include a statement immediately above their signatures to the effect that:

- They have relied on the exemptions set out in Part I or Part II of Schedule 8 that entitle them to deliver abbreviated financial statements.

- A statement of the grounds on which, in the directors' opinion, the company is entitled to the exemptions.

[8 Sch 7(1)].

23.24 An example of such a statement is as follows:

> *"Advantage has been taken of the exemptions for small/medium-sized companies conferred by Part I/Part II of Schedule 8 of the Companies Act 1985, because in the directors' opinion, the company is entitled to benefit from those exemptions as a small/medium-sized company."*

Auditors' responsibilities

23.25 Where the directors propose to rely on the exemptions that entitle them to deliver abbreviated financial statements, the auditors must *provide the directors* with a report that states whether:

- In the auditors' opinion, the company is entitled to those exemptions.

- The documents to be proposed to be delivered in accordance with Schedule 8 have been properly prepared.

[8 Sch 8(1)].

23.26 The directors must also include, with the documents that they deliver to the Registrar of Companies, *a special auditors' report*. This report must state that, in the auditors' opinion:

- The company is entitled to the exemptions claimed in the directors' statement.
- The abbreviated financial statements to be delivered have been properly prepared in accordance with Schedule 8.

[8 Sch 8(2)].

23.27 The special auditors' report must also reproduce the full text of the auditors' report under section 235 that was made in respect of the full financial statements the company prepared for shareholders. If the report under section 235 was qualified, any further material necessary to understand the qualification must be included. [8 Sch 8(3)].

23.28 The provisions of section 236 (signature of auditors' report) applies to the special auditors' report as stated above. [8 Sch 8(4)].

23.29 An example of a special report is as follows:

Auditors' report to the directors of GAAP UK Limited under Schedule 8 paragraph 8 of the Companies Act 1985.

We have examined the abbreviated financial statements on pages x to x together with the full financial statements of GAAP UK Limited for the year ended 31st December 19xx. The scope of our work for the purpose of this report was limited to confirming that the company is entitled to the exemptions conferred by Part I/Part II of Schedule 8 and that the abbreviated financial statements have been properly prepared in accordance with Schedule 8 from the full financial statements.

In our opinion the company is entitled to the exemptions conferred by Part I/Part II of Schedule 8 and the abbreviated financial statements have been properly prepared in accordance with Schedule 8.

We reported as auditors of GAAP UK Limited to the members on (date) on the company's full financial statements prepared under section 226 of the Companies Act 1985 for the year ended 31st December 19xx and our audit opinion was as follows:

(insert full text of audit opinion)

Chartered Accountants

(Address)

(Date)

23.30 For the purpose of making the two required auditors' reports, it will usually be sufficient if the auditors perform their normal audit work on the main financial statements and also review the abbreviated financial statements. Auditors are not required to perform an audit as such of the abbreviated financial statements. Such financial statements are, anyway, unlikely to give a true and fair view.

23.31 Where the auditors have qualified their report on the main financial statements, they will need to ensure that the subject matter of their qualification is not relevant in assessing the criteria for exemption. Where the effect of the subject matter of the qualification cannot take at least two of the criteria for exemption over the exemption limits, then there is no problem, and the auditors can issue a standard special report that contains the text of the qualified report.

23.32 The importance of a qualification in the auditors' report on the financial statements the company has prepared for its shareholders may not be obvious from the abbreviated financial statements themselves. For instance, the qualification in question may refer to a note to the financial statements given to shareholders, but this note may not be reproduced in a small company's abbreviated financial statements. In this situation, the auditors' report should include sufficient information that makes it clear that the note concerned has not been reproduced.

23.33 If abbreviated financial statements were delivered to the Registrar of Companies with a qualified special report, it would appear that the directors would be in breach of the Act.

Chapter 24

DORMANT COMPANIES

Chapter 24

DORMANT COMPANIES

Introduction

24.1 Section 250 of the Act makes certain provisions regarding dormant companies. In particular, it allows a company to resolve not to appoint auditors when it becomes dormant.

24.2 For this purpose, a 'dormant company' is defined as a company that had no significant accounting transaction during the period in question. A 'significant accounting transaction' is defined as any transaction that section 221 requires the company to enter into its accounting records (for example, receiving or expending money, or buying or selling goods), except for one that results from a subscriber to the memorandum taking shares in the company under his undertaking given in the memorandum. [Sec 250(3)].

24.3 Where a company has been dormant for any period, it ceases to be dormant if any significant accounting transaction occurs. [Sec 250(3)].

Exemption available

24.4 A dormant company may exclude the application of section 384 of the Act (company to appoint auditors at general meeting) by passing a special resolution resolving that auditors shall not be appointed. This resolution may be passed only at a general meeting of the company at which copies of its latest financial statements (which have been prepared in accordance with section 226) are laid (in accordance with section 241) before the company in general meeting. [Sec 250(1)(b)].

24.5 A company may only pass such a resolution provided that the following three conditions are satisfied:

- The directors must have been entitled under section 246 during the year to take advantage of the exemptions available to small companies when preparing the company's financial statements. The only exception to this relates to a company that was not entitled to benefit from those exemptions solely because it was a member of an ineligible group (see chapter 23 para 23.4). In this situation, the company will be treated for the purpose of this part of the Act as if it had been so qualified.

- The financial statements that are being laid must not be required under section 227 to include group accounts for the year in question.

- The company must have been dormant since the end of the previous financial year.

[Sec 250(1)(b)].

24.6 If, for example, a company has reserves and pays a dividend to its parent company, it will have a significant accounting transaction in any year in which it accounts for the dividend. This means that it cannot then be dormant, and it must appoint auditors.

24.7 Although section 250 of the Act empowers dormant companies to pass a special resolution enabling them to avoid the statutory requirement to appoint auditors, it is important also that they check that the resolution would not contravene any provision in the company's articles of association. Companies that have adopted Table A (other than in the latest form which took effect from 1 July 1985) as their articles, and many other companies (especially those incorporated before 1967) will have a clause in their articles that requires them to appoint auditors. Section 250 does not automatically override such a clause, because it relates only to the statutory requirement in section 384 to appoint auditors.

24.8 In this situation, the company should, in addition to passing the special resolution under section 250, consider whether it needs to pass a special resolution amending its articles by removing the clause concerning the appointment of auditors.

24.9 If a company has not appointed auditors in previous financial years by relying on the exemption in section 250, but it has overlooked its articles, the company should:

- Ratify, by special resolution, its previous decision not to appoint auditors.

- Amend, by special resolution, its articles, and remove the clause that requires it to appoint auditors.

- Pass a new special resolution resolving not to appoint auditors. This resolution will then be effective until such time as the company ceases to be dormant.

24.10 Where a company has not yet held its first general meeting at which financial statements are laid, it may exempt itself from the obligation to appoint auditors by passing a special resolution at any time before that general meeting. It can do this only if it has been dormant from the time it was formed until the time the resolution is passed. [Sec 250(1)(a)].

24.11 A company may not take advantage of the exemptions outlined in paragraphs 24.4 and 24.10 above if it is either a public company, a banking or insurance company, or an authorised person under the Financial Services Act 1986. [Sec 250(2)].

24.12 The resolution need be passed only in the first year in which the company wishes to take advantage of the exemption. The company does not have to repeat the resolution in subsequent years. It will, however, have both to appoint auditors and to have financial statements audited in a year when the company ceases to qualify as a dormant company (see para 24.16).

24.13 Any company wanting to take advantage of these provisions of the Act should include a statement, such as the one set out below, either in the notice of the meeting or in the directors' report attached to the financial statements that are to be laid before the next general meeting of the company. The notice of meeting must state verbatim the resolution to be proposed, and state that it is intended to propose it as a special resolution. [Sec 378].

Auditors

In accordance with section 250 of the Companies Act 1985, a special resolution resolving that auditors shall not be appointed will be put to the annual general meeting.

24.14 The following example illustrates the situation in which a special resolution should be passed.

Example

A parent company prepares its financial statements to 31st December each year. On 30th June 1989, one of its subsidiaries ceased trading and no significant accounting transactions took place thereafter. The next annual general meeting of the subsidiary is on 31st March 1990. The directors wish to take advantage of the exemption not to appoint auditors.

In order to qualify as a dormant company and, therefore, not appoint auditors, the following steps must be followed. The directors must prepare the financial statements of the subsidiary for the year ended 31st December 1989. In addition, the directors must be able to claim the exemptions available to small companies under section 246 when preparing those financial statements. These financial statements must be audited and laid before the general meeting on 31st March 1990. As the company had been dormant since 31st December 1989, a resolution not to appoint auditors can be tabled and passed at that meeting. The resolution remains effective for the financial year 1990 and thereafter, provided the company remains dormant in each of the financial years commencing with 1990.

Additional matters relating to dormant companies

24.15 There are certain additional matters that are relevant to a dormant company that is exempt, at the end of its financial year, from the obligation to appoint auditors. These additional matters are as follows:

- A dormant company need only send a copy of its financial statements without an audit report to those persons entitled to receive copies of the financial statements under sections 238 and 239 (right to receive or demand the financial statements). [Sec 250(4)(a)].

- An auditors' report need not be laid before the company in general meeting. [Sec 250(4)(b)].

- An auditors' report need not be delivered to the Registrar of Companies. Where this is so, the directors must include a statement immediately above their signatures on the balance sheet to the effect that the company was dormant throughout the financial year in question. [Sec 250(4)(c)]. The directors' statement could take the following form:

  The company was dormant (within the meaning of section 250 of the Companies Act 1985) throughout the year ended 31 December 1989.

- The company is entitled to claim the exemptions available to small companies under section 246 when preparing its individual financial statements for the year in question. This requirement applies even where the dormant company is a member of an ineligible group. [Sec 250(4)(d)]. Therefore, the directors of a dormant company need only deliver an abbreviated balance sheet to the Registrar of Companies. (see further chapter 23 paras 23.13 to 23.20).

- Furthermore, the following are not required:

  - The directors' statement that is required under Schedule 8, paragraph 7 (company is entitled to rely, and has relied, on exemptions for small and medium-sized companies) (see chapter 23 para 23.23).

  - The special report of the auditors required by Schedule 8, paragraph 8 (see chapter 23 para 23.26).

  [8 Sch 9].

Ceasing to qualify as a dormant company

24.16 Where a company ceases, for any reason, to qualify as a dormant company, the directors may appoint auditors at any time before the next general meeting at which the company's financial statements prepared under section 226 of the Act are laid before the company. Where this applies, those auditors hold office until the conclusion of that meeting. [Sec 388A(3)].

Agency companies

24.17 An agency company that acts for either a disclosed or an undisclosed principal may be able to take advantage of the exemption for dormant companies. However, because a company may be treated as dormant only if it is not required to record any transaction in its accounting records, it may not qualify as a dormant company if it is involved in any one or more of the following activities:

- Receiving and expending monies.
- Disposing of assets.
- Dealing in goods or stocks that it holds.

24.18 With any of the activities set out above, it will be a matter of fact as to whether a particular agency company performs any such activity. In the first instance, it is necessary to look to the agency agreement for guidance. This agreement defines the relationship between the principal company and the agency company, and it sets out the tasks the respective companies are to perform.

24.19 When considering the agreement, the following points may assist in determining whether the agency company is in fact 'dormant':

- Receiving and expending monies

  An agency company that is merely required to account to its principal for the amount (or the net amount) of the monies it has received for its principal in the course of the agency, is the owner of the monies it receives when acting as agent. The agency company should enter such receipts in its own accounting records. Where, however, the agency company is obliged to hand over to its principal the very monies it receives as agent, it will receive those monies as a trustee for its principal. It will then not be obliged to record those receipts in its own accounting records. Where the agent is a trustee, the agency company must pay the monies it receives on behalf of the principal into a separate bank account belonging to the principal.

  As regards expenditure, it is not sufficient that the principal indemnifies the agency company against any liabilities the company incurs in the course of acting as agent. The agency company must contract with third parties solely in its capacity as agent, and without assuming any liability on the resultant contract. It does not so contract if it does not disclose its principal. If the agency company does assume a liability on the contract, it would have a significant accounting transaction, and so it would not qualify as 'dormant'.

- Disposing of assets

  An agency company might not, in fact, own any assets. However, care should be taken in situations where the agency company remains the legal owner of property. Provided that the agency agreement passed all the beneficial interests in freehold or leasehold property to the principal, and left only the legal title to that property in the name of the agency company, the subsequent transfer of that title would not constitute a transfer of assets. This is because a bare legal title that is held to the order of the principal cannot be said to be an asset of the agent.

- Dealing in goods or stocks that the agency company holds

  If the agent's sole business is that of trading for and on behalf of the principal, the agent is unlikely to 'hold' any stocks of its own.

24.20 It would, therefore, appear that there is no reason in principle why agency companies, in appropriate circumstances, should not qualify to be treated as dormant companies. Whether the agency company actually qualifies for the exemption available to dormant companies will, however, be a matter of fact in the light of both the appropriate agency agreement and the actual relationship between the two parties. Suppose, for example, that a parent company owns an agency company, but there is no formal agency agreement. The agency company may be able to avoid an audit if there was a minute that confirmed its status. Although there would be no formal documentation between the companies, the arrangement would be both effective and clear.

Chapter 25

COMPLETION OF FINANCIAL STATEMENTS AND THEIR PUBLICATION

Chapter 25

COMPLETION OF FINANCIAL STATEMENTS AND THEIR PUBLICATION

Introduction

25.1 When a company has prepared its annual financial statements in accordance with the provisions of the Act, the directors of the company are required to approve, sign and lay the financial statements and reports before the company in general meeting. A private company, however, may elect to dispense with laying its financial statements and reports before the company in general meeting. The directors of the company are also required to deliver the financial statements and reports to persons entitled to receive them and to the Registrar of Companies. There are also rules that companies have to comply with when they publish their financial statements. In addition, there are provisions for the revision of defective financial statements or reports. These and other requirements are considered in more detail in this chapter.

Directors' duties

Preparation and approval of financial statements

25.2 The directors have a duty to prepare annual financial statements for the company under section 226(1) of the Act, and this obligation is discussed in chapter 2.

25.3 The board of directors has to approve the company's financial statements and they must be signed on behalf of the board by a director of the company. [Sec 233(1)].

25.4 In addition, a director is required to sign, on behalf of the board of directors, a copy of the company's balance sheet that is to be delivered to the Registrar of Companies. [Sec 233(4)].

25.5 Every copy of the balance sheet that is laid before the company in general meeting, or that is otherwise circulated, published or issued, should state the name of the person who signed the balance sheet on behalf of the board. [Sec 233(3)].

25.6 In addition to the legal requirement, SSAP 17 requires that the financial statements should disclose the date on which the board of directors approved the financial statements. The date of approval will normally be the date on which the board of directors formally approves a set of documents as the financial statements. The date of approval for consolidated financial statements is the date on which the parent company's directors formally approve them.

25.7 The requirements of both the Act and SSAP 17 will be satisfied if the directors minute their approval of the financial statements at a board meeting and include, at the foot of the balance sheet, a note along the following lines:

"The financial statements on pages X to Y were approved by the board of directors on (date) and are signed on its behalf by:

(Name)

Director "

25.8 The pages of the financial statements that are being approved should normally include, where applicable, any supplementary accounts or other financial statements (such as a value added statement or current cost information). The reason for this is that the directors should acknowledge their responsibility for any such financial information that is presented.

25.9 Alternatively, a similar statement may be included in the directors' report (for example, see Table 88). But when this alternative presentation is adopted, the Act still requires a director to sign the balance sheet of the company.

Table 88: Illustration of a company that includes the note of approval by the board of directors of the financial statements in its directors' report.

Extract from The Savoy Hotel PLC Directors' Report and Annual Accounts 31st December 1988.

APPROVAL OF ACCOUNTS

The accounts on pages 12 to 25 were approved on 11th April, 1989, by the Board of Directors, who authorised two Directors to sign the accounts on behalf of the Board.

25.10 The Act also requires the directors' report to be approved by the board of directors and signed by one director or by the company's secretary. The approval and signing of directors' reports are considered further in chapter 20 paragraphs 20.42 to 20.44.

25.11 Where a parent company prepares consolidated financial statements in accordance with the Act, it is not required to include its own profit and loss account in the group's consolidated financial statements (see further 'Manual of Accounting - volume II' chapter 4). In this situation, the company's individual profit and loss account must be approved by the board of directors and signed on behalf of the board by a director of the company in accordance with section 233(1). [Sec 230(3)].

Presentation of financial statements at general meetings

25.12 The directors have a duty to present the financial statements of the company to the shareholders each year at a general meeting of the company. [Sec 241(1)].

25.13 The financial statements do not necessarily have to be laid before the shareholders at the annual general meeting. Another general meeting will suffice. In practice, however, most companies do lay their annual financial statements before the shareholders at their annual general meeting. The financial statements presented at that meeting should include:

- The company's profit and loss account and balance sheet.
- The directors' report.
- The auditors' report.
- The company's consolidated financial statements (if the company has subsidiaries).
- The statement of source and application of funds (if applicable).

[Sec 241(1); SSAP 10 para 10].

25.14 However, a private company may elect to dispense with laying its financial statements and reports before the company in general meeting (see para 25.20). [Sec 252(1)].

Delivery of financial statements to the Registrar of Companies

Individual companies

25.15 The directors of the company also have a duty to send to the Registrar of Companies a copy of the financial statements of the company (see also para 25.38). Where that copy of the financial statements is not in English, a certified translation of the financial statements also has to be delivered to the Registrar of Companies. [Sec 242(1)]. In addition (and provided that the appropriate rate of exchange to sterling on the balance sheet date is disclosed in the financial statements), the Registrar of Companies will accept, for filing, a UK company's financial statements that have been prepared in a foreign currency.

Consolidated financial statements not prepared

25.16 Where a company is exempt from the requirements to prepare consolidated financial statements, a copy of the ultimate parent company's financial statements must be appended to the company's financial statements delivered to the Registrar of Companies. This requirement applies where the company is itself a wholly-owned subsidiary of a EC parent or the EC parent holds more than 50 per cent of the shares in the company and no notice has been served on the company to prepare consolidated financial statements. [Sec 228(1)]. If the EC parent does not prepare its financial statements in English, a certified translation of the EC parent's financial statements into English must be appended (see further 'Manual of accounting - volume II' chapter 2). [Sec 228(2)(f)].

Subsidiaries excluded from consolidation

25.17 Special rules apply where a parent company has a subsidiary undertaking which is excluded from consolidation under section 229(4) on the grounds that its activities are different from those of the rest of the group, and the subsidiary is either a body corporate incorporated outside Great Britain without an established place of business in Great Britain or an unincorporated undertaking. [Sec 243(1)]. These provisions are further explained in 'Manual of Accounting - volume II' chapter 3.

25.18 A copy of the excluded undertaking's latest individual financial statements and, if it is a parent, its latest consolidated financial statements, should be appended to the company's annual financial statements delivered to the Registrar of Companies. A copy of the auditors' report should also be appended if the financial statements are required by law to be audited. [Sec 243(2)]. Other requirements that must be complied with are as follows:

- The financial statements must be for a period ending not more than 12 months before the end of the financial year for which the parent company financial statements are made up.

- If any document required to be appended is in a language other than English, a certified translation of that document should accompany it.

[Sec 243(3)(4)].

25.19 The above requirements are, however, subject to the following qualifications.

- No financial statements need be specially prepared to satisfy the above requirements, and if no financial statements satisfying the above requirements are prepared none need to be appended.

- A document need not be appended if it is not otherwise required to be published, or made available for public inspection, anywhere in the world. The reason for not appending it should, however, be given in this circumstance.

- If an undertaking and all its subsidiary undertakings are excluded from consolidation under section 229(4), on the grounds that their activities are different from those of the rest of the group, the financial statements of those subsidiary undertakings that are included in its consolidated financial statements need not be appended (see further 'Manual of Accounting - volume II' chapter 3).

[Sec 243(5)].

Exemptions available to private companies

25.20 As stated in paragraph 25.14 above, a private company may elect (by elective resolution in accordance with section 379A), to dispense with laying its financial statements before the company in general meeting. [Sec 252(1)]. This does not remove the requirement to send such reports and accounts to members. That is to say, such companies still have to prepare financial statements and send them to members. They are exempt from presenting them at a general meeting.

25.21 As a consequence, where such an election has been made and is in force, the following sections of the Act that refer to laying financial statements and other statements before members should be read as meaning the *sending* of such statements to members, debenture holders and those persons entitled to receive notice of general meetings:

- Section 235(1) (financial statements on which auditors are to report).

- Section 270(3) and (4) (financial statements by reference to which distributions are to be justified).

- Section 320(2) (financial statements relevant for determining a company's net assets for the purposes of determining whether approval is required for certain transactions).

- Section 271(4) (statement made by auditor where his opinion has been qualified and the company is proposing to pay a dividend).

[Sec 252(3)].

For instance, section 235(1) above refers to the requirement for auditors to report on all annual financial statements that are to be laid before the company in general meeting. Where an election is in force this would be read as still requiring the auditors to report on all annual financial statements that are to be sent to members.

25.22 The Act sets out the period during which the election applies. In the year that the election is made it applies to the financial statements for that year and to all subsequent years. [Sec 252(2)]. If the election is revoked, the financial statements for that year and subsequent financial years must comply with normal requirements for the laying and delivering of financial statements under section 241. [Sec 252(4)].

25.23 Where an election under section 252 is in force, copies of the financial statements must be sent to shareholders and others entitled to receive them, not less than 28 days before the end of the period allowed for laying and delivering accounts and reports. Where they are sent to a member of the company, they should be accompanied by a notice informing him of his right to require the financial statements to be laid before a general meeting. [Sec 253(1)]. If a default is made in complying with this section, the company and every officer who is in default is guilty of an offence and is liable to a fine.

25.24 A member or an auditor of the company has the right, by giving notice at the company's registered office, to require that a general meeting be held in order to lay the financial statements before the company. The notice must be sent to the company within 28 days beginning with the day on which the financial statements are sent out. [Sec 253(2)].

25.25 If the directors do not proceed within 21 days from the date the notice is deposited with the company, the member or auditor may proceed to call a meeting himself. [Sec 253(3]. Where a meeting is convened by the member or auditor it should be held within three months from the date the notice was deposited and should be convened in a similar manner as meetings convened by directors. [Sec 253(4)].

25.26 Where the directors do not convene a meeting, the person who deposited the notice may recover any reasonable expenses from the company that he incurs in convening the meeting himself. The company can recoup such expenses from the remuneration of the defaulting directors. [Sec 253(5)].

25.27 The directors are deemed not to have duly convened a meeting if the date chosen is more than 28 days after the date of the notice convening it. [Sec 253(6)]. Effectively this appears to give the directors 49 days in which to hold the meeting, since they have 21 days in which to proceed to convene a meeting after the notice is deposited by a shareholder or auditor.

Subsequent events

25.28 As discussed in chapter 20 paragraphs 20.6 to 20.10, the directors' report must give details of any significant events that occur between the end of the financial year and the date on which the directors approve the financial statements. SSAP 17 contains a similar requirement.

25.29 SSAP 17 says that it relates only to those events that occur before the date on which the directors approve the financial statements. However, the standard goes on to say that, *"If (events occurring after that date) are material the directors should consider publishing the relevant information so that users of financial statements are not misled"*. [SSAP 17 para 4]. Also, if the company is either listed on The International Stock Exchange or traded on the USM, The International Stock Exchange's Continuing Obligations or the USM's General Undertaking (as appropriate) require the company to inform the Quotations Department of The International Stock Exchange of any significant events that occur at any time that affect the company. [CO 5, GU 1].

25.30 If the auditors become aware of any significant event that has occurred between the date on which the directors approve the financial statements and the date of the relevant general meeting, they should consider whether they should advise the company's directors to disclose that event or exercise their rights to speak at the meeting.

Persons entitled to receive the financial statements

25.31 Every member of the company, every debenture holder of the company, and every person who is entitled to receive notice of general meetings is entitled to receive a copy of the annual financial statements. A copy must be sent to them not less than 21 days before the date of the meeting at which the financial statements are to be presented. [Sec 238(1)].

25.32 A copy must also be given to the company's auditors. [Sec 390(1)]. In addition, the company's bankers may require that they should receive copies of the company's financial statements, and this requirement could be an enforceable term of either a loan agreement or a facility agreement.

25.33 In addition to the right that a member has to be sent a copy of the annual financial statements (as mentioned in para 25.31), every member of the company is entitled (on demand and without charge) to be given, within seven days, a copy of the company's last financial statements that were laid before the company in general meeting. [Sec 239(1)].

25.34 Copies of a company's financial statements, however, need not be sent to:

- A person who is not entitled to receive notices of general meetings, and of whose address the company is unaware.
- More than one of the joint holders of shares or debentures, none of whom is entitled to receive such notices.
- Joint holders of shares or debentures who are not entitled to receive such notices, where the other joint holders are so entitled.

[Sec 238(2)].

25.35 If the company does not have a share capital, copies of the financial statements are not required to be sent to anyone who is not entitled to receive notice of the company's general meetings. [Sec 238(3)].

25.36 If all of the members who are entitled to vote at the general meeting are in agreement, the financial statements may be sent to members and others less than 21 days before the general meeting. [Sec 238(4)].

25.37 If the company is either listed on The International Stock Exchange or traded on the USM, the financial statements must be given to the members within six months from the end of the relevant accounting period. [CO 20; GU 8].

Period allowed for filing

25.38 As stated in paragraph 25.15 above, a company must deliver to the Registrar of Companies a copy of the company's annual financial statements. These financial statements must be sent to the Registrar of Companies before the end of the period allowed for laying and delivery those financial statements. [Sec 242(2)]. An unlimited company, however, does not have to file its financial statements with the Registrar of Companies under certain conditions (see para 25.45). Reference to financial statements means the company's annual accounts and reports.

25.39 The period allowed for filing financial statements with the Registrar of Companies is:

- Ten months after the end of the relevant accounting reference period for a private company.

- Seven months after the end of that period for a public company.

[Sec 244(1)].

25.40 However, the period allowed for filing may be extended or shortened in the following situations outlined in the paragraphs that follow.

25.41 If a company's first accounting reference period exceeds 12 months, the period allowed is the later of:

- Ten months (private company) or seven months (public company) from the first anniversary of the incorporation of the company.

- Three months from the end of the accounting reference period.

[Sec 244(2)].

Example

A public company is incorporated on 1st August 1989, and its first accounting reference period ends on 31st December 1990 (that is, 17 months later). The company must deliver its financial statements to the Registrar of Companies by 31st March 1991. This is because the period allowed is the later of three months after the end of the accounting reference period, that is 31st March 1991 and seven months from the first anniversary of the inception of the company, that is 28th February 1991.

25.42 If the directors of a company that carries on part of its business overseas or has interests overseas (that is, the business is carried on outside the UK, the Channel Islands and the Isle of Man) have notified the Registrar of Companies of this business, or of the interests, before the end of the period allowed for laying and delivering financial statements (see paras 25.39 and 25.41), then they may claim an extension to the period allowed for filing. This extension is for a further three months. [Sec 244(3)].

25.43 A company may shorten its accounting reference period by notifying the Registrar of Companies. Section 225 of the Act sets out the procedures a company must follow to shorten its accounting reference period (see chapter 2 para 2.38). Where a company takes advantage of section 225 and shortens its accounting reference period, the period it is allowed for filing its financial statements that cover this shortened period will be the longer of:

- The period allowed as described in paragraphs 25.39 and 25.41 above.

- Three months after the date on which the notice was given to the Registrar of Companies to change the accounting reference date.

[Sec 244(4)].

25.44 The Secretary of State may also, for any special reason, extend the period a company is allowed for filing its financial statements on application made to him before the expiration of that period. He does this by notifying the company, in writing, of the period of the extension. [Sec 244(5)].

Unlimited companies

25.45 An unlimited company's directors are not required to file a copy of the company's financial statements with the Registrar of Companies if the company was not, at any time during the relevant accounting reference period, any one of the following:

- A subsidiary of a limited company.
- A parent company of a limited company.
- Subject to rights exercisable by or on behalf of two or more limited undertakings which if exercised by one of them, would have made the company a subsidiary undertaking of it.
- A company carrying on a business as the promoter of a trading stamp scheme (under the Trading Stamp Act 1964).

[Sec 254(1)(2)(3)].

Liabilities for contravention

Liability for approving defective financial statements

25.46 All financial statements (including consolidated financial statements) that are approved by the board of directors, must comply with the requirements of the Act. However, if those financial statements do not comply with the Act, then every director of the company who is party to their approval and who knows that they do not comply, or is reckless as to whether they comply, is guilty of an offence and liable to a fine. For this purpose, every director of the company at the time the financial statements are approved is taken to be a party to their approval unless the director shows that he took all reasonable steps to prevent their approval (see appendix IV). [Sec 233(5)]. (See also paras 25.76 to 25.87 for revision of defective financial statements.)

Liability if the balance sheet is not signed

25.47 The company and those of its officers that are in default will be liable to a fine if either of the following applies:

- A director has not signed the company's financial statements or the copy delivered to the Registrar of Companies.

- Copies of the balance sheet have been laid before the company in general meeting or otherwise circulated, published or issued, and these copies do not include the director's signature, or the statement of the signatory's name (see appendix IV).

[Sec 233(6)].

<u>Liability for not sending financial statements to those people entitled to receive them</u>

25.48 Where the company does not comply with the requirements set out in paragraphs 25.31 to 25.36 above, the company and every officer who is in default will be liable to a fine (see appendix IV). [Sec 238(5)].

<u>Liability for not laying and filing financial statements</u>

25.49 If a company's directors either fail to present the financial statements at a general meeting or fail to file the financial statements with the Registrar of Companies within the period allowed (as set out in paras 25.12 and 25.38), then those persons who were the directors of the company immediately before the end of that period will be both guilty of an offence and liable to a fine. If they continue to contravene the Act's requirements, they will also be liable to a daily default fine (see appendix IV). [Sec 241(2), 242(2)]. As a defence, a director in this situation may use proof that he took all reasonable steps to ensure that the requirements had been complied with. [Sec 241(3), 242(4)]. However, it is no defence that the financial statements had not been prepared. [Sec 241(4), 242(5)].

25.50 In addition, if a company has not complied with the filing requirements of section 242(1) of the Act within the period allowed for filing financial statements, then any member of the company, or any creditor of the company, or the Registrar of Companies may serve notice on the company requiring the company to comply with the filing requirements. If the company's directors fail to make good the default within 14 days after this notice has been served, then the person who served the notice may apply to the court to make an order instructing the directors to comply with the filing requirements within a time the court specifies. The court order may also require the directors to bear the cost of the application. [Sec 242(3)].

25.51 Furthermore, if a company has not complied with the filing requirements of section 242(1) of the Act within the period allowed for filing financial statements, the company is liable to a civil penalty recoverable by the Registrar of Companies. The amount of the penalty, which is detailed in appendix IV, will vary according to whether the default has been committed by a private or a public company. The penalty cannot be avoided on the grounds that the financial statements have not been prepared. [Sec 242A(4)].

25.52 The Company Directors (Disqualification) Act 1986 has broadened the scope of the law. If a director is persistently in default in filing any returns, accounts or other document with the Registrar of Companies, he may be disqualified. Default will be conclusively proven if he has three or more defaults in the five years ending with the date of the application.

Liability for not giving copies of financial statements to shareholders or debenture holders on demand

25.53 If a shareholder or holder of the company's debentures has asked for a copy of the company's last financial statements and he does not receive a copy within seven days, the company and any officer of it who is in default will be liable to a fine, and for continued contravention, to a daily default fine. The entitlement is to a copy in addition to any which he might be entitled to receive under normal procedures under section 238 (see para 25.33). [Sec 239(2)]. If in proceedings concerning such an offence the issue arises whether a person had already been given a copy of the financial statements, the defendant bears the burden of proof (see appendix IV). [Sec 239(4)].

Publication of financial statements

25.54 A company will be regarded as 'publishing' financial statements if it either publishes, or issues or circulates them, or otherwise makes them available for public inspection in a manner calculated to invite members of the public generally (or any class of members of the public) to read it. [Sec 240(4)]. There are four types of financial statements that may be published by a company. Their definitions and the rules for publication are discussed in the paragraphs that follow.

Full financial statements

25.55 Full financial statements are referred to in the Act as the company's 'statutory accounts'. 'Statutory accounts' means the company's full financial statements that are required to be delivered to the Registrar of Companies under section 242. [Sec 240(5)]. Statutory accounts are referred to hereafter as statutory financial statements.

25.56 Section 240 of the Act sets out the requirements that companies have to comply with when they publish their financial statements. Any company's statutory financial statements that are to be published should include the auditors' report under section 235. [Sec 240(1)]. Also, if section 227 requires the company to prepare consolidated financial statements, then the published financial statements should include those consolidated financial statements. [Sec 240(2)].

25.57 If any of these requirements of section 240 are not complied with, then the company and any officer of it who is in default will be liable to a fine (see appendix IV). [Sec 240(6)].

Abbreviated financial statements

25.58 Abbreviated (previously referred to in the Act as 'modified') financial statements are not full financial statements. They are normally prepared by small and medium-sized companies that have taken advantage of the exemption afforded by section 246(1) of the Act not to file full financial statements with the Registrar of Companies (see also chapter 23). Abbreviated financial statements are also 'statutory accounts' as defined in section 240(5) of the Act.

25.59 If the financial statements that are being published are 'abbreviated', they should include the auditors' special report that paragraph 8 of Schedule 8 requires. [8 Sch 10]. This report is discussed further in paragraphs 23.26 to 23.33 of chapter 23.

Summary financial statements

25.60 The Companies Act 1989 introduced summary financial statements, which listed public companies ('listed' should be interpreted as meaning admitted to the Official List of The International Stock Exchange) are able to send to shareholders instead of the full financial statements otherwise required under section 238(1). [Sec 251(1)]. Summary financial statements are not statutory accounts.

25.61 Copies of the full financial statements must, however, be sent to any shareholder who wishes to receive them. The Secretary of State has issued The Companies (Summary Financial Statement) Regulations under SI 1990/515 indicating the manner in which it is to be ascertained whether a member of the company wishes to receive them. [Sec 251(2)].

25.62 Summary financial statements are derived from the company's annual financial statements. [Sec 251(3)]. Their exact form and content are specified in SI 1990/515. A summary financial statement will have to:

- State that it is only a summary of information in the company's annual financial statements.
- Contain a statement by the auditors that the summary financial statement is consistent with the annual financial statements and complies with the requirements of section 251 and SI 1990/515.

- State whether the auditors' report on the annual financial statements was unqualified or qualified, and if it was qualified, set out the report in full together with any further material required to understand the qualification.

- State whether the auditors' report on the annual financial statements contained a statement under either of the following sections, and if so, set out the statement in full.

  - Section 237(2), where accounting records or returns have been inadequate, or the financial statements have not agreed with the records or returns.

  - Section 237(3), where necessary information and explanations have not been received.

[Sec 251(4)].

25.63 Summary financial statements do not have to comply with the normal requirements for the publication of financial statements under section 240. [Sec 251(7)].

25.64 Default in complying with section 251, or SI 1990/515, render the company and every officer of it who is in default, guilty of an offence and liable to a fine. [Sec 251(6)].

25.65 The conditions that must be complied with before a company can issue summary financial statements and their form and content are considered further in 'Manual of accounting - volume II' chapter 4.

Non-statutory accounts

25.66 Non-statutory (previously referred to in the Act as 'abridged') accounts are not full financial statements. 'Non-statutory accounts' means any balance sheet or profit and loss account of the company or the group that either relates to, or purports to deal with, a company's or group's full financial year. [Sec 240(5)(a)(b)]. This means that where a full-year's figures and a narrative explanation of those figures are recognisable as either a balance sheet or a profit and loss account of the company or the group, the rules that relate to non-statutory accounts are likely to apply.

25.67 Where a company publishes non-statutory accounts, those accounts must be accompanied by a statement that indicates:

- That the non-statutory accounts are not full financial statements.

- Whether or not the full financial statements have been delivered to the Registrar of Companies.

- Whether or not the auditors have reported on the full financial statements.

- Whether or not the auditors' report was qualified and contained a statement under either of the following sections:

  - Section 237(2), where accounting records or returns have been inadequate, or the financial statements have not agreed with the records or returns.

  - Section 237(3), where necessary information and explanations have not been received.

[Sec 240(3)].

25.68 Published non-statutory accounts should not include the auditors' report that has been made in connection with the full financial statements in accordance with section 235 (see para 25.56). [Sec 240(3)].

25.69 Interim statements that either a listed company or a company traded on the USM must issue are *prima facie* not considered to be non-statutory accounts. The reason for this is that the information they give relates to a six-month period, and not to a full year. Where, however, the interim statement includes, for comparative purposes, figures that relate to a full-year period, the company needs to consider the rules relating to non-statutory accounts. In these circumstances, much depends on whether the full-year's comparative information is sufficiently comprehensive to be recognisable as either a balance sheet or a profit and loss account. Where the information can be so recognised, the provisions that relate to non-statutory accounts apply.

25.70 In contrast to interim statements, preliminary results that either listed companies or companies traded on the USM must issue are *prima facie* considered to be non-statutory accounts. This is because the preliminary results either relate to, or purport to deal with, a company's full financial year. Furthermore, the information that The International Stock Exchange's Continuing Obligations and the USM's General Undertaking respectively require listed companies and companies traded on the USM to give on a preliminary basis is capable of being recognised as a balance sheet or a profit and loss account. The historical cost form of the statement includes (for example) figures for turnover, profit before and after extraordinary items and dividends, as well as 'any supplementary information which in the opinion of the directors is necessary for a reasonable appreciation of the results of the period' (see further chapter 6 paras 6.59 to 6.62). Consequently, where either a listed company or a company traded on the USM publishes a preliminary statement, the provisions that relate to non-statutory accounts apply.

25.71 Another possible example of non-statutory accounts is the special report that some companies prepare for employees. Much depends on whether the report either relates to, or purports to deal with, the company's activities during a full financial year, and also on whether it takes the form of a balance sheet or a profit and loss account.

25.72 It is not likely, however, that either five-year or ten-year summaries would be considered to be non-statutory accounts. The reason for this is that the purpose of such a summary is not to deal with a company's activities for any particular year. Rather its purpose is to put the company's current position in a larger perspective and to provide pointers for the future.

25.73 Where a company publishes non-statutory accounts, a statement along one or other of the following lines should be included in those accounts:

"The non-statutory balance sheet/income statement for the year 199* is an extract from the latest published financial statements that have been delivered to the Registrar of Companies, and on which the auditors' report was unqualified and did not contain a statement under either section 237(2) of the Companies Act 1985 (accounting records or returns inadequate or accounts not a agreeing with records and returns), or section 237(3) (failure to obtain necessary information and explanations)."

"The non-statutory balance sheet/income statement for the year 199* is an extract from the latest financial statements. These financial statements have not yet been delivered to the Registrar of Companies, nor have the auditors yet reported on them."

25.74 Where published non-statutory accounts deal with more than one year (for example, preliminary announcements that must include comparative figures for the previous year), the one document may contain two sets of non-statutory accounts. Where this applies, the wording of the above statements should, be adapted to cover both sets of accounts.

25.75 A company that does not comply with the requirements for the publication of non-statutory accounts outlined above and any officer who is in default will be liable to a fine (see appendix IV). [Sec 240(6)].

Revision of defective accounts and reports

25.76 Revision of defective financial statements was one of the recommendations made by the Dearing Committee and has been implemented by the Companies Act 1989. Financial statements may be voluntarily revised by the directors of the company, or the Secretary of State or a person authorised by him may apply to the court to have them revised (see also chapter 3 para 3.23).

Revision by the directors

25.77 If it appears to the directors of a company that any financial statements (including the directors' report) did not comply with the requirements of the Act, they may prepare revised financial statements or a revised report. [Sec 245(1)]. Where copies of the previous financial statements or report have been laid before the company in general meeting or delivered to the Registrar of Companies, the revisions must be confined to:

- Correcting those aspects in which the previous financial statements did not comply with the requirements of the Act.

- Making any necessary consequential alterations.

[Sec 245(2)].

25.78 Furthermore, the Secretary of State is empowered to make regulations by SI applying the provisions of the Act. The regulations will be able to cover, *inter alia:*

- Different provision according to whether the previous financial statements and reports are replaced or are supplemented by a document indicating the corrections to be made.

- The functions of the auditors in relation to the revised financial statements.

- The steps that should be taken by the directors where the previous financial statements have been:

  - Sent out to members and others under section 238(1).

  - Laid before the company in general meeting.

  - Delivered to the Registrar of Companies.

- Application of other provisions of the Act, including those creating criminal offences.

[Sec 245(3)(4)].

25.79 The regulations can also cover situations where a summary financial statement based on the previous financial statements has been sent to members under section 251. [Sec 245(4)].

Revision ordered by the Secretary of State or by a person authorised by the Secretary of State

25.80 If copies of a company's financial statements have been sent out under section 238 (see para 25.31), or a copy of the financial statements has been laid before the company in general meeting, or delivered to the Registrar of Companies, and the Secretary of State considers that the financial statements may not comply with the Act, he can give notice to the directors of a company indicating areas of concern. [Sec 245A(1)]. The notice must specify a period of not less than one month for the directors to provide an explanation of the financial statements or prepare a revision. [Sec 245A(2)].

25.81 If the Secretary of State does not receive a satisfactory explanation or the financial statements are not appropriately revised, within the time limit set, or within any longer period that he can set at his discretion, he can apply to the court. [Sec 245A(3)].

25.82 The above provisions apply equally to revised financial statements. The Secretary of State can, therefore, request changes to financial statements more than once. [Sec 245A(4)].

25.83 Where a company's financial statements do not comply with the Act, an application can be made to the court by either the Secretary of State (having first complied with section 245A, see paras 25.80 and 25.81) or a person authorised by the Secretary of State (see para 25.87). Such an application is for a declaration that the financial statements of the company do not comply with the requirements of the Act, and that the company's directors should prepare revised financial statements. [Sec 245B(1)]. Notice of the application, together with a general statement of the matters at issue, should also be given to the Registrar of Companies for registration. [Sec 245B(2)].

25.84 If the court orders the preparation of revised financial statements, it can give directions regarding:

- The auditing of the revised financial statements.

- The revision of the directors' report or revision of any summary financial statement.

- The steps to be taken by the directors to bring the order to the notice of those people likely to rely on the previous financial statements.

- Any other matters as the court thinks fit.

[Sec 245B(3)].

25.85 If the court finds that the financial statements, or the revised financial statements, did not comply with the requirements of the Act, it may order that all or part of the following costs shall be borne by those directors who were party to the approval of the defective financial statements:

- The costs (or in Scotland, expenses) of the application.

- Any reasonable expenses incurred by the company in connection with or in consequence of the preparation of revised financial statements.

[Sec 245B(4)].

25.86 Every director of the company at the time the financial statements were approved will be taken to be party to their approval unless he took all reasonable steps to prevent their being approved. [Sec 245B(4)].

25.87 The Secretary of State can authorise any person to make an application to the court under section 245B who appears:

- To have an interest in, and have satisfactory procedures for, securing compliance by companies with the accounting requirements of the Act.

- To have satisfactory procedures for receiving and investigating complaints about the annual financial statements of companies.

- Otherwise to be a fit and proper person to be authorised.

[Sec 245C(1)].

CHECKLIST TO THE REQUIREMENT OF UK GAAP PART I - COMPANIES

This is the first part of the checklist to the requirements of UK GAAP. Part II is reproduced as appendix I of 'Manual of Accounting - volume II'. The checklist is designed to assist a company incorporated in the UK or a group whose parent is incorporated in the UK to ensure that the statutory measurement and disclosure requirements of the Companies Act 1985 (as amended by the Companies Act 1989) have been complied with. The checklist also covers the measurement and disclosure requirements of all SSAPs, the International Stock Exchange's Continuing Obligations for listed companies, and the International Stock Exchange's General Undertaking for companies traded on the USM.

Whilst every effort has been made to make the checklist comprehensive, reference should be made to the source documents on any point of doubt or difficulty.

The checklist is not applicable to banking companies or insurance companies or groups who choose to prepare their financial statements under the rules set out in Schedule 9 to the Act. Nor does it apply to overseas companies. Also, the checklist does not cover special provisions for investment companies that are laid down by Part V of Schedule 4 to the Act.

The accounting provisions of the Companies Act 1989 dealt with in this checklist apply to financial statements starting on or after 23rd December 1989. Consequently, the checklist does not apply to companies or groups whose financial statements start prior to 23rd December 1989.

To comply with the Act, a company or group must adopt one of the balance sheet formats and one of the profit and loss account formats that are set out in Schedule 4 (as amended by Schedule 4A for groups) to the Act. Unless additional disclosures are required, an item that appears in those formats is not specifically referred to in this checklist.

Reference should be made also to the company's articles of association for any special requirements regarding the presentation of financial statements. Furthermore, a company or group may be subject to other legislation that contains accounting requirements.

Each step in the checklist is accompanied by a reference to the appropriate provisions or regulation. The content of the complete checklist is given below, of which only that shown under Part I is reproduced in this appendix.

The contents of the checklist are divided into the following eight sections:

Part I - companies

1. General requirements
2. Directors' report
3. Accounting policies
4. Profit and loss account and related notes
5. Balance sheet and related notes
6. Statement of source and application of funds

Part II - groups

7. Group accounts and accounting for business combinations
8. Summary financial statements

The detailed content of Part I is given on the next page.

CHECKLIST CONTENT PART I

1. General requirements

1.1 Accounting principles
1.2 A true and fair view
1.3 Format of financial statements
1.4 Corresponding amounts
1.5 Disclosure in the event of non-compliance with a SSAP
1.6 The auditors' statutory duties

2. Directors' report

2.1 Principal activities
2.2 Fair review of the business
2.3 Future developments
2.4 Post balance sheet events
2.5 Research and development
2.6 Results and dividend
2.7 Fixed assets
2.8 Charitable and political donations
2.9 Insurance of officers and auditors
2.10 Accounting standards
2.11 Close company status
2.12 Acquisition of own shares
2.13 Directors
2.14 Directors' interests in shares
2.15 Other interests in shares
2.16 Contracts with corporate substantial shareholders
2.17 Vendor placings
2.18 Employees
2.19 General rules

3. Accounting policies

4. Profit and loss account and related notes

4.1 Turnover
4.2 Expenditure
4.3 Disaggregated information
4.4 Employees
4.5 Directors' emoluments
4.6 Depreciation
4.7 Other income and expenditure items
4.8 Pension costs
4.9 Income and share of results of associated companies
4.10 Profit or loss before taxation
4.11 Taxation
4.12 Dividends
4.13 Exceptional and extraordinary items

4.14 Prior year adjustments
4.15 Reserves
4.16 Earnings per share
4.17 Foreign currency translation

5. Balance sheet and related notes

5.1 Assets - general rules
 Determining purchase price or production cost
 Capitalisation of interest
 Alternative accounting rules
 Assets included at a fixed amount
 Foreign currency translation
 Other general rules
5.2 Fixed assets
 Cost and valuation
 Depreciation
 Government grants
 Movements
5.3 Intangible fixed assets
 Development costs
 Research and development facilities
 Concessions, patents, etc.
 Goodwill
5.4 Tangible fixed assets
 Land and buildings
 Investment properties
5.5 Leases and hire purchase contracts
 Lessees
 Sale and leaseback transactions - lessees
 Lessors
5.6 Investments
 Fixed asset investments and current asset investments
 Significant shareholdings (excluding subsidiaries and associated undertakings)
 Associated companies
 Investments in subsidiaries
 Merger relief
 Details of parents
 Consolidated financial statements
5.7 Current assets
 Stocks and fungible assets
 Long-term contracts
 Debtors
 Loans for acquisition of own shares
 Foreign currency translation
5.8 Loans to and transactions with directors
5.9 Loans to and transactions with officers
5.10 Creditors and other liabilities
 General disclosure

Debentures
Foreign currency translation
Dividends
Leasing obligations
Pension costs

5.11 Provisions for liabilities and charges
General disclosure
Deferred taxation

5.12 Guarantees and other financial commitments

5.13 Contingencies

5.14 Share capital

5.15 Reserves

5.16 Post balance sheet events

5.17 Date of approval

6. Statement of source and applications of funds

1. GENERAL REQUIREMENTS

1.1 Accounting principles

1.1.1	Have the amounts to be included in the financial statements been determined in accordance with the following accounting principles:	4 Sch 9
	(a) Going concern?	4 Sch 10 SSAP 2 para 14
	(b) Consistency?	4 Sch 11 SSAP 2 para 14
	(c) Prudence?	4 Sch 12 SSAP 2 para 14
	Note: In particular only profits realised at the balance sheet date should be included in the profit and loss account and all liabilities and losses that have arisen or are likely to arise in respect of the financial year to which the financial statements relate (or a previous financial year) shall be taken into account, including those which only become apparent between the balance sheet date and the date on which it is signed on behalf of the board of directors.	4 Sch 12(a) (b)
	(d) Accruals?	4 Sch 13 SSAP 2 para 14
	(e) Separate determination of the amount of each individual asset and liability?	4 Sch 14
1.1.2	If the answer to 1.1.1 is no, because the directors consider that there are special reasons for departing from them, are particulars of, the reasons for, and the effect of the departure given?	4 Sch 15 SSAP 2 para 17

1.2 A true and fair view

1.2.1	The overriding requirement is that the profit or loss account must give a true and fair view of the profit or loss for the year and the balance sheet must give a true and fair view of the state of affairs at the end of the year. Therefore, in order to give a true and fair view:	Sec 226(2) Sec 227(3)
	(a) Has additional information to that which the Act requires been give where it is needed for the financial statements to give a true and fair view?	Sec 226(4) Sec 227(5)
	(b) Where there are special circumstances, such that compliance with a requirement of the Act would not result in a true and fair view, has the company or group departed from that requirement?	Sec 226(5) Sec 227(6) CO 20

1.2.2	Where 1.2.1(b) applies, are particulars of, the reasons for, and the effect of, the departure given?	Sec 226(5) Sec 227(6)

> Note: In special circumstances, accounting for transactions in accordance with their legal form may not be consistent with their economic substance. If it is considered that to account for the transactions in accordance with their legal form would not be to give a true and fair view, even with additional disclosure, consideration should be given to accounting for them in a manner that is consistent with their economic effect, albeit this may result in a departure from the requirements of Schedule 4 to the Act. Full disclosure of any such departure, and reasons for it, should always be given.

1.3 Format of financial statements

1.3.1	Have one of the profit and loss account formats and one of the balance sheet formats set out in Schedule 4 to the Act been adopted?	4 Sch 1(1)
1.3.2	Are the format for the profit and loss account and the format for the balance sheet the same as those used in the preceding year?	4 Sch 2(1)
1.3.3	If the answer to 1.3.2 is no, does a note disclose both that the directors have adopted a different format and their special reason for doing this?	4 Sch 2(2)
1.3.4	Are the items in both the profit and loss account and the balance sheet shown in the order and under the headings and sub-headings set out in the chosen format?	4 Sch 1(1)

Notes:	
(a) Greater detail is permitted.	4 Sch 3(1)
(b) Additional headings and sub-headings are permitted except that preliminary expenses, expenses of, and commission on any issue of shares or debentures, and costs of research may not be treated as assets in the balance sheet.	4 Sch 3(2) SSAP 13 para 24
(c) Headings and sub-headings are not required where there is no relevant amount in both the current and the preceding year.	4 Sch 3(5), 4(3)
(d) Items preceded in the formats by an Arabic numeral may be combined if immaterial, or if combination results in greater clarity and the breakdown is given in the notes.	4 Sch 3(4)
(e) The directors shall adapt the arrangement and the headings and sub-headings of items preceded by an Arabic numeral where the special nature of the business requires such adaption.	4 Sch 3(3)
(f) The letters, Roman numerals, and Arabic numerals that appear in the formats set out in the Act are not required to be shown in published financial statements.	4 Sch 1(2)

1.3.5	Are assets not offset against liabilities and vice versa, and is income not offset against expenditure and vice versa?	4 Sch 5

> Notes:
> (a) This does not preclude the aggregation of debtor and creditor balances with the same party, so as to arrive at a net indebtedness.
> (b) The full amount of bank loans and overdrafts should be shown, unless there is a legal right of set off, in which case the relevant accounts should be netted.

1.4 Corresponding amounts

1.4.1 Are corresponding amounts for the immediately preceding year given for all items in the financial statements except where corresponding amounts are specifically not required? 4 Sch 4(1), 58(2)(3)

> Notes: Corresponding amounts are specifically not required for the following items :
> (a) Particulars of the company's shareholdings in other undertakings.
> (b) Particulars of loans and other dealings in favour of directors and others.
> (c) Particulars of additions, disposals, transfers of fixed assets and the depreciation charge.
> (d) Particulars of amounts transferred to and from reserves and provisions.
> (e) Details of the accounting treatment of acquisitions.

1.4.2 Where the corresponding amount is not comparable with the current amount: 4 Sch 4(2), 58(2)

(a) Has the corresponding amount been adjusted?

(b) Have particulars of, and the reason for, the adjustment in 1.4.2(a) been disclosed?

1.5 Disclosure in the event of non-compliance with a SSAP

1.5.1 If there is a departure from a SSAP, and if its effect is material, is such a departure referred to in:

(a) The financial statements, giving particulars of the departure, the reasons for it and its effect? SSAP's explanatory foreword 4 Sch 36A

(b) The audit report, in all cases where the auditors do not concur with the departure? Auditing standard 103 paras 1,10

1.6 The auditors' statutory duties

1.6.1 If the information in the directors' report is not consistent with the financial statements is that fact stated in the audit report? Sec 235(3)

1.6.2 Have the auditors stated the fact in their report if they are not satisfied that : Sec 237(1) (2)

(a) The company has kept proper accounting records?

(b) They have been provided with proper returns adequate for their audit from branches they did not visit?

(c) The financial statements are in agreement with the accounting records?

1.6.3	Have the auditors stated in their report where necessary that they have failed to obtain, to the best of their knowledge and belief, all the information and explanations that are necessary for the purposes of their audit?	Sec 237(3)
1.6.4	Where the details required concerning emoluments and other benefits of directors (that is steps 4.5, 5.8 and 5.9) are not disclosed in the financial statements, have the auditors included in their audit report, so far as they are reasonably able to do so, a statement giving the required particulars?	Sec 237(4)
1.6.5	If the auditors have qualified their opinion on the financial statements and if the company proposes to pay a dividend, have the auditors made an additional statement to the members of the company as to whether the subject matter of the qualification is material in determining the legality of the proposed dividend?	Sec 271(3)(4)

2 THE DIRECTORS' REPORT

2.1 Principal activities

2.1.1 Is a description given of the principal activities of the company (and its subsidiaries) during the year and of any significant changes in those activities? Sec 234(2)

2.2 Fair review of the business

2.2.1 Is a fair review given of the development of the business of the company (and its subsidiary undertakings) during the year and of their position at the end of the financial year? Sec 234(1)(a)

2.3 Future developments

2.3.1 Is an indication given of likely future developments in the business of the company (and its subsidiary undertakings)? 7 Sch 6(b) Sec 234(4)

2.4 Post balance sheet events

2.4.1 Are particulars disclosed of any important events affecting the company (or its subsidiary undertakings) that have occurred since the end of the year? 7 Sch 6(a) Sec 234(4)

2.5 Research and development

2.5.1 Is an indication given of any activities of the company (and its subsidiary undertakings) in the field of research and development? 7 Sch 6(c) Sec 234(4)

2.6 Results and dividends

2.6.1 Is the amount, if any, the directors recommend should be paid by way of dividend disclosed? Sec 234(1)(b)

2.6.2 Is the amount, if any, the directors propose to transfer to reserves disclosed? Sec 234(1)(b)

2.6.3 If the company is listed, or if it is traded on the USM, is an explanation given of any material difference between the trading results for the year and any published forecast made by the company? CO 21(b) GU 10(b)

2.7 Fixed assets

2.7.1 Are particulars of any significant changes in the fixed assets of the company (and its subsidiary undertakings) during the year disclosed? 7 Sch 1(1) Sec 234(4)

2.7.2 Is the difference (as precisely as practicable) at the year end between the market value and the balance sheet value of land disclosed if, in the opinion of the directors, the difference is of such significance that it should be drawn to the attention of the members or the debenture holders? 7 Sch 1(2) Sec 234(4)

> Note: Under section 3 of the Interpretation Act 1889, 'land' means any interest in 'land and buildings'.

2.8 Charitable and political donations

2.8.1	Is the amount of money, if any, given by the company and its subsidiaries to UK charities and the amount given for UK political purposes disclosed (if together they exceed £200)?	7 Sch 3 - 5, Sec 234(4)
2.8.2	In the case of any individual political contributions exceeding £200, is the name of the recipient or political party concerned and the amount disclosed?	7 Sch 3,4 Sec 234(4)
	Note: Not applicable to directors' reports of wholly-owned subsidiaries of companies incorporated in Great Britain.	7 Sch 3(1) Sec 234(4)

2.9 Insurance of officers and auditors

2.9.1	Where the company has purchased or maintained any insurance during the year for any officers or auditors against liabilities in relation to the company, has this fact been stated.	7 Sch 5A Sec 310(3) (a)

2.10 Accounting standards

2.10.1	If the company is listed, or if it is traded on the USM, is a statement given by the directors as to the reasons for any significant departure from applicable standard accounting practices?	CO 21(a) GU 10(a)

2.11 Close company status

2.11.1	If the company is listed, or if it is traded on the USM, is a statement given of whether or not, so far as the directors are aware, the company is a close company for taxation purposes and whether there has been any change in that respect since the end of the year?	CO 21(j) GU 10(j)

2.12 Acquisition of own shares

2.12.1	In respect of purchases by the company of its own shares during the year are the following disclosed: (a) The number and nominal value of shares purchased? (b) The percentage of called-up capital that shares of the description purchased represent? (c) The aggregate consideration paid? (d) The reasons for the purchase?	7 Sch 8(a)(e)
2.12.2	In respect of acquisitions (other than purchases) by the company or by another person, of its own shares, or in respect of a lien or charge on those shares, are the following disclosed: (a) The number and nominal value of shares acquired or charged during the year, and the percentage of called-up capital that shares of the description acquired or charged represent? (b) The maximum number and nominal value of shares acquired or charged that were held at any time during the year? (c) The number and nominal value of shares acquired or charged that were disposed of or cancelled during the year?	7 Sch 8(b)-(g)

(d) The consideration received in respect of disposals during the year where the shares were originally acquired for money or money's worth?

(e) The amount of any charge?

Note: Acquisitions (other than purchases) by the company of its own shares comprise: (a) Shares acquired by forfeiture, by surrender in lieu of forfeiture or by way of gift. (b) In the case of a public company, shares any person acquires with the financial assistance of the company and in respect of which the company has a beneficial interest. (c) Shares that a nominee of the company acquires from a third party without the company providing any financial assistance and in respect of which the company has a beneficial interest. (d) Shares over which the company takes a lien or a charge (express or implied) for any amount payable in respect of those shares.	7 Sch 7

2.12.3 If the company is listed, are particulars given of any shareholders' authority existing at the year end for the purchase by the company of its own shares? CO 21(p)

2.12.4 In the case of such purchases made otherwise than through the market or by tender or partial offer to all shareholders, are the names of the sellers of such shares purchased, or proposed to be purchased, by the company during the year disclosed? CO 21(p)

2.12.5 Are particulars given of purchases or options or contracts to make purchases of own shares entered into since the end of the year? CO 21(p)

Note: The particulars to be given are those in 2.12.1 and 2.12.2 above.

2.13 Directors

2.13.1 Are the names disclosed of persons who were directors of the company at any time during the year together with, for listed companies and companies traded on the USM, the identity of independent non-executive directors and a short biographical note on each. Sec 234(2) CO 21(t)

2.13.2 If the company is listed, is the unexpired period disclosed (if greater than one year) of any service contract of each director proposed for re-election at the annual general meeting (or, if he does not have a service contract of more than one year's duration, a statement to that effect)? CO 43(c)

2.14 Directors' interests in shares

2.14.1 Are the interests given of each person who was a director at the end of the year in shares or debentures of either the company or any other body corporate in the group at both the beginning of the year (or date of appointment, if later) and the end of the year? 7 Sch 2 CO 21(h) GU 10(h)

Notes: (a) Details to be according to the register kept by the company. (b) Interests of a director include interests of his spouse or infant child. (c) If a director has no such interests at the end of the year, there should be a statement to that effect.	 Sec 328(1)

(d) If a director has no interests at the end of the year, no details are required of any interests at the beginning of the year (whether or not he had any), unless the company is listed or it is traded on the USM.
(e) The information may be given in a note to the financial statements. 7 Sch 2(1)
(f) Details required in the register of directors' shareholdings include shadow directors. Consequently, it is appropriate to disclose the required information for such directors.
(g) The main exemptions are:

(i) Directors' nominee shareholdings in wholly-owned subsidiaries. Sec 324(6)
(ii) Interests of directors of wholly-owned subsidiaries of companies incorporated in Great Britain who are also directors of the holding company. SI 1985/802
(iii) Interests of directors of wholly-owned subsidiaries of companies incorporated outside Great Britain in companies incorporated outside Great Britain. SI 1985/802

(h) Other exemptions are set out in SI 1985/802 7 Sch 2(1)
(i) Directors' interests may be given in the notes to the financial statements.
(j) If the company is listed, or traded on the USM, interests in shares in the company and its subsidiaries should distinguish between beneficial and non-beneficial interests and particulars should be given of the extent of any duplication that occurs. CO 21(h) GU 10(h)
(k) If a director has an interest in the company's shares in the form of an option, this interest should be disclosed. 7 Sch 2A 13 Sch 6(1) Sec 324 (2)(d) 328 (2)(a)

2.14.2 Where a director has exercised a right (which includes an option) during the period to subscribe for shares in, or debentures of the company or another body corporate in the same group, has the number of shares exercised and the amount of debentures taken up for each such body been disclosed? 7 Sch 2B

Note: The notes to 2.14.1 also apply to 2.14.2.

2.14.3 If the company is listed, or if it is traded on the USM, are any changes in directors' interests between the end of the year and a date not more than one month prior to the date of the notice of meeting, or the fact that there have been no changes disclosed? CO 21(h) GU 10(h)

2.15 Other interests in shares

2.15.1 If the company is listed, or if it is traded on the USM, are particulars of, and the amount of, an interest of any person (other than a director) in 3 per cent or more of the nominal value of any class of voting capital at a date not more than one month prior to the date of the notice of meeting, or the fact that there are no such interests disclosed? CO 21(i) GU 10(i)

Note: Details to be according to the register kept by the company under section 211.

2.16 Contracts with corporate substantial shareholders

2.16.1 If the company is listed, are particulars disclosed of any contract of significance between the company, or one of its subsidiaries, and a corporate substantial shareholder? CO 21(l)

> Notes:
> (a) A 'contract of significance' is one which represents in amount or value a sum equal to 1 per cent or more of:
>
> (i) In the case of a capital transaction or a transaction of which the principal purpose is the granting of credit, the net assets of the company.
> (ii) In other cases, the total purchases, sales, payments or receipts, as the case may be, of the company.
> Where the company has subsidiaries, then comparison should be made on a consolidated basis.
>
> (b) A 'corporate substantial shareholder' means any body corporate entitled to exercise or control the exercise of 30 per cent or more of the voting power at general meetings of the company, or one which is in a position to control the composition of a majority of the board of directors.

2.16.2 If the company is listed, are particulars disclosed of any contract for the provision of services to the company or any of its subsidiaries by a corporate substantial shareholder except in the circumstances given in the note to this question? CO 21(m)

> Note: Such a contract need not be disclosed if it is a contract for the provision of services which it is the principal business of the shareholder to provide and it is not a 'contract of significance'.

2.17 Vendor placings

2.17.1 If the company is listed, are particulars disclosed of the participation of the company's parent company in any vendor consideration placing made during the year? CO 22

2.18 Employees

2.18.1 Is a statement given of the company's policy during the year in respect of: 7 Sch 9

(a) Applications for employment from disabled persons?
(b) Persons that become disabled during their employment?
(c) Training, career development and promotion of disabled persons?

> Notes:
> (a) Not applicable to employees who work wholly outside the UK.
> (b) Not applicable to directors' reports of companies that employ on average 250 or fewer persons in the UK.

2.18.2 Is a description given of the action that the company has taken during the year to introduce, maintain or develop arrangements aimed at: 7 Sch 11

(a) Providing employees systematically with information on matters of concern to them as employees?

(b) Consulting employees or their representatives on a regular basis so that the views of employees can be taken into account in making decisions that are likely to affect their interests?

(c) Encouraging the involvement of employees in the company's performance through an employees' share scheme or by some other means?

(d) Achieving a common awareness on the part of all employees of the financial and economic factors that affect the performance of the company?

> Notes:
> (a) Not applicablc to employees who work wholly outside the UK.
> (b) Not applicable to directors' reports of companies that employ on average 250 or fewer persons in the UK.

2.19 General rules

2.19.1 Where the shareholders are sent a notice of a meeting which includes any business other than routine business at an AGM and an explanatory circular does not accompany the notice, is an explanation given of the business if it is to be considered on the same day as the AGM? CO 32

2.19.2 Does the directors' report refer to the resolution to reappoint the auditors at the AGM?

> Note: There is no statutory requirement to include a note on the reappointment of auditors, but it is normal practice to do so.

2.19.3 Has the directors' report been approved by the board of directors and signed on its behalf by a director or secretary of the company? Sec 234A

3. ACCOUNTING POLICIES

3.1	Have the significant accounting policies adopted been stated, in particular, the policies in respect of:	4 Sch 36 SSAP 2 para 18
	(a) Depreciation and diminution in value of assets (including for each major class of depreciable fixed asset, the depreciation method used, and the useful economic lives or the depreciation rates used)?	4 Sch 36 SSAP 12 para 25
	(b) Deferred development expenditure?	SSAP 13 para 30
	(c) The valuation of stocks and long-term contracts, and in particular the method of ascertaining turnover and attributable profit?	SSAP 9 para 32
	(d) Deferred taxation?	SSAP 15
	(e) The basis of translating amounts denominated in foreign currencies and the treatment of exchange differences?	4 Sch 58(1) SSAP 20 para 59
	(f) Accounting for finance leases and for operating leases by lessees (including hire purchase contracts with similar characteristics)?	SSAP 21 para 57
	(g) Accounting for finance leases and operating leases by lessors and, in detail, the policy for accounting for finance lease income (including hire purchase contracts with similar characteristics)?	SSAP 21 para 60(a)
	(h) Goodwill?	SSAP 22 para 39
	(i) Pension costs and, if different, the funding policy?	SSAP 24 para 87,88
3.2	Have the accounting policies been applied consistently within the same financial statements and from one financial year to the next?	4 Sch 11

4. PROFIT AND LOSS ACCOUNT AND RELATED NOTES

Note: If a parent company prepares a consolidated profit and loss account that complies with the requirements of the Act and shows in the notes to the company's balance sheet the company's profit or loss for the year, the company's own profit and loss account may be omitted from the group's consolidated financial statements. The company's profit and loss account must, however, be approved by the board of directors. (See further Part II of the checklist in 'Manual of Accounting - volume II').	Sec 230(1), (3)

4.1 Turnover

4.1.1 Is turnover stated exclusive of trade discounts, VAT and other taxes based on turnover? — SSAP 5 para 8

4.1.2 Does turnover include ascertainable turnover for long-term contracts in progress? — SSAP 9 para 7

4.1.3 Does turnover exclude the investing company's share of any turnover of associated companies? — SSAP 1 para 23

Note: An associated company's turnover should not be aggregated with the company's turnover, but where it is material, it should be disclosed separately. See also steps 5.6.6 to 5.6.21.	SSAP 1 para 23

4.2 Expenditure

4.2.1 Do all items of expenditure include any irrecoverable VAT on that expenditure? — SSAP 5 para 9

4.3 Disaggregated information

4.3.1 Where two or more classes of business are carried on that, in the opinion of the directors, differ substantially, are the following disclosed: — 4 Sch 55(1)(3)(4)

(a) A description of each class?

(b) The amount of turnover attributable to each class?

(c) The amount of profit or loss before taxation?

4.3.2 Where geographically defined markets are supplied that, in the opinion of the directors, differ substantially, is the amount of turnover attributable to each market disclosed? — 4 Sch 55(2)(3)(4) CO 21(c) GU 10(c)

4.3.3 If a company is listed, or is traded on the USM and the geographical analysis of net turnover is given by continent, has the net turnover related to one continent been further analysed where 50 per cent of the overseas operations relate to that continent? — CO 21(c)

4.3.4 If the company is listed, or if it is traded on the USM, and the contribution to profit or loss from a specific market is substantially out of line with the normal ratio of profit to turnover, is the geographical analysis of contribution to trading results disclosed? CO 21(c) GU 10(c)

4.3.5 Where the directors consider that disclosure of disaggregated information would be seriously prejudicial to the interests of the company or group, is there a statement that the information is not disclosed? 4 Sch 55(5)

> Note: The reason for non-disclosure is not required. 4 Sch 55(5)

4.4 Employees

4.4.1 Is the average number of employees (including directors, and employees working wholly or mainly outside the UK) in the year disclosed both in total and by category of employee? 4 Sch 56(1)(2)(3)

> Note:
> (a) The directors may select whatever categories they consider appropriate, but in doing so they should have regard to the manner in which the company's or group's activities are organised. 4 Sch 56(5)
> (b) The average should be calculated by reference to weekly numbers of persons employed under contracts of employment. 4 Sch 56(2)(3)

4.4.2 Is the aggregate of each of the following amounts disclosed in respect of the employees included in step 4.4.1: 4 Sch 56(4) 94

(a) Wages and salaries paid or payable?

(b) Social security costs incurred?

(c) Other pension costs incurred?

4.5 Directors' emoluments

4.5.1 Are directors' emoluments (divided in each case between amounts receivable in respect of services as director of the company or of any of its subsidiaries, and amounts receivable otherwise in respect of the management of the affairs of the company or any of its subsidiaries) disclosed as follows:

(a) Aggregate emoluments? 6 Sch 1

(b) Aggregate directors' and past directors' pensions? 6 Sch 7

(c) Aggregate of compensation paid to directors or past directors for loss of office, including retirement, divided between that receivable from the company, its subsidiaries and any other persons? 6 Sch 8

(d) Aggregate amount of consideration paid to or receivable by third parties for making available the services of a person as a director? 6 Sch 9

Notes	
(a) In consolidated financial statements, the provisions apply only to directors of the parent company.	
(b) Disclosure must include sums paid by, or receivable from the following, (but excluding sums for which the recipient has to account): (i) The company. (ii) Subsidiary undertakings. (iii) Any other person.	6 Sch 10(2)
(c) Aggregate emoluments in 4.5.1(a) includes in addition to a director's normal emoluments: (i) Fees and percentages. (ii) Sums paid by way of expense allowance (so far as those sums are chargeable to UK income tax). (iii) Contributions paid in respect of him under any pension scheme. (iv) The estimated money value of any other benefits received by him otherwise than in cash. (v) Emoluments received in respect of a person accepting office as a director.	6 Sch 1(4)
(d) In 4.5.1(b) pensions include those payable to nominees, dependants or connected persons, but exclude pensions payable under a pension scheme where the contributions are substantially adequate for the maintenance of the scheme.	6 Sch 7(2)
(e) In 4.5.1(b), (c) and (d), the amounts disclosed include benefits otherwise than in cash based on their estimated money value. Where such benefits exist, the nature of the benefit must be disclosed separately for each category.	6 Sch 7(4), 8(3), 9(2)
(f) For 4.5.1(c) above, the payment to a director of compensation is illegal unless particulars and the amount of the proposed payment have been disclosed to and approved by the company in general meeting. This does not apply, however, to bona fide payments representing damages for breach of contract or consideration for the premature termination of a service contract, or a pension in respect of past services.	Sec 312, 316(3)
(g) In 4.5.1(d) reference to third parties is to persons other than the director himself or a person connected with him or body corporate controlled by him, and the company or any of its subsidiaries.	6 Sch 9(3)

4.5.2	Are the following disclosed:	
	(a) The number of directors whose emoluments fall into each of the bands, £0-£5,000, £5,001-£10,000, etc. in multiples of £5,000?	6 Sch 4(2)
	(b) The chairman's emoluments, or the emoluments of each person for the period during which he acted as chairman?	6 Sch 3(1) (2) (3), 4(4)
	(c) The emoluments (but not the name) of the highest-paid director (or directors, if equal) if in excess of the chairman's emoluments?	6 Sch 4(3)
	(d) The number of directors who have waived rights to receive emoluments during the year, and the aggregate amount waived?	6 Sch 6
	(e) If the company is listed, or if it is traded on the USM, particulars of any arrangement under which a director has waived or agreed to waive, emoluments from the company or any of its subsidiaries?	CO 21(n) GU 10(k)

Notes:	
(a) Individual bands in 4.5.2(a) need not be shown if no director falls within that band in either period, directors with no emoluments should still be included..	
(b) The requirements in 4.5.2(a) to (d) do not apply to those companies that are neither parent companies nor subsidiaries and the aggregate directors' emoluments do not exceed £60,000.	6 Sch 2
(c) Exclude from 4.5.2(a) to (c) above directors whose duties were wholly or mainly discharged outside the UK.	6 Sch 3(4), 4(5)
(d) In calculating emoluments 4.5.2(a) to (c), exclude contributions to pension schemes.	6 Sch 5
(e) The requirement in 4.5.2(e) applies both to emoluments which accrued during the year and to future emoluments.	
(f) In consolidated financial statements, the provisions apply only to directors of the parent company.	

4.6 Depreciation

Note: See also 5.2.5 to 5.2.16.

4.6.1 Where profit and loss account Format 1 or 3 is adopted:

(a) Are 'cost of sales', 'distribution costs' and 'administrative expenses' stated after deducting provisions for depreciation and diminution in value of related assets?	4 Sch Format Note 14
(b) Is the amount of provisions for depreciation and diminution in value of tangible and intangible fixed assets disclosed?	4 Sch Format Note 17 SSAP 12 para 25

4.6.2 Are the following amounts of provisions for diminution in value disclosed:

(a) The amount in respect of a temporary diminution in value of fixed asset investments?	4 Sch 19(1)
(b) The amount in respect of a permanent diminution in value of any fixed asset?	4 Sch 19(2) SSAP 12 para 19
(c) The amount written back because it is no longer required?	4 Sch 19(3) SSAP 12 para 19

4.6.3	Where a fixed asset has been revalued, has the depreciation charge included in the profit and loss account been based on the carrying amount of the asset?	4 Sch 32(1) SSAP 12 para 6
4.6.4	Does the depreciation charge exclude 'supplementary' depreciation (that is, depreciation in excess of the normal charge for depreciation based on the carrying amount of the asset) and is any appropriation of profits specifically designated for the replacement of fixed assets shown as a reserve movement?	SSAP 12 para 16

4.6.5	Where the investing company does not prepare consolidated financial statements and is not a wholly-owned subsidiary, does depreciation exclude the investing company's share of any depreciation of associated companies?	SSAP 1 para 23

> Note: See also steps 5.6.6 to 5.6.21

4.6.6	Has the amount of any goodwill amortised through the profit and loss account during the year been disclosed?	SSAP 22 para 45(a)

4.7 Other income and expenditure items

4.7.1	Is income from fixed asset investments and interest, derived from group undertakings disclosed separately from income and interest derived from other sources?	4 Sch Format Note 15

> Note: This will not apply to income derived from subsidiary undertakings included in a consolidated profit and loss account.

4.7.2	For lessors, is the aggregate amount of rentals receivable disclosed in the year from leases and hire purchase contracts analysed between finance leases and operating leases?	SSAP 21 para 60(b)

> Note: See also step 5.5

4.7.3	Is interest and similar charges payable to group companies disclosed separately from other interest and similar charges payable?	4 Sch Format Note 16

4.7.4 Is interest payable on and any similar charges disclosed in respect of each of the three categories: — 4 Sch 53(2)

(a) Bank loans and overdrafts, and other loans that are repayable:

- Not repayable by instalments and due wholly within 5 years of the balance sheet date?
- Repayable by instalments wholly within 5 years of the balance sheet date?

(b) Loans of any other kind made to the company (that is, repayable wholly or partly beyond 5 years)?

> Note: Not applicable to interest and similar charges payable on loans from other group undertakings.

4.7.5	Is the amount of income from listed investments including tax credits in the case of franked investment income disclosed?	4 Sch 53(4) SSAP 8 para 25
4.7.6	Is the amount, where substantial, of the revenue from rents (after deduction of ground rents, rates and other out goings) disclosed?	4 Sch 53(5)
4.7.7	Is the auditors' remuneration including expenses disclosed?	390A(3)(4)

> Note: A statutory instrument specifying further disclosures is expected in Autumn 1990.

4.7.8 For lessees, is the total operating lease rentals (including rentals in respect of hire purchase contracts that have similar characteristics to an operating lease) charged as an expense in the profit and loss account disclosed, analysed between hire of plant and machinery and other operating leases? 4 Sch 53(6) SSAP 21 para 55

> Note: See also step 5.5

4.7.9 For lessees, is the aggregate amount of finance charges allocated to the profit and loss account in respect of finance leases and hire purchase contracts disclosed? SSAP 21 para 53

> Note: See also step 5.5

4.7.10 Are any amounts set aside for the redemption of the following disclosed: 4 Sch 53(3)
(i) Share capital?
(ii) Loans?

4.7.11 Are dividends receivable from UK resident companies stated at the amount of cash received or receivable plus the tax credit? SSAP 8 para 25

4.7.12 Is the amount of research and development expenditure charged in the profit and loss account disclosed, analysed between the current year's expenditure and amounts amortised from deferred expenditure? SSAP 13 para 31

> Note: This disclosure is only required where the company is either a plc or a banking or insurance company (or holding company that has one of those companies as a subsidiary) or it exceeds the criteria for determining a medium-size company under the Act multiplied by ten. SSAP 13 para 22

4.8 Pension Costs

> Note: SSAP 24 applies where the employer has a legal or contractual commitment under a pension scheme or one implicit in the employer's actions, to provide, or contribute to, pensions for his employees. The same principles apply whether the scheme is funded or unfunded. SSAP 24 para 73

4.8.1 If the company operates a defined contribution scheme, is the charge against profits the amount of contributions payable to the scheme in respect of the accounting period? SSAP 24 para 78

> Notes:
> (a) See also steps 5.10.25 to 5.10.33
> (b) A 'defined contribution scheme' is a pension scheme in which the benefits are directly determined by the value of contributions paid in respect of each member. Normally the rate of contribution is specified in the rules of the scheme. SSAP 24 para 62

4.8.2 If the company operates a defined benefit scheme, is the pension cost an amount calculated using actuarial valuation methods consistent with the requirements of SSAP 24? SSAP 24 para 79

> Note: See also steps 5.10.25 to 5.10.33.

4.8.3 Is the method for providing for expected pension costs (in the light of the current actuarial assumptions) such that the regular pension cost is a substantially level percentage of the current and expected future pensionable payroll? SSAP 24 para 79

> Notes:
> (a) 'Regular cost' is the consistent ongoing cost recognised under the actuarial method used. SSAP 24 para 72
> (b)'Pensionable payroll/earnings' are the earnings on which benefits and/or contributions are calculated. One or more elements of earnings (for example, overtime) may be excluded, and/or there may be a reduction to take account of all or part of the state scheme benefits which the member is deemed to receive. SSAP 24 para 69

4.8.4 Subject to exceptions mentioned in steps 4.8.5 to 4.8.9, are variations from the regular pension cost (that is, experience surpluses or deficiencies), including contribution holidays, spread over the expected remaining service lives of current employees in the scheme? SSAP 24 para 80, 81

> Notes:
> (a) A period representing the average remaining service lives may be used if desired. SSAP 24 para 80
> (b) An 'experience surplus or deficiency' is that part of the excess or deficiency of the actuarial value of assets over the actuarial value of liabilities, on the basis of the valuation method used, which arises because events have not coincided with the actuarial assumptions made for the last valuation. SSAP 24 para 63
> (c) The 'average remaining service life' is a weighted average of the expected future service lives of the current members of the scheme up to their normal retirement dates or expected dates of earlier withdrawal or death in service. The weights can have regard to periods of service, salary levels of scheme members and future anticipated salary growth, in a manner which the actuary considers appropriate having regard to the actuarial method and assumptions used. SSAP 24 para 58

4.8.5 If there has been a significant reduction in the normal level of contributions to, or a refund from, a pension scheme has this been recognised when it occurs in the following circumstances:

(a) Where a surplus or deficiency resulting from a significant reduction in the number of employees is eliminated (except when this is caused by an extraordinary event, see step 4.13.13)? SSAP 24 para 81

(b) Where a refund is subject to deduction of tax in accordance with the provisions of the Finance Act 1986 (or equivalent legislation)? SSAP 24 para 83

Note: The Finance Act 1986 stipulates that a pension scheme will lose part of its tax exemptions if its surplus exceeds 5 per cent of the scheme's liabilities. One method that a trustee and employer may use, to reduce a surplus to less than 5 per cent, is to make a cash payment to the employer. This cash payment is liable to tax at 40 per cent. Furthermore, the Social Security Bill 1990 proposes to index benefits by reference to the RPI.	Finance Act 1986

4.8.6 If significant additional contributions have been paid and the resulting material deficit has been recognised over a shorter period than the expected average remaining service lives of employees, has this been accepted because a major event or transaction has occurred that has not been allowed for in the actuarial assumptions? SSAP 24 para 82

4.8.7 In the period when an 'ex gratia' pension is granted, is the capital cost (to the extent that it is not covered by a surplus) recognised? SSAP 24 para 84

Note: An 'ex gratia' pension or 'discretionary' or 'ex gratia increase' in a pension is one which the employer has no legal, contractual or implied commitment to provide.	SSAP 24 para 60

4.8.8 When discretionary or ex gratia increases in pensions are granted and allowances have not been made in the actuarial assumptions, has the capital cost (to the extent that it is not covered by a surplus) been recognised in the period the pension is granted? SSAP 24 para 85

4.8.9 If on implementing SSAP 24 for the first time a cumulative adjustment arises in respect of prior years, has the adjustment been dealt with in accordance with the transitional provisions in one of the following ways: SSAP 24 para 92

(a) In accordance with the other provisions of the standard (that is, by allocating the adjustment over the expected average remaining service lives)?

(b) In accordance with SSAP 6 as a prior year adjustment?

4.8.10 Has the way in which the transitional provisions have been applied been disclosed? SSAP 24 para 92

Note: This applies in the period in which SSAP 24 is first implemented.

4.9 Income and share of results of associated companies

4.9.1 Do the financial statements of the company include only dividends received and receivable from associates in its own profit and loss account? SSAP 1 para 18

Note: Steps 4.9.2 to 4.9.4 below relate to the treatment of associated companies in the financial statements of a company that is not a member of a group and therefore has to deal with the associate in its individual financial statements, or where the company is not a wholly-owned subsidiary and does not prepare consolidated financial statements. For undertakings that are required to prepare consolidated financial statements the provisions that apply to consolidating associated undertakings on an equity basis are dealt with in section 7.13 of Part II of the checklist included in 'Manual of Accounting - volume II'

4.9.2 Does an investing company that does not prepare consolidated financial statements and which is not a wholly-owned subsidiary, prepare a separate profit and loss account which includes the investing company's share of profits less losses of associated companies before tax? SSAP 1 para 24

> Note: This basis need not be applied to those interests in partnerships and non-corporate joint ventures where it is appropriate to account for a proportionate share of individual assets and liabilities as well as profits or losses.

4.9.3 Where under 4.9.2 a separate profit and loss account is not prepared does the company add the required information in supplementary form to its own profit and loss account in such a way that its share of the profits of the associated companies is not treated as realised for the purposes of the Act? SSAP 1 para 24

4.9.4 If the results of one or more associated companies are very material in the context of the investing company, is there separate disclosure of items such as total turnover, total depreciation charges and total profits less losses before taxation of the associated companies concerned? SSAP 1 para 23

> Note: When judging materiality, regard should also be had to the scale of the associated company's operations in relation to those of the investing company.

4.10 Profit or loss before taxation

4.10.1 Is the amount of the profit or loss on ordinary activities before taxation disclosed? 4 Sch 3(6)

4.11 Taxation

4.11.1 If the rate of corporation tax is not known for the whole or part of the year, has the latest known rate been used, and disclosed? SSAP 8 para 23

4.11.2 Are the following elements of the taxation charge separately disclosed: 4 Sch 54(1)(3) SSAP 8 para 22

(a) UK corporation tax, showing separately the extent of any relief from double taxation, and the basis of computation?

(b) Transfers to or from the deferred taxation account? SSAP 15 para 33

(c) UK income tax, and the basis of computation?

(d) Tax attributable to franked investment income?

(e) Taxation imposed outside the UK on profits, income and (so far as charged to revenue) capital gains relieved and unrelieved, specifying that part of unrelieved overseas taxation which arises from the payment of dividends? SSAP 8 para 22(b)

(f) The amount, if any, of irrecoverable ACT that is unrelieved as a result of the payment or proposed payment of dividends?

	Note: Elements 4.11.2(a), (b), (c) and (e) must be stated separately in respect of ordinary activities and extraordinary items.	4 Sch 54(3) SSAP 15 para 34
4.11.3	Where the investing company does not prepare consolidated financial statements and is not a wholly-owned subsidiary, does its separate proforma profit and loss account (which includes the associate) or additional note information disclose, in taxation, the tax attributed to its share of profits of associated companies?	SSAP 1 para 20
	Note: See also steps 5.6.6 to 5.6.21.	
4.11.4	Has deferred taxation been provided on the liability method to the extent that it is probable that a liability (or asset) will crystallise?	SSAP 15 paras 24,25
4.11.5	Is tax deferred or accelerated by the effect of timing differences only accounted for to the extent that it is probable that a liability (or asset) will crystallise?	SSAP 15 paras 26 to 28
4.11.6	Is the provision for deferred tax liabilities reduced by any deferred tax debit balances arising from separate categories of timing differences and any ACT that is available for offset against those liabilities?	SSAP 15 para 29
	Note: See also steps 5.11.4 to 5.11.12	
4.11.7	Is the amount of unprovided deferred tax in respect of the year disclosed in a note and analysed into its major components?	SSAP 15 para 35
4.11.8	Where the company is a member of a group, does it take account when accounting for deferred tax of any group relief that may be available to it and any charge that may be made for that relief and are these assumptions stated?	SSAP 15 para 43
4.11.9	Are adjustments to the deferred taxation account that result from a change in the rate of taxation separately disclosed as part of the taxation charge for the year?	SSAP 15 para 36
	Note: This will be so unless the change in rate is associated with a fundamental change in the basis of taxation, or with a significant change in government fiscal policy, when the adjustment should be treated as an extraordinary item.	
4.11.10	Is deferred tax in respect of the remittance of overseas earnings accounted for in accordance with the provisions noted above?	SSAP 15 para 44
4.11.11	If the answer to 4.11.10 is no, is there a statement that deferred tax is not provided on earnings retained overseas?	SSAP 15 para 44
4.11.12	Are any special circumstances that affect the liability in respect of taxation of profits, income or capital gains either for the year or for succeeding years (for example, tax losses utilised or carried forward) disclosed?	4 Sch 54(2)

4.12 Dividends

4.12.1 Is the aggregate amount disclosed of any dividends paid or proposed? — 4 Sch 3(7)(b)

4.12.2 Do these dividends exclude the related ACT or the attributable tax credit? — SSAP 8 para 24

> Notes:
> (a) A company cannot pay a dividend unless it has profits available for the purpose. — Sec 263(1)
> (b) Profits available for the purpose are accumulated realised profits less accumulated realised losses, less (in the case of a public company) accumulated net unrealised losses. (Such profits and losses may be either revenue or capital in origin.) — Sec 263(3) 264(1) 280(3)
> (c) The Act does not define 'realised' and 'unrealised' but it does give some guidance in specific cases. (See Sec 263(5), 269, 276.)

4.12.3 If the company is listed, or it is traded on the USM, are particulars of any arrangement under which a shareholder has waived, or agreed to waive, any dividends (including future dividends) disclosed? — CO 21(o) GU 10(l)

4.13 Exceptional and extraordinary items

4.13.1 Does the profit and loss account show separately and in the following order: — SSAP 6 para 34

(a) The profit or loss on ordinary activities?
(b) The extraordinary profit or loss recognised in the financial statements for the year?
(c) The profit or loss for the financial year?
(d) Dividends proposed or paid?

4.13.2 Are the nature and size of material amounts charged or credited that relate to any preceding year (for example, the normal recurring corrections and adjustments of accounting estimates made in prior years) disclosed? — 4 Sch 57(1) SSAP 6 para 16

4.13.3 Are material items of an abnormal size or incidence that are derived from the ordinary activities of the business (that is exceptional items) included in arriving at the profit or loss on ordinary activities? — 4 Sch 57(3) SSAP 6 para 29, 36

4.13.4 Are exceptional items described as such and shown (with an adequate explanation) either in a note to the financial statements or separately on the face of the profit and loss account (where this is necessary for the financial statements to give a true and fair view)? — 4 Sch 57(3) SSAP 6 para 36

4.13.5 Do extraordinary items comprise only those items that derive from events or transactions outside the ordinary activities of the business and that are both material and expected not to recur frequently or regularly? — SSAP 6 para 30

> Note: Material profits or losses on disposal of fixed assets should be treated as exceptional or extraordinary according to the nature of the event which gave rise to the disposal. — SSAP 6 para 15

4.13.6 Is the amount of each extraordinary item shown individually either on the face of the profit or loss account or in the notes? — SSAP 6 para 37

4.13.7	Is there an adequate description given of each extraordinary item to enable its nature to be understood?	4 Sch 57(2) SSAP 6 para 37
4.13.8	Is the tax on extraordinary items disclosed?	SSAP 6 para 37
4.13.9	Is the tax shown as attributable to extraordinary items the difference between the tax on the profit or loss on ordinary activities as if the extraordinary items did not exist, and the tax charge on the profit or loss for the financial year after extraordinary items?	SSAP 6 para 38 SSAP 15 para 34
4.13.10	If there is a change in the basis of taxation or a significant change in Government fiscal policy are any significant deferred tax adjustments that arise because of that change shown as extraordinary items?	SSAP 6 para 10
4.13.11	Where the investing company does not prepare consolidated financial statements and is not a wholly-owned subsidiary, is its share of the aggregate extraordinary items of associated companies included with other extraordinary items in a separate profit and loss account or additional note disclosure?	SSAP 1 para 21,24
4.13.12	Where material, is the amount included in 4.13.11 separately disclosed?	SSAP 1 para 21

Note: See steps 5.6.6 to 5.6.21

4.13.13	Where there has been a significant change in the normal level of pension contributions to eliminate a deficiency or surplus resulting from a reduction in the number of employees due to an extraordinary event (for example, closure of a business segment), has the resulting charge or credit been included in extraordinary items?	SSAP 24 para 81

Notes: See also steps 4.8 and 5.10.25 to 5.10.33.

4.13.14	Are the following disclosed in respect of each material disposal of a business or business segment: (a) The profit or loss on disposal? (b) The amount of purchase goodwill attributable to the business or business segment disposed of and how it has been treated in determining the profit or loss on disposal? (c) The accounting treatment adopted and the amount of the proceeds in situations where no profit or loss is recorded on a disposal because the proceeds have been accounted for as a reduction in the cost of acquisition?	SSAP 22 para 52

Note: The provisions in 4.13.14 should apply to all disposals where the relevant information is obtained and in all cases where disposals relate to acquisitions made after 1st January 1989. Where in relation to acquisitions made prior to that date, it is impossible or impracticable to ascertain the attributable goodwill on disposal, this should be stated and the reasons given. SSAP 22 para 53

4.14 Prior year adjustments

4.14.1 Do prior year adjustments comprise only those material adjustments applicable to prior years that arise from changes in accounting policies or from the correction of fundamental errors? SSAP 6 para 31

4.14.2 Are prior year adjustments (less attributable taxation) accounted for by restating prior years with the result that the opening balance of retained profits is adjusted accordingly? SSAP 6 para 39

4.14.3 Is the effect of the change on the results of the preceding year disclosed, where practicable? SSAP 6 para 39

4.15 Reserves

4.15.1 Are transfers to or from reserves disclosed? 4 Sch 3(7)(a)

4.15.2 Where the statement of movement on all reserves does not immediately follow the profit and loss account, is there a reference on the face of the profit and loss account to where this statement can be found? SSAP 6 paras 25, 35

4.15.3 Are all profits and losses included in the profit and loss account unless they are specifically permitted, or required by either an accounting standard or the law to be taken directly to reserves? SSAP 6 para 3

4.16 Earnings per share

Notes:
(a) SSAP 3 applies only to listed companies. Companies traded on the USM are now required also to disclose their earnings per share. SSAP 3 para 13
(b) Appendix 1 to SSAP 3 contains detailed guidance on how to calculate earnings per share in certain circumstances.

4.16.1 Are earnings per share shown on the face of the profit and loss account on the net basis? SSAP 3 para 14

Note: The net basis is after charging against profit any irrecoverable ACT or unrelieved overseas tax arising as a result of dividends paid or proposed.

4.16.2 Where materially different, are earnings per share shown also on the nil distribution basis? SSAP 3 paras 9, 14

4.16.3 Is the basis of calculating earnings per share disclosed? (In particular, the amount of the earnings and the number of equity shares used in the calculation.) SSAP 3 para 15

4.16.4 Where a company has, at the balance sheet date, contracted to issue further shares after the end of the year, or where it has already issued shares that do not rank for dividend until future years, and the effect will be to dilute basic earnings per share by 5 per cent or more, are fully diluted earnings per share also shown on the face of the profit and loss account, and is the basis of their calculation disclosed? SSAP 3 para 16

4.16.5 Is equal prominence given to basic and fully diluted earnings per share? SSAP 3 para 16

Notes:
(a) A company has "contracted to issue further shares after the end of the year" where it has issued debentures, loan stock or preference shares that are convertible into equity shares or where it has granted options or it has issued warrants to subscribe for equity shares or where it has agreed to issue shares as deferred consideration. SSAP 3 para 16
(b) The corresponding amount for fully diluted earnings per share is required only if the assumptions on which the amount was based still apply. SSAP 3 para 16

4.17 Foreign currency translation

4.17.1 Have foreign currency transactions completed during the year been translated at one of the following rates: SSAP 20 para 46

(a) If the transaction is to be settled at a contracted rate, that rate?
(b) At the rate ruling on the date the transaction occurred?

Note:
(a) If rates do not fluctuate significantly, an average rate for the period may be used instead of the rate ruling on the date the transaction occurred.
(b) A trading transaction that is covered by a related or matching forward contract may be translated either at the rate specified in the contract or at the rate ruling on the date the transaction occurred. (A company should, however, apply consistently the policy it adopts in respect of such trading transactions).

4.17.2 Have exchange gains and losses on foreign currency transactions completed in the year and on foreign currency monetary assets and liabilities outstanding at the balance sheet date been reported as part of the profit or loss for the year from ordinary activities? SSAP 20 para 49

Note: Exchange gains and losses that result from transactions that themselves fall to be treated as extraordinary items should be included as part of such items.

4.17.3 If the profit and loss account includes unrealised gains on long-term monetary items outstanding at the balance sheet date, are particulars of, the reasons for, and the effect of, the departure from the valuation principles of the Act given? 4 Sch 15

4.17.4 Have net amounts of exchange gains or losses on foreign currency borrowings less deposits been stated, identifying separately: SSAP 20 para 60

(a) Amounts offset in reserves?

(b) The net amount charged/credited to the profit and loss account?

5. BALANCE SHEET AND RELATED NOTES

5.1 Assets - general rules

Determining purchase price or production cost

5.1.1	Does the purchase price of an asset comprise the actual price paid together with any expenses incidental to its acquisition?	4 Sch 26(1) SSAP 9 para 18
5.1.2	Does the production cost of an asset comprise the purchase price of raw materials and consumables used, together with the amount of costs incurred that are directly attributable to the production of that asset?	4 Sch 26(2) SSAP 9 paras 17,19, 20
5.1.3	Where the production cost of an asset includes a reasonable proportion of costs incurred that are only indirectly attributable to the production of that asset, are these included only to the extent that they relate to the period of production?	4 Sch 26(3)

Capitalisation of interest

5.1.4	Where the production cost of an asset includes interest on capital borrowed to finance the production of that asset, is the fact that interest is included, and the amount of interest included, disclosed?	4 Sch 26(3)
5.1.5	If the company is listed, or if it is traded on the USM, is the amount of interest capitalised during the year, and an indication of the amount and treatment of any related tax relief, disclosed?	CO 21(g) GU 10(g)

Alternative accounting rules

5.1.6 Where any of the alternative accounting rules have been adopted, are the following disclosed: — 4 Sch 33

(a) The items affected and the basis of valuation adopted?

(b) In respect of each balance sheet item affected (except stocks) one of the following:

(i) The aggregate cost and aggregate accumulated depreciation on an historical cost basis?

(ii) The difference between the aggregate cost and aggregate accumulated depreciation as stated and what they would have been on an historical cost basis?

5.1.7 Where any of the alternative accounting rules have been adopted, has the profit or loss on revaluation been transferred to the revaluation reserve? — 4 Sch 34(1) SSAP 6 para 22

Note: The revaluation reserve may be shown under another name.	4 Sch 34(2)

Assets included at fixed amount

5.1.8 Are assets under the items 'Tangible fixed assets' and 'Raw materials and consumables' which are constantly being replaced included at a fixed quantity and value only if both their overall value is not material to assessing the state of affairs and their quantity, value and composition are not subject to material variation? 4 Sch 25

Foreign currency translation

5.1.9 Have foreign currency transactions completed during the year been translated at one of the following rates: SSAP 20 para 46

(a) If the transaction is to be settled at a contracted rate, that rate?
(b) At the rate ruling on the date the transaction occurred?

> Notes:
> (a) If rates do not fluctuate significantly, an average rate for the period may be used instead of the rate ruling on the date the transaction occurred.
> (b) A trading transaction that is covered by a related or matching forward contract may be translated either at the rate specified in the contract or at the rate ruling on the date the transaction occurred. (A company should, however, apply consistently the policy it adopts in respect of such trading transactions.)

Other general rules

5.1.10 Where the amount repayable on any debt owed by a company is greater than the value of the consideration received, and the difference is treated as an asset: 4 Sch 24
(a) Is the difference being written off by reasonable amounts each year so that it will be completely written off before the debt is repaid?

(b) Is the amount of the difference at the year end separately disclosed?

5.1.11 Does the cost of an asset include any irrecoverable VAT on that asset? SSAP 5 para 9

5.1.12 Where there is no record of the purchase price or production cost of an asset (or such record can be obtained only with unreasonable expense or delay), is the asset included at its earliest known value? 4 Sch 28

5.1.13 Where the purchase price or production cost is determined by using 'the earliest known value' for the first time, are particulars given? 4 Sch 51(1)

5.2 Fixed assets

Cost and valuation

5.2.1 Unless any of the alternative accounting rules are adopted, are fixed assets included at purchase price or production cost less any provision for depreciation or diminution in value? 4 Sch 16, 17

5.2.2 Where any of the alternative accounting rules are adopted, have fixed assets been valued on the following bases:

	(a) Intangible fixed assets (except goodwill) at their current cost?	4 Sch 31(1)
	(b) Tangible fixed assets either at market value as at the date of their last valuation or at their current cost?	4 Sch 31(2)
	(c) Fixed asset investments either at market value as at the date of their last valuation or at a value determined on any basis that the directors consider is appropriate in the circumstances?	4 Sch 31(3)
5.2.3	Where the basis applied in 5.2.2(c) is other than market value, are particulars of the method adopted and the reasons for adopting it disclosed?	4 Sch 31(3)
5.2.4	Where any fixed assets (other than listed investments) are included at a valuation, are the following disclosed:	
	(a) The years (so far as they are known to the directors) in which the assets were valued?	4 Sch 43
	(b) The respective values?	4 Sch 43
	(c) In the case of assets valued during the year:	4 Sch 43
	(i) Either the names or qualifications of the valuers? (ii) The bases of valuation used?	SSAP 19 para 12
	Depreciation	
5.2.5	Where any fixed asset has a limited useful economic life, is the purchase price or production cost or valuation, less the estimated residual value, written off systematically over that life?	4 Sch 18, 32(1) SSAP 12 para 15, 22 SSAP 13 para 25

Notes:	
(a) The useful economic life of an asset is the period over which the present owner will derive economic benefit from its use.	SSAP 12 para 11
(b) Leasehold investment properties should be depreciated at least over the period when the unexpired term of the lease is 20 years or less. Other investment properties should not be depreciated. (Steps 5.4.5 to 5.4.11 cover investment properties)	SSAP 12 para 14 SSAP 19 para 10

5.2.6	Are the depreciation methods used the ones that are the most appropriate having regard to the types of asset and their use in the business?	SSAP 12 para 15
5.2.7	If there is a change from one method of providing depreciation to another, does the new method give a fairer presentation of the results and of the financial position?	SSAP 12 para 21
5.2.8	Where the method of providing depreciation has changed, has the net book amount been written off over the remaining useful economic life, commencing with the period in which the change is made?	SSAP 12 para 21
5.2.9	In the year a method is changed, is the effect and the reason for the change disclosed, where it is material?	SSAP 12 para 26
5.2.10	Are the useful economic lives of assets reviewed regularly?	SSAP 12 para 18

5.2.11 Are identical asset lives used for the calculation of depreciation both on an historical cost basis and on any bases that reflect the effects of changing prices? SSAP 12 para 17

5.2.12 Where the estimated useful economic life of an asset is revised, and to charge the unamortised cost/valuation over the revised remaining useful life would materially distort future results, is: SSAP 12 para 18

(a) The adjustment to the accumulated depreciation dealt with as an exceptional item in arriving at the profit on ordinary activities?

(b) The nature and amount of the adjustment disclosed?

5.2.13 If there has been a diminution in value of any fixed asset and this diminution is expected to be permanent, has: 4 Sch 19(2)
(a) Provision been made and disclosed? SSAP 12 para 19

(b) The remaining balance then been written off over the remaining useful economic life of the asset? SSAP 13 para 29

5.2.14 Where the reasons for any provision for a diminution in value of a fixed asset cease to exist to any extent, has the provision been written back to that extent and disclosed? 4 Sch 19(3) SSAP 12 para 19

5.2.15 Where an asset is revalued, is the depreciation charge prior to the revaluation only written back to the profit and loss account to the extent that it relates to a provision for permanent diminution in value (see 5.2.13) which is subsequently found to be unnecessary? SSAP 12 para 22

5.2.16 In the year that assets are revalued, is the effect on the depreciation charge disclosed, if material? SSAP 12 para 27

Government grants

5.2.17 Are grants relating to fixed assets credited to revenue over the expected useful life of the asset by one of the following methods: SSAP 4 para 9

(a) Reducing the cost of the asset by the amount of the grant?

(b) Treating the grant as a deferred credit and making annual transfers to revenue?

5.2.18 If method in 5.2.17(b) is adopted, is the amount of the deferred credit shown separately in the balance sheet (under the heading 'Accruals and deferred income')?

Movements

5.2.19 In respect of the cost/valuation of fixed assets under any heading, are the following disclosed: 4 Sch 42(1)(2)

(a) The aggregate cost/valuation of fixed assets at the beginning of the year? SSAP 13 para 32

(b) Any revisions to the amount in respect of a valuation during the year?

(c) Acquisitions during the year?

(d) Disposals during the year?

(e) Any reclassification of assets to, or from, that heading during the year?

(f) The aggregate cost/valuation at the end of the year? SSAP 12 para 25

Note: Corresponding amounts are not required.	4 Sch 58(3)

5.2.20 In respect of provisions for depreciation or diminution in value of fixed assets under any heading, are the following disclosed: 4 Sch 42(3) SSAP 13 para 27

(a) The cumulative provisions at the beginning of the year?

(b) Any such provisions made during the year?

(c) Any adjustments made as a result of disposals of assets during the year?

(d) Any other adjustments made during the year?

(e) The cumulative provisions at the end of the year? SSAP 12 para 25

Note: Corresponding amounts are not required.	4 Sch 58(3)

5.3 Intangible fixed assets

Development costs

5.3.1 Are development costs capitalised only where all of the following conditions apply: 4 Sch 20(1) SSAP 13 para 25

(a) There is a clearly defined project?

(b) The related expenditure is separately identifiable?

(c) The outcome of the project has been assessed with reasonable certainty as to both its technical feasibility and its ultimate commercial viability?

(d) All costs (including future costs to be incurred) are reasonably expected to be more than covered by related future revenues?

(e) Adequate resources exist, or are reasonably expected to be available, to enable the project to be completed, and to provide any consequential increases in working capital?

5.3.2 Are development costs capitalised only to the extent that their recovery can reasonably be regarded as assured? SSAP 13 para 26

5.3.3 In respect of capitalised development costs, are the following disclosed? 4 Sch 20(2)

(a) The period over which the costs are being, or are to be, written off?

(b) The reasons for capitalising the costs?

(c) Where appropriate, a statement that the directors have decided not to treat unamortised development costs as a realised loss when calculating distributable profits, and the special circumstances that justify their decision? — Sec 269(2)(b)

Research and development facilities

5.3.4 Is the cost of fixed assets acquired or constructed to provide facilities for research and development activities over a number of years capitalised and written off over the useful life of those assets? — SSAP 13 para 23

Concessions, patents, etc.

5.3.5 Are amounts in respect of concessions, patents, licences, trade marks and similar rights and assets included in the balance sheet only if one of the following applies: — 4 Sch Format Note 2

(a) The assets were acquired for valuable consideration and do not represent goodwill?

(b) The assets were created by the company?

Goodwill

5.3.6 Is goodwill capitalised only to the extent that it was acquired for valuable consideration? — 4 Sch Format Note 3

5.3.7 Where the company has recognised amounts of goodwill as a result of acquisitions during the year, do the financial statements disclose separately, where material, the goodwill arising from each acquisition? — SSAP 22 para 44

5.3.8 Where the company amortises purchased goodwill, does the company show purchased goodwill as a separate item under intangible fixed assets in the balance sheet until the company has fully written off the purchased goodwill? — 4 Sch Format SSAP 22 para 45

> Note: 4 Sch 3(4) permits a company to combine goodwill with another intangible asset sub-heading in either of the two following circumstances:
> (a) Where the individual amounts combined are not material to an assessment of the state of affairs of the company.
> (b) Where the combination facilitates the assessment of the state of affairs of the company. (A note to the financial statements must disclose the individual amounts of any items combined in this way.)
> SSAP 22 does not specifically permit a company to combine goodwill with another item in either of these two circumstances. However, the preliminary paragraph of SSAP 22 says that a company need not apply the Standard to immaterial items.

5.3.9 Where the company amortises purchased goodwill, does the company disclose the movement on the goodwill account during the year? Does this disclosure including the following: — 4 Sch 42 SSAP 22 para 45(a)

(a) The cost of goodwill at the beginning and at the end of the year?
(b) The accumulated amortisation at the beginning and at the end of the year?
(c) The net book value of goodwill at the beginning and at the end of the year?

(d) The amount of goodwill that the company has amortised through the profit and loss account during the year?

5.3.10 Where the company amortises purchased goodwill, does the company disclose the period it has selected for amortising the goodwill that relates to each major acquisition? 4 Sch 21(4) SSAP 22 para 45(b)

5.3.11 Where the company amortises goodwill, does the company disclose the reasons for choosing the period it has selected for amortising the goodwill? 4 Sch 21(4)

5.3.12 Where a company's accounting treatment of goodwill that existed at the time the Standard came into effect differs from the policy it has followed in respect of all other goodwill, does the company disclose the following: SSAP 22 para 46

(a) The accounting treatment of goodwill that existed at the time the Standard came into effect?

(b) The amounts involved?

> Note: The disclosures in 5.3.13 to 5.3.18 apply separately for each material acquisition and in aggregate for other acquisitions that are material in total.

5.3.13 Where an acquisition has taken place during the period, is the fair value of the consideration and the amount of purchased goodwill separately disclosed? SSAP 22 para 47

> Note: The disclosure should identify the method of dealing with goodwill arising and whether it has been set off against the merger reserve or other reserves or has been carried forward as an intangible asset.

5.3.14 Where an acquisition has taken place during the period, do the financial statements contain a table showing the book values, originally carried by the acquired company, and the fair values of each major category of assets and liabilities acquired? SSAP 22 para 48

> Note: The reasons for the adjustments to fair values should be explained and analysed between: (a) revaluations; (b) provisions for future trading losses; (c) other provisions; (d) bringing accounting policies into line with those of the acquiring company; (e) any other major item.

5.3.15 Where there are provisions in respect of acquisitions, are movements disclosed and analysed between amounts used, released unused or applied for other purposes? SSAP 22 para 49

5.3.16 Where, for an acquisition in the year, the fair value of either the consideration or the assets could be determined only on a provisional basis, has that fact been stated and the reasons given? SSAP 22 para 50

5.3.17 Where there are subsequent material adjustments to provisional fair values (and where goodwill has also been adjusted), have those adjustments been disclosed and explained? SSAP 22 para 50

5.3.18 In respect of each material disposal of a previously acquired business or business segment, have each of the following been disclosed: SSAP 22 para 52

(a) The profit or loss on the disposal?

(b) The amount of purchased goodwill attributable to the business or business segment disposed of and how it has been treated in determining the profit or loss on disposal?

(c) The accounting treatment adopted and the amount of the proceeds in situations where no profit or loss is recorded on disposal because the proceeds have been accounted for as a reduction in the cost of the acquisition?

Note: It might be impossible or impracticable to ascertain the attributable goodwill on a disposal of a business or business segment which was acquired before 1 January 1989. If so, the fact and the reasons should be stated.	SSAP 22 para 53

5.4 Tangible fixed assets

Land and buildings

5.4.1	Is the division of the net book amount of land and buildings between freehold, long leases (50 or more years to run) and short leases disclosed?	4 Sch 44, 83
5.4.2	Is freehold land only amortised to the extent that it is subject to depletion by, for example, the extraction of minerals?	SSAP 12 para 23
5.4.3	Are provisions made against the value of freehold land where circumstances adversely affect its value, for example, changes in the desirability of its location?	SSAP 12 para 23
5.4.4	Are buildings depreciated over their useful economic lives?	SSAP 12 para 24

Investment properties

Note: SSAP 19 does not apply to investment properties owned by charities.	SSAP 19 para 9

5.4.5	Are investment properties included in the balance sheet at their open market value?	SSAP 19 para 11
5.4.6	Are investment properties only depreciated where they are held under leases with an unexpired term of 20 years or less?	SSAP 19 para 10
5.4.7	Are changes in the value of investment properties disclosed as a movement on an investment revaluation reserve?	SSAP 19 para 13

Note: Not applicable to the long-term business of insurance companies where changes in value are dealt with in the relevant fund account.	SSAP 19 para 14

5.4.8	If a deficit on revaluation exceeds the balance on the investment revaluation reserve, has the excess been charged in the profit and loss account?	SSAP 19 para 13

> Note: For investment trust companies and property unit trusts it may not be appropriate to deal with deficits in the profit and loss account. In such cases they should be shown prominently elsewhere in the financial statements.

5.4.9 If the persons making the revaluation are employees or officers of the company that owns the property, is this fact disclosed? — SSAP 19 para 12

5.4.10 Are both the carrying value of investment properties and the investment revaluation reserve displayed prominently? — SSAP 19 para 15

5.4.11 Are particulars given of the departure from the specific requirement in the Act to provide depreciation on any fixed asset that has a limited useful economic life together with the reasons for, and the effect of, the departure? — SSAP 19 para 17, Sec 226(5) 227(6)

> Note: The DTI has agreed the text of a note that meets the requirements of section 228 of the Act (see chapter 8 para 8.43 of this book).

5.5 Leases and hire purchase contracts

> Note: Hire purchase contracts that are of a financing nature should be accounted for on a similar basis to finance leases. Other hire purchase contracts should be accounted for on a similar basis to operating leases. — SSAP 21 para 31

Lessees

5.5.1 Are finance leases recorded in the balance sheet as an asset and as an obligation to pay future rentals? At the inception of the lease, are both the asset and the liability recorded at the present value of the minimum lease payments derived by discounting them at the interest rate implicit in the lease? — SSAP 21 para 32

> Notes:
> (a) In practice, the fair value of the asset will often be a sufficiently close approximation to the present value of the minimum lease payments. — SSAP 21 para 33
> (b) Where the minimum lease payments are less than the fair value of the asset because of the benefit to the lessor of regional development and other grants and capital allowances, the amount capitalised should be restricted to the minimum lease payments. — SSAP 21 para 34

5.5.2 Are finance lease rentals payable apportioned between the finance charge and a reduction of the outstanding obligation for future amounts payable? — SSAP 21 para 35

5.5.3 Is the total finance charge allocated to accounting periods during the finance lease term so as to produce a constant periodic rate of charge on the remaining balance of the obligation for each accounting period (or a reasonable approximation thereto)? — SSAP 21 para 35

5.5.4 Is an asset leased under a finance lease depreciated over the shorter of the lease term and its useful life? — SSAP 21 para 36

Note: The lease term includes the optional secondary rental period where it is reasonable to assume that the lessee will exercise the option.	SSAP 21 para 19

5.5.5 Is an asset under a hire purchase contract, which has the characteristics of a finance lease, depreciated over its useful life? — SSAP 21 para 36

5.5.6 Is the rental under operating leases charged on a straight-line basis over the lease term, unless another systematic and rational basis is more appropriate? — SSAP 21 para 37

5.5.7 Are the gross amount of assets held under finance leases and the related accumulated depreciation disclosed by each major class of asset? — SSAP 21 para 49

5.5.8 If the answer to 5.5.7 is no because the amounts are integrated with owned fixed assets, is the net amount of assets held under finance leases disclosed? — SSAP 21 para 50

5.5.9 Is the total depreciation allocated for the period in respect of assets held under finance leases disclosed by each major class of asset? — SSAP 21 para 49

5.5.10 If the answer to 5.5.8 is no because the amounts are integrated with owned fixed assets, is the total depreciation allocated for the period in respect of assets held under finance leases disclosed? — SSAP 21 para 50

Note: See also steps 3(f), 4.7.8 and 4.7.9, 5.10.22 to 5.10.24, and 5.12.3 to 5.12.5.

Sale and leaseback transactions - lessees

5.5.11 Where the sale and leaseback transaction results in the seller/lessee entering into a finance lease, is any apparent profit or loss deferred and amortised over the shorter of the lease term and the useful life of the asset? — SSAP 21 para 46

5.5.12 Where the sale and leaseback transaction results in the seller/lessee entering into an operating lease: — SSAP 21 para 47

(a) If the sale price is at a fair value, is any profit or loss recognised immediately?

(b) If the sale price is below fair value but any future rentals are set at market rates, is any profit or loss recognised immediately?

(c) If the sale price in 5.5.12(b) is below fair value, and the future rentals are below market price, is any loss arising deferred to the extent that it represents a reduction of future rentals and amortised over the shorter of the remainder of the lease term and the period during which rentals are chargeable?

(d) If the sale price is above fair value, is the excess deferred and amortised over the shorter of the remainder of the lease term and the period to the next rent review?

Lessors

Note: Steps 5.5.13 to 5.5.21 apply equally to sale and leaseback transactions	SSAP 21 para 48

5.5.13 Is the amount due from the lessee under a finance lease recorded in the balance sheet as a debtor at the amount of the net investment in the lease after making provisions for such items as bad and doubtful rentals receivable? SSAP 21 para 38

5.5.14 Have the total gross earnings for finance leases been allocated to accounting periods to give a constant periodic rate of return on the lessor's net cash investment in the lease in each period? SSAP 21 para 39

5.5.15 As an alternative to 5.5.14, has an allocation first been made out of gross earnings of an amount equal to the lessor's estimated cost of finance included in the net cash investment calculation, with the balance being recognised on a systematic basis? SSAP 21 para 40

> Notes:
> (a) In the case of a hire purchase contract, allocation of gross earnings so as to give a constant periodic rate of return on the finance company's net investments will in most cases be a suitable approximation to an allocation based on the net cash investment in the lease. SSAP 21 para 39
> (b) In arriving at the constant periodic rate of return a reasonable approximation may be made. SSAP 21 para 39

5.5.16 Have tax free grants available to the lessor against the purchase price of assets acquired for finance leasing been spread over the period of the lease? SSAP 21 para 41

5.5.17 Has the income in each period resulting from the spreading of such grants been dealt with in one of the following ways: SSAP 21 para 41

(a) By treating it as non-taxable income?

(b) By grossing up the grant and including the grossed-up amount in arriving at the profit before tax?

(c) If 5.5.17(b) has been adopted, is the amount by which the profit before tax and the tax charge have been increased, as a result of grossing-up the grant, been disclosed?

> Notes:
> (a) In the case of a finance lease, the tax free grants should effectively be spread on a constant rate of return basis.
> (b) In the case of an operating lease, the tax free grants should be spread on a straight-line basis.

5.5.18 Are assets held for use as operating leases recorded as fixed assets and depreciated over their useful lives? SSAP 21 para 42

5.5.19 Is rental income (excluding charges for services such as insurance and maintenance) recognised for operating leases on a straight-line basis over the period of the lease (even if the payments are not made on such a basis), unless another systematic and rational basis is more representative of the time pattern in which the benefit from the leased asset is receivable? SSAP 21 para 42

> Note: Initial direct costs incurred by a lessor in arranging a lease may be apportioned over the period of the lease on a systematic and rational basis. SSAP 21 para 44

5.5.20 In respect of assets held for use in operating leases, are the following disclosed: SSAP 21 para 59

(a) The gross amount?
(b) The accumulated depreciation charge?

5.5.21 For a manufacturer or dealer lessor, is the selling profit under a finance lease restricted to the excess of the fair value of the asset over the manufacturer's or dealer lessor's cost less any grants receivable by the manufacturer or dealer towards the purchase, construction or use of the asset? SSAP 21 para 45

> Note: A manufacturer or dealer lessor should not recognise a selling profit under an operating lease.

5.6 Investments

Fixed asset investments and current asset investments

5.6.1 In respect of investments under any heading, are the following disclosed: 4 Sch 45, 84

(a) The amount that is attributable to investments listed on a recognised stock exchange?

(b) The amount of other listed investments?

(c) The total amount of all listed investments?

(d) The aggregate market value of listed investments (unless the investments are included in the balance sheet at market value)?

(e) Both the market value and the stock exchange value of listed investments where the market value is higher?

> Notes:
> (a) In step 5.6.1(a) the only 'recognised stock exchange' in Great Britain is The International Stock Exchange.
> (b) In step 5.6.1(e) the market value of listed investments may be higher than their stock exchange quoted value, for example, where the investor owns a substantial or controlling interest which is expected to command a premium over the price available for small parcels of shares.

5.6.2 If the company is holding any of its own shares, is the nominal value of those shares disclosed? 4 Sch Format Note 4

Significant shareholdings (excluding subsidiaries and associated undertakings)

5.6.3 For shareholdings in an undertaking at the balance sheet date where: 5 Sch 7, 23, 26

(i) The investing company's or group's holding exceeds 10 per cent of the nominal value of any class of shares in the undertaking.

(ii) The aggregate amount of the shareholding in that undertaking exceeds 10 per cent of the total assets as stated in the investing company's or the group's balance sheet, are the following disclosed:

(a) The name of the undertaking? 5 Sch 8(1), 24(1), 27(1)

(b) Its country of incorporation, if outside Great Britain? 5 Sch 8(2)(a), 24(2)(a), 27(2)(a)

(c) Its country of registration (England and Wales or Scotland) if incorporated in Great Britain? 5 Sch 8(2)(b), 24(2)(b), 27(2)(b)

(d) If unincorporated, the address of its principal place of business? 5 Sch 8(2)(c), 24(2)(c), 27(2)(c)

(e) The identity of, and the proportion of, the nominal value of the allotted shares of each class (whether equity or not) held? 5 Sch 8(3), 24(4), 27(4)

Notes:
(a) The information required by 5.6.3 need not be given in respect of an undertaking which is established under the law of a country outside the UK, or which carries on business outside the UK, if in the directors' opinion such disclosure would be seriously prejudicial to the business of the undertaking, or to the business of the parent or any of its subsidiaries, and the Secretary of State agrees that the information need not be disclosed. Where advantage is taken of this exemption, it should be stated in the notes to the financial statements. Sec 231(3)(4)
(b) Where disclosure of the information required by 5.6.3 would lead in the directors' opinion to disclosure of excessive length, the information need only be given in respect of the undertakings whose results or financial position, in the directors' opinion, principally affect the figures shown in the company's financial statements. Where advantage is taken of this provision, the notes to the company's financial statements should state that the information is only given for those undertakings that in the directors' opinion principally affect the figures shown in the financial statements. Furthermore, the full information including that given in the financial statements must be annexed to the next annual return. Sec 231(5)(6)
(c) Corresponding amounts are not required. 4 Sch 58(3)

5.6.4 For shareholdings in an undertaking at the balance sheet date where the investing company's or group's holding exceeds in nominal value 20 per cent of the nominal value of the shares of that undertaking, are the following disclosed (if material): 5 Sch 9(1)(4), 23(1), 25(1)(3), 26(1), 28(1)(3)

(a) The aggregate amount of the capital and reserves of that undertaking as at the end of its financial year ending with, or last before, the financial year of the investing company? 5 Sch 9(1)(a)(5), 25(1)(a)(4) 28(1)(a)(4)

(b) The profit or loss of that undertaking for its financial year ending with, or last before, the financial year of the investing company? 5 Sch 9(1)(b)(5), 25(1)(b)(4) 28(1)(b)(4)

Notes:
(a) The information in 5.6.4 is not required if the company is exempt from preparing group accounts because it is itself a subsidiary included in the accounts of a larger group and the investment is included in, or in a note to, the investing company's financial statements by way of the equity method of valuation. 5 Sch 9(2),
(b) The information in 5.6.4 is not required if it is immaterial. 5 Sch 9(4), 25(3), 28(3)
(c) An undertaking need not disclose the information required by 5.6.4 if the undertaking is not required to deliver a copy of its balance sheet for its relevant financial year and does not publish that balance sheet in Great Britain or elsewhere and the company's holding is less than 50 per cent of the nominal value of the shares in the undertaking. 5 Sch 9(3), 25(2), 28(2)
(d) The information required by 5.6.4 need not be given in respect of an undertaking which is established under the law of a country outside the UK, or which carries on business outside the UK, if in the directors' opinion such disclosure would be seriously prejudicial to the business of the undertaking, or to the business of the parent or any of its subsidiaries, and the Secretary of State agrees that the information need not be disclosed. Where advantage is taken of this exemption, it should be stated in the notes to the financial statements. Sec 231(3)(4)
(e) Where disclosure of the information required by 5.6.4 would lead in the directors' opinion to disclosure of excessive length, the information need only be given in respect of the undertakings whose results or financial position, in the directors' opinion, principally affect the figures shown in the company's financial statements. Where advantage is taken of this provision, the notes to the company's financial statements should state that the information is only given for those subsidiaries that in the directors' opinion principally affect the figures shown in the financial statements. Furthermore, the full information including that given in the financial statements must be annexed to the next annual return. Sec 231(5)(6)

5.6.5 If the company is listed, or if it is traded on the USM, and the group has an interest of 20 per cent or more in the equity capital of another company (not being a subsidiary), are the following disclosed in respect of each such company. CO 21(e) GU 10(e)

(a) The principal country of operation?

(b) Particulars of its issued share and debt securities?

(c) The percentage of each class of debt securities attributable to the company's interest (direct or indirect)?

(d) The total amount of its reserves if the company is traded on the USM?

Notes:
(a) If the number of such holdings is large, particulars in respect of those of less importance may be omitted if the company is listed.
(b) 'Debt securities' means debenture or loan stock, debentures, bonds and notes whether secured or unsecured. Yellow book definitions

Associated companies

> Note: Steps 5.6.6 to 5.6.21 below relate to the treatment of associated companies in the financial statements of a company that is not a member of a group and therefore has to deal with the associate in its individual financial statements, or where the company is not a wholly-owned subsidiary and does not prepare consolidated financial statements. For undertakings that are members of a group that are required to prepare consolidated financial statements, the provisions that apply to consolidating associated undertakings on an equity basis are dealt with in section 7.13 of Part II of the checklist included in 'Manual of Accounting - volume II'.

5.6.6 Where the interest of the investing company is not effectively that of a partner in a joint venture or consortium and it amounts to 20 per cent or more of the equity voting rights but it is not treated as an associated company, are the accounting treatment adopted and the reasons for adopting this treatment stated? SSAP 1 para 38

> Note: The Standard specifies that "in those cases where disclosure of the reason would be harmful to the business, the directors may omit the information, after consultation with their auditors".

5.6.7 Where the interest of the investing company amounts to less than 20 per cent of the equity voting rights but the interest is treated as an associated company, is the basis on which significant influence is exercised stated? SSAP 1 para 38

5.6.8 In respect of each of the principal associated companies, are the following disclosed: SSAP 1 para 49

(a) Its name?
(b) The proportion of its issued shares of each class held by the investing group?
(c) An indication of the nature of its business?

5.6.9 Is the interest in associated companies shown in the investing company's own balance sheet either at a valuation or at cost less amounts written off? SSAP 1 para 25

5.6.10 Does the company prepare a separate proforma balance sheet, or give equivalent additional note information, which discloses the following: SSAP 1 para 35, 26

(a) Its share of the net assets other than goodwill of the associated companies stated, where possible, after attributing fair values to the net assets at the time each interest was acquired?

(b) Its share of any goodwill in the associated companies' own financial statements?

(c) The premium paid, or discount, on the acquisition of the interest (to the extent that it has not been written off)?

> Note: Item (a) must be disclosed separately, but items (b) and (c) may be combined.

5.6.11 Where there has been a permanent impairment in the value of items (b) and (c) in step 5.6.10, have they been written down and is the amount written off in the period separately disclosed? SSAP 1 para 32

5.6.12 Where an associated company has a deficiency of net assets but is still regarded as a long-term investment and is supported in some way by its shareholders, is the investing company's share of the deficiency of net assets reflected in the proforma balance sheet? SSAP 1 para 33

5.6.13 Where an investment is made in an unincorporated entity and a liability could arise in excess of that resulting from taking account only of the investing company's share of net assets (for example, as a result of joint and several liability in a partnership), has the investing company considered whether it would be prudent either to include an additional provision or to recognise a contingent liability for this excess in its own financial statements? SSAP 1 para 34

5.6.14 If the interests in associated companies are very material in the context of the company, is more detailed information given about the associated companies' tangible assets, intangible assets and liabilities? SSAP 1 para 30

> Note: When judging materiality, regard should also be had to the scale of the associated company's operations in relation to those of the investing company.

5.6.15 Do the associated companies prepare their financial statements either to the same date as, or to a date that is not more than six months before, or shortly after, the date of the investing company's financial statements? SSAP 1 para 36

5.6.16 If financial statements of associated companies used are not coterminous with those of the investing company and the effect is material, are the facts and the dates of the year ends disclosed? SSAP 1 para 37

5.6.17 If the investing company has used financial statements already issued by the associated company, has it ensured that later information has not materially affected the view shown by those financial statements? SSAP 1 para 37

> Note: If the associated company is listed on a recognised stock exchange, only published financial information should be disclosed. SSAP 1 para 36

5.6.18 Where the effect is material, has the investing company made adjustments to the information it discloses to exclude such items as unrealised profits on stocks transferred to or from associated companies and to achieve reasonable consistency with company's accounting policies? SSAP 1 para 39

5.6.19 Where an associated company has subsidiary or associated companies, is the investing company's share of the results and net assets based on the group financial statements of the associated company? SSAP 1 para 42

5.6.20 Has the effective date for both the acquisition and the disposal of an interest, or part interest, in an associated company been taken as the earlier of either the date on which consideration passes or the date on which an offer becomes unconditional? SSAP 1 para 44

5.6.21 Have steps 4.1.3, 4.6.5, 4.9.1 to 4.9.4, 4.11.3, and 4.13.11 been completed?

Investments in subsidiaries

5.6.22 If the company is listed, or if it is traded on the USM, is the name of the principal country in which each subsidiary operates disclosed (this applies also to companies that prepare consolidated financial statements)? CO 21(d) GU 10(d)

5.6.23 Are the aggregate amounts of each of the following disclosed by way of subdivision of the relevant item in the balance sheet or in a note: 4 Sch 59

(a) Amounts owed to or by, and any interest in, any parent undertaking or fellow subsidiary undertaking?
(b) Amounts owed to or by, and any interest in, any subsidiary undertaking?

Note: In consolidated financial statements, 5.6.23(b) applies only to subsidiaries not consolidated. 4A Sch 1(2)

5.6.24 For investing companies that do not prepare consolidated financial statements, are the following disclosed for each subsidiary at the balance sheet date: 5 Sch 1, 2 SSAP 14 para 33

(a) The name of the subsidiary?

(b) Its country of incorporation, if outside Great Britain?

(c) Its country of registration (England and Wales or Scotland) if it is incorporated in Great Britain?

(d) If it is unincorporated, the address of its principal place of business.

(e) If the reason for not preparing consolidated financial statements is that all the subsidiaries fall within the exclusions provided for in section 229 of the Act, are the relevant exclusions stated in respect of each subsidiary?

(f) The identity, and proportion of the nominal value of the shares, of each class held by:

(i) The company and its nominees?
(ii) Subsidiaries and their nominees?

(g) The aggregate amount of the capital and reserves of the subsidiary as at the end of its financial year ending with, or last before, the financial year of the holding company? 5 Sch 3(1a) (5)

(h) The profit or loss of the subsidiary for its financial year ending with, or last before, the financial year of the holding company? 5 Sch 3(1b)

(i) For each principal subsidiary, an indication of the nature of its business? SSAP 14 para 33

Notes:
(a) The information in (g) and (h) is not required if one of the following apples: 5 Sch 3(2) (3)(4)

(i) The company is exempt from preparing group accounts because it is itself a subsidiary included in the accounts of a larger EC group.

(ii) The subsidiary undertaking is not required to deliver a copy of its balance sheet for its relevant financial year and does not publish that balance sheet in Great Britain or elsewhere and the company's holding is less than 50 per cent of the nominal value of the shares in the undertaking.
(iii) It is not material.

(b) The information required by 5.6.24 need not be given in respect of an undertaking which is established under the law of a country outside the UK, or which carries on business outside the UK, if in the directors' opinion such disclosure would be seriously prejudicial to the business of the undertaking, or to the business of the parent of any of its subsidiaries, and the Secretary of State agrees that the information need not be disclosed. Where advantage is taken of this exemption, it should be stated in the note to the financial statements. Sec 231(3) (4)

(c) Where disclosure of the information required by 5.6.24 would lead in the directors' opinion to disclosure of excessive length, the information need only be given in respect of (i) the undertakings whose results or financial position, in the directors' opinion, principally affect the figures shown in the company's financial statements and (ii) undertakings excluded from consolidation. Where advantage is taken of this provision, the notes to the company's financial statements should state that the information is only given for those subsidiaries that in the directors' opinion principally affect the figures shown in the financial statements. Furthermore, the full information including that given in the financial statements must be annexed to the next annual return. Sec 231(5) (6) CO 21(d)

5.6.25 Where the investing company is not required to prepare consolidated financial statements does it disclose the following regarding its subsidiary undertakings: 5 Sch 5(1)

(a) Any qualifications contained in the auditors' report on the financial statements of subsidiary undertakings for financial years ending with or during the financial year of the company?

(b) Any note contained in the subsidiary's financial statements to call attention to a matter which, apart from the note, would properly have been referred to in such a qualification?

Note: It is not necessary to make the disclosure required by 5.6.25 if the matter is covered by the company's own financial statements and is immaterial from the point of view of its members. 5 Sch 5(1)

5.6.26 Where the information required by 5.6.25 is not available, is a statement to that effect given? 5 Sch 5(3)

5.6.27 Where the investing company is not required to prepare consolidated financial statements is the aggregate amount of the total investment of the company in the shares of subsidiary undertakings stated by way of the equity method of valuation unless the following two provisions both apply: 5 Sch 5(2)

(a) The company is exempt from the requirement to prepare consolidated financial statements because its financial statements are included in those of a larger group (that is, section 228).
(b) The directors state their opinion that the aggregate value of the

assets of the company consisting of shares in, or amounts owing (whether on account of a loan or otherwise) from, the company's subsidiary undertakings is not less that the aggregate of the amounts at which those assets are stated or included in the company's balance sheet.

5.6.28 Where the information required by 5.6.27 is not available, is a statement to that effect given? 5 Sch 5(3)

Merger relief

5.6.29 Where the company has entered into an arrangement to which merger relief applies under section 131 of the Act in the current year or in either of the two preceding years, has section 7.7 of Part II of the checklist been completed which is included in 'Manual of Accounting - volume II'?

Details of parents

5.6.30 Where the company is a subsidiary of another has section 7.15 of Part II of the checklist been completed which is included in 'Manual of Accounting - volume II'?

Consolidated financial statements

5.6.31 If the company has subsidiaries, has Part II of the checklist been completed which is included in 'Manual of Accounting - volume II'?

5.7 Current assets

5.7.1 Unless the alternative accounting rules are adopted, is each current asset included at the lower of purchase price (or production cost) and net realisable value? 4 Sch 16, 22, 23(1) SSAP 9 para 26

5.7.2 Does production cost exclude distribution costs? 4 Sch 26(4)

5.7.3 Where the reasons for a provision to reduce purchase price or production cost to net realisable value cease to exist to any extent, has the provision been written back to that extent? 4 Sch 23(2)

5.7.4 If current assets are not included at the lower of purchase price or production cost and net realisable value, then where the alternative accounting rules are adopted, have current assets been valued on the following bases:

(a) Current asset investments at their current cost? 4 Sch 31(4)

(b) Stocks at their current cost ? 4 Sch 31(5)

Stocks and fungible assets

> Note: Fungible assets are assets that are substantially indistinguishable one from another (for example, identical shares in a particular company). 4 Sch 27(6)

5.7.5 Is the purchase price or production cost of stocks and fungible assets determined using FIFO, weighted average price or any other similar method? 4 Sch 27(1) (2)(6) SSAP 9 para 4 Appendix I paras 11-15

5.7.6	Is the method chosen one which appears to the directors to be appropriate in the circumstances of the company?	4 Sch 27(1)
5.7.7	Where the purchase price or production cost of stocks and fungible assets is determined using one of the methods referred to in step 5.7.5 and it is materially different from the replacement cost (or, if more appropriate, the most recent actual purchase price or production cost) of those stocks or fungible assets, is the amount of the difference disclosed for each category?	4 Sch 27(3)(4)(5)
5.7.8	Are stocks sub-classified in the balance sheet or in the notes to the financial statements so as to indicate the amounts held in each of the following categories:	SSAP 9 para 27 4 Sch Formats
	(a) Raw materials and consumables?	
	(b) Work in progress?	
	(c) Finished goods and goods for resale?	
	(d) Payments on account?	
	Long-term contracts	
5.7.9	Are long-term contracts assessed on a contract by contract basis?	SSAP 9 para 28
5.7.10	Are turnover and related costs on long-term contracts reflected in the profit and loss account as the contract activity progresses and is turnover ascertained in a manner appropriate to the stage of completion of the contract, the business and the industry in which it operates?	SSAP 9 para 28
5.7.11	Where it is considered that the outcome of the long-term contract can be assessed with reasonable certainty has attributable profit been added to turnover?	SSAP 9 para 29
	Note: Attributable profit is that part of the profit currently estimated to arise over the duration of the contract, after allowing for estimated remedial and maintenance costs and increases in costs so far as not recoverable under the terms of the contract, that fairly reflects the profit attributable to that part of the work performed at the accounting date.	SSAP 9 para 23
5.7.12	In respect of long-term contracts are the following disclosed:	SSAP 9 para 30
	(a) If recorded turnover exceeds payments on account, the excess classified as 'amounts recoverable on contracts' separately disclosed within debtors?	
	(b) Where payments on account exceed turnover and any balance of costs of the long-term contract, the excess classified as 'payments on account' separately disclosed within creditors?	
	(c) The amount of long-term contracts, at cost incurred, net of amounts transferred to cost of sales, after deducting foreseeable losses and payments on account not matched with turnover classified as 'long-term contract balances' separately disclosed within stocks?	

(d) Long-term contract balances analysed between the following:

(i) Net cost less foreseeable losses?
(ii) Applicable payments on account?

(e) The amount of provision or accrual for foreseeable losses that exceeds costs incurred (after transfers to cost of sales) included within either provisions for liabilities and charges or creditors as appropriate?

> Notes:
> (a) Payments on account include all sums received and receivable at the accounting date in respect of contracts in progress.
> (b) Foreseeable losses are losses that are currently estimated to arise over the duration of the contract (after allowing for estimated remedial and maintenance costs and increases in costs so far as not recoverable under the terms of the contract). This estimate is required irrespective for the following:
> (i) Whether or not work has yet commenced on such contracts.
> (ii) The proportion of work carried out at the accounting date.
> (iii) The amount of profits expected to arise on other contracts.

SSAP 9 para 25 Note (a) para 24 Note (b)

Debtors

5.7.13 For each item included under debtors, is the amount falling due after more than one year separately disclosed? 4 Sch Note 5

5.7.14 Is a lessor's net investment at the balance sheet date in the following disclosed: SSAP 21 para 58

(a) Finance leases?
(b) Hire purchase contracts?

5.7.15 Is the cost of assets acquired by a lessor, whether by purchase or by finance lease, for the purpose of letting under finance leases disclosed? SSAP 21 para 60(c)

> Note: See steps 5.5.13 to 5.5.21

5.7.16 Where pension contributions paid exceed the cumulative pension cost, has the excess been shown as a prepayment? SSAP 24 para 86

> Notes: See also steps 5.10.25 to 5.10.33.

Loans for acquisition of own shares

5.7.17 Is the aggregate amount of any outstanding loans disclosed in respect of financial assistance for acquisition of own shares and authorised by sections 153(4)(b), (bb) or (c) or 155? 4 Sch 51(2)

Foreign currency translation

5.7.18 Have foreign currency transactions completed during the year been translated at one of the following rates: SSAP 20 para 46

(a) If the transaction is to be settled at a contracted rate, that rate?

(b) At the rate ruling on the date the transaction occurred?

Notes:
(a) If rates do not fluctuate significantly, an average rate for the period may be used instead of the rate ruling on the date the transaction occurred.
(b) A trading transaction that is covered by a related or matching forward contract may be translated either at the rate specified in the contract or at the rate ruling on the date the transaction occurred. (A company should, however, apply consistently the policy it adopts in respect of such trading transactions.)

5.7.19 Have foreign currency monetary assets outstanding at the balance sheet date been translated at one of the following rates: SSAP 20 para 48

(a) The rate fixed under the terms of the relevant transaction?
(b) The closing rate?

Note: SSAP 20 para 48
(a) If there is a related or matching forward contract in respect of a trading transaction, translation may be either at the rate specified in the contract or at the closing rate. (A company should, however, apply consistently the policy it adopts in respect of such trading transactions.)
(b) See also steps 3.1(e), 4.17, 5.10.12 to 5.10.16.

5.8 Loans to and transactions with directors

Notes:
Special provisions apply to recognised banks and to money-lending companies and the provisions are not dealt with here (see chapters 21 and 22 of this book).
If loans or other transactions with directors or connected persons have been entered into, or subsisted, during the course of the year, the notes to the financial statements must contain the disclosures set out below in respect of: 6 Sch 15(a), 16(a)
(a) Any transaction or arrangement of a kind described in section 330 (see notes below) entered into by the company (or in the case of a holding company by a subsidiary of the company) for a person who at any time during the year was a director of the company, or of its holding company, or was connected with such a director. 6 Sch 15(b), 16(b)
(b) An agreement by the company (or in the case of a holding company by a subsidiary of the company) to enter into such a transaction or arrangement. 6 Sch 15(c), 16(c)
(c) Any other transaction with the company (or, in the case of a holding company with a subsidiary of the company) in which a person, who at any time during the year was a director of the company or of its holding company, had directly or indirectly, a material interest. 6 Sch 17(1)
(A director is also treated as being interested in a transaction between a company and any of his connected persons).

5.8.1 Do the notes contain the following particulars of loans to and transactions with directors: 6 Sch 15, 16

(a) The principal terms of the transaction? 6 Sch 22(1)

(b) A statement that the transaction was made during the year, or that it subsisted during the year? 6 Sch 22(2)(a)

(c) The name of the person for whom the transaction was made and, where that person is connected with a director, the name of the director? 6 Sch 22(2)(b)

(d) If the transaction or arrangement is one in which the director has a material interest, the name of the director and the nature of that interest? 6 Sch 22(2)(c)

(e) In respect of a loan, or an agreement for a loan, or an arrangement within section 330(6) or (7) relating to a loan: 6 Sch 22(2)(d)

(i) The amount of the liability for both the principal and the interest outstanding at both the beginning and the end of the year?

(ii) The maximum amount of the liability during the year?

(iii) The amount of interest which, having fallen due, has not been paid?

(iv) The amount of any provision that the company has made against the failure of the borrower to repay the whole, or any part, of the principal or the interest?

(f) In respect of a guarantee, or security, or an arrangement within section 330(6) relating to a guarantee or security: 6 Sch 22(2)(e)

(i) The amount for which the company (or its subsidiary) was liable under the guarantee, or in respect of the security, both at the beginning and at the end of the year?
(ii) The maximum amount for which the company (or its subsidiary) may become liable?
(iii) Any amount paid, and any liability incurred, by the company (or its subsidiary) in fulfilling the guarantee or discharging the security?

(g) In the case of any other transaction the value of the transaction or the value of any transaction to which the agreement relates? 6 Sch 22(2)(f)

Notes:
(a) The transactions of the kind described in section 330 include:

(i) A loan.
(ii) A quasi-loan.
(iii) A credit transaction.
(iv) A guarantee or provision of security in connection with a loan, quasi-loan or credit transaction.
(v) An assignment of any rights, obligations or liabilities to the company under a transaction which, if it had been entered into by the company, would have fallen within (i), (ii), (iii) or (iv) above.
(vi) An arrangement by the company for another person to enter into such a transaction.

(b) The disclosure requirements do not apply to the following transactions:

(i) A transaction, between one company and another company in which a director of the first company or its subsidiary or holding company is interested only by virtue of his being a director of the other. 6 Sch 18(a)

(ii) A contract of service between a company and one of its directors or a director of its holding company or between a director of a company and any of that company's subsidiaries.	6 Sch 18(b)
(iii) A transaction, which was not entered into during the year in question and which did not subsist at any time during that year.	6 Sch 18(e)
(iv) Any credit transaction, guarantee, security, agreement or arrangement falling within section 330 (6) or (7) that is made in connection with a credit transaction, where the aggregate amount outstanding in respect of all such transactions does not exceed £5,000 for the director and his connected persons during the year.	6 Sch 24(1) (2)
(v) A transaction (covered by 6 Sch 1(c) or 2(c)) between a company and a director of the company or of its holding company or a person connected with such a director in which the director has an interest and the majority of the directors (other than the director) of the company which is preparing the financial statements in question are of the opinion that the interest is not material.	6 Sch 17(2)
(vi) A transaction between a director and his company or another company within the group, provided it was entered into in the ordinary course of the company's business and at arms length.	6 Sch 20
(vii) A transaction between member of a group of companies that would have been disclosable only because a director is associated with both contracting companies (provided there are no minority interests).	6 Sch 21
(viii) A transaction or arrangement (covered by 6 Sch 1(c) or 2(c)) and in which a director has a material interest if (a) the value of each such transaction made in that year in which the director had a material interest, and (b) the value of each such transaction previously made less the amount by which the liabilities of the person for whom the transaction was made have been reduced, at no time during the year exceeded £1,000 or, if more, the lower of £5,000 and 1 per cent of the value of the net assets of the company preparing the financial statements as at the end of the year.	6 Sch 25
(c) Corresponding amounts are not required.	4 Sch 58(3)(c)
(d) In consolidated financial statements, the above provisions apply only to directors of the holding company.	

5.8.2 If the company is listed, are particulars of any contracts of significance subsisting during, or at the end of, the year in which a director of the company is, or was (for International Stock Exchange purposes) materially interested, or the fact that there are no such contracts, disclosed? CO 21(k)

Notes:	
(a) When complying with this requirement, companies should have regard to the relevant provisions of the Act.	
(b) For International Stock Exchange purposes a 'contract of significance' is one which represents in amount or value a sum equal to 1 per cent or more of:	CO 21(l)
(i) In the case of a capital transaction of which the principal purpose is the granting of credit, the net assets of the company.	
(ii) In other cases, the total purchases, sales, payments or receipts, as the case may be of the company.	

5.9 Loans to and transactions with officers

5.9.1 In respect of transactions, arrangements and agreements made by the company, and, in the case of a holding company, by its subsidiary, for persons who were, at any time during the year, officers, but not directors, of the company, do the notes contain the following particulars: Sec 232 (1) (2) 6 Sch 28, 29(1)

(a) The aggregate amounts outstanding at the end of the year of:

(i) Loans (including guarantees, securities, arrangements and agreements relating to loans)?
(ii) Quasi-loans (including guarantees, securities, arrangements and agreements relating to quasi-loans)?
(iii) Credit transactions (including guarantees, securities, arrangements and agreements relating to credit transactions)?

(b) The number of officers that each of the aggregate amounts in 5.9.1(a) cover?

Notes:
(a) Where the aggregate amount outstanding at the end of the year under transactions, arrangements and agreements made for the officer does not exceed £2,500, the amount may be excluded from the aggregate amounts disclosed under 5.9.1(a). 6 Sch 29(2)
(b) Corresponding amounts are not required. 4 Sch 58(3)
(c) In consolidated financial statements, the provisions apply only to officers of the holding company.

5.10 Creditors and other liabilities

General disclosure

5.10.1 If balance sheet Format 2 is used, is the amount falling due within one year and after more than one year shown separately for each item included under creditors and in aggregate for all items? 4 Sch Note 13

5.10.2 In respect of each item included under creditors, are the following disclosed: 4 Sch 48(1)
(a) The aggregate amount of debts that are payable or repayable otherwise than by instalments and fall due more than five years after the balance sheet date?

(b) The aggregate amount of debts that are payable or repayable by instalments, any of which fall due more than five years after the balance sheet date?

(c) The aggregate amount of the instalments in (b) that fall due more than five years after the balance sheet date?

5.10.3 In relation to each debt within step 5.10.2, is one of the following disclosed: 4 Sch 48(2) (3)

(a) The terms of payment or repayment and the rate of interest payable?
(b) If the above statement would be excessively long, a general indication of the terms of payment or repayment and the rates of interest payable?

5.10.4 If the company is listed, or it is traded on the USM, a statement detailing the aggregate amounts repayable: CO 21(f) GU 10(f)

(a) In one year or less, or on demand.
(b) Between one and two years.
(c) Between two and five years.
(d) In five years or more.
In respect of:

(i) Bank loans and overdrafts?
(ii) Other borrowings?

5.10.5 In respect of each item shown under creditors, are the following disclosed: 4 Sch 48(4)
(a) The aggregate amount in respect of which any security has been given?
(b) An indication of the nature of the securities given?

5.10.6 Is the amount for creditors in respect of taxation and social security shown separately from the amount for other creditors? 4 Sch Note 9

Debentures

5.10.7 Is there separate disclosure of the amount of convertible debenture loans? 4 Sch Note 7

5.10.8 In respect of debentures issued during the year, are the following disclosed: 4 Sch 41(1)
(a) The reason for making the issue?
(b) The classes of debentures issued?
(c) For each class:

(i) The amount issued?
(ii) The consideration received by the company?

5.10.9 Are particulars disclosed of any redeemed debentures that the company has power to reissue? 4 Sch 41(2)

5.10.10 In respect of any of the company's debentures held by a nominee of, or trustee for, the company, are the following disclosed: 4 Sch 41(3)

(a) The nominal amount of the debentures?

(b) The book value of the holding?

5.10.11 Are the number, description and amount of the company's debentures held beneficially by subsidiaries or their nominees disclosed? 5 Sch 6

Foreign currency translation

Note: See also steps 3.1(e), 4.17, 5.7.18 and 5.7.19. Also for translation of financial statements of overseas subsidiaries see section 7.16 of Part II to the checklist in 'Manual of Accounting - volume II'.

5.10.12 Have foreign currency monetary liabilities outstanding at the balance sheet date been translated at one of the following rates: SSAP 20 para 48

(a) The rate fixed under the terms of the relevant transaction?

(b) The closing rate?

Note: If there is a related or matching forward contract in respect of a trading transaction, translation may be either at the rate specified in the contract or at the closing rate. (A company should, however, apply consistently the policy it adopts in respect of such trading transactions.)	SSAP 20 para 48

5.10.13 In the exceptional cases where there are doubts as to the convertibility or marketability of the currency of a long-term monetary item outstanding at the balance sheet date, has the company considered whether, on the grounds of prudence, it should restrict the amount of the exchange gain (or the amount by which the gain exceeds past exchange losses on the same items) that it recognises in the profit and loss account? SSAP 20 para 50

5.10.14 Where a company has used foreign currency borrowings to finance, or to provide a hedge against, its foreign equity investments and it denominates the equity investments in the appropriate foreign currency, is the offset procedure used only where both of the following conditions are met: SSAP 20 Para 51

(a) In any year, exchange gains and losses on the translation of borrowings are offset as a reserve movement only to the extent of exchange differences arising on the retranslation of equity investments?

(b) The foreign currency borrowings used in the offset process do not exceed in aggregate the total amount of cash that the investments are expected to be able to generate from profits or otherwise?

5.10.15 If the company has chosen to use the offset procedure, has it applied it consistently from year to year unless the two conditions outlined in 5.10.14 above cease to apply? SSAP 20 para 51

Note: Under the offset procedure, exchange gains/losses on the translation of the foreign equity investments are taken to reserves, and exchange losses/gains on the translation of the foreign currency borrowings are offset as a reserve movement against these exchange gains/losses.

5.10.16 If the company or group is not an exempt company or group, are the following disclosed: SSAP 20 para 60

(a) The net amount of exchange gains and losses on foreign currency borrowings less deposits?
(b) The amount of (a) that is offset in reserves under the offset procedure?
(c) The net amount of (a) that is charged or credited to the profit and loss account?

Note: An exempt company is one that does not prepare its financial statements in accordance with section 228 or section 230 of, and Schedule 4 to, the Act.	SSAP 20 para 35

Dividends

5.10.17 Is the aggregate amount that is recommended for distribution by way of dividend disclosed? 4 Sch 51(3)

5.10.18 Do proposed dividends and dividends declared but not yet payable exclude the related ACT? SSAP 8 para 26

5.10.19 Is the ACT on proposed dividends (whether recoverable or irrecoverable) only carried forward to the extent that it is foreseen that sufficient corporation tax will be assessed on the profits or income of the next accounting period against which the ACT is available for offset? SSAP 15 para 31

5.10.20 If the ACT on proposed dividends is regarded as recoverable, has it been deducted from the deferred taxation account, or, in the absence of such an account, shown under 'Prepayments and accrued income'? SSAP 8 para 27

5.10.21 For arrears of fixed cumulative dividends, are the following disclosed: 4 Sch 49

(a) The amount of the arrears?
(b) The period for which the dividend on each class of shares is in arrears?

Leasing obligations

5.10.22 Is the amount for lessees of obligations related to finance leases (net of finance charges allocated to future periods) disclosed separately from other obligations and liabilities either on the face of the balance sheet or in the notes to the financial statements? SSAP 21 para 51

5.10.23 Are net obligations under finance leases analysed between amounts payable: SSAP 21 para 52

(a) In the next year?
(b) In the second to fifth years inclusive?
(c) In more than five years?

5.10.24 If the answer to 5.10.23 is no because obligations under finance leases are combined on the balance sheet with other obligations and liabilities, is the analysis given in respect of the combined total?

> Note: Where net obligations are not combined on the balance sheet with other obligations and liabilities, the gross obligations can be analysed and the future finance charges separately deducted from the total. See also steps 5.5.1 to 5.5.10

Pension Costs

5.10.25 Where the cumulative pension cost shown in the profit and loss account has not been completely discharged by the payment of contributions, has the excess been shown as a net pension provision in the balance sheet? SSAP 24 para 86

> Note: See also step 4.8.

5.10.26 Has the following been disclosed where the company operates a defined contribution scheme: SSAP 24 para 87

(a) The nature of the scheme (that is, defined contribution)?

(b) The pension cost charge for the period?

(c) Any outstanding or prepaid contributions at the balance sheet date?

5.10.27 Has the following been disclosed where the company operates a defined benefit scheme: SSAP 24 para 88

(a) The nature of the scheme (that is, defined benefit)?

(b) Whether it is funded of unfunded?

(c) Whether the pension cost and provision (or asset) are assessed in accordance with the advice of a professionally qualified actuary and, if so, the date of the most recent formal actuarial valuation or later formal review used for this purpose?

(d) Whether the actuary is an employee or officer of the reporting company, or of a group of which it is a member?

(e) The pension cost charge for the period together with explanations of significant changes in the charge compared to that in the previous accounting period?

(f) Any provisions or prepayments in the balance sheet resulting from a difference between the amounts recognised as cost and the amounts funded or paid directly?

(g) The amount of any deficiency on a current funding level basis, including the action, if any, being taken to deal with it in the current and future accounting periods?

(h) Any commitment to make additional payments over a limited number of years?

(i) The accounting treatment adopted in respect of a refund made in accordance with the provisions of the Finance Act 1986 (or equivalent legislation) where a credit appears in the financial statements in relation to it?

(j) Details of the expected effects on future costs of any material changes in the group's and/or company's pension arrangements?

Notes:

(a) A 'funded scheme' is a pension scheme where the future liabilities for benefits are provided for by the accumulation of assets held externally to the employing company's business. SSAP 24 para 65

(b) The Finance Act 1986 stipulates that a pension scheme will lose part of its tax exemptions if its surplus exceeds 5 per cent of the scheme's liabilities. One method that a trustee and employer may use, to reduce a surplus to less than 5 per cent, is to make a cash payment to the employer. This cash payment is liable to tax at 40 per cent. Finance Act 1986

5.10.28 For a defined benefit scheme, is an outline of the results of the most recent formal actuarial valuation or later formal review of the scheme on an ongoing basis disclosed and does this include disclosure of: SSAP 24 para 88

(a) The actuarial method used and a brief description of the main actuarial assumptions?

(b) The market value of scheme assets at the date of their valuation or review?

(c) The level of funding expressed in percentage terms?

(d) Comments on any material actuarial surplus or deficiency indicated by (c) above?

Notes:	
(a) An 'ongoing actuarial valuation' is a valuation in which it is assumed that the pension scheme will continue in existence and (where appropriate) that new members will be admitted. The liabilities allow for expected increases in earnings.	SSAP 24 para 67
(b) The 'level of funding' is the proportion at a given date of the actuarial value of liabilities for pensioners' and deferred pensioners' benefits and for members' accrued benefits that is covered by the actuarial value of assets. For this purpose the actuarial value of future combinations is excluded from the value of the assets.	SSAP 24 para 66

5.10.29 Where a company has more than one pension scheme: SSAP 24 para 89

(a) Has disclosure been made on a combined basis (unless disclosure of information about individual schemes is necessary for a proper understanding of the financial statements)?

(b) Has no set-off occurred between schemes, such that a current funding level basis deficiency in one scheme is not set off against a surplus in another?

5.10.30 If a subsidiary company is a member of a group scheme, has the following disclosure been made: SSAP 24 para 90

(a) That the company is a member of a group scheme?

(b) The nature of the group scheme?

(c) That the contributions are based on pension costs across the group as a whole, if appropriate?

5.10.31 A subsidiary that is a member of a group scheme is exempt from disclosing the requirements of steps 5.10.27(g) and 5.10.28. Instead, is the name of the parent company stated whose financial statements contain particulars of the actuarial valuation of the group scheme? SSAP 24 para 90

Note: This exemption only applies if the parent company is registered in the UK or the Republic of Ireland.	SSAP 24 para 90

5.10.32 In respect of foreign operations where the employer has an obligation to provide pensions, is the pension charge provided in accordance with the requirements of SSAP 24, unless one of the following applies: SSAP 24 para 91

(a) An adjustment has been made on consolidation to bring the pension charge onto a basis consistent with the provisions of SSAP 24?

(b) This is impractical because of the difficulty and cost of obtaining the necessary actuarial information?

5.10.33 In respect of all pension schemes of foreign operations that do not comply with the provisions of SSAP 24 and where no consolidation adjustment has been made, has the amount charged to the profit and loss account and the basis of the charge been disclosed? SSAP 24 para 91

5.11 Provisions for liabilities and charges

General disclosure

5.11.1	In respect of provisions under any heading or sub-heading where there has been (i) a transfer to the provision, or (ii) a transfer from the provision otherwise than for the purpose for which the provision was established, are the following disclosed: (a) The amount of the provision at the beginning of the year? (b) The amount and the source of transfers to the provision? (c) The amount and the application of transfers from the provision? (d) The amount of the provision at the end of the year?	4 Sch 46
	Note: Corresponding amounts are not required.	4 Sch 58(3)
5.11.2	Are particulars disclosed separately of each material provision that is included under the heading 'Other provisions'?	4 Sch 46(3)
5.11.3	If a business has been acquired during the year have steps 7.9.16 to 7.9.30 of Part II of the checklist been completed?	
	Notes: (a) When a business is acquired, in steps 7.9.16 to 7.9.30 read 'business' for 'subsidiary', 'company's financial statements' for 'consolidated financial statements', and 'purchased goodwill' for 'goodwill arising on consolidation'. (b) Part II of the checklist is reproduced in 'Manual of Accounting - volume II'.	

Deferred taxation

5.11.4	Is the amount of any provision for deferred taxation stated separately from the amount of any provision for other taxation?	4 Sch 47
5.11.5	Are the deferred tax balances and their major components disclosed?	SSAP 15 para 37
5.11.6	Are transfers to and from deferred tax disclosed in a note?	SSAP 15 para 38
5.11.7	Is the total amount of any unprovided deferred tax disclosed in a note analysed by its major components?	SSAP 15 para 40
5.11.8	Where amounts of deferred tax arise that relate to movements on reserves, are the amounts transferred to or from deferred tax shown separately as part of such movements?	SSAP 15 para 39
5.11.9	Are debit balances on the deferred taxation account carried forward only to the extent that they are expected to be recoverable without replacement by equivalent debit balances?	SSAP 15 para 30
	Note: Debit balances in respect of ACT other than on dividends payable or proposed at the balance sheet date (see steps 4.11.1 to 4.11.12) should be written off unless recovery is assured beyond reasonable doubt. Such recovery will normally only be assured where the debit balances are recoverable out of corporation tax arising on profits or income of the next accounting period, without replacement by equivalent debit balances.	SSAP 15 para 32

5.11.10 Where the financial statements disclose the value of an asset by way of note and that value differs from the book value of the asset, does the note also disclose the tax implications that would result if the asset was sold at that value? SSAP 15 para 42

5.11.11 Where the potential amount of deferred tax on a revalued asset is not shown because the revaluation does not constitute a timing difference, is this fact, and the fact that the tax has not been quantified, disclosed? SSAP 15 para 41

5.11.12 Where deferred tax is not provided on earnings retained overseas, is this fact stated? SSAP 15 para 44

5.12 Guarantees and other financial commitments

5.12.1 Are particulars (including the amount secured, where practicable) of any charge on the assets to secure the liabilities of any other person disclosed? 4 Sch 50(1)

5.12.2 Are the following amounts of capital expenditure disclosed: 4 Sch 50(3)

(a) Contracted but not provided for?
(b) Authorised but not contracted for?

5.12.3 Is the amount for lessees of any commitments at the balance sheet date in respect of finance leases which have been entered into but where inception occurs after the year end disclosed? SSAP 21 para 54

> Note: See also steps 5.5.1 to 5.5.10.

5.12.4 Are the payments that the lessee is committed to make in respect of operating leases during the next year disclosed? Is this amount analysed between payments where the commitment expires: SSAP 21 para 56

(a) In that year?
(b) In the second to fifth years inclusive?
(c) In more than five years?

5.12.5 Is the analysis in 5.12.4 given separately for leases of land and buildings and for other operating leases?

> Note: See also steps 5.5.1 to 5.5.10.

5.12.6 Are particulars of the following pension commitments disclosed: 4 Sch 50(5)

(a) Those included under any provision in the balance sheet?
(b) Those for which no provision has been made?
(c) Those in (a) and (b) in respect of pensions payable to past directors?

5.12.7 Are particulars disclosed of any other financial commitments that have not been provided for and that are relevant to the assessment of the state of affairs? 4 Sch 50(5)

5.12.8 Is there separate disclosure of commitments in steps 5.12.1, 5.12.2, 5.12.6 and 5.12.7 that are undertaken on behalf of or for the benefit of: 4 Sch 59A
(a) Any holding company or fellow subsidiary?
(b) Any subsidiary?

5.12.9 Are the commitments in 5.12.8 shown separately from other commitments and are those related to 5.12.8(a) shown separately from those in 5.12.8(b)? 4 Sch 59A

5.13 Contingencies

5.13.1 Have material contingent losses been accrued where it is probable that a future event will confirm a loss that can be estimated with reasonable accuracy at the date on which the financial statements are approved by the board of directors? SSAP 18 para 15

5.13.2 Except where the possibility of loss is remote, have material contingent losses not accrued been disclosed? SSAP 18 para 16

5.13.3 Have material contingent gains been disclosed only where it is probable that the gain will be realised? SSAP 18 para 17

5.13.4 In respect of each contingency (or group of similar transactions) that require disclosure, are the following disclosed: SSAP 18 paras 18, 21 4 Sch 50(2)

(a) The nature of the contingency?

(b) The uncertainties that are expected to affect the ultimate outcome?

(c) A prudent estimate of the financial effect (made at the date on which the financial statements are approved by the board of directors), or a statement that it is not practicable to make such an estimate?

5.13.5 In addition, in respect of any contingent liability not provided for, are the following disclosed: 4 Sch 50(2)
(a) Its legal nature?
(b) Whether any valuable security has been provided and if so, what?

5.13.6 If an estimate of the financial effect of a contingency is disclosed, does this take into account the probable outcome of any related counter-claim or claim by or against a third party such that only the potential financial effect is disclosed? SSAP 18 paras 6, 19

5.13.7 In the case of a contingent loss, has the potential financial effect that is disclosed been reduced by: SSAP 18 para 19

(a) Any amounts accrued?
(b) Any amounts where the possibility of loss is remote?

5.13.8 Has the estimate of the financial effect been disclosed before taking account of taxation, and have the taxation implications of the contingency crystallising been explained where this is necessary for a proper understanding of the financial position? SSAP 18 para 20

5.13.9 Is there separate disclosure of contingent liabilities that are undertaken on behalf of or for the benefit of: 4 Sch 59A
(a) Any holding company or fellow subsidiary?
(b) Any subsidiary?

5.13.10 Are contingent liabilities in 5.13.9 shown separately from other commitments and are those related to 5.13.9(a) shown separately from those in 5.13.9(b)? 4 Sch 59A

5.14 Share capital

5.14.1 Is the authorised share capital disclosed? 4 Sch 38(1)(a)

5.14.2 Where more than one class of shares has been allotted, are the number and the aggregate nominal value of each class of shares allotted disclosed? 4 Sch 38(1)(b)

5.14.3 Are the amounts of allotted share capital and the amount of called-up share capital that has been paid up separately disclosed? 4 Sch Note 12

5.14.4 In respect of allotted redeemable shares, are the following disclosed: 4 Sch 38(2)

(a) The earliest and the latest dates on which the company has power to redeem them?

(b) Whether they must be redeemed in any event or at the option of the company or of the shareholder?
(c) The premium, if any, payable on redemption (or, if none, a statement to that effect)?

5.14.5 Where a class of preference shares (or participating or preferred ordinary shares) was issued before 6 April 1973 and indicates a fixed rate of dividend, is the new effective rate of dividend that is paid to shareholders also incorporated in the description of the shares? SSAP 8 para 28

5.14.6 In respect of shares allotted during the year, are the following disclosed: 4 Sch 39

(a) The reason for making the allotment?
(b) The classes of shares allotted?
(c) For each class:

(i) The number allotted?
(ii) The aggregate nominal value?
(iii) The consideration received by the company?

5.14.7 In respect of any issue for cash, by listed companies, or companies traded on the USM, of securities having an equity element (not made to the company's shareholders in proportion to their equity shareholding) and which has not been specifically authorised by the company's shareholders, are the following disclosed: CO 21(q)

(a) The names of the allottees, if less than six in number, and in the case of six or more allottees a generic description of them?

(b) The market price of the securities concerned on a named date, being the date on which the terms of the issue were fixed?

5.14.8 In respect of any option to subscribe for shares and of any other right to require the allotment of shares to any person, are the following disclosed: 4 Sch 40

(a) The number, description and amount of shares involved?
(b) The period during which the option or right is exercisable?
(c) The price to be paid for the shares?

5.14.9 Are the number, description and amount of the company's shares held beneficially by subsidiaries or their nominees disclosed? 5 Sch 6

5.15 Reserves

5.15.1 In respect of reserves under any heading or sub-heading where there has been a transfer to or from the reserve, are the following disclosed: 4 Sch 46

(a) The amount of the reserve at the beginning of the year?
(b) The amount and the source of transfers to the reserve?
(c) The amount and the application of transfers from the reserve?
(d) The amount of the reserve at the end of the year?

> Note: Corresponding amounts are not required. 4 Sch 58(3)

5.15.2 Does an investing company that is not part of a group, or is not a wholly-owned subsidiary, disclose the following in respect of associated companies in either its additional proforma financial statements or additional note information :

(a) The investing company's share of the post-acquisition accumulated reserves of the associated companies and any movements on those reserves (including amounts that have not passed through the proforma profit and loss account)? SSAP 1 para 31

(b) Where applicable, the fact that the accumulated reserves of overseas associated companies would be subject to further tax on distribution? SSAP 1 para 31

(c) The extent of any significant restrictions on the ability of an associated company to distribute its retained profits (other than those shown as non-distributable)? SSAP 1 para 40

> Note: See steps 5.6.6 to 5.6.21.

5.15.3 Are amounts only transferred from the revaluation reserve: 4 Sch 34(3)

(a) To the profit and loss account where the amount concerned has previously been charged to the profit and loss account or it represents a realised profit?

(b) On capitalisation?

(c) Where to the extent that the amounts originally transferred to that reserve are no longer necessary for the purposes of the valuation method used? 4 Sch para 34(3)

> Note: 'Capitalisation' in 5.15.3(b) means applying an amount standing to the credit of the revaluation reserve in wholly or partly paying up unissued shares in the company to be allotted to members of the company as fully or partly paid up shares. 4 Sch 34(3A)

5.15.4 Is the treatment for taxation purposes of amounts credited or debited to the revaluation reserve disclosed? 4 Sch 34(4)

5.15.5 Is the net movement on reserves that arises from exchange differences disclosed? SSAP 20 para 60

> Note: See also steps 3.1(e), 4.17, 5.7.18 and 5.7.19, and 5.10.12 to 5.10.16..

5.16 Post balance sheet events

Notes:	
(a) Financial statements should be prepared on the basis of conditions existing at the balance sheet date.	SSAP 17 para 21
(b) See also step 2.4.	

5.16.1 Do amounts included in the financial statements take account of a material post balance sheet event where: SSAP 17 para 22

(a) It is an adjusting event?
(b) It indicates that the application of the going concern concept to the whole or a material part of the company is inappropriate?

5.16.2 Has a material post balance sheet event been disclosed where: SSAP 17 para 23

(a) It is a non-adjusting event of such materiality that its non-disclosure would affect the ability of the users of the financial statements to reach a proper understanding of the financial position?
(b) It is the reversal or maturity of transactions entered into to alter the appearance of the balance sheet (that is, 'window dressing')?

5.16.3 In respect of each material post balance sheet event that requires disclosure, are the following disclosed: SSAP 17 para 24

(a) The nature of the event?
(b) An estimate of the financial effect, or a statement that it is not practicable to make such an estimate?

5.16.4 Has the estimate of the financial effect been disclosed before taking account of taxation, and have the taxation implications been explained where this is necessary for a proper understanding of the financial position? SSAP 17 para 25

5.17 Date of approval

5.17.1 Is the date on which the financial statements were approved by the board of directors disclosed and has a director signed the company's balance sheet? Sec 233(1)(4) SSAP 17 para 26

6 STATEMENT OF SOURCE AND APPLICATION OF FUNDS

6.1	Where an entity has turnover or gross income of £25,000 or more per annum, do the financial statements include a statement of source and application of funds?	SSAP 10 paras 9,10
	Note: Where group accounts are prepared, the statement should reflect the operations of the group.	SSAP 10 para 12
6.2	Does the statement show the profit or loss for the year together with the adjustments required for items that did not use (or provide) funds in the year?	SSAP 10 para 11
6.3	Are the following other sources and applications of funds also shown where material: (a) Dividends paid? (b) Acquisitions and disposals of fixed assets? (c) Funds raised by increasing, or expended in repaying or redeeming, medium or long-term loans or the issued capital of the company? (d) The increase or decrease in working capital sub-divided into its components, and movements in net liquid funds?	SSAP 10 para 11
	Notes: (a) There should be a minimum of 'netting off'. The figures should generally be identifiable in the profit and loss account, or in the balance sheet or in the related notes. If adjustments to those figures are necessary, details should be given to enable the related figures to be located.	SSAP 10 para 4
	(b) The effects of acquiring, or disposing of, a subsidiary should be reflected.	SSAP 10 para 5

Appendix II

MODEL SET OF FINANCIAL STATEMENTS UNDER UK GAAP

The financial statements that follow are the consolidated financial statements of the GAAP UK plc group of companies.

These financial statements, prepared under Schedule 4 and Schedule 4A to the Companies Act 1985, illustrate the more common disclosure requirements of the Act. They also include many of the disclosure requirements contained in Statements of Standard Accounting Practice, The Stock Exchange's Continuing Obligations for listed companies and The Stock Exchange's General Undertakings for companies traded on the USM.

The suggested disclosure throughout is intended for guidance only, and would not necessarily be applicable to all groups of companies.

The abbreviations used in this appendix are notated in the same way as they have been throughout the book, except that the notation for a 'section' of the Companies Act 1985 is 's'. All of the references given in the appendix are discussed in detail elsewhere in volume I or volume II of the book. The Table of legislation and of other regulations indicates where in this book these references are considered. In many places it would be misleading to give a specific example of wording. Consequently, in these situations a description of the requirements is given in italics.

GAAP UK plc
Report and Financial Statements
For the year ended 31 December 1990

Contents

Directors' Report

s 234(1) The directors present their report and the consolidated financial statements of GAAP UK plc for the year ended 31 December 1990.

Principal activities and business review

This review should include:

s 234(2) (a) *A description of the principal activities of the company and its subsidiaries during the year and of any significant changes in those activities.*

s 234(1)(a) (b) *A fair review of the development of the company's and its subsidiaries' business during the year and of their position at the end of the year.*

7 Sch 6(b)
s 234(4) (c) *An indication of likely future developments in the business of the company and its subsidiaries.*

Results and dividends

The profit for the year after taxation and extraordinary items amounted to £ . It is recommended that this amount be dealt with as follows:

		£
s 234(1)(b)	Preference dividends	
	Ordinary dividends - Interim paid	
	- Final proposed	
s 234(1)(b)	Transfer to reserves	£

The directors recommend a final dividend of p per ordinary share.

CO 21(b)
GU 10(b) *This section must include (where applicable) an explanation of any material difference between the trading results and any published forecast made by the company.*

Post-balance-sheet events

7 Sch 6(a)
s 234(4) *Particulars of any important events affecting the company and its subsidiaries that have occurred since the end of the year must be given (see note 30).*

Research and development

7 Sch 6(c)
s 234(4) *The report must include an indication of any activities of the company and its subsidiaries in the field of research and development. (See also note 8.)*

Significant changes in fixed assets

7 Sch 1(1)
s 234(4)
Particulars have to be given of any significant changes in the fixed assets of the company and its subsidiaries during the year.

Market value of land and buildings

7 Sch 1(2)
s 234(4)
If, in the directors' opinion, the difference between the book amount and the market value of land and buildings is of such significance that it should be drawn to the members' and debenture holders' attention, it must be disclosed.

Directors

s 234(2)
CO 21(e)
The names must be given of persons who were directors of the company at any time during the year and indicate for listed and USM companies the identity of independent non-executive directors and a short biographical note on each.

Custom
This section will also probably include the director's title (for example, chairman, managing director), changes in the board of directors since the end of the year and the rotation of directors at the annual general meeting.

Directors' service contracts

CO 43(c)
The unexpired period of the service contract of each director of the company proposed for re-election at the annual general meeting is as follows:

	Unexpired period
Name of director	

OR

There are no directors' service contracts in existence.

Directors' interests in shares and debentures

7 Sch 2(1)
(2), 2B
CO 21(h)
The directors of the company who held office at 31 December 1990 had the following interests in (including options to subscribe for) the shares and the debentures of group companies:

	Name of and description of shares or debentures	31 December 1990 No. of Shares	31 December 1990 Debentures £	1 January 1990 (or date of appointment if later) No. of Shares	1 January 1990 (or date of appointment if later) Debentures £
Name of each director					
Beneficial interests					
Non-beneficial interests					

CO 21(h)
GU 10(h)
(references to beneficial and non-beneficial interests)

7 Sch 2(1)
The particulars set out above may alternatively be included in the notes to the financial statements.

CO 21(h) GU 10(h) Between 31 December 1990 and (*a date not more than one month prior to the date of the notice of the meeting*) there have been the following changes in the interests of the directors in the shares of the company:

OR

Between 31 December 1990 and (*a date not more than one month prior to the date of the notice of the meeting*) there have been no changes in the interests of the directors in the shares of the company.

Substantial shareholders

CO 21(i) GU 10(i) On (*a date not more than one month prior to the date of the notice of the meeting*), the following were interested in 3% or more of the company's ordinary share capital.

	Number of shares	Percentage
Name		

OR

As at (*a date not more than one month prior to the date of the notice of the meeting*), no person has reported to the company an interest in 3% or more of its ordinary share capital.

Contracts of significance with corporate substantial shareholders

CO 21(l) *Particulars must be given of any contract of significance between the company or one of its subsidiaries and any corporate substantial shareholder.*

Acquisition of the company's own shares

7 Sch 8 *The report should include in respect of purchases during the year:*

(a) *The number and the nominal value of shares purchased.*
(b) *The percentage of the called-up capital that shares of the description purchased represent.*
(c) *The aggregate consideration paid.*
(d) *The reasons for the purchase.*

7 Sch 8 *The report should include in respect of other acquisitions by the company, and of acquisitions by persons with financial assistance from the company where the company has a beneficial interest in those shares:*

(a) *The maximum number and the nominal value of shares acquired that were held at any time during the year.*
(b) *The number and the nominal value of shares acquired that were either disposed of or cancelled during the year.*
(c) *The consideration received in respect of disposals during the*

year where the shares involved were originally acquired either for money or money's worth.

(d) *The percentage of the called-up capital that shares of the description acquired or charged represent.*

(e) *The amount of any charge.*

CO 21(p) *Details should also be included of particulars of any shareholders' authority for the purchase by the company of its own shares existing at the end of the year. For such purchases made otherwise than through the market or by tender or by partial offer to all shareholders, the names of the sellers of the shares purchased should be given also.*

For such purchases, or options or contracts to make such purchases that have been entered into since the end of the year covered by this report, the equivalent information to that required by paragraph 8 of Schedule 7 to the Act (detailed above) must be disclosed.

Charitable and political contributions

7 Sch 3-5 During the year, the group has made the following contributions:

United Kingdom Charitable organisations	£
	£
United Kingdom political organisations (*State name of party concerned*)	
Individuals (*state names*)	
Total of other contributions under £200 each	
	£

The details outlined above are not required if charitable and political contributions in the UK do not exceed £200 in aggregate. For political contributions, the name of the recipient is required for individual amounts that exceed £200.

Employment of disabled persons

7 Sch 9 *A statement must be given of the company's policy in respect of:*

(a) *Applications for employment from disabled perons.*

(b) *Employees who become disabled.*

(c) *The training, career development and promotion of disabled persons.*

This statement is not required, however, if the company employs on average 250 or fewer persons in the UK.

Employee involvement

7 Sch 11 *The report should describe the action that the company has taken during the year to introduce, maintain or develop arrangements aimed at employee involvement. However, this statement*

is not required if the company employs on average 250 or fewer persons in the UK.

Taxation status

CO 21(j) GU 10(j) The company is not a close company within the provisions of the Income and Corporation Taxes Act 1970.

Insurance of officers and auditors

7 Sch 5A s 310(3)(a) *Particulars must be given of any insurance that the company has taken out or maintained during the period for its directors, officers or auditors.*

Auditors

Custom In accordance with section 384 of the Companies Act 1985, a resolution proposing the reappointment of (*name*) as auditors to the company will be put to the annual general meeting.

s 234A BY ORDER OF THE BOARD

Name

Director or Secretary

Date

Auditors' Report
To the members of GAAP UK plc

Auditing Standard 102 — We have audited the financial statements on pages to in accordance with Auditing Standards.

ss 235, 236 SSAP 10 — In our opinion the financial statements give a true and fair view of the state of affairs of the company and the group at 31 December 1990 and of the profit and source and application of funds of the group for the year then ended and have been properly prepared in accordance with the Companies Act 1985.

Name

Chartered Accountants

Address

Date

s 237(1)(2)(3) — *The auditors must state the relevant facts in their audit report where they are of the opinion that:*

(a) *The company has not kept proper accounting records.*
(b) *They have not received adequate returns from branches they did not visit.*
(c) *The financial statements are not in agreement with the accounting records and returns.*
(d) *They have not obtained all the information and explanations they consider necessary for their audit.*

s 237(4) — *Where the relevant details are not disclosed in the financial statements, the auditors must include in their report, so far as they are able to do so, a statement that gives the required particulars of:*

(a) *Emoluments of directors.*
(b) *Transactions with directors and officers.*

s 235(3) — *If the auditors are of the opinion that the information relating to the year given in the directors' report is not consistent with the financial statements, they must state that fact in their audit report.*

s 271(3)(4) — *Where the auditors qualify their audit report, and the company proposes to pay a dividend, they will have to state in writing whether the subject matter of their qualification is material in determining whether the company can lawfully make the proposed distribution. (They could give this additional statement to the members of the company as a separate statement. But that statement would have to be laid before the company at a general meeting.)*

Statement of Accounting Policies

4 Sch 36 SSAP 2 para 18	The accounting policies that the group has adopted to determine the amounts included in respect of material items shown in the balance sheet, and also to determine the profit or loss are shown below.
	This will probably include accounting policies in respect of:
	Basis of accounting
	The basis of accounting adopted (namely, historical cost, or modified historical cost, or current cost).
	Basis of consolidation
SSAP 14 SSAP 23 para 21 4A Sch 1(1), 2, 3 s 223(5)	*The basis of consolidation (for example, whether acquisition accounting or merger accounting or a combination of these methods is used, whether all subsidiaries are consolidated, whether all subsidiaries prepare their accounts to the same date as the holding company, whether uniform accounting policies are adopted by all companies in the group). The treatment of subsidiaries acquired or disposed of during the year.*
SSAP 22 para 39	*The treatment of goodwill arising on consolidation.*
	Associated undertakings
SSAP 1 para 18	*The definition and treatment of associated undertakings.*
	Research and development
4 Sch 20(2) SSAP 13 para 30	*The fact that research expenditure is written off in the year of expenditure. The basis and the reasons for capitalising development costs, and the period over which they are being written off, or the fact that development costs are written off in the year of expenditure.*
	Intangible fixed assets (excluding goodwill)
4 Sch 17, 18 SSAP 12 paras 22, 25	*The basis for capitalising patents and trade marks and the amortisation policy adopted.*
	Purchased goodwill
4 Sch 21(4) SSAP 22 paras 39, 41	*The treatment of purchased goodwill. If purchased goodwill is capitalised, the period over which it is being written off, and the directors' reasons for choosing that period.*

Tangible fixed assets

4 Sch 17, 18, 19 SSAP 12 paras 22, 25

The basis on which tangible fixed assets are stated (normally cost or valuation, less depreciation), the depreciation policy adopted, the rates of depreciation used and the useful economic lives used. The treatment of permanent diminutions in value of fixed assets.

Investment properties

SSAP 19

The basis on which investment properties are included in the balance sheet.

Leased assets and obligations

SSAP 21 para 57

For lessees, the policy adopted for accounting for operating leases and finance leases. This disclosure should include also the equivalent policies in respect of hire purchase contracts that have characteristics similar to leases. (If part of the group's business was that of a lessor, then its policy for accounting for operating leases and finance leases would need to be given. These model financial statements do not deal with the accounting disclosure required by SSAP 21 for lessors.)

Government grants

SSAP 4 para 9

The treatment of Government grants.

Fixed asset investments

4 Sch 19

The basis on which fixed asset investments are stated. The treatment of any temporary or permanent diminutions in value of fixed asset investments.

Stocks and long-term contracts

SSAP 9 para 32

The bases that have been used to determine the balance sheet value. In particular, the bases used to calculate cost, net realisable value, turnover, attributable profit and foreseeable losses.

Deferred taxation

SSAP 15

The basis and the method for providing deferred taxation.

Pension schemes

SSAP 24 paras 87, 88

The nature of the pension schemes. The accounting policy, and the funding policy if different from the accounting policy, indicating the basis on which amounts are charged to the profit and loss account. The policy in respect of any deficiency revealed by an actuarial valuation.

Foreign currency amounts

4 Sch 58(1) SSAP 20 para 59	*The basis of translating amounts denominated in foreign currencies. The basis of translating the financial statements of overseas subsidiaries. The treatment of translation differences.*

Turnover

s 262(1) SSAP 5 para 8	*The basis on which turnover is stated.*

Departures from Accounting Standards

4 Sch 36A CO 21(a) GU 10(a)	*If any of the above accounting policies represent a significant departure from standard accounting practice, the directors' reasons for the departure must be given in the directors' report and the particulars of such a departure and the reason for it must be given in the financial statements.*

Consolidated Profit and Loss Account
For the year ended 31 December 1990

Based on the profit and loss account format 1 shown in Schedule 4 to the Companies Act 1985 as amended by Schedule 4A to the Companies Act 1989.

		Notes	1990	1989
			£	£
	Turnover	2		
4 Sch Note 14	Cost of sales			
	Gross profit			
4 Sch Note 14	Other operating expenses	3		
	Trading profit			
4A Sch 21(3)	Income from interests in associated undertakings			
	Investment income	5		
	Amounts written off investments	6		
	Interest payable and similar charges	7		
4 Sch 3(6)	Profit on ordinary activities before taxation	8		
	Taxation	9		
	Profit on ordinary activities after taxation			
4A Sch 17(3) SSAP 14 para 35	Minority interests			
	Profit before extraordinary items			
SSAP 6 para 15	Extraordinary items	10		
SSAP 6 para 34	Profit for the financial year	11		
4 Sch 3(7)(b) SSAP 6 para 34	Dividends	12		
4 Sch 3(7)(a)	Retained profit for year		£	£
SSAP 3 paras 14, 15	**Earnings per share**	13		
	Net basis		p	p
	Nil basis		p	p
	Fully diluted		p	p

SSAP 6 paras 25, 35 — Movements on reserves are set out in note 27

Balance Sheets
At 31 December 1990

Based on the balance sheet format 1 shown in Schedule 4 to the Companies Act 1985 as amended by Schedule 4A to the Companies Act 1989.

		Notes	Group 1990	Group 1989	Company 1990	Company 1989
			£	£	£	£
	Fixed Assets					
	Intangible assets	15				
	Tangible assets	16				
	Investments	17				
	Current Assets					
	Stocks	20				
	Debtors	21				
	Investments	22				
	Cash at bank and in hand					
	Current Liabilities					
	Creditors: amounts falling due within one year	23				
4 Sch Note 11	Net Current Assets					
	Total Assets less Current Liabilities					
	Creditors: amounts falling due after more than one year (including loans)	23				
	Provisions for liabilities and charges					
	Deferred taxation	24				
	Pensions	25				
	Net Assets		£	£	£	£
	Capital and Reserves					
	Called-up share capital	26				
	Share premium account	27				
	Revaluation reserve	27				
	Merger reserve	27				
	Other reserves	27				
	Profit and loss account	27				
	Shareholders' funds					
4A Sch 17(2) SSAP 14 para 34	Minority interests					
			£	£	£	£

s 233(1)(4)
SSAP 17
para 26

The financial statements on pages to were approved by the board of directors on (*date*) and were signed on its behalf:

Name Director

Consolidated Statement of Source and Application of Funds For the year ended 31 December 1990

	1990 £	1989 £
Source of funds		
Profit on ordinary activities before taxation less minority interests		
Extraordinary items before taxation		
Adjustments for items not involving the movement of funds:		
Depreciation and amounts written off fixed assets		
Profit on disposals of fixed assets		
Exchange differences on consolidation		
Minority interests in retained profits		
Profits retained in associated undertakings		
Total funds generated from operations		
Funds from other sources		
Proceeds of disposals of tangible fixed assets		
Proceeds of disposals of fixed asset investments		
Debentures issued in part consideration of the acquisition of a subsidiary*		
Shares issued in part consideration of the acquisition of a subsidiary*		
Total source of funds		
Application of Funds		
Development costs incurred		
Purchase of tangible fixed assets*		
Purchase of goodwill on acquisition of subsidiary*		
Purchase of fixed asset investments		
Loan repayments		
Tax paid		
Dividends paid by parent company		
Dividends paid to minority shareholders		
Total application of funds		
Net source of funds	£	£
The net source of funds is represented by the following increase in working capital:		
Stocks*		
Debtors*		
Creditors falling due within one year*		
Movements in net liquid funds:		
Current asset investments		
Cash at bank and in hand		
Bank overdraft*		
Increase in working capital	£	£

*See Note 33 for a summary of the effect of the acquisition of the subsidiary.

Notes to the Financial Statements
For the year ended 31 December 1990

s 230 1. As permitted by section 230 of the Companies Act 1985, the holding company's profit and loss account has not been included in these financial statements.

2. Turnover and profit on ordinary activities before taxation

		Turnover		Profit on ordinary activities before taxation	
		1990 £	1989 £	1990 £	1989 £
4 Sch 55 (1)(3)(4)	*Description of classes of business*				
		£	£	£	£
4 Sch 55 (2)(3)(4) CO 21(c) GU 10(c)	*Geographical markets supplied*				
		£	£	£	£

OR

The analysis of turnover by geographical market and the analysis of turnover and profit before taxation by class of business has not been given.

SSAP 14 para 30 SSAP 23 para 22 As a result of the acquisition of a material subsidiary (see note 18), turnover increased by £ and the profit on ordinary activities before taxation increased by £

3. Other operating expenses

		1990 £	1989 £
4 Sch Format 1	Distributions costs		
	Administrative expenses		
	Other operating income		
		£	£

4. Directors and employees

Employees

4 Sch 56(1) The average weekly number of persons (including directors)

employed by the group during the year was:

	1990 Number	1989 Number
Categories		
	______	______
	______	______

The directors may select the categories of employees disclosed, which could be for example by product group or by type of work.

		1990 £	1989 £
4 Sch 56 (4), 94	Staff costs (for the above persons):		
	Wages and salaries		
	Social Security costs		
	Other pension costs		
		£	£

Directors' remuneration

6 Sch 1, 7, 8, 9 The remuneration paid to the directors of GAAP UK plc was:

	1990 £	1989 £
Fees		
Other emoluments (including pension contributions, benefits in kind and golden hellos)		
Pensions paid to former directors		
Compensation for loss of office		
Consideration paid to third parties for services of directors		
	£	£

6 Sch 3, 4 Fees and other emoluments disclosed above (excluding pension contributions) include amounts paid to:

	1990	1989
The chairman	£	£
The highest-paid director	£	£

6 Sch 4(2) The number of directors (including the chairman and the highest-paid director) who received fees and other emoluments (excluding pension contributions) in the following ranges was:

	1990 Number	1989 Number
£0 — £5,000		
£5,001 — £10,000		
etc		

6 Sch 6
CO 21(n)
GU 10(k) Emoluments amounting to £ (1989: £) have been waived by (*number*) (1989: *number*) directors.

5. Investment income

		1990 £	1989 £
4 Sch format 1	Income from other participating interests		
	Income from other fixed asset investments		
	Other interest receivable and similar income		
		£	£

4 Sch 53(4) SSAP 8 para 25	Income from investments includes £ (1989: £) from listed investments.
4 Sch format Note 15	*Income derived from group undertakings has to be shown separately from income derived from other sources.*

6. Amounts written off investments

		1990 £	1989 £
4 Sch 19(1)(2) SSAP 12 para 19	Amounts written off fixed asset investments as a result of:		
	A permanent diminution in value		
	A temporary diminution in value		
4 Sch 23(1)	Amounts written off current asset investments		
4 Sch 19(3), 23(2)	Amounts written off fixed asset or current asset investments in prior years written back as no longer necessary:		
	Fixed assets		
	Current assets		
		£	£

7. Interest payable and similar charges

		1990 £	1989 £
4 Sch 53(2)	On bank loans, overdrafts and other loans:		
	Repayable within 5 years, not by instalments		
	Repayable within 5 years, by instalments		
	Repayable wholly or partly in more than 5 years		
SSAP 21 para 53	On finance leases and hire purchase contracts		
		£	£

8. **Profit on ordinary activities before taxation**

Reference		1990 £	1989 £
	Profit on ordinary activities before taxation is stated after crediting:		
4 Sch 53(5)	Rents receivable (net of outgoings)		
	And after charging:		
SSAP 22 para 45(a)	Goodwill amortisation		
4 Sch 18, Note 17 SSAP 12 para 25 SSAP 21 para 50	Depreciation of assets and amounts written off assets as a result of a permanent diminution in their value: Depreciation charge for the year:		
	– intangible fixed assets		
	– tangible owned fixed assets		
	– tangible fixed assets held under finance leases and hire purchase contracts		
4 Sch 19(2)	Amounts written off fixed assets as a result of a permanent diminution in their value		
4 Sch 19(3)	Amounts written off fixed assets in prior years written back as no longer necessary		
SSAP 13 para 22	Research and development expenditure:		
	– deferred expenditure amortised		
	– current years' expenditure		
4 Sch 57(3) SSAP 6 para 14	Exceptional item: Provision made against a major contract		
390A (3)(4)	Auditors' remuneration (including expenses)		
4 Sch 53(6)	Hire of plant and machinery – operating leases		
SSAP 21 para 55	Hire of other assets – operating leases		

SSAP 13 para 22 — *Disclosure of research and development expenditure is only required where the company is a plc or a banking or insurance company or it exceeds the criteria for determining a medium-size company under the Act multiplied by ten.*

4 Sch 53(6) SSAP 21 para 55 — Amounts charged to revenue in respect of sums payable for the hire of plant and machinery under finance leases and hire purchase contracts are shown above separately under the headings of depreciation £ and finance charges £ – total £ (1989: £) (see note 7).

4A Sch 14 — The cumulative amount of goodwill resulting from acquisitions in the year and in earlier years which has been written off is £ (1989: £).

9. **Taxation**

		1990 £	1989 £
4 Sch 54	UK corporation tax at %:		
SSAP 8	Current		
para 22	Deferred		
SSAP 15	Tax credits on franked investment income		
para 33	Irrecoverable advance corporation tax		
	Double taxation relief		
	Overseas taxation		
	Under-provision in respect of prior years:		
	Current		
	Deferred		
SSAP 1	Associated undertakings		
para 20		£	£

SSAP 15 para 35 — The taxation charge for the year has been reduced by £ (1989: £) in respect of the excess of tax allowances over depreciation, and other timing differences on which, in accordance with the group's accounting policy, no deferred taxation has been provided.

10. **Extraordinary items**

		1990 £	1989 £
4 Sch	Extraordinary income:		
Format 1	Surplus on disposal of freehold land and		
SSAP 6	buildings including £ transferred		
paras 15,	from the revaluation reserve (see note 27)		
37	Share of associated undertaking's extraordinary income		
SSAP 1	Extraordinary charges:		
para 21	Closure costs		
SSAP 22	Loss on disposal of subsidiary		
para 52			
	Extraordinary profit		
4 Sch 54(3)	Taxation on the above:		
SSAP 6	UK corporation tax at %:		
para 37	Current		
	Deferred		
		£	£

SSAP 22 para 52 — The loss on disposal resulted from the sale of (*company name*) a subsidiary during the year. Goodwill of £ was written off directly to reserves in 1984 and has not been taken into account in determining the loss on sale.

11. **Profit for the financial year**

		1990	1989
		£	£
s 230(1)(3) SSAP 1 para 22	Dealt with in the accounts of the holding company		
	Retained by subsidiary companies		
	Retained by associated companies		
		£	£

12. **Dividends**

		1990	1989
		£	£
4 Sch 3(7)(b)	Preference paid		
	Ordinary:		
	Interim paid of p per share		
	Final proposed of p per share		
		£	£

CO 21(o)
GU 10(l)
Particulars must also be given where there are any arrangements under which a shareholder has waived, or agreed to waive, any dividends.

13. **Earnings per ordinary share**

SSAP 3
paras 14,
16,
Appendix 1
para 31
The calculation of earnings per share on the net basis is based on the profit on ordinary activities after taxation but before extraordinary items and after deducting preferrence dividends, namely, £ (1989: £) and on (*number*) (1989: *number*) ordinary shares, being the weighted average number of ordinary shares in issue and ranking for dividend during the year.

The calculation of earnings per share on the nil basis is based on adjusted profits of £ (1989: £), after adding irrecoverable advance corporation tax, and on (*number*) (1989: *number*) ordinary shares.

The calculation of fully diluted earnings per ordinary share is based on (*number*) (1989: *number*) ordinary shares, allowing for the full exercise of outstanding share purchase options (see note 26), and adjusted profit of £ (1989: £), after adding interest deemed to be earned from investing the proceeds of such share options in 2½% Consolidated Stock.

14. Prior-year adjustment

SSAP 6 paras 16, 39

A narrative description is normally given of the cause of a prior year adjustment. Prior year adjustments are made for changes in accounting policy or fundamental errors. The effect of the prior year adjustment should be disclosed. (See also note 27.)

15. Intangible fixed assets

		Development costs	Patents and trademarks	Goodwill on consolidation	Total
		£	£	£	£
	Group				
SSAP 13	Cost				
para 32	1 January 1990				
4 Sch	Exchange differences				
Notes 2, 3	Additions				
	Disposals				
	At 31 December 1990				
4 Sch 42(3)	Amounts written off				
	At 1 January 1990				
	Exchange differences				
	Charge for the year				
	Eliminated in respect of disposals				
	At 31 December 1990				
	Net book value				
	At 31 December 1990	£	£	£	£
	At 31 December 1989	£	£	£	£

If GAAP UK plc owned any intangible fixed assets, similar information would be required in respect of those assets.

S 269

Where appropriate, the note should include a statement that capitalised development costs have not been treated as a realised loss, and the special circumstances that the directors have relied upon.

16. Tangible fixed assets

		Investment properties £	Land and buildings £	Plant and machinery £	Fixtures fittings tools and equipment £	Total £
	Group					
4 Sch 42(1)	Cost or valuation					
	At 1 January 1990					
	Exchange differences					
	Surplus on revaluation					
	Additions					
	In respect of new subsidiary					
	Disposals					
	At 31 December 1990					
4 Sch 42(3)	Depreciation					
	At 1 January 1990					
	Exchange differences					
	Adjustment on revaluation					
	In respect of new subsidiary					
	Charge for the year					
	Provision for diminution in value					
	Eliminated in respect of disposals					
	At 31 December 1990					
	Net book value					
	At 31 December 1990	£	£	£	£	£
	At 31 December 1989	£	£	£	£	£
	Cost or valuation at 31 December 1990 is represented by:					
	Valuation in *year*					
	Cost					
		£	£	£	£	£

Where a company has made payments on account of tangible fixed assets or is in the course of constructing tangible fixed assets, it must show the amounts involved in a separate column.

SSAP 21 para 50 — The net book value of tangible fixed assets includes an amount of £ (1989: £) in respect of assets held under finance leases and hire purchase contracts.

4 Sch 33(2), 43 SSAP 19 para 12 — Investment properties were revalued at their open market value at 31 December 1990 by (*name*), a director of the subsidiary that owns the investment properties.

s 226(4)(5) SSAP 19 paras 11, 13	In accordance with SSAP 19, investment properties are revalued annually and the aggregate surplus or deficit is transferred to the revaluation reserve. Depreciation is not provided in respect of freehold investment properties, and leasehold investment properties where the unexpired term of the lease is more than 20 years. The directors consider that this accounting policy results in the financial statements giving a true and fair view. Depreciation is only one of the many factors reflected in the annual valuation and the amount that might otherwise have been shown cannot be separately identified or quantified.
4 Sch 33(2), 43	Land and buildings in the UK were revalued on the basis of an open market valuation for existing use at 31 December 1990 by (*name*), Chartered Surveyors.
4 Sch 33(3) (4)	If investment properties and land and buildings had not been revalued they would have been included at the following amounts:

		Investment properties		Land and buildings	
		1990	1989	1990	1989
	Group				
	Cost	£	£	£	£
	Aggregate depreciation based on cost	£	£	£	£
4 Sch 44	Investment properties and land and buildings at net book value comprise:				

	Investment properties		Land and buildings	
	1990	1989	1990	1989
	£	£	£	£
Freeholds				
Long leaseholds				
Short leaseholds				
	£	£	£	£

If GAAP UK plc had any tangible fixed assets, similar information would be required in respect of those assets.

17. **Fixed asset investments**

		Associated undertakings £	Other participating interests £	Loans £	Other investments £	Total £
	Group					
4 Sch 42(1)	Cost or valuation					
	At 1 January 1990					
	Additions					
	Disposals					
	At 31 December 1990					

		Associated undertakings £	Other participating interests £	Loans £	Other investments £	Total £
4 Sch 42(3)	Amounts written off					
	At 1 January 1990					
	Amounts written off in the year					
	Amounts written off in prior years writen back					
	Eliminated in respect of disposals					
	Net book value					
	At 31 December 1990	£	£	£	£	£
	At 31 December 1989	£	£	£	£	£

4 Sch 45(1) Investments at net book value include:

	Associated undertakings 1990 £	Associated undertakings 1989 £	Other participating interests 1990 £	Other participating interests 1989 £	Other investments 1990 £	Other investments 1989 £
Investments listed on a recognised investment exchange						
Other listed investments						
	£	£	£	£	£	£
Aggregate market value of listed investments	£	£	£	£	£	£

		1990 £	1989 £	1990 £	1989 £	1990 £	1989 £
SSAP 1 para 26	Interests in associated undertakings:						
	Share of associated undertakings' net assets (excluding goodwill)						
	Share of associated undertakings' goodwill						
	Premium paid on acquisition of interests in associated undertakings						
	Total interests in associated undertakings	£	£	£	£	£	£

GAAP UK plc

		Interests in group undertakings £	Joint venture £	Participating interests £	Other investments £	Total £
4 Sch 42(1)	Cost or valuation					
	At 1 January 1990					
	Surplus on revaluation					
	Additions (see note 18)					
	Disposals (see note 10)					
	At 31 December 1990					
4 Sch 42(3)	Amounts written off					
	At 1 January 1990					
	Amounts written off in year					
	Amounts written off in prior years written back					
	Eliminated in respect of disposals					
	At 31 December 1990					

	Interests in group undertakings £	Joint venture £	Participating interests £	Other investments £	Total £
Net book value					
At 31 December 1990	£	£	£	£	£
At 31 December 1989	£	£	£	£	£

Participating interests include interests in associated undertakings and other participating interests.

4 Sch 31(3) 33(2) Investments in group undertakings are stated at the group's share of the net assets of the group undertakings. The directors have adopted this basis for valuing the investments in group undertakings because they consider that it more fairly represents the investment of GAAP UK plc in group undertakings.

4 Sch 33(3) (4) If investments in group undertakings had not been revalued they would have been included at the following amounts:

	1990 £	1989 £
Cost		
Aggregate amounts written off		
Total	£	£

Listed investments

		Participating interests		Other investments	
		1990 £	1989 £	1990 £	1989 £
4 Sch 45(1)	Investments at net book value include:				
	Investments listed on a recognised investment exchange				
	Other listed investments				
		£	£	£	£

4 Sch 45(2) (a)(b) Listed investments include certain investments for which the market value is considered to be higher than the stock exchange value. The market value of these investments is £ and their stock exchange value £

Group and GAAP UK plc

The group holds more than 10% of the equity of the following undertakings:

Interests in group undertakings

5 Sch 15, 16

Name of undertaking	Country of* incorporation or registration	Description of shares held	Proportion of nominal value of issued shares held by the company %	the group %
A				
B				
C				

5 Sch 15(4) s 229 All the above companies are included in the consolidation except company C (*state reason*).

5 Sch 17 *If company C is not included in the consolidated financial statements by way of the equity method of accounting, disclosure of the aggregate capital and reserves of company C at 31 December 1990 and its profit or loss of the year then ended is required.*

5 Sch 18 *A statement of any qualifications in the auditors' report on company C's financial statements for the year ending with or during the year of the company that are material from the point of view of GAAP UK plc and that are not covered in the consolidated financial statements is required. If this information is not obtainable, a statement to that effect should be given.*

5 Sch 19 *Where the financial year of any subsidiary is other than 31 December 1990, the names of the subsidiaries, their year ends (or the earliest or latest of those dates) and the reasons why the year ends do not coincide with that of GAAP UK plc should be stated.*

5 Sch 15(c) * *If unincorporated, the address of its principal place of business should be stated.*

Joint venture

5 Sch 21(1) The company directly owns 60% of the business of an unincorporated joint venture (name) which is included in the consolidation on a proportional basis. Its principal place of business is in the UK (address).

5 Sch 21(2) *Where the financial year of the joint venture is other than 31 December 1990, the date on which its financial statements last ended before 31 December 1990 should be stated.*

Significant interests

Details of those undertakings in which the company and the group holds more than a 10% interest are set out below:

Associated undertakings

5 Sch 22
SSAP 1
para 49

Name of undertaking	Country of* incorporation or registration	Description of shares held	Proportion of nominal value of issued shares held by	
			the company %	the group %

SSAP 1
para 49(b)

An indication of the nature of the business of each associated undertaking should also be given.

5 Sch 22(c)

* *If unincorporated, the address of its principal place of business should be stated.*

Other significant interests

5 Sch 22
SSAP 1
para 49

Name of undertaking	Country of* incorporation or registration	Description of shares held	Proportion of nominal value of issued shares held by	
			the company %	the group %

SSAP 1
para 38

The 25% holding in (company) is not treated as an associated undertaking because GAAP UK plc is not in a position to exercise significant influence over that company.

5 Sch
25(1), 28(1)

At 31 December 1990, the aggregate capital and reserves of that company was £ (1989: £). The profit of that company for the year ended 31 December 1990 was £ (1989: £).

5 Sch 24(c)
27(c)

* *If unincorporated, the address of its principal place of business should be stated.*

18. **Acquisition of subsidiary**

4A Sch 13
SSAP 23
paras 21, 22
SSAP 22
paras 44, 47

On (*date*) the group acquired the whole of the issued share capital of (*name of subsidiary*) for a total consideration of £ . The consideration was satisfied by the issue of (*number*) ordinary shares of p each having a value of £ and the issue of £ of % debenture stock 1994/99. The total fair value of the consideration was £ . The company has taken merger relief on the issue of its shares and the group has used acquisition accounting to account for the purchase.

4A Sch 13

The subsidiary made a profit of £ from (*date*) the beginning of the subsidiary's financial year to the date of acquisition and made a profit of £ for the previous financial year.

SSAP 22 para 47 — In accordance with the group's accounting policy, the goodwill arising on consolidation of £ has been written off against the merger reserve arising on consolidation.

4A Sch 13 SSAP 22 para 48 — The table that follows analyses the book values and fair values of the net assets acquired.

	Book value	Revaluation	Provisions for trading losses	Other provisions	Accounting policy alignment	Other major items	Fair value to the group
	£	£	£	£	£	£	£
Fixed assets							
Intangibles						(f)	
Tangibles		(a)					
Investments		(b)					
Current assets							
Stocks			(c)	(d)	(e)		
Debtors							
Investments							
Cash at bank							
Total assets							
Liabilities							
Provisions:							
Pensions							
Taxation						(g)	
Other			(c)				
Creditors							
Debentures							
Bank loans							
Trade creditors							
Other creditors							
Accruals							
Total liabilities							
Net assets acquired	£	£	£	£	£	£	
Fair value of consideration							
Goodwill							£

Adjustments	Explanations
1. Revaluations	
Note a	Increases in value of freehold properties since last revaluation.
Note b	Increases in value of shares of USM investment since purchase.
2. Provisions for trading losses	
Note c	Losses expected to be incurred prior to closing down small tools division.
3. Other provisions	
Note d	Write-down following reassess-

		ment of realisable value of stock which is more than one year old.
	4. Accounting policy alignment Note e	Change of stock valuation from weighted average cost to FIFO which is used by the group.
	5. Other items Note f	Recognition of intangibles – relating to publishing titles and brands acquired.
	Note g	Adjustment to deferred tax arising from the incorporation of fair values.

19. **Capital commitments**

		Group 1990	Group 1989	Company 1990	Company 1989
4 Sch 50(3)	Capital expenditure that has been contracted for but has not been provided for in the financial statements	£	£	£	£
	Capital expenditure that has been authorised by the directors but has not yet been contracted for	£	£	£	£
SSAP 21 para 54	Commitments under finance leases entered into, but not yet provided for in the financial statements	£	£	£	£

20. **Stocks**

		Group 1990 £	Group 1989 £	Company 1990 £	Company 1989 £
SSAP 9 para 27	Stocks comprise:				
	Raw materials and consumables				
	Work in progress				
	Finished goods				
SSAP 9 para 30(c)	Long-term contracts				
	Net cost less foreseeable losses				
4 Sch Note 8	*Less:* Applicable payments on account				
		£	£	£	£

4 Sch 26(3)(b) CO 21(g) GU 10(g)	The cost of long-term contracts includes interest amounting to £ (1989: £) on capital borrowed to finance production. Payments received on account in excess of the value of the work done on the related contract are included in creditors.
4 Sch 27(3) (4)	The replacement cost of raw materials and consumables is greater than the balance sheet value of raw materials and consumables by £ (1989: £). The replacement cost of work in progress is greater than the balance sheet value of work in progress by £ (1989: £).

21. Debtors

		Group		Company	
		1990	1989	1990	1989
		£	£	£	£
	Amounts falling due within one year:				
	Trade debtors				
	Amounts recoverable on contracts				
	Amounts owed by group undertakings				
	Amounts owed by associated undertakings				
	Amounts owed by undertakings in which the company has a participating interest				
	Other debtors				
4 Sch Note 6	Prepayments and accrued income				
4 Sch Note 5	Amounts falling due after more than one year:				
	Amounts owed by group undertakings				
	Amounts owed by associated undertakings				
	Amounts owed by undertakings in which the company has a participating interest				
	Other debtors				
		£	£	£	£

22. **Current asset investments**

		Group		Company	
		1990	1989	1990	1989
		£	£	£	£
4 Sch 45(1)	Investments listed on a recognised investment exchange				
	Other listed investments				
		£	£	£	£

4 Sch 45(2) (a) Listed investments include certain investments for which the market value is considered to be higher than the stock exchange value. The market value of these investments is £ and their stock exchange value £

23. **Creditors**

		Group		Company	
		1990	1989	1990	1989
		£	£	£	£
	Amounts falling due within one year:				
	Current instalments due on debenture loans				
	Bank overdrafts				
SSAP 21 para 51	Obligations under finance leases				
4 Sch Note 8	Payments received on account				
	Trade creditors				
	Bills of exchange payable				
	Amounts owed to group undertakings				
	Amounts owed to associated undertakings				
	Amounts owed to undertakings in which the company has a participating interest				
4 Sch 51(3)	Dividends payable				
SSAP 8 para 26	Corporation tax				
4 Sch Note 9	Other taxation and social security payable				
	Other creditors				
4 Sch Note 10	Accruals and deferred income				
		£	£	£	£

4 Sch 48(4) Bank overdrafts amounting to £ (1989: £) are secured by a floating charge on all the assets of the company.

		Group		Company	
		1990	1989	1990	1989
		£	£	£	£
	Amounts falling due after more than one year:				
	Debenture loans				
	Bank loans				
SSAP 21 para 51	Obligations under finance leases				
	Amounts owed to group undertakings				
	Amounts owed to associated undertakings				
	Amounts owed to undertakings in which the company has a participating interest				
		£	£	£	£

Debenture loans

4 Sch 48(1) (4)	Repayable otherwise than by instalments in more than five years:				
	% first mortgage debenture stock 2005 secured on the land and buildings, repayable at par on 1 April 2005				
	Repayable by instalments:				
	% debenture stock 1994/99 secured on the land and buildings, repayable at par by equal annual instalments from 1 April 1994. Instalments amounting to £ are repayable in more than five years				
		£	£	£	£

CO 21(f) GU 10(f)	Debenture loans are repayable as follows:				
	In one year or less				
	Between one and two years				
	Between two and five years				
	In five years or more				
		£	£	£	£

		Group 1990 £	Group 1989 £	Company 1990 £	Company 1989 £
	Bank loans and obligations under finance leases				
4 Sch 48(1) to (4)	Repayable otherwise than by instalments in more than five years:				
	Bank loans at % per annum secured by a floating charge on all the assets of the company, repayable on demand after 1 April 1998				
	Repayable by instalments:				
	Bank loans at % per annum repayable in three equal annual instalments from 1 April 1992				
	Finance leases				
		£	£	£	£
CO 21(f) GU 10(f) SSAP 21 para 52	Bank loans and obligations under finance leases are repayable as follows:				
	In one year or less, or on demand				
	Between one and two years				
	Between two and five years				
	In five years or more				
		£	£	£	£

24. Deferred taxation

Deferred taxation provided in the financial statements, and the total potential liability including the amounts for which provision has been made, are as follows:

		Amount provided 1990 £	Amount provided 1989 £	Total potential liability 1990 £	Total potential liability 1989 £
	Group				
SSAP 15 paras 37 to 42	Tax effect of timing differences because of:				
	Excess of tax allowances over depreciation				
	Other				
SSAP 8 para 27	*Less:* Advance corporation tax				
SSAP 15 para 42	Tax effect of timing differences on revaluation of:				
	Land and buildings				
	Investment properties				
		£	£	£	£

4 Sch 46(2) SSAP 15 para 38	The movements on the group provision for deferred taxation are as follows:	
		£
	Provision at 1 January 1990	
	Utilised in the year	
	Transfer from profit and loss account	
	Provision at 31 December 1990	£

If GAAP UK plc had any deferred taxation, similar information would be required in respect of that deferred taxation.

25. **Pensions**

		Group	Company
		£	£
4 Sch 50(5)	At 1 January 1990		
	Profit and loss account charge		
	Contributions paid to pension schemes		
	At 31 December 1990	£	£

SSAP 24 para 88

The group operates a number of pension schemes in the UK and overseas. The major schemes, which cover 85% of scheme members are defined benefit schemes. The assets of the schemes are held in separate trustee administered funds.

The total pension cost to the group was £ (1989: £) of which £ (1989: £) related to overseas schemes. The pension cost relating to the UK schemes is assessed in accordance with the advice of an independent qualified actuary using the (*specify method*). The latest actuarial assessment of these schemes was at 31 December 1989. The assumption made in the valuation were that the investment return would be (*specify percentage*) per annum, salary increases would average (*specify percentage*) per annum and the net present and future pensions would increase at the rate of (*specify percentage*) per annum. The cost has fallen as a result of the amortisation of an experience surplus shown by the latest valuation.

At the date of the latest actuarial valuation, the market value of the assets of the UK scheme was £ and the actuarial value of the assets was sufficient to cover (*specify percentage*) of the benefits which had accrued to members, after allowing for expected future increases in earnings. This surplus will be eliminated by 1992 as a result of a pension holiday taken by the group on the recommendation of the actuary.

26. Called-up share capital

		1990 £	1989 £
	Authorised		
4 Sch 38(1) (a) SSAP 8 para 28	(*Number*) ordinary share of p each (*Number*) 10% (now 7% plus tax credit) redeemable preference shares of £1 each		
		£	£

		1990 £	1989 £
	Allotted, called up and fully paid		
4 Sch 38(1) (b) 4 Sch Note 12 SSAP 8 para 28	(*Number*) ordinary share of p each (*Number*) 10% (now 7% plus tax credit) redeemable preference shares of £1 each		
		£	£

4 Sch 38(2) The 10% (now 7% plus tax credit) redeemable preference shares must be redeemed by three equal annual instalments commencing on 1 January 1992 at a premium of 10p per £1 share.

Allotment during the year

4 Sch 39 As part of the acquisition of (*name of new subsidiary*), GAAP UK plc made an allotment of (*number*) ordinary shares at p each (see note 18).

Contingent rights to the allotment of shares

4 Sch 40 Options have been granted to subscribe for ordinary shares of GAAP UK plc as follows:

Number and description of shares	Subscription price per share	Period within which options exercisable

Details of directors' interests in shares and debentures of group companies are included in the directors' report.

27. Share premium account and reserves

		Share premium account £	Revaluation reserve £	Merger reserve £	Other reserves £	Profit and loss account £
	Group					
4 Sch 46(2) SSAP 6 para 35	At 1 January 1990 as previously reported					
SSAP 6 para 39	Prior year adjustment (note 14)					
	As restated					
	Premium on allotment during the year					
	Merger reserve on acquisition					
	Goodwill written off (see note 18)					
	Surplus arising on revaluation of investment properties and land and buildings					
	Transfer from revaluation reserve to profit and loss account					
	Retained profit for the year					
	At 31 December 1990	£	£	£	£	£
SSAP 1 para 31	GAAP UK plc and subsidiaries					
	Associated undertakings					
		£	£	£	£	£
	GAAP UK plc					
4 Sch 46(2)	At 1 January 1990					
	Premium on allotment during year					
	Surplus arising on revaluation of investments in subsidiaries					
	Retained profit for the year					
	At 31 December 1990	£	£	£	£	£

SSAP 19 para 13 The revaluation reserve includes £ (1989: £) in respect of surpluses on the annual revaluation of investment properties.

4 Sch 34(4) No provision has been made for the additional United Kingdom taxation that would accrue if the investment properties, land and buildings or the investments in subsidiaries were disposed of at their revalued amounts. The potential liability to such taxation is disclosed in Note 24.

The transfer from the revaluation reserve to the profit and loss account includes £ transferred to extraordinary items (see note 10) being the realisation of a revaluation surplus on the disposal of freehold land and buildings. The balance of the transfer represents the difference between the depreciation charge for the year based on revalued amounts and the depreciation charge for the year based on cost.

SSAP 1 para 31 SSAP 14 para 36 SSAP 15 para 44

Included in the group profit and loss account is an amount of £ (1989: £) in respect of profits retained in (*country*), the remittance of which is subject to approval by the (*country's*) authorities. No deferred taxation has been provided on these earnings as they are not expected to be remitted to the UK in the near future.

Not statutory

The amount of the reserves of GAAP UK plc that may not legally be distributed under section 264 of the Companies Act 1985 is £ (1989: £).

28. **Contingent liabilities**

		Group		Company	
		1990	1989	1990	1989
		£	£	£	£
4 Sch 50(2) SSAP 18 paras 16	Bills discounted with recourse	£	£	£	£
4 Sch 50(6) (b)	Guarantee in respect of bank overdraft of a subsidiary	–	–	£	£

29. **Other financial commitments**

4 Sch 50(5)

GAAP UK plc has agreed to enter into a joint venture with (*name*). The initial contribution to the joint venture will amount to £ . The total contribution to the joint venture is not expected to exceed £

SSAP 21 para 56

At 31 December 1990 the company had annual commitments under non-cancellable operating leases as follows:

	1990		1989	
	Land and buildings	Other	Land and buildings	Other
	£	£	£	£
Expiring within one year				
Expiring between two and five years inclusive				
Expiring in over five years				
	£	£	£	£

The majority of the company's leases of land and buildings are subject to rent review periods ranging between three and five years.

30. **Subsequent events**

SSAP 17 paras 23, 24

On (*date*), a subsidiary's factory was badly damaged by fire. The costs of repair are not expected to exceed insurance proceeds. Accordingly, no provision has been made in these financial statements.

31. Transactions with directors

6 Sch 22 During the year, the company made a loan for house purchase of £ to (*name*), a director, following his transfer to London. The loan is repayable by 24 monthly instalments. The maximum amount outstanding during the year was £ . At 31 December 1990, the amount outstanding (excluding accrued interest) was £ . The amount of interest outstanding at 31 December 1990 was £

32. Transactions with officers

6 Sch 32 Included in other debtors are loans to (*number*) officers amounting to £ and quasi-loans to (*number*) officers amounting to £

33. Consolidated statement of source and application of funds

SSAP 10 Appendix 1 The figures in the consolidated statement of source and application of funds include the following amounts that relate to the effect of the acquisition of a subsidiary:

	£	£
Assets acquired:		
Tangible fixed assets		
Stocks		
Debtors		
Less: Bank overdraft		
Creditors		
Current taxation		
Net assets of subsidiary		
Less: Minority interest		
Goodwill		
Total consideration		£
Discharged by:		
Allotment of ordinary shares		
Issue of debentures		
		£

The movement in creditors falling due within one year comprises the following:

	1990	1989
		£
Current instalments due on loans		
Payments received on account		
Trade creditors		
Bills of exchange payable		
Other taxation and social security payable		
Other creditors		
Accruals and deferred income		
	£	£

GAAP UK plc
Summary of accounts, for the five years ended 31 December 1990

	1990 £	1989 £	1988 £	1987 £	1986 £
Sales and results					
Turnover	£	£	£	£	£
Profit before taxation					
Taxation					
Profit after taxation					
Minority interests					
Profit after taxation, before extraordinary items					
Extraordinary items					
Attributable profit/(loss)					
Dividends					
Retained profit/(loss)	£	£	£	£	£
Net assets employed					
Fixed assets					
Net current assets					
Non-current liabilities					
Provisions for liabilities and charges including deferred tax and pensions					
	£	£	£	£	£
Ratios					
Profit before taxation as a percentage of sales	%	%	%	%	%
Profit before taxation as a percentage of net assets employed	%	%	%	%	%
Earnings per ordinary share	p	p	p	p	p
Dividends	p	p	p	p	p

The Statement is not required by statute, but it is customary for listed companies and companies traded on the USM to give this information.

Appendix III

SUMMARY OF EC COMPANY LAW AND RELATED DIRECTIVES

The UK's membership of the European Community has had a significant effect on UK company law. The Council of the European Community has a specific duty to coordinate (or 'harmonize') the company law of the Community to make it equivalent in its effects throughout the Member States (Article 54(g) of the Treaty of Rome). It also has a general duty to issue Directives harmonising the provisions directly affecting the establishing or functioning of the common market laid down in the laws, regulations or by other administrative actions of the Members States (Article 100). The Council has used these powers to introduce a number of measures, some of which have been adopted into Community and national law, whilst others are still under discussion.

The European Community law-making process is lengthy, and it takes years, rather than months, for agreement to be reached on the measures to be adopted. Each new Regulation, Directive, etc. is examined and amended by various Community bodies and by all the individual Member States before the Council finally approves it. Even then, it is unlikely that all the Member States will implement a measure into their national laws until at least two years after the Council has approved it.

The principal company law measures of the EC that the Council has already approved, and those that it is still discussing, are briefly described below.

Directives already adopted in UK law

1st Company Law Directive - Publicity requirements, *ultra vires* and nullity [68/151/EEC]

This Directive deals with the disclosure and the public inspection of company documents and the protection of third parties. It was enacted in the UK in January 1973 by section 9 of the European Communities Act.

Section 9 has been repealed and the provisions are now contained in the Companies Act 1985 sections 18, 35, 36(4), 42, 351, 711 and Schedule 22. The Companies Act 1989 section 108 substitutes for section 35, new sections 35 and 35A which are intended to clarify the *ultra vires* position in certain respects.

2nd Company Law Directive - Formation of companies and capital and dividend requirements [77/91/EEC]

This Directive deals with the formation of public limited liability companies, the maintenance and alteration of their capital, and the payment of dividends. It was enacted in the UK in December 1980 by sections 1 to 45 and 76 to 78 of the Companies Act 1980.

These sections have been consolidated into the Companies Act 1985.

4th Company Law Directive - Company accounts [78/660/EEC]

This Directive requires that annual accounts of certain types of companies should be presented in a standard format and give a true and fair view. It was enacted in the UK for accounting periods beginning on or after 15th June 1982 by sections 1 to 21 of, and Schedules 1 and 2 to, the Companies Act 1981.

The sections have been consolidated into the Companies Act 1985 Part VII and Schedules 4, 5 and 7.

Directive coordinating the conditions for admission of securities to listing [79/279/EEC]

The Directive coordinates the conditions for the admission of securities for listing on an official stock exchange, and was implemented in the UK with effect from 1st January 1985 by the Stock Exchange (Listing) Regulations 1984 (SI 1984/716). This regulation together with the two directives listed immediately below were included in the revision to The International Stock Exchange's 'Yellow Book'. The requirements of the new Yellow book affect all announcements made by listed companies concerning accounting periods ending after 31st December 1984. The 1984 Regulations were replaced by the Financial Services Act 1986 Part IV.

Directive on listing particulars [80/390/EEC]

This Directive coordinates the requirements for drawing up, scrutinising and distributing the listing particulars that are required for securities to be admitted to an official stock exchange listing, and was implemented in the UK with effect from 1st January 1985 by the Stock Exchange (Listing) Regulations 1984 (SI 1984/716). The 1984 Regulations were replaced by the Financial Services Act 1986 Part IV.

Directive on continuing disclosure of information [82/121/EEC]

This Directive deals with the information to be published on a regular basis by companies whose shares have been admitted for listing on an official stock exchange. This was implemented in the UK with the effect from 1st January 1985 by the Stock Exchange (Listing) Regulations 1984 (SI 1984/716). The 1984 Regulations were replaced by the Financial Services Act 1986 Part IV.

3rd Company Law Directive - Internal mergers [78/855/EEC]

This Directive deals with mergers between public limited companies within the same Member State. The Council adopted the Directive in October 1978, but deferred the deadline for the implementation of the Directive until January 1986. This date then coincided with the implementation of the 6th Directive (described below).

The Directive, which was implemented by The Companies (Mergers and Divisions) Regulations 1987 No 1991, inserting section 427A and Schedule 15A into the Companies Act 1985 and has had little impact in the UK, because few mergers fall within its scope. The Regulations came into force on 1st January 1988. The Directive safeguarding employees' rights which is applied to such transactions by the 3rd Directive was implemented by the Transfer of Undertakings (Protection of Employment) Regulations 1981 No 1794.

6th Company Law Directive - Division of companies [82/891/EEC]

The Directive complements the 3rd Directive. It deals with a public limited company that transfers all of its assets and liabilities to a number of limited companies in exchange for the issue of shares to the shareholders of the divided company.

The Directive was adopted by the Council in December 1982. Like the 3rd Directive this has now been implemented and has been incorporated in the Companies Act 1985 as section 427A and Schedule 15A.

7th Company Law Directive - Group accounts [84/349/EEC]

This Directive deals with the preparation, the content and the publication of group accounts. It was adopted by the Council in June 1983. Members States had until the end of 1987 to implement it, and they need to apply its provisions by 1990.

The Directive has now been implemented by Part I of the Companies Act 1989. Part I has effect from 1st April 1990 and applies to accounting periods beginning on or after 23rd December 1989.

8th Company Law Directive - Auditors [84/253/EEC]

This Directive sets out the minimum standards for the education, the training and the qualification of auditors. The Directive was adopted by the Council in April 1984. Members States are required to implement the Directive by 1988, but they need not apply its provisions until 1990. Part II of the Companies Act 1989 implements this Directive.

Directive to revise the amounts expressed in ECU in the 4th Directive (regarding modified individual accounts)

This Directive provides for a revision of the thresholds for the balance sheet total and the net turnover that are relevant when determining whether a company qualifies as either a small or a medium-sized company.

The Directive was adopted by the Council in November 1984. The Companies (Modified Accounts) Amendment Regulations 1986 (S.I. 1986 No 1865), amending section 248(1) and (2) of the Companies Act 1985, increased the figures respectively from £5.75m to £8m and £2.8m to £3.9m in respect of medium companies and from 1.4m to 2.m and £700,000 to £975,000 in respect of small companies with effect from 30th November 1986.

Directive on unit trusts [85/611/EEC]

This directive, adopted on 20th December 1985, on the coordination of laws etc. relating to undertakings for collective investment in transferable securities (the so-called UCITS Directive), enables unit trusts and similar undertakings to market their units throughout the Community. It has been implemented in the UK by the Financial Services Act 1986 and by five statutory instruments (SI 1989/1535, SI 1989/1583, SI 1989/1584, SI 1989/1585 and SI 1989/1586) *inter alia* bringing into force on 1st October 1989 sections 24 and 86 of the Financial Services Act 1986 and prescribing Regulations under section 86.

EC Council Regulation 1985 for a European Economic Interest Grouping

This Regulation was adopted by the Council of Ministers on 25th July 1985. It introduces the EEIG, which is a new legal form of undertaking, into Community law in order to encourage cooperation between those undertakings that carry on similar business across national frontiers. It enables those undertakings to set up common non-profit-making support activities, and to operate with unlimited liability.

The Regulation applies from 1st July 1989 and has been supplemented in the United Kingdom by The European Economic Interest Grouping Regulations 1989 (SI 1989/638). The status of legal personality was left to each member state and under UK law an EEIG is a body corporate to which certain provisions of the Companies Act 1985 apply.

Directive on mutual recognition of listing particulars [80/390/EEC]

This was adopted on 22nd June 1987 and provides for the mutual recognition of listing particulars required to be published on admission to official Stock Exchange listing and for the Community to enter in reciprocal agreements with non-member states on the recognition of listing particulars. On 6th February 1990 the Council of the International Stock Exchange approved the changes to the requirements for the regulation of the UK primary markets outlined in the 1989 Consultative Document published by the Quotations Committee of the International Stock Exchange. These changes include those necessary to implement this directive and they take effect from 12th February 1990. There is also a proposed directive amending requirements in respect of the mutual recognition of stock exchange listing particulars.

Directives that have been adopted by the council, but have not yet been implemented in the UK

Directive on the annual accounts and consolidated accounts of banks and other financial institutions [86/635/EEC]

The 4th Company Law Directive mentioned above provides that Member States need not apply the provisions of that Directive to the financial statements of banks and other financial institutions. The United Kingdom took advantage of this provision. Consequently, this later Directive makes provision for the harmonisation of the annual financial statements of banks and other financial institutions. It was adopted on 8th December 1986 and Member States are required to bring into force the laws, regulations and administrative provisions necessary to comply with the Directive by 31st December 1990. The provisions are to apply to financial statements for financial years beginning on or after 1st January 1993. The DTI issued a consultative document in July 1989.

Directive on prospectuses [89/298/EEC]

A directive (adopted 17th April 1989) co-ordinating the requirements for drawing up, scrutiny and distribution of the prospectus to be published when transferable securities are offered to the public for the first time is due to be implemented by April 1991. It also provides for the mutual recognition of prospectuses drawn up in accordance with the Listing Particulars Directive mentioned above, both as public offer prospectuses and as listing particulars.

Directive on mutual recognition of professional qualifications [89/48/EEC]

This directive, adopted in December 1988, on a general system for the recognition of higher education diplomas is aimed at establishing a system of mutual recognition of professional qualifications, and is to be implemented by 4th January 1991. It requires professional qualifications obtained in one member state to be recognised by all the others. The requirement includes both university and related qualifications and other qualifications such as those of a solicitor or an accountant. Details of how the directive will be implemented in the UK and in the other Member States have yet to be finalised. Professional bodies in the UK are being consulted by the DTI. Another directive is proposed to provide for the general recognition of vocational training.

Directive on insider dealing [89/592/EEC]

Adopted in November 1989 this directive sets out the minimum standards for the prevention of insider dealing in Member States. Implementation is to be by 1st June 1992 and it is not thought that it will necessitate major changes in the scope of UK legislation. The DTI published a consultative document, The Law on Insider Dealing, in December 1989, and it is thought that the Government will take this opportunity to simplify and update the law.

The 2nd Banking Directive [89/646/EEC]

This directive together with the Solvency Ratio Directive and the Directive on own Funds (all adopted in December 1989) are designed to assist in the creation of a single market in banking services by the end of 1992, and they fit into a wider pattern of measures relating to the establishment of a free single market in financial services. These include the directives on investment services and other directives covering deposit protection, large exposures, consolidated reporting and insider trading. The EC intends that the three banking directives mentioned above should be fully in force by 1st January 1993.

11th Company Law Directive - Disclosure requirements in respects of branches opened in a Member States [89/666/EEC]

The directive provides for the disclosure of specified documents and particulars (for example, the names of persons authorised to represent the company, accounts, the appointment of a liquidator) of a branch opened in one Member State by a company governed by the law of another Member State; separate provision is made for branches opened by companies from third countries. Its object is to place branches of foreign companies in the same position as subsidiaries in the context of the harmonisation of company law. It also amends the

4th and 7th Directives. National legislation implementing the directive has to be brought into force by 1st January 1992.

12th Company Law Directive - Single member private limited companies [89/667/EEC]

This was adopted on 21st December 1989. The effect of the directive is to require Member States to allow private limited companies to be formed with a single member by 1st January 1992. Member States will also have to permit single member companies when shares come to be held by a single person, but need not apply these provisions until 1st January 1993.

Merger Control Regulation [No 4064/89]

This regulation, adopted on 21st December 1989, should not be confused with the Draft 13th Directive on mergers. The new Regulation will come into effect on 21st September 1990. The directive requires prior notification to the Commission of certain mergers and covers partial mergers and joint ventures which are in effect mergers. It distinguishes between larger mergers which will be the responsibility of the Commission, and smaller mergers which will be regulated at national level.

Proposals for Directives and other instruments still under discussion by EC institutions

Proposal for a European company statute

This Regulation provides for the incorporation of a European company - a Societas Europea - under Community law. The draft was adopted by the Commission in July 1989 and submitted to the Council on 25th August 1989. The DTI issued a Consultative Document in December 1989.

Proposals relating to the 4th and 7th Company Law Directives - annual accounts and small and medium sized companies (SMEs)

Two proposals relating to these directives were discussed by a Council working group in February 1990. The first aims to extend the scope of these directives to certain partnerships and unlimited companies; the second aims to reduce the reporting burden on certain SMEs, and to make them mandatory on all Member States. It is thought that the Council intends to take these proposals forward in parallel.

Draft 5th Directive - Company structure and employee participation

This directive concerns the structure of public limited companies and the powers and duties of their board members and auditors, and would require companies employing 1,000 or more to permit employees to participate in management. It proposes a two-tier board system (supervisory board and management board), but companies which choose a single tier board must have a majority of non-executive directors who appoint and dismiss the executive directors. As its proposals were opposed by some Member States, including the UK, the Commission submitted an Amended Proposal to the Council in August 1983. In January 1990 the Department of Trade and Industry published a Consultative Document on the Amended Proposal for a 5th Directive. It is expected that discussion on the proposal will take several years.

Draft Vredeling Directive

This is a proposal on procedures for informing and consulting the employees of undertakings with complex structures, in particular transnational undertakings. It proposes that the head offices of large companies and other major employers (such as leading building societies and large professional partnerships) should inform and consult employees of subsidiaries or separate establishments through local management about proposed decisions likely to affect employees. Consultations are not yet concluded.

Draft Proposal for a 9th Company Law Directive - Conduct of groups of companies

It is proposed that this draft directive would provide for a harmonised legal structure for the 'unified management' of a public limited company and any other undertaking which had a controlling interest in it, whether or not that undertaking was itself a company. It would also prescribe rules for the conduct of groups through employee participation. It also proposes the harmonisation of the law of plcs in certain other areas.

Draft 10th Company Law Directive - Cross border mergers

On 25th April 1988 the EC Commission submitted their draft regulation relating to merger control for approval by the Council of Ministers. The draft regulation was entitled 'A regulation on the control of concentrations between undertakings'. The draft requires pre-notification to the Commission of all relevant mergers. The term concentration (or merger) would apply in two situations. Firstly, where two or more undertakings merge and secondly, where control, for example by purchase of shares, is acquired. The proposal would import many provisions from the 3rd Directive.

Draft Directive on the annual accounts of insurance undertakings

The 4th Directive also excluded insurance companies from its scope. An amended proposal was submitted by the Commission to the Council on 30th August 1989. There is also a draft investment services directive and a proposal (revised September 1989) for a directive on compulsory winding-up of insurance undertakings.

Draft Bankruptcy Convention

This draft convention provides for the harmonisation throughout the Community of bankruptcy proceedings, liquidation proceedings of insolvent companies and analogous proceedings. The proposal has been agreed subject to some reservations by certain Member States, but certain constitutional points have been raised which are currently being considered by the Council. There is also a draft proposal for a directive on the dissolution and liquidation of limited companies, in effect, on members' voluntary winding up.

Draft Convention on the mutual recognition of companies and bodies corporate.

The object of this draft convention is to ensure that companies and other business associates formed under the law of one member state are recognised in other Member States. The proposal has run into serious difficulties, and indeed some Member States have challenged the fundamental need to have it at all. No agreement is expected on the convention in the foreseeable future. The convention has been under reconsideration by an *ad hoc* working group.

Draft 13th Directive - Takeovers and other general bids)

This proposal from the Commission was referred to the Council in December 1989. The DTI published a Consultative Document in January 1990. Its intention is to permit takeovers in the context of a single market.

Appendix IV

SUMMARY OF MAXIMUM PENALTIES FOR OFFENCES UNDER THE ACCOUNTING PROVISIONS OF THE COMPANIES ACT 1985

This appendix refers throughout to the 'statutory maximum fine' which is currently £2,000.

Section	Who is liable	Maximum punishment
151(3)	A company that gives financial assistance for the acquisition of its own shares, and every officer of that company who is in default.	On indictment: (a) Where the company is convicted, a fine. (b) Where an officer of the company is convicted, 2 years imprisonment or a fine, or both. On summary conviction: (a) Where the company is convicted, the statutory maximum fine. (b) Where an officer of the company is convicted, 6 months imprisonment or the statutory maximum fine, or both.
156(6)	A company that fails to register a statutory declaration under section 155 and every officer of that company who is in default.	On summary conviction, the statutory maximum fine and a daily default fine (where applicable) of one-fiftieth of the statutory maximum.
156(7)	A director who makes a statutory declaration under section 155, without having reasonable grounds for the opinion expressed in it.	On indictment, 2 years imprisonment or a fine, or both. On summary conviction, 6 months imprisonment or the statutory maximum fine, or both.
221(5) or 222(4)	Every officer, who is in default, of a company that fails to keep accounting records.	On indictment, 2 years imprisonment or a fine, or both. On summary conviction, 6 months imprisonment or the statutory maximum fine, or both.

222(6)	An officer of a company who fails to secure compliance with, or intentionally causes default under, section 222(5) (preservation of accounting records for requisite number of years).	On indictment, 2 years imprisonment or a fine, or both. On summary conviction, 6 months imprisonment or the statutory maximum fine, or both.
231(7)	A company that fails to annex to its annual return certain particulars required by Schedule 5 that are not included in its annual accounts, and every officer of that company who is in default.	On summary conviction, a fine of one-fifth of the statutory maximum, and (where applicable) a daily default fine of one-fiftieth of the statutory maximum.
232(4)	A director or an officer of a company who is in default in giving notice of matters relating to himself for purposes of Schedule 6 Part I.	On summary conviction, a fine of one-fifth of the statutory maximum.
233(5)	A director of a company who is a party to the approval of defective financial statements and who knows that the financial statements do not conform with the requirements of the Act.	Directors are individually liable: (a) On indictment, to a fine. (b) On summary conviction, to the statutory maximum fine.
233(6)	A company that lays or delivers an unsigned balance sheet or circulates copies of the balance sheet without signatures, and every officer of that company who is in default.	On summary conviction, a fine of one-fifth of the statutory maximum.
234(5)	Directors of a company whose directors' report does not comply with the Part VII of the Act.	Directors are individually liable: (a) On indictment, to a fine. (b) On summary conviction, to the statutory maximum fine.
234A(4)	A company that lays, circulates or delivers a directors' report without the required signature, and every officer of that company who is in default.	On summary conviction, a fine of one-fifth of the statutory maximum.

236(4)	A company that lays, circulates or delivers an auditors' report without the required signature, and every officer of that company who is in default.	On summary conviction, a fine of one-fifth of the statutory maximum.
238(5)	A company that fails to send its annual accounts, directors' report and auditors' report to those entitled to receive them, and every officer of that company who is in default.	On indictment, a fine. On summary conviction, the statutory maximum fine.
239(3)	A company that fails to supply a copy of its accounts and reports to a shareholder on his demand, and every officer of that company who is in default.	On summary conviction, a fine of one-fifth of the statutory maximum, and (where applicable) a daily default fine of one-fiftieth of the statutory maximum.
240(6)	A company and any officer that fails to comply with the requirements of section 240 in connection with the publication of full individual or group statutory accounts or non-statutory accounts.	On summary conviction, a fine of one-fifth of the statutory maximum.
241(2) or 242(2)	A director who is in default regarding his duty to lay and deliver the company's annual accounts, directors' report and auditors' report.	On summary conviction, the statutory maximum fine, and (where applicable) a daily default fine of one-tenth of the statutory maximum.
251(6)	A company and any officer that fails to comply with the requirements of section 251 in connection with the publication of summary financial statements.	On summary conviction, a fine of one-fifth of the statutory maximum.
314(3)	A director who fails to comply with section 314 (duty to disclose compensation payable on a takeover, etc), or a person who fails to include the required particulars in a notice he has to give of such matters.	On summary conviction, a fine of one-fifth of the statutory maximum.

317(7)	A director who fails to disclose an interest in a contract.	On indictment, a fine. On summary conviction, the statutory maximum fine.
318(8)	A company that is in default in complying with section 318(1) or (5) (directors' service contracts to be kept at an appropriate place), or that is 14 days in default in complying with section 318(4) (notice to Registrar as to where copies of contracts and memoranda are kept), or that refuses inspection as required under section 318(7).	On summary conviction, a fine of one-fifth of the statutory maximum, and (where applicable) a daily default fine of one-fiftieth of the statutory maximum.
323(2)	A director who deals in options to buy or sell a listed company's shares or debentures.	On indictment, 2 years imprisonment or a fine, or both. On summary conviction, 6 months imprisonment or the statutory maximum fine, or both.
324(7)	A director who fails to notify his interest in a company's shares, or who makes a false statement in a purported notification.	On indictment, 2 years imprisonment or a fine, or both. On summary conviction, 6 months imprisonment or the statutory maximum fine, or both.
326(2), (3),(4), (5).	A company that commits various defaults in connection with a company's register of directors' interests, and any officer who is in default.	On summary conviction, a fine of one-fifth of the statutory maximum, and, except in the case of section 326(5), a daily default fine (where applicable) of one-fiftieth of the statutory maximum.
328(6)	A director who fails to notify the company that members of his family have, or have exercised, options to buy shares or debentures, or who makes a false statement in a purported notification.	On indictment, 2 years imprisonment or a fine, or both. On summary conviction, 6 months imprisonment or the statutory maximum fine, or both.

329(3)	A company that fails to notify an investment exchange of an acquisition of its securities by a director, and any officer of the company who is in default.	On summary conviction, a fine of one-fifth of the statutory maximum, and (where applicable) a daily default fine of one-fiftieth of the statutory maximum.
342(1)	A director of a relevant company who authorises or permits a company to enter into a transaction or arrangement, knowing or suspecting it to contravene section 330 (loans to directors etc.)	On indictment, 2 years imprisonment or a fine, or both. On summary conviction, 6 months imprisonment or the statutory maximum fine, or both.
342(2)	A relevant company that enters into a transaction or an arrangement for a director in contravention of section 330.	On indictment, 2 years imprisonment or a fine, or both. On summary conviction, 6 months imprisonment or the statutory maximum fine, or both.
342(3)	A person who procures a relevant company to enter into a transaction or an arrangement knowing or suspecting it to be contrary to section 330	On indictment, 2 years imprisonment or a fine, or both. On summary conviction, 6 months imprisonment or the statutory maximum fine, or both.
343(8)	A director of a company that fails to maintain a register of transactions, etc. made with and for directors and not disclosed in the company's accounts or that fails to make the register available at the registered office or at the company's meeting.	On indictment, a fine. On summary conviction, a fine of the statutory maximum.
458	A person who is a party to carrying on a company's business with intent to defraud creditors, or for any fraudulent purpose.	On indictment, 7 years imprisonment or a fine, or both. On summary conviction, 6 months imprisonment or the statutory maximum fine, or both.

Appendix V

COUNSEL'S OPINIONS ON 'TRUE AND FAIR'

The Accounting Standards Committee—Joint Opinion

1. The Accounting Standards Committee ("ASC") from time to time issues Statements of Standard Accounting Practice ("SSAPs"). These are declared in the Explanatory Foreword to be "methods of accounting approved. . . for application to all financial accounts intended to give a true and fair view of financial position and profit or loss." They are not intended to be "a comprehensive code of rigid rules" but departures from them should be disclosed and explained. The Committee also noted in its Explanatory Foreword that "methods of financial accounting evolve and alter in response to changing business and economic needs. From time to time new accounting standards will be drawn at progressive levels, and established standards will be reviewed with the object of improvement in the light of new needs and developments."

2. The ASC has recently undertaken a review of the standard setting process and decided that future standards will "deal only with those matters which are of major and fundamental importance and affect the generality of companies" but that, as in the past, the standards will apply "to all accounts which are intended to show a true and fair view of financial position and profit or loss". A SSAP is therefore a declaration by the ASC, on behalf of its constituent professional bodies, that save in exceptional circumstances, accounts which do not comply with the standard will not give a true and fair view.

3. But the preparation of accounts which give a true and fair view is not merely a matter of compliance with professional standards. In many important cases it is a requirement of law. Since 1947 all accounts prepared for the purpose of compliance with the Companies Acts have been required to "give a true and fair view": s 13(1) of the Companies Act 1947, re-enacted as s 149(1) of the Companies Act 1948. In 1978 the concept of a true and fair view was adopted by the EEC Council in its Fourth Directive "on the annual accounts of certain types of companies". The Directive combined the requirement of giving a true and fair view with extremely detailed provisions about the form and contents of the accounts but the obligation to give a true and fair view was declared to be overriding. Accounts must not comply with the detailed requirements if this would prevent them from giving a true and fair view. Parliament gave effect to the Directive, by passing the Companies Act 1981. This substitutes a new s 149(2) in the 1948 Act [*that is now Section 226(2) of the Companies Act 1985*], reproducing

the old s 149(1) in substantially similar words. The detailed requirements of the Directive appear as a new Eighth Schedule to the 1948 Act [*now Schedule 4 to the Companies Act 1985*]. The old s 149(1) (now renumbered 149A(1)) and the old Eighth Schedule (now Sch 8A) are retained for the accounts of banking, insurance [and shipping] companies. [*These are now Section 255(1) of, and Schedule 9 to, the Companies Act 1985.*] So far as the requirement to give a true and fair view is concerned, a difference between 149(2) and 149A(1) is that the former has come into the law via Brussels, whereas the latter has no EEC pedigree.

4. "True and fair view" is thus a legal concept and the question of whether company accounts comply with s 149(2) (or s 149A(1)) can be authoritatively decided only by a court. This gives rise to a number of questions about the relationship between the legal requirement and the SSAPs issued by the ASC, which also claim to be authoritative statements on what is a true and fair view. What happens if there is a conflict between the professional standards demanded by the ASC and the decisions of the courts on the requirements of the Companies Acts? Furthermore, the ASC issues new SSAPs "at progressive levels" and reviews established ones. How is this consistent with a statutory requirement of a true and fair view which has been embodied in the law in the same language sinced 1947? Can the issue of a new SSAP make it unlawful to prepare accounts in a form which would previously have been lawful? How can the ASC have power to legislate in this way?

5. To answer these questions it is necessary first to examine the nature of the "true and fair view" concept as used in the Companies Act. It is an abstraction or philosophical concept expressed in simple English. The law uses many similar concepts, of which "reasonable care" is perhaps the most familiar example. It is a common feature of such concepts that there is seldom any difficulty in understanding what they mean but frequent controversy over their application to particular facts. One reason for this phenomenon is that because such concepts represent a very high level of abstraction which has to be applied to an infinite variety of concrete facts, there can never be a sharply defined line between, for example, what is reasonable care and what is not. There will always be a penumbral area in which views may reasonably differ.

6. The courts have never attempted to define "true and fair" in the sense of offering a paraphrase in other languages and in our opinion have been wise not to do so. When a concept can be expressed in ordinary English words, we do not think that it illuminates their meaning to attempt to frame a definition. We doubt, for example, whether the man on the Clapham omnibus has really contributed very much to the understanding of "reasonable care" or that accountants have found it helpful to ask themselves how this imaginary passenger would have prepared a set of accounts. It is much more useful to illustrate the concept in action, for example, to explain why certain accounts do or do not give a true and fair view.

7. It is however important to observe that the application of the concept involves judgment in questions of degree. The information contained in accounts must be accurate and comprehensive (to mention two of the most obvious elements which contribute to a true and fair view) to within acceptable limits. What is acceptable and how is this to be achieved? Reasonable businessmen and accountants may differ over the degree of accuracy or comprehensiveness which in particular cases the accounts should attain. Equally, there may sometimes be room for differences over the method to adopt in order to give a true and fair view, cases in which there may be more than one "true and fair view" of the same financial position. Again, because "true and fair view" involves questions of degree, we think that cost-effectiveness must play a part in deciding the amount of information which is sufficient to make accounts true and fair.

8. In the end, as we have said, the question of whether accounts give a true and fair view in compliance with the Companies Act must be decided by a judge. But the courts look for guidance on this question to the ordinary practices of professional accountants. This is not merely because accounts are expressed in a language which judges find difficult to understand. This may sometimes be true but it is a minor reason for the importance which the courts attach to evidence of accountancy practice. The important reason is inherent in the nature of the "true and fair" concept. Accounts will not be true and fair unless the information they contain is sufficient in quantity and quality to satisfy the reasonable expectations of the readers to whom they are addressed. On this question, accountants can express an informed professional opinion on what, in current circumstances, it is thought that accounts should reasonably contain. But they can do more than that. The readership of accounts will consist of businessmen, investors, bankers and so forth, as well as professional accountants. But the expectations of the readers will have been moulded by the practices of accountants because by and large they will expect to get what they ordinarily get and that in turn will depend upon the normal practices of accountants.

9. For these reasons, the courts will treat compliance with accepted accounting principles as *prima facie* evidence that the accounts are true and fair. Equally, deviation from accepted principles will be *prima facie* evidence that they are not. We have not been able to find reported cases on the specific question of whether accounts are true and fair, although the question has been adverted to in the course of judgments on other matters; see for example *Willingale v. International Commercial Bank Ltd* [1978] A.C.834. There are however some cases on the analogous question arising in income tax cases of whether profit or loss has been calculated in accordance with "the correct principles of commercial accountancy" and there is a helpful statement of principle (approved in subsequent cases in the Court of Appeal) by Pennycuick V-C in *Odeon Associated Theatres Ltd v. Jones (Inspector of Taxes)* [1971] 1 W.L.R. 442 at 454:

"In order to ascertain what are the correct principles [the court] has

> recourse to the evidence of accountants. That evidence is conclusive on the practice of accountants in the sense of the principles on which accountants act in practice. That is a question of pure fact, but the court itself has to make a final decision as to whether that practice corresponds to the correct principles of commercial accountancy. No doubt in the vast proportion of cases the court will agree with the accountants but it will not necessarily do so. Again, there may be a divergency of views between the accountants, or there may be alternative principles, none of which can be said to be incorrect, or of course there may be no accountancy evidence at all. . . At the end of the day the court must determine what is the correct principle of commercial accountancy to be applied."

10. This is also in our opinion the relationship between generally accepted accounting principles and the legal concept of "true and fair". The function of the ASC is to formulate what it considers should be generally accepted accounting principles. Thus the value of a SSAP to a court which has to decide whether accounts are true and fair is two-fold. First, it represents an important statement of professional opinion about the standards which readers may reasonably expect in accounts which are intended to be true and fair. The SSAP is intended to crystallise professional opinion and reduce penumbral areas in which divergent practices exist and can each have claim to being "true and fair". Secondly, because accountants are professionally obliged to comply with a SSAP, it creates in the readers an expectation that the accounts will be in conformity with the prescribed standards. This is in itself a reason why accounts which depart from the standard without adequate justification or explanation may be held not to be true and fair. The importance of expectations was emphasised by the Court of Appeal in what may be regarded as a converse case, *Re Press Caps* [1949] Ch.434. An ordinary historic cost balance sheet was said to be "true and fair" notwithstanding that it gave no information about the current value of freehold properties because, it was said, no one familiar with accounting conventions would expect it to include such information.

11. A SSAP therefore has no direct legal effect. It is simply a rule of professional conduct for accountants. But in our opinion it is likely to have an indirect effect on the content which the courts will give to the "true and fair" concept. The effect of a SSAP may therefore be to make it likely that accounts which would previously have been considered true and fair will no longer satisfy the law. Perhaps the most dramatic example arises out of the recent statement by the ASC in connection with its review of SSAP 16 "Current Cost Accounting". The Statement puts forward for discussion the proposition that "where a company is materially affected by changing prices, pure HC accounts do not give a true and fair view". If this proposition were embodied in a new SSAP and accepted by the courts, the legal requirements of a true and fair view will have undergone a revolutionary change.

12. There is no inconsistency between such a change brought about by changing professional opinion and the rule that words in a statute must

be construed in accordance with the meaning which they bore when the statute was passed. The *meaning* of true and fair remains what it was in 1947. It is the *content* given to the concept which has changed. This is something which constantly happens to such concepts. For example, the Bill of Rights 1688 prohibited "cruel and unusual punishments". There has been no change in the meaning of "cruel" since 1688. The definition in Dr Johnson's Dictionary of 1755 ("pleased with hurting others, inhuman, hard-hearted, without pity, barbarous") is much the same as in a modern dictionary. But changes in society mean that a judge in 1983 would unquestionably characterise punishments as "cruel" which his predecessor of 1688 would not have thought o come within this description. The meaning of the concept remains the same; the facts to which it is applied have changed.

13. The possibility of changing accounting standards has been recognised both by the courts and the legislature. In *Associated Portland Cement Manufacturers Ltd v. Price Commission* [1975] I.C.R.27, esp. at 45-6, the court recognised changes since 1945 in the permissible methods of calculating depreciation. Similarly para 90 of the new Eighth Schedule to the Companies Act 1948 refers to "principles generally accepted. . . at the time when those accounts are prepared."

14. We therefore see no conflict between the functions of the ASC in formulating standards which it declares to be essential to true and fair accounts and the function of the courts in deciding whether the accounts satisfy the law. The courts are of course not bound by a SSAP. A court may say that accounts which ignore them are nevertheless true and fair. But the immediate effect of a SSAP is to strengthen the likelihood that a court will hold that compliance with the prescribed standard is necessary for the accounts to give a true and fair view. In the absence of a SSAP, a court is unlikely to reject accounts drawn up in accordance with principles which command some respectable professional support. The issue of a SSAP has the effect, for the two reasons which we have given in para 10, of creating a *prima facie* presumption that accounts which do not comply are not true and fair. This presumption is then strengthened or weakened by the extent to which the SSAP is actually accepted and applied. Universal acceptance means that it is highly unlikely that a court would accept accounts drawn up according to different principles. On the other hand, if there remains a strong body of professional opinion which consistently opts out of applying the SSAP, giving reasons which the ASC may consider inadequate, the *prima facie* presumption against such accounts is weakened.

15. We therefore do not think that the ASC should be concerned by the possibility that a court may hold that compliance with one of its SSAPs is not necessary for the purposes of the Companies Acts. This possibility is inherent in the fact that the courts are not bound by professional opinion. The function of the ASC is to express their professional judgment on the standards which in their opinion are required.

16. There are two further points to be considered. The first is the relationship between the "true and fair" requirement and the detailed provisions of the new Eighth Schedule. The Act is quite explicit on this point: the true and fair view is overriding. Nevertheless it may be said that the detailed requirements offer some guidance as to the principles which Parliament considered would give a true and fair view. In particular, the Schedule plainly regards historic cost accounting as the norm and current cost accounting as an optional alternative. In these circumstances, is a court likely to follow a SSAP which declares that for certain companies, historic cost accounts *cannot* give a true and fair view? In our opinion, whatever reasons there may be for taking one view or the other, the provisions of the Eighth Schedule are no obstacle to accepting such a SSAP. As we have already pointed out, the provisions of the Schedule are static whereas the concept of a true and fair view is dynamic. If the latter is overriding, it is not impossible that the effect in time will be to render obsolete some of the provisions of the Schedule. But we think that this is what must have been intended when overriding force was given to a concept with a changing content.

17. Lastly, there is the effect of the adoption of "true and fair view" by the EEC. Because s 149(2) of the 1948 Act now gives effect to a Directive, it must (unlike s 149A(1)) be construed in accordance with any decision of the European Court on the meaning of Article 2.3 of the Directive. In practice we do not think that this is likely to affect the evolution of the concept in England. Just as the concept may have a different content at different times, so it may have a different content in different countries. Although the European Court may seek to achieve some uniformity by laying down minimum standards for the accounts of all EEC countries, it seems to use that they are unlikely to disapprove of higher standards being required by the professional bodies of individual states and in consequence, higher legal criteria for what is a true and fair view being adopted in the national courts of some member states.

18. So for example Article 33 of the Directive gives member states the right to "permit or require" companies to use current cost accounting instead of historic cost principles. In the UK, as we have said, current cost accounts are permitted by the Eighth Schedule but the only circumstances in which they may be required is if a court should decide, on the basis of prevailing principles, that they were necessary to give a true and fair view. In Germany, on the other hand, the equivalent of the Eighth Schedule does not even permit current cost accounts. In Germany therefore, the only way they could be permitted would be if the German court applied "true and fair view" as an overriding requirement. For the reasons given in para 16, we do not regard it as illogical or impossible that even a German court may take this view. But having regard to the Directive, we think it is very unlikely that the European Court would decide as a matter of community law that there are circumstances in which historic cost accounts do not give a true and fair view. Developments of this kind are more likely to be left to national courts to make in the light of local professional opinion.

Leonard Hoffman
M. H. Arden

Lincoln's Inn
13 September 1983

The Joint Opinion that follows was given in relation to the Statement of Intent issued by the ASC on the proposed revision of SSAP 16. However, this Opinion has a more general application to the relationship between SSAPs and the 'true and fair' concept. In particular, it discusses the question of cost-effectiveness and whether a SSAP should apply to all companies.

The Accounting Standards Committee—Supplementary Joint Opinion

1. This Opinion is intended to be supplementary to our Joint Opinion dated 13 September 1983. We do not propose to repeat the contents of that Opinion more than is necessary in order to make this one intelligible. The two Opinions should therefore be read together.

2. The ASC proposed to issue a Statement of Intent concerning the future of SSAP 16 "Current Cost Accounting". In summary, the proposal is that all public limited companies ("PLCs") other than insurance companies, property companies and investment-based companies ("value-based companies") should show the effects of changing prices when these effects are material, but this should be indicated in a note and not in separate current cost accounts. The present position is that SSAP 16 applies only to large and quoted companies (as therein defined) and does not apply to value-based companies, whatever their size. The ASC is not satisfied that a method has yet been developed for producing useful information about the effects of changing prices on the businesses of private companies and value-based companies at a cost that can be justified. It is therefore commissioning further work on the application of current cost accounting to these companies. However, the ASC draws attention to the principal factors which have led them to their conclusion that significant benefits result from the disclosure of current cost information by PLCs, including the large number and wide range of users of their accounts and in many cases the sophistication of those users. These factors generally do not apply to private companies. The benefits of providing information about the effects of changing prices on the businesses of private companies are therefore likely to be significantly less than in the case of PLCs.

3. The Statement of Intent therefore recognises that while in principle and subject to cost-effectiveness, all accounts should, in order to give a true and a fair view, show the effects of changing prices when such effects are material, there are practical difficulties about devising cost-effective methods for implementing this principle in the case of certain companies.

4. This practical approach has been criticised on the ground that if a footnote about the effects of changing prices is regarded as necessary for accounts to give a true and fair view, this requirement should apply to all sets of accounts. Questions of cost and expediency are said to be irrelevant to whether or not the accounts give a true and fair view and it is argued that there can be no justification for the ASC distinguishing between different kinds of companies.

5. We think that this criticism is misconceived. In the first place, questions of cost-effectiveness are in our opinion relevant to whether accounts give a true and fair view or not. "True and fair view" is not an absolute and unique concept. If that was what the legislature had meant, it would no doubt have said "the true and fair view". More than one view may be true and fair and whether a particular set of accounts satisfies this test or not involves questions of degree and a consideration of many factors relating both to the affairs of the particular business and the reasonable expectations of the people likely to use the accounts. In paragraph 7 of our Joint Opinion we said:

> "Again, because 'true and fair view' involves questions of degree, we think that cost-effectiveness must play a part in deciding the amount of information which is sufficient to make accounts true and fair."

Some elaboration of this statement may be useful. The information contained in accounts may vary in its comprehensiveness, usefulness and degree of precision. These are all factors which bear upon the question of whether the accounts are "true and fair". The accounts must satisfy criteria of acceptability in regard to each of these and other matters. But the question of whether it is necessary for particular kinds of information to be included must take into account the cost and difficulty of providing such information. There is in our opinion nothing illogical in saying: "This information would be useful to (say) investors in assessing the condition of the business. If it could be provided relatively easily, we think that fairness to investors demands that it should be included. *Prima facie* therefore, accounts which do not include such information would not be true and fair. On the other hand, if the information could be provided only with great expense and difficulty, we do not think that it would be reasonable to insist upon it. Therefore we would accept accounts without such information as still being true and fair."[1]

6. In our earlier Opinion we mentioned for another purpose the analogy of the legal concept of reasonable care. On this point too, we think that reasonable care provides a useful comparison. The question of

[1] In saying this we have in mind expense and difficulty applicable to any company of that kind. We are not saying that it would be right to take into account the difficulty which a particular company might have in providing certain information, e.g. because its records had been badly maintained. There is again an analogy here with "reasonable care" (see paragraph 6) in which difficulties or handicaps peculiar to an individual are usually disregarded on the ground that a person suffering from such a difficulty or handicap should not have undertaken the activity which gave rise to the risk.

whether a person has taken reasonable care to guard against some danger depends upon weighing a number of factors, including the likelihood that the risk may materialise, the seriousness of the loss or injury which may be caused if the risk does materialise, the importance of the activity giving rise to the risk, and the cost of taking various kinds of precautions. As Lord Wilberforce put it, more succinctly than we have done:

> "What is reasonable depends on the nature and degree of the danger. It also depends upon the difficulty and expense of guarding against it."[2]

This process of weighing risks against the difficulty and expense of guarding against them would apply equally to the question of whether an accountant had taken reasonable care in the preparation of a set of accounts. And although the question of whether reasonable care has been taken in the preparation of accounts is not the same as whether they are true and fair, we think that the questions of "reasonableness" and "fairness" have enough in common to make the analogy a valid one.

7. At this point the critic may say: "Well, I can see that questions of cost-effectiveness may enter into the decision on whether accounts are true and fair and that information about the effects of price changes may have to be given in the accounts of some companies but not others. But the SSAP should still be capable of expression in general terms. How can one justify an arbitrary dividing line which requires such information in the accounts of one company which happens to be a PLC and does not require it in the accounts of a private company of the same size and carrying on a substantially similar business?"

8. This criticism in our opinion misses the true function of SSAPs, which is to reduce the level of abstraction at which rules of good accounting practice are expressed. The more abstract the rule, the more pure and universally applicable it is, but the less useful it is to the practitioner seeking to apply it to the facts of a particular case. If universality were all that one wanted, the proposition that accounts should be true and fair would be sufficient. The point of a SSAP is to concretise that proposition, while recognising that every case must depend upon its own facts and that any rules expressed at a lower level of abstraction must to a greater or lesser extent be "rules of thumb". This point is made with great clarity in the Explanatory Foreword. We therefore see nothing illogical in a SSAP which gives guidance to the profession by taking a (necessarily) arbitrary but practical dividing line and saying that for PLCs which are not value-based companies it will ordinarily be assumed that the public benefit from the provision of information about the effects of changing prices will be sufficient to justify the cost of providing such information, whereas this will not be assumed, or will not yet be assumed, in the case of private or value-based companies.

[2] *Herrington v. British Railways Board* [1972] A.C.877, 920.

9. We said in our earlier opinion that "true and fair" was a dynamic concept and that its detailed content could change by degrees over time. We also said that one of the functions of the ASC was to initiate and promote such changes. A SSAP in accordance with the draft Statement of Intent seems to us to give effect to that function.

Leonard Hoffman
M. H. Arden

Lincoln's Inn
20 March 1984

The two preceding opinions are reproduced with the kind permission of Accountancy, The Accounting Standards Committee, Leonard Hoffman and Mary H. Arden.

The Institute of Chartered Accountants of Scotland—Opinion

I have been asked to consider the meaning of the term 'true and fair view' from the Scottish point of view, in the light of the Joint Opinion given by English leading Counsel to the Accounting Standards Committee dated 14th September 1983.

In their Opinion English Counsel examine the nature of the 'true and fair' view concept as used in the Companies Acts in some detail. They draw attention to the fact that the Courts have never attempted to define this term, in the sense of offering a paraphrase of it, and go on to say that the application of the concept involves judgment in questions of degree. Turning to the relationship between the legal concept of 'true and fair' on the one hand and generally accepted accounting principles on the other, they say that the Courts will treat compliance with accepted accounting principles as *prima facie* evidence that the accounts are true and fair, and that equally deviation from accepted principles will be *prima facie* evidence that they are not. This leads them to consider the problem of the effect upon the 'true and fair view' concept of a new Statement of Standard Accounting Practice. ('SSAP'). Their answer to it is to say that there is no inconsistency between a change in the legal requirements for a true and fair view resulting from a new SSAP and the rule that words in a statute must be construed in accordance with the meaning which they bore when the statute was passed. As they put it, 'The *meaning* of true and fair remains what it was in 1947. It is the *content* given to the concept which has changed.' Thus the concept of the 'true and fair view' is, they say, dynamic, with a changing content as accounting practices are revised and developed with time. The importance of this conclusion is revealed when they recognise, in paragraph 16 of their Opinion, that since the 'true and fair' view requirement in section 149(2) of the Companies Act 1948 [*now Section 226(6) of the Companies Act 1985*] as amended overrides the provisions of the new Schedule 8 [*now Schedule 4*] to the Act, it may have the effect in time of rendering obsolete some of the detailed provisions of the Schedule.

Had I been approaching the matter afresh I would have reached the same conclusions as English Counsel have done, for substantially the same reasons. While the various authorities to which they refer in the course of their discussion are cases decided in the English Courts, the principles upon which their opinion is based are all familiar to a Scottish lawyer, and the statutes are of course applicable with equal force in both countries. It is equally true of Scotland to say that the Courts have not attempted to provide a definition of the term 'true and fair view', although there have been a number of recent cases where the sufficiency of a company's accounts in that regard have come under consideration. In each case the question whether or not they present a 'true and fair view' is a question of fact, which the Court will decide in the light of the evidence including evidence of current accounting practice. As in England, the Court is likely to pay close attention to the evidence of accountants without feeling bound by that evidence: cf. Lord Advocate v. Ruffle, 1979 SC 351. The statement of principle by Pennycuick V-C in Odeon Associated Theatres v. Jones (1971) 1 WLR 442 at p. 454, which English Counsel quote in paragraph 9 of their Opinion, as explained by Lord Denning MR. in Heather v. P.E. Consulting Group Limited (1973) Ch. 189, is familiar in this country, and has been referred to in the Scottish Court on a number of occasions particularly in tax cases.

The distinction which English Counsel draw between the meaning of the term 'true and fair' on the one hand and its content on the other is entirely sound in my opinion. This is because the answer to the question whether a true and fair view is given by the accounts inevitably involves questions of fact and degree, which must always be decided by reference to the state of affairs generally at the time when the accounts were prepared. An analogy can be drawn with other concepts used by the law, such as 'reasonable care' and 'reasonably practicable'. The latter expression, for instance, is used in a variety of provisions to be found in the Factories Act 1961 and its subordinate legislation. The meaning of the phrase, no doubt, must be taken to have remained the same since the date of the enactment, but it is well established in Scotland as well as in England that when it comes to considering whether in any particular case measures which might have been taken so as to avoid the accident were or were not reasonably practicable regard must be had to the state of current knowledge and invention. In my opinion an argument to the effect that the question whether a particular set of accounts gave a true and fair view had to be decided with reference to principles of accounting which, while current in 1947 or 1948, had become obsolete by the time the accounts were prepared only has to be stated to be seen to be unacceptable. I agree with English Counsel that it is reasonable to think that the reason why overriding force was given by the Companies Act 1981 to the concept of the 'true and fair view' is that it was recognised that this was a dynamic concept with a changing content, capable of rendering obsolete any particular provision in the Schedule which had become inconsistent with current practice.

For these reasons I am of opinion that the guidance which English Counsel have given to the Accounting Standards Committee can be accepted as being in accordance with the Scottish approach.

J. A. D. Hope
Edinburgh, 22 December 1983

This legal opinion is reproduced with the kind permission of The Institute of Chartered Accountants of Scotland and J. A. D. Hope.

Appendix VI

DIRECTORS' LOANS DECISION TABLES

Decision table 1: Loans – relevant company

(To be read in conjunction with Chapter 21 of this book.)

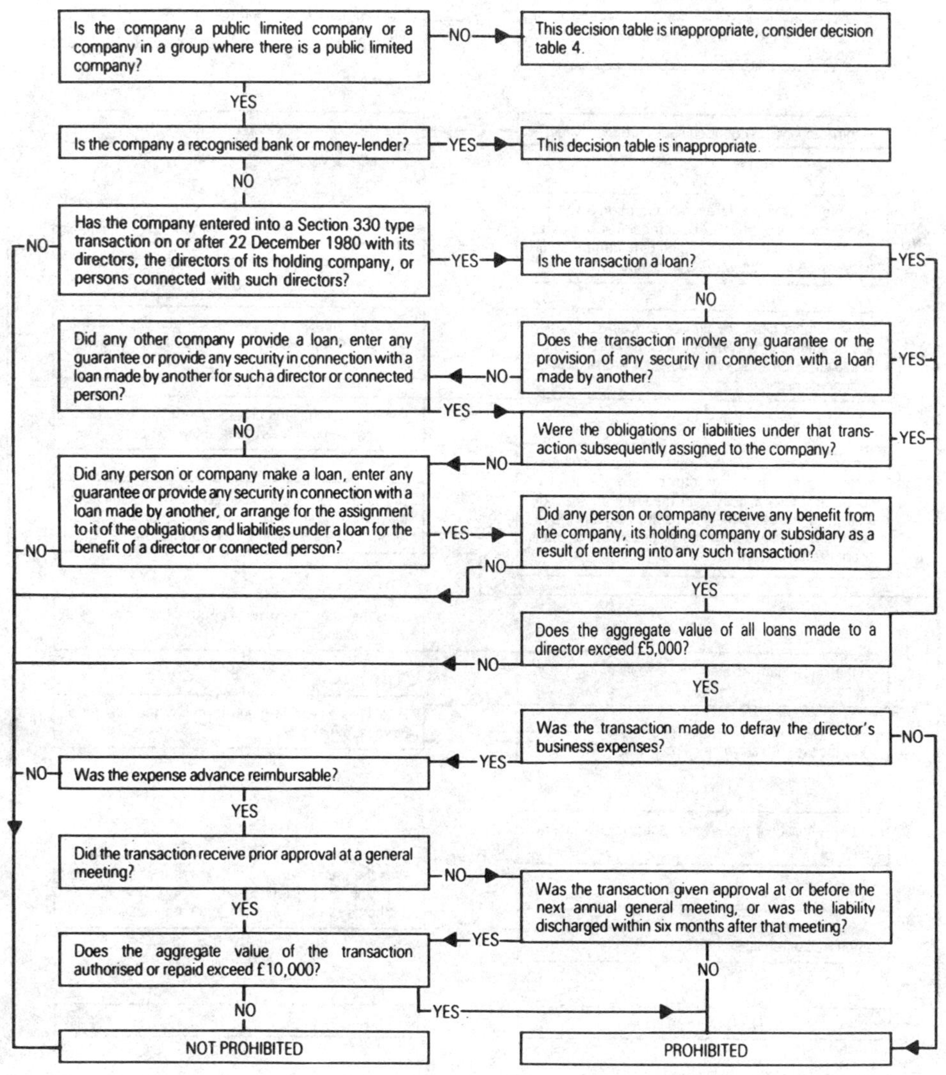

Decision table 2: Quasi-loans – relevant company

(To be read in conjunction with Chapter 21 of this book.)

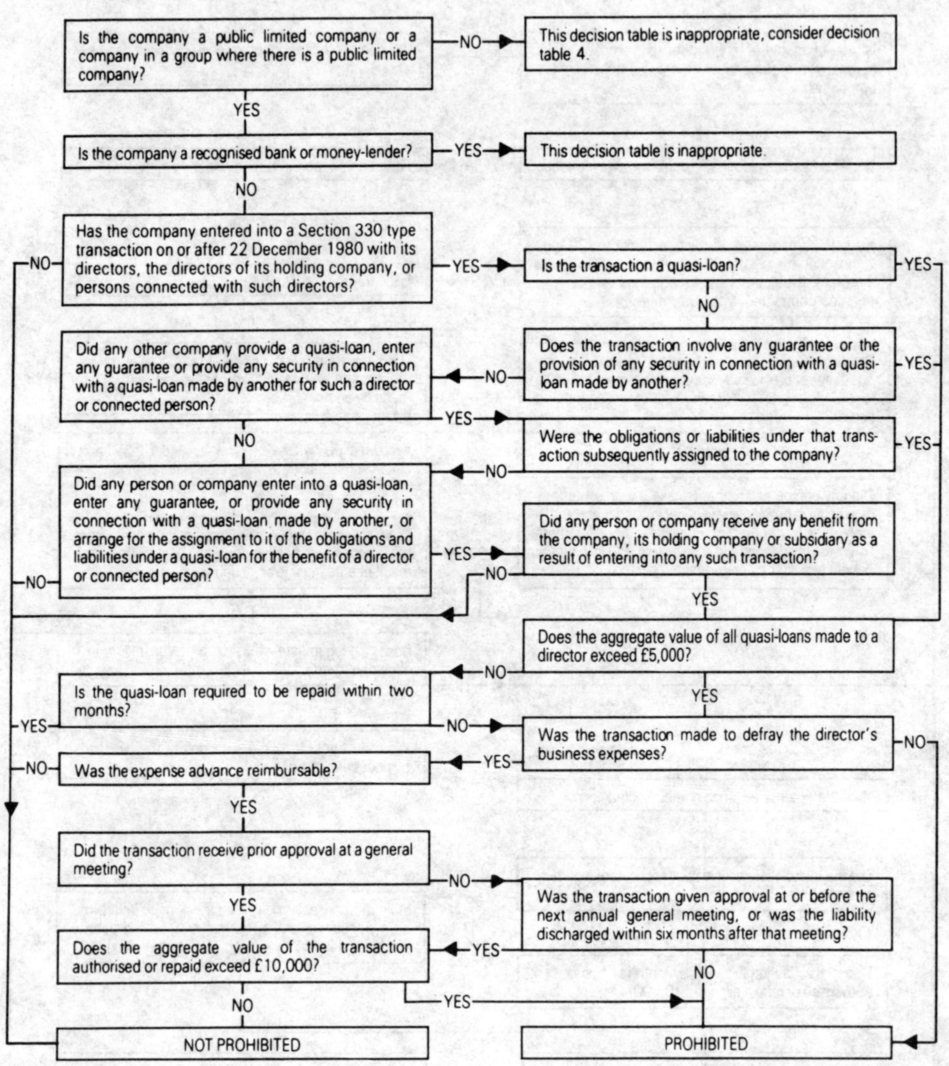

Decision table 3: Credit transactions – relevant company

(To be read in conjunction with Chapter 21 of this book.)

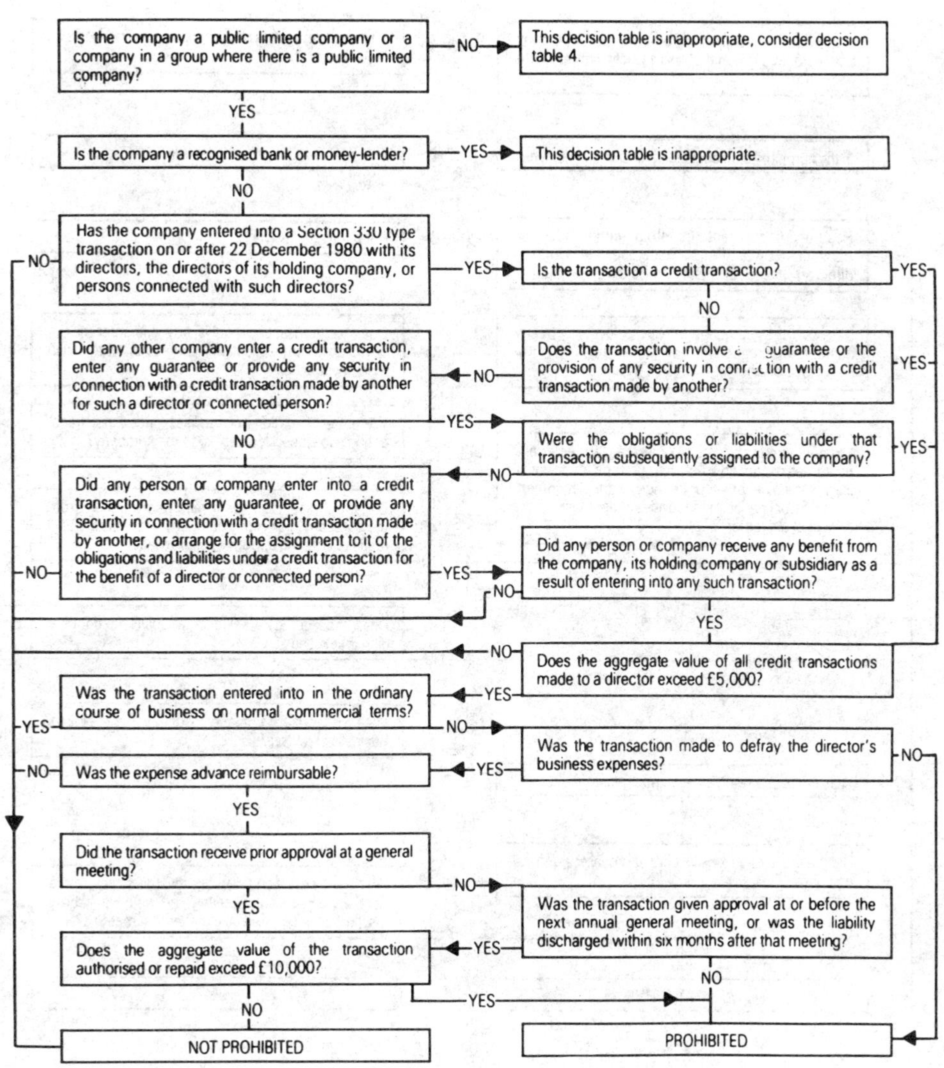

Decision table 4: Loans – non-relevant company

(To be read in conjunction with Chapter 21 of this book.)

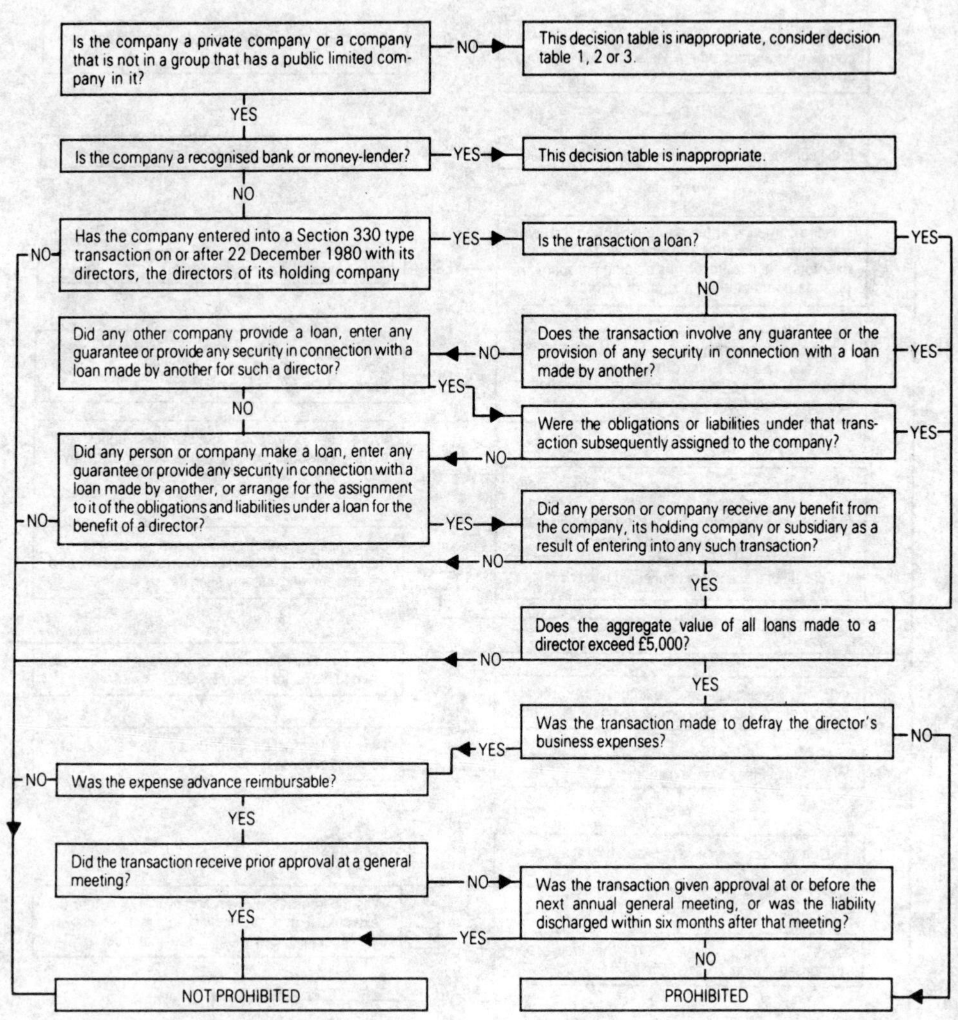

Appendix VII

TEXT OF TR 481 AND TR 482

Technical Release 481, The Determination of Realised Profits and Disclosure of Distributable Profits in the Context of the Companies Acts 1948 to 1981, and Technical Release 482, The Determination of Distributable Profits in the Context of the Companies Acts 1948 to 1981, were issued in September 1982 by the Consultative Committee of Accountancy Bodies (CCAB), whose members are as follows: The Institute of Chartered Accountants in England and Wales; The Institute of Chartered Accountants of Scotland; The Institute of Chartered Accountants in Ireland; The Chartered Association of Certified Accountants; The Institute of Cost and Management Accountants; and The Chartered Institute of Public Finance and Accountancy.

Set out below is the complete text of Technical Release 481 and Technical Release 482. These Technical Releases refer to the Companies Acts 1948 to 1981. The appropriate references to the Companies Act 1985 that correspond to those references to the previous Acts that are included in the text are as follows:

Reference to previous Act		Reference to Companies Act 1985	
Companies Act 1948, s 56		Sec 130	
s 57		(Repealed by Companies Act 1980)	
s 58		(Repealed by Companies Act 1981)	
s 149		Sec 226	
s 152		Sec 227	
new Schedule 8 para:	12	Sch 4 para:	12
	13		13
	15		15
	19		19
	20		20
	34		34
	61 to 66		Sch 4A
	87		Sch 4 para: 88
	88		89
	90		Sec 262 (3)
Schedule 8A		Sch 9	
Companies Act 1967, s 14		Sec 235	
Companies Act 1976, s 1		Sec 241 and 242	

Companies Act 1980, Part III	Part VIII
s 39	Sec 263 and 275
s 40	Sec 264
s 41	Sec 265 to 267
s 42	Sec 268
s 42A	Sec 269
s 43	Sec 270 to 275
s 43A	Sec 276
s 45	Sec 263 and 280
s 87	Sec 264
Companies Act 1981, s 53	Sec 170
s 60	Sec 274

Technical Release 481

Explanatory note

The Consultative Committee of Accountancy Bodies wishes to draw readers' attention to the fact that the attached (*sic*) guidance statement does not deal with the special problems arising in connection with the determination of realised profits in the context of foreign currency translation. It is intended that these problems should be dealt with in the future by the issue of an accounting standard on foreign currency translation. (*Such a standard has since been issued as SSAP 20.*)

The following statement of guidance on the determination of realised profits and disclosure of distributable profits in the context of the Companies Acts 1948 to 1981 is issued by the Councils of the member bodies of the Consultative Committee of Accountancy Bodies. The guidance given in this statement may need to be amended as the law is interpreted in particular cases, or as existing Accounting Standards are revised and new Standards are issued.

The statement and its appendix have been considered and approved by Counsel. They are, however, not definitive. Interpretation of the law rests ultimately with the courts.

References to the '1948 Act', the '1980 Act' and the '1981 Act' are to the Companies Acts 1948, 1980 and 1981 respectively.

References to the 'new Schedule 8' are to Schedule 8 to the 1948 Act as inserted by Section 1(2) of the 1981 Act, and as set out in Schedule 1 to the 1981 Act.

Realised profits: The statutory framework

1. The term 'realised profits' was introduced into UK company law statutes as a result of the implementation of the 2nd and 4th EEC directives on company law in the Companies Act 1980 (Part III) and

the Companies Act 1981 (Part I) respectively:

(1) Part III of the 1980 Act imposes statutory restrictions on the distribution of profits and assets by companies. These restrictions include a prohibition on the distribution of unrealised profits.*

(2) Paragraph 12(a) of the new Schedule 8 requires that 'Only profits realised at the balance sheet date shall be included in the profit and loss account'. Paragraph 34(4) contains a similar requirement applicable to transfers from the revaluation reserve to the profit and loss account. These requirements are extended to consolidated accounts by paragraphs 61 to 66 of the new Schedule 8. They do not apply to accounts prepared under Schedule 8A to the 1948 Act.

*There is an exception to this rule where distributions are made in kind (see Section 43A of the 1980 Act, as inserted by Section 85 of the 1981 Act).

2. The new Schedule 8 states that 'references to realised profits . . . are references to such profits . . . as fall to be treated as realised profits . . . in accordance with principles generally accepted with respect to the determination for accounting purposes of realised profits at the time when those accounts are prepared' (new Schedule 8, para. 90, extended to the 1980 Act by reason of Section 21(1) of the 1981 Act). The term 'principles generally accepted' for the determination of realised profits is not defined in the Act.

3. This statement gives guidance as to the interpretation of 'principles generally accepted' for the determination of realised profits in the context of these statutory requirements. Both the statutory requirements and the following guidance must throughout be viewed in the context of Section 149 of the 1948 Act, as amended by Section 1 of the 1981 Act, which states that the requirement for company accounts to give a true and fair view overrides all other provisions of the Companies Acts 1948 to 1981 as to the matters to be included in a company's accounts. Section 152 of the 1948 Act, as amended by Section 2 of the 1981 Act, imposes a corresponding requirement for group accounts.

'Principles generally accepted' for realised profits

4. 'Principles generally accepted' for the determination of realised profits should be considered in conjunction with, inter alia, the legal principles laid down in the new Schedule 8, statements of standard accounting practice ('SSAPs'), and in particular the fundamental accounting concepts referred to in SSAP 2 'Disclosure of accounting policies'. As stated in the Explanatory Foreword to Accounting Standards, SSAPs describe methods of accounting for all accounts intended to give a true and fair view. They must therefore, where

applicable, be considered to be highly persuasive in the interpretation of 'principles generally accepted' for the determination of realised profits.

5. Accounting thought and practice develop over time. This is recognised in the statutory requirement that realised profits should be determined 'in accordance with principles generally accepted . . . at the time when those accounts are prepared'. Because of this, the guidance set out in this statement is itself liable to amendment from time to time.

6. In determining whether a profit is realised, particular regard should be had to the statutory accounting principles at paragraphs 12 and 13 of the new Schedule 8, and to the parallel fundamental accounting concepts of 'prudence' and 'accruals' as set out in SSAP 2.

7. Paragraph 12 of the new Schedule 8 requires that 'The amount of any item shall be determined on a prudent basis' and, in particular, as already noted, that 'only profits realised at the balance sheet date shall be included in the profit and loss account'. SSAP 2 amplifies the prudence concept as follows:

> 'revenues and profits are not anticipated, but are recognised by inclusion in the profit and loss account only when realised in the form either of cash or of other assets the ultimate cash realisation of which can be assessed with reasonable certainty'.

In the light of the new statutory requirements, it should be borne in mind that the phrases 'ultimate cash realisation' and 'assessed with reasonable certainty' are intended to clarify the extent to which a profit can be said to be 'realised' under the prudence concept in circumstances other than where the profit has already been realised in the form of cash. 'Reasonable certainty' is the limiting factor.

8. This approach is consistent with paragraph 13 of the new Schedule 8 which requires that:

> 'All income and charges relating to the financial year to which the accounts relate shall be taken into account, without regard to the date of receipt or payment'.

The statutory requirement corresponds with the accruals concept as explained at paragraph 14(b) of SSAP 2. This states that:

> 'revenue and costs are accrued (that is, recognised as they are earned or incurred, not as money is received or paid), matched with one another so far as their relationship can be established or justifiably assumed, and dealt with in the profit and loss account of the period to which they relate'.

9. In determining realised profits, it is also necessary to comply with paragraph 12(b) of the new Schedule 8, which states that:

> 'all liabilities and losses which have arisen or are likely to arise in

> respect of the financial year to which the accounts relate or a previous financial year shall be taken into account, including those which only become apparent between the balance sheet date and the date on which it is signed on behalf of the board of directors . . . '.

This statutory requirement corresponds with the prudence concept as explained at paragraph 14(d) of SSAP 2. This states that:

> 'provision is made for all known liabilities (expenses and losses) whether the amount of these is known with certainty or is a best estimate in the light of the information available'.

Realised profits: Summary of guidance

10. A profit which is required by statements of standard accounting practice to be recognised in the profit and loss account should normally be treated as a realised profit, unless the SSAP specifically indicates that it should be treated as unrealised. *See Appendix*.

11. A profit may be recognised in the profit and loss account in accordance with an accounting policy which is not the subject of a SSAP, or, exceptionally, which is contrary to a SSAP. Such a profit will normally be a realised profit if the accounting policy adopted is consistent with paragraphs 12 and 13 of the new Schedule 8 and with the accruals and prudence concepts as set out in SSAP 2.

12. Where, in special circumstances, a true and fair view could not be given, even if additional information were provided, without including in the profit and loss account an unrealised profit, the effect of Section 149(3) of the 1948 Act (as amended) is to require inclusion of that unrealised profit notwithstanding paragraph 12(a) of the new Schedule 8. Moreover, paragraph 15 of the new Schedule 8 allows the directors to include an unrealised profit in the profit and loss account where there are special reasons for doing so. Where unrealised profits are thus recognised in the profit and loss account, particulars of this departure from the statutory accounting principle, the reasons for it and its effect are required to be given in a note to the accounts.

Distributable profits

13. The definition of realised profits contained in the new Schedule 8 is extended by Section 21(1) of the 1981 Act to apply to any of the Companies Acts. It therefore applies to the provisions of Part III of the 1980 Act, dealing with distributions. In that context this guidance should be read in conjunction with the statutory rules as to what constitute distributable profits and losses in particular circumstances for the purposes of that part of that Act.

14. It is essential that all companies should keep sufficient records to enable them to distinguish between those reserves which are

distributable and those which are not. While most realised profits will be passed through the profit and loss account, there may be some realised profits which will originally have been brought into the accounts as unrealised profits by way of direct credit to reserves. Similarly, while most unrealised profits will be credited direct to reserves, there may be some unrealised profits passed through the profit and loss account (see paragraph 12 above). Subsequently, when such profits are realised either in whole or in part, a reclassification needs to be made between unrealised and realised profits.

15. There is no legal requirement for a company to distinguish in its balance sheet between distributable and non-distributable reserves as such. However, where material non-distributable profits are included in the profit and loss account or in other reserves which might reasonably be assumed to be distributable, it may be necessary for this to be disclosed and quantified in a note to the accounts in order for them to give a true and fair view.

16. Distributions are made by companies and not by groups. It follows that the profits of a group are only distributable to members of the group's holding company to the extent of the holding company's distributable profits. The concept of distributable profit is not, therefore, strictly applicable to groups. However, it is reasonable to assume that the distributable retained profits of subsidiaries can be distributed to the holding company. Where this is not the case, the requirements of paragraph 36 of SSAP 14 'Group accounts' should be complied with. This states:

> 'If there are significant restrictions on the ability of the holding company to distribute the retained profits of the group (other than those shown as non-distributable) because of statutory, contractual or exchange control restrictions the extent of the restrictions should be indicated.'

Appendix to TR 481

Accounting standards and realised profits: Examples

1. As statements of standard accounting practice are revised and as new standards are issued, it is expected that they will deal with any matters relevant to the determination of realised profits.

2. This has already been done in the case of SSAP 1 'Accounting for Associated Companies', revised in April 1982. This provides an example of the way in which the true and fair view requirements should be satisfied by giving additional information rather than by including unrealised profits in profit and loss account (see paragraph 12 above). As far as an investing company is concerned, the profits of its associated companies are not realised until they are passed on as dividends; the true and fair view, however, requires that they should

be reflected in the investing company's financial statements. There is no problem where group accounts are prepared because specific provision is made for this situation in paragraph 65(1) of the new Schedule 8. Where, however, the investing company does not prepare group accounts, the revised SSAP 1 states that it should show the information required as to its share of the associated company's profit by preparing a separate profit and loss account or by adding the information to its own profit and loss account in supplementary form in such a way that its share of the profits of the associated company is not treated as realised.

3. An example of the principle that profit recognised in accordance with an Accounting Standard should normally be treated as realised (see paragraph 10 above) is provided by SSAP 9 'Stocks and work in progress'. This requires that long-term contract work in progress should be stated in periodic financial statements at cost plus any attributable profit, less any foreseeable losses and progress payments received and receivable. There was initially some concern as to whether profit thus recognised on long-term contract work in progress would be construed as realised profit within the provisions of the Companies Acts. However, the relevant principles of recognising profits in SSAP 9 are based on the concept of 'reasonable certainty' as to the eventual outcome and are not in conflict with the statutory accounting principles. Such profits should be treated as realised profits. The Department of Trade does not dissent from this view.

Technical Release 482

Guidance statement issued in September 1982 on behalf of the Councils of the constituent members of the Consultative Committee of Accountancy Bodies, on the determination of distributable profits. This statement gives guidance on the interpretation of Part III of the Companies Act 1980 and on the determination of the maximum amount of profit which can be legally distributed under that Act.

It should be emphasised that it does not seek to deal with the many commercial factors which need to be taken into account before a company decides on the amount of a distribution to be recommended to its shareholders. It should also be borne in mind that its guidance relates solely to the determination of profits legally available for distribution and that it does not give guidance on the recognition of profit in the accounts.

This statement should be read in conjunction with the guidance statement issued by the Councils of the constituent members of the CCAB on 'The determination of realised profits and disclosure of distributable profits in the context of the Companies Acts 1948 to 1981', issued in September 1982.

This statement has been considered and approved by Counsel.

However, it is not definitive. Interpretation of the law rests ultimately with the courts.

References to the '1948 Act', the '1967 Act', the '1980 Act' and the '1981 Act' are to the Companies Acts 1948, 1967, 1980 and 1981 respectively. Section references without ascription refer to the 1980 Act.

References to the 'new Schedule 8' are to Schedule 8 to the 1948 Act as inserted by S 1(2) of the 1981 Act, and as set out in Schedule 1 to the 1981 Act.

Introduction

1. The 1980 Act restricts distributions of both public and private companies. Previously the determination of legally distributable reserves and profits was governed only by a company's articles of association, Sections 56 to 58 of the 1948 Act, and a significant body of case law. After the commencement of the provisions of the 1980 Act, a company must restrict its distributions to those permitted by the 1980 Act, subject to any further restrictions imposed under its memorandum or articles of association.

2. In general, companies are only able to make distributions out of realised profits less realised losses, but further restrictions are imposed on public companies (see paragraph 6 below). The 1980 Act also includes special provisions for certain investment companies and insurance companies (ss 41 and 42): these are not discussed in this guidance statement.

Provision of the Companies Act 1980 (as amended)

Distribution

3. A 'distribution' is defined (s 45(2)) as 'every description of distribution of a company's assets to members of the company, whether in cash or otherwise, except distributions made by way of –

(*a*) an issue of shares as fully or partly paid bonus shares;

(*b*) redemption or purchase of any of the company's own shares out of capital (including a new issue of shares) or out of unrealised profits;

(*c*) reduction of share capital; and

(*d*) a distribution of assets to members of the company on its winding-up.

Profits available for distribution

4. A company may only make a distribution out of profits available for that purpose (s 39(1)). A company's profits available for distribution are stated to be its accumulated, realised profits (so far as not previously distributed or capitalised) less its accumulated, realised losses (so far as not previously written off in a reduction or reorganisation of its share capital) (s 39(2)). Realised losses may not be offset against unrealised profits. Public companies are subject to a further restriction (see paragraph 6 below).

5. A company may only distribute an unrealised profit when the distribution is in kind and the unrealised profit arises from the writing up of the asset being distributed (s 43A, as inserted by s 85 of the 1981 Act).

Public companies

6. A further restriction is placed on distributions by public companies (s 40). A public company may only make a distribution if, after giving effect to such distribution, the amount of its net assets (as defined in s 87(4)(c)) is not less than the aggregate of its called up share capital and undistributable reserves. This means that a public company must deduct any net unrealised losses from net realised profits before making a distribution, whereas a private company need not make such a deduction (see also paragraphs 29 to 31 below).

7. Under Section 40(2) the following are undistributable reserves:

(*a*) share premium account (see also s 56 of the 1948 Act as amended by the 1981 Act);

(*b*) capital redemption reserve (see also s 53 of the 1981 Act);

(*c*) the excess of accumulated, unrealised profits, over the accumulated, unrealised losses so far as not previously written off in a reduction or reorganisation of its share capital;

(*d*) any other reserve which the company is prohibited from distributing by any enactment, or by its memorandum or articles of association (or equivalent).

Section 40 only applies to public companies. However, because of the effect of Section 39(2) of the 1980 Act, Section 56 of the 1948 Act, and Section 53 of the 1981 Act, none of the above mentioned reserves is distributable by private companies. (The restrictions which are placed upon public companies which have distributed or utilised unrealised profits prior to the commencement of the Act are discussed at paragraph 30 below).

Relevant accounts

8. Whether or not a distribution may be made within the terms of the 1980 Act is determined by reference to 'relevant items' as stated in the 'relevant accounts'. A 'relevant item' is defined by s 43(8) as profits, losses, assets, liabilities, provisions, share capital and reserves. Thus, valuations or contingencies included in notes to the financial statements, but not incorporated in the accounts themselves, have no effect on the amount of distributable profit. There is no requirement that distributions can only be made out of distributable profits described as such in the accounts.

9. The 'relevant accounts' (annual, interim or initial) are defined in Section 43(2) and, except for the initial or interim accounts of private companies, must be properly prepared in accordance with Section 43(8).

10. Annual accounts must be accompanied by an audit report complying with Section 14 of the 1967 Act, and must have been laid before the company in general meeting in accordance with Section 1 of the 1976 Act (s 43(3)). Interim and initial accounts of public companies (there is no such requirement for private companies) must have been delivered to the Registrar of Companies (s 43(5)(b) and s 43(6)(d)). Initial accounts of public companies must be accompanied by a report by the auditor stating whether in his opinion the accounts have been properly prepared (s 43(6)(b)). The interim accounts need not be accompanied by an audit report.

11. There are requirements in Section 43(3)(c) and Section 43(6)(c), where an auditor has issued a qualified report on either annual or initial accounts as appropriate, that before a distribution may be made in reliance on those accounts the auditor must issue an additional statement. In this statement he must express an opinion whether the subject of his qualification is material for the purposes of determining whether the proposed distribution complies with the requirements of the Act.

Adjustments to relevant accounts

12. Adjustments to distributable profits calculated from the relevant accounts are required where one or more distributions have already been made 'in pursuance of determinations made by reference to' those accounts (s 43(7)). Adjustments are also required where a company has, since those accounts were prepared, provided financial assistance for the purchase of its own shares which depletes its net assets or made certain payments in respect of or in connection with the purchase of its own shares (s 60(1) of the 1981 Act).

Basis for calculating profits available for distribution

13. The starting point in determining profits available for distribution, the 'accumulated, realised profits . . . less accumulated, realised losses', will be the profit or loss recognised in the relevant accounts. That is the accumulated balance on the profit and loss account. This figure may require adjustment to take into account any items which are required to be excluded in the determination of distributable profits (e.g. see paragraph 21 below). The amount so arrived at will require further adjustment for any items taken to reserve accounts which may properly be included in the determination of distributable profits. For example, an unrealised profit on an asset revaluation will originally be credited direct to a revaluation reserve. On a subsequent disposal of the asset part or all of the profit is clearly realised notwithstanding the fact that it may not have been passed through the profit and loss account.

14. If an item has not been recognised in the relevant accounts, it cannot be taken into account in determining the profits or net assets available for distribution.

Aspects requiring special consideration

Realised losses

15. Section 39(4) as amended states that certain provisions are to be treated as a realised loss. These are provisions of any kind mentioned in paragraphs 87(1) and 88 of the new Schedule 8, namely:

> '. . . any amount written off by way of providing for depreciation or diminution in value of assets' and ' . . . any amount retained as reasonably necessary for the purpose of providing for any liability or loss which is likely to be incurred, or certain to be incurred but uncertain as to amount or as to the date on which it will arise.'

16. Section 39(4) as amended makes one specific exception to the rule that any provision of any kind mentioned in these paragraphs is to be treated as a realised loss, namely a provision arising on a revaluation of a fixed asset when all the fixed assets, or all fixed assets other than goodwill, have been revalued (see paragraph 19 below).

17. In view of the requirement of s 39(4), any loss recognised in the profit and loss account will normally be a realised loss. (An exception to this rule at s 39(5) is discussed at paragraph 21 below.)

Revaluation of assets

18. A surplus over original cost recognised on revaluation of any asset is unrealised. There is no statutory requirement specifying whether the

balance, if any, of the surplus that represents the writing back of past depreciation or of provisions for diminution in value should be regarded as realised or unrealised. Moreover, there is at present no unanimity of opinion as to whether such a surplus, to the extent that it represents the writing back of a realised loss, particularly where the realised loss arises from past depreciation, constitutes a realised profit. In view of the division of opinion on this matter, and in the absence of any statutory rule or clearly decisive precedent in case law, it is considered inappropriate to offer guidance on the question in this statement. Where reliance is placed on such a profit being realised in order to make a distribution, it may be appropriate for the directors of the company to seek legal advice. To the extent that the surplus represents the writing back of an unrealised loss, it should be treated as an unrealised profit.

19. A deficit on the revaluation of an asset (unless offsetting a previous unrealised surplus on the same asset) gives rise to a provision and is required to be treated as a realised loss. A realised loss thus created cannot be reduced by being offset wholly or partially against revaluation surpluses on other assets, whether or not of the same class. However, there is an exception to the general rule where a provision for diminution in value of a fixed asset arises on a revaluation of all the fixed assets (other than goodwill) (s 39(4) as amended). Although not explicitly stated, the Act implies that such a provision may be treated as unrealised, and therefore that it does not reduce the profits available for distribution.

20. For the purpose of s 39(4), a 'revaluation' of all the fixed assets may comprise actual revaluations of some of the fixed assets combined with consideration by the directors of the value of the remaining fixed assets. However, if an actual revaluation of all the fixed assets has not occurred, the directors must be satisfied that the aggregate value of all fixed assets 'considered' but not actually revalued is not less than the aggregate amount at which they are for the time being stated in the company's accounts (s 39(4A): see paragraph 45(2) of Schedule 3 to the 1981 Act). If the accounts include 'revalued' fixed assets which have been 'considered', but which have not been subject to an actual revaluation, certain additional information is required to be disclosed for the 'revaluation' to be valid (s 43(7A): see paragraph 47 (c) of Schedule 3 to the 1981 Act).

Revalued fixed assets and depreciation

21. Provisions for depreciation of revalued fixed assets require special treatment to the extent that these provisions exceed the amounts which would have been provided if an unrealised profit had not been made on revaluation (s 39(5)). For the purpose of calculating the amount of profit which is legally available for distribution, s 39(5) requires an amount equivalent to this excess depreciation to 'be treated . . . as a realised profit', thereby reducing the provision for this

purpose to that relating to the original cost of the asset. As a result, while the depreciation of a surplus on a fixed asset revaluation will affect the published profits, it will not normally affect the amount of a company's distributable profits, provided of course that this revaluation surplus has not been capitalised ('capitalisation' in this context is defined at s 45(3)).

Disposal of revalued assets

22. On the disposal of a revalued asset any surplus over cost immediately becomes realised. Any loss which has been treated as unrealised (see paragraph 20 above) should on disposal of the asset be redesignated as a realised loss.

Development costs

23. Development costs carried forward in accordance with SSAP 13 'Accounting for research and development' will not normally affect distributable profits. Although Section 42A(1) (inserted by s 84 of the 1981 Act) requires that development costs shown as an asset should be treated as a realised loss, this requirement does not apply (s 42A(3)) if the directors justify the costs carried forward not being treated as a realised loss. This they will normally be able to do if the costs are carried forward in accordance with SSAP 13. Such justification must be included in the note on capitalised development costs required by paragraph 20(2) of the new Schedule 8.

Holding company

24 It should be noted that although the whole of the distributable profits of a subsidiary are (subject to the interests of minority shareholders and tax on distributions) available to the holding company, the latter cannot distribute these profits to its own shareholders until such time as they are recognised in the accounts of the holding company.

25. It is not normal practice to take credit for dividends from investments unless the amounts are declared prior to the investing company's year-end. However, dividends receivable from subsidiaries and associates in respect of accounting periods ending on or before that of the holding company are normally accrued in the holding company's accounts even if declared after the holding company's year-end. Such dividends should be treated as realised by the holding company whether they are paid or passed through a current account, provided that, in the latter case, an appropriate reassessment of the realisable value of the current account balance is made.

26. Exchange control or other restrictions may affect the ability of overseas subsidiaries to remit dividends to the UK. In accordance with

the prudence concept such dividends receivable should be treated as realised only when their eventual receipt can be assessed with reasonable certainty.

27. Whilst there is no legal requirement for a holding company to take into account its share of the net losses (if any) of its subsidiaries in determining its distributable profits, the holding company may need to make a provision against a permanent diminution in the value of its investment in any such subsidiary (paragraph 19(2) of the new Schedule 8).

Current cost accounts

28. It will normally make no difference to a company's legally distributable profit whether its relevant accounts are drawn up under the historical or the current cost convention. Where net assets under the current cost convention exceed net assets under the historical cost convention, the difference consists of net unrealised profits which form part of the current cost reserve. The remainder of the current cost reserve consists of an amount equal to the cumulative current cost adjustments charged in the profit and loss account each year. According to SSAP 16 this amount is regarded as realised (in the case of the depreciation adjustment the 1980 Act specifically requires it to be so treated). This part of the current cost reserve, being realised, is legally distributable even though there would be a reduction in the operating capability of the business as a result of making such a distribution, which might, therefore, be commercially inadvisable.

Transitional provisions

Determination of distributable profits at the commencement date

29. Where the directors of a company are, after making all reasonable enquiries, unable to determine whether a particular profit or loss made before the commencement date of the 1980 Act is realised or unrealised, they may treat such a profit as realised and such a loss as unrealised (s39(7)). Such a position will occur when there are no records of the original cost of an asset or the original amount of a liability.

30. Where a public company has distributed or utilised (otherwise than by capitalisation) unrealised profits prior to the commencement date of the 1980 Act and such profits have not subsequently been realised, an amount equal to the unrealised profits so distributed or utilised falls to be included as part of the undistributable reserves (s 40(2) and s 45(4)). This prevents a public company which has so distributed or utilised unrealised profits in the past from making any further distribution until the shortfall has been made good.

31. If, prior to the commencement of the 1980 Act, a company has realised losses (insofar as they have not been previously written off in either a reduction or a reorganisation of capital), such losses must be made good before making any distribution (s 39(2)).

32. The part of the 1980 Act dealing with distributable profits came into operation as follows (s 45(6)):

New public companies	On their registration under Part I of the 1980 Act.
Existing public companies	On their re-registration as a public limited company under Part I of the 1980 Act, or on 22 June 1982 (18 months after the appointed day), whichever is the earlier.
Private companies	22 June 1982.

EC 4TH COMPANY LAW DIRECTIVE

Fourth Council Directive*

of 25 July 1978

based on Article 54(3)(g) of the Treaty on the annual accounts of certain types of companies

(78/660/EEC)

The Council of the European Communities,

Having regard to the Treaty establishing the European Economic Community, and in particular Article 54(3)(g) thereof,

Having regard to the proposal from the Commission,

Having regard to the opinion of the European Parliament,[1]

Having regard to the opinion of the Economic and Social Committee,[2]

Whereas the coordination of national provisions concerning the presentation and content of annual accounts and annual reports, the valuation methods used therein and their publication in respect of certain companies with limited liability is of special importance for the protection of members'and third parties;

Whereas simultaneous coordination is necessary in these fields for these forms of company because, on the one hand, these companies' activities frequently extend beyond the frontiers of their national territories and, on the other, they offer no safeguards to third parties beyond the amounts of their net assets; whereas, moreover, the necessity for and the urgency of such coordination have been recognized and confirmed by Article 2(1)(f) of Directive 68/151/EEC;[3]

---

* OJ No. L 222, 14.8.1978, p. 11.
1. OJ No. C 129, 11.12.1972, p. 38.
2. OJ No. C 39, 7.6.1973, p. 31.
3. OJ No. L 65, 14.3.1968, p. 8.

Whereas it is necessary, moreover, to establish in the Community minimum equivalent legal requirements as regards the extent of the financial information that should be made available to the public by companies that are in competition with one another;

Whereas annual accounts must give a true and fair view of a company's assets and liabilities, financial position and profit or loss; whereas to this end a mandatory layout must be prescribed for the balance sheet and the profit and loss account and whereas the minimum content of the notes on the accounts and the annual report must be laid down; whereas, however, derogations may be granted for certain companies of minor economic or social importance;

Whereas the different methods for the valuation of assets and liabilities must be coordinated to the extent necessary to ensure that annual accounts disclose comparable and equivalent information;

Whereas the annual accounts of all companies to which this Directive applies must be published in accordance with Directive 68/151/EEC; whereas, however, certain derogations may likewise be granted in this area for small and medium-sized companies;

Whereas annual accounts must be audited by authorized persons whose minimum qualifications will be the subject of subsequent coordination; whereas only small companies may be relieved of this audit obligation;

Whereas, when a company belongs to a group, it is desirable that group accounts giving a true and fair view of the activities of the group as a whole be published; whereas, however, pending the entry into force of a Council Directive on consolidated accounts, derogations from certain provisions of this Directive are necessary;

Whereas, in order to meet the difficulties arising from the present position regarding legislation in certain Member States, the period allowed for the implementation of certain provisions of this Directive must be longer than the period generally laid down in such cases,

Has adopted this Directive:

Article 1

1. The coordination measures prescribed by this Directive shall apply to the laws, regulations and administrative provisions of the Member States relating to the following types of companies:

- in Germany:
  die Aktiengesellschaft, die Kommanditgesellschaft auf Aktien, die Gesellschaft mit beschränkter Haftung;

- in Belgium:
  la société anonyme / de naamloze vennootschap, la société en commandite par actions / de commanditaire vennootschap op aandelen, la société de personnes à responsabilité limitée / de personenvennootschap met beperkte aansprakelijkheid:

- in Denmark:
  aktieselskaber, kommanditaktieselskaber, anpartsselskaber;

- in France:
  la société anonyme, la société en commandite par actions, la société à responsabilité limitée;

- in Ireland:
  public companies limited by shares or by guarantee, private companies limited by shares or by guarantee;

- in Italy:
  la società per azioni, la società in accomandita per azioni, la società a responsabilità limitata;

- in Luxembourg:
  la société anonyme, la société en commandite par actions, la société à responsabilité limitée;

- in the Netherlands:
  de naamloze vennootschap, de besloten vennootschap met beperkte aansprakelijkheid;

- in the United Kingdom:
  public companies limited by shares or by guarantee, private companies limited by shares or by guarantee.

2. Pending subsequent coordination, the Member States need not apply the provisions of this Directive to banks and other financial institutions or to insurance companies.

Section 1

General provisions

Article 2

1. The annual accounts shall comprise the balance sheet, the profit and loss account and the notes on the accounts. These documents shall constitute a composite whole.

2. They shall be drawn up clearly and in accordance with the provisions of this Directive.

3. The annual accounts shall give a true and fair view of the company's assets, liabilities, financial position and profit or loss.

4. Where the application of the provisions of this Directive would not be sufficient to give a true and fair view within the meaning of paragraph 3, additional information must be given.

5. Where in exceptional cases the application of a provision of this Directive is incompatible with the obligation laid down in paragraph 3, that provision must be departed from in order to give a true and fair view within the meaning of paragraph 3. Any such departure must be disclosed in the notes on the accounts together with an explanation of the reasons for it and a statement of its effect on the assets, liabilities, financial position and profit or loss. The Member States may define the exceptional cases in question and lay down the relevant special rules.

6. The Member States may authorize or require the disclosure in the annual accounts of other information as well as that which must be disclosed in accordance with this Directive.

Section 2

General provisions concerning the balance sheet and the profit and loss account

Article 3

The layout of the balance sheet and of the profit and loss account, particularly as regards the form adopted for their presentation, may not be changed from one financial year to the next. Departures from this principle shall be permitted in exceptional cases. Any such departure must be disclosed in the notes on the accounts together with an explanation of the reasons therefor.

Article 4

1. In the balance sheet and in the profit and loss account the items prescribed in Articles 9, 10 and 23 to 26 must be shown separately in the order indicated. A more detailed subdivision of the items shall be authorized provided that the layouts are complied with. New items may be added provided that their contents are not covered by any of the items prescribed by the layouts. Such subdivision or new items may be required by the Member States.

2. The layout, nomenclature and terminology of items in the balance sheet and profit and loss account that are preceded by Arabic numerals must be adapted where the special nature of an undertaking so requires. Such adaptations may be required by the Member States of undertakings forming part of a particular economic sector.

3. The balance sheet and profit and loss account items that are preceded by Arabic numerals may be combined where:

(a) they are immaterial in amount for the purpose of Article 2(3); or

(b) such combination makes for greater clarity, provided that the items so combined are dealt with separately in the notes on the accounts. Such combination may be required by the Member States.

4. In respect of each balance sheet and profit and loss account item the figure relating to the corresponding item for the preceding financial year must be shown. The Member States may provide that, where these figures are not comparable, the figure for the preceding year must be adjusted. In any case, non-comparability and any adjustment of the figures must be disclosed in the notes on the accounts, with relevant comments.

5. Save where there is a corresponding item for the preceding financial year within the meaning of paragraph 4, a balance sheet or profit and loss account item for which there is no amount shall not be shown.

Article 5

1. By way of derogation from Article 4(1) and (2), the Member States may prescribe special layouts for the annual accounts of investment companies and of financial holding companies provided that these layouts give a view of these companies equivalent to that provided for in Article 2(3).

2. For the purposes of this Directive, 'investment companies' shall mean only:

(a) those companies the sole object of which is to invest their funds in various securities, real property and other assets with the sole aim of spreading investment risks and giving their shareholders the benefit of the results of the management of their assets;

(b) those companies associated with investment companies with fixed capital if the sole object of the companies so associated is to acquire fully paid shares issued by those investment companies without prejudice to the provisions of Article 20(1)(h) of Directive 77/91/EEC.[1]

3. For the purposes of this Directive, 'financial holding companies' shall mean only those companies the sole subject of which is to acquire holdings in other undertakings, and to manage such holdings and turn them to profit, without involving themselves directly or indirectly in the management of those undertakings, the aforegoing without prejudice to their rights as shareholders. The limitations imposed on the activities of these companies must be such that compliance with them can be supervised by an administrative or judicial authority.

Article 6

The Member States may authorize or require adaptation of the layout of the balance sheet and profit and loss account in order to include the appropriation of profit or the treatment of loss.

Article 7

Any set-off between asset and liability items, or between income and expenditure items, shall be prohibited.

Section 3

Layout of the balance sheet

Article 8

For the presentation of the balance sheet, the Member States shall prescribe one or both of the layouts prescribed by Articles 9 and 10. If a Member State prescribes both, it may allow companies to choose between them.

Article 9

Assets

A. Subscribed capital unpaid

– of which there has been called

1. OJ No. L 26, 31.1.1977, p. 1.

(unless national law provides that called-up capital be shown under 'Liabilities'. In that case, the part of the capital called but not yet paid must appear as an asset either under A or under D (II)(5)).

B. Formation expenses

– as defined by national law, and in so far as national law permits their being shown as an asset. National law may also provide for formation expenses to be shown as the first item under 'Intangible assets'.

C. Fixed assets

I. Intangible assets
1. Costs of research and development, in so far as national law permits their being shown as assets.
2. Concessions, patents, licences, trade marks and similar rights and assets, if they were:
   (a) acquired for valuable consideration and need not be shown under C (I) (3); or
   (b) created by the undertaking itself, in so far as national law permits their being shown as assets.
3. Goodwill, to the exxtent that it was acquired for valuable consideration.
4. Payments on account.

II. Tangible assets
1. Land and buildings.
2. Plant and machinery.
3. Other fixtures and fittings, tools and equipment.
4. Payments on account and tangible assets in course of construction.

III. Financial assets
1. Shares in affiliated undertakings.
2. Loans to affiliated undertakings.
3. Participating interests.
4. Loans to undertakings with which the company is linked by virtue of participating interests.
5. Investments held as fixed assets.
6. Other loans.
7. Own shares (with an indication of their normal value or, in

the absence of a nominal value, their accounting par value) to the extent that national law permits their being shown in the balance sheet.

D. Current assets

I. Stocks
1. Raw materials and consumables.
2. Work in progress.
3. Finished goods and goods for resale.
4. Payments on account.

II. Debtors
(Amounts becoming due and payable after more than one year must be shown separately for each item.)
1. Trade debtors.
2. Amounts owed by affiliated undertakings.
3. Amounts owed by undertakings with which the company is linked by virtue of participating interests.
4. Other debtors.
5. Subscribed capital called but not paid (unless national law provides that called-up capital be shown as an asset under A).
6. Prepayments and accrued income (unless national law provides for such items to be shown as an asset under E).

III. Investments
1. Shares in affiliated undertakings.
2. Own shares (with an indication of their nominal value or, in the absence of a nominal value, their accounting par value) to the extent that national law permits their being shown in the balance sheet.
3. Other investments.

IV. Cash at bank and in hand

E. Prepayments and accrued income

(unless national law provides for such items to be shown as an asset under D(II)(6)).

F. Loss for the financial year

(unless national law provides for it to be shown under A(VI) under 'Liabilities').

Liabilities

A. Capital and reserves

I. Subscribed capital
(unless national law provides for called-up capital to be shown under this item. In that case, the amounts of subscribed capital and paid-up capital must be shown separately).

II. Share premium account

III. Revaluation reserve

IV. Reserves
1. Legal reserve, in so far as national law requires such a reserve.
2. Reserve for own shares, in so far as national law requires such a reserve, without prejudice to Article 22(1)(b) of Directive 77/91/EEC.
3. Reserves provided for by the articles of association.
4. Other reserves.

V. Profit or loss brought forward

VI. Profit or loss for the financial year
(unless national law requires that this item be shown under F under 'Assets' or under E under 'Liabilities').

B. Provisions for liabilities and charges

1. Provisions for pensions and similar obligations.
2. Provisions for taxation.
3. Other provisions.

C. Creditors

(Amounts becoming due and payable within one year and amounts becoming due and payable after more than one year must be shown separately for each item and for the aggregate of these items.)

1. Debenture loans, showing convertible loans separately.
2. Amounts owed to credit institutions.
3. Payments received on account of orders in so far as they are not shown separately as deductions from stocks.
4. Trade creditors.
5. Bills of exchange payable.
6. Amounts owed to affiliated undertakings.
7. Amounts owed to undertakings with which the company is linked by virtue of participating interests.
8. Other creditors including tax and social security.

9. Accruals and deferred income (unless national law provides for such items to be shown under D under 'Liabilities').

D. Accruals and deferred income

(unless national law provides for such items to be shown under C (9) under 'Liabilities').

E. Profit for the financial year

(unless national law provides for it to be shown under A(VI) under 'Liabilities').

Article 10

A. Subscribed capital unpaid

– of which there has been called

(unless national law provides that called-up capital be shown under L. In that case, the part of the capital called but not yet paid must appear either under A or under D(II)(5)).

B. Formation expenses

– as defined by national law, and in so far as national law permits their being shown as an asset. National law may also provide for formation expenses to be shown as the first item under 'Intangible assets'.

C. Fixed assets

I. Intangible assets
1. Costs of research and development, in so far as national law permits their being shown as assets.
2. Concessions, patents, licences, trade marks and similar rights and assets, if they were:
   (a) acquired for valuable consideration and need not be shown under C (I)(3); or
   (b) created by the undertaking itself, in so far as national law permits their being shown as assets.
3. Goodwill, to the extent that it was acquired for valuable consideration.
4. Payments on account.

II. Tangible assets
1. Land and buildings.
2. Plant and machinery.
3. Other fixtures and fittings, tools and equipment.

4. Payments on account and tangible assets in course of construction.

III. Financial assets
1. Shares in affiliated undertakings.
2. Loans to affiliated undertakings.
3. Participating interests.
4. Loans to undertakings with which the company is linked by virtue of participating interests.
5. Investments held as fixed assets.
6. Other loans.
7. Own shares (with an indication of their nominal value or, in the absence of a nominal value, their accounting par value) to the extent that national law permits their being shown in the balance sheet.

D. Current assets

I. Stocks
1. Raw materials and consumables.
2. Work in progress.
3. Finished goods and goods for resale.
4. Payments on account.

II. Debtors
(Amounts becoming due and payable after more than one year must be shown separately for each item.)
1. Trade debtors.
2. Amounts owed by affiliated undertakings.
3. Amounts owed by undertakings with which the company is linked by virtue of participating interests.
4. Other debtors.
5. Subscribed capital called but not paid (unless national law provides that called-up capital be shown under A).
6. Prepayments and accrued income (unless national law provides that such items be shown under E).

III. Investments
1. Shares in affiliated undertakings.
2. Own shares (with an indication of their nominal value or, in the absence of a nominal value, their accounting par value) to the extent that national law permits their being shown in the balance sheet.

3. Other investments.

IV. Cash at bank and in hand

E. Prepayments and accrued income

(unless national law provides for such items to be shown under D (II)(6)).

F. Creditors: amounts becoming due and payable within one year

1. Debenture loans, showing convertible loans separately.
2. Amounts owed to credit institutions.
3. Payments received on account of orders in so far as they are not shown separately as deductions from stocks.
4. Trade creditors.
5. Bills of exchange payable.
6. Amounts owed to affiliated undertakings.
7. Amounts owed to undertakings with which the company is linked by virtue of participating interests.
8. Other creditors including tax and social security.
9. Accruals and deferred income (unless national law provides for such items to be shown under K).

G. Net current assets / liabilities

(taking into account prepayments and accrued income when shown under E and accruals and deferred income when shown under K).

H. Total assets less current liabilities

I. Creditors: amounts becoming due and payable after more than one year

1. Debenture loans, showing convertible loans separately.
2. Amounts owed to credit institutions.
3. Payments received on account of orders in so far as they are not shown separately as deductions from stocks.
4. Trade creditors.
5. Bills of exchange payable.
6. Amounts owed to affiliated undertakings.
7. Amounts owed to undertakings with which the company is linked by virtue of participating interests.
8. Other creditors including tax and social security.

9. Accruals and deferred income (unless national law provides for such items to be shown under K).

J. Provisions for liabilities and charges

1. Provisions for pensions and similar obligations.
2. Provisions for taxation.
3. Other provisions.

K. Accruals and deferred income

(unless national law provides for such items to be shown under F (9) or I (9) or both).

L. Capital and reserves

I. Subscribed capital
(unless national law provides for called-up capital to be shown under this item. In that case, the amounts of subscribed capital and paid-up capital must be shown separately).

II. Share premium account

III. Revaluation reserve

IV. Reserves
1. Legal reserves, in so far as national law requires such a reserve.
2. Reserve for own shares, in so far as national law requires such a reserve, without prejudice to Article 22 (1)(b) of Directive 77/91/EEC.
3. Reserves provided for by the articles of association.
4. Other reserves.

V. Profit or loss brought forward

VI. Profit or loss for the financial year

Article 11

The Member States may permit companies which on their balance sheet dates do not exceed the limits of two of the three following criteria:
- balance sheet total: 1,000,000 EUA,
- net turnover: 2,000,000 EUA,
- average number of employees during the financial year:50,

to draw up abridged balance sheets showing only those items preceded by letters and roman numerals in Articles 9 and 10, disclosing separately the information required in brackets in D (II) under 'Assets' and C under 'Liabilities' in Article 9 and in D (II) in Article 10, but in total for each.

Article 12

1. Where on its balance sheet date, a company exceeds or ceases to exceed the limits of two of the three criteria indicated in Article 11, that fact shall affect the application of the derogation provided for in that Article only if it occurs in two consecutive financial years.

2. For the purposes of translation into national currencies, the amounts in European units of account specified in Article 11 may be increased by not more than 10 percent.

3. The balance sheet total referred to in Article 11 shall consist of the assets in A to E under 'Assets' in the layout prescribed in Article 9 or those in A to E in the layout prescribed in Article 10.

Article 13

1. Where an asset or liability relates to more than one layout item, its relationship to other items must be disclosed either under the item where it appears or in the notes on the accounts, if such disclosure is essential to the comprehension of the annual accounts.

2. Own shares and shares in affiliated undertakings may be shown only under the items prescribed for that purpose.

Article 14

All commitments by way of guarantee of any kind must, if there is no obligation to show them as liabilities, be clearly set out at the foot of the balance sheet or in the notes on the accounts, and a distinction made between the various types of guarantee which national law recognizes; specific disclosure must be made of any valuable security which has been provided. Commitments of this kind existing in respect of affiliated undertakings must be shown separately.

Section 4

Special provisions relating to certain balance sheet items

Article 15

1. Whether particular assets are to be shown as fixed assets or current assets shall depend upon the purpose for which they are intended.

2. Fixed assets shall comprise those assets which are intended for use on a continuing basis for the purposes of the undertaking's activities.

3. (a) Movements in the various fixed asset items shall be shown in the balance sheet or in the notes on the accounts. To this end there shall be shown separately, starting with the purchase price or production cost, for each fixed asset item, on the one hand, the additions, disposals and transfers during the financial year and, on the other, the cumulative value adjustments at the balance sheet date and the rectifications made during the financial year to the value adjustment of previous financial years. Value adjustments shall be shown either in the balance sheet, as clear deductions from the relevant items, or in the notes on the accounts.
(b) If, when annual accounts are drawn up in accordance with this Directive for the first time, the purchase price or production cost of a fixed asset cannot be determined without undue expense or delay, the residual value at the beginning of the financial year may be treated as the purchase price or production cost. Any application of this provision must be disclosed in the notes on the accounts.
(c) Where Article 33 is applied, the movements in the various fixed asset items referred to in subparagraph (a) of this paragraph shall be shown starting with the purchase price or production cost resulting from revaluation.

4. Paragraph 3 (a) and (b) shall apply to the presentation of 'Formation expenses'.

Article 16

Rights to immovables and other similar rights as defined by national law must be shown under 'Land and buildings'.

Article 17

For the purposes of this Directive, 'participating interest' shall mean rights in the capital of other undertakings, whether or not represented by certificates, which, by creating a durable link with those undertakings, are intended to contribute to the company's activities. The holding of part of the capital of another company shall be presumed to constitute a participating interest where it exceeds a percentage fixed by the Member States which may not exceed 20 percent.

Article 18

Expenditure incurred during the financial year but relating to a subsequent financial year, together with any income which, though relating to the financial year in question, is not due until after its expiry must be shown under 'Prepayments and accrued income'. The Member States may, however, provide that such income shall be included in 'Debtors'. Where such income is material, it must be disclosed in the notes on the accounts.

Article 19

Value adjustments shall comprise all adjustments intended to take account of reductions in the values of individual assets established at the balance sheet date whether that reduction is final or not.

Article 20

1. Provisions for liabilities and charges are intended to cover losses or debts the nature of which is clearly defined and which at the date of the balance sheet are either likely to be incurred, or certain to be incurred but uncertain as to amount or as to the date on which they will arise.

2. The Member States may also authorize the creation of provisions intended to cover charges which have their origin in the financial year under review or in a previous financial year, the nature of which is clearly defined and which at the date of the balance sheet are either likely to be incurred, or certain to be incurred but uncertain as to amount or as to the date on which they will arise.

3. Provisions for liabilities and charges may not be used to adjust the values of assets.

Article 21

Income receivable before the balance sheet date but relating to a subsequent financial year, together with any charges which, though relating to the financial year in question, will be paid only in the course of a subsequent financial year, must be shown under 'Accruals and deferred income'. The Member States may, however, provide that such charges shall be included in 'Creditors'. Where such charges are material, they must be disclosed in the notes on the accounts.

Section 5

Layout of the profit and loss account

Article 22

For the presentation of the profit and loss account, the Member States shall prescribe one or more of the layouts provided for in Articles 23 to 26. If a Member State prescribes more than one layout, it may allow companies to choose from among them.

Article 23

1. Net turnover.
2. Variation in stocks of finished goods and in work in progress.

3. Work performed by the undertaking for its own purposes and capitalized.
4. Other operating income.
5. (a) Raw materials and consumables.
   (b) Other external charges.
6. Staff costs:
   (a) wages and salaries;
   (b) social security costs, with a separate indication of those relating to pensions.
7. (a) Value adjustments in respect of formation expenses and of tangible and intangible fixed assets.
   (b) Value adjustments in respect of current assets, to the extent that they exceed the amount of value adjustments which are normal in the undertaking concerned.
8. Other operating charges.
9. Income from participating interests, with a separate indication of that derived from affiliated undertakings.
10. Income from other investments and loans forming part of the fixed assets, with a separate indication of that derived from affiliated undertakings.
11. Other interests receivable and similar income, with a separate indication of that derived from affiliated undertakings.
12. Value adjustments in respect of financial assets and of investments held as current assets.
13. Interest payable and similar charges, with a separate indication of those concerning affiliated undertakings.
14. Tax on profit or loss on ordinary activities.
15. Profit or loss on ordinary activities after taxation.
16. Extraordinary income.
17. Extraordinary charges.
18. Extraordinary profit or loss.
19. Tax on extraordinary profit or loss.
20. Other taxes not shown under the above items.
21. Profit or loss for the financial year.

Article 24

A. Charges

1. Reduction in stocks of finished goods and in work in progress:
2. (a) raw materials and consumables;
   (b) other external charges.
3. Staff costs:
   (a) wages and salaries;
   (b) social security costs, with a separate indication of those relating to pensions.
4. (a) Value adjustments in respect of formation expenses and of tangible and intangible fixed assets.
   (b) Value adjustments in respect of current assets, to the extent that they exceed the amount of value adjustments which are

normal in the undertaking concerned.

5. Other operating charges.
6. Value adjustments in respect of financial assets and of investments held as current assets.
7. Interest payable and similar charges, with a separate indication of those concerning affiliated undertakings.
8. Tax on profit or loss on ordinary activities.
9. Profit or loss on ordinary activities after taxation.
10. Extraordinary charges.
11. Tax on extraordinary profit or loss.
12. Other taxes not shown under the above items.
13. Profit or loss for the financial year.

B. Income

1. Net turnover.
2. Increase in stocks of finished goods and in work in progress.
3. Work performed by the undertaking for its own purposes and capitalized.
4. Other operating income.
5. Income from participating interests, with a separate indication of that derived from affiliated undertakings.
6. Income from other investments and loans forming part of the fixed assets, with a separate indication of that derived from affiliated undertakings.
7. Other interest receivable and similar income, with a separate indication of that derived from affiliated undertakings.
8. Profit or loss on ordinary activities after taxation.
9. Extraordinary income.
10. Profit or loss for the financial year.

Article 25

1. Net turnover.
2. Cost of sales (including value adjustments).
3. Gross profit or loss.
4. Distribution costs (including value adjustments).
5. Administrative expenses (including value adjustments).
6. Other operating income.
7. Income from participating interests, with a separate indication of that derived from affiliated undertakings.
8. Income from other investments and loans forming part of the fixed assets, with a separate indication of that derived from affiliated undertakings.
9. Other interest receivable and similar income, with a separate indication of that derived from affiliated undertakings.
10. Value adjustments in respect of financial assets and of investments held as current assets.
11. Interest payable and similar charges, with a separate indication of those concerning affiliated undertakings.

12. Tax on profit or loss on ordinary activities.
13. Profit or loss on ordinary activities after taxation.
14. Extraordinary income.
15. Extraordinary charges.
16. Extraordinary profit or loss.
17. Tax on extraordinary profit or loss.
18. Other taxes not shown under the above items.
19. Profit or loss for the financial year.

Article 26

A. *Charges*

1. Cost of sales (including value adjustments).
2. Distribution costs (including value adjustments).
3. Administrative expenses (including value adjustments).
4. Value adjustments in respect of financial assets and of investments held as current assets.
5. Interest payable and similar charges, with a separate indication of those concerning affiliated undertakings.
6. Tax on profit or loss on ordinary activites.
7. Profit of loss on ordinary activities after taxation.
8. Extraordinary charges.
9. Tax on extraordinary profit or loss.
10. Other taxes not shown under the above items.
11. Profit or loss for the financial year.

B. *Income*

1. Net turnover.
2. Other operating income.
3. Income from participating interests, with a separate indication of that derived from affiliated undertakings.
4. Income from other investments and loans forming part of the fixed assets, with a separate indication of that derived from affiliated undertakings.
5. Other interest receivable and similar income, with a separate indication of that derived from affiliated undertakings.
6. Profit or loss on ordinary activities after taxation.
7. Extraordinary income.
8. Profit or loss for the financial year.

Article 27

The Member States may permit companies which on their balance sheet dates do not exceed the limits of two of the three following criteria:
– balance sheet total: 4 million EUA,
– net turnover: 8 million EUA,
– average number of employees during the financial year: 250

to adopt layouts different from those prescribed in Articles 23 to 26 within the following limits:
(a) in Article 23: 1 to 5 inclusive may be combined under one item called 'Gross profit or loss';
(b) in Article 24: A(1), A(2) and B(1) to B(4) inclusive may be combined under one item called 'Gross profit or loss';
(c) in Article 25: (1), (2), (3) and (6) may be combined under one item called 'Gross profit or loss';
(d) in Article 26: A(1), B(1) and B(2) may be combined under one item called 'Gross profit or loss'.

Article 12 shall apply.

Section 6

Special provisions relating to certain items in the profit and loss account

Article 28

The net turnover shall comprise the amounts derived from the sale of products and the provision of services falling within the company's ordinary activities, after deduction of sales rebates and of value added tax and other taxes directly linked to the turnover.

Article 29

1. Income and charges that arise otherwise than in the course of the company's ordinary activities must be shown under 'Extraordinary income and extraordinary charges'.

2. Unless the income and charges referred to in paragraph 1 are immaterial for the assessment of the results, explanations of their amount and nature must be given in the notes on the accounts. The same shall apply to income and charges relating to another financial year.

Article 30

The Member States may permit taxes on the profit or loss on ordinary activities and taxes on the extraordinary profit or loss to be shown in total as one item in the profit and loss account before 'Other taxes not shown under the above items'. In that case, 'Profit or loss on ordinary activities after taxation' chall be omitted from the layouts prescribed in Articles 23 to 26.

Where this derogation is applied, companies must disclose in the notes on the accounts the extent to which the taxes on the profit or loss affect the profit or loss on ordinary activities and the 'Extraordinary profit or loss'.

Section 7

Valuation rules

Article 31

1. The Member States shall ensure that the items shown in the annual accounts are valued in accordance with the following general principles:
(a) the company must be presumed to be carrying on its business as a going concern;
(b) the methods of valuation must be applied consistently from one financial year to another;
(c) valuation must be made on a prudent basis, and in particular:
  (aa) only profits made at the balance sheet date may be included,
  (bb) account must be taken of all foreseeable liabilities and potential losses arising in the course of the financial year concerned or of a previous one, even if such liabilities or losses become apparent only between the date of the balance sheet and the date on which it is drawn up,
  (cc) account must be taken of all depreciation, whether the result of the financial year is a loss or a profit;
(d) account must be taken of income and charges relating to the financial year, irrespective of the date of receipt or payment of such income or charges;
(e) the components of asset and liability must be valued separately;
(f) the opening balance sheet for each financial year must correspond to the closing balance sheet for the preceding financial year.

2. Departures from these general principles shall be permitted in exceptional cases. Any such departures must be disclosed in the notes on the accounts and the reasons for them given together with an assessment of their effect on the assets, liabilities, financial position and profit or loss.

Article 32

The items shown in the annual accounts shall be valued in accordance with Articles 34 to 42, which are based on the principle of purchase price or production cost.

Article 33

1. The Member States may declare to the Commission that they reserve the power, by way of derogation from Article 32 and pending subsequent coordination, to permit or require in respect of all companies or any classes of companies:

(a) valuation by the replacement value method for tangible fixed assets with limited useful economic lives and for stocks;
(b) valuation by methods other that that provided for in (a) which are designed to take account of inflation for the items shown in annual accounts, including capital and reserves;
(c) revaluation of tangible fixed assets and financial fixed assets.

Where national law provides for valuation methods as indicated in (a), (b) and (c), it must define their content and limits and the rules for their application.

The application of any such method, the balance sheet and profit and loss account items concerned and the method by which the values shown are calculated shall be disclosed in the notes on the accounts.

2. (a) Where paragraph 1 is applied, the amount of the difference between valuation by the method used and valuation in accordance with the general rule laid down in Article 32 must be entered in the revaluation reserve under 'Liabilities'. The treatment of this item for taxation purposes must be explained either in the balance sheet or in the notes on the accounts.
For the purposes of the application of the last subparagraph of paragraph 1, companies shall, whenever the amount of the reserve has been changed in the course of the financial year, publish in the notes on the acounts *inter alia* a table showing:
– the amount of the revaluation reserve at the beginning of the financial year,
– the revaluation differences transferred to the revaluation reserve during the financial year,
– the amounts capitalized or otherwise transferred from the revaluation reserve during the financial year, the nature of any such transfer being disclosed,
– the amount of the revaluation reserve at the end of the financial year.

(b) The revaluation reserve may be capitalized in whole or in part at any time.

(c) The revaluation reserve must be reduced to the extent that the amounts transferred thereto are no longer necessary for the implementation of the valuation method used and the achievement of its purpose.
The Member States may lay down rules governing the application of the revaulation reserve, provided that transfers to the profit and loss account from the revaluation reserve may be made only to the extent that the amounts transferred have been entered as charges in the profit and loss account or reflect increases in value which have been actually realized. These amounts must be disclosed separately in the profit and loss account. No part of the revaluation reserve may be distributed, either directly or indirectly,

unless it represents gains actually realized.

(d) Save as provided under (b) and (c) the revaluation reserve may not be reduced.

3. Value adjustments shall be calculated each year on the basis of the value adopted for the financial year in question, save that by way of derogation from Articles 4 and 22, the Member States may permit or require that only the amount of the value adjustments arising as a result of the application of the general rule laid down in Article 32 be shown under the relevant items in the layouts prescribed in Articles 23 to 26 and that the difference arising as a result of the valuation method adopted under this Article be shown separately in the layouts. Furthermore, Articles 34 to 42 shall apply *mutatis mutandis*.

4. Where paragraph 1 is applied, the following must be disclosed, either in the balance sheet or in the notes on the accounts, separately for each balance sheet item as provided for in the layouts prescribed in Article 9 and 10, except for stocks, either:

(a) the amount at the balance sheet date of the valuation made in accordance with the general rule laid down in Article 32 and the amount of the cumulative value adjustments; or

(b) the amount at the balance sheet date of the difference between the valuation made in accordance with this Article and that resulting from the application of Article 32 and, where appropriate, the cumulative amount of the additional value adjustments.

5. Without prejudice to Article 52 the Council shall, on a proposal from the Commission and within seven years of the notification of this Directive, examine and, where necessary, amend this article in the light of economic and monetary trends in the Community.

Article 34

1. (a) Where national law authorizes the inclusion of formation expenses under 'Assets', they must be written off within a maximum period of five years.

(b) In so far as formation expenses have not been completely written off, no distribution of profits shall take place unless the amount of the reserves available for distribution and profits brought forward is at least equal to that of the expenses not written off.

2. The amounts entered under 'Formation expenses' must be explained in the notes on the accounts.

Article 35

1. (a) Fixed assets must be valued at purchase price or production cost, without prejudice to (b) and (c) below.

(b) The purchase price or production cost of fixed assets with limited useful economic lives must be reduced by value adjustments calculated to write off the value of such assets systematically over their useful economic lives.

(c) (aa) Value adjustments may be made in respect of financial fixed assets, so that they are valued at the lower figure to be attributed to them at the balance sheet date.

(bb) Value adjustments must be made in respect of fixed assets, whether their useful economic lives are limited or not, so that they are valued at the lower figure to be attributed to them at the balance sheet date if it is expected that the reduction in their value will be permanent.

(cc) The value adjustments referred to in (aa) and (bb) must be charged to the profit and loss account and disclosed separately in the notes on the accounts if they have not been shown separately in the profit and loss account.

(dd) Valuation at the lower of the values provided for in (aa) and (bb) may not be continued if the reasons for which the value adjustments were made have ceased to apply.

(d) If fixed assets are the subject of exceptional value adjustments for taxation purposes alone, the amount of the adjustments and the reasons for making them shall be indicated in the notes on the accounts.

2. The purchase price shall be calculated by adding to the price paid the expenses incidental thereto.

3. (a) The production cost shall be calculated by adding to the purchasing price of the raw materials and consumables the costs directly attributable to the product in question.

(b) A reasonable proportion of the costs which are only indirectly attributable to the product in question may be added into the production costs to the extent that they relate to the period of production.

4. Interest on capital borrowed to finance the production of fixed assets may be included in the production costs to the extent that it relates to the period of production. In that event, the inclusion of such interest under 'Assets' must be disclosed in the notes on the accounts.

Article 36

By way of derogation from Article 35 (1)(c)(cc), the Member States may allow investment companies within the meaning of Article 5 (2) to set off value adjustments to investments directly against 'Capital and reserves'. The amounts in question must be shown separately under 'Liabilities' in the balance sheet.

Article 37

1. Article 34 shall apply to costs of research and development. In exceptional cases, however, the Member States may permit derogations from Article 34 (1)(a). In that case, they may also provide for derogations from Article 34 (1)(b), Such derogations and the reasons for them must be disclosed in the notes on the accounts.

2. Article 34 (1)(a) shall apply to goodwill. The Member States may, however, permit companies to write goodwill off systematically over a limited period exceeding five years provided that this period does not exceed the useful economic life of the asset and is disclosed in the notes on the accounts together with the supporting reasons therefore.

Article 38

Tangible fixed assets, raw materials and consumables which are constantly being replaced and the overall value of which is of secondary importance to the undertaking may be shown under 'Assets' at a fixed quantity and value, if the quantity, value and composition thereof do not vary materially.

Article 39

1. (a) Current assets must be valued at purchase price or production cost, without prejudice to (b) and (c) below.
   (b) Value adjustments shall be made in respect of current assets with a view to showing them at the lower market value or, in particular circumstances, another lower value to be attributed to them at the balance sheet date.
   (c) The Member States may permit exceptional value adjustments where, on the basis of a reasonable commercial assessment, these are necessary if the valuation of these items is not to be modified in the near future because of fluctuations in value. The amount of these value adjustments must be disclosed separately in the profit and loss account or in the notes on the accounts.
   (d) Valuation at the lower value provided for in (b) and (c) may not be continued if the reasons for which the value adjustments were made have ceased to apply.
   (e) If current assets are the subject of exceptional value adjustments for taxation purposes alone, the amount of the adjustments and the reasons for making them must be disclosed in the notes on the accounts.

2. The definitions of purchase price and of production cost given in Article 35 (2) and (3) shall apply. The Member States may also apply Article 35 (4). Distribution costs may not be included in production costs.

Article 40

1. The Member States may permit the purchase price or production cost of stocks of goods of the same gategory and all fungible items including investments to be calculated either on the basis of weighted average prices or by the 'first in, first out' (FIFO) method, the 'last in, first out' (LIFO) method, or some similar method.

2. Where the value shown in the balance sheet, following application of the methods of calculation specified in paragraph 1, differs materially, at the balance sheet date, from the value on the basis of the last known market value prior to the balance sheet date, the amount of that difference must be disclosed in total by category in the notes on the accounts.

Article 41

1. Where the amount repayable on account of any debt is greater than the amount received, the difference may be shown as an asset. It must be shown separately in the balance sheet or in the notes on the accounts.

2. The amount of this difference must be written off by a reasonable amount each year and completely written off no later than the time of repayment of the debt.

Article 42

Provisions for liabilities and charges may not exceed in amount the sums which are necessary.
The provisions shown in the balance sheet under 'Other provisions' must be disclosed in the notes on the accounts if they are material.

Section 8

Contents of the notes on the accounts

Article 43

1. In addition to the information required under other provisions of this Directive, the notes on the accounts must set out information in respect of the following matters at least:
(1) the valuation methods applied to the various items in the annual accounts, and the methods employed in calculating the value

adjustments. For items included in the annual accounts which are or were originally expressed in foreign currency, the bases of conversion used to express them in local currency must be disclosed;

(2) the name and registered office of each of the undertakings in which the company, either itself or through a person acting in his own name but on the company's behalf, holds at least a percentage of the capital which the Member States cannot fix at more than 20 percent, showing the proportion of the capital held, the amount of capital and reserves, and the profit or loss for the latest financial year of the undertaking concerned for which accounts have been adopted. This information may be omitted where for the purposes of Article 2 (3) it is of negligible importance only. The information concerning capital and reserves and the profit or loss may also be omitted where the undertaking concerned does not publish its balance sheet and less than 50 percent of its capital is held (directly or indirectly) by the company;

(3) the number and the nominal value or, in the absence of a nominal value, the accounting par value of the shares subscribed during the financial year within the limits of an authorized capital, without prejudice as far as the amount of this capital is concerned to Article 2 (1)(e) of Directive 68/151/EEC or to Article 2(c) of Directive 77/91/EEC;

(4) where there is more than one class of shares, the number and the nominal value of, in the absence of a nominal value, the accounting par value of each class;

(5) the existence of any participation certificates, convertible debentures or similar securities or rights, with an indication of their number and the rights they confer;

(6) amounts owed by the company becoming due and payable after more than five years as well as the company's entire debts covered by valuable security furnished by the company with an indication of the nature and form of the security. This information must be disclosed separately for each creditors item, as provided for in the layouts prescribed in Articles 9 and 10;

(7) the total amount of any financial commitments that are not included in the balance sheet, in so far as this information is of assistance in assessing the financial position. Any commitments concerning pensions and affiliated undertakings must be disclosed separately;

(8) the net turnover within the meaning of Article 28, broken down by categories of activity and into geographical markets in so far as, taking account of the manner in which the sale of products and the provision of services falling within the company's ordinary activities are organized, these categories and markets differ substantially from one another;

(9) the average number of persons employed during the financial year, broken down by categories and, if they are not disclosed separately in the profit and loss account, the staff costs relating

to the financial year, broken down as provided for in Article 23 (6);

(10) the extent to which the calculation of the profit or loss for the financial year has been affected by a valuation of the items which, by way of derogation from the principles enunciated in Articles 31 and 34 to 42, was made in the financial year in question or in an earlier financial year with a view to obtaining tax relief. Where the influence of such a valuation on future tax charges is material, details must be disclosed;

(11) the difference between the tax charged for the financial year and for earlier financial years and the amount of tax payable in respect of those years, provided that this difference is material for the purposes of future taxation. This amount may also be disclosed in the balance sheet as a cumulative amount under a separate item with an appropriate heading;

(12) the amount of the emoluments granted in respect of the financial year to the members of the administrative, managerial and supervisory bodies by reason of their responsibilities, and any commitments arising or entered into in respect of retirement pensions for former members of those bodies, with an indication of the total for each category;

(13) the amount of advances and credits granted to the members of the administrative, managerial and supervisory bodies, with indications of the interest rates, main conditions and any amounts repaid, as well as commitments entered into on their behalf by way of guarantees of any kind, with an indication of the total for each category.

2. Pending subsequent coordination, the Member States need not apply paragraph 1 (2) to financial holding companies within the meaning of Article 5 (3).

Article 44

The Member States may permit the companies referred to in Article 11 to draw up abridged notes on their accounts without the information required in Article 43 (1)(5) to (12). However, the notes must disclose the information specified in Article 43 (1)(6) in total for all the items concerned.
Article 12 shall apply.

Article 45

1. The Member States may allow the disclosures prescribed in Article 43 (1)(2):

(a) to take the form of a statement deposited in accordance with Article 3 (1) and (2) of Directive 68/151/EEC; this must be disclosed in the notes on the accounts;

(b) to be omitted when their nature is such that they would be seriously prejudicial to any of the undertakings to which Article

43 (1)(2) relates. The Member States may make such omissions subject to prior administrative or judicial authorization. Any such omission must be disclosed in the notes on the accounts.

2. Paragraph 1 (b) shall also apply to the information prescribed by Article 43 (1)(8).
The Member States may permit the companies referred to in Article 27 to omit the disclosures prescribed by Article 43 (1)(8). Article 12 shall apply.

Section 9

Contents of the annual report

Article 46

1. The annual report must include at least a fair review of the development of the company's business and of its position.

2. The report shall also give an indication of:
(a) any important events that have occurred since the end of the financial year;
(b) the company's likely future development;
(c) activities in the field of research and development;
(d) the information concerning acquisitions of own shares prescribed by Article 22 (2) of Directive 77/91/EEC.

Section 10

Publication

Article 47

1. The annual accounts, duly approved, and the annual report, together with the opinion submitted by the person responsible for auditing the accounts, shall be published as laid down by the laws of each Member State in accordance with Article 3 of Directive 68/151/EEC.

The laws of a Member State may, however, permit the annual report not to be publsihed as stipulated above. In that case, it shall be made available to the public at the company's registered office in the Member State concerned. It must be possible to obtain a copy of all or part of any such report free of charge upon request.

2. By way of derogation from paragraph 1, the Member States may permit the companies referred to in Article 11 to publish:

(a) abridged balance sheets showing only those items preceded by letters and roman numerals in Articles 9 and 10, disclosing separately the information required in brackets in D (II) under 'Assets' and C under 'Liabilities' in Article 9 and in D (II) in Article 10, but in total for all the items concerned; and
(b) abridged notes on their accounts without the explanations required in Article 43 (1)(5) to (12). However, the notes must disclose the information specified in Article 43 (1)(6) in total for all the items concerned.

Article 12 shall apply.

In addition, the Member States may relieve such companies from the obligation to publish their profit and loss accounts and annual reports and the opinions of the persons responsible for auditing the accounts.

3. The Member States may permit the companies mentioned in Article 27 to publish:

(a) abridged balance sheets showing only those items preceded by letters and roman numerals in articles 9 and 10 disclosing separately, either in the balance sheet or in the notes on the accounts:
   - C(I)(3), C(II)(1), (2), (3) and (4), C(III)(1), (2), (3), (4) and (7), D(II)(2), (3) and (6) and D(III)(1) and (2) under 'Assets' and C(1), (2), (6), (7) and (9) under 'Liabilities' in Article 9,
   - C(I)(3), C(II)(1), (2), (3) and (4), C(III)(1), (2), (3), (4) and (7), D(II)(2), (3) and (6), D(III)(1) and (2), F(1), (2), (6), (7) and (9) and (I)(1), (2), (6), (7) and (9) in Article 10,
   - the information required in brackets in D(II) under 'Assets' and C under 'Liabilities' in Article 9, in total for all the items concerned and separately for D(II)(2) and (3) under 'Assets' and C(1), (2), (6), (7) and (9) under 'Liabilities',
   - the information required in brackets in D(II) in Article 10, in total for all the items concerned, and separately for D(II)(2) and (3);
(b) abridged notes on their accounts without the information required in Article 43 (1)(5), (6), (8), (10) and (11). However, the notes on the accounts must give the information specified in Article 43(1)(6) in total for all the items concerned.

This paragraph shall be without prejudice to paragraph 1 in so far as it relates to the profit and loss account, the annual report and the opinion of the person responsible for auditing the accounts.
Article 12 shall apply.

Article 48

Whenever the annual accounts and the annual report are published in full, they must be reproduced in the form and text on the basis of which the person responsible for auditing the accounts has drawn up his opinion. They must be accompanied by the full text of his report.

If the person responsible for auditing the accounts has made any qualifications or refused to report upon the accounts, that fact must be disclosed and the reasons given.

Article 49

If the annual accounts are not published in full, it must be indicated that the version published is abridged and reference must be made to the register in which the accounts have been filed in accordance with Article 47 (1). Where such filing has not yet been effected, the fact must be disclosed. The report issued by the person responsible for auditing the accounts may not accompany this publication, but it must be disclosed whether the report was issued with or without qualification, or was refused.

Article 50

The following must be published together with the annual accounts, and in like manner:
- the proposed appropriation of the profit or treatment of the loss,
- the appropriation of the profit or treatment of the loss,

where these items do not appear in the annual accounts.

Section 11

Auditing

Article 51

1. (a) Companies must have their annual accounts audited by one or more persons authorized by national law to audit accounts.
   (b) The person or persons responsible for auditing the accounts must also verify that the annual report is consistent with the annual accounts for the same financial year.

2. The Member States may relieve the companies referred to in Article 11 from the obligation imposed by paragraph 1.
Article 12 shall apply.

3. Where the exemption provided for in paragraph 2 is granted the Member States shall introduce appropriate sanctions into their laws for cases in which the annual accounts or the annual reports of such companies are not drawn up in accordance with the requirements of this Directive.

Section 12

Final provisions

Article 52

1. A Contact Committee shall be set up under the auspices of the Commission. Its function shall be:
(a) to facilitate, without prejudice to the provisions of Articles 169 and 170 of the Treaty, harmonized application of this Directive through regular meetings dealing in particular with practical problems arising in connection with its application;
(b) to advise the Commission, if necessary, on additions or amendments to this Directive.

2. The Contact Committee shall be composed of representatives of the Member States and representatives of the Commission. The chairman shall be a representative of the Commission. The Commission shall provide the secretariat.

3. The Committee shall be convened by the chairman either on his own initiative or at the request of one of its members.

Article 53

1. For the purposes of this Directive, the European unit of account shall be that defined by Commission Decision No. 3289/75/ECSC of 18 December 1975.[1] The equivalent in national currency shall be calculated initially at the rate obtaining on the date of adoption of this Directive.

2. Every five years the Council, acting on a proposal from the Commission, shall examine and, if need be, revise the amounts expressed in European units of account in this Directive, in the light of economic and monetary trends in the Community.

Article 54

This Directive shall not affect laws in the Member States requiring that the annual accounts of companies not falling within their jurisdiction be filed in a register in which branches of such companies are listed.

Article 55

1. The Member States shall bring into force the laws, regulations and administrative provisions necessary for them to comply with this Directive within two years of its notification. They shall forthwith inform the Commission thereof.

---

1. OJ No. L 327, 19.12.1975, p. 4.

2. The Member States may stipulate that the provisions referred to in paragraph 1 shall not apply until 18 months after the end of the period provided for in that paragraph.

That period of 18 months may, however, be five years:
(a) in the case of unregistered companies in the United Kingdom and Ireland;
(b) for purposes of the application of Articles 9 and 10 and Articles 23 to 26 concerning the layouts for the balance sheet and the profit and loss account, where a Member State has brought other layouts for these documents into force not more than three years before the notification of this Directive;
(c) for purposes of the application of this Directive as regards the calculation and disclosure in balance sheets of depreciation relating to assets covered by the asset items mentioned in Article 9, C(II)(2) and (3), and Article 10, C(II)(2) and (3);
(d) for purposes of the application of Article 47(1) of this Directive except as regards companies already under an obligation of publication under Article 2(1)(f) of Directive 68/151/EEC. In this case the second subparagraph of Article 47(1) of this Directive shall apply to the annual accounts and to the opinion drawn up by the person responsible for auditing the accounts;
(e) for purposes of the application of Article 51(1) of this Directive.

Furthermore, this period of 18 months may be extended to eight years for companies the principal object of which is shipping and which are already in existence on the entry into force of the provisions referred to in paragraph 1.

3. The Member States shall ensure that they communicate to the Commission the texts of the main provisions of national law which they adopt in the field covered by this Directive.

Article 56

The obligation to show in the annual accounts the items prescribed by Articles 9, 10 and 23 to 26 which relate to affiliated undertakings, and the obligation to provide information concerning these undertakings in accordance with Article 13(2), 14 or 43(1)(7), shall enter into force at the same time as a Council Directive on consolidated accounts.

Article 57

1. Until the entry into force of a Council Directive on consolidated accounts, and without prejudice to the provisions of directives 68/151/EEC and 77/91/EEC, the Member States need not apply to the dependent companies of any group governed by their national laws the provisions of this Directive concerning the content, auditing and publication of the annual accounts of such dependent companies where the following conditions are fulfilled:

(a) the dominant company must be subject to the laws of a Member State;
(b) all shareholders or members of the dependent company must have declared their agreement to the exemption from such obligation; this declaration must be made in respect of every financial year;
(c) the dominant company must have declared that it guarantees the commitments entered into by the dependent company;
(d) the declarations referred to in (b) and (c) must be published by the dependent company in accordance with the first subparagraph of Article 47(1);
(e) the annual accounts of the dependent company must be consolidated in the group's annual accounts;
(f) the exemption concerning the preparation, auditing and publication of the annual accounts of the dependent company must be disclosed in the notes on the group's annual accounts.

2. Articles 47 and 51 shall apply to the group's annual accounts.

3. Articles 2 to 46 shall apply as far as possible to the group's annual accounts.

Article 58

1. Until the entry into force of a Council Directive on consolidated accounts, and without prejudice to the provisions of Directive 77/91/EEC, the Member States need not apply to the dominant companies of groups governed by their national laws the provisions of this Directive concerning the auditing and publication of the profit and loss accounts of such dominant companies where the following conditions are fulfilled:
(a) this exemption must be published by the dominant company in accordance with Article 47(1);
(b) the annual accounts of the dominant company must be consolidated in the group's annual accounts;
(c) the exemption concerning the auditing and publication of the profit and loss account of the dominant company must be mentioned in the notes on the group's annual accounts;
(d) the profit or loss of the dominant company, determined in accordance with the principles of this Directive, must be shown in the balance sheet of the dominant company.

2. Articles 47 and 51 shall apply to the group's annual accounts.

3. Articles 2 to 46 shall apply as far as possible to the group's annual accounts.

Article 59

Pending subsequent coordination, the Member States may permit the valuation of holdings in affiliated undertakings by the equity method provided the following conditions are fulfilled:

(a) the use of this method of valuation must be disclosed in the notes on the accounts of a company having such holdings;

(b) the amount of any differences existing when such holdings were acquired between their purchase price and the percentage of the capital which they represent, including the affiliated undertaking's reserves, profit and loss and profits and losses brought forward, must be shown separately in the balance sheet or in the notes on the accounts of a company having such holdings;

(c) the purchase price of these holdings shall be increased or reduced in the balance sheet of a company having such holdings by the profits or losses realized by the affiliated undertaking according to the percentage of capital held;

(d) the amounts specified in subparagraph (c) shall be shown each year in the profit and loss account of a company having such holdings as a separate item with an appropriate heading;

(e) when an affiliated undertaking distributes dividends to a company having such holdings, their book values shall be reduced accordingly;

(f) when the amounts shown in the profit and loss account in accordance with subparagraph (d) exceed the amounts of dividends already received or the payment of which can be claimed, the amount of the differences must be placed in a reserve which cannot be distributed to shareholders.

Article 60

Pending subsequent coordination, the Member States may prescribe that investments in which investment companies within the meaning of article 5(2) have invested their funds shall be valued on the basis of their market value.

In that case, the Member States may also waive the obligation on investment companies with valuable capital to show separately the value adjustments referred to in Article 36.

Article 61

Until the entry into force of a Council Directive on consolidated accounts, the Member States need not apply to the dominant companies of groups governed by their national laws the provisions of Article 43(1)(2) concerning the amount of capital and reserves and the profits and losses of the undertakings concerned if the national accounts of such undertakings are consolidated into the group's annual accounts or if the holdings in those undertakings are valued by the equity method.

Article 62

This Directive is addressed to the Member States.

Done at Brussels, 25 July 1978.

For the Council

The President

K. von DOHNANYI

Appendix IX

STATEMENTS OF ACCOUNTING PRACTICE AND EXPOSURE DRAFTS

SSAP 1	Accounting for associated companies	Revised April 1982
SSAP 2	Disclosure of accounting policies	Issued Nov. 1971
SSAP 3	Earnings per share	Revised Aug. 1984
SSAP 4	The accounting treatment of government grants	Issued April 1974
SSAP 5	Accounting for value added tax	Issued April 1974
SSAP 6	Extraordinary items and prior year adjustments	Revised Aug. 1986
SSAP 8	The treatment of taxation under the imputation system in the accounts of companies	Revised Dec. 1977
SSAP 9	Stocks and long-term contracts	Revised Sept. 1988
SSAP 10	Statements of source and application of funds	Revised June 1978
SSAP 12	Accounting for depreciation	Revised Jan. 1987
SSAP 13	Accounting for research and development	Revised Jan. 1989
SSAP 14	Group accounts	Issued Sept. 1978
SSAP 15	Accounting for deferred taxation	Revised May 1985
SSAP 17	Accounting for post balance sheet events	Issued Aug. 1980
SSAP 18	Accounting for contingencies	Issued Aug. 1980
SSAP 19	Accounting for investment properties	Issued Nov. 1981

SSAP 20	Foreign currency translation	Issued April 1983
SSAP 21	Accounting for leases and hire purchase contracts	Issued Aug. 1984
SSAP 22	Accounting for goodwill	Revised July 1989
SSAP 23	Accounting for acquisitions and mergers	Issued April 1985
SSAP 24	Accounting for pension costs	Issued May 1988
ED 42	Accounting for special purpose transactions	Issued March 1988
ED 43	The accounting treatment of government grants	Issued June 1988
ED 45	Segmental reporting	Issued Nov. 1988
ED 46	Disclosure of related party transactions	Issued April 1989
ED 47	Accounting for goodwill	Issued Feb. 1990
ED 47	Accounting for acquisitions and mergers	Issued Feb. 1990

Tolley's Companies Legislation

Extracts of accounting provisions

Those sections of, and Schedules to, the Act that are reproduced in full are indicated on the Arrangement of Sections by an asterisk.

The first edition of Tolley's Companies Legislation incorporates all relevant companies legislation (excluding insolvency) up to and including the Companies Act 1989, together with statutory instruments. It not only includes current provisions but also superseded provisions to the extent that these have applied at some time since the Companies Act 1985 came into force. Amending or repealing legislation is both given effect to in the original legislation and referred to in the text of the Act or statutory instrument where it occurs. This includes the Commencement Orders up to and including No 5 (SI 1990 No 713) issued on 23 March 1990.

Free of charge supplements will be issued to subscribers with details of commencement dates of the Companies Act 1989 provisions if these are not known at the time of publication.

TOLLEY PUBLISHING CO. LTD.

Abbreviations

BNA	=	Business Names Act 1985
CA 1989	=	Companies Act 1989
CC(CP)A	=	Companies Consolidation (Consequential Provisions) Act 1985
CDDA	=	Company Directors Disqualification Act 1986
CS(ID)A	=	Company Securities (Insider Dealing) Act 1985
FSA	=	Financial Services Act 1986
FTA	=	Fair Trading Act 1973
Pt	=	Part
Reg	=	Regulation
s	=	Section
Sch	=	Schedule
4 Sch 10	=	4th Schedule, paragraph 10
Sec	=	Section
SI	=	Statutory Instrument

Companies Act 1985

1985 Chapter 6 — Royal Assent 11 March 1985 incorporating Companies Act 1989, Chapter 40 — Royal Assent 16 November 1989

ARRANGEMENT OF SECTIONS

Part I Formation and Registration of Companies; Juridical Status and Membership

CHAPTER I COMPANY FORMATION

Part III Capital Issues

CHAPTER I ISSUES BY COMPANIES REGISTERED, OR TO BE REGISTERED, IN GREAT BRITAIN

The prospectus

Registration of prospectus

Liabilities and offences in connection with prospectus

Supplementary

CHAPTER II ISSUES BY COMPANIES INCORPORATED, OR TO BE INCORPORATED, OUTSIDE GREAT BRITAIN

Part IV Allotment of Shares and Debentures

General provisions as to allotment

Part V Share Capital, its Increase, Maintenance and Reduction

CHAPTER I GENERAL PROVISIONS ABOUT SHARE CAPITAL

117* Public company share capital requirements.
118* The authorised minimum.
119 Provision for different amounts to be paid on shares.
120 Reserve liability of limited company.
121 Alteration of share capital (limited companies).
122 Notice to registrar of alteration.
123 Notice to registrar of increased share capital.
124 Reserve capital of unlimited company.

CHAPTER II CLASS RIGHTS

125 Variation of class rights.
126 Saving for court's powers under other provisions.
127 Shareholders' right to object to variation.
128 Registration of particulars of special rights.
129 Registration of newly created class rights.

CHAPTER III SHARE PREMIUMS

130* Application of share premiums.
131* Merger relief.
132* Relief in respect of group reconstructions.
133* Provisions supplementing ss 131, 132.
134* Provision for extending or restricting relief from s 130.

CHAPTER IV REDUCTION OF SHARE CAPITAL

135* Special resolution for reduction of share capital.
136 Application to court for order of confirmation.
137 Court order confirming reduction.
138 Registration of order and minute of reduction.
139 Public company reducing capital below authorised minimum.
140 Liability of members on reduced shares.
141 Penalty for concealing name of creditor, etc.

CHAPTER V MAINTENANCE OF CAPITAL

142* Duty of directors on serious loss of capital.
143* General rule against company acquiring own shares.
144* Acquisition of shares by company's nominee.
145* Exceptions from s 144.
146* Treatment of shares held by or for public company.
147* Matters arising out of compliance with s 146(2).
148* Further provisions supplementing ss 146, 147.
149* Sanctions for non-compliance.
150* Charges of public companies on own shares.

CHAPTER VI FINANCIAL ASSISTANCE BY A COMPANY FOR ACQUISITION OF ITS OWN SHARES

Provisions applying to both public and private companies

151* Financial assistance generally prohibited.
152* Definitions for this Chapter.
153* Transactions not prohibited by s 151.
154* Special restriction for public companies.

Private companies

155* Relaxation of s 151 for private companies.
156* Statutory declaration under s 155.
157* Special resolution under s 155.
158* Time for giving financial assistance under s 155.

CHAPTER VII REDEEMABLE SHARES; PURCHASE BY A COMPANY OF ITS OWN SHARES

Redemption and purchase generally

159* Power to issue redeemable shares.
159A* Terms and manner of redemption.
160* Financing, etc., of redemption.
161 Stamp duty on redemption of shares [repealed].
162* Power of company to purchase own shares.
163 Definitions of "off-market" and "market" purchase.
164 Authority for off-market purchase.
165 Authority for contingent purchase contract.
166 Authority for market purchase.
167 Assignment or release of company's right to purchase own shares.
168 Payments apart from purchase price to be made out of distributable profits.
169 Disclosure by company of purchase of own shares.
170* The capital redemption reserve.

Redemption or purchase of own shares out of capital (private companies only)

171 Power of private companies to redeem or purchase own shares out of capital.
172 Availability of profits for purposes of s 171.
173 Conditions for payment out of capital.
174 Procedure for special resolution under s 173.
175 Publicity for proposed payment out of capital.
176 Objections by company's members or creditors.
177 Powers of court on application under s 176.

Supplementary

178 Effect of company's failure to redeem or purchase.
179 Power for Secretary of State to modify this Chapter.
180 Transitional cases arising under this Chapter; and savings.
181 Definitions for Chapter VII.

CHAPTER VIII MISCELLANEOUS PROVISIONS ABOUT SHARES AND DEBENTURES

Share and debenture certificates, transfers and warrants

182 Nature, transfer and numbering of shares.
183 Transfer and registration.
184 Certification of transfers.
185 Duty of company as to issue of certificates.
186 Certificate to be evidence of title.
187 Evidence of grant of probate or confirmation as executor.
188 Issue and effect of share warrant to bearer.
189 Offences in connection with share warrants (Scotland).

Debentures

190 Register of debenture holders.
191 Right to inspect register.
192 Liability of trustees of debentures.
193 Perpetual debentures.
194 Power to re-issue redeemed debentures.
195 Contract to subscribe for debentures.
196 Payment of debts out of assets subject to floating charge (England and Wales).
197 Debentures to bearer (Scotland).

Part VI Disclosure of Interests in Shares

Individual and group acquisitions

198 Obligation of disclosure: the cases in which it may arise and "the relevant time".
199 Interests to be disclosed.
200 "Percentage level" in relation to notifiable interests.
201 The notifiable percentage [repealed].
202 Particulars to be contained in notification.
203 Notification of family and corporate interests.
204 Agreement to acquire interests in a particular company.
205 Obligation of disclosure arising under s 204.
206 Obligation of persons acting together to keep each other informed.
207 Interests in shares by attribution.
208 Interests in shares which are to be notified.
209 Interests to be disregarded.
210 Other provisions about notification under this Part.
210A Power to make further provision by regulations.

Registration and investigation of share acquisitions and disposals

211 Register of interests in shares.
212 Company investigations.
213 Registration of interests disclosed under s 212.
214 Company investigation on requisition by members.
215 Company report to members.
216 Penalty for failure to provide information.
217 Removal of entries from register.

240* Requirements in connection with publication of accounts.

Laying and delivering of accounts and reports

241* Accounts and reports to be laid before company in general meeting.
242* Accounts and reports to be delivered to the registrar.
242A* Civil penalty for failure to deliver accounts.
243* Accounts of subsidiary undertakings to be appended in certain cases.
244* Period allowed for laying and delivering accounts and reports.

Revision of defective accounts and reports

245* Voluntary revision of annual accounts or directors' report.
245A* Secretary of State's notice in respect of annual accounts.
245B* Application to court in respect of defective accounts.
245C* Other persons authorised to apply to court.

CHAPTER II EXEMPTIONS, EXCEPTIONS AND SPECIAL PROVISIONS

Small and medium-sized companies and groups

246* Exemptions for small and medium-sized companies.
247* Qualification of company as small or medium-sized.
248* Exemption for small and medium-sized groups.
249* Qualification of group as small or medium-sized.

Dormant companies

250* Resolution not to appoint auditors.

Listed public companies

251* Provision of summary financial statement to shareholders.

Private companies

252* Election to dispense with laying of accounts and reports before general meeting.
253* Right of shareholder to require laying of accounts.

Unlimited companies

254* Exemption from requirement to deliver accounts and reports.

Banking and insurance companies and groups

255* Special provisions for banking and insurance companies.
255A* Special provisions for banking and insurance groups.
255B* Modification of disclosure requirements in relation to banking company or group.
255C* Directors' report where accounts prepared in accordance with special provisions.
255D* Power to apply provisions to banking partnerships.

CHAPTER III SUPPLEMENTARY PROVISIONS

Accounting standards

256* Accounting standards.

Power to alter accounting requirements

257* Power of Secretary of State to alter accounting requirements.

Parent and subsidiary undertakings

258* Parent and subsidiary undertakings.

Other interpretation provisions

259* Meaning of "undertaking" and related expressions.
260* Participating interests.
261* Notes to the accounts.
262* Minor definitions.
262A* Index of defined expressions.

Part VIII Distribution of Profits and Assets

Limits of company's power of distribution

263* Certain distributions prohibited.
264* Restriction on distribution of assets.
265* Other distributions by investment companies.
266* Meaning of "investment company".
267* Extension of ss 265, 266 to other companies.
268* Realised profits of insurance company with long term business.
269* Treatment of development costs.

Relevant accounts

270* Distribution to be justified by reference to company's accounts.
271* Requirements for last annual accounts.
272* Requirements for interim accounts.
273* Requirements for initial accounts.
274* Method of applying s 270 to successive distributions.
275* Treatment of assets in the relevant accounts.
276* Distributions in kind.

Supplementary

277* Consequences of unlawful distribution.
278* Saving for provision in articles operative before Act of 1980.
279* Distributions by banking or insurance companies.
280* Definitions for Part VIII.
281* Saving for other restraints on distribution.

Part IX A Company's Management; Directors and Secretaries; their Qualifications, Duties and Responsibilities

Officers and registered office

282 Directors.
283 Secretary.
284 Acts done by person in dual capacity.
285 Validity of acts of directors.
286 Qualifications of company secretaries.
287 Registered office.
288 Register of directors and secretaries.
289 Particulars of directors to be registered under s 288.
290 Particulars of secretaries to be registered under s 288.

Provisions governing appointment of directors

291 Share qualification of directors.
292 Appointment of directors to be voted on individually.
293 Age limit for directors.
294 Duty of director to disclose his age.

Disqualification

295-302 [Repealed].

Removal of directors

303 Resolution to remove director.
304 Director's right to protest removal.

Other provisions about directors and officers

305 Directors' names on company correspondence, etc.
306 Limited company may have directors with unlimited liability.
307 Special resolution making liability of directors unlimited.
308 Assignment of office by directors.
309 Directors to have regard to interests of employees.
310* Provisions exempting officers and auditors from liability.

Part X Enforcement of Fair Dealing by Directors

Restrictions on directors taking financial advantage

311* Prohibition on tax-free payments to directors.
312* Payment to director for loss of office, etc.
313* Company approval for property transfer.
314* Director's duty of disclosure on takeover, etc.
315* Consequences of non-compliance with s 314.
316* Provisions supplementing ss 312-315.
317* Directors to disclose interest in contracts.
318* Directors' service contracts to be open to inspection.
319* Director's contract of employment for more than 5 years.
320* Substantial property transactions involving directors, etc.
321* Exceptions from s 320.

357 Non-compliance with ss 353, 354, 356; agent's default.
358 Power to close register.
359 Power of court to rectify register.
360 Trusts not to be entered on register in England and Wales.
361 Register to be evidence.
362 Overseas branch registers.

CHAPTER III ANNUAL RETURN

363 Duty to deliver annual returns.
364 Contents of annual return: general.
364A Contents of annual return: particulars of share capital and shareholders.
365 Supplementary provisions: regulations and interpretation.

CHAPTER IV MEETINGS AND RESOLUTIONS

Meetings

366 Annual general meeting.
366A Election by private company to dispense with annual general meetings.
367 Secretary of State's power to call meeting in default.
368 Extraordinary general meeting on members' requisition.
369 Length of notice for calling meetings.
370 General provisions as to meetings and votes.
371 Power of court to order meeting.
372 Proxies.
373 Right to demand a poll.
374 Voting on a poll.
375 Representation of corporations at meetings.

Resolutions

376 Circulation of members' resolutions.
377 In certain cases, compliance with s 376 not required.
378* Extraordinary and special resolutions.
379* Resolution requiring special notice.
379A* Elective resolution of private company.
380 Registration, etc. of resolutions and agreements.
381 Resolution passed at adjourned meeting.

Written resolutions of private companies

381A Written resolutions of private companies.
381B Rights of auditors in relation to written resolution.
381C Written resolutions: supplementary provisions.

Records of proceedings

382 Minutes of meetings.
382A Recording of written resolutions.
383 Inspection of minute books.

CHAPTER V AUDITORS

Appointment of auditors

384* Duty to appoint auditors.
385* Appointment at general meeting at which accounts laid.
385A* Appointment by private company which is not obliged to lay accounts.
386* Election by private company to dispense with annual appointment.
387* Appointment by Secretary of State in default of appointment by company.
388* Filling of casual vacancy.
388A* Dormant company exempt from obligation to appoint auditors.
389 Qualification for appointment as auditors [repealed].

Rights of auditors

389A* Rights to information.
390* Right to attend company meetings, etc.

Remuneration of auditors

390A* Remuneration of auditors.
390B* Remuneration of auditors or their associates for non-audit work.

Removal, resignation, etc. of auditors

391* Removal of auditors.
391A* Rights of auditors who are removed or not re-appointed.
392* Resignation of auditors.
392A* Rights of resigning auditors.
393* Termination of appointment of auditors not appointed annually.
394* Statement by person ceasing to hold office as auditor.
394A* Offences of failing to comply with s 394.

Part XII Registration of Charges

Registration in the companies charges register

395 Introductory provisions.
396 Charges requiring registration.
397 The companies charges register.
398 Company's duty to deliver particulars of charge for registration.
399 Effect of failure to deliver particulars for registration.
400 Late delivery of particulars.
401 Delivery of further particulars.
402 Effect of omissions and errors in registered particulars.
403 Memorandum of charge ceasing to affect company's property.
404 Exclusion of voidness as against unregistered charges.
405 Restrictions on voidness by virtue of this Part.
406 Effect of exercise of power of sale.
407 Effect of voidness on obligation secured.

Additional information to be registered

408 Particulars of taking up of issue of debentures.
409 Notice of appointment of receiver or manager, etc.
410 Notice of crystallisation of floating charge, etc.

Copies of instruments and register to be kept by company

411	Duty to keep copies of instruments and register.
412	Inspection of copies and register.
413	Power to make further provision by regulations.
414	Date of creation of charge.
415	Prescribed particulars and related expressions.
416	Notice of matters disclosed on register.
417	Power of court to dispense with signature.
418	Regulations.
419	Minor definitions.
420	Index of defined expressions.
421-424	[Repealed].

Part XIII Arrangements and Reconstructions

425	Power of company to compromise with creditors and members.
426	Information as to compromise to be circulated.
427	Provisions for facilitating company reconstruction or amalgamation.
427A	Application of ss 425-427 to mergers and divisions of public companies.

Part XIIIA Takeover Offers

428	"Takeover offers".
429	Rights of offeror to buy out minority shareholders.
430	Effect of notice under s 429.
430A	Right of minority shareholder to be bought out by offeror.
430B	Effect of requirement under s 430A.
430C	Applications to the court.
430D	Joint offers.
430E	Associates.
430F	Convertible securities.

Part XIV Investigation of Companies and their Affairs; Requisition of Documents

Appointment and functions of inspectors

431	Investigation of a company on its own application or that of its members.
432	Other company investigations.
433	Inspectors' powers during investigation.
434	Production of documents and evidence to inspectors.
435	Power of inspector to call for directors' bank accounts [repealed].
436	Obstruction of inspectors treated as contempt of court.
437	Inspectors' reports.
438	Power to bring civil proceedings on company's behalf.
439	Expenses of investigating a company's affairs.
440	Power of Secretary of State to present winding-up petition [repealed].
441	Inspectors' report to be evidence.

Other powers of investigation available to Secretary of State

442	Power to investigate company ownership.
443	Provisions applicable on investigation under s 442.
444	Power to obtain information as to those interested in shares, etc.

Part XIX Receivers and Managers (England and Wales)

488-500 [Repealed].

Part XX Winding Up of Companies Registered under this Act or the former Companies Acts

CHAPTERS I-V

501-650 [Repealed].

CHAPTER VI MATTERS ARISING SUBSEQUENT TO WINDING UP

651 Power of court to declare dissolution of company void.
652 Registrar may strike defunct company off register.
653 Objection to striking off by person aggrieved.
654 Property of dissolved company to be bona vacantia.
655 Effect on s 654 of company's revival after dissolution.
656 Crown disclaimer of property vesting as bona vacantia.
657 Effect of Crown disclaimer under s 656.
658 Liability for rentcharge on company's land after dissolution.

CHAPTER VII

659-664 [Repealed].

Part XXI Winding Up of Unregistered Companies

665-674 [Repealed].

Part XXII Bodies Corporate subject, or becoming subject, to this Act (otherwise than by original formation under Part I)

CHAPTER I COMPANIES FORMED OR REGISTERED UNDER FORMER COMPANIES ACTS

675 Companies formed and registered under former Companies Acts.
676 Companies registered but not formed under former Companies Acts.
677 Companies re-registered with altered status under former Companies Acts.
678 Companies registered under Joint Stock Companies Acts.
679 Northern Ireland and Irish companies.

CHAPTER II COMPANIES NOT FORMED UNDER COMPANIES LEGISLATION, BUT AUTHORISED TO REGISTER

680* Companies capable of being registered under this Chapter.
681 Procedural requirements for registration.
682 Change of name on registration.
683 Definition of "joint stock company".
684 Requirements for registration by joint stock companies.
685 Registration of joint stock company as public company.
686 Other requirements for registration.
687 Name of company registering.
688 Certificate of registration under this Chapter.
689 Effect of registration.

Part XXV Miscellaneous and Supplementary Provisions

Part XXVI Interpretation

Part XXVII Final Provisions

SCHEDULES

PART I FORMATION AND REGISTRATION OF COMPANIES; JURIDICAL STATUS AND MEMBERSHIP

CHAPTER I COMPANY FORMATION

Memorandum of association

1 Mode of forming incorporated company

(1) Any two or more persons associated for a lawful purpose may, by subscribing their names to a memorandum of association and otherwise complying with the requirements of this Act in respect of registration, form an incorporated company, with or without limited liability.

(2) A company so formed may be either—

(a) a company having the liability of its members limited by the memorandum to the amount, if any, unpaid on the shares respectively held by them ("a company limited by shares");
(b) a company having the liability of its members limited by the memorandum to such amount as the members may respectively thereby undertake to contribute to the assets of the company in the event of its being wound up ("a company limited by guarantee"); or
(c) a company not having any limit on the liability of its members ("an unlimited company").

(3) A "public company" is a company limited by shares or limited by guarantee and having a share capital, being a company—

(a) the memorandum of which states that it is to be a public company, and
(b) in relation to which the provisions of this Act or the former Companies Acts as to the registration or re-registration of a company as a public company have been complied with on or after 22nd December 1980;

and a "private company" is a company that is not a public company.

(4) With effect from 22nd December 1980, a company cannot be formed as, or become, a company limited by guarantee with a share capital.

23 Membership of holding company

[(1) Except as mentioned in this section, a body corporate cannot be a member of a company which is its holding company and any allotment or transfer of shares in a company to its subsidiary is void.

(2) The prohibition does not apply where the subsidiary is concerned only as personal representative or trustee unless, in the latter case, the holding company or a subsidiary of it is beneficially interested under the trust.

For the purpose of ascertaining whether the holding company or a subsidiary is so interested, there shall be disregarded—

(a) any interest held only by way of security for the purposes of a transaction entered into by the holding company or subsidiary in the ordinary course of a business which includes the lending of money;
(b) any such interest as is mentioned in Part I of Schedule 2.

(3) The prohibition does not apply where the subsidiary is concerned only as a market maker.

For this purpose a person is a market maker if—

(a) he holds himself out at all normal times in compliance with the rules of a recognised investment exchange other than an overseas investment exchange (within the meaning of the Financial Services Act 1986) as willing to buy and sell securities at prices specified by him, and
(b) he is recognised as so doing by that investment exchange.

(4) Where a body corporate became a holder of shares in a company—

(a) before 1st July 1948, or
(b) on or after that date and before the commencement of section 129 of the Companies Act 1989, in circumstances in which this section as it then had effect did not apply,

but at any time after the commencement of that section falls within the prohibition in subsection (1) above in respect of those shares, it may continue to be a member of that company; but for so long as that prohibition would apply, apart from this subsection, it has no right to vote in respect of those shares at meetings of the company or of any class of its members.

(5) Where a body corporate becomes a holder of shares in a company after the commencement of that section in circumstances in which the prohibition in subsection (1) does not apply, but subsequently falls within that prohibition in respect of those shares, it may continue to be a member of that company; but for so long as that prohibition would apply, apart from this subsection, it has no right to vote in respect of those shares at meetings of the company or of any class of its members.

(6) Where a body corporate is permitted to continue as a member of a company by virtue of subsection (4) or (5), an allotment to it of fully paid shares in the company may be validly made by way of capitalisation of reserves of the company; but for so long as the prohibition in subsection (1) would apply, apart from subsection (4) or (5), it has no right to vote in respect of those shares at meetings of the company or of any class of its members.

(7) The provisions of this section apply to a nominee acting on behalf of a subsidiary as to the subsidiary itself.

(8) In relation to a company other than a company limited by shares, the references in this section to shares shall be construed as references to the interest of its members as such, whatever the form of that interest.][1]

---

1 Substituted by CA 1989, s 129 with effect from a date to be appointed.

CHAPTER III A COMPANY'S CAPACITY, FORMALITIES OF CARRYING ON BUSINESS

[35A Power of directors to bind the company

(1) In favour of a person dealing with a company in good faith, the power of the board of directors to bind the company, or authorise others to do so, shall be deemed to be free of any limitation under the company's constitution.

(2) For this purpose—

(a) a person "deals with" a company if he is a party to any transaction or other act to which the company is a party;

(b) a person shall not be regarded as acting in bad faith by reason only of his knowing that an act is beyond the powers of the directors under the company's constitution; and

(c) a person shall be presumed to have acted in good faith unless the contrary is proved.

(3) The references above to limitations on the directors' powers under the company's constitution include limitations deriving—

(a) from a resolution of the company in general meeting or a meeting of any class of shareholders, or

(b) from any agreement between the members of the company or of any class of shareholders.

(4) Subsection (a) does not affect any right of a member of the company to bring proceedings to restrain the doing of an act which is beyond the powers of the directors; but no such proceedings shall lie in respect of an act to be done in fulfilment of a legal obligation arising from a previous act of the company.

(5) Nor does that subsection affect any liability incurred by the directors, or any other person, by reason of the directors' exceeding their powers.

(6) The operation of this section is restricted by section 30B(1) of the Charities Act 1960 and section 112(3) of the Companies Act 1989 in relation to companies which are charities; and section 322A below (invalidity of certain transactions to which directors or their associates are parties) has effect notwithstanding this section.][1]

---

[1] Inserted by CA 1989, s 108 with effect from a date to be appointed.

PART II RE-REGISTRATION AS A MEANS OF ALTERING A COMPANY'S STATUS

Private company becoming public

43 Re-registration of private company as public

(1) Subject to this and the following five sections, a private company (other than a company not having a share capital) may be re-registered as a public company if—

(a) a special resolution that it should be so re-registered is passed; and
(b) an application for re-registration is delivered to the registrar of companies, together with the necessary documents.

A company cannot be re-registered under this section if it has previously been re-registered as unlimited.

(2) The special resolution must—

(a) alter the company's memorandum so that it states that the company is to be a public company; and
(b) make such other alterations in the memorandum as are necessary to bring it (in substance and in form) into conformity with the requirements of this Act with respect to the memorandum of a public company (the alterations to include compliance with section 25(1) as regards the company's name); and
(c) make such alterations in the company's articles as are requisite in the circumstances.

(3) The application must be in the prescribed form and be signed by a director or secretary of the company; and the documents to be delivered with it are the following—

(a) a printed copy of the memorandum and articles as altered in pursuance of the resolution;
(b) a copy of a written statement by the company's auditors that in their opinion the relevant balance sheet shows that at the balance sheet date the amount of the company's net assets (within the meaning given to that expression by section 264(2)) was not less than the aggregate of its called-up share capital and undistributable reserves;
(c) a copy of the relevant balance sheet, together with a copy of an unqualified report (defined in section 46) by the company's auditors in relation to that balance sheet;
(d) if section 44 applies, a copy of the valuation report under subsection (2)(b) of that section; and
(e) a statutory declaration in the prescribed form by a director or secretary of the company—
   (i) that the special resolution required by this section has been passed and that the conditions of the following two sections (so far as applicable) have been satisfied, and
   (ii) that, between the balance sheet date and the application for re-registration, there has been no change in the company's financial position that has resulted in the amount of its net assets becoming less than the aggregate of its called-up share capital and undistributable reserves.

(4) "Relevant balance sheet" means a balance sheet prepared as at a date not more than 7 months before the company's application under this section.

(5) A resolution that a company be re-registered as a public company may change the company name by deleting the word "company" or the words "and company", or its or their equivalent in Welsh ("cwmni", "a'r cwmni"), including any abbreviation of them.

CHAPTER II ISSUES BY COMPANIES INCORPORATED, OR TO BE INCORPORATED, OUTSIDE GREAT BRITAIN

Amount to be paid for shares; the means of payment

101 Shares to be allotted as at least one-quarter paid-up

(1) A public company shall not allot a share except as paid up at least as to one-quarter of its nominal value and the whole of any premium on it.

(2) Subsection (1) does not apply to shares allotted in pursuance of an employees' share scheme.

(3) If a company allots a share in contravention of subsection (1), the share is to be treated as if one-quarter of its nominal value, together with the whole of any premium on it, had been received.

(4) But the allottee is liable to pay the company the minimum amount which should have been received in respect of the share under subsection (1) (less the value of any consideration actually applied in payment up, to any extent, of the share and any premium on it), with interest at the appropriate rate.

(5) Subsections (3) and (4) do not apply to the allotment of bonus shares, unless the allottee knew or ought to have known the shares were allotted in contravention of subsection (1).

PART V SHARE CAPITAL, ITS INCREASE, MAINTENANCE AND REDUCTION

CHAPTER I GENERAL PROVISIONS ABOUT SHARE CAPITAL

117 Public company share capital requirements

(1) A company registered as a public company on its original incorporation shall not do business or exercise any borrowing powers unless the registrar of companies has issued it with a certificate under this section or the company is re-registered as a private company.

(2) The registrar shall issue a company with such a certificate if, on an application made to him by the company in the prescribed form, he is satisfied that the nominal value of the company's allotted share capital is not less than the authorised minimum, and there is delivered to him a statutory declaration complying with the following subsection.

(3) The statutory declaration must be in the prescribed form and be signed by a director or secretary of the company; and it must—

(a) state that the nominal value of the company's allotted share capital is not less than the authorised minimum;
(b) specify the amount paid up, at the time of the application, on the allotted share capital of the company;
(c) specify the amount, or estimated amount, of the company's preliminary expenses and the persons by whom any of those expenses have been paid or are payable; and
(d) specify any amount or benefit paid or given, or intended to be paid or given, to any promoter of the company, and the consideration for the payment or benefit.

(4) For the purposes of subsection (2), a share allotted in pursuance of an employees' share scheme may not be taken into account in determining the nominal value of the company's allotted share capital unless it is paid up at least as to one-quarter of the nominal value of the share and the whole of any premium on the share.

(5) The registrar may accept a statutory declaration delivered to him under this section as sufficient evidence of the matters stated in it.

(6) A certificate under this section in respect of a company is conclusive evidence that the company is entitled to do business and exercise any borrowing powers.

(7) If a company does business or exercises borrowing powers in contravention of this section, the company and any officer of it who is in default is liable to a fine.

(8) Nothing in this section affects the validity of any transaction entered into by a company; but, if a company enters into a transaction in contravention of this section and fails to comply with its obligations in that connection within 21 days from being called upon to do so, the directors of the company are jointly and severally liable to indemnify the other party to the transaction in respect of any loss or damage suffered by him by reason of the company's failure to comply with those obligations.

118 The authorised minimum

(1) In this Act, "the authorised minimum" means £50,000, or such other sum as the Secretary of State may by order made by statutory instrument specify instead.

(2) An order under this section which increases the authorised minimum may—

(a) require any public company having an allotted share capital of which the nominal value is less than the amount specified in the order as the authorised minimum to increase that value to not less than that amount or make application to be re-registered as a private company;

(b) make, in connection with any such requirement, provision for any of the matters for which provision is made by this Act relating to a company's registration, re-registration or change of name, to payment for any share comprised in a company's capital and to offers of shares in or debentures of a company to the public, including provision as to the consequences (whether in criminal law or otherwise) of a failure to comply with any requirement of the order; and

(c) contain such supplemental and transitional provisions as the Secretary of State thinks appropriate, make different provision for different cases and, in particular, provide for any provision of the order to come into operation on different days for different purposes.

(3) An order shall not be made under this section unless a draft of it has been laid before Parliament and approved by resolution of each House.

CHAPTER III SHARE PREMIUMS

130 Application of share premiums

(1) If a company issues shares at a premium, whether for cash or otherwise, a sum equal to the aggregate amount or value of the premiums on those shares shall be transferred to an account called "the share premium account".

(2) The share premium account may be applied by the company in paying up unissued shares to be allotted to members as fully paid bonus shares, or in writing off—

(a) the company's preliminary expenses; or
(b) the expenses of, or the commission paid or discount allowed on, any issue of shares or debentures of the company,

or in providing for the premium payable on redemption of debentures of the company.

(3) Subject to this, the provisions of this Act relating to the reduction of a company's share capital apply as if the share premium account were part of its paid up share capital.

(4) Sections 131 and 132 below give relief from the requirements of this section, and in those sections references to the issuing company are to the company issuing shares as above mentioned.

Cross references. See Sec 131(2); Sec 132(2); Sec 134; CC(CP)A 1985, s 12 (share premiums—retrospective relief).

---

131 Merger relief

(1) With the exception made by section 132([8][2]) (group reconstruction) this section applies where the issuing company has secured at least a 90 per cent. equity holding in another company in pursuance of an arrangement providing for the allotment of equity shares in the issuing company on terms that the consideration for the shares allotted is to be provided—

(a) by the issue or transfer to the issuing company of equity shares in the other company, or
(b) by the cancellation of any such shares not held by the issuing company.

(2) If the equity shares in the issuing company allotted in pursuance of the arrangement in consideration for the acquisition or cancellation of equity shares in the other company are issued at a premium, section 130 does not apply to the premiums on those shares.

(3) Where the arrangement also provides for the allotment of any shares in the issuing company on terms that the consideration for those shares is to be provided by the issue or transfer to the issuing company of non-equity shares in the other company or by the cancellation of any such shares in that company not held by the issuing company, relief under subsection (2) extends to any shares in the issuing company allotted on those terms in pursuance of the arrangement.

(4) Subject to the next subsection, the issuing company is to be regarded for purposes of this section as having secured at least a 90 per cent. equity holding in another company in pursuance of such an arrangement as is mentioned in subsection (1) if in consequence of an acquisition or cancellation of equity shares in that company (in pursuance of that arrangement) it holds equity shares in that company (whether all or any of those shares were acquired in pursuance of that arrangement, or not) of an aggregate nominal value equal to 90 per cent. or more of the nominal value of that company's equity share capital.

(5) Where the equity share capital of the other company is divided into different classes of shares, this section does not apply unless the requirements of subsection (1) are satisfied in relation to each of those classes of shares taken separately.

(6) Shares held by a company which is the issuing company's holding company or subsidiary, or a subsidiary of the issuing company's holding company, or by its or their nominees, are to be regarded for purposes of this section as held by the issuing company.

(7) In relation to a company and its shares and capital, the following definitions apply for purposes of this section—

(a) "equity shares" means shares comprised in the company's equity share capital; and

(b) "non-equity shares" means shares (of any class) not so comprised;

and "arrangement" means any agreement, scheme or arrangement (including an arrangement sanctioned under section 425 (company compromise with members and creditors) or section [110 of the Insolvency Act][1] (liquidator accepting shares etc. as consideration for sale of company property)).

(8) The relief allowed by this section does not apply if the issue of shares took place before 4th February 1981.

---

[1] Substituted by IA 1986, s 439(1), 13 Sch Part I with effect from 29 December 1986 (see IA 1986, s 443 and SI 1986 No 1924).
Previously '582'.

[2] Substituted by CA 1989, 19 Sch 1 with effect from 1 March 1990 (SI 1990 No 142) but deemed always to have had effect.
Previously '4'.

Cross references. See Sec 132(8); Sec 133 (supplementary provisions).

---

132 Relief in respect of group reconstructions

(1) This section applies where the issuing company—

(a) is a wholly-owned subsidiary of another company ("the holding company"), and

(b) allots shares to the holding company or to another wholly-owned subsidiary of the holding company in consideration for the transfer to the issuing company of assets other than cash, being assets of any company ("the transferor company") which is a member of the group of companies which comprises the holding company and all its wholly-owned subsidiaries.

(2) Where the shares in the issuing company allotted in consideration for the transfer are issued at a premium, the issuing company is not required by section 130 to transfer any amount in excess of the minimum premium value to the share premium account.

(3) In subsection (2), "the minimum premium value" means the amount (if any) by which the base value of the consideration for the shares allotted exceeds the aggregate nominal value of those shares.

(4) For the purposes of subsection (3), the base value of the consideration for the shares allotted is the amount by which the base value of the assets transferred exceeds the base value of any liabilities of the transferor company assumed by the issuing company as part of the consideration for the assets transferred.

(5) For the purposes of subsection (4)—

(a) the base value of the assets transferred is to be taken as—
  (i) the cost of those assets to the transferor company, or
  (ii) the amount at which those assets are stated in the transferor company's accounting records immediately before the transfer,

whichever is the less; and

(b) the base value of the liabilities assumed is to be taken as the amount at which they are stated in the transferor company's accounting records immediately before the transfer.

(6) The relief allowed by this section does not apply (subject to the next subsection) if the issue of shares took place before the date of the coming into force of the Companies (Share Premium Account) Regulations 1984 (which were made on 21st December 1984).

(7) To the extent that the relief allowed by this section would have been allowed by section 38 of the Companies Act 1981 as originally enacted (the text of which section is set out in Schedule 25 to this Act), the relief applies where the issue of shares took place before the date of the coming into force of those Regulations, but not if the issue took place before 4th February 1981.

(8) Section 131 does not apply in a case falling within this section.

Cross references. See Sec 133 (supplementary provisions).

---

133 Provisions supplementing ss 131, 132

(1) An amount corresponding to one representing the premiums or part of the premiums on shares issued by a company which by virtue of sections 131 or 132 of this Act, or section 12 of the Consequential Provisions Act, is not included in the company's share premium account may also be disregarded in determining the amount at which any shares or other consideration provided for the shares issued is to be included in the company's balance sheet.

(2) References in this Chapter (however expressed) to—

(a) the acquisition by a company of shares in another company; and
(b) the issue or allotment of shares to, or the transfer of shares to or by, a company,

include (respectively) the acquisition of any of those shares by, and the issue or allotment or (as the case may be) the transfer of any of those shares to or by, nominees of that company; and the reference in section 132 to the company transferring the shares is to be construed accordingly.

(3) References in this Chapter to the transfer of shares in a company include the transfer of a right to be included in the company's register of members in respect of those shares.

(4) In sections 131 to 133 "company", except in references to the issuing company, includes any body corporate.

134 Provision for extending or restricting relief from s 130

(1) The Secretary of State may by regulations in a statutory instrument make such provision as appears to him to be appropriate—

(a) for relieving companies from the requirements of section 130 in relation to premiums other than cash premiums, or

(b) for restricting or otherwise modifying any relief from those requirements provided by this Chapter.

(2) Regulations under this section may make different provision for different cases or classes of case and may contain such incidental and supplementary provisions as the Secretary of State thinks fit.

(3) No such regulations shall be made unless a draft of the instrument containing them has been laid before Parliament and approved by a resolution of each House.

CHAPTER IV REDUCTION OF SHARE CAPITAL

135 Special resolution for reduction of share capital

(1) Subject to confirmation by the court, a company limited by shares or a company limited by guarantee and having a share capital may, if so authorised by its articles, by special resolution reduce its share capital in any way.

(2) In particular, and without prejudice to subsection (1), the company may—

(a) extinguish or reduce the liability on any of its shares in respect of share capital not paid up; or

(b) either with or without extinguishing or reducing liability on any of its shares, cancel any paid-up share capital which is lost or unrepresented by available assets; or

(c) either with or without extinguishing or reducing liability on any of its shares, pay off any paid-up share capital which is in excess of the company's wants;

and the company may, if and so far as is necessary, alter its memorandum by reducing the amount of its share capital and of its shares accordingly.

(3) A special resolution under this section is in this Act referred to as "a resolution for reducing share capital".

CHAPTER V MAINTENANCE OF CAPITAL

142 Duty of directors on serious loss of capital

(1) Where the net assets of a public company are half or less of its called-up share capital, the directors shall, not later than 28 days from the earliest day on which that fact is known to a director of the company, duly convene an extraordinary general meeting of the company for a date not later than 56 days from that day for the purpose of considering whether any, and if so what, steps should be taken to deal with the situation.

(2) If there is a failure to convene an extraordinary general meeting as required by subsection (1), each of the directors of the company who—

(a) knowingly and wilfully authorises or permits the failure, or

(b) after the expiry of the period during which that meeting should have been convened, knowingly and wilfully authorises or permits the failure to continue,

is liable to a fine.

(3) Nothing in this section authorises the consideration, at a meeting convened in pursuance of subsection (1), of any matter which could not have been considered at that meeting apart from this section.

143 General rule against company acquiring own shares

(1) Subject to the following provisions, a company limited by shares or limited by guarantee and having a share capital shall not acquire its own shares, whether by purchase, subscription or otherwise.

(2) If a company purports to act in contravention of this section, the company is liable to a fine, and every officer of the company who is in default is liable to imprisonment or a fine, or both; and the purported acquisition is void.

(3) A company limited by shares may acquire any of its own fully paid shares otherwise than for valuable consideration; and subsection (1) does not apply in relation to—

(a) the redemption or purchase of shares in accordance with Chapter VII of this Part,

(b) the acquisition of shares in a reduction of capital duly made,

(c) the purchase of shares in pursuance of an order of the court under section 5 (alteration of objects), section 54 (litigated objection to resolution for company to be re-registered as private) or Part XVII (relief to members unfairly prejudiced), or

(d) the forfeiture of shares, or the acceptance of shares surrendered in lieu, in pursuance of the articles, for failure to pay any sum payable in respect of the shares.

144 Acquisition of shares by company's nominee

(1) Subject to section 145, where shares are issued to a nominee of a company mentioned in section 143(1), or are acquired by a nominee of such a company from a third person as partly paid up, then, for all purposes—

(a) the shares are to be treated as held by the nominee on his own account; and

(b) the company is to be regarded as having no beneficial interest in them.

(2) Subject to that section, if a person is called on to pay any amount for the purpose of paying up, or paying any premium on, any shares in such a company which were issued to him, or which he otherwise acquired, as the company's nominee and he fails to pay that amount within 21 days from being called on to do so, then—

(a) if the shares were issued to him as subscriber to the memorandum by virtue of an undertaking of his in the memorandum, the other subscribers to the memorandum, or
(b) if the shares were otherwise issued to or acquired by him, the directors of the company at the time of the issue or acquisition,

are jointly and severally liable with him to pay that amount.

(3) If in proceedings for the recovery of any such amount from any such subscriber or director under this section it appears to the court—

(a) that he is or may be liable to pay that amount, but
(b) that he has acted honestly and reasonably and, having regard to all the circumstances of the case, he ought fairly to be excused from liability,

the court may relieve him, either wholly or partly, from his liability on such terms as the court thinks fit.

(4) Where any such subscriber or director has reason to apprehend that a claim will or might be made for the recovery of any such amount from him, he may apply to the court for relief; and the court has the same power to relieve him as it would have had in proceedings for the recovery of that amount.

145 Exceptions from s 144

(1) Section 144(1) does not apply to shares acquired otherwise than by subscription by a nominee of a public company, where a person acquires shares in the company with financial assistance given to him directly or indirectly by the company for the purpose of or in connection with the acquisition, and the company has a beneficial interest in the shares.

(2) Section 144(1) and (2) do not apply—

(a) to shares acquired by a nominee of a company when the company has no beneficial interest in those shares, or
(b) to shares issued in consequence of an application made before 22nd December 1980, or transferred in pursuance of an agreement to acquire them made before that date.

(3) Schedule 2 to this Act has effect for the interpretation of references in this section to a company having, or not having, a beneficial interest in shares.

146 Treatment of shares held by or for public company

(1) Except as provided by section 148, the following applies to a public company—

(a) where shares in the company are forfeited, or surrendered to the company in lieu, in pursuance of the articles, for failure to pay any sum payable in respect of the shares;
(b) where shares in the company are acquired by it (otherwise than by any of the methods mentioned in section 143(3)(a) to (d)) and the company has a beneficial interest in the shares;

(c) where the nominee of the company acquires shares in the company from a third person without financial assistance being given directly or indirectly by the company and the company has a beneficial interest in the shares; or

(d) where a person acquires shares in the company with financial assistance given to him directly or indirectly by the company for the purpose of or in connection with the acquisition, and the company has a beneficial interest in the shares.

Schedule 2 to this Act has effect for the interpretation of references in this subsection to the company having a beneficial interest in shares.

(2) Unless the shares or any interest of the company in them are previously disposed of, the company must, not later than the end of the relevant period from their forfeiture or surrender or, in a case within subsection (1)(b), (c) or (d), their acquisition—

(a) cancel them and diminish the amount of the share capital by the nominal value of the shares cancelled, and

(b) where the effect of cancelling the shares will be that the nominal value of the company's allotted share capital is brought below the authorised minimum, apply for re-registration as a private company, stating the effect of the cancellation.

(3) For this purpose "the relevant period" is—

(a) 3 years in the case of shares forfeited or surrendered to the company in lieu of forfeiture, or acquired as mentioned in subsection (1)(b) or (c);

(b) one year in the case of shares acquired as mentioned in subsection (1)(d).

(4) The company and, in a case within subsection (1)(c) or (d), the company's nominee or (as the case may be) the other shareholder must not exercise any voting rights in respect of the shares; and any purported exercise of those rights is void.

Cross references. See Secs 147 and 148.

---

147 Matters arising out of compliance with s 146(2)

(1) The directors may take such steps as are requisite to enable the company to carry out its obligations under section 146(2) without complying with sections 135 and 136 (resolution to reduce share capital; application to court for approval).

(2) The steps taken may include the passing of a resolution to alter the company's memorandum so that it no longer states that the company is to be a public company; and the resolution may make such other alterations in the memorandum as are requisite in the circumstances.

Such a resolution is subject to section 380 (copy to be forwarded to registrar within 15 days).

(3) The application for re-registration required by section 146(2)(b) must be in the prescribed form and be signed by a director or secretary of the company, and must be delivered to the registrar of companies together with a printed copy of the memorandum and articles of the company as altered by the resolution.

(4) If the registrar is satisfied that the company may be re-registered under section 146, he shall retain the application and other documents delivered with it and issue the company with a certificate of incorporation appropriate to a company that is not a public company; and—

(a) the company by virtue of the issue of the certificate becomes a private company, and the alterations in the memorandum and articles set out in the resolution take effect accordingly, and

(b) the certificate is conclusive evidence that the requirements of sections 146 to 148 in respect of re-registration and of matters precedent and incidental to it have been complied with, and that the company is a private company.

148 Further provisions supplementing ss 146, 147

(1) Where, after shares in a private company—

(a) are forfeited in pursuance of the company's articles or are surrendered to the company in lieu of forfeiture, or

(b) are acquired by the company (otherwise than by such surrender or forfeiture, and otherwise than by any of the methods mentioned in section 143(3)), the company having a beneficial interest in the shares, or

(c) are acquired by the nominee of a company in the circumstances mentioned in section 146(1)(c), or

(d) are acquired by any person in the circumstances mentioned in section 146(1)(d),

the company is re-registered as a public company, sections 146 and 147, and also section 149, apply to the company as if it had been a public company at the time of the forfeiture, surrender or acquisition, but with the modification required by the following subsection.

(2) That modification is to treat any reference to the relevant period from the forfeiture, surrender or acquisition as referring to the relevant period from the re-registration of the company as a public company.

(3) Schedule 2 to this Act has effect for the interpretation of the reference in subsection (1)(b) to the company having a beneficial interest in shares.

(4) Where a public company or a nominee of a public company acquires shares in the company or an interest in such shares, and those shares are (or that interest is) shown in a balance sheet of the company as an asset, an amount equal to the value of the shares or (as the case may be) the value to the company of its interest in them shall be transferred out of profits available for dividend to a reserve fund and are not then available for distribution.

149 Sanctions for non-compliance

(1) If a public company required by section 146(2) to apply to be re-registered as a private company fails to do so before the end of the relevant period referred to in that subsection, section 81 (restriction on public offers) applies to it as if it were a private company such as is mentioned in that section; but, subject to this, the company continues to be treated for the purpose of this Act as a public company until it is so re-registered.

(2) If a company when required to do so by section 146(2) (including that subsection as applied by section 148(1)) fails to cancel any shares in accordance with paragraph (a) of that subsection or to make an application for re-registration in accordance with paragraph (b) of it, the company and every officer of it who is in default is liable to a fine and, for continued contravention, to a daily default fine.

150 Charges of public companies on own shares

(1) A lien or other charge of a public company on its own shares (whether taken expressly or otherwise), except a charge permitted by any of the following subsections, is void.

This is subject to section 6 of the Consequential Provisions Act (saving for charges of old public companies on their own shares).

(2) In the case of any description of company, a charge on its own shares is permitted if the shares are not fully paid and the charge is for any amount payable in respect of the shares.

(3) In the case of a company whose ordinary business—

(a) includes the lending of money, or
(b) consists of the provision of credit or the bailment (in Scotland, hiring) of goods under a hire purchase agreement, or both,

a charge of the company on its own shares is permitted (whether the shares are fully paid or not) if it arises in connection with a transaction entered into by the company in the ordinary course of its business.

(4) In the case of a company which is re-registered or is registered under section 680 as a public company, a charge on its own shares is permitted if the charge was in existence immediately before the company's application for re-registration or (as the case may be) registration.

This subsection does not apply in the case of such a company as is referred to in section 6(3) of the Consequential Provisions Act (old public company remaining such after 22nd March 1982, not having applied to be re-registered as public company).

CHAPTER VI FINANCIAL ASSISTANCE BY A COMPANY FOR ACQUISITION OF ITS OWN SHARES

Provisions applying to both public and private companies

151 Financial assistance generally prohibited

(1) Subject to the following provisions of this Chapter, where a person is acquiring or is proposing to acquire shares in a company, it is not lawful for the company or any of its subsidiaries to give financial assistance directly or indirectly for the purpose of that acquisition before or at the same time as the acquisition takes place.

(2) Subject to those provisions, where a person has acquired shares in a company and any liability has been incurred (by that or any other person), for the purpose of that acquisition, it is not lawful for the company or any of its subsidiaries to give financial assistance directly or indirectly for the purpose of reducing or discharging the liability so incurred.

(3) If a company acts in contravention of this section, it is liable to a fine, and every officer of it who is in default is liable to imprisonment or a fine, or both.

Cross references. See Sec 153 (transactions not prohibited by Sec 151); Sec 154 (special restriction for public companies); Sec 155 (relaxation of Sec 151 for private companies).

152 Definitions for this Chapter

(1) In this Chapter—

(a) "financial assistance" means—

(i) financial assistance given by way of gift,

(ii) financial assistance given by way of guarantee, security or indemnity, other than an indemnity in respect of the indemnifier's own neglect or default, or by way of release or waiver,

(iii) financial assistance given by way of a loan or any other agreement under which any of the obligations of the person giving the assistance are to be fulfilled at a time when in accordance with the agreement any obligation of another party to the agreement remains unfulfilled, or by way of the novation of, or the assignment of rights arising under, a loan or such other agreement, or

(iv) any other financial assistance given by a company the net assets of which are thereby reduced to a material extent or which has no net assets;

(b) "distributable profits", in relation to the giving of any financial assistance—

(i) means those profits out of which the company could lawfully make a distribution equal in value to that assistance, and

(ii) includes, in a case where the financial assistance is or includes a non-cash asset, any profit which, if the company were to make a distribution of that asset, would under section 276 (distributions in kind) be available for that purpose,

and

(c) "distribution" has the meaning given by section 263(2).

(2) In subsection (1)(a)(iv), "net assets" means the aggregate of the company's assets, less the aggregate of its liabilities ("liabilities" to include any provision for liabilities or charges within paragraph 89 of Schedule 4).

(3) In this Chapter—

(a) a reference to a person incurring a liability includes his changing his financial position by making an agreement or arrangement (whether enforceable or unenforceable, and whether made on his own account or with any other person) or by any other means, and
(b) a reference to a company giving financial assistance for the purpose of reducing or discharging a liability incurred by a person for the purpose of the acquisition of shares includes its giving such assistance for the purpose of wholly or partly restoring his financial position to what it was before the acquisition took place.

153 Transactions not prohibited by s 151

(1) Section 151(1) does not prohibit a company from giving financial assistance for the purpose of an acquisition of shares in it or its holding company if—

(a) the company's principal purpose in giving that assistance is not to give it for the purpose of any such acquisition, or the giving of the assistance for that purpose is but an incidental part of some larger purpose of the company, and
(b) the assistance is given in good faith in the interests of the company.

(2) Section 151(2) does not prohibit a company from giving financial assistance if—

(a) the company's principal purpose in giving the assistance is not to reduce or discharge any liability incurred by a person for the purpose of the acquisition of shares in the company or its holding company, or the reduction or discharge of any such liability is but an incidental part of some larger purpose of the company, and
(b) the assistance is given in good faith in the interests of the company.

(3) Section 151 does not prohibit—

(a) a distribution of a company's assets by way of dividend lawfully made or a distribution made in the course of the company's winding up,
(b) the allotment of bonus shares,
(c) a reduction of capital confirmed by order of the court under section 137,
(d) a redemption or purchase of shares made in accordance with Chapter VII of this Part,
(e) anything done in pursuance of an order of the court under section 425 (compromises and arrangements with creditors and members),
(f) anything done under an arrangement made in pursuance of section [110 of the Insolvency Act][1] (acceptance of shares by liquidator in winding up as consideration for sale of property), or
(g) anything done under an arrangement made between a company and its creditors which is binding on the creditors by virtue of [Part I of the Insolvency Act][2].

(4) Section 151 does not prohibit—

(a) where the lending of money is part of the ordinary business of the company, the lending of money by the company in the ordinary course of its business,
(b) [the provision by a company, in good faith in the interests of the company, of financial assistance for the purposes of an employees' share scheme,][4]

[(bb) without prejudice to paragraph (b), the provision of financial assistance by a company or any of its subsidiaries for the purposes of or in connection with anything done by the company (or [a company in the same group][5]) for the purpose of enabling or facilitating transactions in shares in the first-mentioned company between, and involving the acquisition of beneficial ownership of those shares by, any of the following persons—

(i) the bona fide employees or former employees of that company or of another company in the same group; or

(ii) the wives, husbands, widows, widowers, children or step-children under the age of eighteen of any such employees or former employees.][3]

(c) the making by a company of loans to persons (other than directors) employed in good faith by the company with a view to enabling those persons to acquire fully paid shares in the company or its holding company to be held by them by way of beneficial ownership.

(5) [For the purposes of subsection (4)(bb) a company is in the same group as another company if it is a holding company or subsidiary of that company, or a subsidiary of a holding company of that company.][6]

---

1 Substituted by IA 1986, s 439(1), 13 Sch Part I with effect from 29 December 1986 (see IA 1986, s 443 and SI 1986 No 1924).
Previously '582'.

2 Substituted by IA 1986, s 439(1), 13 Sch Part I as above.
Previously '[chapter II of Part II of the Insolvency Act 1985][a]'.
a Substituted by IA 1985, s 109, 6 Sch 8 with effect from 29 December 1986 (see SI 1986 No 1924).
Previously 'section 601 (winding-up imminent or in progress)'.

3 Inserted by FSA 1986, s 196(1)-(3) with effect from 1 December 1987 (see SI 1987 No 1997).

4 Substituted by CA 1989, s 132 with effect from 1 April 1990 (SI 1990 No 355).
Previously 'the provision by a company in accordance with an employees' share scheme of money for the acquisition of fully paid shares in the company or its holding company,'.

5 Substituted by CA 1989, 18 Sch 33 with effect from a date to be appointed.
Previously 'a company connected with it'.

6 Substituted by CA 1989, 18 Sch 33 with effect from a date to be appointed.
Previously
'[For the purposes of subsection (4)(bb) a company is connected with another company if—
(a) they are in the same group; or
(b) one is entitled, either alone or with any other company in the same group, to exercise or control the exercise of a majority of the voting rights attributable to the share capital which are exercisable in all circumstances at any general meeting of the other company or of its holding company;
and in this section "group", in relation to a company, means that company, any other company which is its holding company or subsidiary and any other company which is a subsidiary of that holding company.][a]'.
a Inserted by FSA 1986, s 196(1)-(3) with effect from 1 December 1987 (see SI 1987 No 1997).

---

154 Special restriction for public companies

(1) In the case of a public company, section 153(4) authorises the giving of financial assistance only if the company has net assets which are not thereby reduced or, to the extent that those assets are thereby reduced, if the assistance is provided out of distributable profits.

(2) For this purpose the following definitions apply—

(a) "net assets" means the amount by which the aggregate of the company's assets exceeds the aggregate of its liabilities (taking the amount of both assets and liabilities to be as stated in the company's accounting records immediately before the financial assistance is given);

(b) "liabilities" includes any amount retained as reasonably necessary for the purpose of providing for any liability or loss which is either likely to be incurred, or certain to be incurred but uncertain as to amount or as to the date on which it will arise.

Private companies

155 Relaxation of s 151 for private companies

(1) Section 151 does not prohibit a private company from giving financial assistance in a case where the acquisition of shares in question is or was an acquisition of shares in the company or, if it is a subsidiary of another private company, in that other company if the following provisions of this section, and sections 156 to 158, are complied with as respects the giving of that assistance.

(2) The financial assistance may only be given if the company has net assets which are not thereby reduced or, to the extent that they are reduced, if the assistance is provided out of distributable profits.

Section 154(2) applies for the interpretation of this subsection.

(3) This section does not permit financial assistance to be given by a subsidiary, in a case where the acquisition of shares in question is or was an acquisition of shares in its holding company, if it is also a subsidiary of a public company which is itself a subsidiary of that holding company.

(4) Unless the company proposing to give the financial assistance is a wholly-owned subsidiary, the giving of assistance under this section must be approved by special resolution of the company in general meeting.

(5) Where the financial assistance is to be given by the company in a case where the acquisition of shares in question is or was an acquisition of shares in its holding company, that holding company and any other company which is both the company's holding company and a subsidiary of that other holding company (except, in any case, a company which is a wholly-owned subsidiary) shall also approve by special resolution in general meeting the giving of the financial assistance.

(6) The directors of the company proposing to give the financial assistance and, where the shares acquired or to be acquired are shares in its holding company, the directors of that company and of any other company which is both the company's holding company and a subsidiary of that other holding company shall before the financial assistance is given make a statutory declaration in the prescribed form complying with the section next following.

Cross references. See Sec 156; Sec 157 (special resolution under Sec 155); Sec 158 (time for giving financial assistance under Sec 155).

156 Statutory declaration under s 155

(1) A statutory declaration made by a company's directors under section 155(6) shall contain such particulars of the financial assistance to be given, and of the business of the company of which they are directors, as may be prescribed, and shall identify the person to whom the assistance is to be given.

(2) The declaration shall state that the directors have formed the opinion, as regards the company's initial situation immediately following the date on which the assistance is proposed to be given, that there will be no ground on which it could then be found to be unable to pay its debts; and either—

(a) if it is intended to commence the winding up of the company within 12 months of that date, that the company will be able to pay its debts in full within 12 months of the commencement of the winding up, or
(b) in any other case, that the company will be able to pay its debts as they fall due during the year immediately following that date.

(3) In forming their opinion for purposes of subsection (2), the directors shall take into account the same liabilities (including contingent and prospective liabilities) as would be relevant under section [122 of the Insolvency Act][1] (winding up by the court) to the question whether the company is unable to pay its debts.

(4) The directors' statutory declaration shall have annexed to it a report addressed to them by their company's auditors stating that—

(a) they have enquired into the state of affairs of the company, and
(b) they are not aware of anything to indicate that the opinion expressed by the directors in the declaration as to any of the matters mentioned in subsection (2) of this section is unreasonable in all the circumstances.

(5) The statutory declaration and auditors' report shall be delivered to the registrar of companies—

(a) together with a copy of any special resolution passed by the company under section 155 and delivered to the registrar in compliance with section 380, or
(b) where no such resolution is required to be passed, within 15 days after the making of the declaration.

(6) If a company fails to comply with subsection (5), the company and every officer of it who is in default is liable to a fine and, for continued contravention, to a daily default fine.

(7) A director of a company who makes a statutory declaration under section 155 without having reasonable grounds for the opinion expressed in it is liable to imprisonment or a fine, or both.

---

[1] Substituted by IA 1986, s 439(1), 13 Sch Part I with effect from 29 December 1986 (see IA 1986, s 443 and SI 1986 No 1924).
Previously '517'.

---

157 Special resolution under s 155

(1) A special resolution required by section 155 to be passed by a company approving the giving of financial assistance must be passed on the date on which the directors of that company make the statutory declaration required by that section in connection with the giving of that assistance, or within the week immediately following that date.

(2) Where such a resolution has been passed, an application may be made to the court for the cancellation of the resolution—

(a) by the holders of not less in the aggregate than 10 per cent. in nominal value of the company's issued share capital or any class of it, or
(b) if the company is not limited by shares, by not less than 10 per cent. of the company's members;

but the application shall not be made by a person who has consented to or voted in favour of the resolution.

(3) Subsections (3) to (10) of section 54 (litigation to cancel resolution under section 53) apply to applications under this section as to applications under section 54.

(4) A special resolution passed by a company is not effective for purposes of section 155—

(a) unless the declaration made in compliance with subsection (6) of that section by the directors of the company, together with the auditors' report annexed to it, is available for inspection by members of the company at the meeting at which the resolution is passed,

(b) if it is cancelled by the court on an application under this section.

158 Time for giving financial assistance under s 155

(1) This section applies as to the time before and after which financial assistance may not be given by a company in pursuance of section 155.

(2) Where a special resolution is required by that section to be passed approving the giving of the assistance, the assistance shall not be given before the expiry of the period of 4 weeks beginning with—

(a) the date on which the special resolution is passed, or

(b) where more than one such resolution is passed, the date on which the last of them is passed,

unless, as respects that resolution (or, if more than one, each of them), every member of the company which passed the resolution who is entitled to vote at general meetings of the company voted in favour of the resolution.

(3) If application for the cancellation of any such resolution is made under section 157, the financial assistance shall not be given before the final determination of the application unless the court otherwise orders.

(4) The assistance shall not be given after the expiry of the period of 8 weeks beginning with—

(a) the date on which the directors of the company proposing to give the assistance made their statutory declaration under section 155, or

(b) where that company is a subsidiary and both its directors and the directors of any of its holding companies made such a declaration, the date on which the earliest of the declarations is made,

unless the court, on an application under section 157, otherwise orders.

CHAPTER VII REDEEMABLE SHARES; PURCHASE BY A COMPANY OF ITS OWN SHARES

Redemption and purchase generally

159 Power to issue redeemable shares

(1) Subject to the provisions of this Chapter, a company limited by shares or limited by guarantee and having a share capital may, if authorised to do so by its articles, issue shares which are to be redeemed or are liable to be redeemed at the option of the company or the shareholder.

(2) No redeemable shares may be issued at a time when there are no issued shares of the company which are not redeemable.

(3) Redeemable shares may not be redeemed unless they are fully paid; and the terms of redemption must provide for payment on redemption.

[159A Terms and manner of redemption

(1) Redeemable shares may not be issued unless the following conditions are satisfied as regards the terms and manner of redemption.

(2) The date on or by which, or dates between which, the shares are to be or may be redeemed must be specified in the company's articles or, if the articles so provide, fixed by the directors, and in the latter case the date or dates must be fixed before the shares are issued.

(3) Any other circumstances in which the shares are to be or may be redeemed must be specified in the company's articles.

(4) The amount payable on redemption must be specified in, or determined in accordance with, the company's articles, and in the latter case the articles must not provide for the amount to be determined by reference to any person's discretion or opinion.

(5) Any other terms and conditions of redemption shall be specified in the company's articles.

(6) Nothing in this section shall be construed as requiring a company to provide in its articles for any matter for which provision is made by this Act.][1]

---

1 Inserted by CA 1989, s 133 with effect from a date to be appointed.

---

160 Financing etc. of redemption

(1) Subject to the next subsection and to sections 171 (private companies redeeming or purchasing own shares out of capital) and 178(4) (terms of redemption or purchase enforceable in a winding up)—

(a) redeemable shares may only be redeemed out of distributable profits of the company or out of the proceeds of a fresh issue of shares made for the purposes of the redemption; and

(b) any premium payable on redemption must be paid out of distributable profits of the company.

(2) If the redeemable shares were issued at a premium, any premium payable on their redemption may be paid out of the proceeds of a fresh issue of shares made for the purposes of the redemption, up to an amount equal to—

(a) the aggregate of the premiums received by the company on the issue of the shares redeemed, or

(b) the current amount of the company's share premium account (including any sum transferred to that account in respect of premiums on the new shares),

whichever is the less; and in that case the amount of the company's share premium account shall be reduced by a sum corresponding (or by sums in the aggregate corresponding) to the amount of any payment made by virtue of this subsection out of the proceeds of the issue of the new shares.

(3) [. . .][1]

(4) Shares [redeemed under this Chapter][2] shall be treated as cancelled on redemption, and the amount of the company's issued share capital shall be diminished by the nominal value of those shares accordingly; but the redemption of shares by a company is not to be taken as reducing the amount of the company's authorised share capital.

(5) Without prejudice to subsection (4), where a company is about to redeem shares, it has power to issue shares up to the nominal value of the shares to be redeemed as if those shares had never been issued.

---

1 Deleted by CA 1989, s 133 with effect from a date to be appointed.
Previously 'Subject to the following provisions of this Chapter, redemption of shares may be effected on such terms and in such manner as may be provided by the company's articles'.

2 Substituted by CA 1989, s 133 with effect from a date to be appointed.
Previously 'redeemed under this section'.

---

162 Power of company to purchase own shares

(1) Subject to the following provisions of this Chapter, a company limited by shares or limited by guarantee and having a share capital may, if authorised to do so by its articles, purchase its own shares (including any redeemable shares).

(2) [Sections 159, 160 and 161 apply to the purchase by a company under this section of its own shares as they apply to the redemption of redeemable shares.][1]

(3) A company may not under this section purchase its shares if as a result of the purchase there would no longer be any member of the company holding shares other than redeemable shares.

---

1 Substituted by CA 1989, s 133 with effect from a date to be appointed.
Previously
'Sections 159 to 161 apply to the purchase by a company under this section of its own shares as they apply to the redemption of redeemable shares, save that the terms and manner of purchase need not be determined by the articles as required by section 160(3).'

---

170 The capital redemption reserve

(1) Where under this Chapter shares of a company are redeemed or purchased wholly out of the company's profits, the amount by which the company's issued share capital is diminished in accordance with section 160(4) on cancellation of the shares redeemed or purchased shall be transferred to a reserve, called "the capital redemption reserve".

(2) If the shares are redeemed or purchased wholly or partly out of the proceeds of a fresh issue and the aggregate amount of those proceeds is less than the aggregate nominal value of the shares redeemed or purchased, the amount of the difference shall be transferred to the capital redemption reserve.

(3) But subsection (2) does not apply if the proceeds of the fresh issue are applied by the company in making a redemption or purchase of its own shares in addition to a payment out of capital under section 171.

(4) The provisions of this Act relating to the reduction of a company's share capital apply as if the capital redemption reserve were paid-up share capital of the company, except that the reserve may be applied by the company in paying up its unissued shares to be allotted to members of the company as fully paid bonus shares.

PART VII ACCOUNTS AND AUDIT

CHAPTER I PROVISIONS APPLYING TO COMPANIES GENERALLY

[*Accounting records*

221 Duty to keep accounting records

(1) Every company shall keep accounting records which are sufficient to show and explain the company's transactions and are such as to—

(a) disclose with reasonable accuracy, at any time, the financial position of the company at that time, and

(b) enable the directors to ensure that any balance sheet and profit and loss account prepared under this Part complies with the requirements of this Act.

(2) The accounting records shall in particular contain—

(a) entries from day to day of all sums of money received and expended by the company, and the matters in respect of which the receipt and expenditure takes place, and

(b) a record of the assets and liabilities of the company.

(3) If the company's business involves dealing in goods, the accounting records shall contain—

(a) statements of stock held by the company at the end of each financial year of the company,

(b) all statements of stocktakings from which any such statement of stock as is mentioned in paragraph (a) has been or is to be prepared, and

(c) except in the case of goods sold by way of ordinary retail trade, statements of all goods sold and purchased, showing the goods and the buyers and sellers in sufficient detail to enable all these to be identified.

(4) A parent company which has a subsidiary undertaking in relation to which the above requirements do not apply shall take reasonable steps to secure that the undertaking keeps such accounting records as to enable the directors of the parent company to ensure that any balance sheet and profit and loss account prepared under this Part complies with the requirements of this Act.

(5) If a company fails to comply with any provision of this section, every officer of the company who is in default is guilty of an offence unless he shows that he acted honestly and that in the circumstances in which the company's business was carried on the default was excusable.

(6) A person guilty of an offence under this section is liable to imprisonment or a fine, or both.][1]

---

1 Inserted by CA 1989, s 2 with effect from 1 April 1990 (SI 1990 No 355) subject to the transitional and saving provisions in Arts 6 to 9 of that Order.

[222 Where and for how long records to be kept

(1) A company's accounting records shall be kept at its registered office or such other place as the directors think fit, and shall at all times be open to inspection by the company's officers.

(2) If accounting records are kept at a place outside Great Britain, accounts and returns with respect to the business dealt with in the accounting records so kept shall be sent to, and kept at, a place in Great Britain, and shall at all times be open to such inspection.

(3) The accounts and returns to be sent to Great Britain shall be such as to—

(a) disclose with reasonable accuracy the financial position of the business in question at intervals of not more than six months, and

(b) enable the directors to ensure that the company's balance sheet and profit and loss account comply with the requirements of this Act.

(4) If a company fails to comply with any provision of subsections (1) to (3), every officer of the company who is in default is guilty of an offence, and liable to imprisonment or a fine or both, unless he shows that he acted honestly and that in the circumstances in which the company's business was carried on the default was excusable.

(5) Accounting records which a company is required by section 221 to keep shall be preserved by it—

(a) in the case of a private company, for three years from the date on which they are made, and

(b) in the case of a public company, for six years from the date on which they are made.

This is subject to any provision contained in rules made under section 411 of the Insolvency Act 1986 (company insolvency rules).

(6) An officer of a company is guilty of an offence, and liable to imprisonment or a fine or both, if he fails to take all reasonable steps for securing compliance by the company with subsection (5) or intentionally causes any default by the company under that subsection.][1]

---

1 Inserted by CA 1989, s 2 with effect from 1 April 1990 (SI 1990 No 355) subject to the transitional and saving provisions in Arts 6 to 9 of that Order.

[*A company's financial year and accounting reference periods*

223 A company's financial year

(1) A company's "financial year" is determined as follows.

(2) Its first financial year begins with the first day of its first accounting reference period and ends with the last day of that period or such other date, not more than seven days before or after the end of that period, as the directors may determine.

(3) Subsequent financial years begin with the day immediately following the end of the company's previous financial year and end with the last day of its next accounting reference period or such other date, not more than seven days before or after the end of that period, as the directors may determine.

(4) In relation to an undertaking which is not a company, references in this Act to its financial year are to any period in respect of which a profit and loss account of the undertaking is required to be made up (by its constitution or by the law under which it is established), whether that period is a year or not.

(5) The directors of a parent company shall secure that, except where in their opinion there are good reasons against it, the financial year of each of its subsidiary undertakings coincides with the company's own financial year.][1]

1 Inserted by CA 1989, s 3 with effect from 1 April 1990 (SI 1990 No 355) subject to the transitional and saving provisions in Arts 6 to 9 of that Order.

[224 Accounting reference periods and accounting reference date

(1) A company's accounting reference periods are determined according to its accounting reference date.

(2) A company may, at any time before the end of the period of nine months beginning with the date of its incorporation, by notice in the prescribed form given to the registrar specify its accounting reference date, that is, the date on which its accounting reference period ends in each calendar year.

(3) Failing such notice, a company's accounting reference date is—

(a) in the case of a company incorporated before [1st April 1990][2], 31st March;

(b) in the case of a company incorporated after [1st April 1990][3], the last day of the month in which the anniversary of its incorporation falls.

(4) A company's first accounting reference period is the period of more than six months, but not more than 18 months, beginning with the date of its incorporation and ending with its accounting reference date.

(5) Its subsequent accounting reference periods are successive periods of twelve months beginning immediately after the end of the previous accounting reference period and ending with its accounting reference date.

(6) This section has effect subject to the provisions of section 225 relating to the alteration of accounting reference dates and the consequences of such alteration.][1]

1 Inserted by CA 1989, s 3 with effect from 1 April 1990 (SI 1990 No 355) subject to the transitional and saving provisions in Arts 6 to 9 of that Order.

2 Substituted by SI 1990 No 355, Art 15 with effect from 1 April 1990.
Previously 'the commencement of section 3 of the Companies Act 1989'.

3 Substituted by SI 1990 No 355, Art 15 with effect from 1 April 1990.
Previously 'the commencement of that section'.

[225 Alteration of accounting reference date

(1) A company may by notice in the prescribed form given to the registrar specify a new accounting reference date having effect in relation to the company's current accounting reference period and subsequent periods.

(2) A company may by notice in the prescribed form given to the registrar specify a new accounting reference date having effect in relation to the company's previous accounting reference period and subsequent periods if—

(a) the company is a subsidiary undertaking or parent undertaking of another company and the new accounting reference date coincides with the accounting reference date of that other company, or

(b) an administration order under Part II of the Insolvency Act 1986 is in force.

A company's "previous accounting reference period" means that immediately preceding its current accounting reference period.

(3) The notice shall state whether the current or previous accounting reference period—

(a) is to be shortened, so as to come to an end on the first occasion on which the new accounting reference date falls or fell after the beginning of the period, or
(b) is to be extended, so as to come to an end on the second occasion on which that date falls or fell after the beginning of the period.

(4) A notice under subsection (1) stating that the current accounting reference period is to be extended is ineffective, except as mentioned below, if given less than five years after the end of an earlier accounting reference period of the company which was extended by virtue of this section.

This subsection does not apply—

(a) to a notice given by a company which is a subsidiary undertaking or parent undertaking of another company and the new accounting reference date coincides with that of the other company, or
(b) where an administration order is in force under Part II of the Insolvency Act 1986,

or where the Secretary of State directs that it should not apply, which he may do with respect to a notice which has been given or which may be given.

(5) A notice under subsection (2)(a) may not be given if the period allowed for laying and delivering accounts and reports in relation to the previous accounting reference period has already expired.

(6) An accounting reference period may not in any case, unless an administration order is in force under Part II of the Insolvency Act 1986, be extended so as to exceed 18 months and a notice under this section is ineffective if the current or previous accounting reference period as extended in accordance with the notice would exceed that limit.][1]

---

1 Inserted by CA 1989, s 3 with effect from 1 April 1990 (SI 1990 No 355) subject to the transitional and saving provisions in Arts 6 to 9 of that Order.

[*Annual accounts*

226 Duty to prepare individual company accounts

(1) The directors of every company shall prepare for each financial year of the company—

(a) a balance sheet as at the last day of the year, and
(b) a profit and loss account.

Those accounts are referred to in this Part as the company's 'individual accounts'.

(2) The balance sheet shall give a true and fair view of the state of affairs of the company as at the end of the financial year; and the profit and loss account shall give a true and fair view of the profit or loss of the company for the financial year.

(3) A company's individual accounts shall comply with the provisions of Schedule 4 as to the form and content of the balance sheet and profit and loss account and additional information to be provided by way of notes to the accounts.

(4) Where compliance with the provisions of that Schedule, and the other provisions of this Act as to the matters to be included in a company's individual accounts or in notes to those accounts, would not be sufficient to give a true and fair view, the necessary additional information shall be given in the accounts or in a note to them.

(5) If in special circumstances compliance with any of those provisions is inconsistent with the requirement to give a true and fair view, the directors shall depart from that provision to the extent necessary to give a true and fair view.

Particulars of any such departure, the reasons for it and its effect shall be given in a note to the accounts.][1]

1 Inserted by CA 1989, s 4 with effect from 1 April 1990 (SI 1990 No 355) subject to the transitional and saving provisions in Arts 6 to 9 of that Order.

[227 Duty to prepare group accounts

(1) If at the end of a financial year a company is a parent company the directors shall, as well as preparing individual accounts for the year, prepare group accounts.

(2) Group accounts shall be consolidated accounts comprising—

(a) a consolidated balance sheet dealing with the state of affairs of the parent company and its subsidiary undertakings, and

(b) a consolidated profit and loss account dealing with the profit or loss of the parent company and its subsidiary undertakings.

(3) The accounts shall give a true and fair view of the state of affairs as at the end of the financial year, and the profit or loss for the financial year, of the undertakings included in the consolidation as a whole, so far as concerns members of the company.

(4) A company's group accounts shall comply with the provisions of Schedule 4A as to the form and content of the consolidated balance sheet and consolidated profit and loss account and additional information to be provided by way of notes to the accounts.

(5) Where compliance with the provisions of that Schedule, and the other provisions of this Act, as to the matters to be included in a company's group accounts or in notes to those accounts, would not be sufficient to give a true and fair view, the necessary additional information shall be given in the accounts or in a note to them.

(6) If in special circumstances compliance with any of those provisions is inconsistent with the requirement to give a true and fair view, the directors shall depart from that provision to the extent necessary to give a true and fair view.

Particulars of any such departure, the reasons for it and its effect shall be given in a note to the accounts.][1]

1 Inserted by CA 1989, s 5 with effect from 1 April 1990 (SI 1990 No 355) subject to the transitional and saving provisions in Arts 6 to 9 of that Order.

[228 Exemption for parent companies included in accounts of larger group

(1) A company is exempt from the requirement to prepare group accounts if it is itself a subsidiary undertaking and its immediate parent undertaking is established under the law of a member State of the European Economic Community, in the following cases—

(a) where the company is a wholly-owned subsidiary of that parent undertaking;

(b) where that parent undertaking holds more than 50 per cent. of the shares in the company and notice requesting the preparation of group accounts has not been served on the company by shareholders holding in aggregate—

(i) more than half of the remaining shares in the company, or

(ii) 5 per cent. of the total shares in the company.

Such notice must be served not later than six months after the end of the financial year before that to which it relates.

(2) Exemption is conditional upon compliance with all of the following conditions—

(a) that the company is included in consolidated accounts for a larger group drawn up to the same date, or to an earlier date in the same financial year, by a parent undertaking established under the law of a member State of the European Economic Community;

(b) that those accounts are drawn up and audited, and that parent undertaking's annual report is drawn up, according to that law, in accordance with the provisions of the Seventh Directive (83/349/EEC);

(c) that the company discloses in its individual accounts that it is exempt from the obligation to prepare and deliver group accounts;

(d) that the company states in its individual accounts the name of the parent undertaking which draws up the group accounts referred to above and—

(i) if it is incorporated outside Great Britain, the country in which it is incorporated,

(ii) if it is incorporated in Great Britain, whether it is registered in England and Wales or in Scotland, and

(iii) if it is unincorporated, the address of its principal place of business;

(e) that the company delivers to the registrar, within the period allowed for delivering its individual accounts, copies of those group accounts and of the parent undertaking's annual report, together with the auditors' report on them; and

(f) that if any document comprised in accounts and reports delivered in accordance with paragraph (e) is in a language other than English, there is annexed to the copy of that document delivered a translation of it into English, certified in the prescribed manner to be a correct translation.

(3) The exemption does not apply to a company any of whose securities are listed on a stock exchange in any member State of the European Economic Community.

(4) Shares held by directors of a company for the purpose of complying with any share qualification requirement shall be disregarded in determining for the purposes of subsection (1)(a) whether the company is a wholly-owned subsidiary.

(5) For the purposes of subsection (1)(b) shares held by a wholly-owned subsidiary of the parent undertaking, or held on behalf of the parent undertaking or a wholly-owned subsidiary, shall be attributed to the parent undertaking.

(6) In subsection (3) "securities" includes—

(a) shares and stock,
(b) debentures, including debenture stock, loan stock, bonds, certificates of deposit and other instruments creating or acknowledging indebtedness,
(c) warrants or other instruments entitling the holder to subscribe for securities falling within paragraph (a) or (b), and
(d) certificates or other instruments which confer—
(i) property rights in respect of a security falling within paragraph (a), (b) or (c),
(ii) any right to acquire, dispose of, underwrite or convert a security, being a right to which the holder would be entitled if he held any such security to which the certificate or other instrument relates, or
(iii) a contractual right (other than an option) to acquire any such security otherwise than by subscription.][1]

---

1 Inserted by CA 1989, s 5 with effect from 1 April 1990 (SI 1990 No 355) subject to the transitional and saving provisions in Arts 6 to 9 of that Order.

[229 Subsidiary undertakings included in the consolidation

(1) Subject to the exceptions authorised or required by this section, all the subsidiary undertakings of the parent company shall be included in the consolidation.

(2) A subsidiary undertaking may be excluded from consolidation if its inclusion is not material for the purpose of giving a true and fair view; but two or more undertakings may be excluded only if they are not material taken together.

(3) In addition, a subsidiary undertaking may be excluded from consolidation where—

(a) severe long-term restrictions substantially hinder the exercise of the rights of the parent company over the assets or management of that undertaking, or
(b) the information necessary for the preparation of group accounts cannot be obtained without disproportionate expense or undue delay, or
(c) the interest of the parent company is held exclusively with a view to subsequent resale and the undertaking has not previously been included in consolidated group accounts prepared by the parent company.

The reference in paragraph (a) to the rights of the parent company and the reference in paragraph (c) to the interest of the parent company are, respectively, to rights and interests held by or attributed to the company for the purposes of section 258 (definition of "parent undertaking") in the absence of which it would not be the parent company.

(4) Where the activities of one or more subsidiary undertakings are so different from those of other undertakings to be included in the consolidation that their inclusion would be incompatible with the obligation to give a true and fair view, those undertakings shall be excluded from consolidation.

This subsection does not apply merely because some of the undertakings are industrial, some commercial and some provide services, or because they carry on industrial or commercial activities involving different products or provide different services.

(5) Where all the subsidiary undertakings of a parent company fall within the above exclusions, no group accounts are required.][1]

1 Inserted by CA 1989, s 5 with effect from 1 April 1990 (SI 1990 No 355) subject to the transitional and saving provisions in Arts 6 to 9 of that Order.

[230 Treatment of individual profit and loss account where group accounts prepared

(1) The following provisions apply with respect to the individual profit and loss account of a parent company where—

(a) the company is required to prepare and does prepare group accounts in accordance with this Act, and

(b) the notes to the company's individual balance sheet show the company's profit or loss for the financial year determined in accordance with this Act.

(2) The profit and loss account need not contain the information specified in paragraphs 52 to 57 of Schedule 4 (information supplementing the profit and loss account).

(3) The profit and loss account must be approved in accordance with section 233(1) (approval by board of directors) but may be omitted from the company's annual accounts for the purposes of the other provisions below in this Chapter.

(4) The exemption conferred by this section is conditional upon its being disclosed in the company's annual accounts that the exemption applies.][1]

1 Inserted by CA 1989, s 5 with effect from 1 April 1990 (SI 1990 No 355) subject to the transitional and saving provisions in Arts 6 to 9 of that Order.

[231 Disclosure required in notes to accounts: related undertakings

(1) The information specified in Schedule 5 shall be given in notes to a company's annual accounts.

(2) Where the company is not required to prepare group accounts, the information specified in Part I of that Schedule shall be given; and where the company is required to prepare group accounts, the information specified in Part II of that Schedule shall be given.

(3) The information required by Schedule 5 need not be disclosed with respect to an undertaking which—

(a) is established under the law of a country outside the United Kingdom, or

(b) carries on business outside the United Kingdom,

if in the opinion of the directors of the company the disclosure would be seriously prejudicial to the business of that undertaking, or to the business of the company or any of its subsidiary undertakings, and the Secretary of State agrees that the information need not be disclosed.

This subsection does not apply in relation to the information required under paragraph 5(2), 6 or 20 of that Schedule.

(4) Where advantage is taken of subsection (3), that fact shall be stated in a note to the company's annual accounts.

(5) If the directors of the company are of the opinion that the number of undertakings in respect of which the company is required to disclose information under any provision of Schedule 5 to this Act is such that compliance with that provision would result in information of excessive length being given, the information need only be given in respect of—

(a) the undertakings whose results or financial position, in the opinion of the directors, principally affected the figures shown in the company's annual accounts, and

(b) undertakings excluded from consolidation under section 229(3) or (4).

This subsection does not apply in relation to the information required under paragraph 10 or 29 of that Schedule.

(6) If advantage is taken of subsection (5)—

(a) there shall be included in the notes to the company's annual accounts a statement that the information is given only with respect to such undertakings as are mentioned in that subsection, and

(b) the full information (both that which is disclosed in the notes to the accounts and that which is not) shall be annexed to the company's next annual return.

For this purpose the "next annual return" means that next delivered to the registrar after the accounts in question have been approved under section 233.

(7) If a company fails to comply with subsection (6)(b), the company and every officer of it who is in default is liable to a fine and, for continued contravention, to a daily default fine.][1]

---

[1] Inserted by CA 1989, s 6 with effect from 1 April 1990 (SI 1990 No 355) subject to the transitional and saving provisions in Arts 6 to 9 of that Order.

Cross references. See 4 Sch 63.

[232 Disclosure required in notes to accounts: emoluments and other benefits of directors and others

(1) The information specified in Schedule 6 shall be given in notes to a company's annual accounts.

(2) In that Schedule—

Part I relates to the emoluments of directors (including emoluments waived), pensions of directors and past directors, compensation for loss of office to directors and past directors and sums paid to third parties in respect of directors' services,

Part II relates to loans, quasi-loans and other dealings in favour of directors and connected persons, and

Part III relates to transactions, arrangements and agreements made by the company or a subsidiary undertaking for officers of the company other than directors.

(3) It is the duty of any director of a company, and any person who is or has at any time in the preceding five years been an officer of the company, to give notice to the company of such matters relating to himself as may be necessary for the purposes of Part I of Schedule 6.

(4) A person who makes default in complying with subsection (3) commits an offence and is liable to a fine.][1]

---

[1] Inserted by CA 1989, s 6 with effect from 1 April 1990 (SI 1990 No 355) subject to the transitional and saving provisions in Arts 6 to 9 of that Order.

[*Approval and signing of accounts*

233 Approval and signing of accounts

(1) A company's annual accounts shall be approved by the board of directors and signed on behalf of the board by a director of the company.

(2) The signature shall be on the company's balance sheet.

(3) Every copy of the balance sheet which is laid before the company in general meeting, or which is otherwise circulated, published or issued, shall state the name of the person who signed the balance sheet on behalf of the board.

(4) The copy of the company's balance sheet which is delivered to the registrar shall be signed on behalf of the board by a director of the company.

(5) If annual accounts are approved which do not comply with the requirements of this Act, every director of the company who is party to their approval and who knows that they do not comply or is reckless as to whether they comply is guilty of an offence and liable to a fine.

For this purpose every director of the company at the time the accounts are approved shall be taken to be a party to their approval unless he shows that he took all reasonable steps to prevent their being approved.

(6) If a copy of the balance sheet—

(a) is laid before the company, or otherwise circulated, published or issued, without the balance sheet having been signed as required by this section or without the required statement of the signatory's name being included, or

(b) is delivered to the registrar without being signed as required by this section,

the company and every officer of it who is in default is guilty of an offence and liable to a fine.][1]

---

1 Inserted by CA 1989, s 7.

(a) in respect of subsections (1)-(4)(6) with effect from 1 April 1990 (SI 1990 No 355) subject to the transitional and saving provisions in Arts 6 to 9 of that Order.

Cross references. See 4 Sch 63.

[*Directors' report*

234 Duty to prepare directors' report

(1) The directors of a company shall for each financial year prepare a report—

(a) containing a fair review of the development of the business of the company and its subsidiary undertakings during the financial year and of their position at the end of it, and

(b) stating the amount (if any) which they recommend should be paid as dividend and the amount (if any) which they propose to carry to reserves.

(2) The report shall state the names of the persons who, at any time during the financial year, were directors of the company, and the principal activities of the company and its subsidiary undertakings in the course of the year and any significant change in those activities in the year.

(3) The report shall also comply with Schedule 7 as regards the disclosure of the matters mentioned there.

(4) In Schedule 7—

Part I relates to matters of a general nature, including changes in asset values, directors' shareholdings and other interests and contributions for political and charitable purposes,

Part II relates to the acquisition by a company of its own shares or a charge on them,

Part III relates to the employment, training and advancement of disabled persons,

Part IV relates to the health, safety and welfare at work of the company's employees, and

Part V relates to the involvement of employees in the affairs, policy and performance of the company.

(5) In the case of any failure to comply with the provisions of this Part as to the preparation of a directors' report and the contents of the report, every person who was a director of the company immediately before the end of the period for laying and delivering accounts and reports for the financial year in question is guilty of an offence and liable to a fine.

(6) In proceedings against a person for an offence under this section it is a defence for him to prove that he took all reasonable steps for securing compliance with the requirements in question.][1]

---

1 Inserted by CA 1989, s 8 with effect from 1 April 1990 (SI 1990 No 355) subject to the transitional and saving provisions in Arts 6 to 9 of that Order.

Cross references. See 4 Sch 63.

[234A Approval and signing of directors' report

(1) The directors' report shall be approved by the board of directors and signed on behalf of the board by a director or the secretary of the company.

(2) Every copy of the directors' report which is laid before the company in general meeting, or which is otherwise circulated, published or issued, shall state the name of the person who signed it on behalf of the board.

(3) The copy of the directors' report which is delivered to the registrar shall be signed on behalf of the board by a director or the secretary of the company.

(4) If a copy of the directors' report—

(a) is laid before the company, or otherwise circulated, published or issued, without the report having been signed as required by this section or without the required statement of the signatory's name being included, or

(b) is delivered to the registrar without being signed as required by this section,

the company and every officer of it who is in default is guilty of an offence and liable to a fine.][1]

---

1 Inserted by CA 1989, s 8 with effect from 1 April 1990 (SI 1990 No 355) subject to the transitional and saving provisions in Arts 6 to 9 of that Order.

[*Auditors' report*

235 Auditors' report

(1) A company's auditors shall make a report to the company's members on all annual accounts of the company of which copies are to be laid before the company in general meeting during their tenure of office.

(2) The auditors' report shall state whether in the auditors' opinion the annual accounts have bcen properly prepared in accordance with this Act, and in particular whether a true and fair view is given—

(a) in the case of an individual balance sheet, of the state of affairs of the company as at the end of the financial year,
(b) in the case of an individual profit and loss account, of the profit or loss of the company for the financial year,
(c) in the case of group accounts, of the state of affairs as at the end of the financial year, and the profit or loss for the financial year, of the undertakings included in the consolidation as a whole, so far as concerns members of the company.

(3) The auditors shall consider whether the information given in the directors' report for the financial year for which the annual accounts are prepared is consistent with those accounts; and if they are of opinion that it is not they shall state that fact in their report.][1]

1 Inserted by CA 1989, s 9 with effect from 1 April 1990 (SI 1990 No 355) subject to the transitional and saving provisions in Arts 6 to 9 of that Order.

[236 Signature of auditors' report

(1) The auditors' report shall state the names of the auditors and be signed by them.

(2) Every copy of the auditors' report which is laid before the company in general meeting, or which is otherwise circulated, published or issued, shall state the names of the auditors.

(3) The copy of the auditors' report which is delivered to the registrar shall state the names of the auditors and be signed by them.

(4) If a copy of the auditors' report—

(a) is laid before the company, or otherwise circulated, published or issued, without the required statement of the auditors' names, or
(b) is delivered to the registrar without the required statement of the auditors' names or without being signed as required by this section,

the company and every officer of it who is in default is guilty of an offence and liable to a fine.

(5) References in this section to signature by the auditors are, where the office of auditor is held by a body corporate or partnership, to signature in the name of the body corporate or partnership by a person authorised to sign on its behalf.][1]

1 Inserted by CA 1989, s 9 with effect from 1 April 1990 (SI 1990 No 355) subject to the transitional and saving provisions in Arts 6 to 9 of that Order.

[237 Duties of auditors

(1) A company's auditors shall, in preparing their report, carry out such investigations as will enable them to form an opinion as to—

(a) whether proper accounting records have been kept by the company and proper returns adequate for their audit have been received from branches not visited by them, and

(b) whether the company's individual accounts are in agreement with the accounting records and returns.

(2) If the auditors are of opinion that proper accounting records have not been kept, or that proper returns adequate for their audit have not been received from branches not visited by them, or if the company's individual accounts are not in agreement with the accounting records and returns, the auditors shall state that fact in their report.

(3) If the auditors fail to obtain all the information and explanations which, to the best of their knowledge and belief, are necessary for the purposes of their audit, they shall state that fact in their report.

(4) If the requirements of Schedule 6 (disclosure of information: emoluments and other benefits of directors and others) are not complied with in the annual accounts, the auditors shall include in their report, so far as they are reasonably able to do so, a statement giving the required particulars.][1]

---

1 Inserted by CA 1989, s 9 with effect from 1 April 1990 (SI 1990 No 355) subject to the transitional and saving provisions in Arts 6 to 9 of that Order.

[*Publication of accounts and reports*

238 Persons entitled to receive copies of accounts and reports

(1) A copy of the company's annual accounts, together with a copy of the directors' report for that financial year and of the auditors' report on those accounts, shall be sent to—

(a) every member of the company,

(b) every holder of the company's debentures, and

(c) every person who is entitled to receive notice of general meetings,

not less than 21 days before the date of the meeting at which copies of those documents are to be laid in accordance with section 241.

(2) Copies need not be sent—

(a) to a person who is not entitled to receive notices of general meetings and of whose address the company is unaware, or

(b) to more than one of the joint holders of shares or debentures none of whom is entitled to receive such notices, or

(c) in the case of joint holders of shares or debentures some of whom are, and some not, entitled to receive such notices, to those who are not so entitled.

(3) In the case of a company not having a share capital, copies need not be sent to anyone who is not entitled to receive notices of general meetings of the company.

(4) If copies are sent less than 21 days before the date of the meeting, they shall, notwithstanding that fact, be deemed to have been duly sent if it is so agreed by all the members entitled to attend and vote at the meeting.

(5) If default is made in complying with this section, the company and every officer of it who is in default is guilty of an offence and liable to a fine.

(6) Where copies are sent out under this section over a period of days, references elsewhere in this Act to the day on which copies are sent out shall be construed as references to the last day of that period.][1]

---

1 Inserted by CA 1989, s 10 with effect from 1 April 1990 (SI 1990 No 355) subject to the transitional and saving provisions in Arts 6 to 9 of that Order.

[239 Right to demand copies of accounts and reports

(1) Any member of a company and any holder of a company's debentures is entitled to be furnished, on demand and without charge, with a copy of the company's last annual accounts and directors' report and a copy of the auditors' report on those accounts.

(2) The entitlement under this section is to a single copy of those documents, but that is in addition to any copy to which a person may be entitled under section 238.

(3) If a demand under this section is not complied with within seven days, the company and every officer of it who is in default is guilty of an offence and liable to a fine and, for continued contravention, to a daily default fine.

(4) If in proceedings for such an offence the issue arises whether a person had already been furnished with a copy of the relevant document under this section, it is for the defendant to prove that he had.][1]

---

1 Inserted by CA 1989, s 10 with effect from 1 April 1990 (SI 1990 No 355) subject to the transitional and saving provisions in Arts 6 to 9 of that Order.

[240 Requirements in connection with publication of accounts

(1) If a company publishes any of its statutory accounts, they must be accompanied by the relevant auditors' report under section 235.

(2) A company which is required to prepare group accounts for a financial year shall not publish its statutory individual accounts for that year without also publishing with them its statutory group accounts.

(3) If a company publishes non-statutory accounts, it shall publish with them a statement indicating—

(a) that they are not the company's statutory accounts,
(b) whether statutory accounts dealing with any financial year with which the non-statutory accounts purport to deal have been delivered to the registrar,
(c) whether the company's auditors have made a report under section 235 on the statutory accounts for any such financial year, and
(d) whether any report so made was qualified or contained a statement under section 237(2) or (3) (accounting records or returns inadequate, accounts not agreeing with records and returns or failure to obtain necessary information and explanations);

and it shall not publish with the non-statutory accounts any auditors' report under section 235.

(4) For the purposes of this section a company shall be regarded as publishing a document if it publishes, issues or circulates it or otherwise makes it available for public inspection in a manner calculated to invite members of the public generally, or any class of members of the public, to read it.

(5) References in this section to a company's statutory accounts are to its individual or group accounts for a financial year as required to be delivered to the registrar under section 242; and references to the publication by a company of "non-statutory accounts" are to the publication of—

(a) any balance sheet or profit and loss account relating to, or purporting to deal with, a financial year of the company, or

(b) an account in any form purporting to be a balance sheet or profit and loss account for the group consisting of the company and its subsidiary undertakings relating to, or purporting to deal with, a financial year of the company,

otherwise than as part of the company's statutory accounts.

(6) A company which contravenes any provision of this section, and any officer of it who is in default, is guilty of an offence and liable to a fine.][1]

---

[1] Inserted by CA 1989, s 10 with effect from 1 April 1990 (SI 1990 No 355) subject to the transitional and saving provisions in Arts 6 to 9 of that Order.

[*Laying and delivering of accounts and reports*

241 Accounts and reports to be laid before company in general meeting

(1) The directors of a company shall in respect of each financial year lay before the company in general meeting copies of the company's annual accounts, the directors' report and the auditors' report on those accounts.

(2) If the requirements of subsection (1) are not complied with before the end of the period allowed for laying and delivering accounts and reports, every person who immediately before the end of that period was a director of the company is guilty of an offence and liable to a fine and, for continued contravention, to a daily default fine.

(3) It is a defence for a person charged with such an offence to prove that he took all reasonable steps for securing that those requirements would be complied with before the end of that period.

(4) It is not a defence to prove that the documents in question were not in fact prepared as required by this Part.][1]

---

[1] Inserted by CA 1989, s 11 with effect from 1 April 1990 (SI 1990 No 355) subject to the transitional and saving provisions in Arts 6 to 9 of that Order.

Cross references. SI 1985 No 854 (translation of documents into English).

[242 Accounts and reports to be delivered to the registrar

(1) The directors of a company shall in respect of each financial year deliver to the registrar a copy of the company's annual accounts together with a copy of the directors' report for that year and a copy of the auditors' report on those accounts.

If any document comprised in those accounts or reports is in a language other than English, the directors shall annex to the copy of that document delivered a translation of it into English, certified in the prescribed manner to be a correct translation.

(2) If the requirements of subsection (1) are not complied with before the end of the period allowed for laying and delivering accounts and reports, every person who immediately before the end of that period was a director of the company is guilty of an offence and liable to a fine and, for continued contravention, to a daily default fine.

(3) Further, if the directors of the company fail to make good the default within 14 days after the service of a notice on them requiring compliance, the court may on the application of any member or creditor of the company or of the registrar, make an order directing the directors (or any of them) to make good the default within such time as may be specified in the order.

The court's order may provide that all costs of and incidental to the application shall be borne by the directors.

(4) It is a defence for a person charged with an offence under this section to prove that he took all reasonable steps for securing that the requirements of subsection (1) would be complied with before the end of the period allowed for laying and delivering accounts and reports.

(5) It is not a defence in any proceedings under this section to prove that the documents in question were not in fact prepared as required by this Part.][1]

---

[1] Inserted by CA 1989, s 11 with effect from 1 April 1990 (SI 1990 No 355) subject to the transitional and saving provisions in Arts 6 to 9 of that Order.

[242A Civil penalty for failure to deliver accounts

(1) Where the requirements of section 242(1) are not complied with before the end of the period allowed for laying and delivering accounts and reports, the company is liable to a civil penalty.

This is in addition to any liability of the directors under section 242.

(2) The amount of the penalty is determined by reference to the length of the period between the end of the period allowed for laying and delivering accounts and reports and the day on which the requirements are complied with, and whether the company is a public or private company, as follows:—

Length of period	*Public company*	*Private company*
Not more than 3 months.	£500	£100
More than 3 months but not more than 6 months.	£1,000	£250
More than 6 months but not more than 12 months.	£2,000	£500
More than 12 months.	£5,000	£1,000

(3) The penalty may be recovered by the registrar and shall be paid by him into the Consolidated Fund.

(4) It is not a defence in proceedings under this section to prove that the documents in question were not in fact prepared as required by this Part.][1]

1 Inserted by CA 1989, s 11 with effect from a date to be appointed.

[243 Accounts of subsidiary undertakings to be appended in certain cases

(1) The following provisions apply where at the end of the financial year a parent company has as a subsidiary undertaking—

(a) a body corporate incorporated outside Great Britain which does not have an established place of business in Great Britain, or
(b) an unincorporated undertaking,

which is excluded from consolidation in accordance with section 229(4) (undertaking with activities different from the undertakings included in the consolidation).

(2) There shall be appended to the copy of the company's annual accounts delivered to the registrar in accordance with section 242 a copy of the undertaking's latest individual accounts and, if it is a parent undertaking, its latest group accounts.

If the accounts appended are required by law to be audited, a copy of the auditors' report shall also be appended.

(3) The accounts must be for a period ending not more than twelve months before the end of the financial year for which the parent company's accounts are made up.

(4) If any document required to be appended is in a language other than English, the directors shall annex to the copy of that document delivered a translation of it into English, certified in the prescribed manner to be a correct translation.

(5) The above requirements are subject to the following qualifications—

(a) an undertaking is not required to prepare for the purposes of this section accounts which would not otherwise be prepared, and if no accounts satisfying the above requirements are prepared none need be appended;
(b) a document need not be appended if it would not otherwise be required to be published, or made available for public inspection, anywhere in the world, but in that case the reason for not appending it shall be stated in a note to the company's accounts;
(c) where an undertaking and all its subsidiary undertakings are excluded from consolidation in accordance with section 229(4), the accounts of such of the subsidiary undertakings of that undertaking as are included in its consolidated group accounts need not be appended.

(6) Subsections (2) to (4) of section 242 (penalties, etc. in case of default) apply in relation to the requirements of this section as they apply in relation to the requirements of subsection (1) of that section.][1]

1 Inserted by CA 1989, s 11 with effect from 1 April 1990 (SI 1990 No 355) subject to the transitional and saving provisions in Arts 6 to 9 of that Order.

[244 Period allowed for laying and delivering accounts and reports

(1) The period allowed for laying and delivering accounts and reports is—

(a) for a private company, 10 months after the end of the relevant accounting reference period, and
(b) for a public company, 7 months after the end of that period.

This is subject to the following provisions of this section.

(2) If the relevant accounting reference period is the company's first and is a period of more than 12 months, the period allowed is—

(a) 10 months or 7 months, as the case may be, from the first anniversary of the incorporation of the company, or

(b) 3 months from the end of the accounting reference period,

whichever last expires.

(3) Where a company carries on business, or has interests, outside the United Kingdom, the Channel Islands and the Isle of Man, the directors may, in respect of any financial year, give to the registrar before the end of the period allowed by subsection (1) or (2) a notice in the prescribed form—

(a) stating that the company so carries on business or has such interests, and

(b) claiming a 3 month extension of the period allowed for laying and delivering accounts and reports;

and upon such a notice being given the period is extended accordingly.

(4) If the relevant accounting period is treated as shortened by virtue of a notice given by the company under section 225 (alteration of accounting reference date), the period allowed for laying and delivering accounts is that applicable in accordance with the above provisions or 3 months from the date of the notice under that section, whichever last expires.

(5) If for any special reason the Secretary of State thinks fit he may, on an application made before the expiry of the period otherwise allowed, by notice in writing to a company extend that period by such further period as may be specified in the notice.

(6) In this section "the relevant accounting reference period" means the accounting reference period by reference to which the financial year for the accounts in question was determined.][1]

---

1 Inserted by CA 1989, s 11 with effect from 1 April 1990 (SI 1990 No 355) subject to the transitional and saving provisions in Arts 6 to 9 of that Order.

[*Revision of defective accounts and reports*

245 Voluntary revision of annual accounts or directors' report

(1) If it appears to the directors of a company that any annual accounts of the company, or any directors' report, did not comply with the requirements of this Act, they may prepare revised accounts or a revised report.

(2) Where copies of the previous accounts or report have been laid before the company in general meeting or delivered to the registrar, the revisions shall be confined to—

(a) the correction of those respects in which the previous accounts or report did not comply with the requirements of this Act, and

(b) the making of any necessary consequential alterations.

(3) The Secretary of State may make provision by regulations as to the application of the provisions of this Act in relation to revised annual accounts or a revised directors' report.

(4) The regulations may, in particular—

(a) make different provision according to whether the previous accounts or report are replaced or are supplemented by a document indicating the corrections to be made;
(b) make provision with respect to the functions of the company's auditors in relation to the revised accounts or report;
(c) require the directors to take such steps as may be specified in the regulations where the previous accounts or report have been—
  (i) sent out to members and others under section 238(1),
  (ii) laid before the company in general meeting, or
  (iii) delivered to the registrar,
or where a summary financial statement based on the previous accounts or report has been sent to members under section 251;
(d) apply the provisions of this Act (including those creating criminal offences) subject to such additions, exceptions and modifications as are specified in the regulations.

(5) Regulations under this section shall be made by statutory instrument which shall be subject to annulment in pursuance of a resolution of either House of Parliament.][1]

1 Inserted by CA 1989, s 12 with effect from a date to be appointed.

[245A Secretary of State's notice in respect of annual accounts

(1) Where copies of a company's annual accounts have been sent out under section 238, or a copy of a company's annual accounts has been laid before the company in general meeting or delivered to the registrar, and it appears to the Secretary of State that there is, or may be, a question whether the accounts comply with the requirements of this Act, he may give notice to the directors of the company indicating the respects in which it appears to him that such a question arises, or may arise.

(2) The notice shall specify a period of not less than one month for the directors to give him an explanation of the accounts or prepare revised accounts.

(3) If at the end of the specified period, or such longer period as he may allow, it appears to the Secretary of State that no satisfactory explanation of the accounts has been given and that the accounts have not been revised so as to comply with the requirements of this Act, he may if he thinks fit apply to the court.

(4) The provisions of this section apply equally to revised annual accounts, in which case the references to revised accounts shall be read as references to further revised accounts.][1]

1 Inserted by CA 1989, s 12 with effect from a date to be appointed.

[245B Application to court in respect of defective accounts

(1) An application may be made to the court—

(a) by the Secretary of State, after having complied with section 245A, or
(b) by a person authorised by the Secretary of State for the purposes of this section,

for a declaration or declarator that the annual accounts of a company do not comply with the requirements of this Act and for an order requiring the directors of the company to prepare revised accounts.

(2) Notice of the application, together with a general statement of the matters at issue in the proceedings, shall be given by the applicant to the registrar for registration.

(3) If the court orders the preparation of revised accounts, it may give directions with respect to—

(a) the auditing of the accounts,
(b) the revision of any directors' report or summary financial statement, and
(c) the taking of steps by the dirctors to bring the making of the order to the notice of persons likely to rely on the previous accounts,

and such other matters as the court thinks fit.

(4) If the court finds that the accounts did not comply with the requirements of this Act it may order that all or part of—

(a) the costs (or in Scotland expenses) of and incidental to the application, and
(b) any reasonable expenses incurred by the company in connection with or in consequence of the preparation of revised accounts,

shall be borne by such of the directors as were party to the approval of the defective accounts.

For this purpose every director of the company at the time the accounts were approved shall be taken to have been a party to their approval unless he shows that he took all reasonable steps to prevent their being approved.

(5) Where the court makes an order under subsection (4) it shall have regard to whether the directors party to the approval of the defective accounts knew or ought to have known that the accounts did not comply with the requirements of this Act, and it may exclude one or more directors from the order or order the payment of different amounts by different directors.

(6) On the conclusion of proceedings on an application under this section, the applicant shall give to the registrar for registration an office copy of the court order or, as the case may be, notice that the application has failed or been withdrawn.

(7) The provisions of this section apply equally to revised annual accounts, in which case the references to revised accounts shall be read as references to further revised accounts.][1]

---

1 Inserted by CA 1989, s 12 with effect from a date to be appointed.

[245C Other persons authorised to apply to court

(1) The Secretary of State may authorise for the purposes of section 245B any person appearing to him—

(a) to have an interest in, and to have satisfactory procedures directed to securing, compliance by companies with the accounting requirements of this Act,
(b) to have satisfactory procedures for receiving and investigating complaints about the annual accounts of companies, and
(c) otherwise to be a fit and proper person to be authorised.

(2) A person may be authorised generally or in respect of particular classes of case, and different persons may be authorised in respect of different classes of case.

(3) The Secretary of State may refuse to authorise a person if he considers that his authorisation is unnecessary having regard to the fact that there are one or more other persons who have been or are likely to be authorised.

(4) Authorisation shall be by order made by statutory instrument which shall be subject to annulment in pursuance of a resolution of either House of Parliament.

(5) Where authorisation is revoked, the revoking order may make such provision as the Secretary of State thinks fit with respect to pending proceedings.

(6) Neither a person authorised under this section, nor any officer, servant or member of the governing body of such a person, shall be liable in damages for anything done or purporting to be done for the purposes of or in connection with—

(a) the taking of steps to discover whether there are grounds for an application to the court,
(b) the determination whether or not to make such an application, or
(c) the publication of its reasons for any such decision,

unless the act or omission is shown to have been in bad faith.][1]

---

1 Inserted by CA 1989, s 12 with effect from a date to be appointed.

[CHAPTER II EXEMPTIONS, EXCEPTIONS AND SPECIAL PROVISIONS

Small and medium-sized companies and groups

246 Exemptions for small and medium-sized companies

(1) A company which qualifies as a small or medium-sized company in relation to a financial year—

(a) is exempt from the requirements of paragraph 36A of Schedule 4 (disclosure with respect to compliance with accounting standards), and
(b) is entitled to the exemptions provided by Schedule 8 with respect to the delivery to the registrar under section 242 of individual accounts and other documents for that financial year.

(2) In that Schedule—

Part I relates to small companies,

Part II relates to medium-sized companies, and

Part III contains supplementary provisions.

(3) A company is not entitled to the exemptions mentioned in subsection (1) if it is, or was at any time within the financial year to which the accounts relate—

(a) a public company,
(b) a banking or insurance company, or
(c) an authorised person under the Financial Services Act 1986,

or if it is or was at any time during that year a member of an ineligible group.

(4) A group is ineligible if any of its members is—

(a) a public company or a body corporate which (not being a company) has power under its constitution to offer its shares or debentures to the public and may lawfully exercise that power,
(b) an authorised institution under the Banking Act 1987,
(c) an insurance company to which Part II of the Insurance Companies Act 1982 applies, or
(d) an authorised person under the Financial Services Act 1986.

(5) A parent company shall not be treated as qualifying as a small company in relation to a financial year unless the group headed by it qualifies as a small group, and shall not be treated as qualifying as a medium-sized company in relation to a financial year unless that group qualifies as a medium-sized group (see section 249).][1]

---

1 Inserted by CA 1989, s 13 with effect from 1 April 1990 (SI 1990 No 355) subject to the transitional and saving provisions in Arts 6 to 9 of that Order.

[247 Qualification of company as small or medium-sized

(1) A company qualifies as small or medium-sized in relation to a financial year if the qualifying conditions are met—

(a) in the case of the company's first financial year, in that year, and
(b) in the case of any subsequent financial year, in that year and the preceding year.

(2) A company shall be treated as qualifying as small or medium-sized in relation to a financial year—

(a) if it so qualified in relation to the previous financial year under subsection (1); or

(b) if it was treated as so qualifying in relation to the previous year by virtue of paragraph (a) and the qualifying conditions are met in the year in question.

(3) The qualifying conditions are met by a company in a year in which it satisfies two or more of the following requirements—

Small company

1. Turnover	Not more than £2 million
2. Balance sheet total	Not more than £975,000
3. Number of employees	Not more than 50

Medium-sized company

1. Turnover	Not more than £8 million
2. Balance sheet total	Not more than £3.9 million
3. Number of employees	Not more than 250.

(4) For a period which is a company's financial year but not in fact a year the maximum figures for turnover shall be proportionately adjusted.

(5) The balance sheet total means—

(a) where in the company's accounts Format 1 of the balance sheet formats set out in Part I of Schedule 4 is adopted, the aggregate of the amounts shown in the balance sheet under the headings corresponding to items A to D in that Format, and

(b) where Format 2 is adopted, the aggregate of the amounts shown under the general heading "Assets".

(6) The number of employees means the average number of persons employed by the company in the year (determined on a weekly basis).

That number shall be determined by applying the method of calculation prescribed by paragraph 56(2) and (3) of Schedule 4 for determining the corresponding number required to be stated in a note to the company's accounts.][1]

1 Inserted by CA 1989, s 13 with effect from 1 April 1990 (SI 1990 No 355) subject to the transitional and saving provisions in Arts 6 to 9 of that Order.

[248 Exemption for small and medium-sized groups

(1) A parent company need not prepare group accounts for a financial year in relation to which the group headed by that company qualifies as a small or medium-sized group and is not an ineligible group.

(2) A group is ineligible if any of its members is—

(a) a public company or a body corporate which (not being a company) has power under its constitution to offer its shares or debentures to the public and may lawfully exercise that power,

(b) an authorised institution under the Banking Act 1987,

(c) an insurance company to which Part II of the Insurance Companies Act 1982 applies, or

(d) an authorised person under the Financial Services Act 1986.

(3) If the directors of a company propose to take advantage of the exemption conferred by this section, it is the auditors' duty to provide them with a report stating whether in their opinion the company is entitled to the exemption.

(4) The exemption does not apply unless—

(a) the auditors' report states that in their opinion the company is so entitled, and

(b) that report is attached to the individual accounts of the company.][1]

---

1 Inserted by CA 1989, s 13 with effect from 1 April 1990 (SI 1990 No 355) subject to the transitional and saving provisions in Arts 6 to 9 of that Order.

[249 Qualification of group as small or medium-sized

(1) A group qualifies as small or medium-sized in relation to a financial year if the qualifying conditions are met—

(a) in the case of the parent company's first financial year, in that year, and
(b) in the case of any subsequent financial year, in that year and the preceding year.

(2) A group shall be treated as qualifying as small or medium-sized in relation to a financial year—

(a) if it so qualified in relation to the previous financial year under subsection (1); or
(b) if it was treated as so qualifying in relation to the previous year by virtue of paragraph (a) and the qualifying conditions are met in the year in question.

(3) The qualifying conditions are met by a group in a year in which it satisfies two or more of the following requirements—

Small group

1. Aggregate turnover	Not more than £2 million net (or £2.4 million gross)
2. Aggregate balance sheet total	Not more than £1 million net (or £1.2 million gross)
3. Aggregate number of employees	Not more than 50

Medium-sized group

1. Aggregate turnover	Not more than £8 million net (or £9.6 million gross)
2. Aggregate balance sheet total	Not more than £3.9 million net (or £4.7 million gross)
3. Aggregate number of employees	Not more than 250.

(4) The aggregate figures shall be ascertained by aggregating the relevant figures determined in accordance with section 247 for each member of the group.

In relation to the aggregate figures for turnover and balance sheet total, "net" means with the set-offs and other adjustments required by Schedule 4A in the case of group accounts and "gross" means without those set-offs and other adjustments; and a company may satisfy the relevant requirement on the basis of either the net or the gross figure.

(5) The figures for each subsidiary undertaking shall be those included in its accounts for the relevant financial year, that is—

(a) if its financial year ends with that of the parent company, that financial year, and
(b) if not, its financial year ending last before the end of the financial year of the parent company.

(6) If those figures cannot be obtained without disproportionate expense or undue delay, the latest available figures shall be taken.][1]

---

1 Inserted by CA 1989, s 13 with effect from 1 April 1990 (SI 1990 No 355) subject to the transitional and saving provisions in Arts 6 to 9 of that Order.

Cross references. See SI 1986 No 1865 (transitional provisions—small and medium-sized companies).

[*Dormant companies*

250 Resolution not to appoint auditors

(1) A company may by special resolution make itself exempt from the provisions of this Part relating to the audit of accounts in the following cases—

(a) if the company has been dormant from the time of its formation, by a special resolution passed before the first general meeting of the company at which annual accounts are laid;
(b) if the company has been dormant since the end of the previous financial year and—
  (i) is entitled in respect of its individual accounts for that year to the exemptions conferred by section 246 on a small company, or would be so entitled but for being a member of an ineligible group, and
  (ii) is not required to prepare group accounts for that year,

by a special resolution passed at a general meeting of the company at which the annual accounts for that year are laid.

(2) A company may not pass such a resolution if it is—

(a) a public company,
(b) a banking or insurance company, or
(c) an authorised person under the Financial Services Act 1986.

(3) A company is "dormant" during a period in which no significant accounting transaction occurs, that is, no transaction which is required by section 221 to be entered in the company's accounting records; and a company ceases to be dormant on the occurrence of such a transaction.

For this purpose there shall be disregarded any transaction arising from the taking of shares in the company by a subscriber to the memorandum in pursuance of an undertaking of his in the memorandum.

(4) Where a company is, at the end of a financial year, exempt by virtue of this section from the provisions of this Part relating to the audit of accounts—

(a) sections 238 and 239 (right to receive or demand copies of accounts and reports) have effect with the omission of references to the auditors' report;
(b) no copies of an auditors' report need be laid before the company in general meeting;

(c) no copy of an auditors' report need be delivered to the registrar, and if none is delivered, the copy of the balance sheet so delivered shall contain a statement by the directors, in a position immediately above the signature required by section 233(4), that the company was dormant throughout the financial year; and

(d) the company shall be treated as entitled in respect of its individual accounts for that year to the exemptions conferred by section 246 on a small company notwithstanding that it is a member of an ineligible group.

(5) Where a company which is exempt by virtue of this section from the provisions of this Part relating to the audit of accounts—

(a) ceases to be dormant, or

(b) would no longer qualify (for any other reason) to make itself exempt by passing a resolution under this section,

it shall thereupon cease to be so exempt.][1]

---

1 Inserted by CA 1989, s 14 with effect from 1 April 1990 (SI 1990 No 355) subject to the transitional and saving provisions in Arts 6 to 9 of that Order.

[*Listed public companies*

251 Provision of summary financial statement to shareholders

(1) A public company whose shares, or any class of whose shares, are listed need not, in such cases as may be specified by regulations made by the Secretary of State, and provided any conditions so specified are complied with, send copies of the documents referred to in section 238(1) to members of the company, but may instead send them a summary financial statement.

In this subsection "listed" means admitted to the Official List of The International Stock Exchange of the United Kingdom and the Republic of Ireland Limited.

(2) Copies of the documents referred to in section 238(1) shall, however, be sent to any member of the company who wishes to receive them; and the Secretary of State may by regulations make provision as to the manner in which it is to be ascertained whether a member of the company wishes to receive them.

(3) The summary financial statement shall be derived from the company's annual accounts and the directors' report and shall be in such form and contain such information as may be specified by regulations made by the Secretary of State.

(4) Every summary financial statement shall—

(a) state that it is only a summary of information in the company's annual accounts and the directors' report;

(b) contain a statement by the company's auditors of their opinion as to whether the summary financial statement is consistent with those accounts and that report and complies with the requirements of this section and regulations made under it;

(c) state whether the auditors' report on the annual accounts was unqualified or qualified, and if it was qualified set out the report in full together with any further material needed to understand the qualification;

(d) state whether the auditors' report on the annual accounts contained a statement under—

(i) section 237(2) (accounting records or returns inadequate or accounts not agreeing with records and returns), or

(ii) section 237(3) (failure to obtain necessary information and explanations),

and if so, set out the statement in full.

(5) Regulations under this section shall be made by statutory instrument which shall be subject to annulment in pursuance of a resolution of either House of Parliament.

(6) If default is made in complying with this section or regulations made under it, the company and every officer of it who is in default is guilty of an offence and liable to a fine.

(7) Section 240 (requirements in connection with publication of accounts) does not apply in relation to the provision to members of a company of a summary financial statement in accordance with this section.][1]

---

1 Inserted by CA 1989, s 15 with effect from 1 March 1990 (SI 1990 No 142) but subject to the notes below.

Notes

(a) The provisions above inserted by CA 1989, s 15 apply with respect to a financial year for which a company's accounts are prepared under the provisions of the unamended Part VII (see below) as if

(i) the references in subsections (1) and (2) above to section 238(1) were references to section 240(1) of the unamended Part VII;

(ii) the references therein to the company's annual accounts were references to the documents referred to in section 239(a) and (d) of the unamended Part VII;

(iii) the reference in subsection (4)(d) thereof to section 237(3) was a reference to section 237(4) of the unamended Part VII; and

(iv) the reference in subsection (7) thereof to section 240 was a reference to section 255 of the unamended Part VII.

(b) The repeal of the existing section 251 by CA 1989, s 15 does not affect the continued operation of any regulations previously made thereunder.

(SI 1990 No 142, Art 8).

(c) The provisions in (a) and (b) above are revoked with effect from 1 April 1990 (SI 1990 No 355) and superceded by the transitional and saving provisions reproduced above Sec 221 above.

Regulations. The Companies (Modified Accounts) Amendment Regulations 1986 (SI 1986 No 1865).

[*Private companies*

252 Election to dispense with laying of accounts and reports before general meeting

(1) A private company may elect (by elective resolution in accordance with section 379A) to dispense with the laying of accounts and reports before the company in general meeting.

(2) An election has effect in relation to the accounts and reports in respect of the financial year in which the election is made and subsequent financial years.

(3) Whilst an election is in force, the references in the following provisions of this Act to the laying of accounts before the company in general meeting shall be read as references to the sending of copies of the accounts to members and others under section 238(1)—

(a) section 235(1) (accounts on which auditors are to report),

(b) section 270(3) and (4) (accounts by reference to which distributions are justified), and

(c) section 320(2) (accounts relevant for determining company's net assets for purposes of ascertaining whether approval required for certain transactions);

and the requirement in section 271(4) that the auditors' statement under that provision be laid before the company in general meeting shall be read as a requirement that it be sent to members and others along with the copies of the accounts sent to them under section 238(1).

(4) If an election under this section ceases to have effect, section 241 applies in relation to the accounts and reports in respect of the financial year in which the election ceases to have effect and subsequent financial years.][1]

---

1 Inserted by CA 1989, s 16 with effect from 1 April 1990 (SI 1990 No 355) subject to the transitional and saving provisions in Arts 6 to 9 of that Order.

[253 Right of shareholder to require laying of accounts

(1) Where an election under section 252 is in force, the copies of the accounts and reports sent out in accordance with section 238(1)—

(a) shall be sent not less than 28 days before the end of the period allowed for laying and delivering accounts and reports, and

(b) shall be accompanied, in the case of a member of the company, by a notice informing him of his right to require the laying of the accounts and reports before a general meeting;

and section 238(5) (penalty for default) applies in relation to the above requirements as to the requirements contained in that section.

(2) Before the end of the period of 28 days beginning with the day on which the accounts and reports are sent out in accordance with section 238(1), any member or auditor of the company may by notice in writing deposited at the registered office of the company require that a general meeting be held for the purpose of laying the accounts and reports before the company.

(3) If the directors do not within 21 days from the date of the deposit of such a notice proceed duly to convene a meeting, the person who deposited the notice may do so himself.

(4) A meeting so convened shall not be held more than three months from that date and shall be convened in the same manner, as nearly as possible, as that in which meetings are to be convened by directors.

(5) Where the directors do not duly convene a meeting, any reasonable expenses incurred by reason of that failure by the person who deposited the notice shall be made good to him by the company, and shall be recouped by the company out of any fees, or other remuneration in respect of their services, due or to become due to such of the directors as were in default.

(6) The directors shall be deemed not to have duly convened a meeting if they convene a meeting for a date more than 28 days after the date of the notice convening it.][1]

---

1 Inserted by CA 1989, s 16 with effect from 1 April 1990 (SI 1990 No 355) subject to the transitional and saving provisions in Arts 6 to 9 of that Order.

[*Unlimited companies*

254 Exemption from requirement to deliver accounts and reports

(1) The directors of an unlimited company are not required to deliver accounts and reports to the registrar in respect of a financial year if the following conditions are met.

(2) The conditions are that at no time during the relevant accounting reference period—

(a) has the company been, to its knowledge, a subsidiary undertaking of an undertaking which was then limited, or

(b) have there been, to its knowledge, exercisable by or on behalf of two or more undertakings which were then limited, rights which if exercisable by one of them would have made the company a subsidiary undertaking of it, or

(c) has the company been a parent company of an undertaking which was then limited.

The references above to an undertaking being limited at a particular time are to an undertaking (under whatever law established) the liability of whose members is at that time limited.

(3) The exemption conferred by this section does not apply if at any time during the relevant accounting period the company carried on business as the promoter of a trading stamp scheme within the Trading Stamps Act 1964.

(4) Where a company is exempt by virtue of this section from the obligation to deliver accounts, section 240 (requirements in connection with publication of accounts) has effect with the following modifications—

(a) in subsection (3)(b) for the words from 'whether statutory accounts' to 'have been delivered to the registrar' substitute 'that the company is exempt from the requirement to deliver statutory accounts', and

(b) in subsection (5) for 'as required to be delivered to the registrar under section 242' substitute 'as prepared in accordance with this Part and approved by the board of directors'.][1]

---

1 Inserted by CA 1989, s 17 with effect from 1 April 1990 (SI 1990 No 355) subject to the transitional and saving provisions in Arts 6 to 9 of that Order.

[*Banking and insurance companies and groups*

255 Special provisions for banking and insurance companies

(1) A banking or insurance company may prepare its individual accounts in accordance with Part I of Schedule 9 rather than Schedule 4.

(2) Accounts so prepared shall contain a statement that they are prepared in accordance with the special provisions of this Part relating to banking companies or insurance companies, as the case may be.

(3) In relation to the preparation of individual accounts in accordance with the special provisions of this Part relating to banking or insurance companies, the references to the provisions of Schedule 4 in section 226(4) and (5) (relationship between specific requirements and duty to give true and fair view) shall be read as references to the provisions of Part I of Schedule 9.

(4) The Secretary of State may, on the application or with the consent of the directors of a company which prepares individual accounts in accordance with the special provisions of this Part relating to banking or insurance companies, modify in relation to the company any of the requirements of this Part for the purpose of adapting them to the circumstances of the company.

This does not affect the duty to give a true and fair view.][1]

1 Inserted by CA 1989, s 18 with effect from 1 April 1990 (SI 1990 No 355) subject to the transitional and saving provisions in Arts 6 to 9 of that Order.

[255A Special provisions for banking and insurance groups

(1) The parent company of a banking or insurance group may prepare group accounts in accordance with the provisions of this Part as modified by Part II of Schedule 9.

(2) Accounts so prepared shall contain a statement that they are prepared in accordance with the special provisions of this Part relating to banking groups or insurance groups, as the case may be.

(3) References in this Part to a banking group are to a group where—

(a) the parent company is a banking company, or
(b) at least one of the undertakings in the group is an authorised institution under the Banking Act 1987 and the predominant activities of the group are such as to make it inappropriate to prepare group accounts in accordance with the formats in Part I of Schedule 4.

(4) References in this Part to an insurance group are to a group where—

(a) the parent company is an insurance company, or
(b) the predominant activity of the group is insurance business and activities which are a direct extension of or ancillary to insurance business.

(5) In relation to the preparation of group accounts in accordance with the special provisions of this Part relating to banking or insurance groups, the references to the provisions of Schedule 4A in section 227(5) and (6) (relationship between specific requirements and duty to give true and fair view) shall be read as references to those provisions as modified by Part II of Schedule 9.

(6) The Secretary of State may, on the application or with the consent of the directors of a company which prepares group accounts in accordance with the special provisions of this Part relating to banking or insurance groups, modify in relation to the company any of the requirements of this Part for the purpose of adapting them to the circumstances of the company.][1]

1 Inserted by CA 1989, s 18 with effect from 1 April 1990 (SI 1990 No 355) subject to the transitional and saving provisions in Arts 6 to 9 of that Order.

[255B Modification of disclosure requirements in relation to banking company or group

(1) In relation to a company which prepares accounts in accordance with the special provisions of this Part relating to banking companies or groups, the provisions of Schedule 5 (additional disclosure: related undertakings) have effect subject to Part III of Schedule 9.

(2) In relation to a banking company, or the parent company of a banking company, the provisions of Schedule 6 (disclosure: emoluments and other benefits of directors and others) have effect subject to Part IV of Schedule 9.][1]

1 Inserted by CA 1989, s 18 with effect from 1 April 1990 (SI 1990 No 355) subject to the transitional and saving provisions in Arts 6 to 9 of that Order.

[255C Directors' report where accounts prepared in accordance with special provisions

(1) The following provisions apply in relation to the directors' report of a company for a financial year in respect of which it prepares accounts in accordance with the special provisions of this Part relating to banking or insurance companies or groups.

(2) The information required to be given by paragraph 6, 8 or 13 of Part I of Schedule 9 (which is allowed to be given in a statement or report annexed to the accounts), may be given in the directors' report instead.

Information so given shall be treated for the purposes of audit as forming part of the accounts.

(3) The reference in section 234(1)(b) to the amount proposed to be carried to reserves shall be construed as a reference to the amount proposed to be carried to reserves within the meaning of Part I of Schedule 9.

(4) If the company takes advantage, in relation to its individual or group accounts, of the exemptions conferred by paragraph 27 or 28 of Part I of Schedule 9, paragraph 1 of Schedule 7 (disclosure of asset values) does not apply.

(5) The directors' report shall, in addition to complying with Schedule 7, also comply with Schedule 10 (which specifies additional matters to be disclosed).][1]

---

1 Inserted by CA 1989, s 18 with effect from 1 April 1990 (SI 1990 No 355) subject to the transitional and saving provisions in Arts 6 to 9 of that Order.

[255D Power to apply provisions to banking partnerships

(1) The Secretary of State may by regulations apply to banking partnerships, subject to such exceptions, adaptations and modifications as he considers appropriate, the provisions of this Part applying to banking companies.

(2) A "banking partnership" means a partnership which is an authorised institution under the Banking Act 1987.

(3) Regulations under this section shall be made by statutory instrument.

(4) No regulations under this section shall be made unless a draft of the instrument containing the regulations has been laid before Parliament and approved by a resolution of each House.][1]

---

1 Inserted by CA 1989, s 18 with effect from 1 April 1990 (SI 1990 No 355) subject to the transitional and saving provisions in Arts 6 to 9 of that Order.

[CHAPTER III SUPPLEMENTARY PROVISIONS

Accounting standards

256 Accounting standards

(1) In this Part "accounting standards" means statements of standard accounting practice issued by such body or bodies as may be prescribed by regulations.

(2) References in this Part to accounting standards applicable to a company's annual accounts are to such standards as are, in accordance with their terms, relevant to the company's circumstances and to the accounts.

(3) The Secretary of State may make grants to or for the purposes of bodies concerned with—

(a) issuing accounting standards,
(b) overseeing and directing the issuing of such standards, or
(c) investigating departures from such standards or from the accounting requirements of this Act and taking steps to secure compliance with them.

(4) Regulations under this section may contain such transitional and other supplementary and incidental provisions as appear to the Secretary of State to be appropriate.][1]

---

1 Inserted by CA 1989, s 19 with effect from 1 April 1990 (SI 1990 No 355) subject to the transitional and saving provisions in Arts 6 to 9 of that Order.

[*Power to alter accounting requirements*

257 Power of Secretary of State to alter accounting requirements

(1) The Secretary of State may by regulations made by statutory instrument modify the provisions of this Part.

(2) Regulations which—

(a) add to the classes of documents required to be prepared, laid before the company in general meeting or delivered to the registrar,
(b) restrict the classes of company which have the benefit of any exemption, exception or special provision,
(c) require additional matter to be included in a document of any class, or
(d) otherwise render the requirements of this Part more onerous,

shall not be made unless a draft of the instrument containing the regulations has been laid before Parliament and approved by a resolution of each House.

(3) Otherwise, a statutory instrument containing regulations under this section shall be subject to annulment in pursuance of a resolution of either House of Parliament.

(4) Regulations under this section may—

(a) make different provision for different cases or classes of case,
(b) repeal and re-enact provisions with modifications of form or arrangement, whether or not they are modified in substance,
(c) make consequential amendments or repeals in other provisions of this Act, or in other enactments, and

(d) contain such transitional and other incidental and supplementary provisions as the Secretary of State thinks fit.

(5) Any modification by regulations under this section of section 258 or Schedule 10A (parent and subsidiary undertakings) does not apply for the purposes of enactments outside the Companies Acts unless the regulations so provide.][1]

1 Inserted by CA 1989, s 20 with effect from 1 April 1990 (SI 1990 No 355) subject to the transitional and saving provisions in Arts 6 to 9 of that Order.

[*Parent and subsidiary undertakings*

258 Parent and subsidiary undertakings

(1) The expressions "parent undertaking" and "subsidiary undertaking" in this Part shall be construed as follows; and a "parent company" means a parent undertaking which is a company.

(2) An undertaking is a parent undertaking in relation to another undertaking, a subsidiary undertaking, if—

(a) it holds a majority of the voting rights in the undertaking, or
(b) it is a member of the undertaking and has the right to appoint or remove a majority of its board of directors, or
(c) it has the right to exercise a dominant influence over the undertaking—
  (i) by virtue of provisions contained in the undertaking's memorandum or articles, or
  (ii) by virtue of a control contract, or
(d) it is a member of the undertaking and controls alone, pursuant to an agreement with other shareholders or members, a majority of the voting rights in the undertaking.

(3) For the purposes of subsection (2) an undertaking shall be treated as a member of another undertaking—

(a) if any of its subsidiary undertakings is a member of that undertaking, or
(b) if any shares in that other undertaking are held by a person acting on behalf of the undertaking or any of its subsidiary undertakings.

(4) An undertaking is also a parent undertaking in relation to another undertaking, a subsidiary undertaking, if it has a participating interest in the undertaking and—

(a) it actually exercises a dominant influence over it, or
(b) it and the subsidiary undertaking are managed on a unified basis.

(5) A parent undertaking shall be treated as the parent undertaking of undertakings in relation to which any of its subsidiary undertakings are, or are to be treated as, parent undertakings; and references to its subsidiary undertakings shall be construed accordingly.

(6) Schedule 10A contains provisions explaining expressions used in this section and otherwise supplementing this section.][1]

1 Inserted by CA 1989, s 21 with effect from 1 April 1990 (SI 1990 No 355) subject to the transitional and saving provisions in Arts 6 to 9 of that Order.

Cross references. See 10A Sch (parent and subsidiary undertakings (supplementary provisions)).

[*Other interpretation provisions*

259 Meaning of "undertaking" and related expressions

(1) In this Part "undertaking" means—

(a) a body corporate or partnership, or
(b) an unincorporated association carrying on a trade or business, with or without a view to profit.

(2) In this Part references to shares—

(a) in relation to an undertaking with a share capital, are to allotted shares;
(b) in relation to an undertaking with capital but no share capital, are to rights to share in the capital of the undertaking; and
(c) in relation to an undertaking without capital, are to interests—
 (i) conferring any right to share in the profits or liability to contribute to the losses of the undertaking, or
 (ii) giving rise to an obligation to contribute to the debts or expenses of the undertaking in the event of a winding up.

(3) Other expressions appropriate to companies shall be construed, in relation to an undertaking which is not a company, as references to the corresponding persons, officers, documents or organs, as the case may be, appropriate to undertakings of that description.

This is subject to provision in any specific context providing for the translation of such expressions.

(4) References in this Part to "fellow subsidiary undertakings" are to undertakings which are subsidiary undertakings of the same parent undertaking but are not parent undertakings or subsidiary undertakings of each other.

(5) In this Part "group undertaking", in relation to an undertaking, means an undertaking which is—

(a) a parent undertaking or subsidiary undertaking of that undertaking, or
(b) a subsidiary undertaking of any parent undertaking of that undertaking.][1]

---

1 Inserted by CA 1989, s 22 with effect from 1 April 1990 (SI 1990 No 355) subject to the transitional and saving provisions in Arts 6 to 9 of that Order.

[260 Participating interests

(1) In this Part a "participating interest" means an interest held by an undertaking in the shares of another undertaking which it holds on a long-term basis for the purpose of securing a contribution to its activities by the exercise of control or influence arising from or related to that interest.

(2) A holding of 20 per cent. or more of the shares of an undertaking shall be presumed to be a participating interest unless the contrary is shown.

(3) The reference in subsection (1) to an interest in shares includes—

(a) an interest which is convertible into an interest in shares, and
(b) an option to acquire shares or any such interest;

and an interest or option falls within paragraph (a) or (b) notwithstanding that the shares to which it relates are, until the conversion or the exercise of the option, unissued.

(4) For the purposes of this section an interest held on behalf of an undertaking shall be treated as held by it.

(5) For the purposes of this section as it applies in relation to the expression "participating interest" in section 258(4) (definition of "subsidiary undertaking")—

(a) there shall be attributed to an undertaking any interests held by any of its subsidiary undertakings, and
(b) the references in subsection (1) to the purpose and activities of an undertaking include the purposes and activities of any of its subsidiary undertakings and of the group as a whole.

(6) In the balance sheet and profit and loss formats set out in Part I of Schedule 4, "participating interest" does not include an interest in a group undertaking.

(7) For the purposes of this section as it applies in relation to the expression "participating interest"—

(a) in those formats as they apply in relation to group accounts, and
(b) in paragraph 20 of Schedule 4A (group accounts: undertakings to be accounted for as associated undertakings),

the references in subsections (1) to (4) to the interest held by, and the purposes and activities of, the undertaking concerned shall be construed as references to the interest held by, and the purposes and activities of, the group (within the meaning of paragraph 1 of that Schedule).][1]

1 Inserted by CA 1989, s 22 with effect from 1 April 1990 (SI 1990 No 355) subject to the transitional and saving provisions in Arts 6 to 9 of that Order.

[261 Notes to the accounts

(1) Information required by this Part to be given in notes to a company's annual accounts may be contained in the accounts or in a separate document annexed to the accounts.

(2) References in this Part to a company's annual accounts, or to a balance sheet or profit and loss account, include notes to the accounts giving information which is required by any provision of this Act, and required or allowed by any such provision to be given in a note to company accounts.][1]

1 Inserted by CA 1989, s 22 with effect from 1 April 1990 (SI 1990 No 355) subject to the transitional and saving provisions in Arts 6 to 9 of that Order.

[262 Minor definitions

(1) In this Part—

"annual accounts" means—

(a) the individual accounts required by section 226, and
(b) any group accounts required by section 227,

(but see also section 230 (treatment of individual profit and loss account where group accounts prepared));

"annual report", in relation to a company, means the directors' report required by section 234;

"balance sheet date" means the date as at which the balance sheet was made up;

"capitalisation", in relation to work or costs, means treating that work or those costs as a fixed asset;

"credit institution" means an undertaking carrying on a deposit-taking business within the meaning of the Banking Act 1987;

"fixed assets" means assets of a company which are intended for use on a continuing basis in the company's activities, and "current assets" means assets not intended for such use;

"group" means a parent undertaking and its subsidiary undertakings;

"included in the consolidation", in relation to group accounts, or "included in consolidated group accounts", means that the undertaking is included in the accounts by the method of full (and not proportional) consolidation, and references to an undertaking excluded from consolidation shall be construed accordingly;

"purchase price", in relation to an asset of a company or any raw materials or consumables used in the production of such an asset, includes any consideration (whether in cash or otherwise) given by the company in respect of that asset or those materials or consumables, as the case may be;

"qualified", in relation to an auditors' report, means that the report does not state the auditors' unqualified opinion that the accounts have been properly prepared in accordance with this Act or, in the case of an undertaking not required to prepare accounts in accordance with this Act, under any corresponding legislation under which it is required to prepare accounts;

"true and fair view" refers—

(a) in the case of individual accounts, to the requirement of section 226(2), and
(b) in the case of group accounts, to the requirement of section 227(3);

"turnover", in relation to a company, means the amounts derived from the provision of goods and services falling within the company's ordinary activities, after deduction of—

(i) trade discounts,
(ii) value added tax, and
(iii) any other taxes based on the amounts so derived.

(2) In the case of an undertaking not trading for profit, any reference in this Part to a profit and loss account is to an income and expenditure account; and references to profit and loss and, in relation to group accounts, to a consolidated profit and loss account shall be construed accordingly.

(3) References in this Part to "realised profits" and "realised losses", in relation to a company's accounts, are to such profits or losses of the company as fall to be treated as realised in accordance with principles generally accepted, at the time when the accounts are prepared, with respect to the determination for accounting purposes of realised profits or losses.

This is without prejudice to—

(a) the construction of any other expression (where appropriate) by reference to accepted accounting principles or practice, or

(b) any specific provision for the treatment of profits or losses of any description as realised.][1]

[1] Inserted by CA 1989, s 22 with effect from 1 April 1990 (SI 1990 No 355) subject to the transitional and saving provisions in Arts 6 to 9 of that Order.

[262A Index of defined expressions

The following Table shows the provisions of this Part defining or otherwise explaining expressions used in this Part (other than expressions used only in the same section or paragraph)—

accounting reference date and accounting reference period	section 224
accounting standards and applicable accounting standards	section 256
annual accounts	
(generally)	section 262(1)
(includes notes to the accounts)	section 261(2)
annual report	section 262(1)
associated undertaking (in Schedule 4A)	paragraph 20 of that Schedule
balance sheet (includes notes)	section 261(2)
balance sheet date	section 262(1)
banking group	section 255A(3)
capitalisation (in relation to work or costs)	section 262(1)
credit institution	section 262(1)
current assets	section 262(1)
fellow subsidiary undertaking	section 259(4)
financial year	section 223
fixed assets	section 262(1)
group	section 262(1)
group undertaking	section 259(5)
historical cost accounting rules (in Schedule 4)	paragraph 29 of that Schedule
included in the consolidation and related expressions	section 262(1)
individual accounts	section 262(1)
insurance group	section 255A(4)
land of freehold tenure and land of leasehold tenure (in relation to Scotland)	
—in Schedule 4	paragraph 93 of that Schedule
—in Schedule 9	paragraph 36 of that Schedule
lease, long lease and short lease	
—in Schedule 4	paragraph 83 of that Schedule
—in Schedule 9	paragraph 34 of that Schedule
listed investment	
—in Schedule 4	paragraph 84 of that Schedule
—in Schedule 9	paragraph 33 of that Schedule

notes to the accounts	section 261(1)
parent undertaking (and parent company)	section 258 and Schedule 10A
participating interest	section 260
pension costs (in Schedule 4)	paragraph 94(2) and (3) of that Schedule
period allowed for laying and delivering accounts and reports	section 244
profit and loss account	
(includes notes)	section 261(2)
(in relation to a company not trading for profit)	section 262(2)
provision	
—in Schedule 4	paragraphs 88 and 89 of that Schedule
—in Schedule 9	paragraph 32 of that Schedule
purchase price	section 262(1)
qualified	section 262(1)
realised losses and realised profits	section 262(3)
reserve (in Schedule 9)	paragraph 32 of that Schedule
shares	section 259(2)
social security costs (in Schedule 4)	paragraph 94(1) and (3) of that Schedule
special provisions for banking and insurance companies and groups	sections 255 and 255A
subsidiary undertaking	section 258 and Schedule 10A
true and fair view	section 262(1)
turnover	section 262(1)
undertaking and related expressions	section 259(1) to (3).][1]

[1] Inserted by CA 1989, s 22 with effect from 1 April 1990 (SI 1990 No 355) subject to the transitional and saving provisions in Arts 6 to 9 of that Order.

Notes. The original provisions of Part VII above (Secs 221-262) were replaced by CA 1989, ss 1-22 which inserted new sections 221-262A above.

PART VIII DISTRIBUTION OF PROFITS AND ASSETS

Limits of company's power of distribution

263 Certain distributions prohibited

(1) A company shall not make a distribution except out of profits available for the purpose.

(2) In this Part, "distribution" means every description of distribution of a company's assets to its members, whether in cash or otherwise, except distribution by way of—

(a) an issue of shares as fully or partly paid bonus shares,
(b) the redemption or purchase of any of the company's own shares out of capital (including the proceeds of any fresh issue of shares) or out of unrealised profits in accordance with Chapter VII of Part V,
(c) the reduction of share capital by extinguishing or reducing the liability of any of the members on any of the company's shares in respect of share capital not paid up, or by paying off paid up share capital, and
(d) a distribution of assets to members of the company on its winding up.

(3) For purposes of this Part, a company's profits available for distribution are its accumulated, realised profits, so far as not previously utilised by distribution or capitalisation, less its accumulated, realised losses, so far as not previously written off in a reduction or reorganisation of capital duly made.

This is subject to the provision made by sections 265 and 266 for investment and other companies.

(4) A company shall not apply an unrealised profit in paying up debentures, or any amounts unpaid on its issued shares.

(5) Where the directors of a company are, after making all reasonable enquiries, unable to determine whether a particular profit made before 22nd December 1980 is realised or unrealised, they may treat the profit as realised; and where after making such enquiries they are unable to determine whether a particular loss so made is realised or unrealised, they may treat the loss as unrealised.

Cross references. See Secs 270–276 (distributions not contravening provisions).

264 Restriction on distribution of assets

(1) A public company may only make a distribution at any time—

(a) if at that time the amount of its net assets is not less than the aggregate of its called-up share capital and undistributable reserves, and
(b) if, and to the extent that, the distribution does not reduce the amount of those assets to less than that aggregate.

This is subject to the provision made by sections 265 and 266 for investment and other companies.

(2) In subsection (1), "net assets" means the aggregate of the company's assets less the aggregate of its liabilities ("liabilities" to include any provision for liabilities or charges within paragraph 89 of Schedule 4).

(3) A company's undistributable reserves are—

(a) the share premium account,

(b) the capital redemption reserve,
(c) the amount by which the company's accumulated, unrealised profits, so far as not previously utilised by capitalisation of a description to which this paragraph applies, exceed its accumulated, unrealised losses (so far as not previously written off in a reduction or reorganisation of capital duly made), and
(d) any other reserve which the company is prohibited from distributing by any enactment (other than one contained in this Part) or by its memorandum or articles;

and paragraph (c) applies to every description of capitalisation except a transfer of profits of the company to its capital redemption reserve on or after 22nd December 1980.

(4) A public company shall not include any uncalled share capital as an asset in any accounts relevant for purposes of this section.

Cross references. See Secs 270–276 (distributions not contravening provisions).

---

265 Other distributions by investment companies

(1) Subject to the following provisions of this section, an investment company (defined in section 266) may also make a distribution at any time out of its accumulated, realised revenue profits, so far as not previously utilised by distribution or capitalisation, less its accumulated revenue losses (whether realised or unrealised), so far as not previously written off in a reduction or reorganisation of capital duly made—

(a) if at that time the amount of its assets is at least equal to one and a half times the aggregate of its liabilities, and
(b) if, and to the extent that, the distribution does not reduce that amount to less than one and a half times that aggregate.

(2) In subsection (1)(a), "liabilities" includes any provision for liabilities or charges (within the meaning of paragraph 89 of Schedule 4).

(3) The company shall not include any uncalled share capital as an asset in any accounts relevant for purposes of this section.

(4) An investment company may not make a distribution by virtue of subsection (1) unless—

(a) its shares are listed on a [recognised investment exchange other than an overseas investment exchange within the meaning of the Financial Services Act 1986][1], and
(b) during the relevant period it has not—
   (i) distributed any of its capital profits, or
   (ii) applied any unrealised profits or any capital profits (realised or unrealised) in paying up debentures or amounts unpaid on its issued shares.

(5) The "relevant period" under subsection (4) is the period beginning with—

(a) the first day of the accounting reference period immediately preceding that in which the proposed distribution is to be made, or
(b) where the distribution is to be made in the company's first accounting reference period, the first day of that period,

and ending with the date of the distribution.

(6) An investment company may not make a distribution by virtue of subsection (1) unless the company gave to the registrar of companies the requisite notice (that is, notice under section 266(1)) of the company's intention to carry on business as an investment company—

(a) before the beginning of the relevant period under subsection (4), or

(b) in the case of a company incorporated on or after 22nd December 1980, as soon as may have been reasonably practicable after the date of its incorporation.

---

1 Substituted by FSA 1986, s 212(2), 16 Sch 19 with effect from 29 April 1988 (see SI 1988 No 740). Previously 'recognised stock exchange'.

Cross references. See Sec 266; Secs 270–276 (distributions not contravening provisions).

---

266 Meaning of "investment company"

(1) In section 265 "investment company" means a public company which has given notice in the prescribed form (which has not been revoked) to the registrar of companies of its intention to carry on business as an investment company, and has since the date of that notice complied with the requirements specified below.

(2) Those requirements are—

(a) that the business of the company consists of investing its funds mainly in securities, with the aim of spreading investment risk and giving members of the company the benefit of the results of the management of its funds,

(b) that none of the company's holdings in companies (other than those which are for the time being in investment companies) represents more than 15 per cent. by value of the investing company's investments,

(c) that distribution of the company's capital profits is prohibited by its memorandum or articles of association,

(d) that the company has not retained, otherwise than in compliance with this Part, in respect of any accounting reference period more than 15 per cent. of the income it derives from securities.

(3) Notice to the registrar of companies under subsection (1) may be revoked at any time by the company on giving notice in the prescribed form to the registrar that it no longer wishes to be an investment company within the meaning of this section; and, on giving such notice, the company ceases to be such a company.

(4) [Subsections (1A) to (3) of section 842 of the Income and Corporation Taxes Act 1988 apply for the purposes of subsection (2)(b) above as for those of subsection (1)(b) of that section.][1]

---

1 Substituted by FA 1988, s 117(3) with effect for companies' accounting periods ending after 5 April 1988. Previously
'Section 359(2) and (3) of the Income and Corporation Taxes Act 1970 and section 93(6)(b) of the Finance Act 1972 apply for purposes of subsection (2)(b) as for those of section 359(1)(b) of the Act first mentioned.'

267 Extension of ss 265, 266 to other companies

(1) The Secretary of State may by regulations in a statutory instrument extend the provisions of sections 265 and 266 (with or without modifications) to companies whose principal business consists of investing their funds in securities, land or other assets with the aim of spreading investment risk and giving their members the benefit of the results of the management of the assets.

(2) Regulations under this section—

(a) may make different provision for different classes of companies and may contain such transitional and supplemental provisions as the Secretary of State considers necessary, and
(b) shall not be made unless a draft of the statutory instrument containing them has been laid before Parliament and approved by a resolution of each House.

268 Realised profits of insurance company with long term business

(1) Where an insurance company to which Part II of the Insurance Companies Act 1982 applies carries on long term business—

(a) any amount properly transferred to the profit and loss account of the company from a surplus in the fund or funds maintained by it in respect of that business, and
(b) any deficit in that fund or those funds,

are to be (respectively) treated, for purposes of this Part, as a realised profit and a realised loss; and, subject to this, any profit or loss arising in that business is to be left out of account for those purposes.

(2) In subsection (1)—

(a) the reference to a surplus in any fund or funds of an insurance company is to an excess of the assets representing that fund or those funds over the liabilities of the company attributable to its long term business, as shown by an actuarial investigation, and
(b) the reference to a deficit in any such fund or funds is to the excess of those liabilities over those assets, as so shown.

(3) In this section—

(a) "actuarial investigation" means an investigation to which section 18 of the Insurance Companies Act 1982 (periodic actuarial investigation of company with long term business) applies or which is made in pursuance of a requirement imposed by section 42 of that Act (actuarial investigation required by Secretary of State); and
(b) "long term business" has the same meaning as in that Act.

269 Treatment of development costs

(1) Subject as follows, where development costs are shown as an asset in a company's accounts, any amount shown in respect of those costs is to be treated—

(a) under section 263, as a realised loss, and
(b) under section 265, as a realised revenue loss.

(2) This does not apply to any part of that amount representing an unrealised profit made on revaluation of those costs; nor does it apply if—

(a) there are special circumstances in the company's case justifying the directors in deciding that the amount there mentioned is not to be treated as required by subsection (1), and

(b) the note to the accounts required by paragraph 20 of Schedule 4 (reasons for showing development costs as an asset) states that the amount is not to be so treated and explains the circumstances relied upon to justify the decision of the directors to that effect.

Relevant accounts

270 Distribution to be justified by reference to company's accounts

(1) This section and sections 271 to 276 below are for determining the question whether a distribution may be made by a company without contravening sections 263, 264 or 265.

(2) The amount of a distribution which may be made is determined by reference to the following items as stated in the company's accounts—

(a) profits, losses, assets and liabilities,

(b) provisions of any of the kinds mentioned in paragraphs 88 and 89 of Schedule 4 (depreciation, diminution in value of assets, retentions to meet liabilities, etc.), and

(c) share capital and reserves (including undistributable reserves).

(3) Except in a case falling within the next subsection, the company's accounts which are relevant for this purpose are its last annual accounts, that is to say those prepared under Part VII which were laid in respect of the last preceding accounting reference period in respect of which accounts so prepared were laid; and for this purpose accounts are laid if section 241(1) has been complied with in relation to them.

(4) In the following two cases—

(a) where the distribution would be found to contravene the relevant section if reference were made only to the company's last annual accounts, or

(b) where the distribution is proposed to be declared during the company's first accounting reference period, or before any accounts are laid in respect of that period,

the accounts relevant under this section (called "interim accounts" in the first case, and "initial accounts" in the second) are those necessary to enable a reasonable judgment to be made as to the amounts of the items mentioned in subsection (2) above.

(5) The relevant section is treated as contravened in the case of a distribution unless the statutory requirements about the relevant accounts (that is, the requirements of this and the following three sections, as and where applicable) are complied with in relation to that distribution.

Cross references. See Sec 274 (successive distributions).

---

271 Requirements for last annual accounts

(1) If the company's last annual accounts constitute the only accounts relevant under section 270, the statutory requirements in respect of them are as follows.

(2) The accounts must have been properly prepared in accordance with this Act, or have been so prepared subject only to matters which are not material for determining, by reference to items mentioned in section 270(2), whether the distribution would contravene the relevant section; and, without prejudice to the foregoing—

(a) so much of the accounts as consists of a balance sheet must give a true and fair view of the state of the company's affairs as at the balance sheet date, and

(b) so much of the accounts as consists of a profit and loss account must give a true and fair view of the company's profit or loss for the period in respect of which the accounts were prepared.

(3) The auditors must have made their report on the accounts under [section 235][1]; and the following subsection applies if the report is a qualified report, that is to say, it is not a report without qualification to the effect that in the auditors' opinion the accounts have been properly prepared in accordance with this Act.

(4) The auditors must in that case also have stated in writing (either at the time of their report or subsequently) whether, in their opinion, the matter in respect of which their report is qualified is material for determining, by reference to items mentioned in section 270(2), whether the distribution would contravene the relevant section; and a copy of the statement must have been laid before the company in general meeting.

(5) A statement under subsection (4) suffices for purposes of a particular distribution not only if it relates to a distribution which has been proposed but also if it relates to distributions of any description which includes that particular distribution, notwithstanding that at the time of the statement it has not been proposed.

---

1 Substituted by CA 1989, 10 Sch 4 with effect from 1 April 1990 (SI 1990 No 355) subject to the transitional and saving provisions in Arts 6 to 9 of that Order.
Previously 'section 236'.

---

272 Requirements for interim accounts

(1) The following are the statutory requirements in respect of interim accounts prepared for a proposed distribution by a public company.

(2) The accounts must have been properly prepared, or have been so prepared subject only to matters which are not material for determining, by reference to items mentioned in section 270(2), whether the proposed distribution would contravene the relevant section.

(3) "Properly prepared" means that the accounts must comply with [section 226][1] (applying that section and Schedule 4 with such modifications as are necessary because the accounts are prepared otherwise than in respect of an accounting reference period) and any balance sheet comprised in the accounts must have been signed in accordance with [section 233][2]; and, without prejudice to the foregoing—

(a) so much of the accounts as consists of a balance sheet must give a true and fair view of the state of the company's affairs as at the balance sheet date, and

(b) so much of the accounts as consists of a profit and loss account must give a true and fair view of the company's profit or loss for the period in respect of which the accounts were prepared.

(4) A copy of the accounts must have been delivered to the registrar of companies.

(5) If the accounts are in a language other than English and [the second sentence of section 242(1)][3] (translation) does not apply, a translation into English of the accounts, certified in the prescribed manner to be a correct translation, must also have been delivered to the registrar.

---

1 Substituted by CA 1989, 10 Sch 5 with effect from 1 April 1990 (SI 1990 No 355) subject to the transitional and saving provisions in Arts 6 to 9 of that Order reproduced above Sec 221 above.
Previously 'section 228'.

2 Substituted by CA 1989, 10 Sch 5 with effect as in [1] above.
Previously 'section 238'.

3 Substituted by CA 1989, 10 Sch 6 with effect as in [1] above.
Previously 'section 241(3)(b)'.

Cross references. See SI 1985 No 854, Reg 6 (translation of documents into English).

---

273 Requirements for initial accounts

(1) The following are the statutory requirements in respect of initial accounts prepared for a proposed distribution by a public company.

(2) The accounts must have been properly prepared, or they must have been so prepared subject only to matters which are not material for determining, by reference to items mentioned in section 270(2), whether the proposed distribution would contravene the relevant section.

(3) Section 272(3) applies as respects the meaning of "properly prepared".

(4) The company's auditors must have made a report stating whether, in their opinion, the accounts have been properly prepared; and the following subsection applies if their report is a qualified report, that is to say it is not a report without qualification to the effect that in the auditors' opinion the accounts have been so prepared.

(5) The auditors must in that case also have stated in writing whether, in their opinion, the matter in respect of which their report is qualified is material for determining, by reference to items mentioned in section 270(2), whether the distribution would contravene the relevant section.

(6) A copy of the accounts, of the auditors' report under subsection (4) and of the auditors' statement (if any) under subsection (5) must have been delivered to the registrar of companies.

(7) If the accounts are, or the auditors' report under subsection (4) or their statement (if any) under subsection (5) is, in a language other than English and [the second sentence of section 242(1)][1] (translation) does not apply, a translation into English of the accounts, the report or the statement (as the case may be), certified in the prescribed manner to be a correct translation, must also have been delivered to the registrar.

---

1 Substituted by CA 1989, 10 Sch 6 with effect from 1 April 1990 (SI 1990 No 355) subject to the transitional and saving provisions in Arts 6 to 9 of that Order reproduced above Sec 221 above.
Previously 'section 241(3)(b)'.

Cross references. See SI 1985 No 854, Reg 6 (translation of documents into English).

274 Method of applying s 270 to successive distributions

(1) For the purpose of determining by reference to particular accounts whether a proposed distribution may be made by a company, section 270 has effect, in a case where one or more distributions have already been made in pursuance of determinations made by reference to those same accounts, as if the amount of the proposed distribution was increased by the amount of the distributions so made.

(2) Subsection (1) of this section applies (if it would not otherwise do so) to—

(a) financial assistance lawfully given by a public company out of its distributable profits in a case where the assistance is required to be so given by section 154,
(b) financial assistance lawfully given by a private company out of its distributable profits in a case where the assistance is required to be so given by section 155(2),
(c) financial assistance given by a company in contravention of section 151, in a case where the giving of that assistance reduces the company's net assets or increases its net liabilities,
(d) a payment made by a company in respect of the purchase by it of shares in the company (except a payment lawfully made otherwise than out of distributable profits), and
(e) a payment of any description specified in section 168 (company's purchase of right to acquire its own shares, etc.),

being financial assistance given or payment made since the relevant accounts were prepared, as if any such financial assistance or payment were a distribution already made in pursuance of a determination made by reference to those accounts.

(3) In this section the following definitions apply—

"financial assistance" means the same as in Chapter VI of Part V;

"net assets" has the meaning given by section 154(2)(a); and

"net liabilities", in relation to the giving of financial assistance by a company, means the amount by which the aggregate amount of the company's liabilities (within the meaning of section 154(2)(b)) exceeds the aggregate amount of its assets, taking the amount of the assets and liabilities to be as stated in the company's accounting records immediately before the financial assistance is given.

(4) Subsections (2) and (3) of this section are deemed to be included in Chapter VII of Part V for purposes of the Secretary of State's power to make regulations under section 179.

275 Treatment of assets in the relevant accounts

(1) For purposes of sections 263 and 264, a provision of any kind mentioned in paragraphs 88 and 89 of Schedule 4, other than one in respect of a diminution in value of a fixed asset appearing on a revaluation of all the fixed assets of the company, or of all of its fixed assets other than goodwill, is treated as a realised loss.

(2) If, on the revaluation of a fixed asset, an unrealised profit is shown to have been made and, on or after the revaluation, a sum is written off or retained for depreciation of that asset over a period, then an amount equal to the amount by which that sum exceeds the sum which would have been so written off or retained for the depreciation of that asset over that period, if that profit had not been made, is treated for purposes of sections 263 and 264 as a realised profit made over that period.

(3) Where there is no record of the original cost of an asset, or a record cannot be obtained without unreasonable expense or delay, then for the purpose of determining whether the company has made a profit or loss in respect of that asset, its cost is taken to be the value ascribed to it in the earliest available record of its value made on or after its acquisition by the company.

(4) Subject to subsection (6), any consideration by the directors of the value at a particular time of a fixed asset is treated as a revaluation of the asset for the purposes of determining whether any such revaluation of the company's fixed assets as is required for purposes of the exception from subsection (1) has taken place at that time.

(5) But where any such assets which have not actually been revalued are treated as revalued for those purposes under subsection (4), that exception applies only if the directors are satisfied that their aggregate value at the time in question is not less than the aggregate amount at which they are for the time being stated in the company's accounts.

(6) Where section 271(2), 272(2) or 273(2) applies to the relevant accounts, subsections (4) and (5) above do not apply for the purpose of determining whether a revaluation of the company's fixed assets affecting the amount of the relevant items (that is, the items mentioned in section 270(2)) as stated in those accounts has taken place, unless it is stated in a note to the accounts—

(a) that the directors have considered the value at any time of any fixed assets of the company, without actually revaluing those assets,
(b) that they are satisfied that the aggregate value of those assets at the time in question is or was not less than the aggregate amount at which they are or were for the time being stated in the company's accounts, and
(c) that the relevant items in question are accordingly stated in the relevant accounts on the basis that a revaluation of the company's fixed assets which by virtue of subsections (4) and (5) included the assets in question took place at that time.

276 Distributions in kind

Where a company makes a distribution of or including a non-cash asset, and any part of the amount at which that asset is stated in the accounts relevant for the purposes of the distribution in accordance with sections 270 to 275 represents an unrealised profit, that profit is to be treated as a realised profit—

(a) for the purpose of determining the lawfulness of the distribution in accordance with this Part (whether before or after the distribution takes place), and
(b) for the purpose of the application of paragraphs 12(a) and [34(3)(a)][1] of Schedule 4 (only realised profits to be included in or transferred to the profit and loss account) in relation to anything done with a view to or in connection with the making of that distribution.

1 Substituted by CA 1989, 10 Sch 7 with effect from 1 April 1990 (SI 1990 No 355) subject to the transitional and saving provisions in Arts 6 to 9 of that Order.
Previously '34(4)(b)'.

Supplementary

277 Consequences of unlawful distribution

(1) Where a distribution, or part of one, made by a company to one of its members is made in contravention of this Part and, at the time of the distribution, he knows or has reasonable grounds for believing that it is so made, he is liable to repay it (or that part of it, as the case may be) to the company or (in the case of a distribution made otherwise than in cash) to pay the company a sum equal to the value of the distribution (or part) at that time.

(2) The above is without prejudice to any obligation imposed apart from this section on a member of a company to repay a distribution unlawfully made to him; but this section does not apply in relation to—

(a) financial assistance given by a company in contravention of section 151, or

(b) any payment made by a company in respect of the redemption or purchase by the company of shares in itself.

(3) Subsection (2) of this section is deemed included in Chapter VII of Part V for purposes of the Secretary of State's power to make regulations under section 179.

278 Saving for provision in articles operative before Act of 1980

Where immediately before 22nd December 1980 a company was authorised by a provision of its articles to apply its unrealised profits in paying up in full or in part unissued shares to be allotted to members of the company as fully or partly paid bonus shares, that provision continues (subject to any alteration of the articles) as authority for those profits to be so applied after that date.

279 [Distributions by banking or insurance companies

Where a company's accounts relevant for the purposes of this Part are prepared in accordance with the special provisions of Part VII relating to banking or insurance companies, sections 264 to 275 apply with the modifications shown in Schedule 11.][1]

1 Substituted by CA 1989, 10 Sch 8 with effect from 1 April 1990 (SI 1990 No 355) subject to the transitional and saving provisions in Arts 6 to 9 of that Order.
Previously
'Distributions by special category companies
Where a company's accounts relevant for the purposes of this Part are special category, sections 265 to 275 apply with the modifications shown in Schedule 11.'

280 Definitions for Part VIII

(1) The following has effect for the interpretation of this Part.

(2) "Capitalisation", in relation to a company's profits, means any of the following operations (whenever carried out)—

(a) applying the profits in wholly or partly paying up unissued shares in the company to be allotted to members of the company as fully or partly paid bonus shares, or

(b) transferring the profits to capital redemption reserve.

(3) References to profits and losses of any description are (respectively) to profits and losses of that description made at any time and, except where the context otherwise requires, are (respectively) to revenue and capital profits and revenue and capital losses.

281 Saving for other restraints on distribution

The provisions of this Part are without prejudice to any enactment or rule of law, or any provision of a company's memorandum or articles, restricting the sums out of which, or the cases in which, a distribution may be made.

PART IX A COMPANY'S MANAGEMENT; DIRECTORS AND SECRETARIES; THEIR QUALIFICATIONS, DUTIES AND RESPONSIBILITIES

Other provisions about directors and officers

310 Provisions exempting officers and auditors from liability

(1) This section applies to any provision, whether contained in a company's articles or in any contract with the company or otherwise, for exempting any officer of the company or any person (whether an officer or not) employed by the company as auditor from, or indemnifying him against, any liability which by virtue of any rule of law would otherwise attach to him in respect of any negligence, default, breach of duty or breach of trust of which he may be guilty in relation to the company.

(2) Except as provided by the following subsection, any such provision is void.

(3) [This section does not prevent a company—

(a) from purchasing and maintaining for any such officer or auditor insurance against any such liability, or

(b) from indemnifying any such officer or auditor against any liability incurred by him—

(i) in defending any proceedings (whether civil or criminal) in which judgment is given in his favour or he is acquitted, or

(ii) in connection with any application under section 144(3) or (4) (acquisition of shares by innocent nominee) or section 727 (general power to grant relief in case of honest and reasonable conduct) in which relief is granted to him by the court.][1]

---

1 Substituted by CA 1989, s 137 with effect from 1 April 1990 (SI 1990 No 355).
Previously
'A company may, in pursuance of such a provision, indemnify any such officer or auditor against any liability incurred by him in defending any proceedings (whether civil or criminal) in which judgment is given in his favour or he is acquitted, or in connection with any application under section 144(3) or (4) (acquisition of shares by innocent nominee) or section 727 (director in default, but not dishonest or unreasonable), in which relief is granted to him by the court.'

PART X ENFORCEMENT OF FAIR DEALING BY DIRECTORS

Restrictions on directors taking financial advantage

311 Prohibition on tax-free payments to directors

(1) It is not lawful for a company to pay a director remuneration (whether as director or otherwise) free of income tax, or otherwise calculated by reference to or varying with the amount of his income tax, or to or with any rate of income tax.

(2) Any provision contained in a company's articles, or in any contract, or in any resolution of a company or a company's directors, for payment to a director of remuneration as above mentioned has effect as if it provided for payment, as a gross sum subject to income tax, of the net sum for which it actually provides.

312 Payment to director for loss of office etc.

It is not lawful for a company to make to a director of the company any payment by way of compensation for loss of office, or as consideration for or in connection with his retirement from office, without particulars of the proposed payment (including its amount) being disclosed to members of the company and the proposal being approved by the company.

Cross references. See Sec 316(3).

313 Company approval for property transfer

(1) It is not lawful, in connection with the transfer of the whole or any part of the undertaking or property of a company, for any payment to be made to a director of the company by way of compensation for loss of office, or as consideration for or in connection with his retirement from office, unless particulars of the proposed payment (including its amount) have been disclosed to members of the company and the proposal approved by the company.

(2) Where a payment unlawful under this section is made to a director, the amount received is deemed to be received by him in trust for the company.

Cross references. See Sec 316(3)(4).

314 Director's duty of disclosure on takeover, etc.

(1) This section applies where, in connection with the transfer to any persons of all or any of the shares in a company, being a transfer resulting from—

(a) an offer made to the general body of shareholders; or
(b) an offer made by or on behalf of some other body corporate with a view to the company becoming its subsidiary or a subsidiary of its holding company; or
(c) an offer made by or on behalf of an individual with a view to his obtaining the right to exercise or control the exercise of not less than one-third of the voting power at any general meeting of the company; or
(d) any other offer which is conditional on acceptance to a given extent,

a payment is to be made to a director of the company by way of compensation for loss of office, or as consideration for or in connection with his retirement from office.

(2) It is in those circumstances the director's duty to take all reasonable steps to secure that particulars of the proposed payment (including its amount) are included in or sent with any notice of the offer made for their shares which is given to any shareholders.

(3) If—

(a) the director fails to take those steps, or
(b) any person who has been properly required by the director to include those particulars in or send them with the notice required by subsection (2) fails to do so,

he is liable to a fine.

Cross references. See Sec 315; Sec 316(3)(4).

315 Consequences of non-compliance with s 314

(1) If in the case of any such payment to a director as is mentioned in section 314(1)—

(a) his duty under that section is not complied with, or
(b) the making of the proposed payment is not, before the transfer of any shares in pursuance of the offer, approved by a meeting (summoned for the purpose) of the holders of the shares to which the offer relates and of other holders of shares of the same class as any of those shares,

any sum received by the director on account of the payment is deemed to have been received by him in trust for persons who have sold their shares as a result of the offer made; and the expenses incurred by him in distributing that sum amongst those persons shall be borne by him and not retained out of that sum.

(2) Where—

(a) the shareholders referred to in subsection (l)(b) are not all the members of the company, and
(b) no provision is made by the articles for summoning or regulating the meeting referred to in that paragraph,

the provisions of this Act and of the company's articles relating to general meetings of the company apply (for that purpose) to the meeting either without modification or with such modifications as the Secretary of State on the application of any person concerned may direct for the purpose of adapting them to the circumstances of the meeting.

(3) If at a meeting summoned for the purpose of approving any payment as required by subsection (1)(b) a quorum is not present and, after the meeting has been adjourned to a later date, a quorum is again not present, the payment is deemed for the purposes of that subsection to have been approved.

Cross references. See Sec 316(3)(4).

316 Provisions supplementing ss 312 to 315

(1) Where in proceedings for the recovery of any payment as having, by virtue of section 313(2) or 315(1), been received by any person in trust, it is shown that—

(a) the payment was made in pursuance of any arrangement entered into as part of the agreement for the transfer in question, or within one year before or two years after that agreement or the offer leading to it; and

(b) the company or any person to whom the transfer was made was privy to that arrangement,

the payment is deemed, except in so far as the contrary is shown, to be one to which the provisions mentioned above in this subsection apply.

(2) If in connection with any such transfer as is mentioned in any of sections 313 to 315—

(a) the price to be paid to a director of the company whose office is to be abolished or who is to retire from office for any shares in the company held by him is in excess of the price which could at the time have been obtained by other holders of the like shares; or
(b) any valuable consideration is given to any such director,

the excess or the money value of the consideration (as the case may be) is deemed for the purposes of that section to have been a payment made to him by way of compensation for loss of office or as consideration for or in connection with his retirement from office.

(3) References in sections 312 to 315 to payments made to a director by way of compensation for loss of office or as consideration for or in connection with his retirement from office, do not include any bona fide payment by way of damages for breach of contract or by way of pension in respect of past services.

"Pension" here includes any superannuation allowance, superannuation gratuity or similar payment.

(4) Nothing in sections 313 to 315 prejudices the operation of any rule of law requiring disclosure to be made with respect to such payments as are there mentioned, or with respect to any other like payments made or to be made to a company's directors.

317 Directors to disclose interest in contracts

(1) It is the duty of a director of a company who is in any way, whether directly or indirectly, interested in a contract or proposed contract with the company to declare the nature of his interest at a meeting of the directors of the company.

(2) In the case of a proposed contract, the declaration shall be made—

(a) at the meeting of the directors at which the question of entering into the contract is first taken into consideration; or
(b) if the director was not at the date of that meeting interested in the proposed contract, at the next meeting of the directors held after he became so interested;

and, in a case where the director becomes interested in a contract after it is made, the declaration shall be made at the first meeting of the directors held after he becomes so interested.

(3) For purposes of this section, a general notice given to the directors of a company by a director to the effect that—

(a) he is a member of a specified company or firm and is to be regarded as interested in any contract which may, after the date of the notice, be made with that company or firm; or

(b) he is to be regarded as interested in any contract which may after the date of the notice be made with a specified person who is connected with him (within the meaning of section 346 below),

is deemed a sufficient declaration of interest in relation to any such contract.

(4) However, no such notice is of effect unless either it is given at a meeting of the directors or the director takes reasonable steps to secure that it is brought up and read at the next meeting of the directors after it is given.

(5) A reference in this section to a contract includes any transaction or arrangement (whether or not constituting a contract) made or entered into on or after 22nd December 1980.

(6) For purposes of this section, a transaction or arrangement of a kind described in section 330 (prohibition of loans, quasi-loans etc. to directors) made by a company for a director of the company or a person connected with such a director is treated (if it would not otherwise be so treated, and whether or not it is prohibited by that section) as a transaction or arrangement in which that director is interested.

(7) A director who fails to comply with this section is liable to a fine.

(8) This section applies to a shadow director as it applies to a director, except that a shadow director shall declare his interest, not at a meeting of the directors, but by a notice in writing to the directors which is either—

(a) a specific notice given before the date of the meeting at which, if he had been a director, the declaration would be required by subsection (2) to be made; or

(b) a notice which under subsection (3) falls to be treated as a sufficient declaration of that interest (or would fall to be so treated apart from subsection (4)).

(9) Nothing in this section prejudices the operation of any rule of law restricting directors of a company from having an interest in contracts with the company.

318 Directors' service contracts to be open to inspection

(1) Subject to the following provisions, every company shall keep at an appropriate place—

(a) in the case of each director whose contract of service with the company is in writing, a copy of that contract;

(b) in the case of each director whose contract of service with the company is not in writing, a written memorandum setting out its terms; and

(c) in the case of each director who is employed under a contract of service with a subsidiary of the company, a copy of that contract or, if it is not in writing, a written memorandum setting out its terms.

(2) All copies and memoranda kept by a company in pursuance of subsection (1) shall be kept at the same place.

(3) The following are appropriate places for the purposes of subsection (1)—

(a) the company's registered office;

(b) the place where its register of members is kept (if other than its registered office);

(c) its principal place of business, provided that is situated in that part of Great Britain in which the company is registered.

(4) Every company shall send notice in the prescribed form to the registrar of companies of the place where copies and memoranda are kept in compliance with subsection (1), and of any change in that place, save in a case in which they have at all times been kept at the company's registered office.

(5) Subsection (1) does not apply to a director's contract of service with the company or with a subsidiary of it if that contract required him to work wholly or mainly outside the United Kingdom; but the company shall keep a memorandum—

(a) in the case of a contract of service with the company, giving the director's name and setting out the provisions of the contract relating to its duration;

(b) in the case of a contract of service with a subsidiary, giving the director's name and the name and place of incorporation of the subsidiary, and setting out the provisions of the contract relating to its duration,

at the same place as copies and memoranda are kept by the company in pursuance of subsection (1).

(6) A shadow director is treated for purposes of this section as a director.

(7) Every copy and memorandum required by subsection (1) or (5) to be kept shall [. . .][1] be open to inspection of any member of the company without charge.

(8) If—

(a) default is made in complying with subsection (1) or (5), or

(b) an inspection required under subsection (7) is refused, or

(c) default is made for 14 days in complying with subsection (4),

the company and every officer of it who is in default is liable to a fine and, for continued contravention, to a daily default fine.

(9) In the case of a refusal of an inspection required under subsection (7) of a copy or memorandum, the court may by order compel an immediate inspection of it.

(10) Subsections (1) and (5) apply to a variation of a director's contract of service as they apply to the contract.

(11) This section does not require that there be kept a copy of, or memorandum setting out the terms of, a contract (or its variation) at a time when the unexpired portion of the term for which the contract is to be in force is less than 12 months, or at a time at which the contract can, within the next ensuing 12 months, be terminated by the company without payment of compensation.

---

1 Deleted by CA 1989, s 143 with effect from a date to be appointed.
Previously ', during business hours (subject to such reasonable restrictions as the company may in general meeting impose, so that not less than 2 hours in each day be allowed for inspection),'.

319 Director's contract of employment for more than 5 years

(1) This section applies in respect of any term of an agreement whereby a director's employment with the company of which he is a director or, where he is the director of a holding company, his employment within the group is to continue, or may be continued, otherwise than at the instance of the company (whether under the original agreement or under a new agreement entered into in pursuance of it), for a period of more than 5 years during which the employment—

(a) cannot be terminated by the company by notice; or
(b) can be so terminated only in specified circumstances.

(2) In any case where—

(a) a person is or is to be employed with a company under an agreement which cannot be terminated by the company by notice or can be so terminated only in specified circumstances; and
(b) more than 6 months before the expiration of the period for which he is or is to be so employed, the company enters into a further agreement (otherwise than in pursuance of a right conferred by or under the original agreement on the other party to it) under which he is to be employed with the company or, where he is a director of a holding company, within the group,

this section applies as if to the period for which he is to be employed under that further agreement there were added a further period equal to the unexpired period of the original agreement.

(3) A company shall not incorporate in an agreement such a term as is mentioned in subsection (1), unless the term is first approved by a resolution of the company in general meeting and, in the case of a director of a holding company, by a resolution of that company in general meeting.

(4) No approval is required to be given under this section by any body corporate unless it is a company within the meaning of this Act, or is registered under section 680, or if it is a wholly-owned subsidiary of any body corporate, wherever incorporated.

(5) A resolution of a company approving such a term as is mentioned in subsection (1) shall not be passed at a general meeting of the company unless a written memorandum setting out the proposed agreement incorporating the term is available for inspection by members of the company both—

(a) at the company's registered office for not less than 15 days ending with the date of the meeting; and
(b) at the meeting itself.

(6) A term incorporated in an agreement in contravention of this section is, to the extent that it contravenes the section, void; and that agreement and, in a case where subsection (2) applies, the original agreement are deemed to contain a term entitling the company to terminate it at any time by the giving of reasonable notice.

(7) In this section—

(a) "employment" includes employment under a contract for services; and
(b) "group", in relation to a director of a holding company, means the group which consists of that company and its subsidiaries;

and for purposes of this section a shadow director is treated as a director.

Cross references. See Sec 347 (transactions under foreign law); Sec 741 (shadow directors).

320 Substantial property transactions involving directors, etc.

(1) With the exceptions provided by the section next following, a company shall not enter into an arrangement—

(a) whereby a director of the company or its holding company, or a person connected with such a director, acquires or is to acquire one or more non-cash assets of the requisite value from the company; or

(b) whereby the company acquires or is to acquire one or more non-cash assets of the requisite value from such a director or a person so connected,

unless the arrangement is first approved by a resolution of the company in general meeting and, if the director or connected person is a director of its holding company or a person connected with such a director, by a resolution in general meeting of the holding company.

(2) For this purpose a non-cash asset is of the requisite value if at the time the arrangement in question is entered into its value is not less than £1,000 but (subject to that) exceeds £50,000 or 10 per cent. of the company's asset value, that is—

(a) except in a case falling within paragraph (b) below, the value of the company's net assets determined by reference to the accounts prepared and laid under Part VII in respect of the last preceding financial year in respect of which such accounts were so laid; and

(b) where no accounts have been so prepared and laid before that time, the amount of the company's called-up share capital.

(3) For purposes of this section and sections 321 and 322, a shadow director is treated as a director.

Cross references. See Secs 321, 322; Sec 347 (transactions under foreign law); Sec 741 (shadow directors).

321 Exceptions from s 320

(1) No approval is required to be given under section 320 by any body corporate unless it is a company within the meaning of this Act or registered under section 680 or, if it is a wholly-owned subsidiary of any body corporate, wherever incorporated.

(2) Section 320(1) does not apply to an arrangement for the acquisition of a non-cash asset—

(a) if the asset is to be acquired by a holding company from any of its wholly-owned subsidiaries or from a holding company by any of its wholly-owned subsidiaries, or by one wholly-owned subsidiary of a holding company from another wholly-owned subsidiary of that same holding company, or

(b) if the arrangement is entered into by a company which is being wound up, unless the winding up is a members' voluntary winding up.

(3) Section 320(1)(a) does not apply to an arrangement whereby a person is to acquire an asset from a company of which he is a member, if the arrangement is made with that person in his character as a member.

[(4) Section 320(1) does not apply to a transaction on a recognised investment exchange which is effected by a director, or a person connected with him, through the agency of a person who in relation to the transaction acts as an independent broker.

For this purpose an "independent broker" means—

(a) in relation to a transaction on behalf of a director, a person who independently of the director selects the person with whom the transaction is to be effected, and
(b) in relation to a transaction on behalf of a person connected with a director, a person who independently of that person or the director selects the person with whom the transaction is to be effected;

and "recognised", in relation to an investment exchange, means recognised under the Financial Services Act 1986.][1]

---

1 Inserted by CA 1989, 19 Sch 8 with effect from 1 March 1990 (SI 1990 No 142).

Cross references. See Sec 320(3); Sec 347 (transactions under foreign law); Sec 741 (shadow directors).

---

322 Liabilities arising from contravention of s 320

(1) An arrangement entered into by a company in contravention of section 320, and any transaction entered into in pursuance of the arrangement (whether by the company or any other person) is voidable at the instance of the company unless one or more of the conditions specified in the next subsection is satisfied.

(2) Those conditions are that—

(a) restitution of any money or other asset which is the subject-matter of the arrangement or transaction is no longer possible or the company has been indemnified in pursuance of this section by any other person for the loss or damage suffered by it; or
(b) any rights acquired bona fide for value and without actual notice of the contravention by any person who is not a party to the arrangement or transaction would be affected by its avoidance; or
(c) the arrangement is, within a reasonable period, affirmed by the company in general meeting and, if it is an arrangement for the transfer of an asset to or by a director of its holding company or a person who is connected with such a director, is so affirmed with the approval of the holding company given by a resolution in general meeting.

(3) If an arrangement is entered into with a company by a director of the company or its holding company or a person connected with him in contravention of section 320, that director and the person so connected, and any other director of the company who authorised the arrangement or any transaction entered into in pursuance of such an arrangement, is liable—

(a) to account to the company for any gain which he has made directly or indirectly by the arrangement or transaction, and
(b) (jointly and severally with any other person liable under this subsection) to indemnify the company for any loss or damage resulting from the arrangement or transaction.

(4) Subsection (3) is without prejudice to any liability imposed otherwise than by that subsection, and is subject to the following two subsections; and the liability under subsection (3) arises whether or not the arrangement or transaction entered into has been avoided in pursuance of subsection (1).

(5) If an arrangement is entered into by a company and a person connected with a director of the company or its holding company in contravention of section 320, that director is not liable under subsection (3) if he shows that he took all reasonable steps to secure the company's compliance with that section.

(6) In any case, a person so connected and any such other director as is mentioned in subsection (3) is not so liable if he shows that, at the time the arrangement was entered into, he did not know the relevant circumstances constituting the contravention.

Cross references. See Sec 320(3); Sec 347 (transactions under foreign law); Sec 741 (shadow directors).

[322A Invalidity of certain transactions involving directors, etc.

(1) This section applies where a company enters into a transaction to which the parties include—

(a) a director of the company or of its holding company, or
(b) a person connected with such a director or a company with whom such a director is associated,

and the board of directors, in connection with the transaction, exceed any limitation on their powers under the company's constitution.

(2) The transaction is voidable at the instance of the company.

(3) Whether or not it is avoided, any such party to the transaction as is mentioned in subsection (1)(a) or (b), and any director of the company who authorised the transaction, is liable—

(a) to account to the company for any gain which he has made directly or indirectly by the transaction, and
(b) to indemnify the company for any loss or damage resulting from the transaction.

(4) Nothing in the above provisions shall be construed as excluding the operation of any other enactment or rule of law by virtue of which the transaction may be called in question or any liability to the company may arise.

(5) The transaction ceases to be voidable if—

(a) restitution of any money or other asset which was the subject-matter of the transaction is no longer possible, or
(b) the company is indemnified for any loss or damage resulting from the transaction, or
(c) rights acquired bona fide for value and without actual notice of the directors' exceeding their powers by a person who is not party to the transaction would be affected by the avoidance, or
(d) the transaction is ratified by the company in general meeting, by ordinary or special resolution or otherwise as the case may require.

(6) A person other than a director of the company is not liable under subsection (3) if he shows that at the time the transaction was entered into he did not know that the directors were exceeding their powers.

(7) This section does not affect the operation of section 35A in relation to any party to the transaction not within subsection (l)(a) or (b).

But where a transaction is voidable by virtue of this section and valid by virtue of that section in favour of such a person, the court may, on the application of that person or of the company, make such order affirming, severing or setting aside the transaction, on such terms, as appear to the court to be just.

(8) In this section "transaction" includes any act; and the reference in subsection (1) to limitations under the company's constitution includes limitations deriving—

(a) from a resolution of the company in general meeting or a meeting of any class of shareholders, or

(b) from any agreement between the members of the company or of any class of shareholders.][1]

---

1 Inserted by CA 1989, s 109 with effect from a date to be appointed.

Share dealings by directors and their families

323 Prohibition on directors dealing in share options

(1) It is an offence for a director of a company to buy—

(a) a right to call for delivery at a specified price and within a specified time of a specified number of relevant shares or a specified amount of relevant debentures; or

(b) a right to make delivery at a specified price and within a specified time of a specified number of relevant shares or a specified amount of relevant debentures; or

(c) a right (as he may elect) to call for delivery at a specified price and within a specified time or to make delivery at a specified price and within a specified time of a specified number of relevant shares or a specified amount of relevant debentures.

(2) A person guilty of an offence under subsection (1) is liable to imprisonment or a fine, or both.

(3) In subsection (1)—

(a) "relevant shares", in relation to a director of a company, means shares in the company or in any other body corporate, being the company's subsidiary or holding company, or a subsidiary of the company's holding company, being shares as respects which there has been granted a listing on a stock exchange (whether in Great Britain or elsewhere);

(b) "relevant debentures", in relation to a director of a company, means debentures of the company or of any other body corporate, being the company's subsidiary or holding company or a subsidiary of the company's holding company, being debentures as respects which there has been granted such a listing; and

(c) "price" includes any consideration other than money.

(4) This section applies to a shadow director as to a director.

(5) This section is not to be taken as penalising a person who buys a right to subscribe for shares in, or debentures of, a body corporate or buys debentures of a body corporate that confer upon the holder of them a right to subscribe for, or to convert the debentures (in whole or in part) into, shares of that body.

Cross references. See Sec 327 (extension to spouses and children).

---

324 Duty of director to disclose shareholdings in own company

(1) A person who becomes a director of a company and at the time when he does so is interested in shares in, or debentures of, the company or any other body corporate, being the company's subsidiary or holding company or a subsidiary of the company's holding company, is under obligation to notify the company in writing—

(a) of the subsistence of his interests at that time; and
(b) of the number of shares of each class in, and the amount of debentures of each class of, the company or other such body corporate in which each interest of his subsists at that time.

(2) A director of a company is under obligation to notify the company in writing of the occurrence, while he is a director, of any of the following events—

(a) any event in consequence of whose occurrence he becomes, or ceases to be, interested in shares in, or debentures of, the company or any other body corporate, being the company's subsidiary or holding company or a subsidiary of the company's holding company;
(b) the entering into by him of a contract to sell any such shares or debentures;
(c) the assignment by him of a right granted to him by the company to subscribe for shares in, or debentures of, the company; and
(d) the grant to him by another body corporate, being the company's subsidiary or holding company or a subsidiary of the company's holding company, of a right to subscribe for shares in, or debentures of, that other body corporate, the exercise of such a right granted to him and the assignment by him of such a right so granted;

and notification to the company must state the number or amount, and class, of shares or debentures involved.

(3) Schedule 13 has effect in connection with subsections (1) and (2) above; and of that Schedule—

(a) Part I contains rules for the interpretation of, and otherwise in relation to, those subsections and applies in determining, for purposes of those subsections, whether a person has an interest in shares or debentures;
(b) Part II applies with respect to the periods within which obligations imposed by the subsections must be fulfilled; and
(c) Part III specifies certain circumstances in which obligations arising from subsection (2) are to be treated as not discharged;

and subsections (1) and (2) are subject to any exceptions for which provision may be made by regulations made by the Secretary of State by statutory instrument.

(4) Subsection (2) does not require the notification by a person of the occurrence of an event whose occurrence comes to his knowledge after he has ceased to be a director.

(5) An obligation imposed by this section is treated as not discharged unless the notice by means of which it purports to be discharged is expressed to be given in fulfilment of that obligation.

(6) This section applies to shadow directors as to directors; but nothing in it operates so as to impose an obligation with respect to shares in a body corporate which is the wholly-owned subsidiary of another body corporate.

(7) A person who—

(a) fails to discharge, within the proper period, an obligation to which he is subject under subsection (1) or (2), or
(b) in purported discharge of an obligation to which he is so subject, makes to the company a statement which he knows to be false, or recklessly makes to it a statement which is false,

is guilty of an offence and liable to imprisonment or a fine, or both.

(8) Section 732 (restriction on prosecutions) applies to an offence under this section.

Cross references. See Sec 325; Sec 328 (extension to spouses and children).

Regulations. See The Companies (Disclosure of Directors' Interests) (Exceptions) Regulations 1985 (SI 1985 No 802).

325 Register of directors' interests notified under s 324

(1) Every company shall keep a register for the purposes of section 324.

(2) Whenever a company receives information from a director given in fulfilment of an obligation imposed on him by that section, it is under obligation to enter in the register, against the director's name, the information received and the date of the entry.

(3) The company is also under obligation, whenever it grants to a director a right to subscribe for shares in, or debentures of, the company to enter in the register against his name—

(a) the date on which the right is granted,
(b) the period during which, or time at which, it is exercisable,
(c) the consideration for the grant (or, if there is no consideration, that fact), and
(d) the description of shares or debentures involved and the number or amount of them, and the price to be paid for them (or the consideration, if otherwise than in money).

(4) Whenever such a right as is mentioned above is exercised by a director, the company is under obligation to enter in the register against his name that fact (identifying the right), the number or amount of shares or debentures in respect of which it is exercised and, if they were registered in his name, that fact and, if not, the name or names of the person or persons in whose name or names they were registered, together (if they were registered in the names of two persons or more) with the number or amount of the shares or debentures registered in the name of each of them.

(5) Part IV of Schedule 13 has effect with respect to the register to be kept under this section, to the way in which entries in it are to be made, to the right of inspection, and generally.

(6) For purposes of this section, a shadow director is deemed a director.

Cross references. See Sec 328(9); 13 Sch.

326 Sanctions for non-compliance

(1) The following applies with respect to defaults in complying with, and to contraventions of, section 325 and Part IV of Schedule 13.

(2) If default is made in complying with any of the following provisions—

(a) section 325(1), (2), (3) or (4), or
(b) Schedule 13, paragraph 21, 22 or 28,

the company and every officer of it who is in default is liable to a fine and, for continued contravention, to a daily default fine.

(3) If an inspection of the register required under paragraph 25 of the Schedule is refused, or a copy required under paragraph 26 is not sent within the proper period, the company and every officer of it who is in default is liable to a fine and, for continued contravention, to a daily default fine.

(4) If default is made for 14 days in complying with paragraph 27 of the Schedule (notice to registrar of where register is kept), the company and every officer of it who is in default is liable to a fine and, for continued contravention, to a daily default fine.

(5) If default is made in complying with paragraph 29 of the Schedule (register to be produced at annual general meeting), the company and every officer of it who is in default is liable to a fine.

(6) In the case of a refusal of an inspection of the register required under paragraph 25 of the Schedule, the court may by order compel an immediate inspection of it; and in the case of failure to send within the proper period a copy required under paragraph 26, the court may by order direct that the copy be sent to the person requiring it.

Cross references. See 13 Sch.

327 Extension of s 323 to spouses and children

(1) Section 323 applies to—

(a) the wife or husband of a director of a company (not being herself or himself a director of it), and
(b) an infant son or infant daughter of a director (not being himself or herself a director of the company),

as it applies to the director; but it is a defence for a person charged by virtue of this section with an offence under section 323 to prove that he (she) had no reason to believe that his (her) spouse or, as the case may be, parent was a director of the company in question.

(2) For purposes of this section—

(a) "son" includes step-son, and "daughter" includes step-daughter ("parent" being construed accordingly),
(b) "infant" means, in relation to Scotland, pupil or minor, and
(c) a shadow director of a company is deemed a director of it.

328 Extension of s 324 to spouses and children

(1) For the purposes of section 324—

(a) an interest of the wife or husband of a director of a company (not being herself or himself a director of it) in shares or debentures is to be treated as the director's interest; and
(b) the same applies to an interest of an infant son or infant daughter of a director of a company (not being himself or herself a director of it) in shares or debentures.

(2) For those purposes—

(a) a contract, assignment or right of subscription entered into, exercised or made by, or a grant made to, the wife or husband of a director of a company (not being herself or himself a director of it) is to be treated as having been entered into, exercised or made by, or (as the case may be) as having been made to, the director; and

(b) the same applies to a contract, assignment or right of subscription entered into, exercised or made by, or grant made to, an infant son or infant daughter of a director of a company (not being himself or herself a director of it).

(3) A director of a company is under obligation to notify the company in writing of the occurrence while he or she is a director, of either of the following events, namely—

(a) the grant by the company to his (her) spouse, or to his or her infant son or infant daughter, of a right to subscribe for shares in, or debentures of, the company; and

(b) the exercise by his (her) spouse or by his or her infant son or infant daughter of such a right granted by the company to the wife, husband, son or daughter.

(4) In a notice given to the company under subsection (3) there shall be stated—

(a) in the case of the grant of a right, the like information as is required by section 324 to be stated by the director on the grant to him by another body corporate of a right to subscribe for shares in, or debentures of, that other body corporate; and

(b) in the case of the exercise of a right, the like information as is required by that section to be stated by the director on the exercise of a right granted to him by another body corporate to subscribe for shares in, or debentures of, that other body corporate.

(5) An obligation imposed by subsection (3) on a director must be fulfilled by him before the end of 5 days beginning with the day following that on which the occurrence of the event giving rise to it comes to his knowledge; but in reckoning that period of days there is disregarded any Saturday or Sunday, and any day which is a bank holiday in any part of Great Britain.

(6) A person who—

(a) fails to fulfil, within the proper period, an obligation to which he is subject under subsection (3), or

(b) in purported fulfilment of such an obligation, makes to a company a statement which he knows to be false, or recklessly makes to a company a statement which is false,

is guilty of an offence and liable to imprisonment or a fine, or both.

(7) The rules set out in Part I of Schedule 13 have effect for the interpretation of, and otherwise in relation to, subsections (1) and (2); and subsections (5), (6) and (8) of section 324 apply with any requisite modification.

(8) In this section, "son" includes step-son, "daughter" includes step-daughter, and "infant" means, in relation to Scotland, pupil or minor.

(9) For purposes of section 325, an obligation imposed on a director by this section is to be treated as if imposed by section 324.

329 Duty to notify stock exchange of matters notified under preceding sections

(1) Whenever a company whose shares or debentures are listed on a [recognised investment exchange other than an overseas investment exchange within the meaning of the Financial Services Act 1986][1] is notified of any matter by a director in consequence of the fulfilment of an obligation imposed by section 324 or 328, and that matter relates to shares or debentures so listed, the company is under obligation to notify that [investment][2] exchange of that matter; and the [investment][2] exchange may publish, in such manner as it may determine, any information received by it under this subsection.

(2) An obligation imposed by subsection (1) must be fulfilled before the end of the day next following that on which it arises; but there is disregarded for this purpose a day which is a Saturday or a Sunday or a bank holiday in any part of Great Britain.

(3) If default is made in complying with this section, the company and every officer of it who is in default is guilty of an offence and liable to a fine and, for continued contravention, to a daily default fine.

Section 732 (restriction on prosecutions) applies to an offence under this section.

---

1 Substituted by FSA 1986, s 212(2), 16 Sch 20 with effect from 29 April 1988 (see SI 1988 No 740). Previously 'recognised stock exchange'.

2 Substituted by FSA 1986, s 212(2), 16 Sch 20 with effect from 29 April 1988 (see SI 1988 No 740). Previously 'stock'.

Restrictions on a company's power to make loans, etc., to directors and persons connected with them

330 General restriction on loans etc. to directors and persons connected with them

(1) The prohibitions listed below in this section are subject to the exceptions in sections 332 to 338.

(2) A company shall not—

(a) make a loan to a director of the company or of its holding company;
(b) enter into any guarantee or provide any security in connection with a loan made by any person to such a director.

(3) A relevant company shall not—

(a) make a quasi-loan to a director of the company or of its holding company;
(b) make a loan or a quasi-loan to a person connected with such a director;
(c) enter into a guarantee or provide any security in connection with a loan or quasi-loan made by any other person for such a director or a person so connected.

(4) A relevant company shall not—

(a) enter into a credit transaction as creditor for such a director or a person so connected;
(b) enter into any guarantee or provide any security in connection with a credit transaction made by any other person for such a director or a person so connected.

(5) For purposes of sections 330 to 346, a shadow director is treated as a director.

(6) A company shall not arrange for the assignment to it, or the assumption by it, of any rights, obligations or liabilities under a transaction which, if it had been entered into by the company, would have contravened subsection (2), (3) or (4); but for the purposes of sections 330 to 347 the transaction is to be treated as having been entered into on the date of the arrangement.

(7) A company shall not take part in any arrangement whereby—

(a) another person enters into a transaction which, if it had been entered into by the company, would have contravened any of subsections (2), (3), (4) or (6); and

(b) that other person, in pursuance of the arrangement, has obtained or is to obtain any benefit from the company or its holding company or a subsidiary of the company or its holding company.

Cross references. See Sec 340 (value of transactions); Sec 341 (civil remedies for breach of Sec 330); Sec 342 (criminal penalties); Sec 347 (transactions under foreign law); Sec 741 (shadow directors).

331 Definitions for ss 330 ff

(1) The following subsections apply for the interpretation of sections 330 to 346.

(2) "Guarantee" includes indemnity, and cognate expressions are to be construed accordingly.

(3) A quasi-loan is a transaction under which one party ("the creditor") agrees to pay, or pays otherwise than in pursuance of an agreement, a sum for another ("the borrower") or agrees to reimburse, or reimburses otherwise than in pursuance of an agreement, expenditure incurred by another party for another ("the borrower")—

(a) on terms that the borrower (or a person on his behalf) will reimburse the creditor; or

(b) in circumstances giving rise to a liability on the borrower to reimburse the creditor.

(4) Any reference to the person to whom a quasi-loan is made is a reference to the borrower; and the liabilities of a borrower under a quasi-loan include the liabilities of any person who has agreed to reimburse the creditor on behalf of the borrower.

(5) [. . .][1]

(6) "Relevant company" means a company which—

(a) is a public company, or
(b) is a subsidiary of a public company, or
(c) is a subsidiary of a company which has as another subsidiary a public company, or
(d) has a subsidiary which is a public company.

(7) A credit transaction is a transaction under which one party ("the creditor")—

(a) supplies any goods or sells any land under a hire-purchase agreement or a conditional sale agreement;
(b) leases or hires any land or goods in return for periodical payments;
(c) otherwise disposes of land or supplies goods or services on the understanding that payment (whether in a lump sum or instalments or by way of periodical payments or otherwise) is to be deferred.

(8) "Services" means anything other than goods or land.

(9) A transaction or arrangement is made "for" a person if—

(a) in the case of a loan or quasi-loan, it is made to him;
(b) in the case of a credit transaction, he is the person to whom goods or services are supplied, or land is sold or otherwise disposed of, under the transaction;
(c) in the case of a guarantee or security, it is entered into or provided in connection with a loan or quasi-loan made to him or a credit transaction made for him;
(d) in the case of an arrangement within subsection (6) or (7) of section 330, the transaction to which the arrangement relates was made for him; and
(e) in the case of any other transaction or arrangement for the supply or transfer of, or of any interest in, goods, land or services, he is the person to whom the goods, land or services (or the interest) are supplied or transferred.

(10) "Conditional sale agreement" means the same as in the Consumer Credit Act 1974.

---

1 Repealed by Banking Act 1987, s 108(2), 7 Sch Part I with effect from 1 October 1987 (see SI 1987 No 1664).
Previously
'"Recognised bank" means a company which is recognised as a bank for the purposes of the Banking Act 1979.'

Cross references. See Sec 330(5)(6); Sec 331; Sec 340 (value of transactions); Sec 347 (transactions under foreign law); Sec 741 (shadow directors).

---

332 Short-term quasi-loans

(1) Subsection (3) of section 330 does not prohibit a company ("the creditor") from making a quasi-loan to one of its directors or to a director of its holding company if—

(a) the quasi-loan contains a term requiring the director or a person on his behalf to reimburse the creditor his expenditure within 2 months of its being incurred; and
(b) the aggregate of the amount of that quasi-loan and of the amount outstanding under each relevant quasi-loan does not exceed [£5,000][1].

(2) A quasi-loan is relevant for this purpose if it was made to the director by virtue of this section by the creditor or its subsidiary or, where the director is a director of the creditor's holding company, any other subsidiary of that company; and "the amount outstanding" is the amount of the outstanding liabilities of the person to whom the quasi-loan was made.

---

1 Substituted by CA 1989, s 138 with effect from a date to be appointed.
Previously '£1,000'.

Cross references. See Sec 330(5)(6); Sec 331; Sec 340 (value of transactions); Sec 347 (transactions under foreign law); Sec 741 (shadow directors).

---

333 Inter-company loans in same group

In the case of a relevant company which is a member of a group of companies (meaning a holding company and its subsidiaries), paragraphs (b) and (c) of section 330(3) do not prohibit the company from—

(a) making a loan or quasi-loan to another member of that group; or

(b) entering into a guarantee or providing any security in connection with a loan or quasi-loan made by any person to another member of the group,

by reason only that a director of one member of the group is associated with another.

Cross references. See Sec 330(5)(6); Sec 331; Sec 340 (value of transactions); Sec 347 (transactions under foreign law); Sec 741 (shadow directors).

334 Loans of small amounts

Without prejudice to any other provision of sections 332 to 338, paragraph (a) of section 330(2) does not prohibit a company from making a loan to a director of the company or of its holding company if the aggregate of the relevant amounts does not exceed [£5,000][1].

[1] Substituted by CA 1989, s 138 with effect from a date to be appointed. Previously '£2,500'.

Cross references. See Sec 330(5)(6); Sec 331; Sec 339 (relevant amounts); Sec 340 (value of transactions); Sec 347 (transactions under foreign law); Sec 741 (shadow directors).

335 Minor and business transactions

(1) Section 330(4) does not prohibit a company from entering into a transaction for a person if the aggregate of the relevant amounts does not exceed £5,000.

(2) Section 330(4) does not prohibit a company from entering into a transaction for a person if—

(a) the transaction is entered into by the company in the ordinary course of its business; and

(b) the value of the transaction is not greater, and the terms on which it is entered into are no more favourable, in respect of the person for whom the transaction is made, than that or those which it is reasonable to expect the company to have offered to or in respect of a person of the same financial standing but unconnected with the company.

Cross references. See Sec 330(5)(6); Sec 331; Sec 339 (relevant amounts); Sec 340 (value of transactions); Sec 347 (transactions under foreign law); Sec 741 (shadow directors).

336 Transactions at behest of holding company

The following transactions are excepted from the prohibitions of section 330—

(a) a loan or quasi-loan by a company to its holding company, or a company entering into a guarantee or providing any security in connection with a loan or quasi-loan made by any person to its holding company;

(b) a company entering into a credit transaction as creditor for its holding company, or entering into a guarantee or providing any security in connection with a credit transaction made by any other person for its holding company.

Cross references. See Sec 330(5)(6); Sec 331; Sec 340 (value of transactions); Sec 347 (transactions under foreign law); Sec 741 (shadow directors).

337 Funding of director's expenditure on duty to company

(1) A company is not prohibited by section 330 from doing anything to provide a director with funds to meet expenditure incurred or to be incurred by him for the purposes of the company or for the purpose of enabling him properly to perform his duties as an officer of the company.

(2) Nor does the section prohibit a company from doing anything to enable a director to avoid incurring such expenditure.

(3) Subsections (1) and (2) apply only if one of the following conditions is satisfied—

(a) the thing in question is done with prior approval of the company given at a general meeting at which there are disclosed all the matters mentioned in the next subsection;
(b) that thing is done on condition that, if the approval of the company is not so given at or before the next annual general meeting, the loan is to be repaid, or any other liability arising under any such transaction discharged, within 6 months from the conclusion of that meeting;

but those subsections do not authorise a relevant company to enter into any transaction if the aggregate of the relevant amounts exceeds £10,000.

(4) The matters to be disclosed under subsection (3)(a) are—

(a) the purpose of the expenditure incurred or to be incurred, or which would otherwise be incurred, by the director,
(b) the amount of the funds to be provided by the company, and
(c) the extent of the company's liability under any transaction which is or is connected with the thing in question.

Cross references. See Sec 330(5)(6); Sec 331; Sec 339 (relevant amounts); Sec 340 (value of transactions); Sec 347 (transactions under foreign law); Sec 741 (shadow directors).

338 Loan or quasi-loan by money-lending company

(1) There is excepted from the prohibitions in section 330—

(a) a loan or quasi-loan made by a money-lending company to any person; or
(b) a money-lending company entering into a guarantee in connection with any other loan or quasi-loan.

(2) "Money-lending company" means a company whose ordinary business includes the making of loans or quasi-loans, or the giving of guarantees in connection with loans or quasi-loans.

(3) Subsection (1) applies only if both the following conditions are satisfied—

(a) the loan or quasi-loan in question is made by the company, or it enters into the guarantee, in the ordinary course of the company's business; and
(b) the amount of the loan or quasi-loan, or the amount guaranteed, is not greater, and the terms of the loan, quasi-loan or guarantee are not more favourable, in the case of the person to whom the loan or quasi-loan is made or in respect of whom the guarantee is entered into, than that or those which it is reasonable to expect that company to have offered to or in respect of a person of the same financial standing but unconnected with the company.

(4) But subsection (1) does not authorise a relevant company (unless it is [a banking company][1]) to enter into any transaction if the aggregate of the relevant amounts exceeds [£100,000][2].

(5) In determining that aggregate, a company which a director does not control is deemed not to be connected with him.

(6) The condition specified in subsection (3)(b) does not of itself prevent a company from making a loan to one of its directors or a director of its holding company—

(a) for the purpose of facilitating the purchase, for use as that director's only or main residence, of the whole or part of any dwelling-house together with any land to be occupied and enjoyed with it;
(b) for the purpose of improving a dwelling-house or part of a dwelling-house so used or any land occupied and enjoyed with it;
(c) in substitution for any loan made by any person and falling within paragraph (a) or (b) of this subsection,

if loans of that description are ordinarily made by the company to its employees and on terms no less favourable than those on which the transaction in question is made, and the aggregate of the relevant amounts does not exceed [£100,000][2].

---

[1] Substituted by CA 1989, 10 Sch 10 with effect from 1 April 1990 (SI 1990 No 355) subject to the transitional and saving provisions in Arts 6 to 9 of that Order reproduced above Sec 221 above.
Previously '[an authorised institution][a]'.

[a] Substituted by Banking Act 1987, s 108(1), 6 Sch 18(6) with effect from 1 October 1987 (see SI 1987 No 1664).
Previously 'a recognised bank'.

[2] Substituted by CA 1989, s 138 with effect from a date to be appointed.
Previously '£50,000'.

Cross references. See Sec 330(5)(6); Sec 331; Sec 339 (relevant amounts); Sec 340 (value of transactions); Sec 347 (transactions under foreign law); Sec 741 (shadow directors).

---

339 "Relevant amounts" for purposes of ss 334 ff

(1) This section has effect for defining the "relevant amounts" to be aggregated under sections 334, 335(1), 337(3) and 338(4); and in relation to any proposed transaction or arrangement and the question whether it falls within one or other of the exceptions provided by those sections, "the relevant exception" is that exception; but where the relevant exception is the one provided by section 334 (loan of small amount), references in this section to a person connected with a director are to be disregarded.

(2) Subject as follows, the relevant amounts in relation to a proposed transaction or arrangement are—

(a) the value of the proposed transaction or arrangement,
(b) the value of any existing arrangement which—
 (i) falls within subsection (6) or (7) of section 330, and
 (ii) also falls within subsection (3) of this section, and
 (iii) was entered into by virtue of the relevant exception by the company or by a subsidiary of the company or, where the proposed transaction or arrangement is to be made for a director of its holding company or a person connected with such a director, by that holding company or any of its subsidiaries;
(c) the amount outstanding under any other transaction—
 (i) falling within subsection (3) below, and
 (ii) made by virtue of the relevant exception, and
 (iii) made by the company or by a subsidiary of the company or, where the proposed transaction or arrangement is to be made for a director of its holding company or a person connected with such a director, by that holding company or any of its subsidiaries.

(3) A transaction falls within this subsection if it was made—

(a) for the director for whom the proposed transaction or arrangement is to be made, or for any person connected with that director; or
(b) where the proposed transaction or arrangement is to be made for a person connected with a director of a company, for that director or any person connected with him;

and an arrangement also falls within this subsection if it relates to a transaction which does so.

(4) But where the proposed transaction falls within section 338 and is one which [a banking company][1] proposes to enter into under subsection (6) of that section (housing loans, etc.), any other transaction or arrangement which apart from this subsection would fall within subsection (3) of this section does not do so unless it was entered into in pursuance of section 338(6).

(5) A transaction entered into by a company which is (at the time of that transaction being entered into) a subsidiary of the company which is to make the proposed transaction, or is a subsidiary of that company's holding company, does not fall within subsection (3) if at the time when the question arises (that is to say, the question whether the proposed transaction or arrangement falls within any relevant exception), it no longer is such a subsidiary.

(6) Values for purposes of subsection (2) of this section are to be determined in accordance with the section next following; and "the amount outstanding" for purposes of subsection (2)(c) above is the value of the transaction less any amount by which that value has been reduced.

---

1 Substituted by CA 1989, 10 Sch 10 with effect from 1 April 1990 (SI 1990 No 355) subject to the transitional and saving provisions in Arts 6 to 9 of that Order reproduced above Sec 221 above.
Previously '[an authorised institution][a]'.
a Substituted by Banking Act 1987, s 108(1), 6 Sch 18(6) with effect from 1 October 1987 (see SI 1987 No 1664).
Previously 'a recognised bank'.

Cross references. See Sec 330(5)(6); Sec 331; Sec 340 (value of transactions); Sec 347 (transactions under foreign law); Sec 741 (shadow directors).

---

340 "Value" of transactions and arrangements

(1) This section has effect for determining the value of a transaction or arrangement for purposes of sections 330 to 339.

(2) The value of a loan is the amount of its principal.

(3) The value of a quasi-loan is the amount, or maximum amount, which the person to whom the quasi-loan is made is liable to reimburse the creditor.

(4) The value of a guarantee or security is the amount guaranteed or secured.

(5) The value of an arrangement to which section 330(6) or (7) applies is the value of the transaction to which the arrangement relates less any amount by which the liabilities under the arrangement or transaction of the person for whom the transaction was made have been reduced.

(6) The value of a transaction or arrangement not falling within subsections (2) to (5) above is the price which it is reasonable to expect could be obtained for the goods, land or services to which the transaction or arrangement relates if they had been supplied (at the time the transaction or arrangement is entered into) in the ordinary course of business and on the same terms (apart from price) as they have been supplied, or are to be supplied, under the transaction or arrangement in question.

(7) For purposes of this section, the value of a transaction or arrangement which is not capable of being expressed as a specific sum of money (because the amount of any liability arising under the transaction or arrangement is unascertainable, or for any other reason), whether or not any liability under the transaction or arrangement has been reduced, is deemed to exceed £50,000.

Cross references. See Sec 330(5)(6); Sec 331; Sec 347 (transactions under foreign law); Sec 741 (shadow directors).

341 Civil remedies for breach of s 330

(1) If a company enters into a transaction or arrangement in contravention of section 330, the transaction or arrangement is voidable at the instance of the company unless—

(a) restitution of any money or any other asset which is the subject matter of the arrangement or transaction is no longer possible, or the company has been indemnified in pursuance of subsection (2)(b) below for the loss or damage suffered by it, or

(b) any rights acquired bona fide for value and without actual notice of the contravention by a person other than the person for whom the transaction or arrangement was made would be affected by its avoidance.

(2) Where an arrangement or transaction is made by a company for a director of the company or its holding company or a person connected with such a director in contravention of section 330, that director and the person so connected and any other director of the company who authorised the transaction or arrangement (whether or not it has been avoided in pursuance of subsection (1)) is liable—

(a) to account to the company for any gain which he has made directly or indirectly by the arrangement or transaction; and

(b) (jointly and severally with any other person liable under this subsection) to indemnify the company for any loss or damage resulting from the arrangement or transaction.

(3) Subsection (2) is without prejudice to any liability imposed otherwise than by that subsection, but is subject to the next two subsections.

(4) Where an arrangement or transaction is entered into by a company and a person connected with a director of the company or its holding company in contravention of section 330, that director is not liable under subsection (2) of this section if he shows that he took all reasonable steps to secure the company's compliance with that section.

(5) In any case, a person so connected and any such other director as is mentioned in subsection (2) is not so liable if he shows that, at the time the arrangement or transaction was entered into, he did not know the relevant circumstances constituting the contravention.

Cross references. See Sec 330(5)(6); Sec 331; Sec 347 (transactions under foreign law); Sec 741 (shadow directors).

342 Criminal penalties for breach of s 330

(1) A director of a relevant company who authorises or permits the company to enter into a transaction or arrangement knowing or having reasonable cause to believe that the company was thereby contravening section 330 is guilty of an offence.

(2) A relevant company which enters into a transaction or arrangement for one of its directors or for a director of its holding company in contravention of section 330 is guilty of an offence.

(3) A person who procures a relevant company to enter into a transaction or arrangement knowing or having reasonable cause to believe that the company was thereby contravening section 330 is guilty of an offence.

(4) A person guilty of an offence under this section is liable to imprisonment or a fine, or both.

(5) A relevant company is not guilty of an offence under subsection (2) if it shows that, at the time the transaction or arrangement was entered into, it did not know the relevant circumstances.

Cross references. See Sec 330(5)(6); Sec 331; Sec 347 (transactions under foreign law); Sec 741 (shadow directors); 24 Sch (punishment of offences).

343 Record of transactions not disclosed in company accounts

(1) The following provisions of this section—

(a) apply in the case of a company which is, or is the holding company of, [a banking company][1], and

(b) are subject to the exceptions provided by section 344.

(2) Such a company shall maintain a register containing a copy of every transaction, arrangement or agreement of which particulars would, but for [paragraph 2 of Part IV of Schedule 9, be required][2] to be disclosed in the company's accounts or group accounts for the current financial year and for each of the preceding 10 financial years.

(3) In the case of a transaction, arrangement or agreement which is not in writing, there shall be contained in the register a written memorandum setting out its terms.

(4) Such a company shall before its annual general meeting make available at its registered office for not less than 15 days ending with the date of the meeting a statement containing the particulars of transactions, arrangements and agreements which the company would, but for [paragraph 2 of Part IV of Schedule 9, be required][2] to disclose in its accounts or group accounts for the last complete financial year preceding that meeting.

(5) The statement shall be so made available for inspection by members of the company; and such a statement shall also be made available for their inspection at the annual general meeting.

(6) It is the duty of the company's auditors to examine the statement before it is made available to members of the company and to make a report to the members on it; and the report shall be annexed to the statement before it is made so available.

(7) The auditors' report shall state whether in their opinion the statement contains the particulars required by subsection (4); and, where their opinion is that it does not, they shall include in the report, so far as they are reasonably able to do so, a statement giving the required particulars.

(8) If a company fails to comply with any provision of subsections (2) to (5), every person who at the time of the failure is a director of it is guilty of an offence and liable to a fine; but—

(a) it is a defence in proceedings against a person for this offence to prove that he took all reasonable steps for securing compliance with the subsection concerned, and

(b) a person is not guilty of the offence by virtue only of being a shadow director of the company.

(9) For purposes of the application of this section to loans and quasi-loans made by a company to persons connected with a person who at any time is a director of the company or of its holding company, a company which a person does not control is not connected with him.

---

1 Substituted by CA 1989, 10 Sch 10 with effect from 1 April 1990 (SI 1990 No 355) subject to the transitional and saving provisions in Arts 6 to 9 of that Order reproduced above Sec 221 above.
Previously '[an authorised institution][a]'.

a Substituted by Banking Act 1987, s 108(1), 6 Sch 18(6) with effect from 1 October 1987 (see SI 1987 No 1664).
Previously 'a recognised bank'.

2 Substituted by CA 1989, 10 Sch 11 with effect as in [1] above.
Previously 'paragraph 4 of Schedule 6, be required by section 232'.

Cross references. See Sec 330(5)(6); Sec 331; Sec 344; Sec 347 (transactions under foreign law).

---

344 Exceptions from s 343

(1) Section 343 does not apply in relation to—

(a) transactions or arrangements made or subsisting during a financial year by a company or by a subsidiary of a company for a person who was at any time during that year a director of the company or of its holding company or was connected with such a director, or

(b) an agreement made or subsisting during that year to enter into such a transaction or arrangement,

if the aggregate of the values of each transaction or arrangement made for that person, and of each agreement for such a transaction or arrangement, less the amount (if any) by which the value of those transactions, arrangements and agreements has been reduced, did not exceed £1,000 at any time during the financial year.

For purposes of this subsection, values are to be determined as under section 340.

(2) Section 343(4) and (5) do not apply to [a banking company][1] which is the wholly-owned subsidiary of a company incorporated in the United Kingdom.

---

1 Substituted by CA 1989, 10 Sch 10 with effect from 1 April 1990 (SI 1990 No 355) subject to the transitional and saving provisions in Arts 6 to 9 of that Order reproduced above Sec 221 above.
Previously '[an authorised institution][a]'.

a Substituted by Banking Act 1987, s 108(1), 6 Sch 18(6) with effect from 1 October 1987 (see SI 1987 No 1664).
Previously 'a recognised bank'.

Cross references. See Sec 330(5)(6); Sec 331; Sec 741 (shadow directors).

Supplementary

345 Power to increase financial limits

(1) The Secretary of State may by order in a statutory instrument substitute for any sum of money specified in this Part a larger sum specified in the order.

(2) An order under this section is subject to annulment in pursuance of a resolution of either House of Parliament.

(3) Such an order does not have effect in relation to anything done or not done before its coming into force; and accordingly, proceedings in respect of any liability (whether civil or criminal) incurred before that time may be continued or instituted as if the order had not been made.

Cross references. See Sec 330(5)(6); Sec 331; Sec 741 (shadow directors).

---

346 "Connected persons", etc.

(1) This section has effect with respect to references in this Part to a person being "connected" with a director of a company, and to a director being "associated with" or "controlling" a body corporate.

(2) A person is connected with a director of a company if, but only if, he (not being himself a director of it) is—

(a) that director's spouse, child or step-child; or
(b) except where the context otherwise requires, a body corporate with which the director is associated; or
(c) a person acting in his capacity as trustee of any trust the beneficiaries of which include—
 (i) the director, his spouse or any children or step-children of his, or
 (ii) a body corporate with which he is associated, or of a trust whose terms confer a power on the trustees that may be exercised for the benefit of the director, his spouse, or any children or step-children of his, or any such body corporate; or
(d) a person acting in his capacity as partner of that director or of any person who, by virtue of paragraph (a), (b) or (c) of this subsection, is connected with that director; or
(e) a Scottish firm in which—
 (i) that director is a partner,
 (ii) a partner is a person who, by virtue of paragraph (a), (b) or (c) above, is connected with that director, or
 (iii) a partner is a Scottish firm in which that director is a partner or in which there is a partner who, by virtue of paragraph (a), (b) or (c) above, is connected with that director.

(3) In subsection (2)—

(a) a reference to the child or step-child of any person includes an illegitimate child of his, but does not include any person who has attained the age of 18; and
(b) paragraph (c) does not apply to a person acting in his capacity as trustee under an employees' share scheme or a pension scheme.

(4) A director of a company is associated with a body corporate if, but only if, he and the persons connected with him, together—

(a) are interested in shares comprised in the equity share capital of that body corporate of a nominal value equal to at least one-fifth of that share capital; or
(b) are entitled to exercise or control the exercise of more than one-fifth of the voting power at any general meeting of that body.

(5) A director of a company is deemed to control a body corporate if, but only if—

(a) he or any person connected with him is interested in any part of the equity share capital of that body or is entitled to exercise or control the exercise of any part of the voting power at any general meeting of that body; and

(b) that director, the persons connected with him and the other directors of that company, together, are interested in more than one-half of that share capital or are entitled to exercise or control the exercise of more than one-half of that voting power.

(6) For purposes of subsections (4) and (5)—

(a) a body corporate with which a director is associated is not to be treated as connected with that director unless it is also connected with him by virtue of subsection (2)(c) or (d); and

(b) a trustee of a trust the beneficiaries of which include (or may include) a body corporate with which a director is associated is not to be treated as connected with a director by reason only of that fact.

(7) The rules set out in Part I of Schedule 13 apply for the purposes of subsections (4) and (5).

(8) References in those subsections to voting power the exercise of which is controlled by a director include voting power whose exercise is controlled by a body corporate controlled by him; but this is without prejudice to other provisions of subsections (4) and (5).

Cross references. See Sec 330(5)(6); Sec 331; Sec 741 (shadow directors); 13 Sch.

---

347 Transactions under foreign law

For purposes of sections 319 to 322 and 330 to 343, it is immaterial whether the law which (apart from this Act) governs any arrangement or transaction is the law of the United Kingdom, or of a part of it, or not.

Cross references. See Sec 330(6).

PART XI COMPANY ADMINISTRATION AND PROCEDURE

CHAPTER IV MEETINGS AND RESOLUTIONS

Resolutions

378 Extraordinary and special resolutions

(1) A resolution is an extraordinary resolution when it has been passed by a majority of not less than three-fourths of such members as (being entitled to do so) vote in person or, where proxies are allowed, by proxy, at a general meeting of which notice specifying the intention to propose the resolution as an extraordinary resolution has been duly given.

(2) A resolution is a special resolution when it has been passed by such a majority as is required for the passing of an extraordinary resolution and at a general meeting of which not less than 21 days' notice, specifying the intention to propose the resolution as a special resolution, has been duly given.

(3) If it is so agreed by a majority in number of the members having the right to attend and vote at such a meeting, being a majority—

(a) together holding not less than 95 per cent. in nominal value of the shares giving that right; or

(b) in the case of a company not having a share capital, together representing not less than 95 per cent. of the total voting rights at that meeting of all the members,

a resolution may be proposed and passed as a special resolution at a meeting of which less than 21 days' notice has been given.

[A private company may elect (by elective resolution in accordance with section 379A) that the above provisions shall have effect in relation to the company as if for the references to 95 per cent. there were substituted references to such lesser percentage, but not less than 90 per cent., as may be specified in the resolution or subsequently determined by the company in general meeting.][1]

(4) At any meeting at which an extraordinary resolution or a special resolution is submitted to be passed, a declaration by the chairman that the resolution is carried is, unless a poll is demanded, conclusive evidence of the fact without proof of the number or proportion of the votes recorded in favour of or against the resolution.

(5) In computing the majority on a poll demanded on the question that an extraordinary resolution or a special resolution be passed, reference is to be had to the number of votes cast for and against the resolution.

(6) For purposes of this section, notice of a meeting is deemed duly given, and the meeting duly held, when the notice is given and the meeting held in the manner provided by this Act or the company's articles.

---

1 Inserted by CA 1989, s 115 with effect from 1 April 1990 (SI 1990 No 355) subject to the transitional and saving provisions in Schedule 4 of that Order.

---

379 Resolution requiring special notice

(1) Where by any provision of this Act special notice is required of a resolution, the resolution is not effective unless notice of the intention to move it has been given to the company at least 28 days before the meeting at which it is moved.

(2) The company shall give its members notice of any such resolution at the same time and in the same manner as it gives notice of the meeting or, if that is not practicable, shall give them notice either by advertisement in a newspaper having an appropriate circulation or in any other mode allowed by the company's articles, at least 21 days before the meeting.

(3) If, after notice of the intention to move such a resolution has been given to the company, a meeting is called for a date 28 days or less after the notice has been given, the notice is deemed properly given, though not given within the time required.

[379A Elective resolution of private company

(1) An election by a private company for the purposes of—

(a) section 80A (election as to duration of authority to allot shares),
(b) section 252 (election to dispense with laying of accounts and reports before general meeting),
(c) section 366A (election to dispense with holding of annual general meeting),
(d) section 369(4) or 378(3) (election as to majority required to authorise short notice of meeting), or
(e) section 386 (election to dispense with appointment of auditors annually),

shall be made by resolution of the company in general meeting in accordance with this section.

Such a resolution is referred to in this Act as an "elective resolution".

(2) An elective resolution is not effective unless—

(a) at least 21 days' notice in writing is given of the meeting, stating that an elective resolution is to be proposed and stating the terms of the resolution, and
(b) the resolution is agreed to at the meeting, in person or by proxy, by all the members entitled to attend and vote at the meeting.

(3) The company may revoke an elective resolution by passing an ordinary resolution to that effect.

(4) An elective resolution shall cease to have effect if the company is re-registered as a public company.

(5) An elective resolution may be passed or revoked in accordance with this section, and the provisions referred to in subsection (1) have effect, notwithstanding any contrary provision in the company's articles of association.][1]

---

1 Inserted by CA 1989, s 116 with effect from 1 April 1990 (SI 1990 No 355).

CHAPTER V AUDITORS

Note. The original provisions of this Chapter (Secs 384-394) are replaced by CA 1989, ss 119-123 which inserts new Secs 384-394A. The previous provisions of Sec 389 (qualification for appointment as auditors) are replaced by new provisions in CA 1989, ss 24-54.

[*Appointment of auditors*

384 Duty to appoint auditors

(1) Every company shall appoint an auditor or auditors in accordance with this Chapter.

This is subject to section 388A (dormant company exempt from obligation to appoint auditors).

(2) Auditors shall be appointed in accordance with section 385 (appointment at general meeting at which accounts are laid), except in the case of a private company which has elected to dispense with the laying of accounts in which case the appointment shall be made in accordance with section 385A.

(3) References in this Chapter to the end of the time for appointing auditors are to the end of the time within which an appointment must be made under section 385(2) or 385A(2), according to whichever of those sections applies.

(4) Sections 385 and 385A have effect subject to section 386 under which a private company may elect to dispense with the obligation to appoint auditors annually.][1]

1 Inserted by CA 1989, s 119 with effect from 1 April 1990 (SI 1990 No 355) subject to the transitional and saving provisions in Schedule 4 of that Order.

[385 Appointment at general meeting at which accounts laid

(1) This section applies to every public company and to a private company which has not elected to dispense with the laying of accounts.

(2) The company shall, at each general meeting at which accounts are laid, appoint an auditor or auditors to hold office from the conclusion of that meeting until the conclusion of the next general meeting at which accounts are laid.

(3) The first auditors of the company may be appointed by the directors at any time before the first general meeting of the company at which accounts are laid; and auditors so appointed shall hold office until the conclusion of that meeting.

(4) If the directors fail to exercise their powers under subsection (3), the powers may be exercised by the company in general meeting.][1]

1 Inserted by CA 1989, s 119 with effect from 1 April 1990 (SI 1990 No 355) subject to the transitional and saving provisions in Schedule 4 of that Order.

[385A Appointment by private company which is not obliged to lay accounts

(1) This section applies to a private company which has elected in accordance with section 252 to dispense with the laying of accounts before the company in general meeting.

(2) Auditors shall be appointed by the company in general meeting before the end of the period of 28 days beginning with the day on which copies of the company's annual accounts for the previous financial year are sent to members under section 238 or, if notice is given under section 253(2) requiring the laying of the accounts before the company in general meeting, the conclusion of that meeting.

Auditors so appointed shall hold office from the end of that period or, as the case may be, the conclusion of that meeting until the end of the time for appointing auditors for the next financial year.

(3) The first auditors of the company may be appointed by the directors at any time before—

(a) the end of the period of 28 days beginning with the day on which copies of the company's first annual accounts are sent to members under section 238, or

(b) if notice is given under section 253(2) requiring the laying of the accounts before the company in general meeting, the beginning of that meeting;

and auditors so appointed shall hold office until the end of that period or, as the case may be, the conclusion of that meeting.

(4) If the directors fail to exercise their powers under subsection (3), the powers may be exercised by the company in general meeting.

(5) Auditors holding office when the election is made shall, unless the company in general meeting determines otherwise, continue to hold office until the end of the time for appointing auditors for the next financial year; and auditors holding office when an election ceases to have effect shall continue to hold office until the conclusion of the next general meeting of the company at which accounts are laid.][1]

---

1 Inserted by CA 1989, s 119 with effect from 1 April 1990 (SI 1990 No 355) subject to the transitional and saving provisions in Schedule 4 of that Order.

[386 Election by private company to dispense with annual appointment

(1) A private company may elect (by elective resolution in accordance with section 379A) to dispense with the obligation to appoint auditors annually.

(2) When such an election is in force the company's auditors shall be deemed to be re-appointed for each succeeding financial year on the expiry of the time for appointing auditors for that year, unless—

(a) a resolution has been passed under section 250 by virtue of which the company is exempt from the obligation to appoint auditors, or

(b) a resolution has been passed under section 393 to the effect that their appointment should be brought to an end.

(3) If the election ceases to be in force, the auditors then holding office shall continue to hold office—

(a) where section 385 then applies, until the conclusion of the next general meeting of the company at which accounts are laid;

(b) where section 385A then applies, until the end of the time for appointing auditors for the next financial year under that section.

(4) No account shall be taken of any loss of the opportunity of further deemed re-appointment under this section in ascertaining the amount of any compensation or damages payable to an auditor on his ceasing to hold office for any reason.][1]

1 Inserted by CA 1989, s 119 with effect from 1 April 1990 (SI 1990 No 355) subject to the transitional and saving provisions in Schedule 4 of that Order.

[387 Appointment by Secretary of State in default of appointment by company

(1) If in any case no auditors are appointed, re-appointed or deemed to be re-appointed before the end of the time for appointing auditors, the Secretary of State may appoint a person to fill the vacancy.

(2) In such a case the company shall within one week of the end of the time for appointing auditors give notice to the Secretary of State of his power having become exercisable.

If a company fails to give the notice required by this subsection, the company and every officer of it who is in default is guilty of an offence and liable to a fine and, for continued contravention, to a daily default fine.][1]

1 Inserted by CA 1989, s 119 with effect from 1 April 1990 (SI 1990 No 355) subject to the transitional and saving provisions in Schedule 4 of that Order.

[388 Filling of casual vacancies

(1) The directors, or the company in general meeting, may fill a casual vacancy in the office of auditor.

(2) While such a vacancy continues, any surviving or continuing auditor or auditors may continue to act.

(3) Special notice is required for a resolution at a general meeting of a company—

(a) filling a casual vacancy in the office of auditor, or
(b) re-appointing as auditor a retiring auditor who was appointed by the directors to fill a casual vacancy.

(4) On receipt of notice of such an intended resolution the company shall forthwith send a copy of it—

(a) to the person proposed to be appointed, and
(b) if the casual vacancy was caused by the resignation of an auditor, to the auditor who resigned.][1]

1 Inserted by CA 1989, s 119 with effect from 1 April 1990 (SI 1990 No 355) subject to the transitional and saving provisions in Schedule 4 of that Order.

[388A Dormant company exempt from obligation to appoint auditors

(1) A company which by virtue of section 250 (dormant companies: exemption from provisions as to audit of accounts) is exempt from the provisions of Part VII relating to the audit of accounts is also exempt from the obligation to appoint auditors.

(2) The following provisions apply if the exemption ceases.

(3) Where section 385 applies (appointment at general meeting at which accounts are laid), the directors may appoint auditors at any time before the next meeting of the company at which accounts are to be laid; and auditors so appointed shall hold office until the conclusion of that meeting.

(4) Where section 385A applies (appointment by private company not obliged to lay accounts), the directors may appoint auditors at any time before—

(a) the end of the period of 28 days beginning with the day on which copies of the company's annual accounts are next sent to members under section 238, or

(b) if notice is given under section 253(2) requiring the laying of the accounts before the company in general meeting, the beginning of that meeting;

and auditors so appointed shall hold office until the end of that period or, as the case may be, the conclusion of that meeting.

(5) If the directors fail to exercise their powers under subsection (3) or (4), the powers may be exercised by the company in general meeting.][1]

---

1 Inserted by CA 1989, s 119 with effect from 1 April 1990 (SI 1990 No 355) subject to the transitional and saving provisions in Schedule 4 of that Order.

[*Rights of auditors*

389A Rights to information

(1) The auditors of a company have a right of access at all times to the company's books, accounts and vouchers, and are entitled to require from the company's officers such information and explanations as they think necessary for the performance of their duties as auditors.

(2) An officer of a company commits an offence if he knowingly or recklessly makes to the company's auditors a statement (whether written or oral) which—

(a) conveys or purports to convey any information or explanations which the auditors require, or are entitled to require, as auditors of the company, and

(b) is misleading, false or deceptive in a material particular.

A person guilty of an offence under this subsection is liable to imprisonment or a fine, or both.

(3) A subsidiary undertaking which is a body corporate incorporated in Great Britain, and the auditors of such an undertaking, shall give to the auditors of any parent company of the undertaking such information and explanations as they may reasonably require for the purposes of their duties as auditors of that company.

If a subsidiary undertaking fails to comply with this subsection, the undertaking and every officer of it who is in default is guilty of an offence and liable to a fine; and if an auditor fails without reasonable excuse to comply with this subsection he is guilty of an offence and liable to a fine.

(4) A parent company having a subsidiary undertaking which is not a body corporate incorporated in Great Britain shall, if required by its auditors to do so, take all such steps as are reasonably open to it to obtain from the subsidiary undertaking such information and explanations as they may reasonably require for the purposes of their duties as auditors of that company.

If a parent company fails to comply with this subsection, the company and every officer of it who is in default is guilty of an offence and liable to a fine.

(5) Section 734 (criminal proceedings against unincorporated bodies) applies to an offence under subsection (3).][1]

1 Inserted by CA 1989, s 120 with effect from 1 April 1990 (SI 1990 No 355) subject to the transitional and saving provisions in Schedule 4 of that Order.

[390 Right to attend company meetings, etc.

(1) A company's auditors are entitled—

(a) to receive all notices of, and other communications relating to, any general meeting which a member of the company is entitled to receive;
(b) to attend any general meeting of the company; and
(c) to be heard at any general meeting which they attend on any part of the business of the meeting which concerns them as auditors.

(2) In relation to a written resolution proposed to be agreed to by a private company in accordance with section 381A, the company's auditors are entitled—

(a) to receive all such communications relating to the resolution as, by virtue of any provision of Schedule 15A, are required to be supplied to a member of the company,
(b) to give notice in accordance with section 381B of their opinion that the resolution concerns them as auditors and should be considered by the company in general meeting or, as the case may be, by a meeting of the relevant class of members of the company,
(c) to attend any such meeting, and
(d) to be heard at any such meeting which they attend on any part of the business of the meeting which concerns them as auditors.

(3) The right to attend or be heard at a meeting is exercisable in the case of a body corporate or partnership by an individual authorised by it in writing to act as its representative at the meeting.][1]

1 Inserted by CA 1989, s 120 with effect from 1 April 1990 (SI 1990 No 355) subject to the transitional and saving provisions in Schedule 4 of that Order.

[*Remuneration of auditors*

390A Remuneration of auditors

(1) The remuneration of auditors appointed by the company in general meeting shall be fixed by the company in general meeting or in such manner as the company in general meeting may determine.

(2) The remuneration of auditors appointed by the directors or the Secretary of State shall be fixed by the directors or the Secretary of State, as the case may be.

(3) There shall be stated in a note to the company's annual accounts the amount of the remuneration of the company's auditors in their capacity as such.

(4) For the purposes of this section "remuneration" includes sums paid in respect of expenses.

(5) This section applies in relation to benefits in kind as to payments in cash, and in relation to any such benefit references to its amount are to its estimated money value.

The nature of any such benefit shall also be disclosed.][1]

[1] Inserted by CA 1989, s 121 with effect from 1 April 1990 (SI 1990 No 355) subject to the transitional and saving provisions in Schedule 4 of that Order.

[390B Remuneration of auditors or their associates for non-audit work

(1) The Secretary of State may make provision by regulations for securing the disclosure of the amount of any remuneration received or receivable by a company's auditors or their associates in respect of services other than those of auditors in their capacity as such.

(2) The regulations may—

(a) provide that "remuneration" includes sums paid in respect of expenses,
(b) apply in relation to benefits in kind as to payments in cash, and in relation to any such benefit require disclosure of its nature and its estimated money value,
(c) define "associate" in relation to an auditor,
(d) require the disclosure of remuneration in respect of services rendered to associated undertakings of the company, and
(e) define "associated undertaking" for that purpose.

(3) The regulations may require the auditors to disclose the relevant information in their report or require the relevant information to be disclosed in a note to the company's accounts and require the auditors to supply the directors of the company with such information as is necessary to enable that disclosure to be made.

(4) The regulations may make different provision for different cases.

(5) Regulations under this section shall be made by statutory instrument which shall be subject to annulment in pursuance of a resolution of either House of Parliament.][1]

[1] Inserted by CA 1989, s 121 with effect from 1 April 1990 (SI 1990 No 355) subject to the transitional and saving provisions in Schedule 4 of that Order.

[*Removal, resignation, etc. of auditors*

391 Removal of auditors

(1) A company may by ordinary resolution at any time remove an auditor from office, notwithstanding anything in any agreement between it and him.

(2) Where a resolution removing an auditor is passed at a general meeting of a company, the company shall within 14 days give notice of that fact in the prescribed form to the registrar.

If a company fails to give the notice required by this subsection, the company and every officer of it who is in default is guilty of an offence and liable to a fine and, for continued contravention, to a daily default fine.

(3) Nothing in this section shall be taken as depriving a person removed under it of compensation or damages payable to him in respect of the termination of his appointment as auditor or of any appointment terminating with that as auditor.

(4) An auditor of a company who has been removed has, notwithstanding his removal, the rights conferred by section 390 in relation to any general meeting of the company—

(a) at which his term of office would otherwise have expired, or
(b) at which it is proposed to fill the vacancy caused by his removal.

In such a case the references in that section to matters concerning the auditors as auditors shall be construed as references to matters concerning him as a former auditor.][1]

[1] Inserted by CA 1989, s 122 with effect from 1 April 1990 (SI 1990 No 355) subject to the transitional and saving provisions in Schedule 4 of that Order.

[391A Rights of auditors who are removed or not re-appointed

(1) Special notice is required for a resolution at a general meeting of a company—

(a) removing an auditor before the expiration of his term of office, or
(b) appointing as auditor a person other than a retiring auditor.

(2) On receipt of notice of such an intended resolution the company shall forthwith send a copy of it to the person proposed to be removed or, as the case may be, to the person proposed to be appointed and to the retiring auditor.

(3) The auditor proposed to be removed or (as the case may be) the retiring auditor may make with respect to the intended resolution representations in writing to the company (not exceeding a reasonable length) and request their notification to members of the company.

(4) The company shall (unless the representations are received by it too late for it to do so)—

(a) in any notice of the resolution given to members of the company, state the fact of the representations having been made, and
(b) send a copy of the representations to every member of the company to whom notice of the meeting is or has been sent.

(5) If a copy of any such representations is not sent out as required because received too late or because of the company's default, the auditor may (without prejudice to his right to be heard orally) require that the representations be read out at the meeting.

(6) Copies of the representations need not be sent out and the representations need not be read at the meeting if, on the application either of the company or of any other person claiming to be aggrieved, the court is satisfied that the rights conferred by this section are being abused to secure needless publicity for defamatory matter; and the court may order the company's costs on the application to be paid in whole or in part by the auditor, notwithstanding that he is not a party to the application.][1]

[1] Inserted by CA 1989, s 122 with effect from 1 April 1990 (SI 1990 No 355) subject to the transitional and saving provisions in Schedule 4 of that Order.

[392 Resignation of auditors

(1) An auditor of a company may resign his office by depositing a notice in writing to that effect at the company's registered office.

The notice is not effective unless it is accompanied by the statement required by section 394.

(2) An effective notice of resignation operates to bring the auditor's term of office to an end as of the date on which the notice is deposited or on such later date as may be specified in it.

(3) The company shall within 14 days of the deposit of a notice of resignation send a copy of the notice to the registrar of companies.

If default is made in complying with this subsection, the company and every officer of it who is in default is guilty of an offence and liable to a fine and, for continued contravention, a daily default fine.][1]

[1] Inserted by CA 1989, s 122 with effect from 1 April 1990 (SI 1990 No 355) subject to the transitional and saving provisions in Schedule 4 of that Order.

[392A Rights of resigning auditors

(1) This section applies where an auditor's notice of resignation is accompanied by a statement of circumstances which he considers should be brought to the attention of members or creditors of the company.

(2) He may deposit with the notice a signed requisition calling on the directors of the company forthwith duly to convene an extraordinary general meeting of the company for the purpose of receiving and considering such explanation of the circumstances connected with his resignation as he may wish to place before the meeting.

(3) He may request the company to circulate to its members—

(a) before the meeting convened on his requisition, or
(b) before any general meeting at which his term of office would otherwise have expired or at which it is proposed to fill the vacancy caused by his resignation,

a statement in writing (not exceeding a reasonable length) of the circumstances connected with his resignation.

(4) The company shall (unless the statement is received too late for it to comply)—

(a) in any notice of the meeting given to members of the company, state the fact of the statement having been made, and
(b) send a copy of the statement to every member of the company to whom notice of the meeting is or has been sent.

(5) If the directors do not within 21 days from the date of the deposit of a requisition under this section proceed duly to convene a meeting for a day not more than 28 days after the date on which the notice convening the meeting is given, every director who failed to take all reasonable steps to secure that a meeting was convened as mentioned above is guilty of an offence and liable to a fine.

(6) If a copy of the statement mentioned above is not sent out as required because received too late or because of the company's default, the auditor may (without prejudice to his right to be heard orally) require that the statement be read out at the meeting.

(7) Copies of a statement need not be sent out and the statement need not be read out at the meeting if, on the application either of the company or of any other person who claims to be aggrieved, the court is satisfied that the rights conferred by this section are being abused to secure needless publicity for defamatory matter; and the court may order the company's costs on such an application to be paid in whole or in part by the auditor, notwithstanding that he is not a party to the application.

(8) An auditor who has resigned has, notwithstanding his resignation, the rights conferred by section 390 in relation to any such general meeting of the company as is mentioned in subsection (3)(a) or (b).

In such a case the references in that section to matters concerning the auditors as auditors shall be construed as references to matters concerning him as a former auditor.][1]

---

1 Inserted by CA 1989, s 122 with effect from 1 April 1990 (SI 1990 No 355) subject to the transitional and saving provisions in Schedule 4 of that Order.

[393 Termination of appointment of auditors not appointed annually

(1) When an election is in force under section 386 (election by private company to dispense with annual appointment), any member of the company may deposit notice in writing at the company's registered office proposing that the appointment of the company's auditors be brought to an end.

No member may deposit more than one such notice in any financial year of the company.

(2) If such a notice is deposited it is the duty of the directors—

(a) to convene a general meeting of the company for a date not more than 28 days after the date on which the notice was given, and

(b) to propose at the meeting a resolution in a form enabling the company to decide whether the appointment of the company's auditors should be brought to an end.

(3) If the decision of the company at the meeting is that the appointment of the auditors should be brought to an end, the auditors shall not be deemed to be re-appointed when next they would be and, if the notice was deposited within the period immediately following the distribution of accounts, any deemed re-appointment for the financial year following that to which those accounts relate which has already occurred shall cease to have effect.

The period immediately following the distribution of accounts means the period beginning with the day on which copies of the company's annual accounts are sent to members of the company under section 238 and ending 14 days after that day.

(4) If the directors do not within 14 days from the date of the deposit of the notice proceed duly to convene a meeting, the member who deposited the notice (or, if there was more than one, any of them) may himself convene the meeting; but any meeting so convened shall not be held after the expiration of three months from that date.

(5) A meeting convened under this section by a member shall be convened in the same manner, as nearly as possible, as that in which meetings are to be convened by directors.

(6) Any reasonable expenses incurred by a member by reason of the failure of the directors duly to convene a meeting shall be made good to him by the company; and any such sums shall be recouped by the company from such of the directors as were in default out of any sums payable, or to become payable, by the company by way of fees or other remuneration in respect of their services.

(7) This section has effect notwithstanding anything in any agreement between the company and its auditors; and no compensation or damages shall be payable by reason of the auditors' appointment being terminated under this section.][1]

[1] Inserted by CA 1989, s 122 with effect from 1 April 1990 (SI 1990 No 355) subject to the transitional and saving provisions in Schedule 4 of that Order.

[394 Statement by person ceasing to hold office as auditor

(1) Where an auditor ceases for any reason to hold office, he shall deposit at the company's registered office a statement of any circumstances connected with his ceasing to hold office which he considers should be brought to the attention of the members or creditors of the company or, if he considers that there are no such circumstances, a statement that there are none.

(2) In the case of resignation, the statement shall be deposited along with the notice of resignation; in the case of failure to seek re-appointment, the statement shall be deposited not less than 14 days before the end of the time allowed for next appointing auditors; in any other case, the statement shall be deposited not later than the end of the period of 14 days beginning with the date on which he ceases to hold office.

(3) If the statement is of circumstances which the auditor considers should be brought to the attention of the members or creditors of the company, the company shall within 14 days of the deposit of the statement either—

(a) send a copy of it to every person who under section 238 is entitled to be sent copies of the accounts, or
(b) apply to the court.

(4) The company shall if it applies to the court notify the auditor of the application.

(5) Unless the auditor receives notice of such an application before the end of the period of 21 days beginning with the day on which he deposited the statement, he shall within a further seven days send a copy of the statement to the registrar.

(6) If the court is satisfied that the auditor is using the statement to secure needless publicity for defamatory matter—

(a) it shall direct that copies of the statement need not be sent out, and
(b) it may further order the company's costs on the application to be paid in whole or in part by the auditor, notwithstanding that he is not a party to the application;

and the company shall within 14 days of the court's decision send to the persons mentioned in subsection (3)(a) a statement setting out the effect of the order.

(7) If the court is not so satisfied, the company shall within 14 days of the court's decision—

(a) send copies of the statement to the persons mentioned in subsection (3)(a), and
(b) notify the auditor of the court's decision;

and the auditor shall within seven days of receiving such notice send a copy of the statement to the registrar.][1]

[1] Inserted by CA 1989, s 123 with effect from 1 April 1990 (SI 1990 No 355) subject to the transitional and saving provisions in Schedule 4 of that Order.

Cross references. See Sec 394A.

[394A Offences of failing to comply with s 394

(1) If a person ceasing to hold office as auditor fails to comply with section 394 he is guilty of an offence and liable to a fine.

(2) In proceedings for an offence under subsection (1) it is a defence for the person charged to show that he took all reasonable steps and exercised all due diligence to avoid the commission of the offence.

(3) Sections 733 (liability of individuals for corporate default) and 734 (criminal proceedings against unincorporated bodies) apply to an offence under subsection (1).

(4) If a company makes default in complying with section 394, the company and every officer of it who is in default is guilty of an offence and liable to a fine and, for continued contravention, to a daily default fine.][1]

---

1 Inserted by CA 1989, s 123 with effect from 1 April 1990 (SI 1990 No 355) subject to the transitional and saving provisions in Schedule 4 of that Order.

Note. The original provisions of the above Chapter (Secs 384-394) are replaced by CA 1989, ss 119-123 which inserts new Secs 384-394A.

PART XXII BODIES CORPORATE SUBJECT, OR BECOMING SUBJECT, TO THIS ACT (OTHERWISE THAN BY ORIGINAL FORMATION UNDER PART I)

CHAPTER II COMPANIES NOT FORMED UNDER COMPANIES LEGISLATION, BUT AUTHORISED TO REGISTER

680 Companies capable of being registered under this Chapter

(1) With the exceptions and subject to the provisions contained in this section and the next—

(a) any company consisting of two or more members, which was in existence on 2nd November 1862, including any company registered under the Joint Stock Companies Acts, and

(b) any company formed after that date (whether before or after the commencement of this Act), in pursuance of any Act of Parliament (other than this Act), or of letters patent, or being otherwise duly constituted according to law, and consisting of two or more members,

may at any time, on making application in the prescribed form, register under this Act as an unlimited company, or as a company limited by shares, or as a company limited by guarantee; and the registration is not invalid by reason that it has taken place with a view to the company's being wound up.

(2) A company registered in any part of the United Kingdom under the Companies Act 1862, the Companies (Consolidation) Act 1908, the Companies Act 1929 or the Companies Act 1948 shall not register under this section.

(3) A company having the liability of its members limited by Act of Parliament or letters patent, and not being a joint stock company, shall not register under this section.

(4) A company having the liability of its members limited by Act of Parliament or letters patent shall not register in pursuance of this section as an unlimited company or as a company limited by guarantee.

(5) A company that is not a joint stock company shall not register under this section as a company limited by shares.

PART XXVI INTERPRETATION

735 "Company", etc.

(1) In this Act—

(a) "company" means a company formed and registered under this Act, or an existing company;

(b) "existing company" means a company formed and registered under the former Companies Acts, but does not include a company registered under the Joint Stock Companies Acts, the Companies Act 1862 or the Companies (Consolidation) Act 1908 in what was then Ireland;

(c) "the former Companies Acts" means the Joint Stock Companies Acts, the Companies Act 1862, the Companies (Consolidation) Act 1908, the Companies Act 1929 and the Companies Acts 1948 to 1983.

(2) "Public company" and "private company" have the meanings given by section 1(3).

(3) "The Joint Stock Companies Acts" means the Joint Stock Companies Act 1856, the Joint Stock Companies Acts 1856, 1857, the Joint Stock Banking Companies Act 1857 and the Act to enable Joint Stock Banking Companies to be formed on the principle of limited liability, or any one or more of those Acts (as the case may require), but does not include the Joint Stock Companies Act 1844.

(4) The definitions in this section apply unless the contrary intention appears.

[735A Relationship of this Act to Insolvency Act

(1) In this Act "the Insolvency Act" means the Insolvency Act 1986; and in the following provisions of this Act, namely, sections 375(1)(b), 425(6)(a), [. . .][4] 460(2), 675, 676, 677, 699(1), 728 and Schedule 21, paragraph 6(1), the words "this Act" are to be read as including Parts I to VII of that Act, sections 411, 413, 414, 416 and 417 in Part XV of that Act, and also the Company Directors Disqualification Act 1986.

(2) In sections 704(5), 706(1), 707(1), [707A(1),][2] 708(1)(a) and (4), [709(1) and (3),][2], [710A][3], 713(1), 729 and 732(3) references to the Companies Acts include Parts I to VII of the Insolvency Act, sections 411, 413, 414, 416 and 417 in Part XV of that Act, and also the Company Directors Disqualification Act 1986.

(3) Subsections (1) and (2) apply unless the contrary intention appears.][1]

---

1 Inserted by IA 1986, s 439(1), 13 Sch Part II with effect from 29 December 1986 (see IA 1986, s 443 and SI 1986 No 1924).

2 Inserted by CA 1989, s 127 with effect from a date to be appointed.

3 Substituted by CA 1989, s 127 with effect from a date to be appointed. Previously '710(5)'.

4 Repealed by CA 1989, 24 Sch with effect from 21 February 1990 (SI 1990 No 142). Previously '140, 449(1)(a) and (d)'.

[735B Relationship of this Act to Parts IV and V of the Financial Services Act 1986

In sections 704(5), 706(1), 707(1), 707A(1), 708(1)(a) and (4), 709(1) and (3), 710A and 713(1) references to the Companies Acts include Parts IV and V of the Financial Services Act 1986.][1]

1 Inserted by CA 1989, s 127 with effect from a date to be appointed.

[736 "Subsidiary", "holding company" and "wholly-owned subsidiary"

(1) A company is a "subsidiary" of another company, its "holding company", if that other company—

(a) holds a majority of the voting rights in it, or
(b) is a member of it and has the right to appoint or remove a majority of its board of directors, or
(c) is a member of it and controls alone, pursuant to an agreement with other shareholders or members, a majority of the voting rights in it,

or if it is a subsidiary of a company which is itself a subsidiary of that other company.

(2) A company is a "wholly-owned subsidiary" of another company if it has no members except that other and that other's wholly-owned subsidiaries or persons acting on behalf of that other or its wholly-owned subsidiaries.

(3) In this section "company" includes any body corporate.][1]

1 Substituted by CA 1989, s 144 with effect from a date to be appointed. See below for the original provisions.

Cross references. See Secs 736A, 736B; CA 1989, s 144(2)(6).

[736A Provisions supplementing s 736

(1) The provisions of this section explain expressions used in section 736 and otherwise supplement that section.

(2) In section 736(1)(a) and (c) the references to the voting rights in a company are to the rights conferred on shareholders in respect of their shares or, in the case of a company not having a share capital, on members, to vote at general meetings of the company on all, or substantially all, matters.

(3) In section 736(1)(b) the reference to the right to appoint or remove a majority of the board of directors is to the right to appoint or remove directors holding a majority of the voting rights at meetings of the board on all, or substantially all, matters; and for the purposes of that provision—

(a) a company shall be treated as having the right to appoint to a directorship if—
(i) a person's appointment to it follows necessarily from his appointment as director of the company, or
(ii) the directorship is held by the company itself; and
(b) a right to appoint or remove which is exercisable only with the consent or concurrence of another person shall be left out of account unless no other person has a right to appoint or, as the case may be, remove in relation to that directorship.

(4) Rights which are exercisable only in certain circumstances shall be taken into account only—

(a) when the circumstances have arisen, and for so long as they continue to obtain, or
(b) when the circumstances are within the control of the person having the rights;

and rights which are normally exercisable but are temporarily incapable of exercise shall continue to be taken into account.

(5) Rights held by a person in a fiduciary capacity shall be treated as not held by him.

(6) Rights held by a person as nominee for another shall be treated as held by the other; and rights shall be regarded as held as nominee for another if they are exercisable only on his instructions or with his consent or concurrence.

(7) Rights attached to shares held by way of security shall be treated as held by the person providing the security—

(a) where apart from the right to exercise them for the purpose of preserving the value of the security, or of realising it, the rights are exercisable only in accordance with his instructions;

(b) where the shares are held in connection with the granting of loans as part of normal business activities and apart from the right to exercise them for the purpose of preserving the value of the security, or of realising it, the rights are exercisable only in his interests.

(8) Rights shall be treated as held by a company if they are held by any of its subsidiaries; and nothing in subsection (6) or (7) shall be construed as requiring rights held by a company to be treated as held by any of its subsidiaries.

(9) For the purposes of subsection (7) rights shall be treated as being exercisable in accordance with the instructions or in the interests of a company if they are exercisable in accordance with the instructions of or, as the case may be, in the interests of—

(a) any subsidiary or holding company of that company, or
(b) any subsidiary of a holding company of that company.

(10) The voting rights in a company shall be reduced by any rights held by the company itself.

(11) References in any provision of subsections (5) to (10) to rights held by a person include rights falling to be treated as held by him by virtue of any other provision of those subsections but not rights which by virtue of any such provision are to be treated as not held by him.

(12) In this section "company" includes any body corporate.][1]

1 Inserted by CA 1989, s 144 with effect from a date to be appointed.

Cross references. See Sec 736B.

Note. The provisions of Secs 736 and 736A above replaced the original Sec 736.

[736B Power to amend ss 736 and 736A

(1) The Secretary of State may by regulations amend sections 736 and 736A so as to alter the meaning of the expressions "holding company", "subsidiary" or "wholly-owned subsidiary".

(2) The regulations may make different provision for different cases or classes of case and may contain such incidental and supplementary provisions as the Secretary of State thinks fit.

(3) Regulations under this section shall be made by statutory instrument which shall be subject to annulment in pursuance of a resolution of either House of Parliament.

(4) Any amendment made by regulations under this section does not apply for the purposes of enactments outside the Companies Acts unless the regulations so provide.

(5) So much of section 23(3) of the Interpretation Act 1978 as applies section 17(2)(a) of that Act (effect of repeal and re-enactment) to deeds, instruments and documents other than enactments shall not apply in relation to any repeal and re-enactment effected by regulations made under this section.][1]

---

1 Inserted by CA 1989, s 144 with effect from a date to be appointed.

---

737 "Called-up share capital"

(1) In this Act, "called-up share capital", in relation to a company, means so much of its share capital as equals the aggregate amount of the calls made on its shares (whether or not those calls have been paid), together with any share capital paid up without being called and any share capital to be paid on a specified future date under the articles, the terms of allotment of the relevant shares or any other arrangements for payment of those shares.

(2) "Uncalled share capital" is to be construed accordingly.

(3) The definitions in this section apply unless the contrary intention appears.

738 "Allotment" and "paid up"

(1) In relation to an allotment of shares in a company, the shares are to be taken for the purposes of this Act to be allotted when a person acquires the unconditional right to be included in the company's register of members in respect of those shares.

(2) For purposes of this Act, a share in a company is deemed paid up (as to its nominal value or any premium on it) in cash, or allotted for cash, if the consideration for the allotment or payment up is cash received by the company, or is a cheque received by it in good faith which the directors have no reason for suspecting will not be paid, or is a release of a liability of the company for a liquidated sum, or is an undertaking to pay cash to the company at a future date.

(3) In relation to the allotment or payment up of any shares in a company, references in this Act (except sections 89 to 94) to consideration other than cash and to the payment up of shares and premiums on shares otherwise than in cash include the payment of, or any undertaking to pay, cash to any person other than the company.

(4) For the purpose of determining whether a share is or is to be allotted for cash, or paid up in cash, "cash" includes foreign currency.

739 "Non-cash asset"

(1) In this Act "non-cash asset" means any property or interest in property other than cash; and for this purpose "cash" includes foreign currency.

(2) A reference to the transfer or acquisition of a non-cash asset includes the creation or extinction of an estate or interest in, or a right over, any property and also the discharge of any person's liability, other than a liability for a liquidated sum.

740 "Body corporate" and "corporation"

References in this Act to a body corporate or to a corporation do not include a corporation sole, but include a company incorporated elsewhere than in Great Britain.

Such references to a body corporate do not include a Scottish firm.

741 "Director" and "shadow director"

(1) In this Act, "director" includes any person occupying the position of director, by whatever name called.

(2) In relation to a company, "shadow director" means a person in accordance with whose directions or instructions the directors of the company are accustomed to act.

However, a person is not deemed a shadow director by reason only that the directors act on advice given by him in a professional capacity.

(3) For the purposes of the following provisions of this Act, namely—

section 309 (directors' duty to have regard to interests of employees),

section 319 (directors' long-term contracts of employment),

sections 320 to 322 (substantial property transactions involving directors), and

sections 330 to 346 (general restrictions on power of companies to make loans, etc., to directors and others connected with them),

(being provisions under which shadow directors are treated as directors), a body corporate is not to be treated as a shadow director of any of its subsidiary companies by reason only that the directors of the subsidiary are accustomed to act in accordance with its directions or instructions.

742 Expressions used in connection with accounts

[(1) In this Act, unless a contrary intention appears, the following expressions have the same meaning as in Part VII (accounts)—

"annual accounts",

"accounting reference date" and "accounting reference period",

"balance sheet" and "balance sheet date",

"current assets",

"financial year", in relation to a company,

"fixed assets",

"parent company" and "parent undertaking",

"profit and loss account", and

"subsidiary undertaking".

(2) References in this Act to "realised profits" and "realised losses", in relation to a company's accounts, shall be construed in accordance with section 262(3).][1]

---

1 Substituted by CA 1989, 10 Sch 15 with effect from 1 April 1990 (SI 1990 No 355) subject to the transitional and saving provisions in Arts 6 to 9 of that Order reproduced above Sec 221 above.
Previously
'(1) In this Act, unless the contrary intention appears—
(a) "accounting reference period" has the meaning given by sections 224 to 226;
(b) "accounts" includes a company's group accounts (within the meaning of section 229), whether prepared in the form of accounts or not;
(c) "balance sheet date", in relation to a balance sheet, means the date as at which the balance sheet was prepared;
(d) "financial year"—
(i) in relation to a body corporate to which Part VII applies, means a period in respect of which a profit and loss account under section 227 in that Part is made up, and
(ii) in relation to any other body corporate, means a period in respect of which a profit and loss account of the body laid before it in general meeting is made up,
(whether, in either case, that period is a year or not);
(e) any reference to a profit and loss account, in the case of a company not trading for profit, is to its income and expenditure account, and references to profit or loss and, if the company has subsidiaries, references to a consolidated profit and loss account are to be construed accordingly.
(2) Except in relation to special category accounts, any reference to a balance sheet or profit and loss account includes any notes to the account in question giving information which is required by any provision of this Act, and required or allowed by any such provision to be given in a note to company accounts.
(3) In relation to special category accounts, any reference to a balance sheet or profit and loss account includes any notes thereon or document annexed thereto giving information which is required by this Act and is thereby allowed to be so given.
(4) References to special category companies and special category accounts are to be construed in accordance with Chapter II of Part VII.
(5) For the purposes of Part VII, a body corporate is to be regarded as publishing any balance sheet or other account if it publishes, issues or circulates it or otherwise makes it available for public inspection in a manner calculated to invite members of the public generally, or any class of members of the public, to read it.
(6) Expressions which, when used in Schedule 4, fall to be construed in accordance with any provision of Part VII of that Schedule have the same meaning (unless the contrary intention appears) when used in any provision of this Act.'

---

743 "Employees' share scheme"

For purposes of this Act, an employees' share scheme is a scheme for encouraging or facilitating the holding of shares or debentures in a company by or for the benefit of—

(a) the bona fide employees or former employees of the company, the company's subsidiary or holding company or a subsidiary of the company's holding company, or
(b) the wives, husbands, widows, widowers or children or step-children under the age of 18 of such employees or former employees.

Cross references. See CA 1989, 18 Sch 37.

[743A Meaning of "office copy" in Scotland

References in this Act to an office copy of a court order shall be construed, as respects Scotland, as references to a certified copy interlocutor.][1]

---

1 Inserted by CA 1989, 19 Sch 19 with effect from 1 March 1990 (SI 1990 No 142).

744 Expressions used generally in this Act

In this Act, unless the contrary intention appears, the following definitions apply—

"agent" does not include a person's counsel acting as such;

[. . .][7]

"articles" means, in relation to a company, its articles of association, as originally framed or as altered by resolution, including (so far as applicable to the company) regulations contained in or annexed to any enactment relating to companies passed before this Act, as altered by or under any such enactment;

[. . .][5]

[. . .][8]

"bank holiday" means a holiday under the Banking and Financial Dealings Act 1971;

["banking company" means a company which is authorised under the Banking Act 1987;][6]

"books and papers" and "books or papers" include accounts, deeds, writings and documents;

"the Companies Acts" means this Act, the Insider Dealing Act and the Consequential Provisions Act;

"the Consequential Provisions Act" means the Companies Consolidation (Consequential Provisions) Act 1985;

"the court", in relation to a company, means the court having jurisdiction to wind up the company;

"debenture" includes debenture stock, bonds and any other securities of a company, whether constituting a charge on the assets of the company or not;

"document" includes summons, notice, order, and other legal process, and registers;

"equity share capital" means, in relation to a company, its issued share capital excluding any part of that capital which, neither as respects dividends nor as respects capital, carries any right to participate beyond a specified amount in a distribution;

[. . .][9]

"the Gazette" means, as respects companies registered in England and Wales, the London Gazette and, as respects companies registered in Scotland, the Edinburgh Gazette;

[. . .][1]

"hire-purchase agreement" has the same meaning as in the Consumer Credit Act 1974;

"the Insider Dealing Act" means the Company Securities (Insider Dealing) Act 1985;

"insurance company" means the same as in the Insurance Companies Act 1982;

[. . .][10]

"memorandum", in relation to a company, means its memorandum of association, as originally framed or as altered in pursuance of any enactment;

"number", in relation to shares, includes amount, where the context admits of the reference to shares being construed to include stock;

"officer", in relation to a body corporate, includes a director, manager or secretary;

"official seal", in relation to the registrar of companies, means a seal prepared under section 704(4) for the authentication of documents required for or in connection with the registration of companies;

"oversea company" means—

(a) a company incorporated elsewhere than in Great Britain which, after the commencement of this Act, establishes a place of business in Great Britain, and
(b) a company so incorporated which has, before that commencement, established a place of business and continues to have an established place of business in Great Britain at that commencement;

"place of business" includes a share transfer or share registration office;

"prescribed" means—

(a) as respects provisions of this Act relating to winding up, prescribed by general rules [. . .][2], and
(b) otherwise, prescribed by statutory instrument made by the Secretary of State;

"prospectus" means any prospectus, notice, circular, advertisement, or other invitation, offering to the public for subscription or purchase any shares in or debentures of a company;

"prospectus issued generally" means a prospectus issued to persons who are not existing members of the company or holders of its debentures;

[. . .][3]

[. . .][4]

"the registrar of companies" and "the registrar" mean the registrar or other officer performing under this Act the duty of registration of companies in England and Wales or in Scotland, as the case may require;

"share" means share in the share capital of a company, and includes stock (except where a distinction between shares and stock is expressed or implied); and

[. . .][11].

---

1 Repealed by IA 1985, s 235(3), 10 Sch Part II with effect from 1 March 1986 in so far as relating to the making of general rules in England and Wales (SI 1986 No 185) and otherwise as from 29 December 1986 (SI 1986 No 1924).
Previously
'"general rules" means general rules made under section 663, and includes forms;'.

2 Repealed by IA 1985, s 235(3), 10 Sch Part II as [1] above.
Previously 'under section 663'.

3 Repealed by Banking Act 1987, s 108(1), 6 Sch 18(8), 7 Sch Part I with effect from 1 October 1987 (see SI 1987 No 1664).
Previously
'"recognised bank" means a company which is recognised as a bank for the purposes of the Banking Act 1979;'.

4 Repealed by FSA 1986, s 212(3), 17 Sch Part I with effect from 29 April 1988 (see SI 1988 No 740).
Previously
'"recognised stock exchange" means any body of persons which is for the time being a recognised stock exchange for the purposes of the Prevention of Fraud (Investments) Act 1958;'.

5 Deleted by CA 1989, 10 Sch 16 with effect from 1 April 1990 (SI 1990 No 355) subject to the transitional and saving provisions in Arts 6 to 9 of that Order.
Previously '["authorised institution" means a company which is an institution authorised under the Banking Act 1987;][a]'.

[a] Inserted by Banking Act 1987, s 108(1), 6 Sch 18(8) with effect from 1 October 1987 (see SI 1987 No 1664).

6 Inserted by CA 1989, 10 Sch 16 with effect as in [5] above.

7 Repealed by CA 1989, 24 Sch with effect from a date to be appointed.
Previously
'"annual return" means the return to be made by a company under section 363 or 364 (as the case may be);'.

8 Repealed by CA 1989, 24 Sch with effect from a date to be appointed.
Previously
'"authorised minimum" has the meaning given by section 118;'.

9 Repealed by CA 1989, 24 Sch with effect from a date to be appointed.
Previously
'"expert" has the meaning given by section 62;
"floating charge" includes a floating charge within the meaning given by section 462;'.

10 Repealed by CA 1989, 24 Sch with effect from a date to be appointed.
Previously
'"joint stock company" has the meaning given by section 683;'.

11 Repealed by CA 1989, 24 Sch with effect from a date to be appointed.
Previously
'"undistributable reserves" has the meaning given by section 264(3).'.

Notes
(a) The definition of "prospectus issued generally" is repealed by FSA 1986, s 212(3), 17 Sch Part I with effect from 29 April 1988 to the extent that it applies to a prospectus offering for subscription, or to any form of application for, units in a body corporate which is a recognised scheme (SI 1988 No 740).

[744A Index of defined expressions

The following Table shows provisions defining or otherwise explaining expressions for the purposes of this Act generally—

accounting reference date, accounting reference period	sections 224 and 742(1)
acquisition (in relation to a non-cash asset)	section 739(2)
agent	section 744
allotment (and related expressions)	section 738
annual accounts	sections 261(2), 262(1) and 742(1)
annual general meeting	section 366
annual return	section 363
articles	section 744
authorised minimum	section 118
balance sheet and balance sheet date	sections 261(2), 262(1) and 742(1)
bank holiday	section 744
banking company	section 744
body corporate	section 740
books and papers, books or papers	section 744
called-up share capital	section 737(1)
capital redemption reserve	section 170(1)
the Companies Acts	section 744
companies charges register	section 397
company	section 735(1)
the Consequential Provisions Act	section 744
corporation	section 740
the court (in relation to a company)	section 744
current assets	sections 262(1) and 742(1)

debenture	section 744
director	section 741(1)
document	section 744
elective resolution	section 379A
employees' share scheme	section 743
equity share capital	section 744
existing company	section 735(1)
extraordinary general meeting	section 368
extraordinary resolution	section 378(1)
financial year (of a company)	sections 223 and 742(1)
fixed assets	sections 262(1) and 742(1)
floating charge (in Scotland)	section 462
the former Companies Acts	section 735(1)
the Gazette	section 744
hire-purchase agreement	section 744
holding company	section 736
the Insider Dealing Act	section 744
the Insolvency Act	section 735A(1)
insurance company	section 744
the Joint Stock Companies Acts	section 735(3)
limited company	section 1(2)
member (of a company)	section 22
memorandum (in relation to a company)	section 744
non-cash asset	section 739(1)
number (in relation to shares)	section 744
office copy (in relation to a court order in Scotland)	section 743A
officer (in relation to a body corporate)	section 744
official seal (in relation to the registrar of companies)	section 744
oversea company	section 744
overseas branch register	section 362
paid up (and related expressions)	section 738
parent company and parent undertaking	sections 258 and 742(1)
place of business	section 744
prescribed	section 744
private company	section 1(3)
profit and loss account	sections 261(2), 262(1) and 742(1)
prospectus	section 744
public company	section 1(3)
realised profits or losses	sections 262(3) and 742(2)
registered number (of a company)	section 705(1)
registered office (of a company)	section 287
registrar and registrar of companies	section 744
resolution for reducing share capital	section 135(3)
shadow director	section 741(2) and (3)
share	section 744
share premium account	section 130(1)
share warrant	section 188
special notice (in relation to a resolution)	section 379
special resolution	section 378(2)
subsidiary	section 736
subsidiary undertaking	sections 258 and 742(1)

transfer (in relation to a non-cash asset)	section 739(2)
uncalled share capital	section 737(2)
undistributable reserves	section 264(3)
unlimited company	section 1(2)
unregistered company	section 718
wholly-owned subsidiary	section 736(2)][1]

[1] Inserted by CA 1989, 19 Sch 20 with effect from a date to be appointed.

SCHEDULE 4
(Sections 228, 230 and as amended by CA 1989, s 4(2), 1 Sch)

FORM AND CONTENT OF COMPANY ACCOUNTS

PART I GENERAL RULES AND FORMATS

SECTION A GENERAL RULES

1 (1) Subject to the following provisions of this Schedule—

(a) every balance sheet of a company shall show the items listed in either of the balance sheet formats set out below in section B of this Part; and
(b) every profit and loss account of a company shall show the items listed in any one of the profit and loss account formats so set out;

in either case in the order and under the headings and sub-headings given in the format adopted.

(2) Sub-paragraph (1) above is not to be read as requiring the heading or sub-heading for any item to be distinguished by any letter or number assigned to that item in the format adopted.

2 (1) Where in accordance with paragraph 1 a company's balance sheet or profit and loss account for any financial year has been prepared by reference to one of the formats set out in section B below, the directors of the company shall adopt the same format in preparing the accounts for subsequent financial years of the company unless in their opinion there are special reasons for a change.

(2) Particulars of any change in the format adopted in preparing a company's balance sheet or profit and loss account in accordance with paragraph 1 shall be disclosed, and the reasons for the change shall be explained, in a note to the accounts in which the new format is first adopted.

3 (1) Any item required in accordance with paragraph 1 to be shown in a company's balance sheet or profit and loss account may be shown in greater detail than required by the format adopted.

(2) A company's balance sheet or profit and loss account may include an item representing or covering the amount of any asset or liability, income or expenditure not otherwise covered by any of the items listed in the format adopted, but the following shall not be treated as assets in any company's balance sheet—

(a) preliminary expenses;
(b) expenses of and commission on any issue of shares or debentures; and
(c) costs of research.

(3) In preparing a company's balance sheet or profit and loss account the directors of the company shall adapt the arrangement and headings and sub-headings otherwise required by paragraph 1 in respect of items to which an Arabic number is assigned in the format adopted, in any case where the special nature of the company's business requires such adaptation.

(4) Items to which Arabic numbers are assigned in any of the formats set out in section B below may be combined in a company's accounts for any financial year if either—

(a) their individual amounts are not material to assessing the state of affairs or profit or loss of the company for that year; or
(b) the combination facilitates that assessment;

but in a case within paragraph (b) the individual amounts of any items so combined shall be disclosed in a note to the accounts.

(5) Subject to paragraph 4(3) below, a heading or sub-heading corresponding to an item listed in the format adopted in preparing a company's balance sheet or profit and loss account shall not be included if there is no amount to be shown for that item in respect of the financial year to which the balance sheet or profit and loss account relates.

(6) Every profit and loss account of a company shall show the amount of the company's profit or loss on ordinary activities before taxation.

(7) Every profit and loss account of a company shall show separately as additional items—

(a) any amount set aside or proposed to be set aside to, or withdrawn or proposed to be withdrawn from, reserves; and
(b) the aggregate amount of any dividends paid and proposed.

4 (1) In respect of every item shown in a company's balance sheet or profit and loss account the corresponding amount for the financial year immediately preceding that to which the balance sheet or profit and loss account relates shall also be shown.

(2) Where that corresponding amount is not comparable with the amount to be shown for the item in question in respect of the financial year to which the balance sheet or profit and loss account relates, the former amount shall be adjusted and particulars of the adjustment and the reasons for it shall be disclosed in a note to the accounts.

(3) Paragraph 3(5) does not apply in any case where an amount can be shown for the item in question in respect of the financial year immediately preceding that to which the balance sheet or profit and loss account relates, and that amount shall be shown under the heading or sub-heading required by paragraph 1 for that item.

5 Amounts in respect of items representing assets or income may not be set off against amounts in respect of items representing liabilities or expenditure (as the case may be), or vice versa.

SECTION B THE REQUIRED FORMATS FOR ACCOUNTS

Preliminary

6 References in this Part of this Schedule to the items listed in any of the formats set out below are to those items read together with any of the notes following the formats which apply to any of those items, and the requirement imposed by paragraph 1 to show the items listed in any such format in the order adopted in the format is subject to any provision in those notes for alternative positions for any particular items.

7 A number in brackets following any item in any of the formats set out below is a reference to the note of that number in the notes following the formats.

8 In the notes following the formats—

(a) the heading of each note gives the required heading or sub-heading for the item to which it applies and a reference to any letters and numbers assigned to that item in the formats set out below (taking a reference in the case of Format 2 of the balance sheet formats to the item listed under "Assets" or under "Liabilities" as the case may require); and

(b) references to a numbered format are to the balance sheet format or (as the case may require) to the profit and loss account format of that number set out below.

Balance Sheet Formats Format 1

A. Called up share capital not paid (1)

B. Fixed assets

I Intangible assets
1. Development costs
2. Concessions, patents, licences, trade marks and similar rights and assets (2)
3. Goodwill (3)
4. Payments on account

II Tangible assets
1. Land and buildings
2. Plant and machinery
3. Fixtures, fittings, tools and equipment
4. Payments on account and assets in course of construction

III Investments
1. Shares in group [undertakings][1]
2. Loans to group [undertakings][1]
3. [Participating interests][2]
4. Loans to [undertakings in which the company has a participating interest][3]
5. Other investments other than loans
6. Other loans
7. Own shares (4)

C. Current assets

I Stocks
1. Raw materials and consumables
2. Work in progress
3. Finished goods and goods for resale
4. Payments on account

II Debtors (5)
1. Trade debtors
2. Amounts owed by group [undertakings][1]
3. Amounts owed by [undertakings in which the company has a participating interest][3]
4. Other debtors
5. Called up share capital not paid (1)
6. Prepayments and accrued income (6)

III Investments
1. Shares in group [undertakings][1]
2. Own shares (4)
3. Other investments

IV Cash at bank and in hand

D. Prepayments and accrued income (6)

E. Creditors: amounts falling due within one year

1. Debenture loans (7)
2. Bank loans and overdrafts
3. Payments received on account (8)
4. Trade creditors
5. Bills of exchange payable
6. Amounts owed to group [undertakings][1]
7. Amounts owed to [undertakings in which the company has a participating interest][3]
8. Other creditors including taxation and social security (9)
9. Accruals and deferred income (10)

F. Net current assets (liabilities) (11)

G. Total assets less current liabilities

H. Creditors: amounts falling due after more than one year

1. Debenture loans (7)
2. Bank loans and overdrafts
3. Payments received on account (8)
4. Trade creditors
5. Bills of exchange payable
6. Amounts owed to group [undertakings][1]
7. Amounts owed to [undertakings in which the company has a participating interest][3]
8. Other creditors including taxation and social security (9)
9. Accruals and deferred income (10)

I. Provisions for liabilities and charges

1. Pensions and similar obligations
2. Taxation, including deferred taxation
3. Other provisions

J. Accruals and deferred income (10)

K. Capital and reserves

I Called up share capital (12)

II Share premium account

III Revaluation reserve

IV Other reserves

1. Capital redemption reserve
2. Reserve for own shares
3. Reserves provided for by the articles of association
4. Other reserves

V Profit and loss account

---

1 Substituted by CA 1989, 1 Sch 2 with effect from 1 April 1990 (SI 1990 No 355) subject to the transitional and saving provisions in Arts 6 to 9 of that Order.
Previously 'companies'.

2 Substituted by CA 1989, 1 Sch 3 with effect as in [1] above.
Previously 'Shares in related companies'.

3 Substituted by CA 1989, 1 Sch 4 with effect as in [1] above.
Previously 'related companies'.

Balance Sheet Formats Format 2

ASSETS

A. Called up share capital not paid (1)

B. Fixed assets

I Intangible assets
1. Development costs
2. Concessions, patents, licences, trade marks and similar rights and assets (2)
3. Goodwill (3)
4. Payments on account

II Tangible assets
1. Land and buildings
2. Plant and machinery
3. Fixtures, fittings, tools and equipment
4. Payments on account and assets in course of construction

III Investments
1. Shares in group [undertakings][1]
2. Loans to group [undertakings][1]
3. [Participating interests][2]
4. Loans to [undertakings in which the company has a participating interest][3]
5. Other investments other than loans
6. Other loans
7. Own shares (4)

C. Current assets

I Stocks
1. Raw materials and consumables
2. Work in progress
3. Finished goods and goods for resale
4. Payments on account

II Debtors (5)
1. Trade debtors
2. Amounts owed by group [undertakings][1]
3. Amounts owed by [undertakings in which the company has a participating interest][3]
4. Other debtors
5. Called up share capital not paid (1)
6. Prepayments and accrued income (6)

III Investments
1. Shares in group [undertakings][1]
2. Own shares (4)
3. Other investments

IV Cash at bank and in hand

D. Prepayments and accrued income (6)

LIABILITIES

A. Capital and reserves

I Called up share capital (12)

II Share premium account

III Revaluation reserve

IV Other reserves
1. Capital redemption reserve
2. Reserve for own shares
3. Reserves provided for by the articles of association
4. Other reserves

V Profit and loss account

B. Provisions for liabilities and charges
1. Pensions and similar obligations
2. Taxation including deferred taxation
3. Other provisions

C. Creditors (13)
1. Debenture loans (7)
2. Bank loans and overdrafts
3. Payments received on account (8)
4. Trade creditors
5. Bills of exchange payable
6. Amounts owed to group [undertakings][1]
7. Amounts owed to [undertakings in which the company has a participating interest][3]
8. Other creditors including taxation and social security (9)
9. Accruals and deferred income (10)

D. Accruals and deferred income (10)

---

[1] Substituted by CA 1989, 1 Sch 2 with effect from 1 April 1990 (SI 1990 No 355) subject to the transitional and saving provisions in Arts 6 to 9 of that Order.
Previously 'companies'.

[2] Substituted by CA 1989, 1 Sch 3 with effect as in [1] above.
Previously 'Shares in related companies'.

[3] Substituted by CA 1989, 1 Sch 4 with effect as in [1] above.
Previously 'related companies'.

Notes on the balance sheet formats

(1) *Called up share capital not paid*
(Formats 1 and 2, items A and C.II.5.)
This item may be shown in either of the two positions given in Formats 1 and 2.

(2) *Concessions, patents, licences, trade marks and similar rights and assets*
(Formats 1 and 2, item B.I.2.)
Amounts in respect of assets shall only be included in a company's balance sheet under this item if either—
(a) the assets were acquired for valuable consideration and are not required to be shown under goodwill; or
(b) the assets in question were created by the company itself.

(3) *Goodwill*
(Formats 1 and 2, item B.I.3.)

Amounts representing goodwill shall only be included to the extent that the goodwill was acquired for valuable consideration.

(4) *Own shares*
(Formats 1 and 2, items B.III.7 and C.III.2.)
The nominal value of the shares held shall be shown separately.

(5) *Debtors*
(Formats 1 and 2, items C.II.1 to 6.)
The amount falling due after more than one year shall be shown separately for each item included under debtors.

(6) *Prepayments and accrued income*
(Formats 1 and 2, items C.II.6 and D.)
This item may be shown in either of the two positions given in Formats 1 and 2.

(7) *Debenture loans*
(Format 1, items E.1 and H.1 and Format 2, item C.1.)
The amount of any convertible loans shall be shown separately.

(8) *Payments received on account*
(Format 1, items E.3 and H.3 and Format 2, item C.3.)
Payments received on account of orders shall be shown for each of these items in so far as they are not shown as deductions from stocks.

(9) *Other creditors including taxation and social security*
(Format 1, items E.8 and H.8 and Format 2, item C.8.)
The amount for creditors in respect of taxation and social security shall be shown separately from the amount for other creditors.

(10) *Accruals and deferred income*
(Format 1, items E.9, H.9 and J and Format 2, items C.9 and D.)
The two positions given for this item in Format 1 at E.9 and H.9 are an alternative to the position at J, but if the item is not shown in a position corresponding to that at J it may be shown in either or both of the other two positions (as the case may require).
The two positions given for this item in Format 2 are alternatives.

(11) *Net current assets (liabilities)*
(Format 1, item F.)
In determining the amount to be shown for this item any amounts shown under "prepayments and accrued income" shall be taken into account wherever shown.

(12) *Called up share capital*
(Format 1, item K.I and Format 2, item A.I.)
The amount of allotted share capital and the amount of called up share capital which has been paid up shall be shown separately.

(13) *Creditors*
(Format 2, items C.1 to 9.)
Amounts falling due within one year and after one year shall be shown separately for each of these items and their aggregate shall be shown separately for all of these items.

Profit and loss account formats **Format 1** (see note (17) below)

1. Turnover
2. Cost of sales (14)
3. Gross profit or loss
4. Distribution costs (14)
5. Administrative expenses (14)
6. Other operating income
7. Income from shares in group [undertakings][1]
8. Income from [participating interests][2]
9. Income from other fixed asset investments (15)
10. Other interest receivable and similar income (15)
11. Amounts written off investments
12. Interest payable and similar charges (16)
13. Tax on profit or loss on ordinary activities
14. Profit or loss on ordinary activities after taxation
15. Extraordinary income
16. Extraordinary charges
17. Extraordinary profit or loss
18. Tax on extraordinary profit or loss
19. Other taxes not shown under the above items
20. Profit or loss for the financial year

---

[1] Substituted by CA 1989, 1 Sch 2 with effect from 1 April 1990 (SI 1990 No 355) subject to the transitional and saving provisions in Arts 6 to 9 of that Order.
Previously 'companies'.

[2] Substituted by CA 1989, 1 Sch 3 with effect as in [1] above.
Previously 'shares in related companies'.

Profit and loss account formats Format 2

1. Turnover
2. Change in stocks of finished goods and in work in progress
3. Own work capitalised
4. Other operating income
5. (a) Raw materials and consumables
   (b) Other external charges
6. Staff costs:
   (a) wages and salaries
   (b) social security costs
   (c) other pension costs
7. (a) Depreciation and other amounts written off tangible and intangible fixed assets
   (b) Exceptional amounts written off current assets
8. Other operating charges
9. Income from shares in group [undertakings][1]
10. Income from [participating interests][2]
11. Income from other fixed asset investments (15)
12. Other interest receivable and similar income (15)
13. Amounts written off investments
14. Interest payable and similar charges (16)
15. Tax on profit or loss on ordinary activities
16. Profit or loss on ordinary activities after taxation
17. Extraordinary income
18. Extraordinary charges
19. Extraordinary profit or loss
20. Tax on extraordinary profit or loss
21. Other taxes not shown under the above items
22. Profit or loss for the financial year

---

1 Substituted by CA 1989, 1 Sch 2 with effect from 1 April 1990 (SI 1990 No 355) subject to the transitional and saving provisions in Arts 6 to 9 of that Order.
Previously 'companies'.

2 Substituted by CA 1989, 1 Sch 3 with effect as in [1] above.
Previously 'shares in related companies'.

Profit and loss account formats Format 3 (see note (17) below)

A. Charges
1. Cost of sales (14)
2. Distribution costs (14)
3. Administrative expenses (14)
4. Amounts written off investments
5. Interest payable and similar charges (16)
6. Tax on profit or loss on ordinary activities
7. Profit or loss on ordinary activities after taxation
8. Extraordinary charges
9. Tax on extraordinary profit or loss
10. Other taxes not shown under the above items
11. Profit or loss for the financial year

B. Income
1. Turnover
2. Other operating income
3. Income from shares in group [undertakings][1]
4. Income from [participating interests][2]
5. Income from other fixed asset investments (15)
6. Other interest receivable and similar income (15)
7. Profit or loss on ordinary activities after taxation
8. Extraordinary income
9. Profit or loss for the financial year

---

1 Substituted by CA 1989, 1 Sch 2 with effect from 1 April 1990 (SI 1990 No 355) subject to the transitional and saving provisions in Arts 6 to 9 of that Order.
Previously 'companies'.

2 Substituted by CA 1989, 1 Sch 3 with effect as in [1] above.
Previously 'shares in related companies'.

Profit and loss account formats Format 4

A. Charges
1. Reduction in stocks of finished goods and in work in progress
2. (a) Raw materials and consumables
   (b) Other external charges
3. Staff costs:
   (a) wages and salaries
   (b) social security costs
   (c) other pension costs
4. (a) Depreciation and other amounts written off tangible and intangible fixed assets
   (b) Exceptional amounts written off current assets
5. Other operating charges
6. Amounts written off investments
7. Interest payable and similar charges (16)
8. Tax on profit or loss on ordinary activities
9. Profit or loss on ordinary activities after taxation
10. Extraordinary charges
11. Tax on extraordinary profit or loss
12. Other taxes not shown under the above items
13. Profit or loss for the financial year

B. Income
1. Turnover
2. Increase in stocks of finished goods and in work in progress
3. Own work capitalised
4. Other operating income
5. Income from shares in group [undertakings][1]
6. Income from [participating interests][2]
7. Income from other fixed asset investments (15)
8. Other interest receivable and similar income (15)
9. Profit or loss on ordinary activities after taxation
10. Extraordinary income
11. Profit or loss for the financial year

---

1 Substituted by CA 1989, 1 Sch 2 with effect from 1 April 1990 (SI 1990 No 355) subject to the transitional and saving provisions in Arts 6 to 9 of that Order.
Previously 'companies'.

2 Substituted by CA 1989, 1 Sch 3 with effect as in [1] above.
Previously 'shares in related companies'.

Notes on the profit and loss account formats

(14) *Cost of sales: distribution costs: administrative expenses*
(Format 1, items 2, 4 and 5 and Format 3, items A.1, 2 and 3.)
These items shall be stated after taking into account any necessary provisions for depreciation or diminution in value of assets.

(15) *Income from other fixed asset investments: other interest receivable and similar income*
(Format 1, items 9 and 10: Format 2, items 11 and 12: Format 3, items B.5 and 6: Format 4, items B.7 and 8.)
Income and interest derived from group [undertakings][1] shall be shown separately from income and interest derived from other sources.

(16) *Interest payable and similar charges*

(Format 1, item 12: Format 2, item 14: Format 3, item A.5: Format 4, item A.7.)

The amount payable to group [undertakings][1] shall be shown separately.

(17) *Formats 1 and 3*

The amount of any provisions for depreciation and diminution in value of tangible and intangible fixed assets falling to be shown under items 7(a) and A.4(a) respectively in Formats 2 and 4 shall be disclosed in a note to the accounts in any case where the profit and loss account is prepared by reference to Format 1 or Format 3.

---

1 Substituted by CA 1989, 1 Sch 2 with effect from 1 April 1990 (SI 1990 No 355) subject to the transitional and saving provisions in Arts 6 to 9 of that Order.
Previously 'companies'.

PART II ACCOUNTING PRINCIPLES AND RULES

SECTION A ACCOUNTING PRINCIPLES

9 Preliminary

Subject to paragraph 15 below, the amounts to be included in respect of all items shown in a company's accounts shall be determined in accordance with the principles set out in paragraphs 10 to 14.

Accounting principles

10 The company shall be presumed to be carrying on business as a going concern.

11 Accounting policies shall be applied consistently [within the same accounts and][1] from one financial year to the next.

---

1 Inserted by CA 1989, 1 Sch 5 with effect from 1 April 1990 (SI 1990 No 355) subject to the transitional and saving provisions in Arts 6 to 9 of that Order.

---

12 The amount of any item shall be determined on a prudent basis, and in particular—

(a) only profits realised at the balance sheet date shall be included in the profit and loss account; and

(b) all liabilities and losses which have arisen or are likely to arise in respect of the financial year to which the accounts relate or a previous financial year shall be taken into account, including those which only become apparent between the balance sheet date and the date on which it is signed on behalf of the board of directors in pursuance of [section 233][1] of this Act.

---

1 Substituted by CA 1989, 10 Sch 20 with effect from 1 April 1990 (SI 1990 No 355) subject to the transitional and saving provisions in Arts 6 to 9 of that Order.
Previously 'section 238'.

---

13 All income and charges relating to the financial year to which the accounts relate shall be taken into account, without regard to the date of receipt or payment.

14 In determining the aggregate amount of any item the amount of each individual asset or liability that falls to be taken into account shall be determined separately.

15 **Departure from the accounting principles**

If it appears to the directors of a company that there are special reasons for departing from any of the principles stated above in preparing the company's accounts in respect of any financial year they may do so, but particulars of the departure, the reasons for it and its effect shall be given in a note to the accounts.

SECTION B HISTORICAL COST ACCOUNTING RULES

16 **Preliminary**

Subject to section C of this Part of this Schedule, the amounts to be included in respect of all items shown in a company's accounts shall be determined in accordance with the rules set out in paragraphs 17 to 28.

Fixed assets

General rules

17 Subject to any provision for depreciation or diminution in value made in accordance with paragraph 18 or 19 the amount to be included in respect of any fixed asset shall be its purchase price or production cost.

18 In the case of any fixed asset which has a limited useful economic life, the amount of—

(a) its purchase price or production cost; or
(b) where it is estimated that any such asset will have a residual value at the end of the period of its useful economic life, its purchase price or production cost less that estimated residual value;

shall be reduced by provisions for depreciation calculated to write off that amount systematically over the period of the asset's useful economic life.

19 (1) Where a fixed asset investment of a description falling to be included under item B.III of either of the balance sheet formats set out in Part I of this Schedule has diminished in value provisions for diminution in value may be made in respect of it and the amount to be included in respect of it may be reduced accordingly; and any such provisions which are not shown in the profit and loss account shall be disclosed (either separately or in aggregate) in a note to the accounts.

(2) Provisions for diminution in value shall be made in respect of any fixed asset which has diminished in value if the reduction in its value is expected to be permanent (whether its useful economic life is limited or not), and the amount to be included in respect of it shall be reduced accordingly; and any such provisions which are not shown in the profit and loss account shall be disclosed (either separately or in aggregate) in a note to the accounts.

(3) Where the reasons for which any provision was made in accordance with sub-paragraph (1) or (2) have ceased to apply to any extent, that provision shall be written back to the extent that it is no longer necessary; and any amounts written back in accordance with this sub-paragraph which are not shown in the profit and loss account shall be disclosed (either separately or in aggregate) in a note to the accounts.

Rules for determining particular fixed asset items

20 (1) Notwithstanding that an item in respect of "development costs" is included under "fixed assets" in the balance sheet formats set out in Part I of this Schedule, an amount may only be included in a company's balance sheet in respect of development costs in special circumstances.

(2) If any amount is included in a company's balance sheet in respect of development costs the following information shall be given in a note to the accounts—

(a) the period over which the amount of those costs originally capitalised is being or is to be written off; and
(b) the reasons for capitalising the development costs in question.

21 (1) The application of paragraphs 17 to 19 in relation to goodwill (in any case where goodwill is treated as an asset) is subject to the following provisions of this paragraph.

(2) Subject to sub-paragraph (3) below, the amount of the consideration for any goodwill acquired by a company shall be reduced by provisions for depreciation calculated to write off that amount systematically over a period chosen by the directors of the company.

(3) The period chosen shall not exceed the useful economic life of the goodwill in question.

(4) In any case where any goodwill acquired by a company is shown or included as an asset in the company's balance sheet the period chosen for writing off the consideration for that goodwill and the reasons for choosing that period shall be disclosed in a note to the accounts.

Current assets

22 Subject to paragraph 23, the amount to be included in respect of any current asset shall be its purchase price or production cost.

23 (1) If the net realisable value of any current asset is lower than its purchase price or production cost the amount to be included in respect of that asset shall be the net realisable value.

(2) Where the reasons for which any provision for diminution in value was made in accordance with sub-paragraph (1) have ceased to apply to any extent, that provision shall be written back to the extent that it is no longer necessary.

Miscellaneous and supplementary provisions

Excess of money owed over value received as an asset item

24 (1) Where the amount repayable on any debt owed by a company is greater than the value of the consideration received in the transaction giving rise to the debt, the amount of the difference may be treated as an asset.

(2) Where any such amount is so treated—

(a) it shall be written off by reasonable amounts each year and must be completely written off before repayment of the debt; and

(b) if the current amount is not shown as a separate item in the company's balance sheet it must be disclosed in a note to the accounts.

Assets included at a fixed amount

25 (1) Subject to the following sub-paragraph, assets which fall to be included—

(a) amongst the fixed assets of a company under the item "tangible assets"; or

(b) amongst the current assets of a company under the item "raw materials and consumables";

may be included at a fixed quantity and value.

(2) Sub-paragraph (1) applies to assets of a kind which are constantly being replaced, where—

(a) their overall value is not material to assessing the company's state of affairs; and

(b) their quantity, value and composition are not subject to material variation.

Determination of purchase price or production cost

26 (1) The purchase price of an asset shall be determined by adding to the actual price paid any expenses incidental to its acquisition.

(2) The production cost of an asset shall be determined by adding to the purchase price of the raw materials and consumables used the amount of the costs incurred by the company which are directly attributable to the production of that asset.

(3) In addition, there may be included in the production cost of an asset—

(a) a reasonable proportion of the costs incurred by the company which are only indirectly attributable to the production of that asset, but only to the extent that they relate to the period of production; and

(b) interest on capital borrowed to finance the production of that asset, to the extent that it accrues in respect of the period of production;

provided, however, in a case within paragraph (b) above, that the inclusion of the interest in determining the cost of that asset and the amount of the interest so included is disclosed in a note to the accounts.

(4) In the case of current assets distribution costs may not be included in production costs.

27 (1) Subject to the qualification mentioned below, the purchase price or production cost of—

(a) any assets which fall to be included under any item shown in a company's balance sheet under the general item "stocks"; and

(b) any assets which are fungible assets (including investments);

may be determined by the application of any of the methods mentioned in sub-paragraph (2) below in relation to any such assets of the same class.

The method chosen must be one which appears to the directors to be appropriate in the circumstances of the company.

(2) Those methods are—

(a) the method known as "first in, first out" (FIFO);
(b) the method known as "last in, first out" (LIFO);
(c) a weighted average price; and
(d) any other method similar to any of the methods mentioned above.

(3) Where in the case of any company—

(a) the purchase price or production cost of assets falling to be included under any item shown in the company's balance sheet has been determined by the application of any method permitted by this paragraph; and
(b) the amount shown in respect of that item differs materially from the relevant alternative amount given below in this paragraph;

the amount of that difference shall be disclosed in a note to the accounts.

(4) Subject to sub-paragraph (5) below, for the purposes of sub-paragraph (3)(b) above, the relevant alternative amount, in relation to any item shown in a company's balance sheet, is the amount which would have been shown in respect of that item if assets of any class included under that item at an amount determined by any method permitted by this paragraph had instead been included at their replacement cost as at the balance sheet date.

(5) The relevant alternative amount may be determined by reference to the most recent actual purchase price or production cost before the balance sheet date of assets of any class included under the item in question instead of by reference to their replacement cost as at that date, but only if the former appears to the directors of the company to constitute the more appropriate standard of comparison in the case of assets of that class.

(6) For the purposes of this paragraph, assets of any description shall be regarded as fungible if assets of that description are substantially indistinguishable one from another.

Substitution of original stated amount where price or cost unknown

28 Where there is no record of the purchase price or production cost of any asset of a company or of any price, expenses or costs relevant for determining its purchase price or production cost in accordance with paragraph 26, or any such record cannot be obtained without unreasonable expense or delay, its purchase price or production cost shall be taken for the purposes of paragraphs 17 to 23 to be the value ascribed to it in the earliest available record of its value made on or after its acquisition or production by the company.

SECTION C ALTERNATIVE ACCOUNTING RULES

Preliminary

29 (1) The rules set out in section B are referred to below in this Schedule as the historical cost accounting rules.

(2) Those rules, with the omission of paragraphs 16, 21 and 25 to 28, are referred to below in this Part of this Schedule as the depreciation rules; and references below in this Schedule to the historical cost accounting rules do not include the depreciation rules as they apply by virtue of paragraph 32.

30 Subject to paragraphs 32 to 34, the amounts to be included in respect of assets of any description mentioned in paragraph 31 may be determined on any basis so mentioned.

31 Alternative accounting rules

(1) Intangible fixed assets, other than goodwill, may be included at their current cost.

(2) Tangible fixed assets may be included at a market value determined as at the date of their last valuation or at their current cost.

(3) Investments of any description falling to be included under item B.III of either of the balance sheet formats set out in Part I of this Schedule may be included either—

(a) at a market value determined as at the date of their last valuation; or
(b) at a value determined on any basis which appears to the directors to be appropriate in the circumstances of the company;

but in the latter case particulars of the method of valuation adopted and of the reasons for adopting it shall be disclosed in a note to the accounts.

(4) Investments of any description falling to be included under item C.III of either of the balance sheet formats set out in Part I of this Schedule may be included at their current cost.

(5) Stocks may be included at their current cost.

32 Application of the depreciation rules

(1) Where the value of any asset of a company is determined on any basis mentioned in paragraph 31, that value shall be, or (as the case may require) be the starting point for determining, the amount to be included in respect of that asset in the company's accounts, instead of its purchase price or production cost or any value previously so determined for that asset; and the depreciation rules shall apply accordingly in relation to any such asset with the substitution for any reference to its purchase price or production cost of a reference to the value most recently determined for that asset on any basis mentioned in paragraph 31.

(2) The amount of any provision for depreciation required in the case of any fixed asset by paragraph 18 or 19 as it applies by virtue of sub-paragraph (1) is referred to below in this paragraph as the adjusted amount, and the amount of any provision which would be required by that paragraph in the case of that asset according to the historical cost accounting rules is referred to as the historical cost amount.

(3) Where sub-paragraph (1) applies in the case of any fixed asset the amount of any provision for depreciation in respect of that asset—

(a) included in any item shown in the profit and loss account in respect of amounts written off assets of the description in question; or
(b) taken into account in stating any item so shown which is required by note (14) of the notes on the profit and loss account formats set out in Part I of this Schedule to be stated after taking into account any necessary provisions for depreciation or diminution in value of assets included under it;

may be the historical cost amount instead of the adjusted amount, provided that the amount of any difference between the two is shown separately in the profit and loss account or in a note to the accounts.

33 Additional information to be provided in case of departure from historical cost accounting rules

(1) This paragraph applies where the amounts to be included in respect of assets covered by any items shown in a company's accounts have been determined on any basis mentioned in paragraph 31.

(2) The items affected and the basis of valuation adopted in determining the amounts of the assets in question in the case of each such item shall be disclosed in a note to the accounts.

(3) In the case of each balance sheet item affected (except stocks) either—

(a) the comparable amounts determined according to the historical cost accounting rules; or
(b) the differences between those amounts and the corresponding amounts actually shown in the balance sheet in respect of that item;

shall be shown separately in the balance sheet or in a note to the accounts.

(4) In sub-paragraph (3) above, references in relation to any item to the comparable amounts determined as there mentioned are references to—

(a) the aggregate amount which would be required to be shown in respect of that item if the amounts to be included in respect of all the assets covered by that item were determined according to the historical cost accounting rules; and
(b) the aggregate amount of the cumulative provisions for depreciation or diminution in value which would be permitted or required in determining those amounts according to those rules.

34 Revaluation reserve

(1) With respect to any determination of the value of an asset of a company on any basis mentioned in paragraph 31, the amount of any profit or loss arising from that determination (after allowing, where appropriate, for any provisions for depreciation or diminution in value made otherwise than by reference to the value so determined and any adjustments of any such provisions made in the light of that determination) shall be credited or (as the case may be) debited to a separate reserve ("the revaluation reserve").

(2) The amount of the revaluation reserve shall be shown in the company's balance sheet under a separate sub-heading in the position given for the item "revaluation reserve" in Format 1 or 2 of the balance sheet formats set out in Part I of this Schedule, but need not be shown under that name.

[(3) An amount may be transferred from the revaluation reserve—

(a) to the profit and loss account, if the amount was previously charged to that account or represents realised profit, or
(b) on capitalisation;

and the revaluation reserve shall be reduced to the extent that the amounts transferred to it are no longer necessary for the purposes of the valuation method used.

(3A) In sub-paragraph (3)(b) "capitalisation", in relation to an amount standing to the credit of the revaluation reserve, means applying it in wholly or partly paying up unissued shares in the company to be allotted to members of the company as fully or partly paid shares.

(3B) The revaluation reserve shall not be reduced except as mentioned in this paragraph.][1]

(4) The treatment for taxation purposes of amounts credited or debited to the revaluation reserve shall be disclosed in a note to the accounts.

---

1 Substituted by CA 1989, 1 Sch 6 with effect from 1 April 1990 (SI 1990 No 355) subject to the transitional and saving provisions in Arts 6 to 9 of that Order.
Previously
'(3) The revaluation reserve shall be reduced to the extent that the amounts standing to the credit of the reserve are in the opinion of the directors of the company no longer necessary for the purpose of the accounting policies adopted by the company; but an amount may only be transferred from the reserve to the profit and loss account if either—
(a) the amount in question was previously charged to that account; or
(b) it represents realised profit.'

PART III NOTES TO THE ACCOUNTS

35 Preliminary

Any information required in the case of any company by the following provisions of this Part of this Schedule shall (if not given in the company's accounts) be given by way of a note to those accounts.

Disclosure of accounting policies

36 The accounting policies adopted by the company in determining the amounts to be included in respect of items shown in the balance sheet and in determining the profit or loss of the company shall be stated (including such policies with respect to the depreciation and diminution in value of assets).

[36A It shall be stated whether the accounts have been prepared in accordance with applicable accounting standards and particulars of any material departure from those standards and the reasons for it shall be given.][1]

---

1 Inserted by CA 1989, 1 Sch 7 with effect from 1 April 1990 (SI 1990 No 355) subject to the transitional and saving provisions in Arts 6 to 9 of that Order.

Information supplementing the balance sheet

37 Paragraphs 38 to 51 require information which either supplements the information given with respect to any particular items shown in the balance sheet or is otherwise relevant to assessing the company's state of affairs in the light of the information so given.

Share capital and debentures

38 (1) The following information shall be given with respect to the company's share capital—

(a) the authorised share capital; and
(b) where shares of more than one class have been allotted, the number and aggregate nominal value of shares of each class allotted.

(2) In the case of any part of the allotted share capital that consists of redeemable shares, the following information shall be given—

(a) the earliest and latest dates on which the company has power to redeem those shares;
(b) whether those shares must be redeemed in any event or are liable to be redeemed at the option of the company or of the shareholder; and
(c) whether any (and, if so, what) premium is payable on redemption.

39 If the company has allotted any shares during the financial year, the following information shall be given—

(a) the reason for making the allotment;
(b) the classes of shares allotted; and
(c) as respects each class of shares, the number allotted, their aggregate nominal value, and the consideration received by the company for the allotment.

40 (1) With respect to any contingent right to the allotment of shares in the company the following particulars shall be given—

(a) the number, description and amount of the shares in relation to which the right is exercisable;
(b) the period during which it is exercisable; and
(c) the price to be paid for the shares allotted.

(2) In sub-paragraph (1) above "contingent right to the allotment of shares" means any option to subscribe for shares and any other right to require the allotment of shares to any person whether arising on the conversion into shares of securities of any other description or otherwise.

41 (1) If the company has issued any debentures during the financial year to which the accounts relate, the following information shall be given—

(a) the reason for making the issue;
(b) the classes of debentures issued; and
(c) as respects each class of debentures, the amount issued and the consideration received by the company for the issue.

(2) Particulars of any redeemed debentures which the company has power to reissue shall also be given.

(3) Where any of the company's debentures are held by a nominee of or trustee for the company, the nominal amount of the debentures and the amount at which they are stated in the accounting records kept by the company in accordance with section 221 of this Act shall be stated.

Fixed assets

42 (1) In respect of each item which is or would but for paragraph 3(4)(b) be shown under the general item "fixed assets" in the company's balance sheet the following information shall be given—

(a) the appropriate amounts in respect of that item as at the date of the beginning of the financial year and as at the balance sheet date respectively;
(b) the effect on any amount shown in the balance sheet in respect of that item of—
  (i) any revision of the amount in respect of any assets included under that item made during that year on any basis mentioned in paragraph 31;

(ii) acquisitions during that year of any assets;
(iii) disposals during that year of any assets; and
(iv) any transfers of assets of the company to and from that item during that year.

(2) The reference in sub-paragraph (1)(a) to the appropriate amounts in respect of any item as at any date there mentioned is a reference to amounts representing the aggregate amounts determined, as at that date, in respect of assets falling to be included under that item on either of the following bases, that is to say—

(a) on the basis of purchase price or production cost (determined in accordance with paragraphs 26 and 27); or
(b) on any basis mentioned in paragraph 31,

(leaving out of account in either case any provisions for depreciation or diminution in value).

(3) In respect of each item within sub-paragraph (1)—

(a) the cumulative amount of provisions for depreciation or diminution in value of assets included under that item as at each date mentioned in sub-paragraph (1)(a);
(b) the amount of any such provisions made in respect of the financial year;
(c) the amount of any adjustments made in respect of any such provisions during that year in consequence of the disposal of any assets; and
(d) the amount of any other adjustments made in respect of any such provisions during that year;

shall also be stated.

43 Where any fixed assets of the company (other than listed investments) are included under any item shown in the company's balance sheet at an amount determined on any basis mentioned in paragraph 31, the following information shall be given—

(a) the years (so far as they are known to the directors) in which the assets were severally valued and the several values; and
(b) in the case of assets that have been valued during the financial year, the names of the persons who valued them or particulars of their qualifications for doing so and (whichever is stated) the bases of valuation used by them.

44 In relation to any amount which is or would but for paragraph 3(4)(b) be shown in respect of the item "land and buildings" in the company's balance sheet there shall be stated—

(a) how much of that amount is ascribable to land of freehold tenure and how much to land of leasehold tenure; and
(b) how much of the amount ascribable to land of leasehold tenure is ascribable to land held on long lease and how much to land held on short lease.

Investments

45 (1) In respect of the amount of each item which is or would but for paragraph 3(4)(b) be shown in the company's balance sheet under the general item "investments" (whether as fixed assets or as current assets) there shall be stated—

(a) how much of that amount is ascribable to listed investments; and

(b) how much of any amount so ascribable is ascribable to investments as respects which there has been granted a listing on a [recognised investment exchange other than an overseas investment exchange within the meaning of the Financial Services Act 1986][1] and how much to other listed investments.

(2) Where the amount of any listed investments is stated for any item in accordance with sub-paragraph (1)(a), the following amounts shall also be stated—

(a) the aggregate market value of those investments where it differs from the amount so stated; and

(b) both the market value and the stock exchange value of any investments of which the former value is, for the purposes of the accounts, taken as being higher than the latter.

1 Substituted by FSA 1986, s 212(2), 16 Sch 23(a) with effect from 29 April 1988 (see SI 1988 No 740). Previously 'recognised stock exchange'.

Reserves and provisions

46 (1) Where any amount is transferred—

(a) to or from any reserves; or

(b) to any provisions for liabilities and charges; or

(c) from any provision for liabilities and charges otherwise than for the purpose for which the provision was established;

and the reserves or provisions are or would but for paragraph 3(4)(b) be shown as separate items in the company's balance sheet, the information mentioned in the following sub-paragraph shall be given in respect of the aggregate of reserves or provisions included in the same item.

(2) That information is—

(a) the amount of the reserves or provisions as at the date of the beginning of the financial year and as at the balance sheet date respectively;

(b) any amounts transferred to or from the reserves or provisions during that year; and

(c) the source and application respectively of any amounts so transferred.

(3) Particulars shall be given of each provision included in the item "other provisions" in the company's balance sheet in any case where the amount of that provision is material.

Provision for taxation

47 [The amount of any provision for deferred taxation shall be stated separately from the amount of any provision for other taxation.][1]

1 Substituted by CA 1989, 1 Sch 8 with effect from 1 April 1990 (SI 1990 No 355) subject to the transitional and saving provisions in Arts 6 to 9 of that Order.
Previously
'The amount of any provisions for taxation other than deferred taxation shall be stated'.

Details of indebtedness

48 (1) In respect of each item shown under "creditors" in the company's balance sheet there shall be stated—

(a) the aggregate amount of any debts included under that item which are payable or repayable otherwise than by instalments and fall due for payment or repayment after the end of the period of five years beginning with the day next following the end of the financial year; and

(b) the aggregate amount of any debts so included which are payable or repayable by instalments any of which fall due for payment after the end of that period;

and in the case of debts within paragraph (b) above the aggregate amount of instalments falling due after the end of that period shall also be disclosed for each such item.

(2) Subject to sub-paragraph (3), in relation to each debt falling to be taken into account under sub-paragraph (1), the terms of payment or repayment and the rate of any interest payable on the debt shall be stated.

(3) If the number of debts is such that, in the opinion of the directors, compliance with sub-paragraph (2) would result in a statement of excessive length, it shall be sufficient to give a general indication of the terms of payment or repayment and the rates of any interest payable on the debts.

(4) In respect of each item shown under "creditors" in the company's balance sheet there shall be stated—

(a) the aggregate amount of any debts included under that item in respect of which any security has been given by the company; and
(b) an indication of the nature of the securities so given.

(5) References above in this paragraph to an item shown under "creditors" in the company's balance sheet include references, where amounts falling due to creditors within one year and after more than one year are distinguished in the balance sheet—

(a) in a case within sub-paragraph (1), to an item shown under the latter of those categories; and
(b) in a case within sub-paragraph (4), to an item shown under either of those categories;

and references to items shown under "creditors" include references to items which would but for paragraph 3(4)(b) be shown under that heading.

49 If any fixed cumulative dividends on the company's shares are in arrear, there shall be stated—

(a) the amount of the arrears; and
(b) the period for which the dividends or, if there is more than one class, each class of them are in arrear.

Guarantees and other financial commitments

50 (1) Particulars shall be given of any charge on the assets of the company to secure the liabilities of any other person, including, where practicable, the amount secured.

(2) The following information shall be given with respect to any other contingent liability not provided for—

(a) the amount or estimated amount of that liability;
(b) its legal nature; and
(c) whether any valuable security has been provided by the company in connection with that liability and if so, what.

(3) There shall be stated, where practicable—

(a) the aggregate amount or estimated amount of contracts for capital expenditure, so far as not provided for; and
(b) the aggregate amount or estimated amount of capital expenditure authorised by the directors which has not been contracted for.

(4) Particulars shall be given of—

(a) any pension commitments included under any provision shown in the company's balance sheet; and
(b) any such commitments for which no provision has been made;

and where any such commitment relates wholly or partly to pensions payable to past directors of the company separate particulars shall be given of that commitment so far as it relates to such pensions.

(5) Particulars shall also be given of any other financial commitments which—

(a) have not been provided for; and
(b) are relevant to assessing the company's state of affairs.

(6) [. . .][1]

---

1 Repealed by CA 1989, 24 Sch with effect from 1 April 1990 (SI 1990 No 355) subject to the transitional and saving provisions in Arts 6 to 9 of that Order.
Previously
'Commitments within any of the preceding sub-paragraphs undertaken on behalf of or for the benefit of—
(a) any holding company or fellow subsidiary of the company; or
(b) any subsidiary of the company;
shall be stated separately from the other commitments within that sub-paragraph (and commitments within paragraph (a) shall also be stated separately from those within paragraph (b)).'

Miscellaneous matters

51 (1) Particulars shall be given of any case where the purchase price or production cost of any asset is for the first time determined under paragraph 28.

(2) Where any outstanding loans made under the authority of section 153(4)(b) [, (bb)][1] or (c) or section 155 of this Act (various cases of financial assistance by a company for purchase of its own shares) are included under any item shown in the company's balance sheet, the aggregate amount of those loans shall be disclosed for each item in question.

(3) The aggregate amount which is recommended for distribution by way of dividend shall be stated.

---

1 Inserted by CA 1989, 1 Sch 9 with effect from 1 April 1990 (SI 1990 No 355) subject to the transitional and saving provisions in Arts 6 to 9 of that Order.

Information supplementing the profit and loss account

52 Paragraphs 53 to 57 require information which either supplements the information given with respect to any particular items shown in the profit and loss account or otherwise provides particulars of income or expenditure of the company or of circumstances affecting the items shown in the profit and loss account.

Separate statement of certain items of income and expenditure

53 (1) Subject to the following provisions of this paragraph, each of the amounts mentioned below shall be stated.

(2) The amount of the interest on or any similar charges in respect of—

(a) bank loans and overdrafts, and loans made to the company (other than bank loans and overdrafts) which—
  (i) are repayable otherwise than by instalments and fall due for repayment before the end of the period of five years beginning with the day next following the end of the financial year; or
  (ii) are repayable by instalments the last of which falls due for payment before the end of that period; and
(b) loans of any other kind made to the company.

This sub-paragraph does not apply to interest or charges on loans to the company from group [undertakings][1], but, with that exception, it applies to interest or charges on all loans, whether made on the security of debentures or not.

(3) The amounts respectively set aside for redemption of share capital and for redemption of loans.

(4) The amount of income from listed investments.

(5) The amount of rents from land (after deduction of ground rents, rates and other outgoings).

This amount need only be stated if a substantial part of the company's revenue for the financial year consists of rents from land.

(6) The amount charged to revenue in respect of sums payable in respect of the hire of plant and machinery.

(7) [. . .][2]

---

1 Substituted by CA 1989, 1 Sch 2 with effect from 1 April 1990 (SI 1990 No 355) subject to the transitional and saving provisions in Arts 6 to 9 of that Order.
Previously 'companies'.

2 Repealed by CA 1989, 24 Sch with effect as in [1] above.
Previously
'The amount of the remuneration of the auditors (taking "remuneration", for the purposes of this sub-paragraph, as including any sums paid by the company in respect of the auditors' expenses).'

Particulars of tax

54 (1) The basis on which the charge for United Kingdom corporation tax and United Kingdom income tax is computed shall be stated.

(2) Particulars shall be given of any special circumstances which affect liability in respect of taxation of profits, income or capital gains for the financial year or liability in respect of taxation of profits, income or capital gains for succeeding financial years.

(3) The following amounts shall be stated—

(a) the amount of the charge for United Kingdom corporation tax;
(b) if that amount would have been greater but for relief from double taxation, the amount which it would have been but for such relief;
(c) the amount of the charge for United Kingdom income tax; and
(d) the amount of the charge for taxation imposed outside the United Kingdom of profits, income and (so far as charged to revenue) capital gains.

These amounts shall be stated separately in respect of each of the amounts which is or would but for paragraph 3(4)(b) be shown under the following items in the profit and loss account, that is to say "tax on profit or loss on ordinary activities" and "tax on extraordinary profit or loss".

Particulars of turnover

55 (1) If in the course of the financial year the company has carried on business of two or more classes that, in the opinion of the directors, differ substantially from each other, there shall be stated in respect of each class (describing it)—

(a) the amount of the turnover attributable to that class; and

(b) the amount of the profit or loss of the company before taxation which is in the opinion of the directors attributable to that class.

(2) If in the course of the financial year the company has supplied markets that, in the opinion of the directors, differ substantially from each other, the amount of the turnover attributable to each such market shall also be stated.

In this paragraph "market" means a market delimited by geographical bounds.

(3) In analysing for the purposes of this paragraph the source (in terms of business or in terms of market) of turnover or (as the case may be) of profit or loss, the directors of the company shall have regard to the manner in which the company's activities are organised.

(4) For the purposes of this paragraph—

(a) classes of business which, in the opinion of the directors, do not differ substantially from each other shall be treated as one class; and

(b) markets which, in the opinion of the directors, do not differ substantially from each other shall be treated as one market;

and any amounts properly attributable to one class of business or (as the case may be) to one market which are not material may be included in the amount stated in respect of another.

(5) Where in the opinion of the directors the disclosure of any information required by this paragraph would be seriously prejudicial to the interests of the company, that information need not be disclosed, but the fact that any such information has not been disclosed must be stated.

Particulars of staff

56 (1) The following information shall be given with respect to the employees of the company—

(a) the average number of persons employed by the company in the financial year; and

(b) the average number of persons so employed within each category of persons employed by the company.

(2) The average number required by sub-paragraph (1)(a) or (b) shall be determined by dividing the relevant annual number by the number of weeks in the financial year.

(3) The relevant annual number shall be determined by ascertaining for each week in the financial year—

(a) for the purposes of sub-paragraph (1)(a), the number of persons employed under contracts of service by the company in that week (whether throughout the week or not);

(b) for the purposes of sub-paragraph (1)(b), the number of persons in the category in question of persons so employed;

and, in either case, adding together all the weekly numbers.

(4) In respect of all persons employed by the company during the financial year who are taken into account in determining the relevant annual number for the purposes of sub-paragraph (l)(a) there shall also be stated the aggregate amounts respectively of—

(a) wages and salaries paid or payable in respect of that year to those persons;
(b) social security costs incurred by the company on their behalf; and
(c) other pension costs so incurred;

save in so far as those amounts or any of them are stated in the profit and loss account.

(5) The categories of persons employed by the company by reference to which the number required to be disclosed by sub-paragraph (1)(b) is to be determined shall be such as the directors may select, having regard to the manner in which the company's activities are organised.

Miscellaneous matters

57 (1) Where any amount relating to any preceding financial year is included in any item in the profit and loss account, the effect shall be stated.

(2) Particulars shall be given of any extraordinary income or charges arising in the financial year.

(3) The effect shall be stated of any transactions that are exceptional by virtue of size or incidence though they fall within the ordinary activities of the company.

58 General

(1) Where sums originally denominated in foreign currencies have been brought into account under any items shown in the balance sheet or profit and loss account, the basis on which those sums have been translated into sterling shall be stated.

(2) Subject to the following sub-paragraph, in respect of every item stated in a note to the accounts the corresponding amount for the financial year immediately preceding that to which the accounts relate shall also be stated and where the corresponding amount is not comparable, it shall be adjusted and particulars of the adjustment and the reasons for it shall be given.

(3) Sub-paragraph (2) does not apply in relation to any amounts stated by virtue of any of the following provisions of this Act—

[(a) paragraph 13 of Schedule 4A (details of accounting treatment of acquisitions),
(b) paragraphs 2, 8(3), 16, 21(1)(d), 22(4) and (5), 24(3) and (4) and 27(3) and (4) of Schedule 5 (shareholdings in other undertakings),
(c) Parts II and III of Schedule 6 (loans and other dealings in favour of directors and others), and
(d) paragraphs 42 and 46 above (fixed assets and reserves and provisions).][1]

---

1 Substituted by CA 1989, 1 Sch 9 with effect from 1 April 1990 (SI 1990 No 355) subject to the transitional and saving provisions in Arts 6 to 9 of that Order.
Previously
'(a) section 231 as applying Parts I and II of Schedule 5 (proportion of share capital of subsidiaries and other bodies corporate held by the company, etc.),
(b) sections 232 to 234 and Schedule 6 (particulars of loans to directors, etc.), and
(c) paragraphs 42 and 46 above.'

[PART IV SPECIAL PROVISIONS WHERE COMPANY IS A PARENT COMPANY OR SUBSIDIARY UNDERTAKING

59 Dealings with or interests in group undertakings

Where a company is a parent company or a subsidiary undertaking and any item required by Part I of this Schedule to be shown in the company's balance sheet in relation to group undertakings includes—

(a) amounts attributable to dealings with or interests in any parent undertaking or fellow subsidiary undertaking, or
(b) amounts attributable to dealings with or interests in any subsidiary undertaking of the company,

the aggregate amounts within paragraphs (a) and (b) respectively shall be shown as separate items, either by way of subdivision of the relevant item in the balance sheet or in a note to the company's accounts.][1]

---

1 Substituted by CA 1989, 1 Sch 11 with effect from 1 April 1990 (SI 1990 No 355) subject to the transitional and saving provisions in Arts 6 to 9 of that Order.
Previously
'PART IV SPECIAL PROVISIONS WHERE THE COMPANY IS A HOLDING OR SUBSIDIARY COMPANY

Company's own accounts

59 Where a company is a holding company or a subsidiary of another body corporate and any item required by Part I of this Schedule to be shown in the company's balance sheet in relation to group companies includes—

(a) amounts attributable to dealings with or interests in any holding company or fellow subsidiary of the company; or
(b) amounts attributable to dealings with or interests in any subsidiary of the company;

the aggregate amounts within paragraphs (a) and (b) respectively shall be shown as separate items, either by way of subdivision of the relevant item in the balance sheet or in a note to the company's accounts.'

[59A Guarantees and other financial commitments in favour of group undertakings

Commitments within any of sub-paragraphs (1) to (5) of paragraph 50 (guarantees and other financial commitments) which are undertaken on behalf of or for the benefit of—

(a) any parent undertaking or fellow subsidiary undertaking, or
(b) any subsidiary undertaking of the company,

shall be stated separately from the other commitments within that sub-paragraph, and commitments within paragraph (a) shall also be stated separately from those within paragraph (b).][1]

---

1 Inserted by CA 1989, 1 Sch 11 with effect from 1 April 1990 (SI 1990 No 355) subject to the transitional and saving provisions in Arts 6 to 9 of that Order.

60-70 [. . .][1]

---

1 Repealed by CA 1989, 24 Sch with effect from 1 April 1990 (SI 1990 No 355) subject to the transitional and saving provisions in Arts 6 to 9 of that Order.

PART V SPECIAL PROVISIONS WHERE THE COMPANY IS AN INVESTMENT COMPANY

71 (1) Paragraph 34 does not apply to the amount of any profit or loss arising from a determination of the value of any investments of an investment company on any basis mentioned in paragraph 31(3).

(2) Any provisions made by virtue of paragraph 19(1) or (2) in the case of an investment company in respect of any fixed asset investments need not be charged to the company's profit and loss account provided they are either—

(a) charged against any reserve account to which any amount excluded by sub-paragraph (1) from the requirements of paragraph 34 has been credited; or

(b) shown as a separate item in the company's balance sheet under the sub-heading "other reserves".

(3) For the purposes of this paragraph, as it applies in relation to any company, "fixed asset investment" means any asset falling to be included under any item shown in the company's balance sheet under the subdivision "investments" under the general item "fixed assets".

72 (1) Any distribution made by an investment company which reduces the amount of its net assets to less than the aggregate of its called-up share capital and undistributable reserves shall be disclosed in a note to the company's accounts.

(2) For purposes of this paragraph, a company's net assets are the aggregate of its assets less the aggregate of its liabilities (including any provision for liabilities or charges within paragraph 89); and "undistributable reserves" has the meaning given by section 264(3) of this Act.

73 A company shall be treated as an investment company for the purposes of this Part of this Schedule in relation to any financial year of the company if—

(a) during the whole of that year it was an investment company as defined by section 266 of this Act, and

(b) it was not at any time during that year prohibited under section 265(4) of this Act (no distribution where capital profits have been distributed, etc.) from making a distribution by virtue of that section.

74 [. . .][1]

---

1 Repealed by CA 1989, 24 Sch with effect from 1 April 1990 (SI 1990 No 355) subject to the transitional and saving provisions in Arts 6 to 9 of that Order.

PART VI SPECIAL PROVISIONS WHERE THE COMPANY HAS ENTERED INTO ARRANGEMENTS SUBJECT TO MERGER RELIEF

75 [. . .][1]

---

1 Repealed by CA 1989, 24 Sch with effect from 1 April 1990 (SI 1990 No 355) subject to the transitional and saving provisions in Arts 6 to 9 of that Order.

PART VII INTERPRETATION OF SCHEDULE

76 The following paragraphs apply for the purposes of this Schedule and its interpretation.

77-81 [. . .][1]

[1] Repealed by CA 1989, 24 Sch with effect from 1 April 1990 (SI 1990 No 355) subject to the transitional and saving provisions in Arts 6 to 9 of that Order.

Historical cost accounting rules

82 References to the historical cost accounting rules shall be read in accordance with paragraph 29.

Leases

83 (1) "Long lease" means a lease in the case of which the portion of the term for which it was granted remaining unexpired at the end of the financial year is not less than 50 years.

(2) "Short lease" means a lease which is not a long lease.

(3) "Lease" includes an agreement for a lease.

Listed investments

84 "Listed investment" means an investment as respects which there has been granted a listing [on a recognised investment exchange other than an overseas investment exchange within the meaning of the Financial Services Act 1986 or on any stock exchange of repute outside Great Britain][1].

[1] Substituted by FSA 1986, s 212(2), 16 Sch 23(b) with effect from 29 April 1988 (see SI 1988 No 740). Previously 'on a recognised stock exchange, or on any stock exchange of repute (other than a recognised stock exchange) outside Great Britain'.

Loans

85 A loan is treated as falling due for repayment, and an instalment of a loan is treated as falling due for payment, on the earliest date on which the lender could require repayment or (as the case may be) payment, if he exercised all options and rights available to him.

Materiality

86 Amounts which in the particular context of any provision of this Schedule are not material may be disregarded for the purposes of that provision.

87 [. . .][1]

[1] Repealed by CA 1989, 24 Sch with effect from 1 April 1990 (SI 1990 No 355) subject to the transitional and saving provisions in Arts 6 to 9 of that Order.

Provisions

88 (1) References to provisions for depreciation or diminution in value of assets are to any amount written off by way of providing for depreciation or diminution in value of assets.

(2) Any reference in the profit and loss account formats set out in Part I of this Schedule to the depreciation of, or amounts written off, assets of any description is to any provision for depreciation or diminution in value of assets of that description.

89 References to provisions for liabilities or charges are to any amount retained as reasonably necessary for the purpose of providing for any liability or loss which is either likely to be incurred, or certain to be incurred but uncertain as to amount or as to the date on which it will arise.

90-92 [. . .][1]

[1] Repealed by CA 1989, 24 Sch with effect from 1 April 1990 (SI 1990 No 355) subject to the transitional and saving provisions in Arts 6 to 9 of that Order.

Scots land tenure

93 In the application of this Schedule to Scotland, "land of freehold tenure" means land in respect of which the company is the proprietor of the *dominium utile* or, in the case of land not held on feudal tenure, is the owner; "land of leasehold tenure" means land of which the company is the tenant under a lease; and the reference to ground-rents, rates and other outgoings includes feu-duty and ground annual.

Staff costs

94 (1) "Social security costs" means any contributions by the company to any state social security or pension scheme, fund or arrangement.

(2) "Pension costs" includes any other contributions by the company for the purposes of any pension scheme established for the purpose of providing pensions for persons employed by the company, any sums set aside for that purpose and any amounts paid by the company in respect of pensions without first being so set aside.

(3) Any amount stated in respect of either of the above items or in respect of the item "wages and salaries" in the company's profit and loss account shall be determined by reference to payments made or costs incurred in respect of all persons employed by the company during the financial year who are taken into account in determining the relevant annual number for the purposes of paragraph 56(1)(a).

95 [. . .][1]

[1] Repealed by CA 1989, 24 Sch with effect from 1 April 1990 (SI 1990 No 355) subject to the transitional and saving provisions in Arts 6 to 9 of that Order.

SCHEDULE 4A
(Section 5(2), CA 1989)

FORM AND CONTENT OF GROUP ACCOUNTS

Note. This Schedule inserted by CA 1989, s 5(2), 2 Sch with effect from 1 April 1990 (SI 1990 No 355) subject to the transitional and saving provisions in Arts 6 to 9 of that Order.

General rules

2 (1) The consolidated balance sheet and profit and loss account shall incorporate in full the information contained in the individual accounts of the undertakings included in the consolidation, subject to the adjustments authorised or required by the following provisions of this Schedule and to such other adjustments (if any) as may be appropriate in accordance with generally accepted accounting principles or practice.

(2) If the financial year of a subsidiary undertaking included in the consolidation differs from that of the parent company, the group accounts shall be made up—

(a) from the accounts of the subsidiary undertaking for its financial year last ending before the end of the parent company's financial year, provided that year ended no more than three months before that of the parent company, or
(b) from interim accounts prepared by the subsidiary undertaking as at the end of the parent company's financial year.

10 (1) The conditions for accounting for an acquisition as a merger are—

(a) that at least 90 per cent. of the nominal value of the relevant shares in the undertaking acquired is held by or on behalf of the parent company and its subsidiary undertakings,
(b) that the proportion referred to in paragraph (a) was attained pursuant to an arrangement providing for the issue of equity shares by the parent company or one or more of its subsidiary undertakings,
(c) that the fair value of any consideration other than the issue of equity shares given pursuant to the arrangement by the parent company and its subsidiary undertakings did not exceed 10 per cent. of the nominal value of the equity shares issued, and
(d) that adoption of the merger method of accounting accords with generally accepted accounting principles or practice.

(2) The reference in sub-paragraph (1)(a) to the "relevant shares" in an undertaking acquired is to those carrying unrestricted rights to participate both in distributions and in the assets of the undertaking upon liquidation.

13 (1) The following information with respect to acquisitions taking place in the financial year shall be given in a note to the accounts.

(2) There shall be stated—

(a) the name of the undertaking acquired or, where a group was acquired, the name of the parent undertaking of that group, and
(b) whether the acquisition has been accounted for by the acquisition or the merger method of accounting;

and in relation to an acquisition which significantly affects the figures shown in the group accounts, the following further information shall be given.

(3) The composition and fair value of the consideration for the acquisition given by the parent company and its subsidiary undertakings shall be stated.

(4) The profit or loss of the undertaking or group acquired shall be stated—

(a) for the period from the beginning of the financial year of the undertaking or, as the case may be, of the parent undertaking of the group, up to the date of the acquisition, and

(b) for the previous financial year of that undertaking or parent undertaking;

and there shall also be stated the date on which the financial year referred to in paragraph (a) began.

(5) Where the acquisition method of accounting has been adopted, the book values immediately prior to the acquisition, and the fair values at the date of acquisition, of each class of assets and liabilities of the undertaking or group acquired shall be stated in tabular form, including a statement of the amount of any goodwill or negative consolidation difference arising on the acquisition, together with an explanation of any significant adjustments made.

(6) Where the merger method of accounting has been adopted, an explanation shall be given of any significant adjustments made in relation to the amounts of the assets and liabilities of the undertaking or group acquired, together with a statement of any resulting adjustment to the consolidated reserves (including the re-statement of opening consolidated reserves).

(7) In ascertaining for the purposes of sub-paragraph (4), (5) or (6) the profit or loss of a group, the book values and fair values of assets and liabilities of a group or the amount of the assets and liabilities of a group, the set-offs and other adjustments required by this Schedule in the case of group accounts shall be made.

SCHEDULE 5

(Section 6(2), CA 1989)

DISCLOSURE OF INFORMATION: RELATED UNDERTAKINGS

Note. This Schedule substituted by CA 1989, s 6(2), 3 Sch with effect from 1 April 1990 (SI 1990 No 355) subject to the transitional and saving provisions in Arts 6 to 9 of that Order. See after end of Schedule for the previous provisions of 5 Sch.

Cross references. See 4 Sch 63.

PART I COMPANIES NOT REQUIRED TO PREPARE GROUP ACCOUNTS

1 Subsidiary undertakings

(1) The following information shall be given where at the end of the financial year the company has subsidiary undertakings.

(2) The name of each subsidiary undertaking shall be stated.

(3) There shall be stated with respect to each subsidiary undertaking—

(a) if it is incorporated outside Great Britain, the country in which it is incorporated;
(b) if it is incorporated in Great Britain, whether it is registered in England and Wales or in Scotland;
(c) if it is unincorporated, the address of its principal place of business.

(4) The reason why the company is not required to prepare group accounts shall be stated.

(5) If the reason is that all the subsidiary undertakings of the company fall within the exclusions provided for in section 229, it shall be stated with respect to each subsidiary undertaking which of those exclusions applies.

2 Holdings in subsidiary undertakings

(1) There shall be stated in relation to shares of each class held by the company in a subsidiary undertaking—

(a) the identity of the class, and
(b) the proportion of the nominal value of the shares of that class represented by those shares.

(2) The shares held by or on behalf of the company itself shall be distinguished from those attributed to the company which are held by or on behalf of a subsidiary undertaking.

3 Financial information about subsidiary undertakings

(1) There shall be disclosed with respect to each subsidiary undertaking—

(a) the aggregate amount of its capital and reserves as at the end of its relevant financial year, and
(b) its profit or loss for that year.

(2) That information need not be given if the company is exempt by virtue of section 228 from the requirement to prepare group accounts (parent company included in accounts of larger group).

(3) That information need not be given if—

(a) the subsidiary undertaking is not required by any provision of this Act to deliver a copy of its balance sheet for its relevant financial year and does not otherwise publish that balance sheet in Great Britain or elsewhere, and

(b) the company's holding is less than 50 per cent. of the nominal value of the shares in the undertaking.

(4) Information otherwise required by this paragraph need not be given if it is not material.

(5) For the purposes of this paragraph the "relevant financial year" of a subsidiary undertaking is—

(a) if its financial year ends with that of the company, that year, and

(b) if not, its financial year ending last before the end of the company's financial year.

4 Financial years of subsidiary undertakings

Where the financial year of one or more subsidiary undertakings did not end with that of the company, there shall be stated in relation to each such undertaking—

(a) the reasons why the company's directors consider that its financial year should not end with that of the company, and

(b) the date on which its last financial year ended (last before the end of the company's financial year).

Instead of the dates required by paragraph (b) being given for each subsidiary undertaking the earliest and latest of those dates may be given.

5 Further information about subsidiary undertakings

(1) There shall be disclosed—

(a) any qualifications contained in the auditors' reports on the accounts of subsidiary undertakings for financial years ending with or during the financial year of the company, and

(b) any note or saving contained in such accounts to call attention to a matter which, apart from the note or saving, would properly have been referred to in such a qualification,

in so far as the matter which is the subject of the qualification or note is not covered by the company's own accounts and is material from the point of view of its members.

(2) The aggregate amount of the total investment of the company in the shares of subsidiary undertakings shall be stated by way of the equity method of valuation, unless—

(a) the company is exempt from the requirement to prepare group accounts by virtue of section 228 (parent company included in accounts of larger group), and

(b) the directors state their opinion that the aggregate value of the assets of the company consisting of shares in, or amounts owing (whether on account of a loan or otherwise) from, the company's subsidiary undertakings is not less than the aggregate of the amounts at which those assets are stated or included in the company's balance sheet.

(3) In so far as information required by this paragraph is not obtainable, a statement to that effect shall be given instead.

6 **Shares and debentures of company held by subsidiary undertakings**

(1) The number, description and amount of the shares in and debentures of the company held by or on behalf of its subsidiary undertakings shall be disclosed.

(2) Sub-paragraph (1) does not apply in relation to shares or debentures in the case of which the subsidiary undertaking is concerned as personal representative or, subject as follows, as trustee.

(3) The exception for shares or debentures in relation to which the subsidiary undertaking is concerned as trustee does not apply if the company, or any subsidiary undertaking of the company, is beneficially interested under the trust, otherwise than by way of security only for the purposes of a transaction entered into by it in the ordinary course of a business which includes the lending of money.

(4) Schedule 2 to this Act has effect for the interpretation of the reference in sub-paragraph (3) to a beneficial interest under a trust.

Significant holdings in undertakings other than subsidiary undertakings

7 (1) The information required by paragraphs 8 and 9 shall be given where at the end of the financial year the company has a significant holding in an undertaking which is not a subsidiary undertaking of the company.

(2) A holding is significant for this purpose if—

(a) it amounts to 10 per cent. or more of the nominal value of any class of shares in the undertaking, or
(b) the amount of the holding (as stated or included in the company's accounts) exceeds one-tenth of the amount (as so stated) of the company's assets.

8 (1) The name of the undertaking shall be stated.

(2) There shall be stated—

(a) if the undertaking is incorporated outside Great Britain, the country in which it is incorporated;
(b) if it is incorporated in Great Britain, whether it is registered in England and Wales or in Scotland;
(c) if it is unincorporated, the address of its principal place of business.

(3) There shall also be stated—

(a) the identity of each class of shares in the undertaking held by the company, and
(b) the proportion of the nominal value of the shares of that class represented by those shares.

9 (1) Where the company has a significant holding in an undertaking amounting to 20 per cent. or more of the nominal value of the shares in the undertaking, there shall also be stated—

(a) the aggregate amount of the capital and reserves of the undertaking as at the end of its relevant financial year, and

(b) its profit or loss for that year.

(2) That information need not be given if—

(a) the company is exempt by virtue of section 228 from the requirement to prepare group accounts (parent company included in accounts of larger group), and
(b) the investment of the company in all undertakings in which it has such a holding as is mentioned in sub-paragraph (1) is shown, in aggregate, in the notes to the accounts by way of the equity method of valuation.

(3) That information need not be given in respect of an undertaking if—

(a) the undertaking is not required by any provision of this Act to deliver a copy of its balance sheet for its relevant financial year and does not otherwise publish that balance sheet in Great Britain or elsewhere, and
(b) the company's holding is less than 50 per cent. of the nominal value of the shares in the undertaking.

(4) Information otherwise required by this paragraph need not be given if it is not material.

(5) For the purposes of this paragraph the "relevant financial year" of an undertaking is—

(a) if its financial year ends with that of the company, that year, and
(b) if not, its financial year ending last before the end of the company's financial year.

10 Arrangements attracting merger relief

(1) This paragraph applies to arrangements attracting merger relief, that is, where a company allots shares in consideration for the issue, transfer or cancellation of shares in another body corporate ("the other company") in circumstances such that section 130 of this Act (share premium account) does not, by virtue of section 131(2) (merger relief), apply to the premiums on the shares.

(2) If the company makes such an arrangement during the financial year, the following information shall be given—

(a) the name of the other company,
(b) the number, nominal value and class of shares allotted,
(c) the number, nominal value and class of shares in the other company issued, transferred or cancelled, and
(d) particulars of the accounting treatment adopted in the company's accounts in respect of the issue, transfer or cancellation.

(3) Where the company made such an arrangement during the financial year, or during either of the two preceding financial years, and there is included in the company's profit and loss account—

(a) any profit or loss realised during the financial year by the company on the disposal of—
(i) any shares in the other company, or
(ii) any assets which were fixed assets of the other company or any of its subsidiary undertakings at the time of the arrangement, or

(b) any part of any profit or loss realised during the financial year by the company on the disposal of any shares (other than shares in the other company) which was attributable to the fact that there were at the time of the disposal amongst the assets of the company which issued the shares, or any of its subsidiary undertakings, such shares or assets as are described in paragraph (a) above,

then, the net amount of that profit or loss or, as the case may be, the part so attributable shall be shown, together with an explanation of the transactions to which the information relates.

(4) For the purposes of this paragraph the time of the arrangement shall be taken to be—

(a) where as a result of the arrangement the other company becomes a subsidiary undertaking of the company, the date on which it does so or, if the arrangement in question becomes binding only on the fulfilment of a condition, the date on which that condition is fulfilled;

(b) if the other company is already a subsidiary undertaking of the company, the date on which the shares are allotted or, if they are allotted on different days, the first day.

11 Parent undertaking drawing up accounts for larger group

(1) Where the company is a subsidiary undertaking, the following information shall be given with respect to the parent undertaking of—

(a) the largest group of undertakings for which group accounts are drawn up and of which the company is a member, and

(b) the smallest such group of undertakings.

(2) The name of the parent undertaking shall be stated.

(3) There shall be stated—

(a) if the undertaking is incorporated outside Great Britain, the country in which it is incorporated;

(b) if it is incorporated in Great Britain, whether it is registered in England and Wales or in Scotland;

(c) if it is unincorporated, the address of its principal place of business.

(4) If copies of the group accounts referred to in sub-paragraph (1) are available to the public, there shall also be stated the addresses from which copies of the accounts can be obtained.

12 Identification of ultimate parent company

(1) Where the company is a subsidiary undertaking, the following information shall be given with respect to the company (if any) regarded by the directors as being the company's ultimate parent company.

(2) The name of that company shall be stated.

(3) If known to the directors, there shall be stated—

(a) if that company is incorporated outside Great Britain, the country in which it is incorporated;

(b) if it is incorporated in Great Britain, whether it is registered in England and Wales or in Scotland.

(4) In this paragraph "company" includes any body corporate.

13 Constructions of references to shares held by company

(1) References in this Part of this Schedule to shares held by a company shall be construed as follows.

(2) For the purposes of paragraphs 2 to 5 (information about subsidiary undertakings)—

(a) there shall be attributed to the company any shares held by a subsidiary undertaking, or by a person acting on behalf of the company or a subsidiary undertaking; but

(b) there shall be treated as not held by the company any shares held on behalf of a person other than the company or a subsidiary undertaking.

(3) For the purposes of paragraphs 7 to 9 (information about undertakings other than subsidiary undertakings)—

(a) there shall be attributed to the company shares held on its behalf by any person; but

(b) there shall be treated as not held by a company shares held on behalf of a person other than the company.

(4) For the purposes of any of those provisions, shares held by way of security shall be treated as held by the person providing the security—

(a) where apart from the right to exercise them for the purpose of preserving the value of the security, or of realising it, the rights attached to the shares are exercisable only in accordance with his instructions, and

(b) where the shares are held in connection with the granting of loans as part of normal business activities and apart from the right to exercise them for the purpose of preserving the value of the security, or of realising it, the rights attached to the shares are exercisable only in his interests.

PART II COMPANIES REQUIRED TO PREPARE GROUP ACCOUNTS

14 Introductory

In this Part of this Schedule "the group" means the group consisting of the parent company and its subsidiary undertakings.

15 Subsidiary undertakings

(1) The following information shall be given with respect to the undertakings which are subsidiary undertakings of the parent company at the end of the financial year.

(2) The name of each undertaking shall be stated.

(3) There shall be stated—

(a) if the undertaking is incorporated outside Great Britain, the country in which it is incorporated;

(b) if it is incorporated in Great Britain, whether it is registered in England and Wales or in Scotland;

(c) if it is unincorporated, the address of its principal place of business.

(4) It shall also be stated whether the subsidiary undertaking is included in the consolidation and, if it is not, the reasons for excluding it from consolidation shall be given.

(5) It shall be stated with respect to each subsidiary undertaking by virtue of which of the conditions specified in section 258(2) or (4) it is a subsidiary undertaking of its immediate parent undertaking.

That information need not be given if the relevant condition is that specified in subsection (2)(a) of that section (holding of a majority of the voting rights) and the immediate parent undertaking holds the same proportion of the shares in the undertaking as it holds voting rights.

16 Holdings in subsidiary undertakings

(1) The following information shall be given with respect to the shares of a subsidiary undertaking held—

(a) by the parent company, and
(b) by the group;

and the information under paragraphs (a) and (b) shall (if different) be shown separately.

(2) There shall be stated—

(a) the identity of each class of shares held, and
(b) the proportion of the nominal value of the shares of that class represented by those shares.

17 Financial information about subsidiary undertakings not included in the consolidation

(1) There shall be shown with respect to each subsidiary undertaking not included in the consolidation—

(a) the aggregate amount of its capital and reserves as at the end of its relevant financial year, and
(b) its profit or loss for that year.

(2) That information need not be given if the group's investment in the undertaking is included in the accounts by way of the equity method of valuation or if—

(a) the undertaking is not required by any provision of this Act to deliver a copy of its balance sheet for its relevant financial year and does not otherwise publish that balance sheet in Great Britain or elsewhere, and
(b) the holding of the group is less than 50 per cent. of the nominal value of the shares in the undertaking.

(3) Information otherwise required by this paragraph need not be given if it is not material.

(4) For the purposes of this paragraph the "relevant financial year" of a subsidiary undertaking is—

(a) if its financial year ends with that of the company, that year, and
(b) if not, its financial year ending last before the end of the company's financial year.

18 Further information about subsidiary undertakings excluded from consolidation

(1) The following information shall be given with respect to subsidiary undertakings excluded from consolidation.

(2) There shall be disclosed—

(a) any qualifications contained in the auditors' reports on the accounts of the undertaking for financial years ending with or during the financial year of the company, and

(b) any note or saving contained in such accounts to call attention to a matter which, apart from the note or saving, would properly have been referred to in such a qualification,

in so far as the matter which is the subject of the qualification or note is not covered by the consolidated accounts and is material from the point of view of the members of the parent company.

(3) In so far as information required by this paragraph is not obtainable, a statement to that effect shall be given instead.

19 Financial years of subsidiary undertakings

Where the financial year of one or more subsidiary undertakings did not end with that of the company, there shall be stated in relation to each such undertaking—

(a) the reasons why the company's directors consider that its financial year should not end with that of the company, and

(b) the date on which its last financial year ended (last before the end of the company's financial year).

Instead of the dates required by paragraph (b) being given for each subsidiary undertaking the earliest and latest of those dates may be given.

20 Shares and debentures of company held by subsidiary undertakings

(1) The number, description and amount of the shares in and debentures of the company held by or on behalf of its subsidiary undertakings shall be disclosed.

(2) Sub-paragraph (1) does not apply in relation to shares or debentures in the case of which the subsidiary undertaking is concerned as personal representative or, subject as follows, as trustee.

(3) The exception for shares or debentures in relation to which the subsidiary undertaking is concerned as trustee does not apply if the company or any of its subsidiary undertakings is beneficially interested under the trust, otherwise than by way of security only for the purposes of a transaction entered into by it in the ordinary course of a business which includes the lending of money.

(4) Schedule 2 to this Act has effect for the interpretation of the reference in sub-paragraph (3) to a beneficial interest under a trust.

21 Joint ventures

(1) The following information shall be given where an undertaking is dealt with in the consolidated accounts by the method of proportional consolidation in accordance with paragraph 19 of Schedule 4A (joint ventures)—

(a) the name of the undertaking;
(b) the address of the principal place of business of the undertaking;
(c) the factors on which joint management of the undertaking is based; and
(d) the proportion of the capital of the undertaking held by undertakings included in the consolidation.

(2) Where the financial year of the undertaking did not end with that of the company, there shall be stated the date on which a financial year of the undertaking last ended before that date.

22 **Associated undertakings**

(1) The following information shall be given where an undertaking included in the consolidation has an interest in an associated undertaking.

(2) The name of the associated undertaking shall be stated.

(3) There shall be stated—

(a) if the undertaking is incorporated outside Great Britain, the country in which it is incorporated;
(b) if it is incorporated in Great Britain, whether it is registered in England and Wales or in Scotland;
(c) if it is unincorporated, the address of its principal place of business.

(4) The following information shall be given with respect to the shares of the undertaking held—

(a) by the parent company, and
(b) by the group;

and the information under paragraphs (a) and (b) shall be shown separately.

(5) There shall be stated—

(a) the identity of each class of shares held, and
(b) the proportion of the nominal value of the shares of that class represented by those shares.

(6) In this paragraph "associated undertaking" has the meaning given by paragraph 20 of Schedule 4A; and the information required by this paragraph shall be given notwithstanding that paragraph 22(3) of that Schedule (materiality) applies in relation to the accounts themselves.

Other significant holdings of parent company or group

23 (1) The information required by paragraphs 24 and 25 shall be given where at the end of the financial year the parent company has a significant holding in an undertaking which is not one of its subsidiary undertakings and does not fall within paragraph 21 (joint ventures) or paragraph 22 (associated undertakings).

(2) A holding is significant for this purpose if—

(a) it amounts to 10 per cent. or more of the nominal value of any class of shares in the undertaking, or
(b) the amount of the holding (as stated or included in the company's individual accounts) exceeds one-tenth of the amount of its assets (as so stated).

24 (1) The name of the undertaking shall be stated.

(2) There shall be stated—

(a) if the undertaking is incorporated outside Great Britain, the country in which it is incorporated;
(b) if it is incorporated in Great Britain, whether it is registered in England and Wales or in Scotland;
(c) if it is unincorporated, the address of its principal place of business.

(3) The following information shall be given with respect to the shares of the undertaking held by the parent company.

(4) There shall be stated—

(a) the identity of each class of shares held, and
(b) the proportion of the nominal value of the shares of that class represented by those shares.

25 (1) Where the company has a significant holding in an undertaking amounting to 20 per cent. or more of the nominal value of the shares in the undertaking, there shall also be stated—

(a) the aggregate amount of the capital and reserves of the undertaking as at the end of its relevant financial year, and
(b) its profit or loss for that year.

(2) That information need not be given in respect of an undertaking if—

(a) the undertaking is not required by any provision of this Act to deliver a copy of its balance sheet for its relevant financial year and does not otherwise publish that balance sheet in Great Britain or elsewhere, and
(b) the company's holding is less than 50 per cent. of the nominal value of the shares in the undertaking.

(3) Information otherwise required by this paragraph need not be given if it is not material.

(4) For the purposes of this paragraph the "relevant financial year" of an undertaking is—

(a) if its financial year ends with that of the company, that year, and
(b) if not, its financial year ending last before the end of the company's financial year.

26 (1) The information required by paragraphs 27 and 28 shall be given where at the end of the financial year the group has a significant holding in an undertaking which is not a subsidiary undertaking of the parent company and does not fall within paragraph 21 (joint ventures) or paragraph 22 (associated undertakings).

(2) A holding is significant for this purpose if—

(a) it amounts to 10 per cent. or more of the nominal value of any class of shares in the undertaking, or
(b) the amount of the holding (as stated or included in the group accounts) exceeds one-tenth of the amount of the group's assets (as so stated).

27 (1) The name of the undertaking shall be stated.

(2) There shall be stated—

(a) if the undertaking is incorporated outside Great Britain, the country in which it is incorporated;
(b) if it is incorporated in Great Britain, whether it is registered in England and Wales or in Scotland;
(c) if it is unincorporated, the address of its principal place of business.

(3) The following information shall be given with respect to the shares of the undertaking held by the group.

(4) There shall be stated—

(a) the identity of each class of shares held, and

(b) the proportion of the nominal value of the shares of that class represented by those shares.

28 (1) Where the holding of the group amounts to 20 per cent. or more of the nominal value of the shares in the undertaking, there shall also be stated—

(a) the aggregate amount of the capital and reserves of the undertaking as at the end of its relevant financial year, and
(b) its profit or loss for that year.

(2) That information need not be given if—

(a) the undertaking is not required by any provision of this Act to deliver a copy of its balance sheet for its relevant financial year and does not otherwise publish that balance sheet in Great Britain or elsewhere, and
(b) the holding of the group is less than 50 per cent. of the nominal value of the shares in the undertaking.

(3) Information otherwise required by this paragraph need not be given if it is not material.

(4) For the purposes of this paragraph the "relevant financial year" of an outside undertaking is—

(a) if its financial year ends with that of the parent company, that year, and
(b) if not, its financial year ending last before the end of the parent company's financial year.

29 **Arrangements attracting merger relief**

(1) This paragraph applies to arrangements attracting merger relief, that is, where a company allots shares in consideration for the issue, transfer or cancellation of shares in another body corporate ("the other company") in circumstances such that section 130 of this Act (share premium account) does not, by virtue of section 131(2) (merger relief), apply to the premiums on the shares.

(2) If the parent company made such an arrangement during the financial year, the following information shall be given—

(a) the name of the other company,
(b) the number, nominal value and class of shares allotted,
(c) the number, nominal value and class of shares in the other company issued, transferred or cancelled, and
(d) particulars of the accounting treatment adopted in the parent company's individual and group accounts in respect of the issue, transfer or cancellation, and
(e) particulars of the extent to which and manner in which the profit or loss for the financial year shown in the group accounts is affected by any profit or loss of the other company, or any of its subsidiary undertakings, which arose before the time of the arrangement.

(3) Where the parent company made such an arrangement during the financial year, or during either of the two preceding financial years, and there is included in the consolidated profit and loss account—

(a) any profit or loss realised during the financial year on the disposal of—
  (i) any shares in the other company, or
  (ii) any assets which were fixed assets of the other company or any of its subsidiary undertakings at the time of the arrangement, or

(b) any part of any profit or loss realised during the financial year on the disposal of any shares (other than shares in the other company) which was attributable to the fact that there were at the time of the disposal amongst the assets of the company which issued the shares, or any of its subsidiary undertakings, such shares or assets as are described in paragraph (a) above,

then, the net amount of that profit or loss or, as the case may be, the part so attributable shall be shown, together with an explanation of the transactions to which the information relates.

(4) For the purposes of this paragraph the time of the arrangement shall be taken to be—

(a) where as a result of the arrangement the other company becomes a subsidiary undertaking of the company in question, the date on which it does so or, if the arrangement in question becomes binding only on the fulfilment of a condition, the date on which that condition is fulfilled;
(b) if the other company is already a subsidiary undertaking of that company, the date on which the shares are allotted or, if they are allotted on different days, the first day.

30 Parent undertaking drawing up accounts for larger group

(1) Where the parent company is itself a subsidiary undertaking, the following information shall be given with respect to that parent undertaking of the company which heads—

(a) the largest group of undertakings for which group accounts are drawn up and of which that company is a member, and
(b) the smallest such group of undertakings.

(2) The name of the parent undertaking shall be stated.

(3) There shall be stated—

(a) if the undertaking is incorporated outside Great Britain, the country in which it is incorporated;
(b) if it is incorporated in Great Britain, whether it is registered in England and Wales or in Scotland;
(c) if it is unincorporated, the address of its principal place of business.

(4) If copies of the group accounts referred to in sub-paragraph (1) are available to the public, there shall also be stated the addresses from which copies of the accounts can be obtained.

31 Identification of ultimate parent company

(1) Where the parent company is itself a subsidiary undertaking, the following information shall be given with respect to the company (if any) regarded by the directors as being that company's ultimate parent company.

(2) The name of that company shall be stated.

(3) If known to the directors, there shall be stated—

(a) if that company is incorporated outside Great Britain, the country in which it is incorporated;
(b) if it is incorporated in Great Britain, whether it is registered in England and Wales or in Scotland.

(4) In this paragraph "company" includes any body corporate.

32 Construction of references to shares held by parent company or group

(1) References in this Part of this Schedule to shares held by the parent company or the group shall be construed as follows.

(2) For the purposes of paragraphs 16, 22(4) and (5) and 23 to 25 (information about holdings in subsidiary and other undertakings)—

(a) there shall be attributed to the parent company shares held on its behalf by any person; but

(b) there shall be treated as not held by the parent company shares held on behalf of a person other than the company.

(3) References to shares held by the group are to any shares held by or on behalf of the parent company or any of its subsidiary undertakings; but there shall be treated as not held by the group any shares held on behalf of a person other than the parent company or any of its subsidiary undertakings.

(4) Shares held by way of security shall be treated as held by the person providing the security—

(a) where apart from the right to exercise them for the purpose of preserving the value of the security, or of realising it, the rights attached to the shares are exercisable only in accordance with his instructions, and

(b) where the shares are held in connection with the granting of loans as part of normal business activities and apart from the right to exercise them for the purpose of preserving the value of the security, or of realising it, the rights attached to the shares are exercisable only in his interests.

Note. The above Schedule was substituted by CA 1989, 3 Sch with effect from a date to be appointed.

SCHEDULE 6

(Sections 232, 233, 234 and as amended by CA 1989, s 6(4), 4 Sch)

[DISCLOSURE OF INFORMATION: EMOLUMENTS AND OTHER BENEFITS OF DIRECTORS AND OTHERS][1]

1 Substituted by CA 1989, 4 Sch 2 with effect from 1 April 1990 (SI 1990 No 355) subject to the transitional and saving provisions in Arts 6 to 9 of that Order.
Previously
'PARTICULARS IN COMPANY ACCOUNTS OF LOAN AND OTHER TRANSACTIONS FAVOURING DIRECTORS AND OFFICERS'.

Cross references. See 4 Sch 63.

[PART I CHAIRMAN'S AND DIRECTORS' EMOLUMENTS, PENSIONS AND COMPENSATION FOR LOSS OF OFFICE

1 Aggregate amount of directors' emoluments

(1) The aggregate amount of directors' emoluments shall be shown.

(2) This means the emoluments paid to or receivable by any person in respect of—

(a) his services as a director of the company, or
(b) his services while director of the company—
(i) as director of any of its subsidiary undertakings, or
(ii) otherwise in connection with the management of the affairs of the company or any of its subsidiary undertakings.

(3) There shall also be shown, separately, the aggregate amount within sub-paragraph (2)(a) and (b)(i) and the aggregate amount within sub-paragraph (2)(b)(ii).

(4) For the purposes of this paragraph the "emoluments" of a person include—

(a) fees and percentages,
(b) sums paid by way of expenses allowance (so far as those sums are chargeable to United Kingdom income tax),
(c) contributions paid in respect of him under any pension scheme, and
(d) the estimated money value of any other benefits received by him otherwise than in cash,

and emoluments in respect of a person's accepting office as director shall be treated as emoluments in respect of his services as director.][1]

1 Inserted by CA 1989, 4 Sch 3 with effect from 1 April 1990 (SI 1990 No 355) subject to the transitional and saving provisions in Arts 6 to 9 of that Order.

[Details of chairman's and directors' emoluments

2 Where the company is a parent company or a subsidiary undertaking, or where the amount shown in compliance with paragraph 1(1) is £60,000 or more, the information required by paragraphs 3 to 6 shall be given with respect to the emoluments of the chairman and directors, and emoluments waived.][1]

1 Inserted by CA 1989, 4 Sch 3 with effect from 1 April 1990 (SI 1990 No 355) subject to the transitional and saving provisions in Arts 6 to 9 of that Order.

[3 (1) The emoluments of the chairman shall be shown.

(2) The "chairman" means the person elected by the directors to be chairman of their meetings, and includes a person who, though not so elected, holds an office (however designated) which in accordance with the company's constitution carries with it functions substantially similar to those discharged by a person so elected.

(3) Where there has been more than one chairman during the year, the emoluments of each shall be stated so far as attributable to the period during which he was chairman.

(4) The emoluments of a person need not be shown if his duties as chairman were wholly or mainly discharged outside the United Kingdom.][1]

---

1 Inserted by CA 1989, 4 Sch 3 with effect from 1 April 1990 (SI 1990 No 355) subject to the transitional and saving provisions in Arts 6 to 9 of that Order.

[4 (1) The following information shall be given with respect to the emoluments of directors.

(2) There shall be shown the number of directors whose emoluments fell within each of the following bands—

not more than £5,000,

more than £5,000 but not more than £10,000,

more than £10,000 but not more than £15,000,

and so on.

(3) If the emoluments of any of the directors exceeded that of the chairman, there shall be shown the greatest amount of emoluments of any director.

(4) Where more than one person has been chairman during the year, the reference in sub-paragraph (3) to the emoluments of the chairman is to the aggregate of the emoluments of each person who has been chairman, so far as attributable to the period during which he was chairman.

(5) The information required by sub-paragraph (2) need not be given in respect of a director who discharged his duties as such wholly or mainly outside the United Kingdom; and any such director shall be left out of account for the purposes of sub-paragraph (3).][1]

---

1 Inserted by CA 1989, 4 Sch 3 with effect from 1 April 1990 (SI 1990 No 355) subject to the transitional and saving provisions in Arts 6 to 9 of that Order.

[5 In paragraphs 3 and 4 "emoluments" has the same meaning as in paragraph 1, except that it does not include contributions paid in respect of a person under a pension scheme.][1]

---

1 Inserted by CA 1989, 4 Sch 3 with effect from 1 April 1990 (SI 1990 No 355) subject to the transitional and saving provisions in Arts 6 to 9 of that Order.

[6 **Emoluments waived**

(1) There shall be shown—

(a) the number of directors who have waived rights to receive emoluments which, but for the waiver, would have fallen to be included in the amount shown under paragraph 1(1), and
(b) the aggregate amount of those emoluments.

(2) For the purposes of this paragraph it shall be assumed that a sum not receivable in respect of a period would have been paid at the time at which it was due, and if such a sum was payable only on demand, it shall be deemed to have been due at the time of the waiver.][1]

1 Inserted by CA 1989, 4 Sch 3 with effect from 1 April 1990 (SI 1990 No 355) subject to the transitional and saving provisions in Arts 6 to 9 of that Order.

[7 Pensions of directors and past directors

(1) There shall be shown the aggregate amount of directors' or past directors' pensions.

(2) This amount does not include any pension paid or receivable under a pension scheme if the scheme is such that the contributions under it are substantially adequate for the maintenance of the scheme; but, subject to this, it includes any pension paid or receivable in respect of any such services of a director or past director as are mentioned in paragraph 1(2), whether to or by him or, on his nomination or by virtue of dependence on or other connection with him, to or by any other person.

(3) The amount shown shall distinguish between pensions in respect of services as director, whether of the company or any of its subsidiary undertakings, and other pensions.

(4) References to pensions include benefits otherwise than in cash and in relation to so much of a pension as consists of such a benefit references to its amount are to the estimated money value of the benefit.

The nature of any such benefit shall also be disclosed.][1]

1 Inserted by CA 1989, 4 Sch 3 with effect from 1 April 1990 (SI 1990 No 355) subject to the transitional and saving provisions in Arts 6 to 9 of that Order.

[8 Compensation to directors for loss of office

(1) There shall be shown the aggregate amount of any compensation to directors or past directors in respect of loss of office.

(2) This amount includes compensation received or receivable by a director or past director for—

(a) loss of office as director of the company, or
(b) loss, while director of the company or on or in connection with his ceasing to be a director of it, of—
  (i) any other office in connection with the management of the company's affairs, or
  (ii) any office as director or otherwise in connection with the management of the affairs of any subsidiary undertaking of the company;

and shall distinguish between compensation in respect of the office of director, whether of the company or any of its subsidiary undertakings, and compensation in respect of other offices.

(3) References to compensation include benefits otherwise than in cash; and in relation to such compensation references to its amount are to the estimated money value of the benefit.

The nature of any such compensation shall be disclosed.

(4) References to compensation for loss of office include compensation in consideration for, or in connection with, a person's retirement from office.][1]

---

1 Inserted by CA 1989, 4 Sch 3 with effect from a date to be appointed.

[9 Sums paid to third parties in respect of directors' services

(1) There shall be shown the aggregate amount of any consideration paid to or receivable by third parties for making available the services of any person—

(a) as a director of the company, or
(b) while director of the company—
  (i) as director of any of its subsidiary undertakings, or
  (ii) otherwise in connection with the management of the affairs of the company or any of its subsidiary undertakings.

(2) The reference to consideration includes benefits otherwise than in cash; and in relation to such consideration the reference to its amount is to the estimated money value of the benefit.

The nature of any such consideration shall be disclosed.

(3) The reference to third parties is to persons other than—

(a) the director himself or a person connected with him or body corporate controlled by him, and
(b) the company or any of its subsidiary undertakings.][1]

---

1 Inserted by CA 1989, 4 Sch 3 with effect from 1 April 1990 (SI 1990 No 355) subject to the transitional and saving provisions in Arts 6 to 9 of that Order.

[Supplementary

10 (1) The following applies with respect to the amounts to be shown under paragraphs 1, 7, 8 and 9.

(2) The amount in each case includes all relevant sums paid by or receivable from—

(a) the company; and
(b) the company's subsidiary undertakings; and
(c) any other person,

except sums to be accounted for to the company or any of its subsidiary undertakings or, by virtue of sections 314 and 315 of this Act (duty of directors to make disclosure on company takeover; consequence of non-compliance), to past or present members of the company or any of its subsidiaries or any class of those members.

(3) The amount to be shown under paragraph 8 shall distinguish between the sums respectively paid by or receivable from the company, the company's subsidiary undertakings and persons other than the company and its subsidiary undertakings.

(4) References to amounts paid to or receivable by a person include amounts paid to or receivable by a person connected with him or a body corporate controlled by him (but not so as to require an amount to be counted twice).][1]

[1] Inserted by CA 1989, 4 Sch 3 with effect from 1 April 1990 (SI 1990 No 355) subject to the transitional and saving provisions in Arts 6 to 9 of that Order.

[11 (1) The amounts to be shown for any financial year under paragraphs 1, 7, 8 and 9 are the sums receivable in respect of that year (whenever paid) or, in the case of sums not receivable in respect of a period, the sums paid during that year.

(2) But where—

(a) any sums are not shown in a note to the accounts for the relevant financial year on the ground that the person receiving them is liable to account for them as mentioned in paragraph 10(2), but the liability is thereafter wholly or partly released or is not enforced within a period of 2 years; or

(b) any sums paid by way of expenses allowance are charged to United Kingdom income tax after the end of the relevant financial year,

those sums shall, to the extent to which the liability is released or not enforced or they are charged as mentioned above (as the case may be), be shown in a note to the first accounts in which it is practicable to show them and shall be distinguished from the amounts to be shown apart from this provision.][1]

[1] Inserted by CA 1989, 4 Sch 3 with effect from 1 April 1990 (SI 1990 No 355) subject to the transitional and saving provisions in Arts 6 to 9 of that Order.

[12 Where it is necessary to do so for the purpose of making any distinction required by the preceding paragraphs in an amount to be shown in compliance with this Part of this Schedule, the directors may apportion any payments between the matters in respect of which these have been paid or are receivable in such manner as they think appropriate.][1]

[1] Inserted by CA 1989, 4 Sch 3 with effect from 1 April 1990 (SI 1990 No 355) subject to the transitional and saving provisions in Arts 6 to 9 of that Order.

[13 Interpretation

(1) The following applies for the interpretation of this Part of this Schedule.

(2) A reference to a subsidiary undertaking of the company—

(a) in relation to a person who is or was, while a director of the company, a director also, by virtue of the company's nomination (direct or indirect) of any other undertaking, includes (subject to the following sub-paragraph) that undertaking, whether or not it is or was in fact a subsidiary undertaking of the company, and

(b) for the purposes of paragraphs 1 to 7 (including any provision of this Part of this Schedule referring to paragraph 1) is to an undertaking which is a subsidiary undertaking at the time the services were rendered, and for the purposes of paragraph 8 to a subsidiary undertaking immediately before the loss of office as director.

(3) The following definitions apply—

(a) "pension" includes any superannuation allowance, superannuation gratuity or similar payment,

(b) "pension scheme" means a scheme for the provision of pensions in respect of services as director or otherwise which is maintained in whole or in part by means of contributions, and

(c) "contribution", in relation to a pension scheme, means any payment (including an insurance premium) paid for the purposes of the scheme by or in respect of persons rendering services in respect of which pensions will or may become payable under the scheme except that it does not include any payment in respect of two or more persons if the amount paid in respect of each of them is not ascertainable.

(4) References in this Part of this Schedule to a person being "connected" with a director, and to a director "controlling" a body corporate, shall be construed in accordance with section 346.][1]

[1] Inserted by CA 1989, 4 Sch 3 with effect from 1 April 1990 (SI 1990 No 355) subject to the transitional and saving provisions in Arts 6 to 9 of that Order.

[14 Supplementary

This Part of this Schedule requires information to be given only so far as it is contained in the company's books and papers or the company has the right to obtain it from the persons concerned.][1]

[1] Inserted by CA 1989, 4 Sch 3 with effect from 1 April 1990 (SI 1990 No 355) subject to the transitional and saving provisions in Arts 6 to 9 of that Order.

[PART II LOANS, QUASI-LOANS AND OTHER DEALINGS IN FAVOUR OF DIRECTORS][1]

[1] Substituted by CA 1989, 4 Sch 4 with effect from a date to be appointed.
Previously
'PART I MATTERS TO BE DISCLOSED UNDER SECTION 232'

Note. Following the insertion of Part I above by CA 1989, 4 Sch 3, the original paragraphs 1 to 3 and 5 to 14 of Part I are renumbered 15 to 27 and internal cross references are renumbered accordingly.

15 [The group accounts of a holding company, or if it is not required to prepare group accounts its individual accounts,][1] shall contain the particulars required by this Schedule of—

(a) any transaction or arrangement of a kind described in section 330 entered into by the company or by a subsidiary of the company for a person who at any time during the financial year was a director of the company or its holding company, or was connected with such a director;

(b) an agreement by the company or by a subsidiary of the company to enter into any such transaction or arrangement for a person who was at any time during the financial year a director of the company or its holding company, or was connected with such a director; and

(c) any other transaction or arrangement with the company or a subsidiary of it in which a person who at any time during the financial year was a director of the company or its holding company had, directly or indirectly, a material interest.

[1] Substituted by CA 1989, 4 Sch 4 with effect from 1 April 1990 (SI 1990 No 355) subject to the transitional and saving provisions in Arts 6 to 9 of that Order.
Previously 'Group accounts'.

16 The accounts prepared by a company other than a holding company shall contain the particulars required by this Schedule of—

(a) any transaction or arrangement of a kind described in section 330 entered into by the company for a person who at any time during the financial year was a director of it or of its holding company or was connected with such a director;
(b) an agreement by the company to enter into any such transaction or arrangement for a person who at any time during the financial year was a director of the company or its holding company or was connected with such a director; and
(c) any other transaction or arrangement with the company in which a person who at any time during the financial year was a director of the company or of its holding company had, directly or indirectly, a material interest.

17 (1) For purposes of paragraphs 15(c) and 16(c), a transaction or arrangement between a company and a director of it or of its holding company, or a person connected with such a director, is to be treated (if it would not otherwise be so) as a transaction, arrangement or agreement in which that director is interested.

(2) An interest in such a transaction or arrangement is not "material" for purposes of those sub-paragraphs if in the board's opinion it is not so; but this is without prejudice to the question whether or not such an interest is material in a case where the board have not considered the matter.

"The board" here means the directors of the company preparing the accounts, or a majority of those directors, but excluding in either case the director whose interest it is.

[. . .][1]

[1] Deleted by CA 1989, 4 Sch 4 with effect from 1 April 1990 (SI 1990 No 355) subject to the transitional and saving provisions in Arts 6 to 9 of that Order.
Previously
'4 Paragraphs 1 and 2 do not apply, for the purposes of accounts prepared by a company which is, or is the holding company of, [an authorised institution][a], in relation to a transaction or arrangement of a kind described in section 330 or an agreement to enter into such a transaction or arrangement, to which [that authorised institution][b] is a party.'
[a] Substituted by Banking Act 1987, s 108(1), 6 Sch 18(9) with effect from 1 October 1987 (see SI 1987 No 1664).
Previously 'a recognised bank'.
[b] Substituted by Banking Act 1987, s 108(1), 6 Sch 18(9) with effect from 1 October 1987 (see SI 1987 No 1664).
Previously 'that recognised bank'.

18 Paragraphs 15 and 16 do not apply in relation to the following transactions, arrangements and agreements—

(a) a transaction, arrangement or agreement between one company and another in which a director of the former or of its subsidiary or holding company is interested only by virtue of his being a director of the latter;
(b) a contract of service between a company and one of its directors or a director of its holding company, or between a director of a company and any of that company's subsidiaries;
(c) a transaction, arrangement or agreement which was not entered into during the financial year and which did not subsist at any time during that year.

19 Paragraphs 15 and 16 apply whether or not—

(a) the transaction or arrangement was prohibited by section 330;

(b) the person for whom it was made was a director of the company or was connected with a director of it at the time it was made;

(c) in the case of a transaction or arrangement made by a company which at any time during a financial year is a subsidiary of another company, it was a subsidiary of that other company at the time the transaction or arrangement was made.

20 Neither paragraph 15(c) nor paragraph 16(c) applies in relation to any transaction or arrangement if—

(a) each party to the transaction or arrangement which is a member of the same group of companies (meaning a holding company and its subsidiaries) as the company entered into the transaction or arrangement in the ordinary course of business, and

(b) the terms of the transaction or arrangement are not less favourable to any such party than it would be reasonable to expect if the interest mentioned in that sub-paragraph had not been an interest of a person who was a director of the company or of its holding company.

21 Neither paragraph 15(c) nor paragraph 16(c) applies in relation to any transaction or arrangement if—

(a) the company is a member of a group of companies (meaning a holding company and its subsidiaries), and

(b) either the company is a wholly-owned subsidiary or no body corporate (other than the company or a subsidiary of the company) which is a member of the group of companies which includes the company's ultimate holding company was a party to the transaction or arrangement, and

(c) the director in question was at some time during the relevant period associated with the company, and

(d) the material interest of the director in question in the transaction or arrangement would not have arisen if he had not been associated with the company at any time during the relevant period.

The particulars required by this Part

22 (1) Subject to the next paragraph, the particulars required by this Part are those of the principal terms of the transaction, arrangement or agreement.

(2) Without prejudice to the generality of sub-paragraph (1), the following particulars are required—

(a) a statement of the fact either that the transaction, arrangement or agreement was made or subsisted (as the case may be) during the financial year;

(b) the name of the person for whom it was made and, where that person is or was connected with a director of the company or of its holding company, the name of that director;

(c) in a case where paragraph 15(c) or 16(c) applies, the name of the director with the material interest and the nature of that interest;

(d) in the case of a loan or an agreement for a loan or an arrangement within section 330(6) or (7) of this Act relating to a loan—

(i) the amount of the liability of the person to whom the loan was or was agreed to be made, in respect of principal and interest, at the beginning and at the end of the financial year;

(ii) the maximum amount of that liability during that year;

(iii) the amount of any interest which, having fallen due, has not been paid; and

(iv) the amount of any provision (within the meaning of Schedule 4 to this Act) made in respect of any failure or anticipated failure by the borrower to repay the whole or part of the loan or to pay the whole or part of any interest on it;

(e) in the case of a guarantee or security or an arrangement within section 330(6) relating to a guarantee or security—

(i) the amount for which the company (or its subsidiary) was liable under the guarantee or in respect of the security both at the beginning and at the end of the financial year;

(ii) the maximum amount for which the company (or its subsidiary) may become so liable; and

(iii) any amount paid and any liability incurred by the company (or its subsidiary) for the purpose of fulfilling the guarantee or discharging the security (including any loss incurred by reason of the enforcement of the guarantee or security); and

(f) in the case of any transaction, arrangement or agreement other than those mentioned in sub-paragraphs (d) and (e), the value of the transaction or arrangement or (as the case may be) the value of the transaction or arrangement to which the agreement relates.

23 In paragraph 22(2) above, sub-paragraphs (c) to (f) do not apply in the case of a loan or quasi-loan made or agreed to be made by a company to or for a body corporate which is either—

(a) a body corporate of which that company is a wholly-owned subsidiary, or

(b) a wholly-owned subsidiary of a body corporate of which that company is a wholly-owned subsidiary, or

(c) a wholly-owned subsidiary of that company,

if particulars of that loan, quasi-loan or agreement for it would not have been required to be included in that company's annual accounts if the first-mentioned body corporate had not been associated with a director of that company at any time during the relevant period.

[Excluded transactions][1]

24 (1) In relation to a company's accounts for a financial year, compliance with this Part is not required in the case of transactions of a kind mentioned in the following sub-paragraph which are made by the company or a subsidiary of it for a person who at any time during that financial year was a director of the company or of its holding company, or was connected with such a director, if the aggregate of the values of each transaction, arrangement or agreement so made for that director or any person connected with him, less the amount (if any) by which the liabilities of the person for whom the transaction or arrangement was made has been reduced, did not at any time during the financial year exceed £5,000.

(2) The transactions in question are—

(a) credit transactions,

(b) guarantees provided or securities entered into in connection with credit transactions,

(c) arrangements within subsection (6) or (7) of section 330 relating to credit transactions,

(d) agreements to enter into credit transactions.

1 Substituted by CA 1989, 4 Sch 4 with effect from 1 April 1990 (SI 1990 No 355) subject to the transitional and saving provisions in Arts 6 to 9 of that Order.
Previously
'Transactions excluded from section 232'.

25 In relation to a company's accounts for a financial year, compliance with this Part is not required by virtue of paragraph 15(c) or 16(c) in the case of any transaction or arrangement with a company or any of its subsidiaries in which a director of the company or its holding company had, directly or indirectly, a material interest if—

(a) the value of each transaction or arrangement within paragraph 15(c) or 16(c) (as the case may be) in which that director had (directly or indirectly) a material interest and which was made after the commencement of the financial year with the company or any of its subsidiaries, and
(b) the value of each such transaction or arrangement which was made before the commencement of the financial year less the amount (if any) by which the liabilities of the person for whom the transaction or arrangement was made have been reduced,

did not at any time during the financial year exceed in the aggregate £1,000 or, if more, did not exceed £5,000 or 1 per cent. of the value of the net assets of the company preparing the accounts in question as at the end of the financial year, whichever is the less.

For this purpose a company's net assets are the aggregate of its assets, less the aggregate of its liabilities ("liabilities" to include any provision for liabilities or charges within paragraph 89 of Schedule 4).

26 Section 345 of this Act (power of Secretary of State to alter sums by statutory instrument subject to negative resolution in Parliament) applies as if the money sums specified in paragraph 24 or 25 above were specified in Part X.

27 Interpretation

[(1)][3] The following provisions of this Act apply for purposes of this Part of this Schedule—

(a) section 331(2), [. . .][1] and (7), as regards the meaning of "guarantee", [. . .][2] and "credit transaction";
(b) section 331(9), as to the interpretation of references to a transaction or arrangement being made "for" a person;
(c) section 340, in assigning values to transactions and arrangements, and
(d) section 346, as to the interpretation of references to a person being "connected with" a director of a company.

[(2) In this Part of this Schedule "director" includes a shadow director.][3]

1 Repealed by BA 1987, s 108(2), 7 Sch Part I with effect from 1 October 1987 (see SI 1987 No 1664). Previously '(5)'.

2 Repealed by BA 1987, s 108(2), 7 Sch Part I with effect from 1 October 1987 (see SI 1987 No 1664). Previously ' "recognised bank" '.

3 Inserted by CA 1989, 4 Sch 5 with effect from 1 April 1990 (SI 1990 No 355) subject to the transitional and saving provisions in Arts 6 to 9 of that Order.

[PART III OTHER TRANSACTIONS, ARRANGEMENTS AND AGREEMENTS][1]

1 Substituted by CA 1989, 4 Sch 6 with effect from 1 April 1990 (SI 1990 No 355) subject to the transitional and saving provisions in Arts 6 to 9 of that Order reproduced above Sec 221 above.
Previously

'PART II MATTERS TO BE DISCLOSED UNDER SECTION 233'.

Note. Following the insertion of Part I to this Schedule by CA 1989, 4 Sch 3, the original paragraphs 15 to 17 of Part II are renumbered 28 to 30 and internal cross references are renumbered accordingly.

---

28 This Part of this Schedule applies in relation to the following classes of transactions, arrangements and agreements—

(a) loans, guarantees and securities relating to loans, arrangements of a kind described in subsection (6) or (7) of section 330 of this Act relating to loans and agreements to enter into any of the foregoing transactions and arrangements;

(b) quasi-loans, guarantees and securities relating to quasi-loans arrangements of a kind described in either of those subsections relating to quasi-loans and agreements to enter into any of the foregoing transactions and arrangements;

(c) credit transactions, guarantees and securities relating to credit transactions, arrangements of a kind described in either of those subsections relating to credit transactions and agreements to enter into any of the foregoing transactions and arrangements.

29 (1) To comply with this Part of this Schedule, the accounts must contain a statement, in relation to transactions, arrangements and agreements [made by the company or a subsidiary of it for persons who at any time during the financial year were officers of the company (but not directors or shadow directors)][1], of—

(a) the aggregate amounts outstanding at the end of the financial year under transactions, arrangements and agreements within sub-paragraphs (a), (b) and (c) respectively of paragraph 28 above, and

(b) the numbers of officers for whom the transactions, arrangements and agreements falling within each of those sub-paragraphs were made.

(2) This paragraph does not apply to transactions, arrangements and agreements made by the company or any of its subsidiaries for an officer of the company if the aggregate amount outstanding at the end of the financial year under the transactions, arrangements and agreements so made for that officer does not exceed £2,500.

(3) Section 345 of this Act (power of Secretary of State to alter money sums by statutory instrument subject to negative resolution in Parliament) applies as if the money sum specified above in this paragraph were specified in Part X.

---

1 Substituted by CA 1989, 4 Sch 6 with effect from 1 April 1990 (SI 1990 No 355) subject to the transitional and saving provisions in Arts 6 to 9 of that Order.
Previously 'made as mentioned in section 233(1)'.

---

30 The following provisions of this Act apply for purposes of this Part—

(a) section 331(2), (3), [. . .][1] and (7), as regards the meaning of "guarantee", "quasi-loan", [. . .][2] and "credit transaction", and

(b) section 331(9), as to the interpretation of references to a transaction or arrangement being made "for" a person;

and "amount outstanding" means the amount of the outstanding liabilities of the person for whom the transaction, arrangement or agreement was made or, in the case of a guarantee or security, the amount guaranteed or secured.

1 Repealed by BA 1987, s 108(2), 7 Sch Part I with effect from 1 October 1987 (see SI 1987 No 1664). Previously '(5)'.

2 Repealed by BA 1987, s 108(2), 7 Sch Part I with effect from 1 October 1987 (see SI 1987 No 1664). Previously ' "recognised bank" '.

[. . .][1]

1 Deleted by CA 1989, 4 Sch 7 with effect from 1 April 1990 (SI 1990 No 355) subject to the transitional and saving provisions in Arts 6 to 9 of that Order.
Previously
'PART III MATTERS TO BE DISCLOSED UNDER SECTION 234 [AUTHORISED INSTITUTIONS][a]

18 This Part of this Schedule applies in relation to the same classes of transactions, arrangements and agreements as does Part II.

19 To comply with this Part, the accounts must contain a statement, in relation to such transactions, arrangements and agreements made as mentioned in section 234(1), of—

(a) the aggregate amounts outstanding at the end of the financial year under transactions, arrangements and agreements within sub-paragraphs (a), (b) and (c) respectively of paragraph 15 of this Schedule, and

(b) the numbers of persons for whom the transactions, arrangements and agreements falling within each of those sub-paragraphs were made.

20 For the purposes of the application of paragraph 19 in relation to loans and quasi-loans made by a company to persons connected with a person who at any time is a director of the company or of its holding company, a company which a person does not control is not connected with him.

21 The following provisions of this Act apply for purposes of this Part—

(a) section 331(3), as regards the meaning of "quasi-loan";

(b) section 331(9), as to the interpretation of references to a transaction or arrangement being made "for" a person; and

(c) section 346, as to the interpretation of references to a person being connected with a director, or to a director controlling a company;

and "amount outstanding" means the amount of the outstanding liabilities of the person for whom the transaction, arrangement or agreement was made or, in the case of a guarantee or security, the amount guaranteed or secured.'

a Substituted by Banking Act 1987, s 108(1), 6 Sch 18(9) with effect from 1 October 1987 (see SI 1987 No 1664).
Previously 'RECOGNISED BANKS'.

SCHEDULE 7

(Section 235 and as amended by CA 1989, s 8(2), 5 Sch)

MATTERS TO BE DEALT WITH IN DIRECTORS' REPORT

PART I MATTERS OF A GENERAL NATURE

1 Asset values

(1) If significant changes in the fixed assets of the company or of any of its [subsidiary undertakings][1] have occurred in the financial year, the report shall contain particulars of the changes.

(2) If, in the case of such of those assets as consist in interests in land, their market value (as at the end of the financial year) differs substantially from the amount at which they are included in the balance sheet, and the difference is, in the directors' opinion, of such significance as to require that the attention of members of the company or of holders of its debentures should be drawn to it, the report shall indicate the difference with such degree of precision as is practicable.

---

1 Substituted by CA 1989, 5 Sch 2 with effect from 1 April 1990 (SI 1990 No 355) subject to the transitional and saving provisions in Arts 6 to 9 of that Order.
Previously 'subsidiaries'.

Directors' interests

2 [(1) The information required by paragraphs 2A and 2B shall be given in the directors' report, or by way of notes to the company's annual accounts, with respect to each person who at the end of the financial year was a director of the company.

(2) In those paragraphs—

(a) "the register" means the register of directors' interests kept by the company under section 325; and

(b) references to a body corporate being in the same group as the company are to its being a subsidiary or holding company, or another subsidiary of a holding company, of the company.][1]

---

1 Substituted by CA 1989, 5 Sch 3 with effect from 1 April 1990 (SI 1990 No 355) subject to the transitional and saving provisions in Arts 6 to 9 of that Order. See after paragraph 2B below for previous provisions.

[2A (1) It shall be stated with respect to each director whether, according to the register, he was at the end of the financial year interested in shares in or debentures of the company or any other body corporate in the same group.

(2) If he was so interested, there shall be stated the number of shares in and amount of debentures of each body (specifying it) in which, according to the register, he was then interested.

(3) If a director was interested at the end of the financial year in shares in or debentures of the company or any other body corporate in the same group—

(a) it shall also be stated whether, according to the register, he was at the beginning of the financial year (or, if he was not then a director, when he became one) interested in shares in or debentures of the company or any other body corporate in the same group, and

(b) if he was so interested, there shall be stated the number of shares in and amount of debentures of each body (specifying it) in which, according to the register, he was then interested.

(4) In this paragraph references to an interest in shares or debentures have the same meaning as in section 324; and references to the interest of a director include any interest falling to be treated as his for the purposes of that section.

(5) The reference above to the time when a person became a director is, in the case of a person who became a director on more than one occasion, to the time when he first became a director.][1]

---

[1] Inserted by CA 1989, 5 Sch 3 with effect from 1 April 1990 (SI 1990 No 355) subject to the transitional and saving provisions in Arts 6 to 9 of that Order.

[2B (1) It shall be stated with respect to each director whether, according to the register, any right to subscribe for shares in or debentures of the company or another body corporate in the same group was during the financial year granted to, or exercised by, the director or a member of his immediate family.

(2) If any such right was granted to, or exercised by, any such person during the financial year, there shall be stated the number of shares in and amount of debentures of each body (specifying it) in respect of which, according to the register, the right was granted or exercised.

(3) A director's "immediate family" means his or her spouse and infant children; and for this purpose "children" includes step-children, and "infant", in relation to Scotland, means pupil or minor.

(4) The reference above to a member of the director's immediate family does not include a person who is himself or herself a director of the company.][1]

---

[1] Inserted by CA 1989, 5 Sch 3 with effect from 1 April 1990 (SI 1990 No 355) subject to the transitional and saving provisions in Arts 6 to 9 of that Order.

Note. The provisions of paragraphs 2, 2A and 2B above inserted by CA 1989, 5 Sch 3 replaced the former provisions of paragraph 2 which read as follows.

2 (1) The report shall state the following, with respect to each person who, at the end of the financial year, was a director of the company—

(a) whether or not, according to the register kept by the company for the purposes of sections 324 to 328 of this Act (director's obligation to notify his interests in the company and companies in the same group), he was at the end of that year interested in shares in, or debentures of, the company or any other body corporate, being the company's subsidiary or holding company or a subsidiary of the company's holding company;

(b) if he was so interested—

(i) the number and amount of shares in, and debentures of, each body (specifying it) in which, according to that register, he was then interested,

(ii) whether or not (according to that register) he was, at the beginning of that year (or, if he was not then a director, when he became one), interested in shares in, or debentures of, the company or any other such body corporate, and

(iii) if he was, the number and amount of shares in, and debentures of, each body (specifying it) in which, according to that register, he was interested at the beginning of the financial year or (as the case may be) when he became a director.

(2) An interest in shares or debentures which, under sections 324 to 328, falls to be treated as being the interest of a director is so treated for the purposes of this paragraph; and the references above to the time when a person became a director, in the case of a person who became a director on more than one occasion, is to the time when he first became a director.

(3) The particulars required by this paragraph may be given by way of notes to the company's accounts in respect of the financial year, instead of being stated in the directors' report.

Political and charitable gifts

3 (1) The following applies if the company (not being the wholly-owned subsidiary of a company incorporated in Great Britain) has in the financial year given money for political purposes or charitable purposes or both.

(2) If the money given exceeded £200 in amount, there shall be contained in the directors' report for the year—

(a) in the case of each of the purposes for which money has been given, a statement of the amount of money given for that purpose, and

(b) in the case of political purposes for which money has been given, the following particulars (so far as applicable)—

(i) the name of each person to whom money has been given for those purposes exceeding £200 in amount and the amount of money given,

(ii) if money exceeding £200 in amount has been given by way of donation or subscription to a political party, the identity of the party and the amount of money given.

4 (1) Paragraph 3 does not apply to a company which, at the end of the financial year, has subsidiaries which have, in that year, given money as mentioned above, but is not itself the wholly-owned subsidiary of a company incorporated in Great Britain.

(2) But in such a case there shall (if the amount of money so given in that year by the company and the subsidiaries between them exceeds £200) be contained in the directors' report for the year—

(a) in the case of each of the purposes for which money has been given by the company and the subsidiaries between them, a statement of the amount of money given for that purpose, and

(b) in the case of political purposes for which money has been given, the like particulars (so far as applicable) as are required by paragraph 3.

5 (1) The following applies for the interpretation of paragraphs 3 and 4.

(2) A company is to be treated as giving money for political purposes if, directly or indirectly—

(a) it gives a donation or subscription to a political party of the United Kingdom or any part of it; or

(b) it gives a donation or subscription to a person who, to the company's knowledge, is carrying on, or proposing to carry on, any activities which can, at the time at which the donation or subscription was given, reasonably be regarded as likely to affect public support for such a political party as is mentioned above.

(3) Money given for charitable purposes to a person who, when it was given, was ordinarily resident outside the United Kingdom is to be left out of account.

(4) "Charitable purposes" means purposes which are exclusively charitable; and, as respects Scotland, "charitable" is to be construed as if it were contained in the Income Tax Acts.

[5A **Insurance effected for officers or auditors**

Where in the financial year the company has purchased or maintained any such insurance as is mentioned in section 310(3)(a) (insurance of officers or auditors against liabilities in relation to the company), that fact shall be stated in the report.][1]

[1] Inserted by CA 1989, s 137(2) with effect from 1 April 1990 but not to have effect for a directors' report of a company for a financial year commencing on a date prior to 23 December 1989 (SI 1990 No 355).

6 **Miscellaneous**

The directors' report shall contain—

(a) particulars of any important events affecting the company or any of its [subsidiary undertakings][1] which have occurred since the end of the financial year,
(b) an indication of likely future developments in the business of the company and of its [subsidiary undertakings][1], and
(c) an indication of the activities (if any) of the company and its [subsidiary undertakings][1] in the field of research and development.

[1] Substituted by CA 1989, 5 Sch 2 with effect from 1 April 1990 (SI 1990 No 355) subject to the transitional and saving provisions in Arts 6 to 9 of that Order.
Previously 'subsidiaries'.

PART II DISCLOSURE REQUIRED BY COMPANY ACQUIRING ITS OWN SHARES, ETC.

7 This Part of this Schedule applies where shares in a company—

(a) are purchased by the company or are acquired by it by forfeiture or surrender in lieu of forfeiture, or in pursuance of section 143(3) of this Act (acquisition of own shares by company limited by shares), or
(b) are acquired by another person in circumstances where paragraph (c) or (d) of section 146(1) applies (acquisition by company's nominee, or by another with company financial assistance, the company having a beneficial interest), or
(c) are made subject to a lien or other charge taken (whether expressly or otherwise) by the company and permitted by section 150(2) or (4), or section 6(3) of the Consequential Provisions Act (exceptions from general rule against a company having a lien or charge on its own shares).

8 The directors' report with respect to a financial year shall state—

(a) the number and nominal value of the shares so purchased, the aggregate amount of the consideration paid by the company for such shares and the reasons for their purchase;
(b) the number and nominal value of the shares so acquired by the company, acquired by another person in such circumstances and so charged respectively during the financial year;
(c) the maximum number and nominal value of shares which, having been so acquired by the company, acquired by another person in such circumstances or so charged (whether or not during that year) are held at any time by the company or that other person during that year;
(d) the number and nominal value of the shares so acquired by the company, acquired by another person in such circumstances or so charged (whether or not during that year) which are disposed of by the company or that other person or cancelled by the company during that year;

(e) where the number and nominal value of the shares of any particular description are stated in pursuance of any of the preceding sub-paragraphs, the percentage of the called-up share capital which shares of that description represent;

(f) where any of the shares have been so charged the amount of the charge in each case; and

(g) where any of the shares have been disposed of by the company or the person who acquired them in such circumstances for money or money's worth the amount or value of the consideration in each case.

PART III DISCLOSURE CONCERNING EMPLOYMENT, ETC. OF DISABLED PERSONS

9 (1) This Part of this Schedule applies to the directors' report where the average number of persons employed by the company in each week during the financial year exceeded 250.

(2) That average number is the quotient derived by dividing, by the number of weeks in the financial year, the number derived by ascertaining, in relation to each of those weeks, the number of persons who, under contracts of service, were employed in the week (whether throughout it or not) by the company, and adding up the numbers ascertained.

(3) The directors' report shall in that case contain a statement describing such policy as the company has applied during the financial year—

(a) for giving full and fair consideration to applications for employment by the company made by disabled persons, having regard to their particular aptitudes and abilities,

(b) for continuing the employment of, and for arranging appropriate training for, employees of the company who have become disabled persons during the period when they were employed by the company, and

(c) otherwise for the training, career development and promotion of disabled persons employed by the company.

(4) In this Part—

(a) "employment" means employment other than employment to work wholly or mainly outside the United Kingdom, and "employed" and "employee" shall be construed accordingly; and

(b) "disabled person" means the same as in the Disabled Persons (Employment) Act 1944.

PART IV HEALTH, SAFETY AND WELFARE AT WORK OF COMPANY'S EMPLOYEES

10 (1) In the case of companies of such classes as may be prescribed by regulations made by the Secretary of State, the directors' report shall contain such information as may be so prescribed about the arrangements in force in the financial year for securing the health, safety and welfare at work of employees of the company and its subsidiaries, and for protecting other persons against risks to health or safety arising out of or in connection with the activities at work of those employees.

(2) Regulations under this Part may—

(a) make different provision in relation to companies of different classes,

(b) enable any requirements of the regulations to be dispensed with or modified in particular cases by any specified person or by any person authorised in that behalf by a specified authority,

(c) contain such transitional provisions as the Secretary of State thinks necessary or expedient in connection with any provision made by the regulations.

(3) The power to make regulations under this paragraph is exercisable by statutory instrument subject to annulment in pursuance of a resolution of either House of Parliament.

(4) Any expression used in sub-paragraph (1) above and in Part I of the Health and Safety at Work etc. Act 1974 has the same meaning here as it has in that Part of that Act; section 1(3) of that Act applies for interpreting that sub-paragraph; and in sub-paragraph (2) "specified" means specified in regulations made under that sub-paragraph.

PART V EMPLOYEE INVOLVEMENT

11 (1) This Part of this Schedule applies to the directors' report where the average number of persons employed by the company in each week during the financial year exceeded 250.

(2) That average number is the quotient derived by dividing by the number of weeks in the financial year the number derived by ascertaining, in relation to each of those weeks, the number of persons who, under contracts of service, were employed in the week (whether throughout it or not) by the company, and adding up the numbers ascertained.

(3) The directors' report shall in that case contain a statement describing the action that has been taken during the financial year to introduce, maintain or develop arrangements aimed at—

(a) providing employees systematically with information on matters of concern to them as employees,

(b) consulting employees or their representatives on a regular basis so that the views of employees can be taken into account in making decisions which are likely to affect their interests,

(c) encouraging the involvement of employees in the company's performance through an employees' share scheme or by some other means,

(d) achieving a common awareness on the part of all employees of the financial and economic factors affecting the performance of the company.

(4) In sub-paragraph (3) "employee" does not include a person employed to work wholly or mainly outside the United Kingdom; and for the purposes of sub-paragraph (2) no regard is to be had to such a person.

SCHEDULE 8

(Section 13(2), CA 1989)

EXEMPTIONS FOR SMALL AND MEDIUM-SIZED COMPANIES

Note. This Schedule is substituted by CA 1989, 6 Sch with effect from 1 April 1990 (SI 1990 No 355) subject to the transitional and saving provisions in Arts 6 to 9 of that Order. See after the end of the Schedule for the previous provisions.

PART I SMALL COMPANIES

1 Balance sheet

(1) The company may deliver a copy of an abbreviated version of the full balance sheet, showing only those items to which a letter or Roman number is assigned in the balance sheet format adopted under Part I of Schedule 4, but in other respects corresponding to the full balance sheet.

(2) If a copy of an abbreviated balance sheet is delivered, there shall be disclosed in it or in a note to the company's accounts delivered—

(a) the aggregate of the amounts required by note (5) of the notes on the balance sheet formats set out in Part I of Schedule 4 to be shown separately for each item included under debtors (amounts falling due after one year), and

(b) the aggregate of the amounts required by note (13) of those notes to be shown separately for each item included under creditors in Format 2 (amounts falling due within one year or after more than one year).

(3) The provisions of section 233 as to the signing of the copy of the balance sheet delivered to the registrar apply to a copy of an abbreviated balance sheet delivered in accordance with this paragraph.

2 Profit and loss account

A copy of the company's profit and loss account need not be delivered.

3 Disclosure of information in notes to accounts

(1) Of the information required by Part III of Schedule 4 (information to be given in notes to accounts if not given in the accounts themselves) only the information required by the following provisions need be given—

paragraph 36 (accounting policies),

paragraph 38 (share capital),

paragraph 39 (particulars of allotments),

paragraph 42 (fixed assets), so far as it relates to those items to which a letter or Roman number is assigned in the balance sheet format adopted,

paragraph 48(1) and (4) (particulars of debts),

paragraph 58(1) (basis of conversion of foreign currency amounts into sterling),

paragraph 58(2) (corresponding amounts for previous financial year), so far as it relates to amounts stated in a note to the company's accounts by virtue of a requirement of Schedule 4 or under any other provision of this Act.

(2) Of the information required by Schedule 5 to be given in notes to the accounts, the information required by the following provisions need not be given—

paragraph 4 (financial years of subsidiary undertakings),

paragraph 5 (additional information about subsidiary undertakings),

paragraph 6 (shares and debentures of company held by subsidiary undertakings),

paragraph 10 (arrangements attracting merger relief).

(3) Of the information required by Schedule 6 to be given in notes to the accounts, the information required by Part I (directors' and chairman's emoluments, pensions and compensation for loss of office) need not be given.

4 Directors' report

A copy of the directors' report need not be delivered.

PART II MEDIUM-SIZED COMPANIES

5 Profit and loss account

The company may deliver a profit and loss account in which the following items listed in the profit and loss account formats set out in Part I of Schedule 4 are combined as one item under the heading "gross profit or loss"—

Items 1, 2, 3 and 6 in Format 1;

Items 1 to 5 in Format 2;

Items A.1, B.1 and B.2 in Format 3;

Items A.1, A.2 and B.1 to B.4 in Format 4.

6 Disclosure of information in notes to accounts

The information required by paragraph 55 of Schedule 4 (particulars of turnover) need not be given.

PART III SUPPLEMENTARY PROVISIONS

7 Statement that advantage taken of exemptions

(1) Where the directors of a company take advantage of the exemptions conferred by Part I or Part II of this Schedule, the company's balance sheet shall contain—

(a) a statement that advantage is taken of the exemptions conferred by Part I or, as the case may be, Part II of this Schedule, and
(b) a statement of the grounds on which, in the directors' opinion, the company is entitled to those exemptions.

(2) The statements shall appear in the balance sheet immediately above the signature required by section 233.

8 Special auditors' report

(1) If the directors of a company propose to take advantage of the exemptions conferred by Part I or II of this Schedule, it is the auditors' duty to provide them with a report stating whether in their opinion the company is entitled to those exemptions and whether the documents to be proposed to be delivered in accordance with this Schedule are properly prepared.

(2) The accounts delivered shall be accompanied by a special report of the auditors stating that in their opinion—

(a) the company is entitled to the exemptions claimed in the directors' statement, and

(b) the accounts to be delivered are properly prepared in accordance with this Schedule.

(3) In such a case a copy of the auditors' report under section 235 need not be delivered separately, but the full text of it shall be reproduced in the special report; and if the report under section 235 is qualified there shall be included in the special report any further material necessary to understand the qualification.

(4) Section 236 (signature of auditors' report) applies to a special report under this paragraph as it applies to a report under section 235.

9 Dormant companies

Paragraphs 7 and 8 above do not apply where the company is exempt by virtue of section 250 (dormant companies) from the obligation to appoint auditors.

10 Requirements in connection with publication of accounts

(1) Where advantage is taken of the exemptions conferred by Part I or II of this Schedule, section 240 (requirements in connection with publication of accounts) has effect with the following adaptations.

(2) Accounts delivered in accordance with this Schedule and accounts in the form in which they would be required to be delivered apart from this Schedule are both "statutory accounts" for the purposes of that section.

(3) References in that section to the auditors' report under section 235 shall be read, in relation to accounts delivered in accordance with this Schedule, as references to the special report under paragraph 8 above.

SCHEDULE 9
(Section 258 and as amended by CA 1989, s 18(3)(4), 7 Sch)

[SPECIAL PROVISIONS FOR BANKING AND INSURANCE COMPANIES AND GROUPS][1]

1 Substituted by CA 1989, 7 Sch with effect from 1 April 1990 (SI 1990 No 355) subject to the transitional and saving provisions in Arts 6 to 9 of that Order.
Previously
'FORM AND CONTENT OF SPECIAL CATEGORY ACCOUNTS'

[. . .][1]

1 Deleted by CA 1989, 7 Sch with effect from 1 April 1990 (SI 1990 No 355) subject to the transitional and saving provisions in Arts 6 to 9 of that Order.
Previously
'Preliminary
1 Paragraphs 2 to 13 of this Schedule apply to the balance sheet and 14 to 18 to the profit and loss account, and are subject to the exceptions and modifications provided for by Part II of this Schedule in the case of a holding or subsidiary company and by Part III thereof in the case of companies of the classes there mentioned.'

[PART I FORM AND CONTENT OF ACCOUNTS][1]

1 Substituted by CA 1989, 7 Sch with effect from 1 April 1990 (SI 1990 No 355) subject to the transitional and saving provisions in Arts 6 to 9 of that Order.
Previously
'PART I GENERAL PROVISIONS AS TO BALANCE SHEET AND PROFIT AND LOSS ACCOUNT'.

Balance sheet

2 The authorised share capital, issued share capital, liabilities and assets shall be summarised, with such particulars as are necessary to disclose the general nature of the assets and liabilities, and there shall be specified—

(a) any part of the issued capital that consists of redeemable shares, the earliest and latest dates on which the company has power to redeem those shares, whether those shares must be redeemed in any event or are liable to be redeemed at the option of the company or of the shareholder and whether any (and, if so, what) premium is payable on redemption;
(b) so far as the information is not given in the profit and loss account, any share capital on which interest has been paid out of capital during the financial year, and the rate at which interest has been so paid;
(c) the amount of the share premium account;
(d) particulars of any redeemed debentures which the company has power to re-issue.

3 There shall be stated under separate headings, so far as they are not written off,—

(a) the preliminary expenses;
(b) any expenses incurred in connection with any issue of share capital or debentures;
(c) any sums paid by way of commission in respect of any shares or debentures;
(d) any sums allowed by way of discount in respect of any debentures; and
(e) the amount of the discount allowed on any issue of shares at a discount.

SCHEDULE 13
(Sections 324-326, 328 and 346)

PROVISIONS SUPPLEMENTING AND INTERPRETING SECTIONS 324 TO 328

PART I RULES FOR INTERPRETATION OF THE SECTIONS AND ALSO SECTION 346(4) AND (5)

1 (1) A reference to an interest in shares or debentures is to be read as including any interest of any kind whatsoever in shares or debentures.

(2) Accordingly, there are to be disregarded any restraints or restrictions to which the exercise of any right attached to the interest is or may be subject.

4 A person is taken to be interested in shares or debentures if a body corporate is interested in them and—

(a) that body corporate or its directors are accustomed to act in accordance with his directions or instructions, or
(b) he is entitled to exercise or control the exercise of one-third or more of the voting power at general meetings of that body corporate.

As this paragraph applies for the purposes of section 346(4) and (5), "more than one-half" is substituted for "one-third or more".

6 (1) A person is taken to have an interest in shares or debentures if, otherwise than by virtue of having an interest under a trust—

(a) he has a right to call for delivery of the shares or debentures to himself or to his order, or
(b) he has a right to acquire an interest in shares or debentures or is under an obligation to take an interest in shares or debentures;

whether in any case the right or obligation is conditional or absolute.

(2) Rights or obligations to subscribe for shares or debentures are not to be taken, for purposes of sub-paragraph (1), to be rights to acquire, or obligations to take, an interest in shares or debentures.

This is without prejudice to paragraph 1.

TABLE OF LEGISLATION AND OF OTHER REGULATIONS

EXPOSURE DRAFTS

TABLE OF CASES

References are to paragraph numbers of this book.

TABLE OF COMPANIES

References are to paragraph numbers of this book where extracts from the financial statements of these companies are reproduced.

Index

References are to paragraph numbers of this book

Order form

To: Tolley Publishing Company Ltd., Tolley House, 2 Addiscombe Road, Croydon, Surrey CR9 5AF England. Telephone: 081-686 9141

Please send me the following book(s), as shown below. I understand that if, for any reason, I am not satisfied with my order and return the book(s) in saleable condition within 21 days, Tolley will refund my money in full.

If you wish to place a standing order for any book(s) and obtain the benefits of the Tolley Subscriber Service, please tick the relevant standing order box(es). All books placed on standing order are sent post-free within the U.K. Please add 5% towards postage and packing if not placed on standing order.

Title	Price per copy	No. of copies	Standing order	Amount £
			☐	
			☐	
			☐	
			☐	
			☐	
			☐	

Plus VAT (if applicable) ______

Plus 5% postage and packing (if applicable) ______

Total £ ______

Cheque is enclosed for total amount of order £ ______

Please debit Access/Visa* account number

Access VISA Signature ______

*Please delete as necessary

Please send me a copy of the full Tolley catalogue ☐

Name† ______

Firm ______

Position ______

Address† ______

______

______ Post Code ______

Telephone No ______ Date ______

†If paying by credit card, please enter name and address of cardholder

Registered No. 729731 England VAT No. 243 3583 67 Code 262

Tolley